SCRIPTURAL INTERPRETATION IN THE FATHERS

Scriptural Interpretation in the Fathers: Letter and Spirit

edited by

THOMAS FINAN
and
VINCENT TWOMEY

FOUR COURTS PRESS

The book was typeset in New Baskerville 11pt on 12pt
by Seton Music Graphics, Bantry, for
FOUR COURTS PRESS LTD
Kill Lane, Blackrock, Co. Dublin
and in North America by
FOUR COURTS PRESS LTD
c/o ISBS, 5804 NE Hassalo Street, Portland, OR 97213.

A catalogue record for this book
is available from the British Library.

ISBN 1-85182-162-7

Printed in Great Britain
by Cambridge University Press, Cambridge

PATRISTIC HERMENEUTICS

Proceedings of the Second Patristic Conference
at Maynooth 1993

Contents

ILLUSTRATIONS

Preface

Understanding the Word of God expressed in human words has been the source of the life and mission of the People of God from its beginning in the call of Abraham. The incarnation, death and resurrection of the Son of God was the fulfilment of the ancient Scriptures and the beginning of the new. The Fathers of the Church pondered the mysteries contained in Scripture, whose every human word, no matter how obscure, emerges from the depths of divinity. The meaning of human utterance took on a new depth when 'men moved by the Holy Spirit spoke from God' (2 Pet 1:19) and so became the means for the Divine Author to unveil his design for humanity. But already in the New Testament, interpretation was a cause of dispute (cf. 1 Pet 1:18; 2 Pet 3:16). The theological disputes that marked the early Church and shaped both the Church and Christian civilization down to our own day— even when that civilization is secularized—were all essentially disputes about the interpretation of Scripture. Such disputes were matters of life and death—at the personal level, eternal life was at stake, while at the public level the Church's witness to the Truth was often in conflict with the claims or compromises of the State. Some martyrs such as Irenaeus and Cyprian, paid for their teaching with their lives, others like Athanasius and Chrysostom with exile, or even mutilation, as in the case of Maximus Confessor. This was the primary reason for their title: Fathers of the Church. No less significant was their genius, their originality and insight, which remained, and remains, the source of inspiration for all generations. Every renewal of the Church finds its source in the Fathers. The Second Vatican Council was no exception. Indeed one may say that the renewal inaugurated by the Council was primarily due to the painstaking, hidden, and at the time unacknowledged, work of patristic scholars such as Henri de Lubac, who also had the privilege of personally sharing the fate of some of the Fathers.

The aim of *The Patristic Symposium* is, in biblical terms, to go back to those fountains of living water and to attract others to come and drink, in a word, to promote the study of the Fathers here in our own country. Having devoted our first public conference to the relationship between

Neoplatonism and Christianity, we decided to explore the theme of scriptural interpretation in our second conference, held at Maynooth in June 1993. Recent publications testify to the renewed interest in the topic. As it happened, the Pontifical Biblical Commission published its impressive document entitled 'The Interpretation of the Bible in the Church' in September of the same year as our Conference. At its core is a contemporary *relecture* of the patristic heritage concerning the literal and spiritual meanings of Scripture. Indeed, many of the themes of that document were echoed in the Maynooth conference, the proceedings of which we now present. It will be noted that the contributors are either Irish or working in Ireland. This is not to be interpreted as narrow provincialism but must be seen rather in the light of the fact that, since there is no Chair of Patrology in Ireland, and so no focus of theological scholarship in this area, our group, limited though it is in finances and other resources, thought it best to provide some alternative focus for the many Irish scholars working in related disciplines.

Despite the evident constraints of limiting potential contributors to Irish scholars, the main body of the papers presented at the Second Patristic Conference could be said to be representative of the Greek, Latin and Syriac traditions. The first three papers, however, are introductory in nature, opening with an overview of the hermeneutical question from the earliest biblical evidence to the present day. Then follows an examination of the Liturgy as the, often forgotten, primary context for scriptural interpretation. The third introductory paper looks at Philo, one of the major influences, in particular on the Alexandrian tradition of exegesis. We also invited scholars to explore the largely unknown terrain of the early Irish Church and her Fathers. The volume concludes, fittingly, with a paper devoted to the patristic influence on the illustrations of the Book of Kells, which in turn throws light on the early Irish Church's familiarity with, and development of, the thought of the great Church Fathers. Each contribution endeavours to illustrate what the Biblical Commission most recently affirmed, namely that 'the Fathers teach us to read Scripture theologically with an authentic Christian spirit within the heart of a living tradition' (English translation p. 47, slightly modified).

We wish to thank all those who contributed papers or chaired the various sessions of the Conference, as well as the Maynooth Scholastic Trust and other benefactors for the financial support which enabled us to hold the Conference in the first instance. Our thanks are due to the Publications Subcommittee of the College Executive Council, Maynooth, and to the Society of the Divine Saviour for their generous subsidies, without which this publication would never have seen the light of day. We wish also gratefully to acknowledge the permission granted by The Board of Trinity College Dublin to use the illustrations from the Book of Kells. Our sincere thanks are due to the Publisher, Mr Michael Adams and his staff for their patience, efficiency and expertise, Seton Music Graphics,

Bantry, for the typesetting and also Mrs Helen Litton for preparing the index. It is fitting, finally, to pay tribute to the late Professor Thomas March, whose lectures introduced a whole generation of Maynooth students to the Fathers and who contributed a paper on Origen to the Conference. He was called to his eternal reward before he could complete the preparation of his manuscript for publication. Requiescat in pace.

This volume is also the modest contribution of the members of *The Patristic Symposium* to the bicentenary celebrations marking the foundation of the Royal Catholic College of Maynooth. From its inception in 1795 up to about the time of the last Council, the study of Ancient Classics could be said to have been the backbone of its academic programme for future priests. The combination of Classics and clerics inevitably led to the study of the Fathers of the Church. Doctoral theses in Divinity tended to be primarily on patristic themes. Publications included the Handbook of Patrology by Joseph Canon Hamill, selected texts from the works of St John Chrysostom by Cardinal D'Alton, the recently published study of Tertullian by Cahal Brendan Cardinal Daly, as well as studies on Origen and Augustine by Professors Gerard Watson and Thomas Finan. *The Patristic Symposium* originated in, and meets mostly, in Maynooth. It is our wish that Maynooth may, in the not too distant future, establish a Chair of Patristic Studies. That would surely be fitting homage to the patristic tradition at Maynooth and a pledge of its further development.

The Third Patristic Conference is due to be held in Maynooth in June 1996.

The Editors

Apud Maynooth
in annuntiatione Domini
ducentesimo anno a collegio condito.

The Patristic Hermeneutic of Spiritual Freedom and Its Biblical Origins

JAMES McEVOY

In a notable passage of his Confessions St Augustine relates his discovery of the spiritual sense of the Old Testament, made as he listened to the preaching of Bishop Ambrose:

> I was glad also that the old Scriptures of the Law and the Prophets were set before me now, no longer in that light in which they had formerly seemed absurd, when I criticised Your holy ones for thinking this or that which in plain fact they did not think. And it was a joy to hear Ambrose who often repeated to his congregation, as if it were a rule he was most strongly urging upon them, the text: *the letter killeth, but the spirit giveth life.*[1] And he would go on to draw aside the veil of mystery and lay open the spiritual meaning of things which taken literally would have seemed to teach falsehood.
>
> Nothing of what he said struck me as false, although I did not as yet know whether what he said was true.[2]

Augustine presumably thought his readers would be able to identify for themselves the sense of liberation he experienced on learning to read the Old Testament spiritually; he does not enlarge much upon this aspect of his growth towards spiritual freedom, vital though it clearly was. He had long before this made some effort to read the Scriptures for himself (*Conf.* III 5), but although he was drawn to them by that deep reverence for Christ the teacher of wisdom which his upbringing had instilled into him, he felt repelled by the simple-mindedness of much of what he read in the Bible and found it unworthy of comparison with the majesty of Cicero. Did the Old Testament not teach (and did the Catholic Church not accept) that man is made in the image of God—with the result that God must be in the image of man, existing somehow in body and in space? Were there not, in the Old Testament especially, stories of behaviour (of the patriarchs, but more than that, recounted of God himself, with his anger, his vengeance, his jealousy, his changes of heart), which no cultivated man could regard as anything but absurd?

1 Ambrose does employ 2 Cor 3:6 in this sense, in Sermon 19 (PL 17, 663b).
2 The Confessions of St Augustine, trs. F.J. Sheed, London 1944, 64 (Conf. VI 3).

Listening to Ambrose, Augustine felt an embarrassed sense of joy (*gaudens erubui*), as the often shocking letter of the Scriptures was folded back to uncover depths and mysteries hidden beneath: he felt embarrassed, as he realized how groundless had been the objections he had himself propagated against the Church, but he was at the same time joyful to discover that he had been accusing its doctrine in the wrong.

Christianity has always thought of its message—redemption offered gratuitously and universally by God through Jesus Christ the Saviour—as an offer bearing liberation to all who will accept it. Augustine, who details for us his own experience of being set free, and who does so in terms with which we can still broadly identify (*Conf.* VII 5–12), includes in his account of his conversion the above reflection on the liberating power of the spiritual, mystical reading of the Scriptures, in a way that for many of today's readers would require considerable elucidation. Nevertheless, even if his narrative of that clearly very significant, early moment in his conversion is in this respect problematic and obscure for many (even Christian believers) in our own times, we must acknowledge that Augustine himself is completely at one with the great majority of the writers of the first Christian centuries, in regarding the capacity of believers to read the Bible (especially the Old Testament) in a spiritual way as constituting a central and inalienable portion of the experience of Christian liberty, and thus as giving the Church a significant part of its identity as Christian.

The following reflections have the limited aim of exploring some aspects of the relationship between Christian liberty and the spiritual interpretation of the Scriptures.

THE CHRISTIAN DIALECTIC

Among the early Christian writers who practised the interpretation of the Scriptures a theory of how to read the Old Testament in the light of the New was developed. The death and resurrection of Jesus, acclaimed as the Messiah and as Lord, required that the Jewish Scriptures, especially the Prophets, be read in the light of the definitive and unrepeatable event of the death of Jesus, understood as a redemptive intervention of God, and of his resurrection, or his vindication by his Father. The methods of interpretation applied to the Law and the Prophets (regarded as authoritative writings) acquired their focus in Christ. Gradually a genuine, original Christian dialectic emerged. It was expressed in terms already adumbrated in the Gospels and Letters, long before there was anything like a canon of such writings. The dialectic consisted in exploring the differences between the old body of Jewish writings and the new corpus produced by the earliest preachers of the kerygma; differences which in turn were to be appreciated in the light of the overarching unity of the divine plan, which could only be one.

Broadly speaking, the categories of promise and fulfillment (or prophecy and realization) were taken from the Gospel according to Matthew. St Paul supplied the contrast between the letter and the spirit, which so forcibly attracted Augustine. Paul likewise made use of allegory (a feature of the contemporary Greek literary scene) to express the relationship between two covenants, their differences and their interrelationship. It was these ideas which, gradually becoming more thematized, gave rise to the theory of the senses of Scripture. The Fathers and other seminal Christian writers (Origen was not recognized as a Father!) did not start from nothing in their preaching and writing, they rather looked to the New Testament books for precious methodological hints as to how to read the Jewish Scriptures as bearing upon Christ.

It is to the New Testament, then, that we must turn, in order to uncover what the later authors picked up there and tried to develop.

BIBLICAL INTERPRETATION WITHIN THE BIBLE

Since the earliest Christian times it has been recognized that the New Testament contains much that aims to interpret the Jewish Bible, and indeed that Jesus himself interpreted the authoritative books of the Jewish religion for his disciples, both in his preaching and in post-resurrection appearances. Can the matter be pushed back further still, to the Old Testament itself? A recent work has summarized the research of exegetes bearing upon the many and various ways in which portions of the Hebrew scriptures were taken up again within writings which subsequently came themselves to acquire authoritative status, and to be included in the Pharisaic canon of the Jewish scriptures.[3] Not by any means all of the additional and interpretative material is of a purely redactional kind. In Second and Third Isaiah, threats directed by the original prophet against Assyria are repeated literally against new oppressors of Israel. Even within First Isaiah itself (ch. 13 and parts of ch. 14, e.g.) the fall of Babel is invoked, in the face of the actuality of Babylonian oppression during the exile; this addition was made three hundred years after the time of the original prophet. Many examples can be given from pre-exilic prophetic literature of passages which are reworked and interpreted in later but analogous historical circumstances, and then re-introduced into the written, authoritative text, in order to give weight to the message, to lend it actuality, and to respond to Jahweh's injunction, 'Comfort, comfort, my people,

---

3   Henning Graf Reventlow, *Epochen der Bibelauslegung*. Bd I. *Vom Alten Testament bis Origenes*, Munich 1990. Ch. 1 of this work studies 'Biblauslegung innerhalb der Bibel', 11–23. Cf. 'The Old Testament in the Making', by P.R. Ackroyd, in the collective work referred to in the following footnote, 67–113. Only purely illustrative treatment of this topos can be given here, in what is in fact only an essay.

says your God: speak to the heart of Jerusalem...' (Is 40:1f). Nor were the historical books free from re-working. The Books of Chronicles (4–3 c. BC) take the writing of the Deuteronomist as their source for the kings, and a synoptic comparison of the two works reveals numerous omissions, additions and other changes revelatory of the theological interest of the Chronicler(s).

The later writers presuppose that the earlier text is both authoritative and known to their readership; they place themselves in line with its basic theological motifs, even while taking account of the difference in the situation and the hopes of their contemporaries, in a creative reinterpretation of the old which continues to respect the latter's authority and originality. The conclusion may be drawn that within the Old Testament examples may be found of interpretation in the strict sense of the word, namely in those cases where an older, already fixed and authoritative text was actualized and used for idealizing, historicizing or exemplary purposes, by a different and more recent text.

In the intertestamental period an original case of interpretation is presented by the Septuagint Version. The translators' achievement was remarkable, in that they managed to retain and convey the original message of the Bible. It must be acknowledged, however, that the differences between Hebrew and Greek, when added to impulses either coming from or provoked by the hellenized milieu of Alexandria, introduced elements of interpretation which can easily be illustrated in details of language. For instance, the translators limit the anthropmorphic character of some Hebrew expressions (e.g. 'seeing God') and spiritualize and universalize the concept of God ('Sabaoth' becomes 'Pantokrator'). They introduce some Egyptianisms based upon local knowledge. Brief additions, mostly taken from some part of the Bible, are made for purposes of the elucidation of words. Besides that, in its original ordering of the books a Septuagintal theology becomes just visible: Daniel is placed, with the major prophets, at the very end of the Bible. The Septuagint thus has very limited, but none the less quite identifiable elements of interpretation within it.

THE OLD TESTAMENT IN THE NEW

'Christianity is unique among the world religions in being born with a Bible in its cradle'.[4] The Bible in question was not yet canonically circumscribed, but it was sufficiently well defined to be referred to in current formulae, such as 'the Law and the Prophets', 'Moses and the Prophets', or simply 'the Scripture/the Scriptures'. Perhaps more than

---

4   C.F. Evans, 'The New Testament in the Making', in The Cambridge History of the Bible. Vol. I. From the Beginnings to Jerome. Ed. by P.R. Ackroyd and C.F. Evans, Cambridge 1970, 232. See also 'The Interpretation of the Old Testament in the New', by C.K. Barrett, ibid., 377–411.

in former times, exegetes recognize nowadays that for the Apostles and the first believers in Christ the Jewish Bible was the great, indeed the only, work of reference available. Without appealing to it the Apostles would simply not have been able to find any expression for their faith. The significance of the unanimous and unchallenged presupposition in the early Church, that the Bible is a sacred, inspired text, should not escape us; not only Jews believing in Jesus regarded this as a self-evident truth, but in the case of Gentiles the act of converting to the Christian faith meant unquestioning acceptance of the Bible as revelation. (Only with Marcion and perhaps certain Gnostics in the second century would that basic principle be challenged.) The claim of the Christian community upon the the Jewish Bible is as old as the Apostles and the evangelists of the new faith; it is consubstantial with the Church community, and is coeval with its very origin. Before the Church possessed a single writing of its own production, before the letters of Paul began to circulate, and long before any notion of a canonical body of texts surrounding the new faith could arise, this community already had its Bible, its inspired work, to guide it in prayer and to offer it words and formulae in which, and in which alone, the faith in Jesus as the Messiah, the Lord and the Son of God could be given its primordial expression. The Christian writers who followed those first generations would gradually be placed in a position where two series of sacred, canonical books could be compared with one another, as the Old Testament and the New Testament, but this opposition of strict correlatives had no meaning in that earliest time, when the spiritual sense of Scripture could not possibly mean an older text interpreted in the light of a newer one.

If reflection on the Jewish Bible enabled the early community of believers in Jesus as the Christ to articulate its own faith, it in fact did something even more fundamental than that, for it offered it the possibility of reaching an understanding of the very object of that faith. The Apostles were charged with testifying to all that they had witnessed of Jesus, his preaching, his death and his resurrection from the dead; but over and beyond that they had to work out the significance of the words, deeds and experiences to which they testified, by entering into their meaning at the deepest level, the level where the life of the man Jesus brought redemption and offered eternal life. In their effort, first to discern the object of faith, then to give content to it, they had no alternative but to look from Jesus to their Bible, and then back again to Jesus, in an unceasing passage from what they knew by the experience of their Lord to what they knew of God's ways from the sacred writing. Their deepening insight into the meaning of the person of their Lord went hand in hand with a growing appreciation of the Sacred Books, read as bearing a divine promise and as prophesying one who was to be sent by God as the Messiah. The entire sacred writing was therefore read in the light of their Master, as a single great promise, spoken in many ways, of the coming of a unique representative of God. Read in that way, the Apostles and evangelists found that the Bible made complete sense, as it never had done to them beforehand.

It would not be quite exact to say that the early Church produced its own reinterpretation, or new interpretation, of the Jewish Bible, even though perhaps on a greater scale than the other reinterpretations known to us from Jewish milieux; for that would be to put things the wrong way round. The primitive community did not aim at a new interpretation of its own Sacred Books, it simply read them in order to understand in depth the events of which the Apostles had indeed been witnesses, but which they had no other human means to interpret. In a way the intense preoccupation with the Bible which the Apostles pursued had the effect of their seeing in the Sacred Books a means, rather than an end in themselves. The intention of the earliest preachers was to explore the heights and the depths of what had recently occurred, and of the experiences the commuity had undergone in its principal representatives, with and through Jesus, and also after his crucifixion.

The difference between the early Christian reading of the Bible and that of Jewish religious figures and groups (even of those contemporary with Christian origins) is significant—and this can be said without disparaging the latter. Jewish believers all referred to the Scriptures as the manifestation of the word of God. Interpretation of various kinds served this outlook in a variety of ways. *Targum* resulted from the Aramaic paraphrases made of the message conveyed in the ancient language, once it was no longer well understood by the people. Rabbinic *midrash* interpreted the word to make it more assimilable and pointed for the reader or listener. At Qumran, the *pesher* announced that this or that prophetic text had been fulfilled in the community. We have already seen how in the Books of the Prophets later interpretation sought to apply earlier texts to the present situation of the people, revivifying an older curse or promise in the actual circumstances of the speaker or writer. The Christian use of the Bible, however, is neither a reactualization of the sacred texts nor an extension of the unvarying, original meaning identically into the present circumstances; it rather takes the form of a constant reference to the authoritative text in order to deepen understanding of the recent events surrounding Jesus. Christian use of the Bible was led by what had then so recently happened, the events which filled the minds of believers to the point of excluding all else—save, indeed, the Sacred Books that could, and did, offer altogether indispensable help towards building the edifice of that understanding. The specifically Christian use of the Bible did not aim at extending the Torah to circumstances unforeseen or acts not already explicitly covered by it; it did not aim to recall past events in order to grasp their present importance for life under God and in hope. The earliest Christians went from the events they themselves had witnessed back to their prefigurative promise, their prophecy, and their long preparation by a God whose word is also deed (*dabar*). The conviction was always present that the biblical word would serve to express the advent, and the event, of the Christ; the sacred word would serve as the key to unlock the meaning which was altogether given in Christ, and would thus achieve its own finality precisely as a word of promise.

The disciples were horrified at the the ignominious nature of the death Jesus suffered, then disorientated by the empty tomb and overcome with awe at his post-resurrection appearances. The only meaning they could hope to find for these unique events and experiences lay in recourse to the Scriptures. They did not wait for a supplementary special divine revelation to arrive, bearing an explanation of why these things had occurred. Instead they attempted to situate what had taken place in the only context which promised answers to faith, that of the plan of God. They had the word of God, and they followed the constant former example of their own Rabbi, turning in study and prayer to the sacred texts. It is thus that we find them proclaiming from the very beginning, after Pentecost, not only that Jesus of Nazareth died and had risen from the dead, but that He died and rose from the dead 'according to the Scriptures'. It is only by this addition that the witness becomes truly an apostle of the Good News, a believer that God's purpose is the entire meaning of Jesus the Christ. In the course of time the broad spectrum of Christian writings would come to contain a variety of individual ways of reading the traditional Scriptures (think, for example, of the differences in the approach to the Bible of the evangelist Matthew, and the authors of Hebrews and of the Apocalypse); there is total unanimity among them, however, in reading the Sacred Books of Judaism while intending God's action in Jesus: what came about in his death, and even in the terrible manner of it, took place 'according to the Scriptures'.

It was of decisive importance for the Apostles that Jesus himself had referred a series of very significant passages from the Scriptures to his own person. His community of believers did not have to have recourse to free invention, but in the first instance believed what they had heard Him say and seen Him do. Jesus's self-interpretation was the undoubted and assured foundation upon which the kerygma concerning what had taken place 'according to the Scriptures' was bit by bit to be erected. The principal texts which Jesus used in this way may be briefly recalled, beginning with Is 61:1f., which He applied to himself at the start of his public preaching (Lk 4:18–19), as being Himself the one spoken of there 'Who brings good news to the poor and freedom to captives.' For very good reasons He seems to have spoken of his mission often in deliberately oblique ways, one of which identified Him with the 'Son of man' who was awaited in connection with the final judgement (Dn 7:13). At his trial He, according to Mark, answered the High Priest's question, 'Are you the Messiah?' with an affirmative, and a direct reference to 'the Son of man' (Mk 14:62). Jesus justified his cleansing of the Temple (Mk 11:15f.) by a question taken from Is 56:7 and a word of Jeremiah (7:11), thus linking prophetic texts with his own action. He understood his life in the light of the Biblical motif of the suffering Just One. When He speaks of 'the Son of man' (Mk 10:45) He passes on to the thought of one representing 'the many' and giving his life for them (cf. Is 43:3f.; 53:10–12). The blood which Moses scattered over the people of the covenant (Dt 24:8) he made to correspond with his own 'blood of the covenant, which is to be poured out for many' (Mk 14:22–25), when He will die in their place. In the praying of the start of Psalm 22 on the cross we can recognize the same biblical model of the suffering Just One, who in his very moment of suffering places his whole trust in God. Jesus applied the prophetic message to Himself. He looked upon his own death as bringing about the opening of the kingdom of God both to the just and to sinners. Paul, quoting a confession of the faith which he explicitly says he had received, and which recapitulates Jesus's own understanding of his death, will say 'that Christ died for our sins, in acccordance with the Scriptures; that He was buried; and that He was raised to life on the third day, in accordance with the Scriptures' (1 Cor 15:3).

With Jesus Himself, and consequently with the disciples, we encounter a way of reading the Jewish Bible that opens up a new sense of what had been written there. The text is not altered in its substance (although admittedly the particular use of Old Testament texts by writers of the New Testament gives rise upon occasion to some perplexity and uncertainty on the part of exegetes), but the new sense arises from its being related to the person of Jesus, as the Christ, the fulfillment of the promise.

THE NEWNESS OF THE NEW (AND THE OLDNESS OF THE OLD)

The Christian writings which were accorded authority within the different communities, and especially those which were later to be canonized, developed in their different ways the theme of the novelty of what God had done in Christ. Only one dimension of this theme will be evoked here, the one namely that identifies the Church community as a new people, or the people of the New Covenant, or even as 'the Israel of God'. In its multiform development in the earliest Christian writings we can observe a very striking spiritualization of the covenant and of the institutions of the people of Israel which followed upon it.

The Pauline allegory of the Two Covenants

St Paul's Letter to the Galatians may be one of the very earliest documents we have from a Christian hand. The epistle is brief, but it is a veritable digest of the thought of its author, a condensed enunciation of the themes to be found in much more developed form in the Epistle to the Romans, which it seems to have prepared. Its importance for our present purposes is that in it the Apostle thematizes the relationship of the Christian movement to Judaism, and above all to the Covenant of Sinai. He insists that there have been two related dispensations of salvation, the first of which was given to Israel alone, but the second of which, initiated by the saving death of Jesus Christ, is open to all who adhere to him in faith. Paul's opposition to the demand that circumcision be imposed upon believers coming from a Gentile background is complete, because in his eyes to perpetuate the sign of that earlier Covenant would be to ratify the view of the judaizing believers that that Covenant, together with the Torah, constituted the definitive divine plan for the salvation of mankind. This attempt to fit Jesus into a merely prophetic role, and thus to preserve substantial continuity with the Jewish past, and indeed present, by making of gentile converts simple proselytes on the traditional and long-established model, provokes Paul to reaffirm the unique and revolutionary nature of the paschal events, through which the Law has been set aside. It is faith in Christ and that alone which justifies those who believe in Him, and which confers the Spirit of God upon them.

In his celebrated allegory—St Paul uses the term itself—he tries to illustrate both the difference between the two Covenants and their related origin (Ga 4:21–31).[5] Abraham had two wives, of whom Sara was the free-born while Hagar was a slave-girl. Sarah's son was born according to the promise of God, Hagar's on the other hand in the normal way of nature. The two women stand for the two Covenants, which may alternatively be imagined as two cities: Jerusalem standing where it does, while another Jerusalem descends from heaven (to become the mother of Christian believers, as Jerusalem was the mother of the Jewish people; cf Ps 87:5; Is 66.11).

Paul undoubtedly thought of bringing Abraham into his discourse because the patriarch was associated with a divine promise of a universal kind—and promise and fulfillment were of course the primordial categories in which right from the beginning the believers in Christ had thought. Explicit in his allegory is Paul's largely negative attitude to the Torah; implicit, on the other hand, is the origin of Isaac and Ismael from one father. The allegory is constructed by Paul in the full flight of dictation, as an almost graphic device illustrating the Christian dialectic.

Paul is thus fully committed to advocating and ensuring the freedom of the gentile believers in Christ with regard to the entirety of the Jewish law, and in particular to the practice of circumcision. The Law, he argues, had not just negative effects but had at the same time a

5   On the meaning of the word 'allegory' in the grammarians and writers and its reception by early Christian authors in the wake of St Paul, see Henri de Lubac, *Exégèse médiévale. Les quatre sens de l'écriture*, première partie, II, Paris 1959, 373–383.

positive, pedagogical function, for it prepared its children for faith in Christ, acting like a *paidagogos* (the servant who brought the children of his masters to the school and deposited them safely at the door). The law having served its purpose within the divine salvific economy, the freedom of love has come with the new Covenant in Christ. What was obedience, fear and burden has become the sweet yoke of love, or of liberty of spirit that knows neither law nor fear of transgression; what was promised ever since Abraham has come to fruition, in the fruit of the Spirit. Liberty is not solely negative (freedom from the ceremonies and rituals of the Law, or from fear) but positive, and it can even be named: 'love, joy, peace, patience, kindness, goodness, gentleness, fidelity and self-control' (Gal 5:22).

In Paul's eyes spiritual freedom is identical with the love that is the fruit of the Spirit's dwelling in the believer. Liberty is love and love is liberty, and these equivalents stand in the closest relationship to the spiritual sense of the Scriptures (the Jewish Scriptures), which is opened up by the Christ-centered reading of them.

The inner logic of the New Covenant idea

The author of 1 Peter also invoked the idea of two Covenants when he addressed his Christians in terms which seem deliberately to evoke the Book of Exodus (1 Pet 2:9–10). They are to regard themselves as 'a chosen race', even though differently from the chosen people—for the new race is not a nation but has its birth from God (1:2–3). They are 'a royal priesthood', presumably because they attend to the sacred service of the King of Kings. They are 'a consecrated nation, a people set apart'. These expressions are taken from Exodus 19 (the granting of the covenant by Jahweh). A deliberate evocation is made of the Exodus itself: God has just called the believers to be his people and has brought them 'out of darkness into his wonderful light', after the manner in which the Israelites were granted light even in the days of the plague of darkness which covered Egypt. In other words, God has once again called 'a people from within a people' (Dt 4:34) and has brought into existence a kind of new and different Israel, which has emerged through a new exodus from the nation of Israel, and has spiritually crossed the waters to arrive at a new experience of liberation.

The articulation of the New Covenant was borne by the strict logic of the transference of the institutions of Israel the nation, into a spiritual or mystical understanding of the significance of those institutions for the life of the new people of God. The people, land and nationhood of the Old Testament belief were deemed no longer to be the carriers of the divine economy of salvation as a people or a nation, or as inhabiting a particular territory. Physical definitions and ethnic restrictions, together with the territorial ownership which had placed such a heavy mortgage on the implicit universality of the salvation promised through Abraham, must in consequence be considered as types that foreshadowed a purely spiritual understanding of God's redemptive work, in all its newly-realized universality. God had indeed, the Christians felt, raised up children of Abraham, children born of the Promise, from the nations, and God's table itself was now open to those who come to faith in Christ from any ethnic background whatsoever.

The logic of the New Covenant idea is a strict one, for it must spiritualize and universalize one by one the features of the Old Covenant, in order to give to each one and to their totality the finality that was, from this perspective, no less than their due. The New Covenant will have a new Torah (cf. Mt 5:20–48), namely the commandment of Jesus Christ (the new Moses). As the *berith* was ratified by the scattering over the assembled people of the blood of animal victims (Ex 24:8), so there is a new victim whose blood is shed for all (Mk 14:24). A new priest offers the universal sacrifice, with himself as the new paschal lamb-victim (Rev 6:10); and that priesthood of Christ himself is shared in by all the peo- ple (1 Pet 2:9). Sacrifice was performed in the Temple, where Jahweh 'dwelt', hence there must be a new temple for Him to live in and for spiritual offering to be made; it is one built of living stones upon the foundation of the Twelve Apostles (who in Jesus' eyes represented in his new community the twelve tribes of Israel). There will be a New Jerusalem (Gal 4:26; Heb 12:21; Rev 21–22), and within it, at its summit, a new Sion. The pilgrimage to Jerusalem, and with that the pilgrim songs among the Psalms, will be given a metaphorical sense, as the pilgrimage of faith moving to the heavenly city. The motif of new birth (regeneration, Jn 3:5) and the new Adam theme in turn invite the vision of 'a new heavens and a new earth' (Rev 21). The new presence of God in Christ and the Holy Spirit will entail a new *parousia* (literally 'presence'), or new coming of the risen and triumphant Christ at the end. So strict is the logic of this typological symbolism that there must even be a new circumcision (1 Cor 7:19; Gal 5:6; 6:15), that of the Christian heart that carries upon itself the mark of the new Covenant. Finally, just as Israel of old walked in faith and trust towards the promised land, so too the new and universal people is fittingly assigned a new land—reaching to the very ends of the earth (Mt 28:19).

The New Testament spiritual understanding thus raises itself as a vast metaphor upon Israel and its institutions, as upon a literal or physical sense.

While the actual term 'new Israel' does not appear in the books of the New Testament (although the term 'Israel of God' [Gal 6.16] and the opposition between 'Israel of the flesh' and 'true Israel' [Rom 9.6–8; 1 Cor 10.18] do), the notion of the new people's replacing the old is everywhere implicit, and is alone adequate to make sense of the dialectic of Old and New that is intrinsic to the New Testament itself; many of the Fathers of the Church would be quick to perceive this.

The somewhat curious metaphor of the 'circumcised heart' may retain our attention for a moment, for its use (by St Paul) aptly illustrates the difference between, on the one hand, the spiritualization of meaning that took place on a large scale within the Jewish Bible and, on the other hand, the spiritual reading of the Old Testament that runs from end to end throughout the New Testament writings. The prophet Jeremiah already spoke of the 'uncircumcised heart' (4:4; 9:24–25), and even of 'uncircumcised ears' (6:10). In Ezekiel, foreigners are described as being 'uncircumcised in heart and flesh', being strangers to the covenant (44:7; cf. Acts 7:51). In countless passages in the Prophets and the Psalms the practice of animal sacrifice was spiritualized and interiorized, in the form of the self-offering of the 'humble and contrite heart'. It goes without saying that Judaism had no need to await the arrival of the first Christians to discover the metaphorical use of language; it had for centuries been developing a spiritual sense of its own through the spiritual internalization of the Torah, its divinely-given guide to right and holy living, deepening the conscience and inviting individual conversion to a fidelity that would befit a devout heart. The vital relevant difference we can perceive between the Old Testament practice and that of the earliest Christian documents lies in the systematic way in which the latter go about the spiritualization of the Sinai Covenant together with its sequels in historical Jewish life. Now, the logic which so strictly governs this transposition of meaning, or this spiritual sense, is, it may be said once again, that of belief in Jesus as the Christ who died and was raised to life again 'according to the Scriptures.'

EARLY CHRISTIAN HERMENEUTICS AND THE SPIRITUAL SENSE

The claims made by the Fathers and other early Christian writers concerning the levels of meaning present in the Scriptures, and the extremely wide range of interpretation that resulted therefrom in their practice, are not simply a part, or an aspect, of their theological enterprise but are in a sense the whole of it, in so far as the theological expression of the first centuries either was directly homiletic in origin, or at any rate stayed close to the text of the Bible. This range and variety clearly cannot be taken directly into account here. Instead, since Galatians has been mentioned already, some commentaries on that epistle will retain our attention, so that the careful exegesis devoted by certain Christian writers of the patristic age to that New Testament book, and some of the more significant developments they made on the basis of it concerning hermeneutics and Christian liberty, may, if only compendiously and very selectively, be exhibited.

Origen

Jean Daniélou aptly remarked that for Origen

> essentially there are only two meanings in Scripture, the literal and
> the Christological. But the Christological meaning can in turn be
> subdivided into as many sections as there are aspects in Christ him-
> self. Christ may be considered either as an historical person mani-
> fested in the events recorded in the Gospels, or as living a hidden
> life in the 'sacraments' of the Church which is his body, or as appear-
> ing at the parousia at the end of the world and reigning in glory.[6]

Origen himself offers the fundamental clue to his hermeneutics in
his comment on Mt 13:45 ('The kingdom of heaven is like a mer-
chant looking for fine pearls...'):

> The pearl of great price is the Christ of God, the Word, Who is
> far above previous Scriptures and the thoughts expressed in the
> Law and the Prophets. He who has found Him easily under-
> stands all the rest (. . .). I say it without fear (. . .) this pearl which
> he possesses who has given up all and made the entire sacrifice, is
> the One of whom Paul has said, 'I have sacrificed all to win Christ':
> all, meaning the fine pearls; to win Christ, the only precious pearl.[7]

Origen provided the earliest known commentary on Galatians, in his
usual form of homilies, but only a page or two of it survives, and even
then only in the Latin translation of Rufinus.[8] However, he returned
throughout his writings to the allegory of Abraham's two wives, a passage which gave him a critically important scriptural paradigm for his
spiritual interpretation. Indeed, Origen devoted so much attention to
this and several other passages of the epistle that some of the main tendencies and themes of his commentary could in fact be reconstructed.
The following is a brief extract from his defence of the hidden or
mystical sense, made in *De principiis*:

> Now the whole multitude of believers, which believes quite faith-
> fully and simply, is a witness to what great profit lies in the first
> meaning, which I have called narrative. Nor is much argument
> needed, since the point is perfectly clear to everyone. And the
> Apostle Paul has given us a great many examples of that meaning
> which above we have called the soul, as it were, of Scripture (. . .)
> When he writes to the Galatians and rebukes those who are
> apparently reading the Law for themselves but do not understand it,

6   Origen, New York 1955, 161. The best recent, overall discussion of Origen as an
      exegete and speculative thinker is by H. Crouzel, S.J., *Origène*, Paris-Namur 1985.
7   Origen, Commentary on the Gospel of St Matthew, 10, nn. 9–10.
8   Origen, PG 14, 1293–1298.

because they are unaware that there are allegories in the Scriptures, he says to them with a certain amount of chiding, 'Tell me, you who desire to be under the Law, do you not hear the Law? For it is written that Abraham had two sons, one by a slave and one by a free woman (. . .) Now this is an allegory. . .' In this passage we must also consider how carefully the Apostle said what he did (. . .), 'do you not hear the Law?', that is, do you not understand, or do you not know?[9]

Origen therefore justifies his own practice on scriptural authority. He believes, that practically all of Scripture contains a hidden sense, placed there by its author, the Spirit, and accessible only to the reader in whom the Spirit is actively working to uncover for him the spiritual sense of what he is reading; or rather, praying—for Origen's exegesis presupposes that it must be possible to pray every part of the Scriptures 'in the Spirit'. Prayerful attention, he was convinced, would uncover even in passages of the Old Testament whose literal sense was shocking or scandalous, a hidden or mystical meaning placed there by God 'for us'.

St Jerome

Latin commentaries on Galatians begin with Marius Victorinus, Jerome, Augustine, Pelagius and Ambrosiaster. By far the lengthiest and fullest surviving patristic exposition is that which comes from the hand of Jerome,[10] who composed it very early on in his exegetical career, at a time when he greatly admired Origen and made liberal use of his work.[11] Although it is uneven in quality and not infrequently pedantic in tone (as well as being very hard on the Jews), it contains a veritable store of scholarship, and abundant information, especially of a linguistic nature. It has, besides, some very good pages on the intention and achievement of the author of the Epistle. However, even a writer as sympathetic to St Jerome as Père Maurice Testard feels obliged to reproach him in a general way for the excesses of his allegorical practice and his facile delight in etymologies, numerology and other artifices.[12] The same writer does

9   Origen, On First Principles (Washington D.C. translation of the Fathers), 184–185.
10   S. Eusebii Hieronymi, Commentariorum in Epistolam ad Galatas Libri Tres, PL 26, cols. 307–438. The passage quoted in translation is to be found in columns 413–414.
11   Many commentaries on Galatians have been lost and others survive in only fragmentary form. The Clavis Patrum Graecorum, vol. V, 144, lists the Greek commentaries: Origenes (frag.); Eusebius Emesenus (frag.); Theodorus Mopsuestenus (frag.); Severianus Gabalensis (frag.); Chrysostomus; Gennadius Constantinopolitanus (frag.); Theodoretus Episcopus Cyri; Oecumenius (frag.). The numerous Greek catenae on the Epistles of St Paul are listed in the Clavis, vol. IV, 250–258. On Jerome's employment of Origen see M.A. Schatkin, 'The Influence of Origen on Jerome's Commentary on Galatians', in Vigiliae Christianae 24 (1970) 49–58.
12   'On se demande pourquoi Jérôme dépense tant de science, pour perdre pied tout à coup dans l'allégorie et tirer de son texte, au nom de l'argumentation la plus

nevertheless find that Jerome's spiritual exegesis, when taken at its best, succeeds in conveying his sincere religious, pastoral and even mystical inspiration. We may note that the dangers of arbitrary allegorization, even when it remains within the bounds of orthodoxy, were recognized by Jerome himself, at least at those moments where he advocated treading the middle path between an over-literalist tendency and hyper-allegorization.

Among numerous passages which could be quoted from his commentary there is one which imparts to the reader Jerome's attentiveness to the spirituality of the great Old Testament figures who, as he saw it, endeavoured to raise their people from the following of the letter to a spiritual appreciation of the word of God. Moses and the prophets were not 'under the law' (in the sense of Gal 4:18) but were 'led by the Spirit'. Here is a rather free translation of the comment on that verse.

> By the Spirit is meant (. . .) not the spirit of man which is in him but the Holy Spirit. It is through following the Spirit that we become spiritual and cease to be under the law (. . .). The question can be raised in relation to this verse (. . .) whether Moses and the prophets were prompted by the Spirit while living under the Law (the Apostle denies this); or whether they had the Spirit and were not under the Law (which the Apostle affirms here); or, a third possibility, whether they lived under the law and did not have the Spirit (which it would be unpardonable to believe in the case of such great men). Our brief response is as follows. It is not the same thing to be under the Law as to be under it only in a very qualified sense, any more than it is the same thing to be in the likeness of sinful flesh and to be in sinful flesh [cf. Rom 8.3]. Both the prophets and Moses, who walked in the Spirit and lived in the Spirit, lived under the Law only in a qualified sense, for their purpose was to bring benefit to those who were under the Law, and to raise them from the lowly place of the letter to the exalted height of the Spirit.

In this acknowledgement of the spiritual sense present in the Old Testament we can appreciate Jerome's conviction that, even though it unfolds itself in successive historical realizations, God's plan is one, just as his Spirit is.

futile ou la plus fallacieuse, l'enseignement le plus inattendu. C'est là ce qui est grave: saint Jérôme ne semble pas voir la faille qui sépare la science de l'exégèse allégorique telle qu'il la pratique. Or, mis à part les spécialistes, nous sommes peu intéressés aujourd'hui par la science de saint Jérôme—fût-elle du meilleur aloi—car elle est dépassée. Quant aux débordements de l'exégèse allégorique, ils ne nous touchent que si l'auteur, sous l'effet d'une haute inspiration poétique et mystique, laissant là toute prétention de science et son lourd appareil, nous entraîne dans le sillage d'une authentique expérience religieuse. Ce qui est parfois le cas de saint Jérôme.' M. Testard, Saint Jérôme. L'Apôtre savant et pauvre du patriciat romain (Collection d'études anciennes de l'Association G. Budé), Paris 1969, 52–53.

St John Chrysostom

Chrysostom's homilies on Galatians were not to be translated into Latin until the sixteenth century,[13] but they were widely disseminated in the Greek Church, in great part through being paraphrased in an influential catena compiled by Theophylact of Bulgaria.[14] In his comment on Galatians 5:13 Chrysostom reflects incisively on the relationship between the Decalogue and the law of love and liberty. The patristic consensus was by his time firmly established: the ritual and ceremonial aspects of the Torah had ceased to have any value with the coming of Christ, whereas the moral law, essentially the Decalogue, remained normative for the Church's members. Does the Law then not still continue to be in some sense a binding, mandatory regime governing all possible moral action? Chrysostom's view places the issue firmly upon the plane of consciousness. For the person living in faith and responsive to the Spirit of God the moral norms do not constitute an alienating imposition to be enforced by a superior and ever-watchful Power. In a real sense there is for such a believer no law any more; to put it in another way, there is no sense of the moral norms as being commandments which interfere with liberty, or as a sort of boundary of which the individual must be continually and acutely aware lest he be tempted to stray over to the wrong side of it. The fascination with wrong-doing, as St Paul had clearly seen, begins to spell the fall from true freedom.

Here is a superbly fine formulation, one which could scarcely be surpassed, of a quite traditional Christian interpretation of Galatians 5:13. (It is quoted here in whole).[15]

> For, brethren, ye have been called unto liberty; only use not liberty for an occasion to the flesh.'
>
> Henceforward he appears to digress into a moral discourse, and in a new manner, which does not occur in any other of his Epistles. For all of them are divided into two parts, and in the first he discusses doctrine, in the last the rule of life, but here, after having entered upon the moral discourse, he unites with it the doctrinal part. For this passage has reference to doctrine in the controversy with the Manichees. What is the meaning of, 'Use not liberty for an occasion to the flesh'? Christ hath delivered us, he says, from the yoke of bondage, He hath left us free to act as we will, not that we may use our liberty for evil, but that we may have ground for receiving a higher reward, advancing to a higher philosophy. Lest any

13   PG 61, 612–682.
14   See L. Rizzerio, 'Robert Grosseteste, Jean Chrysostome et l'*expositor graecus* (=Théophylacte) dans le commentaire super epistolam ad Galatas' [de Grosseteste], in Recherches de Théologie ancienne et médiévale 59 (1992) 166–209.
15   From the anonymous English version printed in the Library of the Fathers, vol. 5, Oxford/London 1840, 80–81.

one should suspect, from his calling the Law over and over again a yoke of bondage, and grace a deliverance from the curse, that his object in enjoining an abandonment of the Law was that one might live lawlessly, he corrects this notion, and states his object to be, not that our course of life might be lawless, but that our philosophy might surpass the Law. For the bonds of the Law are broken, and I say this not that our standard may be lowered but that it may be exalted. For both he who commits fornication, and he who leads a virgin life, pass the bounds of the Law, but not in the same direction; the one sinks lower, the other rises higher; the one transgresses the law, the other excels it. Thus Paul says that Christ hath removed the yoke from you, not that ye may kick and be wanton, but that though without the yoke ye may proceed at a well-measured pace.

Chrysostom's is an example of spiritual interpretation at its very best. He has the Decalogue in view and reflects on the place it may occupy within the Christian life. But as a good preacher he also keeps his public in mind (for these pages very probably were actually delivered by him). He looks to the spirit, not the letter, since in the precise sense which he intends the Law is not a factor in the living, spiritual consciousness of the just man. If sometimes the Fathers give the impression of having indulged themselves in flights of fancy, or in a recherché quasi-game of free verbal association, all performed in the name of tropological, allegorical, anagogical or mystical interpretation, the sure pastoral instinct, the intention to speak to those hungry and oftentimes beggared sheep whom Chrysostom loved and defended (he paid for that with permanent exile from Constantinople), happily preserved this Church Father, as it did some others, from lapses into sheer exegetical idiosyncrasy.

St Augustine

Five or six years after his conversion (in other words, c. 391) Augustine composed an *Expositio ad Galatas*.[16] It is a somewhat disappointing writing and cannot be compared as regards depth of spiritual appreciation with his exegesis of selected themes from the Epistle (notably the Abraham allegory, and the fruit of the Spirit) as it is found in *De civitate Dei*.[17] In that masterpiece Augustine in a way extended to world history the hermeneutical schema of letter and spirit, for he attempts there to penetrate through and behind the unedifying story of earthly conquests

16 Expositio ad Galatas, CSEL vol. LXXXIV, sect. IV, pars Ia. Ed. I. Divjak, Vienna 1971, 55–141. The Latin text accompanied by a Spanish translation is to be found in Obras de San Augustin. Édition bilingüe, t. XVIII, ed. B. Martin Perez, Madrid 1959, 105–191.
17 Se M. Marin, 'Agostino e l'interpretazione antica di Gal 4:24', in Vetera Christianorum 24 (1987) 5–21.

made out of *libido dominandi*, and the largely meaningless succession of imperial powers, in order to glimpse the quiet but continuous unfolding of the secret, mystical sense, which is the spiritual growth throughout time of the City of God.

If we turn to his work *On the Spirit and the Letter* we can discover Augustine attaching his own deepest hermeneutical conviction to the exegesis of a passage from Galatians.

> The saying, that 'the Scripture hath shut up all under sin, that the promise by faith of Jesus Christ might be given to them that believe' [Gal 3:21], shows the advantage of the 'shutting up'; it is for the purpose presently named: 'before faith came, we were kept in ward under the law, shut up unto the faith which afterwards hath been revealed.' The law was given that grace might be sought; grace was given that the law might be fulfilled. For the non-fulfillment of the Law was not through its own fault, but the fault of the 'mind of the flesh—a fault which the law must exhibit, and grace must heal. 'What the law could not do, in that it was made weak through the flesh, God sent his Son in the likeness of the flesh of sin, and in regard to sin condemned sin in the flesh; that the righteousness of the law might be fulfilled in us, who walk not according to the flesh but according to the spirit' [Rom 8:3ff]. So we read in the prophetic testimony: 'I will consummate upon the house of Israel and upon the house of Judah a new covenant'—'consummate' meaning 'fulfil'—'not according to the covenant that I made for their fathers, in the day that I took their hand to bring them forth from the land of Egypt.'
>
> This was the 'old' covenant, because the other is 'new'; but why should they be distinguished as 'old' and 'new', if through the new covenant is fulfilled the same law which in the old said: 'Thou shalt not covet'? The answer is, that 'they have not continued in my covenant, and I have let them go, saith the Lord.' It is because of the sickness of the old man, which the commands and the threatenings of the letter did nothing to heal, that the former covenant is called old, and the latter new with the newness of the Spirit, which heals the new man from his old failing (. . .). It follows that the laws of God, written by God himself upon the heart, are nothing but the very presence of the Holy Spirit who is the finger of God [Ex 32:16]; the presence by which charity, the fulness of the law and the end of the commandment, is shed abroad in our hearts.[18]

18   The translation comes from Augustine: Later Works. Selected and Translated by John Burnaby (The Library of Christian Classics, vol. VIII), London 1955, 220–221 (sections numbered 34–36 of Latin editions). In a similar vein see section 26 (p. 215), which invokes Galatians: 'Thus it is manifest that the "oldness of the letter," if the "newness of the spirit" be lacking, rather makes men guilty by the knowledge of sin than delivers them from sin (. . .). Not that the law itself is an evil thing but that

Like Origen before him, Augustine considered that any passage of the Scriptures is susceptible of a spiritual interpretation. He does, however, propose a rule to govern the resort to spiritual senses, for he insists that wherever the letter can be understood as promoting the love of God and of the neighbour, to seek out a spiritual sense would be otiose. Inversely, wherever the letter does not overtly speak of love, a hidden meaning bearing the Christian message of love is to be discovered, in and through the letter. It was strictly on the basis of his exegesis that the *Doctor amoris* elaborated his personal views on love and its relationship to liberty, views which are epitomized in the adage *dilige et quod vis fac.* *Amor ordinatus* is free, only when it is released from the particularity of desire, fear and favour, and placed before and within the totality. Liberty, or love, loves, in short, in the way that love ought to love, in other words according to the measure of reality itself, which is not determined by human will but by the unmeasured measure of all things. We are to measure our love according to being, and so to love God without measure, since God is not measured by any other being; to love the neighbour as ourselves, since we are measured together by our creation; and to love the body and bodily creatures less than spiritual. If liberty subverts the order of being then it is no longer liberty, but the slave of something that is itself meant to be the servant of liberty. The finality of lower things is to be of use to human liberty, and the finality of human liberty is the liberating service of the neighbour and of God, or rather of the neighbour (and the self) in God; or, better still, of God in all and all in God. Love 'fulfills the whole law', because love is love only before and within the totality.

THE CONTINUITY OF PATRISTIC AND MEDIEVAL SPIRITUAL EXEGESIS

Ever since the publication, over thirty years ago, of the magisterial study of medieval biblical interpretation by Henri de Lubac, it has become a commonplace to advert to the unbroken continuity linking medieval exegesis with the Fathers.[19] This continuity prevails at the

---

it holds the good commandment in the letter that demonstrates, not in the spirit that brings aid. And if the commandment be done through fear of penalty and not through love of righteousness, it is done in the temper of servitude not freedom—and therefore it is not done at all. For there is no good fruit which does not rise from the root of charity. The man in whom is the "faith that works through love" [Gal 5.6], begins to delight in the law of God after the inward man; and that delight is a gift not of the letter but of the spirit.'

19 H. de Lubac, Exégèse médiévale. Les quatre sens de l'écriture (Théologie 41). Premiére partie, tome 1, Paris 1959; tome 2, 1959; seconde partie, tome 1, 1961; tome 2, 1964. The author points out (Introduction, 23) that the distich in which the later Middle Ages resumed the doctrine of the four senses is first found in Augustine de Dacia, a Dominican, c.1260:

Litera gesta docet, quid credas allegoria,
Moralis quid agas, quo tendas anagogia.

level of both content and method. An illustration of each kind is offered here. The first is taken from a commentary on Galatians belonging to the scholastic period and composed by the Oxford theologian, Robert Grosseteste (d. 1253).[20] Circulated not long before 1235, this work excels its contemporaries by reason of its author's mastery of Greek, which enabled him to reflect in his own composition the characteristic strengths of both Eastern and Western traditions of exegesis. He captures some of the most valuable insights of the tradition going right back to Origen, with the result that his work may be said to stand as in many respects a recapitulation of the exegesis of earlier times.

Here is the comment on Galatians 5:13 ('Serve one another in love'):

> Because they [the opponents of the Apostle] could say, 'If we are free and have been withdrawn from the yoke of slavery to the law, then we ought to serve no-one, nor should we be subjected to any yoke', the Apostle once again rejoins wisely, saying that they must *serve one another* by the *charity* of the Spirit and be subjected to the *sweet yoke* of God and the *light burden* [cf. Mt 2:30], which is charity. This, therefore, is liberty: to do what you will, with a will that is upright and in command of the flesh. Such a will wishes to do to the other what it wishes to be done by the other to itself [cf. Mt 7:12], therefore it serves freely and liberally the utility of each 'other'. This liberty, then, does not exclude but includes the servitude which is of one another, and it places on the neck the sweet yoke of the love of God and neighbour. For this liberty wishes—as is proper—to be loved by all, whence also it loves all in the way that it ought; that is to say, God more than itself, the neighbour as itself, but the body and bodily irrational creatures less than itself. Therefore this liberty does not serve the law of the flesh, it does not serve the elements of the world, it does not serve the will of the flesh; for it cannot serve these, unless by diminishing liberty and subjecting its dignity to something lower and worse that pushes and draws it down. On the other hand, it serves (without being diminished or suffering loss, rather indeed with elevation and increase of itself), the majesty of God, the special utility of the neighbour and the finality of lower things. And so, by serving thus, through charity it fulfills the whole law.

The second example of scholastic exegesis bears on method more than content. It comes from the *reportatio* of St Thomas Aquinas on Galatians 4:24 (the Abraham allegory).[21] A word of introduction may

---

20   The editio princeps, edited by the present writer, will appear under the title Roberti Grosseteste. Expositio in Epistolam ad Galatas, in the Corpus Christianorum/Continuatio Mediaevalis series (Brepols), in 1995.

21   Commentary on St Paul's Epistle to the Galatians, by St Thomas Aquinas. Trans. F. R. Larcher O.P. (Aquinas Scripture Series, vol. 1), Albany N.Y. 1965. The *reportatio*

be of help in seeing the particular relevance of this extract to the theme of the present essay.

That the vocabulary used to designate the different senses in which the Fathers claimed the Bible could be understood should have remained quite variable and fluctuating appears to have troubled those earlier writers but little.[22] Some there admittedly were (especially of the Antiochene school) who wished to confine the practice of spiritual exegesis quite strictly (and indeed to exclude the New Testament entirely from its application). But the great majority of the Fathers at once upheld the practice and yet made no attempt to codify or regulate it, not even to the extent of standardizing the terms used to designate the various tendencies to which it gave rise. Origen, for example, thought predominantly of a moral sense, corrresponding to the soul (the letter being as it were the body of Scripture), and a spiritual or mystical sense, corresponding in his anthopological understanding to the spirit of man. Ambrose speaks of the literal sense and the natural, moral and mystical (or rational) which overlay themselves upon it. Augustine, besides of course the literal, recognizes aetiological, analogical and allegorical senses. Cassian refers to senses beyond the literal in terms of tropological, allegorical and anagogical. Now, the continuity of patristic and scholastic exegetical method was in the thirteenth century to meet with a new mentality, one which was decidedly less tolerant of fluctuations in vocabulary and more insistent upon sober and consistent classification. In his comment upon the Pauline allegory (Gal 4:24) Aquinas enunciates the conclusion which in our own day has rallied the support of the majority of historians of patristic exegesis, which is to say that fundamentally two senses can be distinguished, the literal or historical, which the words of Scripture mean, and the spiritual, which is raised on the basis of the scriptural realities signified by the words. The spiritual sense may then be subdivided, Aquinas suggests, depending on whether it refers to mysteries of Christian faith (the allegorical sense), hope (the anagogical), or love (the moral). His analysis, carried out with characteristic penetration, does not of course resolve any historical questions bearing upon patristic interpretation, but it is worth noting in its own right, and it serves the important purpose of schematic clarification, even for the modern reader. It is excerpted here. After explaining the word 'allegory', he distinguishes two different kinds of meaning which give rise in turn to the two fundamental senses of the Scriptures:

---

on Galatians is the work of Reginald of Piperno, the *socius* of Aquinas for many years and right up to his death, so that its substantial fidelity may be assumed.

22   A very readable introduction to the method and content of patristic exegesis and theology is Boniface Ramsay O.P., Beginning to Read the Fathers, London 1986. Some points from his ch. 2, 'Scripture', are summarized here.

Signification is twofold: one is through words, the other through the things signified by words. Now this is the exclusive characteristic of the sacred writings, since their author is God, in whose power it lies to employ not only words to signify (which man can also do), but things as well (. . .) Consequently this science can have many senses. For the reference by which the words signify something (. . .) pertains to the literal or historical sense, whereas the reference whereby the things signified by the words further signify other things, pertains to the mystical sense.

The mystical or spiritual sense is divided into three types. First, as when the Apostle says that the Old Law is the figure of the New Law; hence, in so far as the things of the Old Law signify things of the New Law, it is the allegorical sense. Then, according to Dionysius in the book on the Heavenly Hierarchy, the New Law is a figure of future glory; accordingly, in so far as things in the New Law and in Christ signify things which are in heaven, it is the anagogical sense. Furthermore, in the New Law the things performed by the Head are examples of things we ought to do (. . .), accordingly in so far as the things which in the New Law were done in Christ (and done in things that signify Christ) are signs of things we ought to do, it is the moral sense.[23]

THE SPIRITUAL SENSE AND THE LITURGY

The late Cardinal de Lubac considered that the role of the earlier (patristic and medieval) spiritual exegesis is inclined to escape us, not because it was unimportant but because it has been completely fulfilled. This thought of his invites the following reflections.

The modern Church enjoys peaceful occupancy of the results secured by the earlier scrutiny of the sacred books. The methods employed by patristic exegesis can sometimes make us smile today, yet those methods and techniques were what the Fathers used in order to find Christ, whom they believed to be hidden throughout the Scriptures. Many nowadays experience difficulty in envisaging the situation which first made allegorical exegesis necessary. In fact de Lubac himself has helped us greatly to see that the whole notion and content of the new faith was at stake in those earliest times of Christianity when only the spiritual reading of the inherited letter offered a way forward.

For the Catholic, the most evident and striking reception of the early exegesis of Scripture is to be found in the liturgy. Throughout its history the Church has adopted and integrated into the celebration of the Eucharist the principle of the symphonic reading of the two Testaments, so that the Christian reading, explicitly of the chosen passages but

23   Ibid., 138–139 (translation adapted).

implicitly of the entire Old Testament, might be exhibited and pro-
secuted.[24] Essential elements of faith are thus manifested, such as the
central place of Christ in revelation and redemption, the paschal mystery
always at work, and the discovery of the Church as the people of the
New Covenant, the New Israel. In the liturgical setting the word of God
is an event taking its place within the history of salvation, rather than the
object of study or the occasion for private meditation. The Constitution
on the Liturgy promulgated by the Second Vatican Council, *Sacrosanc-
tum concilium*, urged in its chapter on the Eucharist (35/1) a reading of
Scripture which would be wider, more varied and better adapted than
that which had prevailed for centuries in the Sunday lectionary. The
same constitution supplied fundamental norms to govern the choice of
biblical pericopes: account was to be taken of the mystery of Christ in its
whole extent; the unity of the history of salvation and the complementar-
ity of the Old and New Testaments were to be underlined; the mysteries
of the faith and the norms of Christian life were to be proposed, and the
realization of the Old Covenant in the preaching, life and suffering of
Jesus Christ pointed to.

The construction of the Roman Breviary is in a way more pointed
still, as the General Instruction, which introduces it, endeavours to
underline.[25] A first kind of spiritual sense is acknowledged, and is so in
a way that would have satisfied Origen himself:

> Whoever sings the psalms properly, meditating as he passes from
> verse to verse, is always prepared to respond in his heart to the
> movements of that Spirit who inspired the psalmists and is present
> to devout men and women ready to accept his grace. Thus the psal-
> mody, though it commands the reverence due to the majesty of
> God, should be conducted in joy and a spirit of charity, as befits the
> freedom of the children of God, and is in harmony with divinely
> inspired poetry and song (no. 35).

The psalms, hymns of praise, help us pray by offering a literal sense of
thanksgiving and joy, or of complaint in times of distress. They possess a
musical and poetic character and are composed in a variety of literary
genres. Each psalm, we are reminded, originated in particular historical
circumstances, but despite that fact a sort of perennial value attaches to

24 On the basic principles and how they were put into practice see André Haquin, 'Le
   lectionnaire biblique des dimanches et des fêtes (1969)' in The Four Gospels.
   Festschrift Frans Neirynck. Ed. F. Van Segbroeck et al. (Bibliotheca Ephemeridum
   Theologicarum Lovaniensium C), Leuven University Press 1992, 2499–2512.
25 The Divine Office. The Liturgy of the Hours According to the Roman Rite. As
   Renewed by Decree of the Second Vatican Council and Promulgated by the
   Authority of Pope Paul VI, London/Glasgow/Sydney/Dublin 1974. 'The General
   Instruction on the Liturgy of the Hours' occupies pp. xix–xcii. Reference is made
   here by section numbers.

their literal sense, which expresses the pain and hope, the misery and the confidence of men of any age and land (no. 107).

> Whoever says the psalms in the name of the Church should pay attention to the full meaning of the psalms, especially that messianic understanding which led the Church to adopt the Psalter. The messianic meaning is made completely manifest in the New Testament; it is in fact declared by Christ our Lord himself when he said to the apostles: 'Everything written about me in the Law of Moses, in the prophets and in the psalms, has to be fulfilled' (Lk 14:44).

The authors of the introduction give un-dogmatic but firm statement to the Christological dimension of the psalms. Although some patristic interpretations were artificial and were based upon mere appropriations, the Church chose the psalms for its liturgy because, even if not every psalm bears a christological reference, the Psalter as a whole is a prophecy about Christ and his Church. This christological reading of the Psalter is underlined by the Liturgy of the Hours, which prefaces each psalm with a heading; 'a phrase [taken] from the New Testment or the Fathers is added as an invitation to pray in a Christian way' (no. 111). Besides, each psalm has its antiphon, which, among other things, 'helps considerably in the typological and festive interpreting of the psalm' (no. 113).

THE JEWISH BIBLE WITHIN THE CHRISTIAN

We have used the phrase, 'the Christian dialectic', to refer to that unity-in-difference of the two Testaments, that inseparable hermeneutical connection whereby the faith of the believer in Christ finds the New already somehow present in the Old and the Old somehow also in the New. The indispensable presence of the Jewish Bible within Christianity, as the lasting basis for the understanding of the New Covenant, is the reason for a permanent relationship to the Jewish parent, and even for a tension that in one sense is unavoidable, and that lies in the Christian claim to be the people of a covenant both 'new and lasting'. The history of exegesis carries many reminders of controversy between Christians and Jews, and examples of the hubris with which some Christians, from the patristic age up to the philosopher G.W.F. Hegel, vaunted the superiority and universality of the New over against the particularity of the Old Covenant, in ways that were bound to antagonize their opponents in debate. Christian writers on the subject do well to remind themselves of the warning issued by Augustine and repeated by Aquinas, that the Church is capable at any time of itself lapsing from the Covenant by ceasing to follow the Spirit in love. With the spectre of anti-Semitism never wholly expelled from lands that were traditionally Christian, the theological statement of what I have called the Christian dialectic always requires sensitivity with regard to Jewish feelings, if it is

to express its own meaning without resorting to caricature or reinforcing negative stereotypes.

CHRISTIAN LIBERTY

The dominant current Western view of freedom is a political one. Liberty
is regarded as a specifically modern experience, or demand, or political
ideal, the meaning of which is, negatively, the absence or removal of all
but the most minimal legal or public constraints upon the thought and
action of the individual, as citizen, economic agent, consumer, member
of associations, and so on; and, positively, certain rights, or claims, including at least those which have been validated by legislative enactment.
Christianity in general, and the Catholic Church in particular, has a firm
sense that it cannot be indifferent to the political dimension of freedom
and that a discernment must be exercised in the light of the Gospel
concerning all possible appropriate means to promote the liberty of
peoples.[26] The Church, however, brings through faith and action a light
which is its very own (though it is intended to benefit all, without exclusion), for it owes its profound sense of liberty, spiritual liberty, to no
human agency or movement or philosophy, but to its own origins as the
community of Jesus Christ. Thus the Christian sense of spiritual liberty is
inseparable from the Christian faith itself, which regards the death of
Christ as universally redemptive from sin, and his resurrection as the
overcoming of the last enemy, death itself. It is perhaps the most urgent
day-to-day challenge facing parents, catechists and pastors at the present
time, how to show by teaching, but especially by the way they live, how
rich, how full of content is this fruit of the Spirit, especially when compared with the prevailing notion that you are free provided you can do as
you please without being impeded by any authority. In some earlier part
of our lives the idea of autonomy, which in essence coincides with the
liberal conception of freedom, is attractive: to do what you like with what
you have (especially if you have a lot of it), is the freedom every adolescent imagines to be complete. The truer sense of freedom that is offered
through faith in Christ implies a free offering of ourselves (after the free
self-sacrifice of Jesus Christ), and spiritual receptiveness to all we can
receive from God, in the form of the 'love that is poured into our hearts
by the Holy Spirit who is given to us' (Rom 5:5).

---

26 Instruction on Christian Freedom and Liberation (Congregation for the
Doctrine of the Faith), Vatican City 1986.

Liturgy: The Context of Patristic Exegesis

PATRICK MC GOLDRICK

Taking the title of this paper fairly literally, I propose to speak rather about liturgy than about patristic exegesis, examining historically and in more general terms the relationship between the liturgy and Scripture. I hope that this will throw some light, direct and indirect, on the context that the liturgy provided for the patristic understanding of the Scriptures and so on the influence it exercised on this understanding.

THE RELATIONSHIP OF SCRIPTURE AND LITURGY: BEGINNINGS

The relationship between Scripture and liturgy is a rich and complex one, because both are rich and complex realities. We can find a good point from which to start in three episodes from the Gospels, three occasions on which Jesus brought word and ritual action closely together.

If the Last Supper was a paschal meal, there would have been a place for the *haggadah*, presumably spoken by Jesus. Moreover, two of the Gospel accounts attribute a discourse to Jesus: John at considerable length, and Luke more economically. The celebration of the Last Supper seemed to call for a word from Jesus that was additional to the normal prayers and to Jesus' own special ritual words.

In John 6 the discourse on the Bread of Life seems to speak both of the bread that was Jesus' word and of the bread that was his flesh. Word and sacrament, it may be hinted, belong harmoniously together.

In Luke 24 Jesus made himself known to the two disciples on the road to Emmaus in the word by which he opened the Scripture and in the breaking of bread. Would the Christian hearer not be reminded of the Eucharist?

These three texts then, involving Jesus himself, suggest an affinity between word and sacrament such that liturgical action invites the accompaniment of the word and the word somehow tends towards sacrament.

'In the beginning was the Word,' John said, not 'in the beginning was Scripture.' There is no doubt that the liturgy had an important role to play in the emergence of the Christian Scriptures. While historically this must have been a complex matter, and many fine distinctions should be made, it is enough for the purpose of this paper to refer in a broad and general way to some early connections between liturgy and Scripture.

a) From the New Testament we know that passages from the Old Testament were read in a Christian sense.[1]

b) The memory of Jesus, his actions, words, etc. and the experience of his disciples were handed on in Christian assemblies, many of them no doubt liturgical. This transmission of his memory was connected with the early Christians' own situations and own lives, and so the tradition grew. Apostolic preaching and tradition of this sort must have been important for the formation of the Scriptures.

c) The letters of Paul were read at and exchanged between Christian assemblies.[2]

Thus the emergence of the Christian liturgy and the emergence of the corpus of Scripture are closely related, so that the early Church includes the word in this form as part of its service of worship. The ritual has its word, its accompanying narrative. From the beginning the word, Scripture, is at home in the liturgical assembly and is not something extraneous or alien or additional.

A couple of sentences from a mid-second-century text of St Justin Martyr can sum up the development. He is describing the Sunday Eucharist of the assembled believers: 'The memoirs of the apostles or the writings of the prophets are read for as long as time allows. When the reader has stopped, the one presiding speaks, admonishing and inviting all to imitate such fine examples.' Prayer follows and then the eucharistic liturgy.[3]

READING OF SCRIPTURE IN THE LITURGICAL ASSEMBLY

So the Church has acquired its Scriptures, written texts, New Testament and Old Testament. How will it use these in the liturgy?

A first answer is: by reading them publicly in the assembly. It will arrange them in many different ways; different numbers of readings, different systems will eventually emerge; different rituals too. And yet there will be notable agreement about the importance of the reading, about the appropriateness of certain books and pericopes for certain seasons

---

1 See, for example, Luke 4:16–21; Acts 4:24–30; 8:26–40; 13:14–40.
2 In addition to these connections, it is sufficient to note here that the synagogue service had an important influence on the developing Christian liturgy of the word; to note also that some acclamations, hymns, prayers, greetings or other formulas from early Christian liturgy were quoted or echoed in the Scriptures; and to note finally that the regularity of the liturgical assembly, the celebration of the Eucharist, and the practice of Baptism were bound to have had some impact on the contents of the Scriptures.
3 Apol. I 67.

or occasions; about the use of the Psalms; about Gospel acclamations; about signs of reverence for the word. There will be universal acknowledgment of the place of the reading of the Scriptures in the liturgy.

This raises a further question: how have the scriptural texts functioned in the liturgy? Different roles can be distinguished. I borrow the enumeration that follows from Paul Bradshaw.[4] The functions are not mutually exclusive; the dominance of one in a particular case does not exclude others.

a) A *didactic* or catechetical function can be recognized, one that starts from the Scriptures themselves. The Scriptures are read to make people familiar with them, to deepen the understanding. This practice may have roots in the liturgy of the synagogue and there are some indications that Christian assemblies adopted early a practice of regular, sustained—you might say, systematic—reading week by week and, perhaps in some places later, day by day. The Christian people must know the most important portions of the Scriptures and so they are formed in the Christian spirit and grow in the knowledge and love of God. Indeed, how else will the great assembly become familiar with the Scripture before the age of printing or even before the mass production of bibles and the spread of literacy? Systems of readings will develop; the lectionary will emerge. A homily or address or commentary or explanation will frequently accompany the reading, required by the primarily didactic function of the reading. In this first case envisaged, the liturgy largely provides the occasion or the context of the reading; the relationship of the reading to the sacramental act that follows will be an indirect one, primarily through the internal effect that it achieves in the participants as it forms them in the Christian spirit.

b) The second function is *anamnetic* and takes its start from the liturgical rite. As an example of this Bradshaw cites the practice in the early Jerusalem cathedral office of reading the same text every Sunday morning throughout the year: the account of the passion and resurrection of Christ. Obviously the primary purpose here is not didactic but rather to recall the resurrection at just the spot where and the time when it was believed to have happened. The rite then was an anamnesis, the reading serving to recall God's great deed and to interpret the meaning of the rite and provide warrant for it. This is just one example of what went on very widely from the fourth century. Before then what we know as the liturgical year had scarcely begun to emerge, and its

---

4   P. F. Bradshaw, 'The Use of the Bible in Liturgy: Some Historical Perspectives,' in *Studia Liturgica* 22 (1992) 36–43. In another article in the same number of this journal, 'Lectionaries—Principles and Problems: A Comparative Analysis,' H. T. Allen Jr in a somewhat similar way identifies six functions of lectionaries (71–77). The greater part of this volume is given over to the papers of the Congress of Societas Liturgica held in Toronto in 1991 on Bible and Liturgy. Much of this material is of interest to our topic.

evolution will obviously be the principal influence on the expansion and the development of this way of using Scripture in the liturgy. No doubt this use will have had some Jewish roots—in connection with the Passover especially—and Christians will have had something similar in their early celebration of the paschal vigil.[5]

Where this is the primary purpose of the scriptural reading, the texts will be specially selected, that is, they will not simply follow the order of regular readings,[6] and they will be more directly related to the sacramental rite that follows them or, better, they will be more obviously part of an integral rite.

Bradshaw warns that didactic and anamnetic functions may both be present together and indeed that over time or for groups at the same time one may yield in priority to the other.

c) The third function, identified by Bradshaw as *paracletic*, starts from the worshippers. What are their needs that are to be met by appropriate Scripture reading? This is primarily a pastoral function. Readings are chosen accordingly for such occasions as funerals, votive Masses, Masses for particular needs, and so on.

d) The final function is *doxological*, to glorify God, a purpose that underlies all public reading of Scripture. The liturgical reading of the Scriptures is always the acknowledgment of the word of God, and hence a confession of God's glory. But this can be the dominant intention— readings have continued to be proclaimed in ancient languages even when these are no longer commonly understood.

In proposing this useful distinction of functions Bradshaw did not intend to confine himself to any particular time but ranged over the whole history of the Christian liturgy. However, all four functions can be recognized within the patristic period. Local and cultural influences will also have come into play, of course, in the way and the circumstances in which these functions were fulfilled and in further determination of them.

What is happening when the Scriptures are read in the liturgy? The word, frequently in origin a spoken word (the prophetic word of the Old Testament, the Gospel word preached by the apostles)—this word, written down and preserved as Scripture, is now restored to its original function and its true status as the living word of God spoken to God's people. As has been suggested earlier, the Scripture is nowhere more at home than in the liturgical assembly. It is for the reader and for the preacher to enable the word to speak today, to be a living and active

---

5   Compare the inclusion of the institution narrative in the celebration of the Eucharist.

6   In his notable work The Origins of the Liturgical Year, New York 1986, T. J. Talley proposes that on occasion the influence may have worked in the opposite direction, that it may have been the course reading of one of the Gospels that occasioned the introduction of elements of the liturgical year.

word, a sword that will apply its sharp edge, cutting into the heart of the community gathered to hear it. The Scripture then is to become word once again through the ministries of the reader and the preacher. On reading from the prophet Isaiah, Jesus said: 'Today this scripture is fulfilled in your hearing.'[7] Something of that remains the aim of the proclamation in the 'today' of the liturgy.

According to Paul De Clerck,[8] there is an act of tradition in the liturgical assembly. Through the proclamation of Scripture the word of God is *received* in faith by the participants as the living word of God; it is *assimilated* in a variety of ways by them, made their own, translated into action, done; and it is actualized by preaching. And so it is *transmitted*. It is not enough, after all, simply to have the Bible. Celebrated in faith, this is the story that gives identity to the Christian people and, in being appropriated and passed on in the liturgy, that takes within itself new assemblies and succeeding generations. Thus the history of salvation continues, the divine plan is worked out, the mystery of Christ is accomplished, God's great deeds are somehow prolonged, when the Scriptures are proclaimed in the liturgical assembly.

From all of this there emerges something of the context of patristic exegesis, something of the dynamics at work when the Fathers addressed themselves to the Scriptures and then to their hearers (or, to put the matter differently, when the Fathers were addressed by the Scriptures and then enabled the participants to be addressed by that same living word).

OTHER USES OF SCRIPTURE IN THE LITURGY

Earlier the question was asked: how does the Church use the Scriptures in the liturgy? A first answer given was: by reading them publicly in the assembly. A second answer may be given in two parts:

a) By taking over psalms and biblical canticles for use as Christian prayers and hymns in its liturgical celebrations.

This happened first with individual psalms, then with the Psalter as a whole and with some Old Testament canticles, and, more gradually, with some of the New Testament canticles. There may have been several related reasons for this and some variety in the interpretation of the fact. In the first place, before these psalms and canticles are the prayer of the Church addressed to God, they are part of the word of God spoken to the Church. Thus in the Mass, for example, the psalm was included in the liturgy of the word not simply to afford an opportunity for response to the readings; it was itself a proclamation of the word of God, as the reading from St Paul or from one of the Gospels

---

7   Lk 4:21.

8   P. De Clerck, ' "In the beginning was the Word": Presidential Address,' *Studia Liturgica* 22 (1992) 10f.

was, and it could be the subject of the homily. A second reason close to this was the fact that these psalms and canticles were viewed differently from non-scriptural compositions, having a quality all their own as part of the word of God. This gave them an authority lacking in popular hymns. It is well known that during the fourth century the Church abandoned almost completely its corpus of early non-biblical hymns because of the use of such compositions in support of heresy, notably Gnosticism and Arianism. As a result the standing of the psalms and other canticles was bound to be enhanced and their use to be increased: they were canonical and therefore trustworthy. A third important and all-pervasive factor at work was the interpretation of the psalms in the light of the mystery of Christ. This is perhaps the most decisive influence in making the Jewish psalter the prayerbook of the Christian Church, and it is too well known to need elaboration here.[9]

b) By using biblical events, phrases, images, references, language in its prayers.

This second way was made relatively easy by the fact that a common text was in use in Greek, and later in Latin, and also because by and large the Fathers shared a rich common biblical culture. The use of the Scriptures in this way varied from a shallow and fairly banal employment of a biblical word or expression, an allusion that set off no deep resonances or suggested no fresh insight, all the way to a profoundly developed and sophisticatedly exploited typology.

TYPOLOGY

Typology requires no explanation in this context. For the purpose of this paper I use the word very broadly here, much as in earlier times. The late Jean Daniélou dealt with this forty years ago in *Bible et liturgie*,[10] a book that still retains its value. Typology has its roots in the Scriptures themselves, which already read some of the events of the Old Testament in the light of Christ and find in them foreshadowings of the good things to come.

The liturgy is shot through with typology. This approach will influence the choice of Old Testament readings to accompany New Testament pericopes and the choice of texts for special occasions. But of more concern here is the way in which many of the prayers of the liturgy reflect this typological approach and develop it skilfully.

9 See B. Fischer, Die Psalmenfrömmigkeit der Martyrerkirche, Freiburg 1949, a work updated and translated several times since; L. G. Walsh, 'The Christian Prayer of the Psalms' in P. Murray O.S.B. (ed.), Studies in Pastoral Liturgy, vol.3, Dublin 1967, 29–73.

10 Paris 1951; English translation, The Bible and the Liturgy, Darton, Longman & Todd, London 1960. For a recent (positive) retrospective appraisal see G. Wainwright, ' "Bible et Liturgie": Daniélou's Work Revisited,' Studia Liturgica 22 (1992) 154–162.

A good example can be seen in the Ordination Prayers of the *Apostolic Tradition* of Hippolytus, probably written in Rome about 215.[11] The prayer for the ordination of a bishop looks back to God's appointment of leaders and priests among the Jewish people, to his provision of ministry for his sanctuary, to the choice He exercised from the beginning. Now God is asked to send upon the candidate the power of the governing Spirit given by God to Jesus Christ and given by Jesus to the Apostles, who established the Church in every place as God's sanctuary. The work of the bishop is characterized as an exercise of the high priesthood and is further described with scriptural phrases and allusions.

Likewise the prayer for the ordination of a presbyter sets the context of God's favour towards his people and appeals to the choice of elders made by Moses at God's command and filled by God with the Spirit He had given to Moses.

For the ordination of a deacon the prayer bases itself on God's sending of Jesus Christ as servant of the divine will and revealer of the divine plan. The deacon in turn is referred to as servant and as chosen for the service of the Church, and the prayer goes on to speak of his service in the sanctuary and to the offering of the appointed high priest (that is, the bishop).

The point is clear. A line is established that runs from the beginning of time through events, figures and institutions (the sanctuary, the offering, the priesthood) of the Old Testament, the event and the person of Jesus Christ, and the present life of the Church. These figures, events and institutions find their focus in Jesus Christ and they are given actuality in the liturgical rite today. What unites all of them and allows the prayer to see them in a single perspective is belief in the continuing action of God carried out in fulfilment of an unfolding salvific design that was revealed and pre-eminently realized in Jesus Christ.

A similar example is found in the ancient Roman blessing of baptismal water, the consecration of the font.[12] Here the symbol of water carries the divine gift of salvation, of life. The prayer cites the primeval waters over which the Spirit was moving (so that water conceives the power of sanctification); the flood, in which by water sin was brought to an end and virtue began; the four rivers that flow [from paradise] to water the whole world; the water that gives joy to God's city; the water given in the desert; the water of Cana changed into wine; the water in which Jesus was baptized; the water that poured from his side. The Holy Spirit is invoked to give fecundity to the water of this font in order that it

11 B. Botte, La Tradition apostolique de saint Hippolyte. Essai de reconstitution, Münster Westfalen ⁵1989, nn. 3,7,8, pp.6–11,20–23,26–27.
12 Liber Sacramentorum Romanae Aeclesiae Ordinis Anni Circuli, herausgegeben von Leo Cunibert Mohlberg OSB, Rome 1960, nn. 445–8, pp.72–4. This text remained in use virtually unchanged until it was revised after the Second Vatican Council.

may bring about all the salvific effects of Baptism (which are also developed).

Water has been God's instrument and sign of salvation from the beginning, so that events and texts of the past can be read in the light of the mystery of Christ and in turn can enable us to understand what God does now in the sacrament of Baptism. Scripture and liturgy are brought into a most harmonious relationship, since ultimately it is the same mystery that both celebrate.

A further example is provided by the ancient Roman prayer, which we still use today, for the consecration of chrism.[13] This prayer begins, as it says, 'in the beginning,' when at God's command the earth brought forth the olive tree and so the oil that provides chrism. With prophetic insight David anticipated the sacraments of God's grace in singing of the joy that the oil would bring us; at the time of the flood the olive branch carried by the dove was the sign of a future gift, announcing the restoration of peace. All of this, the prayer continues, is clearly fulfilled now in Baptism with its water and its oil. God commanded the washing and then the anointing by Moses of Aaron as priest; and chrism attained even greater honour in the baptism of Jesus and the descent of the Holy Spirit in the form of a dove upon Him. So God manifestly fulfilled David's prophecy that Christ would be anointed with the oil of gladness beyond his fellows. The prayer then asks the Father to sanctify the oil, to infuse it with the power of the Holy Spirit through Christ, from whose name chrism takes its name. By chrism God anointed priests, kings, prophets and martyrs. For those to be baptized may it be the chrism of salvation for eternal life.

The line and the continuity of this prayer are even clearer. Past events look towards the future; future fulfilment is seen and anticipated in the past. And all of this is brought to a point in this present rite and in the use of the oil in the Baptism (and in the other sacraments) for which this rite prepares.

A final and somewhat different example can be seen in some of the great eastern anaphoras (on which our Roman Eucharistic Prayer IV was modelled). There the theme of our thanksgiving is the whole sweep of history seen in the light of the economy of salvation.

Is the Eucharist merely the occasion for the use of richly-textured biblical prayers of such magnificent scope? More than that, I should think. Rather, these are prayers that proclaim a history, a design that is celebrated in the Eucharist and finds fulfilment and actuality there, in anticipation of the consummation of all things in Christ in God's kingdom.

I should like to select one point as a particular illustration. In the epiclesis of very many prayers, especially Syrian texts and those influenced

13   Ibid., nn. 386–8, p. 62.

by the Anaphora of James, the eucharistic action of the Spirit is set in the context of, and in relation to, some of the Spirit's actions recounted in Scripture, in particular his coming on Mary and being active in the Incarnation, the descent on Jesus at the Jordan, the coming on the Apostles at Pentecost. This is done in either of two ways: a) by referring explicitly to the scriptural episodes in a brief development on the Spirit at this point; b) by using of the Spirit's coming in the Eucharist such words as 'illapse,' 'descend upon,' 'rest on,' 'hover over,' 'overshadow,' 'dwell in,' 'breath on' (singly or in some combination), which are understood as allusions to the operation of the Spirit in the Scriptures.

So, for example, the Spirit who came upon Mary and formed a body for the Word is to come upon us and upon the mysteries, and by his descent is to make the bread the holy Body of Christ and what is in the cup the Blood of Christ, for the fruit of the Eucharist among the participants. Similarly, as the Spirit rested on the only-begotten Son in the form of a dove in the river Jordan and as He appeared in tongues of fire on the Apostles, so He is to dwell and to rest on us and on the offerings, and by his coming is to make the bread and the wine the Body and Blood of Christ, for the benefit of those who share in the Eucharist. The connection being established between the two sets of actions is closer than simply their common origin in the same agent, the Holy Spirit. The Eucharist can be seen as the actualization of a divine economy revealed and realized in and by Jesus Christ. In the context of the whole Eucharist the epiclesis seeks the realization by the Spirit in the Church of what was accomplished once for all in the paschal mystery of Jesus Christ. The role that the Holy Spirit played in the mysteries of Christ's earthly life, in the resurrection, and on Pentecost, He continues to play in the Eucharist and in making the Eucharist effective in the Church's life.[14]

These are some notable examples from the liturgy of both East and West, the liturgy the Fathers would have celebrated. Its vision was one they would have shared, its sacramental world one they were at ease in, and, of course, many of them composed and adapted the classic prayers of the liturgy. They preached the great mystagogies that were part of the liturgy and explained the liturgy. This typological approach then is one they will develop expertly and energetically. They will recognize a continuity and a progression that stretches from creation, from Adam and Eve and the dominant figures of Genesis through God's mighty deeds in favour of the Chosen People, through the figures of the Old Testament that in their own way pointed to and anticipated Christ, to Christ the fulfilment of the promises, and from Christ through the times of the Church to the consummation of all in the fulness of God's kingdom, in

---

14   This paragraph and the preceding one are taken largely from my article 'The Holy Spirit and the Eucharist,' ITQ 50 (1983/84) 48–66.

which the Church shares even now by anticipation. It is a magnificent vision of faith and it gives the Fathers a perspective in which to read history.[15] The overall continuity which they recognize confirms their sense of the unity in Christ of the two Testaments and of the completion of the Old in the New, a sense elegantly summed up in St Augustine's phrase, *et in vetere novum latet et in novo vetus patet*.[16] Within this they can embrace some of the great, enduring anthropological and religious realities (e.g., sacrifice, guilt, expiation, law). Such an understanding is obviously of enormous hermeneutical importance for their exegesis of the Scriptures. I am aware that some or much of this would be challenged today, but it is not the concern of this paper to deal with such contemporary questioning.[17]

CONCLUSION

The liturgy will not allow us to treat the Scriptures simply as written texts. The reading must be proclaimed by a minister so as to be heard by all present ('heard' in the biblical sense). The setting of the proclamation must be such as to heighten expectation and engage the hearers actively. Because in the final analysis it is Christ who is present and who addresses them. So too, from the beginning the liturgy has had the tradition of preaching and continues to insist on it. The word must be interpreted for and applied to *this* people, *now*.

This word contained in the Scriptures and proclaimed in the Christian assembly is made alive, given its cutting edge in the celebration of the liturgy. The sacrament actualizes it, makes it effective again and again.

Thus the liturgy will not allow us to hear the Scripture as a message from the past or as a record of events and persons long ago. The liturgy insists on bringing that history, that story, down into the present, today, the liturgical *hodie*. Neither will it permit the hearers to remain within the confines of their immediate present. As the liturgy sees it, the

---

15   The liturgy gives expression to this not only in its readings and prayers but also in icons, ritual actions, etc.

16   Quaest. in Hept. II,73 (CSEL 28/2,141); in this original context the verbs are in the present subjunctive.

17   A third answer, of less concern to this paper, can be given to the question, how does the Church use the Scriptures in the liturgy?—by developing rites from events and actions described in its Scriptures. This can range from the establishment of liturgical feasts (e.g., Christmas, Ascension, the Martyrdom of St Stephen) to such imitations and adaptations as the fast of forty days, the washing of the feet, the procession with palms, the ephphetha, some anointings. The development of the liturgy and the popular devotions of Holy Week is interesting and instructive in this regard, as is the tendency through many centuries towards an allegorical or a dramatic interpretation of the Mass with reference to Christ's passion and death. For some expansion of this see Bradshaw, art.cit. 49–52.

Scriptures proclaim a mystery, a mystery that is continuing and is ever actual, a mystery that transcends the limitations of past and present and future, of here and there. This is the mystery that the liturgy engages; every time we celebrate the Sacrament that mystery is actualized for us and we are carried into reaches that lie beyond space and time. This is the understanding that liturgy has of itself, an understanding that the Fathers shared. It must influence their exegesis.

Philo and the Fathers: The Letter and the Spirit

FEARGHUS Ó FEARGHAIL

INTRODUCTION

The profound and far reaching influence that Philo had on the patristic interpretation of biblical texts both through the method of his exegesis and the content of his work has long been noted.[1] For the patristic scholar Philo is *de rigueur*. Biblical exegetes, on the other hand, tend to keep Philo at a distance. Old Testament scholars largely ignore his work, at least for exegetical purposes,[2] while New Testament scholars tend to treat it as a source into which one dips only when the occasion demands, as, for instance, when studying the term *logos* in John's Gospel,[3] the bread of life discourse in Jn 6,[4] or the themes and imagery of Hebrews.[5]

For one schooled in the historical-critical method of biblical interpretation reading Philo is no easy task. While his basic text is that of the Pentateuch, and his characters are biblical figures such as Abraham,

1 Cf. C. Siegfried, Philo von Alexandria als Ausleger des Alten Testaments, Aalen 1970, reprint Jena 1875; P. Heinisch, Der Einfluss Philos auf die älteste Christliche Exegese (Barnabas, Justin und Clemens von Alexandria), Münster 1908; for a more recent bibliography on Philo see E. Gilbert, 'Bibliographia Philoniana 1935–1981', ANRW II, 21.1, ed. W. Hase, Berlin-New York 1984, 47–97, continuing that of H. L. Goodhart, E. R. Goodenough, The Politics of Philo Judaeus, New Haven 1938, 125–348; for patristic scholars, F. Trisoglio, 'Filone Alessandrino e l'esegesi cristiana. Contributo alla conoscenza dell'influsso esercitato da Filone nel IV secolo, specificamente in Gregorio di Nazianzo', Hase, op. cit., II, 21.1, 596 n.2; Studia Philonica begun in 1972 has valuable annotated bibliographical material; so too its successor, St Ph Annual.

2 See, for example, C. Westermann, Genesis 1–11, Neukirchen 1976; the frequent references to Philo in B. S. Childs, Exodus. A Commentary, London 1974, are due to his interest in the history of the exegesis of the text.

3 Cf. C. H. Dodd, The Interpretation of the Fourth Gospel, Cambridge 1953, 54–73, who championed Philonic influence on the Gospel of John; also T. H. Tobin, 'The Prologue of John and Hellenistic Jewish Speculation', CBQ 52 (1992) 252–269.

4 Cf. P. Borgen, Bread from Heaven. An Exegetical Study of the Concept of Manna in the Gospel of John and the Writings of Philo, Supplements to Novum Testamentum, X: Leiden 1981.

5 Cf. C. Spicq, L'Épitre aux Hébreux I, Paris 1952, 39–91; H. W. Attridge, The Epistle to the Hebrews, Philadelphia 1989, who uses Philo consistently throughout his commentary and to good effect.

Isaac, Sarah, Hagar, Joseph and Moses, his narrative is full of philosophical thoughts and ethical exhortations, and his individuals are
symbols often of varying significance. The task is not made easier by his
apparent lack of interest in the context, his seizing on a word or even
half a word in his exegesis, his over-literal approach to the text at times,
his rather arbitrary freedom at othes times, his strange etymologies, his
fascination with numbers, and, most disconcerting of all perhaps, his
pronounced tendency to ramble off in various directions at fairly regular
intervals.[6] At times one gets the impression that the ideas are coming in
a torrent and that he follows wherever they lead.[7] And there is much to
read,[8] ranging from the largely Platonic story of creation, to historical,
legislative, apologetic and philosophical works, to extensive exegetical
commentaries on Genesis. In the latter especially—an ambitious verse
by verse commentary on texts from Gen 2:1–41:24 in twenty four
treatises—allegorical exegesis abounds.

The aspect of Philonic exegesis that is of most interest to patristic
scholars is his allegorizing. This method which greatly influenced a number of patristic writers, originated in the context of a canonized or
authoritative tradition in which interpreters felt obliged to provide
acceptable interpretations for offensive passages of the text in order to
retain them. Homer's anthropomorphic descriptions of gods and their
licentious behaviour were made palatable for a later more enlightened
audience through the medium of allegory. The original text was perceived to say things other than it seemed to say,[9] to contain a deeper
meaning not visible on the surface.[10] The method was developed especially by the Stoics who raised it into 'a rather full-fledged, common
interpretive device'.[11] Allegorical interpretation was also known in Rabbinic Judaism. But while Philo and Rabbinic Judaism have traditions in

6 He is described as an 'inveterate rambler' by F. H. Colson, Philo I, LCL, x, who
   gives the example of Philo's exegesis of Gen 3:14 in Leg. all. III 161–181.
7 In De migr. 35 he describes the ideas falling in a shower from above and being sown
   invisibly, so that under the influence of the divine possession, he has been 'filled with
   corybantic frenzy and been unconscious of anything, place, persons present, myself,
   words spoken, lines written'; tr. Colson; S. Sandmel, Philo of Alexandria. An
   Introduction, New York-Oxford 1979, 78–9, speaks of a 'stream of consciousness'.
8 What survives in Greek represents just over half of what he is known to have
   written. For a description and classification of Philo's writings see S. Sandmel,
   'Philo Judaeus: An Introduction to the Man, his Writings, and his Significance',
   Hase, op. cit., 6–13; P. Borgen, 'Philo of Alexandria', Jewish Writings of the
   Second Temple Period, CRJNT II.2, ed. M. E. Stone, Assen 1984, 233–252.
9 Cf. Heraclitus, Homeric Questions 5.2; Sandmel, op. cit., 17.
10 The basic meaning of *allêgoreô*, first found in Philo, is 'to say another thing', 'to
    say something else': *allo agoreuô*; it is found also in Josephus and Paul; cf. Gal
    4:24; the noun occurs in Cic., Or. 94.
11 Sandmel, op. cit., 13; cf. R. M. Grant, The Letter and the Spirit, New York 1957, 6–8.

common,[12] and while some argue in favour of a greater Jewish influence,[13] it seems generally accepted that Philo is indebted to Hellenistic allegorizing and particularly that of the Stoics. In Dillon's view, Philo makes a very creative use of the Stoic method.[14] The literal meaning of the text also has importance for Philo, and in the context of this volume it seemed appropriate to look at Philo's attitude towards the allegorical and literal interpretation of the text, and its influence on the Fathers. Before doing that let us look briefly at some aspects of the context from which he came.

PHILO AND HIS BACKGROUND

The great cultural and philosophical centre of Alexandria, of which Philo was a native son, already had a well-established religious-philosophical literary tradition in his day.[15] For quite some time Greek-speaking Jews among the substantial Jewish population of the city had sought to bridge the gap between their Jewish faith and their Hellenistic culture, and many were thoroughly hellenized.[16]

The third century B.C. had seen the production of the LXX under Ptolemy II Philadelphus (222–204), and the version was accorded an enormous importance in Alexandria, so much so that an elaborate story about its miraculous translation was in circulation and a festival celebrated this event. The following century saw the tragedian Ezekiel's dramatic poem on the Exodus,[17] the work of the learned Hellenistic-Jewish philosopher Aristobulus, providing perhaps the earliest form of Alexandrian allegorical exegesis, and the so-called *Letter of Aristeas*,

12   Cf. Borgen, op. cit., 125–126; H. A. Wolfson, Philo. Foundations of Religious Philosophy in Judaism, Christianity and Islam, Cambridge Mass. 1968, favours Jewish influence but his Rabbinic citations are often problematic given the difficulty of dating the material.

13   See the comments of B. L. Mack, 'Philo Judaeus and Exegetical Traditions in Alexandria', Hase, op. cit., 250–257.

14   J. Dillon, The Middle Platonists 80 BC to AD 220, Ithaca 1977, 142; cf. G. Reale, R. Radice, Filone di Alessandria. La Filosofia Mosaica, Milan 1987, XXXIII.

15   Born sometime between 20 and 10 BC, of a wealthy and well—connected family, as is clear from Jos., Ant. XX 100, he died possibly about AD 45–50. The only secure dates are 39/40 when he went to Rome as head of a delegation to the emperor and AD 41 when he wrote an account of it in his Embassy to Gaius; in this he describes himself as an old man—*hêmeis hoi gerontes*.

16   Philo appears as a spokesman for those Jews in Alexandria who sought full civil rights, rather than for those happy with their 'intermediate' status, but he was not keen on 'untimely frankness'; cf. De somn. II 83; he was a pacifist with an optimistic long term view; cf. De Mos. II 44.

17   See Eusebius, Praep. ev. IX 29.8a.

probably written in his name, also containing allegorical elements.[18] The
Book of Wisdom with which Philo shares important themes appeared
before the end of the first century.[19]

Philo's education in this 'spiritual centre of the Hellenistic world'[20]
was that of a privileged Hellenistic Jew. He speaks affectionately in his
treatise on the Preliminary Studies of the 'lower instruction' (*hê mesê
paideia*) he received through the 'encyclia'.[21] He probably received tui-
tion from Greek and Egyptian tutors, just as he imagines Moses to
have received (*De Mos.* I 21–24),[22] and he read Greek authors such as
Homer, Euripides and Plato.[23] He was by all accounts a very willing
student, devoted to his books (cf. *De spec. leg.* III 1–6; *Leg. alleg.* II 85;
De fug. 49), but he also enjoyed banquets (*Leg. all.* III 156) and the
theatre (*De prov.* 141) and had an avid interest in sport (*Quod omnis
probus* 26).[24] When he became involved in public life at some stage he
still found time for his studies (*De spec. leg.* III 4–6; cf. *Leg. all.* II 85).
His writings show how much he was influenced by Platonism, Stoicism
(he wrote a treatise on a Stoic proverb: 'every good man is free'), and
Pythagoreanism with its fascination for numbers. He acquired an
extremely good knowledge of the Pentateuch which to all intents and
purposes was his text.[25] For him the Greek version represented a
divinely inspired translation (*De Mos.* II 36–37) which captured the
spirit of Moses, revealing his law to humankind in the garment of the

---

18   M. Hengel, Judaism and Hellenism I, tr. by J. Bowden, London 1974, 69, refers
     to historical romancers of the second century such as Artapanus and Cleodemus
     Malchus, poets such as the elder Philo and the Samaritan Theodotus who dealt
     with historical themes, and the author of the earliest Jewish Sibyllines.
19   Cf. D. Winston, The Wisdom of Solomon, Anchor Bible 43: Garden City 1979, 59–63.
20   Hengel, op. cit., 69.
21   Cf. De congr. 14, 20, etc.; De Mut. 255; see the discussion concerning the 'encyclia'
     in Borgen, op. cit., 116-117 that well-to-do Jews would have been educated at the
     gymnasium may be suggested by De spec. leg. II 230; cf. Hengel, op. cit., 68.
22   D. T. Runia, Philo of Alexandria and the Timaeus of Philo I, Leiden 1986, 35.
23   Dillon, op. cit., 140, holds that Philo used Plato at first hand.
24   Cf. E. Schürer, The History of the Jewish People in the Age of Jesus Christ (175 BC–
     AD 135) III, 2, eds. G. Vermes, F. Miller, M. Goodman, Edinburgh 1987, new edition,
     819 n.27.
25   By comparison there are rare enough references to historical books, Psalms, Pro-
     verbs, Job and the Prophets, the ratio being six to sixty-five pages of the Loeb index,
     though these, too, were holy books for him. The suggestion of I. Heinemann,
     Philons griechische und jüdische Bildung, Breslau 1932, 527 n.4, that Philo's use of
     the Bible reflects synagogal practice in Alexandria is given a favourable hearing by
     Y. Amir, 'Authority and Interpretation of Scripture in the Writings of Philo', Mikra.
     Text, Translation, Reading and Interpretation of the Hebrew Bible in Ancient
     Judaism and Early Christianity, CRJNT II.1, eds. M.J. Mulder, H. Sysling, Assen-
     Maastricht 1990, 422–423.

Greek language (*De Mos.* II 26–44), and differing in no way from the Hebrew original (*De Mos.* II 39–40).[26]

ALEXANDRIAN PREDECESSORS OF PHILO

As is well known, Philo was not the first to interpret Scripture allegorically in an Alexandrian milieu. The mid-second century Aristobulus, who was 'saturated with Greek culture',[27] had recourse to allegory to resolve the problem of anthropomorphisms. He exhorts his readers not to fall into the mythical and human way of thinking about God (2,2). Moses, he wrote, used words relating to outward appearances in order to express something about the arrangements of nature and the constitutions of great matters (Frag. 2,3). He refers to the 'elevated meaning' of the text which escapes those who are devoted to the letter alone. In the case of the 'hand of God' (Ex 13:9) and the descent of God on Sinai (cf. Frag. 2,9–12), the 'elevated meaning' does not go much beyond the Targumic interpretation. But his interpretation of the 'standing' of God of Ex 17:6 does move him appreciably closer to Philo who also treats this text.[28] In the fragments that have survived something of Aristobulus' approach to the literal meaning of the text may be seen. God's descent on Sinai when giving the law and the accompanying phenomena are accepted, though his main interest is in their significance (2,17); likewise in the case of the six-day account of creation with its seventh day of rest (5,11ff.).

The *Letter of Aristeas* (*c.*150 BC–100 BC) provides an example of a more sustained use of allegory. From ritual laws concerning food and drink and unclean animals (148–171) he draws ethical lessons, teaching that one should act righteously and not achieve things by brute force nor lord it over others.[29] But in the allegorizing of these laws, the letter is not

---

26   He had not compared the texts—most likely he could not; cf. M. Hadas, Hellenistic Culture. Fusion and Diffusion, New York 1972, 35; Rabbinic literature pointed out differences between the original and the Greek version; see, for example Megillah 9a, Seder Mo'ed, Babylonian Talmud IV, Soncino ed., London 1938.

27   Cf. A.Y. Collins, 'Aristobulus', The Old Testament Pseudepigrapha II, ed. J. H. Charlesworth, London 1985, 831–834.

28   De somn. I 157–158; II 211–212. Collins, op. cit., 835, comments apropos of Frag. 2,9–12 and 4,3 that the variation in vocabulary and the tentative non-technical character of the method show that Aristobulus represents an early stage in the development both of the allegorical method and of theological reflection on the *Logos*; cf. Hadas, op. cit., 102: 'not full-blown allegorical interpretation such as Philo was later to use'; R. P. C. Hanson, Allegory and Event. A Study of the Sources and Significance of Origen's Interpretation of Scripture, London 1959, 43, describes him as 'trembling on the verge of allegory'.

29   Deduced from the laws forbidding the eating of wild and carnivorous animals and those that dominate by their strength who find food at the expense of the domesticated animals, and prey on others such as pigeons and turtledoves; cf. 143.

emptied of its literal force;[30] for these strict observances 'connected with food and drink and touch and hearing and sight' (142) provide protection for the people, surrounding them with 'unbroken palisades and iron walls' to prevent them mixing with others, to keep them pure in body and soul (139).

The Book of Wisdom has symbolic interpretations, though not the thoroughgoing allegory of Philo.[31] Lot's wife, for instance, is a symbol of the untrusting soul (10:7), the bronze serpent, of salvation (16:5–7), gathering the Manna, a pointer to prayer at dawn (16:28), Egyptian darkness, the equivalent of Hell (17:21). The cosmic interpretation of the priest's robe, albeit in fleeting allusion, is reminiscent of Philo's later treatment of the theme (cf. *De Mos.* II 117–135; *De spec. leg.* I 84–97).

Philo himself indicates the existence of various traditions of allegorical biblical exegesis.[32] The Therapeutai, an ascetic group that lived near Alexandria, practised allegorical interpretation, taking the literal text to contain a deeper underlying meaning (*De vita contempl.* 28).[33] For them the whole Law Book resembled a living creature with the literal ordinances for the body (*sôma*) and its soul (*psuchê*) the invisible mind laid up in its wording (78). Philo refers briefly to the allegorical method of the Essenes, a group he places in Palestinian Syria (*Quod omnis probus* 75, 82). Elsewhere he refers to those who are accustomed to turn literal facts into allegory (*De spec. leg.* II 147; cf. *De Abr.* 200), to allegorical interpretations so dear to the *physikoi* (*De post.* 7),[34] to 'inspired men' who take the contents of the Law Book as outward symbols of hidden truths (*De spec. leg.* III 178). There is mention, too, of 'laws of allegory' (*De spec. leg.* I 287; *De somn.* I 73, 102; *De Abr.* 68).[35] He cites allegorical interpretations which he makes his own (*Quaest. Gen.* I 10) or regards as possible (*Heres* 280). He may include an interpretation without comment (*De Jos.* 125–156), add a

30   Thus Hanson, op. cit., 43; V. Tcherikover, 'The Ideology of the Letter of Aristeas', in *Studies in the Septuagint: Origins, Recensions, and Interpretation. Selected Essays with a Prolegomenon*, ed. S. Jellicoe, New York 1974, 195.

31   Winston, op. cit., 62.

32   See the list of Philo's references to other allegorists in D. Hay, 'Philo's References to other Allegorists', St Ph 6 (1979–80) 42–43.

33   The exposition of the sacred writings at the Sabbath gatherings treated the inner meaning conveyed in allegory ; cf. De vita contempl. 77–78.

34   There is much debate as to whether this term refers to allegorists in general or to Stoic-minded philosophers of nature; see the conflicting views of Hay, op. cit., 46–47, 67–69, and particularly 67 n.37, and J. Pépin, 'Remarques sur la théorie de l'exégèse allégorique chez Philon', Philon d'Alexandrie. Colloquium, Lyon 11–15 Septembre 1966, eds. R. Arnaldez, C. Mondésert, Paris 1967, 131–132; it is possible that *physikoi* has more than a general sense, even if *physikos* exegesis does not.

35   See the references in Siegfried, op. cit., 165, and Heinisch, op. cit., 69–70.

critical note (*De cher.* 25), make some modification (*Heres* 281–283; *De spec. leg.* II 178–180), or reject it altogether (*Quaest. Gen..* I 10; *Leg. all.* I 59).

Some allegorical interpretations cited by Philo may reflect his efforts to enliven and clarify his argument while at the same time attacking those with whom he disagrees—an element of setting up of straw men to shoot them down.[36] But many interpretations suggest the existence of a living, oral tradition of allegorizing. Philo's references to explanations that he himself has heard (*De Abr.* 99; *De spec. leg.* III 178; cf. *De Jos.* 151) point in this direction. So too do the many references to allegorists that present them as contemporaries (note the frequent use of the present tense to express their activity). It is very doubtful if Philo had at his disposal written traditions of allegorical interpretation of the Old Testament comparable to his own writings.[37] References such as those of *De vita contempl.* 29, *Quod omnis probus* 82 or *De spec. leg.* I 8 are less than conclusive.[38] And he himself, as Hay has noted, never directly admits to reliance on written sources.[39]

One possible context for an oral tradition of allegorical interpretation may be found in the exegetical activity pursued in Alexandria and not just in the synagogue homily. On the Sabbath, in particular, and any day when the opportunity arose (*De Mos.* II 215), the Jews occupied themselves with the philosophy of their fathers, dedicating that time to the acquiring of knowledge and the study of truths of nature (*De Mos.* II 211). The ruler expounded the Scriptures and instructed the people in what they should say and do for their edification and betterment in moral principle and conduct (215). Philo's description of their 'places of prayer throughout the cities' as 'schools of prudence and courage and temperance and justice and piety, holiness and every virtue by which duties to God and men are discerned and rightly performed' (211,

36 J. Dillon, 'The Formal Structure of Philo's Allegorical Exegesis', in *Two Treatises of Philo of Alexandria. A Commentary on De gigantibus and Quod Deus sit immutabilis*, eds. D. Winston, J. Dillon, BJS 25: Chico 1983, 84—'a way of attacking the Stoics'; for a somewhat different view see Hay, op. cit., 43 and 63 n.5.

37 See the comments of Hay, op. cit., 43–45, 52, 58–61; also T. H. Tobin, *The Creation of Man: Philo and the History of Interpretation*, CBQMS: Washington 1983, 4–6; Runia, op. cit., 16–17; Reale, Radice, op. cit., XLII n.33.

38 Cited by Hay, op. cit., 65 n.20; the reference to the Therapeutai using 'writings of men of old'—*suggrammata palaiôn andrôn*—who left many memorials of the idea or form used in allegorical interpretations—*tês en tois allêgoroumenois ideais*—is less than clear and may refer more to method than content; *Quod omnis probus* 82 only mentions the tradition of the past, while the four—part explanation of circumcision found in *De spec. leg.* I 8 occurs also in *Quaest. Gen.* III 48 where Philo indicates explicitly that he is leaving it to pass to an allegorical explanation.

39 Hay, op.cit., 65 n.20.

215–16) points to a living oral tradition of interpretation with a purpose to which Philo could readily subscribe. One could imagine interpreters associated with the synagogue being divided into literalists and allegorists or having other hermeneutical preferences in a vibrant interpretive tradition with conflicting views being expressed in ongoing debate. Such a lively context could provide the background for some of Philo's remarks about allegorists including those whose interpretations he rejects.

PHILO: THE LETTER

Turning now to Philo's treatment of the text, let us look first at his attitude towards the literal text. In the main Philo takes seriously the historicity of the biblical narrative. This is evident, for instance, in his treatment of the destruction of Sodom (*De Abr.* 137–141), the flood (*De Mos.* II 60–65), Abraham's separation from Lot (*De Abr.* 212–216), the divine visitation to Abraham (*De Abr.* 118ff), and so on. That Abraham's triple vision is a single vision is clear, he believes, not merely from the laws of allegory but from the literal text (131–147). He describes the ten plagues in detail and many other events from the lives of the patriarchs from which he draws lessons for the reader's edification. His respect for the literal text is particularly evident in his *Quaestiones.*[40]

His respect for the 'letter' is evident also from his advocacy of the literal observance of laws even if he allegorizes them. His treatment of the laws of the Sabbath and circumcision in *De migr.* 91–93 is worth noting. Just because the seventh day is meant to teach 'the power of the unoriginate and the non-action of created beings' does not mean that the laws laid down for its observation are abrogated. It is true, he observes, that receiving circumcision does indeed portray the excision of pleasure and all passions, and the putting away of impious conceit, but that does not mean that the law should be repealed. If one were to pay heed to nothing except what is shown by the inner meaning of things (*hyponoion*), one would be 'ignoring the sanctity of the Temple and a thousand other things'.

Philo compares these 'outward observances' to the body, and their inner meanings to the soul. As one has to take thought for the body because it is the abode of the soul, so one must pay heed to the letter of the laws (*tôn rhêtôn nomôn*). Keeping the former gives one a clearer perception of those things of which they are symbols and avoids

---

40 Cf. Pépin, op. cit., 140–41; Borgen, op. cit., 127–28; Mack, op. cit., 261–262; the oft-quoted reference to Samuel in De ebr. 143–144 should be weighed against Philo's attitude in general, and in any case hardly intends to raise a doubt about Samuel's existence; cf. De somn. I 254; Quod Deus 5–6, 11.

censure. In *De migr.* 89 Philo criticizes those who treat the laws in their literal sense with 'easygoing neglect'. A similar respect for the literal sense is to be found in his treatment of the flood in *De Mos.* II 60–65. Those who find fault with the literal sense are criticized in *De plant.* 70. What was needed was balance—careful attention to both.

On occasion Philo even declares his admiration for the literal narrative. In *De somn.* I 120 his admiration is aroused not only by the lawgiver's allegorical and philosophical teaching, but by the way in which the literal narrative inculcates the practice of toil and endurance. The same is true both of the literal statement and the symbolic interpretation of the giving of names in Genesis; in *Leg. all.* II 14 he specifies that what he admires in the former is its ascription to the first man of the fixing of names. The literal sense of the law of Lev 10:8–10 is also deserving of admiration, it being sensible that men should come to prayer and holy services sober and with full control of themselves (*De ebr.* 130).

There are instances where Philo follows a literal exposition with an allegorical one, or vice versa, without commenting on their relative merits (cf. *De Abr.* 88, 119, 131–32, 217; *De Jos.* 125; *De spec. leg.* II 146–7). This is not infrequently the case in his *Quaestiones*. In his discussion of circumcision and the Sabbath (*De migr.* 89ff.), he remarks that careful attention ought to be given to both. Following his allegorical interpretation of Gen 11:7 and his account of the confusion of tongues in the tower of Babel episode, he admits that those who follow the outward and obvious may also have the truth (*De conf.* 189–90). In *De sobr.* 65 he speaks of the literal story seeming to agree with an interpretation he has just given of Noah's prayer for Japhet in Gen 9:27 (cf. *De sobr.* 59, 62).[41] His remark on the giving of names (*Leg. all.* II 14) has been noted above.

But Philo's admiration for the literal interpretation had its limits. In a number of texts he expresses the view that the literal interpretation is for those who are unable to see the underlying deeper meaning or bear the full truth. Speaking of God anthropomorphically is necessary for those who lack wisdom, those impossible to instruct otherwise, the 'duller folk' (*De somn.* I 234–37).[42] It is for those whose 'natural wit is more dense and dull, or whose early training has been mishandled', those without the power of 'clear vision', needing 'physicians in the shape of admonishers' —all such people may well learn the untruth which will benefit them, he

---

41 Cf. De agric. 157; De spec. leg. II 29, De conf. 189–90; Philo's work is 'double-tracked' ; cf. Amir, op. cit., 444.

42 In Quaest. Gen. IV 168, he describes those who dwell only on the literal as 'untrained, untaught, blinded in soul'.

asserts, if they cannot be brought to wisdom by truth (*Quod Deus* 64).[43] Those who do not love God as pure should fear Him as one who threatens and punishes (69).[44] Earlier in the treatise he had discussed at length the problematic reference to God's anger in Gen 6:7 ('I will blot out man whom I have made from the face of the earth ... because I was wroth in that I made him') and concluded that the lawgiver used such expressions for the training and admonishment (*paideia kai nouthesia*) of those who would not otherwise be brought to their senses (*Quod Deus* 52–54).[45]

PHILO: THE SPIRIT

While the literal interpretation of the sacred text has its own function and importance for Philo, the allegorical interpretation is given more weight. This may be seen in his *Quaestiones* where much more space is given to the allegorical explanation. In *De conf.* 190 he urges the reader not to halt at the literal meaning but to press on to allegorical interpretation and to recognize that the letter is to the oracle as the shadow to the substance. For Philo there is a truth hidden in the text that needs to be expounded. Allegory enables him to draw out this truth.[46]

This deeper, underlying truth is for the generously gifted natures who have truth for their fellow-traveller, those who can contemplate facts stripped of the body and in naked reality (*De Abr.* 236), those who prefer the mental to the sensible and have the power to see it (*De Abr.* 200), those who find 'a moral most pertinent' in the oracles of revelation. It is for those of higher thought and feeling, not those 'of narrow citizenship' (*De somn.* I 39). It is for the few rather than the many.[47] If he should

43   He does accept that those who were 'blind in their understanding' could grow keen-sighted, receiving from the most sacred oracles the gift of eyesight, enabling them to judge the real nature of things and not merely rely on the literal sense; cf. De somn. I 164.

44   The literal meaning of the passage concerning Esau in Gen 25:29f. contains 'a not insignificant reproof of the intemperate man for the admonition of those who can be cured'; cf. Quaest. Gen. IV 168.

45   See the comments of Dillon, op. cit., 303; the problem of reconciling the statements that God is not as a man of Num 23:19 and that like a man he disciplines his son of Dt 8:5 is negotiated by taking the second to be for the instruction of the many; cf. Quod Deus 54; also De somn. I 231–37; Quaest. Gen. II 54.

46   See his description of the practice of the Therapeutai in De vita contempl. 78—unfolding and removing the symbolic coverings... looking through the words as through a mirror . . . enabling one to discern the inward and hidden through the outward and visible.

47   Although in the case of the prescription concerning the garment taken in pledge, mentioned in De somn. I 101, Philo feels that the peculiarities of the wording might lead even the slow-witted to perceive something other than the literal meaning of the passage.

neglect it, Philo beseeches the Sacred Guide to be his prompter, presiding over his steps, anointing his eyes, conducting him to the hidden light of sacred words (*De somn.* I 164). For him, most, if not all, of the 'Law Book' may be allegorized.[48]

Inherent contradictions also require allegorization—a cup of unmixed wine full of mixture (Ps 84:8: *Quod Deus* 77), Hannah's seven sons when she had only one (*Quod Deus* 10–11), Abraham, father of Jacob when he was his grandfather (*De somn.* I 166), or seeing the place from afar—when he was already there (*De post.* 17–20), the Psalmist's reference (46[45]:4) to the river that makes glad the city of God when there is no river there (*De somn.* II 246), Canaan being charged with misdeeds and cursed in Gen 9:25 although he has done no wrong (*De sobr.* 30–34, 44–48).[49]

Philo's all embracing theory of inspiration of the sacred text, a text he considered to be a perfect revelation of divine wisdom, leads him to find indications of an underlying meaning in a wide variety of circumstances.[50] Texts that literally ascribe human characteristics or actions to God or otherwise imply a false assumption about Him, must have an allegorical sense. God does not have human form or parts (*De post.* 1–4, 7).[51] He is not susceptible to passions (*Quod Deus* 52, 59), does not ask questions (*Quod det.* 57),[52] need nourishment (*De plant.* 45), walk (*Quod Deus* 57) or plant a garden (*Leg. all.* I 43).[53] He—the 'infinitely great God'—is not concerned with such a trifling matter as a garment taken in pledge (Ex 22:26–27: *De somn.* I 92–101).[54] He cannot be in thick darkness (*De post.* 14), nor can one hide oneself from Him, since He fills and penetrates all

---

48 Cf. De Jos. 28: *schedon gar ta panta ê ta pleista tês nomothesias allêgoreitai*; also De spec. leg. II 29.

49 He expounds in full the inner interpretation 'in obedience to the suggestions of right reason'; according to Leg. all. II 62, Canaan's fault is that he reported the incident. Equally impossible is that the creation of the world was completed on the sixth day, time being more recent than the world—cf. Leg. all. I 2—or that woman could have been created from the side of man; cf. Gen 2:21; Leg. all. II 19.

50 Cf. Siegfried, op. cit., 168–97; Heinisch, op. cit., 69–125; on the problems of the literal sense of Gen 39:1ff. see De spec. leg. III 236; also De post. 7; De Abr. 99.

51 See also Leg. all. I 43–44; Quod Deus 58.

52 'Literally', he adds, 'such expressions cannot be used for the cause of the first cause'; cf. 58.

53 'Far be it from man's reasoning to be the victim of so great impiety as to suppose that God tills the soil and plants pleasances'—in reference to Gen 2:8; cf. Quod Deus 56.

54 Philo, showing as little understanding of the purpose of the law—to protect the poor and avoid their exploitation—as he does compassion for the poor, feels that the peculiarities of the wording might lead even the slow-witted to perceive something other than the literal meaning of the passage; for his lengthy allegorical treatment of the Law see De somn. I 102–14.

things (*Leg. all.* III 4).[55] Texts which affirm such things literally must be interpreted allegorically (cf. *De plant.* 36).

Philo allegorizes where he considers the literal sense unworthy of the writer as in the lengthy treatment of well-digging in Gen 26:13–22[56] or the description of warfare in Dt 20:5–7;[57] likewise when he perceives the text to be unreasonable as in the case of the law of Num 35:28 governing the length of time to be spent by fugitives in the cities of refuge[58] or Cain, un-aided, building a city for one person.[59] The latter text is also at variance with truth or reality (cf. *De post.* 51), a criterion Philo uses for his allegorical interpretation of Lev 19:23.[60] Philo allegorizes in cases where he perceives the text to be improbable or most unlikely, as in the case of Joseph being sent on an errand by his father when there were any of three hundred servants there to be sent (*Quod det.* 46—evidence of a gentle upbringing perhaps!), the rather mystifying lament of the children of Israel at the death of Pharaoh (*Quod det.* 94–95), the existence of a tree of life when no such trees had appeared on earth nor were likely to (*De opific.* 156). When he can find no reason for treating the camel as unclean (Lev 11:4), he assumes the text must have a deeper meaning (*De agric.* 131).

Scriptural statements that cannot be accepted without allegorization represent only one aspect of Philo's allegorizing and the number of 'unacceptable' texts does not appear to be as high as is often implied. In most cases his exegesis offers an additional underlying sense for the reader.[61] Allegorical meanings are extracted from persons, names, rivers, animals, numbers, syllables and letters.[62] There are examples of allegory being prompted by etymological considerations, the doubling of a word or the use of a superfluous word (cf. *De gig.* 32–34; *De fuga* 54),[63]

---

55   See also Leg. all. III 51.

56   Cf. De somn. I 39.

57   Cf. De agric. 148–58—he concludes that Moses must have had spiritual warfare in mind.

58   Cf. De fuga 106–7; its linkage to the death of the High Priest presents great difficulty for him since it could be so patently unjust.

59   Cf. De post. 49–51.

60   Cleansing the trees makes good sense, he writes, being in accordance with the facts, not so cleansing fruit which is 'out of keeping with the facts', since no gardener cleanses fruit, and must therefore be interpreted allegorically; cf. De plant. 112.

61   Dodd, op. cit., 54, comments that 'we should not think of the allegorical interpretation of Scripture as a mere accommodation for the sake of propaganda. It was for him the true interpretation of the Old Testament, guaranteed as such, not only by its rationality, but also by his own religious experience'.

62   On this and the following remarks see Siegfried, op. cit., 68–196; Heinisch, op. cit., 69–112. The doubling of 'man' in Gen 18:6 LXX, cited in De gig. 32–34, is not in the Hebrew text.

63   As happens in the case of Ex 21:13 where the LXX provides a literal translation of the Hebrew infinitive absolute; cf. H. St. J. Thackeray, A Grammar of the Old Testament in Greek I, Cambridge 1909, 47–50.

the self-evident statement (cf. *Leg. all.* II 89) or the perceived omission (*De somn.* II 300–301). The particular word chosen, the use of singular or plural, of simple or compound, the variation of expression, the presence or absence of the article, the cases used—all are of interest. In short everything about a text carries significance for him. He also permits himself the liberty of altering accents, breathings, punctuation and grammar in the service of allegory.[64]

Philo's reading of the text sometimes causes him difficulty and leads to allegorization, as in Ex 2:23 where he takes the phrase *kai katestenaxan hoi huioi Israêl* with the preceeding *eteleutêsen ho basileus Aiguptou* rather than with the following *apo tôn ergôn* (*Quod det.* 94–5), or in Lev 19:23–25 where he lands himself unnecessarily with the problem of the cleansing of fruit and can only resolve it by allegory.[65]

PHILONIC INFLUENCE

Philonic influence on the New Testament has often been claimed, notably in relation to John's Gospel and the Epistle to the Hebrews.[66] Attention has also been focused on Pauline texts such as 1 Cor 10:1–5 and 15:45–47, Col 1:15–20 and the Letter of James.[67] But establishing dependence is exceedingly difficult, and in any case it seems more likely that the NT writers and Philo were drawing on a common body of tradition.[68]

The Epistle of Barnabas, written probably in Alexandria, uses interpretive methods reminiscent of Philo[69] in addition to typology[70] and gematria, a method of numeral exegesis.[71] The symbolic meanings attributed in

---

64 His manuscripts would not have had word divisions, accents, breathings or punctuation; cf. Heinisch, op. cit., 90; E. Würthwein, The Text of the Old Testament. An Introduction to the Biblia Hebraica, tr. from 4th ed. by E. F. Rhodes, Edinburgh 1979, 70 .

65 See n. 59 above.

66 See nn.3–5 above.

67 Cf. G. D. Fee, The First Epistle to the Corinthians, Grand Rapids 1987, 448–449, 791; J. Gnilka, Der Kolosserbrief, Freiburg 1980, 62, 75; Mayor, op. cit., cxxi–cxxiv.

68 Borgen's study of Jn 6 and the 'bread of life' discourse led him to conclude that John and Philo both used Jewish traditions but with very different methodologies and with different results; see also Attridge, op. cit., 127, who thinks in terms of dipping into a common tradition.

69 Cf. Siegfried, op. cit., 330–332.

70 Popular among the early Fathers who, with the aid of a Christological hermeneutic, found types throughout the OT often in a rather forced fashion; see, for instance, in chs. XI–XII the types of Baptism and the Cross detected in OT references to water, wood and trees; cf. J. Daniélou, Sacramentum Futuri, Paris 1947, for various typologies used by the early Christian writers who were cautious about allegory.

71 Applied to Gen 17:23, it takes the 318 slaves of Abraham's household to symbolize Jesus on the cross, the eighteen computed from I, ten, and H, eight, representing Jesus, the three hundred, T, the cross.

Ch.X to the food laws of Lev 11 recalls *Aristeas* 143–148.[72] His interpretation of the injunction of Dt 14:6 ('Eat of every animal that is cloven
footed and ruminant') recalls the interpretation of the same text found
in *Aristeas* (150–157) and Philo (*De spec. leg.* IV 106; *De agric.* 131–145).
Like Philo he allegorizes the text where he perceives the literal sense to be
impossible, as in the case of Is 28:16.[73] In a remark somewhat reminiscent
of Philo's reference to the literal being for the dull-witted, Barnabas states
that Moses' teaching was intended in a spiritual sense but was received as
really referring to food, owing to the lust of the flesh (X 9).[74] The
complete spiritualization of the rule of circumcision differs from the
approaches of *Aristeas* and Philo, but then for both of these the rule was
still of vital importance, whereas for the Christian Barnabas it had lost its
literal *raison d'être.* For him it could only be circumcision of the heart (IX).

CLEMENT OF ALEXANDRIA

The first Christian to use Philo extensively was the Athenian-born Clement of Alexandria. A deeply religious, erudite man, he was well read in
the writings of the Greek philosophers and especially Plato whom he
frequently cites.[75] He had access to the work of Aristobulus,[76] and Barnabas,[77] and displays, particularly in the *Stromata*, a profound knowledge
of the Scriptures.[78] His writings, though, make little concession to the
reader, and one is occasionally left feeling that the 'method of concealment' which he found in the biblical writings, and of which more anon,
was a method he not infrequently employed in his own narrative.[79]

---

72   The prohibition on eating swine, eagle, hawk, raven and fish with no scales
      teaches that one should not consort with men who are like swine, those who
      plunder and do evil, those who are utterly ungodly.
73   'Is our hope, therefore, on a stone? May it not be?': VI 3.
74   The person shall understand who is 'wise and learned and a lover of his Lord':
      VI 10; wisdom and understanding are divine gifts.
75   Cf. R.B. Tollington, Clement of Alexandria. A Study in Christian Liberalism I,
      London 1914, 164–169.
76   Strom. I 130,1–3, citing Frag. 3,1; Strom. I 148,1, citing Frag. 3,2; Strom. V 107,2
      and Frag. 3,14; Strom. V 107,1–108,1 and Frag. 3,13–16, verses which Clement
      ascribes to Callimachus. He quotes Aristobulus as showing how much older Hebrew
      wisdom was than Greek philosophy and how the latter was indebted to the
      former; cf. Strom. I 72; V 97; he reproduces his allegorical explanation of the
      descent of the Lord on Sinai for the giving of the Law and describes this as an
      allegory according to the Scripture—*hê kata tên graphên allêgoria*; cf. Strom. VI 3.
77   Cited by name in Strom. II 6, 7, 15, 18, 20; V 10; VI 8.
78   See the comment of M. Simonetti, Letteratura cristiana antiqua greca e latina,
      Florence-Milan 1969, 109.
79   Cf. Strom. I 1, where he justifies his method on the basis that the seeds of truth
      should be kept for the husbandmen of faith.

Philo's influence on Clement both from the point of view of content and method is unmistakeable and has been highlighted by Siegfried and Heinisch.[80] Clement is greatly indebted, for instance, to Philo's *Life of Moses*[81] and to his allegorical interpretion of the story of Hagar and Sarah.[82] Abraham's 'buried cakes' (*egkruphiai*) of Gen 18:6 LXX (*De sacrif.* 59, 60 etc.) provide him with a vehicle for his notion of 'concealment' (*Strom.* V 12).[83] He borrows interpretations of names, numbers, persons, places, the tabernacle and its furnishings, laws relating to animals, etymological explanations and many aspects of his teaching (God, *Logos*, sin, etc.), rarely acknowledging the debt which, however, is patently obvious.[84] As with Philo, everything is of significance—every word, syllable, letter, the presence or absence of the article, perceived omis-sions, changes of expression, the inclusion of common or everyday truths.[85] He follows Philo in allegorizing problematic texts—anthropomorphisms (*Strom.* II 16; V 11), affirmations that are deemed unworthy (*Strom.* VII 16), literal impossibilities (*Paed.* I 6), contradictions (*Strom.* III 15).

A Christian dimension is, not unexpectedly, a feature of his exegesis of OT texts. In the case of Isaac, for instance, his name, interpreted as laughter by Philo, now symbolizes the joy resulting from Christ's Passion (*Paed.* I 5),[86] the three hundred and sixty bells of the priest's robe, the Saviour's appearance.[87] Clement applied Philo's method also to the NT, though not to any great extent. Examples include the story of the sinful woman who anointed Jesus, a story about which he felt distinctly uneasy (the anointed feet of the Lord are the Apostles who were anointed by the Holy Spirit, the ointment, Judas, the tears, repentant sinners, and so on),[88] and the Good Samaritan (the neighbour is Christ who rescues us

---

80 Siegfried, op. cit., 343–351; Heinisch, op. cit., 65–125; cf. C. Mondésert, Clément d'Alexandrie, Paris 1944, 172–181, with reference to Philo's influence on Strom. V 32–40.
81 See especially Strom. I 23; also Siegfried, op. cit., 350–351.
82 Strom. I 5, where he cites Philo.
83 Cf. De Caini 60: 'For it is written make "buried cakes" because the sacred story that unveils to us the truth of the Uncreated and his potencies must be buried since the knowledge of divine rights is a trust which not every comer can guard aright': tr. Loeb; Clement, Strom. V 12: 'he ordered "unleavened cakes" to be made so that the truly sacred mystic word . . . ought to be concealed'; cf. Origen, Hom. Gen. IV 1.
84 Cf. Tollinton, op cit. I,212ff.; Siegfried, op. cit. 343–351; the extent of Clement's use of Philo can be gauged from the index of G. Stählin.
85 Job naked from his mother's womb; the adj. 'young' in Zech 9:9; cf. Paed. I 5.
86 Cf. Daniélou, op. cit., 117–118.
87 'Proclaiming and resounding the stupendous manifestation of the Saviour'.
88 Paed. II 8; other examples in Tollinton, op cit. II,214–215—the five barley loaves, the Law, the two fishes, Greek philosophy, etc.

from the world rulers of darkness, Jesus the doctor who applies the oil of the Father's compassion).[89]

Like Philo (*De migr.* 16) Clement distinguished between the literal sense of the text (*tas lexeis kai ta onomata*)—the 'body of the Scriptures' (*sôma tôn graphôn*)—and the underlying senses (*tas dianoias*).[90] He accepts the literal text in the main, including such events as Noah's drunkenness and Lot's indiscretions.[91] He shows respect for the OT Law, describing it as a schoolmaster to bring one to Christ (*Strom.* I 26). Problematic texts are allegorized. But as with Philo there is an underlying meaning for the non-problematic texts that must be brought to light. For Clement, as for Philo, almost (*schedon*) the whole is capable of being interpreted allegorically.[92] But in neither case does allegorization necessarily exclude acceptance of the literal sense.[93] Moreover, as in the case of Philo, allegorical interpretation may unveil more than one meaning or one level of meaning (cf. *Strom.* III 10; IV 6; V 9, 32; VI 84ff.).

Clement uses a number of terms in relation to his notion of 'concealment' (*egkrupsis*). The truth lies concealed underneath the written word, hidden behind the veil (*kalumma, paraptôma*), embedded in enigmas (*ainigmata*), symbols (*symbola*) and parables (*parabolai*).[94] Prophecies and oracles are spoken in 'enigmas', not exhibited incontinently to all but only after certain purifications and previous instruction (*Strom.* V 4). Access is for 'those who have ears', the initiated or consecrated, those who seek the truth through love (*Strom.* VI 15). For the simple believer the plain meaning may suffice. But one cannot be satisfied with the literal (*Quis div. salv.* 5); its hidden truth must be revealed. Those who remain at the literal level only nibble at the word of God (*Strom.* VII 16).

The reasons given by Clement for the use of the 'method of concealment' which he found attested also among the Egyptians and Greeks are manifold—to conceal it from those who might profane it (*Strom.* V 9), or be scandalized or harmed by it (*Strom.* VI 15), to add dignity to the hidden truth (*Strom.* V 9),[95] to lead one to the discovery of the words of

89   Quis div. salv. 28–29; cf. Lampe, in The Cambridge History of the Bible II, ed. G.H.W. Lampe, Cambridge 1969, 172.
90   Strom. VI 15; V 6; V 4; cf. Heinisch, op. cit., 65–67. As has been noted above, Philo used the distinction *sôma*—*psuchê* in his description of the Therapeutai; cf. De vita contempl. 78; De migr. 93; Clement probably took it directly from him; cf. A. van den Hoek, 'The Concept of *sôma tôn graphôn* in Alexandrian Theology', Studia Patristica XIX, ed. E. Livingstone, Louvain 1989, 254.
91   Paed. II 2—Noah; II 9—Lot.
92   Strom. V 6, in reference to 'the Prophets and the Law'.
93   Cf. Paed. III 11; Heinisch, op. cit., 65, cites the example of the serpent of Genesis in Protrept. I—serpent, devil, passion.
94   Cf. Strom. V 4; VI 15.
95   'All things that shine through a veil show the truth grander and more imposing'; cf. Strom. V 9.

salvation by arousing one's curiosity (*Strom.* VI 15), to ensure that underlying truths are not lost (*Strom.* VI 15).

One further point should be made. The interpretive categories used by Clement and Philo are not the same. Whereas Philo divides allegorical interpretation into physical or cosmological and ethical categories, Clement has three, mystical (corresponding to physical), moral (ethical) and prophetic, the latter corresponding to a typological interpretation of which he has many examples.

ORIGEN

Origen, a pupil of Clement's catechetical school at Alexandria (cf. Eusebius, *HE* VI 6), was indebted to Philo both directly and indirectly through Clement.[96] Probably the most influential writer of the early Christian era, he brought to biblical exegesis a systematic approach and a critical spirit,[97] and left a deep imprint on subsequent generations of biblical interpreters.[98] Like Clement, Origen christianized borrowings from Philo, but he went beyond Clement in systematically applying allegorical exegesis to the NT. He also justified his method of allegorization (*De princ.* IV 2,2–3,3). Of his numerous homilies on selected passages, his verse by verse commentaries on biblical books and his scholia on difficult biblical texts, only a fraction survived the vicissitudes of time and circumstance. It is enough, though, to give a good idea of the extent of Philo's influence.[99]

Origen probably refers to Philo's method in his *Commentary on Matthew* (XVII 17) in which he also praises him (XV 3). Indeed while direct borrowings from Philo are not lacking,[100] it is in Origen's application of Philo's method that his debt is most evident. Like Philo and Clement he

96 Hanson, op. cit., 248–249, for example, has noted his debt to Clement's writings.
97 Hanson, op. cit., 179, remarks that by comparison with Clement his method was 'scholarly and almost scientific'. On Origen's critical work on the LXX see G. Sgherri, 'Sulla valutazione origeniana dei LXX', Bib. 58 (1977)1–28; S.P. Brock, 'Origen's Aims as a Textual Critic of the Old Testament', Jellicoe, op. cit., 343–347.
98 Cf. J.W. Trigg, Biblical Interpretation, MFC 9: Washington 1988, 23: 'the single most significant influence in the later development of patristic biblical criticism'.
99 Highlighted particularly by Siegfried, op. cit., 351–362; J. Daniélou, Origen, London and New York 1955, 178–191; see also J. Laporte, 'Sacrifice in Origen in the Light of Philonic Methods', in C. Kannengiesser, W. L. Petersen, Origen of Alexandria. His Work and His Legacy, Notre Dame, Indiana 1988, 250–276; see the comments of G. W. Barkley in his introduction to: Origen. Homilies on Leviticus 1–16, tr. by G.W. Barkley, Washington 1990, 13–14; for a somewhat different perspective, N. de Lange, Origen and the Jews. Studies in Jewish-Christian Relations in Third-Century Palestine, Cambridge 1976, 124–134.
100 Cf. Hanson, op. cit., 249–250 n.8, and references given there.

regarded all Scripture as inspired (*De princ.* IV 1, 6–7). Like them too he took the sacred text to be capable of both literal and allegorical senses (*Contra Celsum* VII 20, 21; *De princ.* III 4). His view that the truth is veiled by the letter is reminiscent of Clement (*De princ.* II 8). He also put forward his view of why the truth is hidden (*De princ.* IV 1, 7). For Origen all Scripture has a spiritual sense, but not all has a bodily sense (*De princ.* III 5). Painstaking research was required to see if one or the other or both were possible (cf. *De princ.* III 5). The circumstances that give rise to allegory and the content of his allegories often parallel those of Philo.[101]

Origen uses the concepts of *sôma* and *psuchê*, body and soul, in relation to the literal and underlying meanings, and parallels it with the incarnation of Christ—as Christ came hidden in a body, so too all divine Scripture (cf. *Hom. Lev.* I 1). He goes beyond Philo and Clement in taking the underlying sense to be capable of both a moral and a spiritual interpretation.[102] The distinction between the two underlying senses, however, is not always evident.

Origen makes clear his respect for the literal text in *De princ.* IV 4 where he lists a number of historical facts reported in the Scriptures as well as a number of commands that are to be taken literally both in the OT and NT, and he notes that instances that are true in terms of the historical narrative far outnumber the purely spiritual texts.[103] The literal meaning of a story is often discussed first by Origen before he goes on to interpret its 'inner truth'.

For him, though, the literal is clearly inferior to the hidden, underlying truth, for which greater perception is required. He describes the literal sense as adequate for simple folk (likewise, Philo and Clement) for whom it may form the limit of their understanding. It still has a positive function for such people since these 'children' who are unable to address God as Father or listen to higher truths might be edified by the flesh of Scripture, that is, the obvious understanding. For these the basic literal narrative of the Gospel is adequate for salvation.[104] In the majority of cases the literal stands, even where it is allegorized. But Origen is scathingly critical of literalists such as the Marcionites whose interpretation he challenged effectively,[105] and he criticizes also the Jews who failed to recognize

---

101 See Siegfried, op. cit., 354–358, who lists occasions such as the doubling of a word or the use of a synonym, and notes similarities in the allegorizing of names, numbers, animals, colours, etc., pointing out also differences in their etymologies.
102 *Hom. Lev.* I 1; in V 5, he speaks of historical, moral and mystical senses corresponding to body, soul and spirit.
103 Cf. Siegfried, op. cit., 351–352; also Hanson, op. cit., 237–242.
104 Cf. Hanson, op. cit., 238 n.1.
105 Id., 136–141.

the Messiah. For hardened hearts, heretics and false teachers, the letter is 'the letter that kills'.

There are cases in the OT where the literal cannot stand—where an unacceptable literal sense necessitates allegorization—statements unworthy of God such as anthropomorphisms,[106] laws which are irrational and impossible to observe (cf. *De princ.* III 2), incoherences, impossibilities, historical errors, things that are scandalous or offensive, or problematic for Christians.[107] In Leviticus, for instance, the literal sense is problematic for Christians given that they can hardly be expected to see the sacrificial laws as applying to them (cf. *Hom. Lev.* I 1; VII 5).

The same is true of the Gospels. From a spiritual point of view they are true in their entirety, but from a literal point of view they may be false.[108] There are many examples of things presented as having happened that did not, and which, therefore, necessitate allegorizing. The vision at Jesus' baptism is a case in point; likewise Jesus being taken to a high mountain by the devil in the Temptation scene. There are commands that are irrational or impossible such as the instruction to greet no one on the way (Lk 10:4) or turn the other cheek (Mt 5:39). The obvious discrepancies among the Evangelists in their accounts of the triumphal entry and the Temple cleansing indicate that these must be allegorized.[109] Origen makes the noteworthy point (*De princ.* IV 15) that elements such as offensive features, impossibilities, etc. have been included as stumbling blocks, divinely furnished to direct the interpreter to allegorize.

GREGORY OF NYSSA AND AMBROSE

To conclude, a brief look at two later writers who were greatly indebted to Philo. The first of these, Gregory of Nyssa (335–395), the youngest of the Cappadocian Fathers and a champion of orthodox faith against Arianism, sought to make the Scriptures relevant to educated Greeks of his time. While Gregory greatly favoured the allegorical method, particularly in his later writings,[110] his approach may legitimately be described

---

106 God does not plant a paradise (IV 16), walk in paradise, have human passions, etc.
107 Cf. Hanson, op. cit., 239–240.
108 J. W. Trigg, Origen, The Bible and Philosophy in the Third-Century Church, London 1985, 153.
109 Cf. Trigg, op. cit., 151–152.
110 Cf. Bardenhewer, op. cit., 296, who notes that his earlier writings paid more attention to the literal. In his Life of Moses II 149 Gregory comments that Moses holding his hands aloft signifies the contemplation of the Law, the loftier insights, his letting them hang to earth, the mean and lowly literal exposition and observance of the law; in II 217 he notes that the contemplation of the spiritual sense agrees with the literal account.

as twin-tracked. This may be illustrated from his two-volume *Life of Moses*. Its format is taken from Philo's work on Moses and it contains many borrowings from Philo.[111] The first volume of this work represents a summary of the literal account, the second his allegorization of the same. In the latter Philo's allegorical method is greatly in evidence.[112]

But there are few texts where the literal meaning is unacceptable and the underlying meaning alone required. The law on 'how to eat' is seen as unnecessary, superfluous or out of place in a revealed law and pointed to the need for a 'higher understanding' (cf. *De vita Mos.* II 105); the despoiling of the Egyptians (*De vita Mos.* II 113) was something morally wrong and required a 'loftier meaning'; likewise the death of the first born of the Egyptians (II 91–92) or the hardening of Pharaoh's heart by God (II 73), something that is unworthy of Him (II 90–94), or Moses seeing God face to face, an anthropomorphism that must have a spiritual sense (II 219–23). The impossibility of duplicating the marvellous deeds of the lives of Moses and other 'honoured men' justifies their allegorical treatment (II 49). Generally speaking, though, allegorization does not exclude the literal text. Indeed in the case of the indiscriminate slaying by the Levites of their fellow-countrymen after the golden calf episode, the literal sense is unexpectedly retained, although discarded by Philo (*De ebr.* 68–70), and from the literal sense a 'useful lesson' is extracted (II 205).[113]

Ambrose, Bishop of Milan (374–397), and a man of vast culture was introduced to Philo by his teacher Simplicianus. Although he rarely cites Philo, his debt to him is evident. One need only compare their respective treatments of Cain, Noah, Abraham,[114] or compare Ambrose's *De fuga saeculi* and Philo's *De fuga*[115]. He actually refers to Philo in his *De paradiso* (4,25), and in his letter to Simplicianus (37/7) he makes liberal

---

111 See, for instance, their treatment (Philo cited first) of the burning bush in De Mos. I 65 and I 20, the Tabernacle in De Mos. II 74 and I 49, the despoiling of the Egyptians in De Mos. I 28 and II 13–15, the Egyptian army in De ebr. 111 and II 122, the brazen serpent in Leg. all. II 71–87, De agric. 94–98 and II 269–277; on the latter see H. Maneschg, Die Erzählung von der ehernen Schlange (Num 21,4–9) in der Auslegung der frühen jüdischen Literatur. Eine traditionsgeschichtliche Studie, Frankfurt-am-Main 1981, 447.
112 Likewise in his works on the Psalms, Ecclesiastes and the Canticle of Canticles.
113 The category 'usefulness' recalling Origen; in II 50 Gregory had stated: 'If the events require dropping from the literal account anything written which is foreign to the sequence of elevated understanding, we pass over this on the grounds that it is useless and unprofitable to our purpose': tr. from Gregory of Nyssa. The Life of Moses, eds. A.J. Malherbe, E. Ferguson, New York 1978, 65.
114 Cf. Siegfried, op. cit., 372–375.
115 See, for example, his treatment of the legislation governing the stay in the cities of refuge; cf. De fuga saeculi 2, 6–13.

use of Philo's *Quod omnis probus liber sit.*[116] But while taking a great deal from Philo, Ambrose adapts it to his own circumstances, 'exorcizing and christianizing' Philo, excising elements not compatible with Christianity.[117]

Ambrose's preference for allegorizing is very evident. He describes literal exegesis of the text as a tree that bears leaves and not fruits (*Ep.* 26,15; cf. *Exp. ad Lucam* VIII 81). In some cases Ambrose contrasts the letter and the spirit,[118] in others, influenced by Origen, he speaks of three senses, literal, moral and logical or mystical.[119] Augustine recalls having heard him preach that the letter kills, the spirit gives life. Drawing aside the mystic veil, he wrote, Ambrose would disclose in spiritual fashion things that seemed perverse when taken literally.[120] There are cases where the literal cannot stand, where, for instance, the letter leaves one perplexed or doubting, as in the legislation governing the length of stay in the cities of refuge (*De fuga saeculi* 2,13), or where it might scandalize part of the faithful (*De par.* 2,11). Here the spiritual sense must be sought. But while according allegory a privileged place in his work, Ambrose does not discard the letter.

Philo's legacy enabled Ambrose to plunder the 'profound secrets' of the biblical text (*De Cain* I 4), that rich paradise where God walks (cf. *Ep.* 49,3), that sea full of profound senses and prophetic enigmas (*Ep.* 2,3) where every word is a potential gold-mine. Philo certainly left his imprint, so much so that one author was moved to describe him as Philo Christianus.[121]

---

116 The use of Philo's treatise is well indicated in Opera Omnia di Sant'Ambrogio. Discorsi e Lettere II/1, ed. G. Banterle, Milan 1988; for numerous other borrowings see Siegfried, op. cit., 376–387, who points out the allegorization of numbers, things, animals, rivers, names, etc.; for the use of other Philonic treatises by Ambrose see the editions of the relevant volumes published by Città Nuova; Trisoglio, op. cit., 693, comments that Ambrose 'lo adoperava senza misura'.

117 H. Savon, 'Saint Ambroise et saint Jérôme, lecteurs de Philon', Hase op. cit., II,21.1, 737–739; Savon argues that Ambrose used Philo with much more liberty than is usually accepted; cf. Opera Omnia di Sant'Ambrogio. Esposizione del Vangelo Secondo Luca I, ed. G. Coppa, Milan-Rome 1978, 29.

118 Cf. Savon, op. cit., 737 n.29; an antithesis appears often in the context of anti-Jewish polemic; cf. Exp. Ps 118,3.26; 6,24; Ep. 38.

119 Savon, op. cit., 737 n.30; cf. De Isaac 4,22–30; Expl. Ps 36,1–2; 118,1,2–3; Exp. Luc. prol. 2–3.

120 Augustine, Conf. V 4,6.

121 Cf. Siegfried, op. cit., 371; also indirectly through Origen; on his debt to Origen see Coppa, op. cit., I, 32–33, 563–564.

A Dark Cloud: Hellenistic Influences on the Scriptural Exegesis of Clement of Alexandria and the Pseudo-Dionysius

DEIRDRE CARABINE

The influence of Platonism and Neoplatonism on Christian thought, especially in the early years of its development, is a theme which has received much scholarly attention. Upon reflection, I began to wonder if, in fact, the reverse could be said: that Christianity had some influence upon Hellenic speculation. However, notwithstanding the attempt by Julian in the fourth century to impose a vast Hellenic religion throughout the Empire, modelled on the hierarchical structures of the Christian Church, the traffic would appear to have been operating along a one-way system.[1] Although Julian's attempt failed, it was not a victory for Christianity over Hellenic thought; in fact the dogmatic form of Iamblichan Neoplatonism adopted by Julian was not, in general, characteristic of the much more open-ended dialectical nature of Platonism. Neither should we be tempted to view the closure of the Platonic school at Athens in 529 as a victory for Christianity; that too, was short-lived,[2] for philosophical ideas in general and Platonic ideas in particular, have continued to exert a powerful influence on Christian intellectualism right down to relatively recent times.

However, the debate still continues among modern scholars regarding the so-called 'hellenization' of Christian thought, a topic which Professor Watson has already noted elsewhere in this volume. Whether one ranges oneself on one or other side of the Hellenic fence, it is nonetheless true that there remains in patristic scholarship even yet, lingering traces of the old method of *Dogmengeschichte*. There is, for example, still a temptation to regard Clement and Origen as 'hellenizers': to see in them a very strong tension between Plato and Scripture, in spite of their own declarations to the contrary.[3] In fact, we find the

---

1   See A. H. Armstrong's comments on Julian's attempt in 'The Way and The Ways. Religious Tolerance and Intolerance in the Fourth Century A.D.', Vigiliae Christianae 38 (1984) 5-8.

2   As Pelikan put it, it was 'more the act of a coroner than an executioner,' J. Pelikan, The Christian Tradition, I: The Emergence of the Catholic Tradition, London/Chicago 1971, 41.

3   Strom. I 19, 94; I 20, 1 and I 20, 100.

Fathers of the first four centuries continuously engaged in a very ener-
getic attempt to show that Platonic philosophy was not a hindrance to
their understanding of the truth contained in the Scriptures, but was, in
fact, a considerable help.

In their practice of tracing Greek philosophical ideas in the Scriptures, especially in the Old Testament, the Fathers were demonstrating
very forceably that the truth of Platonic philosophy itself came from the
Old Testament.[4] Justin, for example, saw Moses as the source for the
Platonic concept of creation in the *Timaeus*, as did Clement;[5] and Origen
traces the ideas contained in the *Phaedrus* to Scripture.[6] Apart from the
attempt to find in Scripture support for philosophical ideas, the earlier
Fathers were also intent on proving the temporal superiority of the
sacred texts. Given that Christianity was a relative innovation, the argument from superior antiquity—the supreme case being the assumed
identity of the Pseudo-Dionysius, an identity which, incidentally symbolizes the meeting of Athens and Rome at the altar to the Unknown
God—can be stated simply enough: Plato learned his wisdom from
Moses, through the agency of Pythagoras. It is in this context that we
find both Justin and Origen assent to the notion that Christ was known
in part even by Socrates.[7]

The anti-philosophical strain in Christian thought, exemplified by
Tertullian, can be traced back to St Paul himself, and scholars have
argued that many of the heretical movements in the first Christian
centuries took root as a direct result of ignoring Paul's warning against
philosophy (the Carpocratians and Nazarenes, for example) and
importing into Christian thought the extraneous concepts of pagan
philosophy.[8] However, for the Fathers themselves it can be said, more or
less with complete conviction, that Platonic philosophy was never
understood to be an alien, external force which resided exclusively in
the gentile world. As Augustine was to note later, 'there are none who
come nearer to us than the Platonists.'[9] Tertullian's famous question:
'what has Athens to do with Jerusalem?' is in effect answered by
Numenius, whom we find expressing the commonly held notion that
Plato learned his wisdom from Moses: 'what is Plato but Moses speaking
Attic?'[10]

In order to evaluate correctly the influence of philosophical speculation on patristic exegesis, we must first of all ascertain which, if in
fact any, philosophical problems and areas of investigation would

---

4   For more specific comments on this theme, see J. Pelikan, op. cit. 31f.
5   I Apol. 59-60 and Prot. VI 70, 1.
6   C. C. VI 19.
7   2 Apol. 10, 8 and C. C. VIII 54.
8   See Col 2:8.
9   De civ. Dei. VIII 5.
10 Tertullian, De praescr. haer. 7; Numenius, Fr. 8.

have had relevance for the Christian exegete. There are, I think, a number of thematic connections which immediately spring to mind, among them the question of divine transcendence.

Platonic speculation was, as any reading of Plotinus or Proclus will demonstrate, very much concerned with the nature of the highest principle, the Father, the Good or the One, and with how this principle could be spoken of and ultimately attained to. Christian thinkers too, were actively seeking answers to this very real problem: witness the very early Christian reliance upon contemporary philosophical terms as descriptive of the transcendence of the divine nature.[11] Philosophy itself was viewed as the supreme spiritual endeavour. The goal of human life was evaluated in terms of attaining to unity and likeness with the One. The constant echo of Plato's *Theaetetus* (176b) penetrated even the logical hard-headedness of Proclus, the last great Athenian Neoplatonist, for the chief focus of his philosophical endeavours was the urgent desire to attain to unity with the One.[12]

Thematically then, at least in very general terms, the Platonist and the Christian were asking much the same sort of questions, although the fact remains that their questions were posed from different perspectives. What then, can be said to differentiate the two from a philosophical viewpoint? Without wishing to sound too dogmatic, I think it valid to suggest that the Platonic approach, as a dialectical interchange of ideas, can be described as non-static and open to continuous revision: no question can ever be answered satisfactorily once and for all. And while the Christian approach cannot be described as static, its dynamism differs from that of Platonism, in that the central tenet of Christian revelation is understood as a gradual unfolding of the truth, an unfolding which deepens as the exegete delves deeper and deeper into the mysteries of the sacred texts.

Although I have described the differences between Christian and Platonist exegesis as dogmatic versus dialectical, the critical independance of the Platonist is itself tempered by insistence upon the supremacy of ancient authority.[13] Even though the Christian exegete was also constrained in terms of asserting the supremacy of the Scriptures, he could exercise his intellectual freedom by choosing from contemporary philosophical ideas whatever supported his own authoritative tradition. The crucial difference between the two, however, was that the Platonist

---

11 Although philosophical terminology was not used solely in support of divine transcendence, it also made its way into dogmatic formulations, for example, the Chalcedonian formulation of the distinction of natures in the person of Christ.

12 Like Plotinus (see Enn. V 5, 12, 7-9 and VI 7, 22, 12-14), Proclus sees the desire and inextinguishable love for the One as the focus for the soul's continual search and, in fact, constitutes all things in their being through their natural striving for the One; see In Parm. VII 54k, 19-21; VII 58k, 16-17; VII 1116 and 1144 and Plat. Theol. I 22.

13 See, for example, Origen's remarks: Contra Celsum VII 71.

had the freedom to disagree with his source, as Plotinus frequently disagreed with Plato. For the Christian exegete, explicit criticism was not possible, since all truth contained in the teaching of Christ, as preached by the Apostles and contained in the Scriptures, was the ultimate authority. However, having said that, it is nonetheless true that the Platonic sentiments in Plato's *Seventh Letter* (341c-d), which is an admirable statement of Platonic scepticism regarding the adequacy of language when dealing with transcendent realities, is expressive of the attitude which gradually became an integral part of the Christian task of scriptural exegesis.

Although the development of the discipline of topology gave the Christian exegete more room to assert the authority of his ancient tradition, he was still constrained to find a harmonious balance within the scriptural texts themselves. Rather than criticize the authority of the Old Testament, for example, in relation to the obviously anthropomorphic representations of God contained there, Origen, the Father of the exegetical tradition, adapted and developed the allegorical method of interpreting sacred texts. For the early Fathers, Scripture was a vibrant world of symbols which veiled the truth of divine reality. The task of scriptural exegesis was illustrative of the continuing attempt to unveil more and more of that truth.[14] However, whatever the differences of approach which distinguish the Christian exegete and the Platonist philosopher, what unites them is that both are deeply committed to the search for truth. This one, vital, shared characteristic can be said to be the primary reason for their close relationship down through the centuries.

In order to narrow the parameters of this discussion, I would like to concentrate specifically on the theme of divine transcendence, and more more especially, how Christian exegesis in this regard was influenced by Hellenistic philosophical speculation. Rather than simply paint a general picture, I have chosen to illustrate my comments with examples from two thinkers: one who stands at the beginning of the Christian exegetical tradition and one very lonely figure who stands on the border between the end of the classical tradition and the beginning of the medieval tradition. Clement of Alexandria illustrates my comments on early Christian exegesis. The great leap I make from the second to the early sixth century takes us into the dark reaches of Dionysian exegesis. However, I have a very good reason for bringing Pseudo-Dionysius into my discussion of patristic exegesis. In the paper I gave at the first Patristic Symposium conference in 1990,[15] I talked about transcendence, incar-

---

14 A. H. Armstrong describes the exegetical task as follows: 'they, so to speak, take hold of it by the scruff of the neck and shake it till it makes sense'; cf. 'Pagan and Christian Traditionalism in the First Three Centuries A.D.' in: Studia Patristica, XV (1984) 431.

15 D. Carabine, 'Gregory of Nyssa on the Incomprehensibility of God' in T. Finan, V. Twomey (eds.), The Relationship between Neoplatonism and Christianity, Dublin 1992, 79-99.

nation and negative theology in Gregory of Nyssa. As the most philosophical of the Cappadocian Fathers, Gregory portrays, I believe, a very tangible Plotinian influence; his speculations also provide a direct thematic link to the Pseudo-Dionysius. In the final part of this paper, I would like to continue that discussion in order to show just how close the Pseudo-Dionysius is to the Fathers of Cappadocia. In that sense I want to attempt some sort of rehabilitation of Dionysian thought in the light of what we term more 'orthodox' patristic exegesis.[16]

CLEMENT OF ALEXANDRIA AND THE PSEUDO-DIONYSIUS

It was the early Christian Apologists, arguing from a monotheistic position, who inaugurated the use of Platonic philosophical terms in order to assert the transcendence, unity and difference of the Christian God in relation to the pagan gods: God was uncreated, unchangeable, invisible, incorruptible, eternal and had no form, sex or limit.[17] It is in the writings of Justin Martyr that we find a Christian philosopher for the first time establishing the validity of using philosophical terms in order to strengthen the biblical formulations of divine transcendence. Justin's doctrine of God, which reveals Philonic and Middle Platonic influences, consolidates the established tradition in Christian writings of attempting to unite Plato and Moses,[18] illustrated by the story that even as a Christian philosopher, Justin wore the *pallium* of the Greek philosopher. According to Justin, God is ungenerate, (a notion which was to remain an integral part of theological and philosophical speculation for some generations to come[19]), and it is a concept which implies ineffability and namelessness, for the naming process involves an ontologically prior namer.[20] As a Christian philosopher who affirms the namelessness of God, Justin must address the question of the apparent contradiction

16 An excellent study of Dionysius and his Christian sources can be found in A. Louth, Denys the Areopagite, London 1989.

17 See D. W. Palmer, 'Atheism, Apologetic and Negative Theology in the Greek Apologists of the Second Century', Vigiliae Christianae 37 (1983) 243. The kind of language (which is more than simple anti-anthropomorphism) to be found in the early Christian writers is much less specific than that of the fourth-century Fathers, precisely because the former used philosophical terms primarily as a means of establishing the unity of God.

18 I give a very short outline of Justin's theology here; for more detailed discussion see E. R. Goodenough, The Theology of Justin Martyr, Amsterdam 1968, 123-128, who stresses the Philonic background of Justin, and L. W. Barnard, Justin Martyr. His Life and Thought, Cambridge 1967, 75-84, who sees Justin as more Middle Platonic than Philonic.

19 There are numerous references to *agennêtos* in Justin's writings, see for example, I Apol. 14, 25, 49 and II Apol. 6 and 12. Goodenough notes the difference between *agennêtos* which Justin uses, and *agenêtos*, the philosophical term meaning no beginning, see 128f.

20 I Apol. 63 and II Apol. 6.

of the many names given to God in the sacred texts. Accordingly, he understands the names, 'Father', 'Maker', 'Creator' and 'Lord' not as real names, but as terms of address: expressions for that which can barely be defined, and which are derived from God's activities.[21] While Justin Martyr was the first Christian philosopher to assert the transcendence of God using negative philosophical terms, his use of such terms was the means whereby later Christian philosophers were able to differentiate God from the pagan gods (by the fourth century it is not any longer the difference between the Christian God and other gods that is argued for through the use of negative terms, but the identity of God's own nature itself). However, Justin did not attempt by means of philosophical negations to make God into the 'philosophic Absolute'. Divine transcendence can never be divorced from divine immanence, or from the reality of the Incarnation, for the invisible Father is revealed through the visible Son. It is to the writings of Clement of Alexandria that I now turn my attention in order to see how Clement deals with the question of divine transcendence. Here I limit my remarks to some of the relevant passages from Book V of the *Stromata*.[22]

In general terms, Clement of Alexandria's underlying aim would appear to be the reconciliation of Pythagoras and Plato with Moses, but it could also be said, with regard to divine transcendence, that he is attempting to reconcile Plato and St Paul. Having argued most persuasively that the highest truth, the wisdom of God, is perceived by the mind alone (it cannot be apprehended by the science of demonstration[23]), Clement paraphrases that important passage from Plato's *Seventh Letter* in order to demonstrate that God's wisdom is veiled in symbol and mystery: 'for the God of the universe, who is above all speech, all conception, all thought, can never be committed to writing, being inexpressible even by his own power'.[24]

Clement's importance for the development of the theology of negation by later Christian thinkers is based upon the fact that he does not simply repeat the philosophical negations which were to be found in Justin and the other second-century writers; he goes much further.[25] Accordingly, God has no attributes whatsoever: those mentioned in the Old Testament texts are to be understood solely in an allegorical

21 II Apol. 6.
22 For more detailed discussion see S. R. C. Lilla, Clement of Alexandria, Oxford 1971, 212ff; J. Hochstaffl, Negative Theologie, Munich 1976, 82-105, and R. Mortley, From Word to Silence II. The Way of Negation Christian and Greek, Bonn 1986, 36-41.
23 Strom. V 12.
24 Strom. V 10; trans. from A. Cleveland Coxe, Fathers of the Second Century, The Ante-Nicene Fathers Series, Michigan 1975, ii, 460; see Ep. VII (341c-d).
25 H. Chadwick has remarked that Clement goes as far as it is possible to go towards the apotheosis of the *alpha* privative, see 'Philo and the Beginning of Christian Thought', in The Cambridge History of Later Greek and Early Medieval Philosophy, ed. A. H. Armstrong, Cambridge 1967, 179.

sense.[26] Like Justin, Clement stresses the notion of God's ungeneracy; he needs nothing, is always equal, immortal and ageless.[27] The Final Cause is above space and time; he has no name or conception; he is inexpressible, uncircumscribable and invisible.[28] God has no genus, species, difference, individual or number; he is ineffable and one (neither having parts nor being divisible); he is infinite (without dimension and limit); he has no form and no name.[29] Clement also follows Justin's conclusion regarding the names given to God: 'One', 'Good', 'Mind', 'Absolute Being', 'Father', 'God', 'Creator', 'Lord', are used as points of reference. No single name can circumscribe God, but all names, taken together indicate the power of God. Clement also couples the ideas of ungeneracy and naming, and argues that since there is nothing prior to the Unbegotten, He cannot be named, for begotten things are things which are named.[30]

It is important to note that although Clement comes very close to the idea that God's transcendence is such that He is essentially unknowable, he never makes this concept actually explicit. For the most part he appears to follow *Timaeus* 28c: the Father is difficult to know.[31] He does mention the altar to the Unknown God (Acts 17:22-23), but says that the Unknown can be known both through divine grace and through the *Logos*.[32] Another idea which is derived from this Platonic text is that the knowledge of God cannot be divulged to the multitude and here Clement uses two very interesting texts to make his point. The first of these is Ex 20:21: Moses enters into the dark cloud alone leaving the multitude behind; the second text Clement uses is Paul's description of the ineffable visions he experienced on being rapt into the third heaven (2 Cor 12: 2-4).[33] According to Clement the cloud represents the fact that God is invisible and ineffable, although the darkness refers to the unbelief and ignorance of the multitude. The mention of the dark cloud of Sinai is a significant one, for it is an idea which will be developed at length by Gregory of Nyssa and, after him, the Pseudo-Dionysius.

My final point concerns Clement's employment of the Platonic method of abstraction. There would appear to be three processes on the path to wisdom: illumination, which is achieved through instruction;[34] purification, which is attained through confession, and finally contemplation, which is achieved through analysis.[35] It is the final 'way' which is of interest to us here, for Clement explains the process of abstraction in much the same way as it is explained by the Platonist, Alcinous. The abstraction from a body of all its physical properties: depth, breadth and

26 V 11.
27 V 11.
28 V 11.
29 V 12.
30 Ibid.

31 V 11.
32 V 12.
33 V 12.
34 V 10.
35 V 11.

length will culminate in the single point, which has only position; taking away position results in the conception of absolute unity. Having used a typically philosophic analogy, Clement then begins to mould the concept of abstraction into a Christian context. He explains that when one is cast into 'the greatness of Christ' and 'the immensity of holiness', one will reach somehow a conception of God, although the knowledge will be knowledge of what God is not, not knowledge of what He is. Although, the exact relationship of the method of abstraction to the casting of one-self into the greatness of Christ is not clear at this point, it is the employment of abstraction leading to 'negative knowledge', which has earned for Clement the status of being the first Christian negative theologian.[36]

Therefore, while it can be said that Clement's understanding of divine transcendence and the concommitant negative theology is closely related to the philosophical negation of the Middle Platonists, it is his use of texts from the New Testament, the framework for his expression of divine transcendence, which puts negative theology firmly on the Christian agenda.[37] The later Fathers have now an expression of negation within the Christian tradition itself upon which they can draw.

I come now to an exposition of some themes in the writings of the Pseudo-Dionysius, that anonymous writer of the final decades of the fifth-century. Although the Proclean and later Neoplatonic influence on Dionysius was obviously important and indeed extremely fruitful, his Patristic inheritance has often been relegated to a place of less significance. The blame for this can be said to be the author's own. Although he was a Christian writer who must have been well schooled in earlier patristic literature, Dionysius never mentions any source by name (with the exception of his master Hierotheus), confining himself to scriptural authority at the risk, of course, of compromising his assumed identity. Therefore, it is extremely difficult to say with complete certainty that Dionysius had read the earlier Fathers of the Greek Church. However, it is possible to establish strong thematic links in the *Corpus Areopagiticum* where the author appears to depend largely on his Christian predecessors in the patristic tradition.[38]

---

36 I find R. Mortley's interpretation of the various levels of unity operative in Clement's exposition of abstraction a little strained in view of the rather inchoate description given by Clement; see From Word to Silence II, 42-43 (see above, note 22).

37 For example, he uses Jn 1:18 and Matt 11:27.

38 H. Ch. Puech's study of the employment of darkness and cloud in Dionysius suggests that between the scriptural concept and the Dionysian interpretation, there stood an intermediary who inspired him, namely Gregory of Nyssa. Puech concludes that this particular aspect of Dionysian thought firmly situates the Mystical Theology 'dans la perspective continue de la tradition patristique', see 'La ténèbre mystique chez le Pseudo-Denys l'Aréopagite et dans la tradition patristique', Études carmélitaines, 23 (1938) 53 and V. Lossky, The Vision of God, trans. A. Moorhouse, London 1973, 100f.

The Areopagite's understanding of the divine nature is well known to contain the apotheosis of negation, for God's essential quality is transcendence (*exêirêmenê*): he is *huperousios* and *huper noun*.[39] Throughout the *Divine Names* and the *Mystical Theology*, Dionysius heaps negation upon negation: the divine nature is invisible, incomprehensible, inscrutable, unsearchable and infinite; there is no perception of it, no image, opinion, name or expression for it, no contact with it.[40] It is neither word, power, mind, life or essence, but is separate from every condition: movement, life, image, opinion, name, word, thought, conception, essence, position, stability and boundary.[41] The great hymn of negations in *Mystical Theology* IV and V is the finest, and indeed most radical statement of divine transcendence in Greek Christian thought, and would, at first sight, have little in common with the revelation of God in the Old and New Testaments. Never before had any Christian writer found it necessary to stress so comprehensively the utterly unknowable and transcendent nature of God. Why then did Dionysius go to such great lengths in his attempts to place the unity of the divine essence beyond the limits of thought and speech? How does such a radical expression of transcendence find its place within Christian exegesis? The central aspect of Dionysian thought is that the transcendent God is known, first and foremost, as the immanent cause of all creation from the orderly arrangement of all things which are, in a sense, projected out of Him. He is known in all things as cause, and yet is distinct from all things as transcendent, a familiar Neoplatonic statement about the One.[42]

One very important aspect of the Dionysian system, indeed the central thesis at the heart of his theology and one which links him directly to the Cappadocian Fathers, is that God is knowable through his works (*energeiai*) or distinctions (*diakriseis*), but He is unknowable in his essence (*ousia*) or unity (*henôsis*). Dionysius, like Augustine, uses the Pauline text, the visible creation makes known the invisible things of God, to suggest that it is by way of creation (the orderly arrangement of all things) that one can be led back to the maker.[43] The visible things of creation, which proceed from the divine ideas, are signs of the invisible, and in their similarity to God they are traces of the divine.[44] In this sense, Dionysius consolidates the Pauline principle at the heart of revelation: the visible things make known the invisible.[45]

What then, can be said about the Dionysian method of exegesis? Theology according to the Areopagite, is the 'science of God', or the

39 See Ep. I (1065A).
40 D. N. I 2 (588C) and I 5 (593A).
41 See D. N. I 5 (593C).
42 D. N. VII 3 (872A).
43 Rom 1:20; see Ep. IX 2 (1108B); see also Ep. X (1117A).
44 C. H. I 2 (121B-C) and D. N. IX 6 (913D-916A).
45 D. N. VII 3 (869C-D) and I 5 (593D).

word of God;[46] it is also a tool for the examination of what Scripture says about the divine nature. Since theology is the word of God, the truth about the divine essence must be confined to what has been revealed in the sacred texts. Accordingly, one must be lifted up, through the manifold forms given in Scripture, to the divine simplicity itself.[47] A correct investigation of Scripture, which is a form of divine manifestation, becomes the means of the ascent to divine unity; the journey of *Logos* descending must be retraced upwards.[48] The theology of Dionysius is, therefore, scripturally based. The sometimes blatant Neoplatonic principles to be found in his reading of the sacred texts is explained by our author in *Epistle* VII where, like Justin and Clement, he reconciles his two sources: philosophy is concerned with the knowledge of beings, and with the same wisdom and knowledge which St Paul sought.[49]

Theology is also the means of differentiating the divine unity, for it refers to the manifested being of God, that is, the divine processions, which come to us wrapped in the sacred veils of Scripture: 'so that what is hidden may be brought out into the open and multiplied, what is unique and undivided may be divided up, and multiple shapes and forms be given to what has neither shape nor form'.[50] Beyond the veiled representations of God the mysteries of God remain simple and unveiled;[51] therefore, we must look beyond the image to the hidden beauty within.[52] The Dionysian ascent, therefore, can be described as the exegetical journey towards unveiled mystery.

It is the aim of the treatise on the *Divine Names* to investigate how we can use the names of special importance which have been given to the nameless in the Oracles. The rationale behind the employment of these many affirmations can be understood as *Logos* descending, of which there can be many words, but these words must be interpreted correctly lest anyone be led to an improper idea of the Transcendent. It is this treatise on the Divine Names which places Dionysius firmly within the Christian Patristic tradition from Justin and Clement, to

46   D. N. II 1 (637A); for a fuller discussion of theology in the Dionysian corpus, see R. Roques, 'Notes sur la notion de theologia chez le Pseudo-Denys l'Aréopagite', Revue d'Ascétique et de mystique 25 (1949) 204, and P. Rorem, Biblical and Liturgical Symbols in the Pseudo-Dionysian Synthesis, Toronto 1984, ch. 2.

47   D. N. I 1 (588A), C. H. II 1 (137A) and I 2 (588C). Dionysius uses the word *logia* rather than *graphē*.

48   D. N. I 1 (588A); VII 4 (872C) and M. Th. III (1033B-C).

49   VII 2 (1080B) and II 2 (640A), trans. from C. Luibhéid and P. Rorem, Pseudo-Dionysius. The Complete Works, London 1987, 60: 'if . . . someone is entirely at loggerheads with scripture, he will be far removed also from what is my philosophy'.

50   Ep. IX 1 (105B-C), trans. 283; see also D. N. II 4 (640D ff); II 5 (641D ff); II 11 (649A-C) and V 1 (816B).

51   M. Th. I 1 (997A). On the concept of veiling in Dionysius, see F. O'Rourke, Pseudo-Dionysius and the Metaphysics of Aquinas, Leiden 1992, 9-10.

52   M. Th. II (1025B).

Eunomius and Gregory of Nyssa, although interest in the question of names is also a Neoplatonic thematic, one which is employed chiefly in the context of theurgy in Iamblichus and Proclus.[53]

The *Divine Names* is a detailed exposition of the different names and titles of God in Scripture: intelligible names, such as Good, Beautiful, Light, Love, Being, Life, Knowledge, Intellect, Word, Wisdom, Power, Justice, Salvation, Redemption, Righteousness, Omnipotent, Eternity, Time, Place, Faith, Truth, Perfect and One; sensible names: sun, cloud, stars, fire, water, wind, dew, stone and rock, and biblical names: 'All Powerful', 'Ancient of Days', 'Peace', 'Holy of Holies', 'King of Kings', 'Lord of Lords' and 'God of Gods'.[54] Dionysius follows the Cappadocian Fathers in making a distinction between different types of divine names: those used for the whole Deity (unified or common names), those denoting cause, and finally, distinctive or differentiated names.[55] He insists, however, that all names must be ascribed to the Divinity in its entirety, even though they pertain solely to the manifestation of God.[56] Names must be understood as symbolic titles, for they are what we say of God, not what God is in Himself; this will become the fundamental reason for their ultimate denial. Dionysius quotes the Angel's rebuke to Manoah from the Book of Judges in support of his claim that man cannot know the name of Him who is celebrated both with no name and with every name.[57] The Areopagite explains that names are given in order to reveal God to finite intelligence: so that we may be drawn upwards and transcend their literal interpretation.[58] We must, he insists, resist the temptation to measure the divine by human standards. For instance, to call the transcendent God, 'life', 'being', 'light' or 'word', points to the fact that the mind lays hold of God as 'life-bearing', 'cause of being', and so on.[59] Therefore, for Dionysius, affirmative theology is imperfect since it proceeds by the way of analogy, and yet it is an important starting point, for it constitutes the rapport between the human and the divine.[60]

Symbolic theology for the Pseudo-Dionysius is concerned with the ascent of the mind from the realm of the sensible to the level of the

---

53 R. Mortley address the Neoplatonic background of the naming process in his chapter on Dionysius in From Word to Silence II (see not 22 above); on the Syriac inheritance of Dionysius on this point see A. Louth, op. cit. 79f. (see note 16 above).

54 Dionysius also considers the application of some philosophical terms: small, great, same, different, equal, unequal, similar, dissimilar—a very definite Neoplatonic theme based ultimately on the Parmenides 137, c f.

55 D. N. II 3 (640B) and II 11 (652A).

56 D. N. II 1 (637C) and II 11 (652A).

57 Jgs 13:17-18; see D. N. I 6 (596A).

58 D. N. VII 1 (865C-D) and XIII 3 (980D).

59 D. N. II 7 (645A).

60 On Dionysian analogy, see V. Lossky, 'La notion des "analogies" chez Pseudo-Denys l'Aréopagite', Archives d'histoire doctrinale et littéraire du moyen âge, 5 (1930) 279-309.

intelligible concept and it is focused upon the manifestation of God in Scripture.[61] In the *Mystical Theology*, Dionysius tells us that the (supposed) treatise, *Symbolic Theology*, is concerned with the interpretation of the anthropomorphic images and attributes said of God in the Oracles which can sometimes appear absurd or shocking, things which are transferred from the sensible to the divine realm: his places, parts, organs, anger, grief, sickness, sleeping and awakening.[62] Scripture, he says, often uses images and pictures derived from the lowest of things: God can be described as a perfume, a corner-stone and even as a lowly worm.[63] 'All this is revealed in the sacred pictures of the Scriptures so that He might lift us in spirit up through the perceptual to the conceptual, from sacred shapes and symbols to the simple peaks of the hierarchies of heaven.'[64] However, the importance of the symbol is its intelligible content and, therefore, the process of metonymy must be reversed: 'to enable the one capable of seeing the beauty hidden within these images to find that they are truly mysterious, appropriate to God and filled with a great theological light'.[65] For example, Dionysius explains that 'drunkenness' in God is nothing else but the ecstatic overflowing of his love and goodness to all creatures.[66] Symbolic theology, therefore, discards the sensible clothing of the symbol in order to unveil and apprehend its significant content, the true task of exegesis. We must, says Dionysius, 'make the holy journey to the heart of the sacred symbols'.[67] The Dionysian illustration of this in liturgical terms can be understood as a movement behind the iconostasis to the unveiled light beyond it; in the same way, Scripture is understood to be a veiling of the divine which must be transcended.[68] At this point, and indeed at many others, Dionysius cautions that the inner secrets veiled by symbol are not to be revealed to the unholy, those who are uninitiated, for it is precisely the function of symbol to protect the inexpressible and invisible from the many.[69] It is only the genuine lover of holiness who is led to leave aside the protective covering of the symbol and enter into the simplicity of the divine nature; knowledge is not for everyone.[70]

---

61 Symbols bear the mark of the divine as manifest images of the ineffeable, Ep. IX 2 (1008c).

62 M. Th. III (1033a-b); Ep. IX (1104b) and D. N. I 8 (597a-b).

63 C. H. II 5 (144d-145a).

64 C. H. I 3 (124a), trans. 147.

65 Ibid.

66 Ep. IX 4 (1112b-c).

67 Ep. IX 2 (1108c), trans. 284. According to Sheldon-Williams, if this process is not undertaken, the methodical science of God will end in idolatry, see 'The Pseudo-Dionysius', 463 and 467.

68 See E. H. III 2 (428c); C. H. I 2 (121b-c) and Ep. IX 1 (1108a-b); on the liturgical aspect of the symbol in Dionysius, see P. Rorem's excellent study (note 49 above).

69 C. H. II 2 (140b); M. Th. I 2 (1000a), and E. H. I 1 (372a).

70 Ep. IX 1 (1105d) and D. N. I 8 (597b-c).

For the Pseudo-Dionysius Moses was the prototype for the journey into union with the *Deus absconditus*. Moses first purifies himself and having separated himself from the unpurified, moves upwards towards the highest ascent, and finally enters alone into the darkness of unknowing through which he is eventually united to the unknown.[71] The process of *aphairesis*, which had already entered into Christian thought through the writings of Clement of Alexandria, is expanded and developed by Dionysius in a most Plotinian fashion; interestingly, it is not a concept which was stressed by the later Neoplatonists. Abstraction involves the removal of all things starting from the lowest and working up to the highest;[72] it is detachment from everything, even the most holy things which are akin to the divine (divine lights, celestial voices and words— even the Scriptures themselves).[73] When the soul has become free from all and released from all, it is then in a worthy state to enter into the divine darkness and to be raised into union with the divine: 'by an undivided and absolute abandonment of yourself and everything, shedding all and freed from all, you will be lifted up to the ray of divine shadow, which is above everything that is'.[74] However, in his exegesis of the Exodus text, Dionysius explains that in order to be raised unknowingly into union with God, Moses first of all sees the place where God is, not God Himself who is invisible. It is when he finally breaks from all that is seen by silencing all intellectual pursuits and becomes an 'eyeless mind' (no longer a knowing subject), that he enters fully into the darkness, being completely united with the transcendent Unknown (no longer a known object): 'being neither oneself nor someone else, one is supremely united by a completely unknowing inactivity of all knowledge, and knows beyond the mind by knowing nothing'.[75] It is, explains Dionysius in very Nyssean (and indeed Plotinian) terms, through not seeing, and not knowing that one truly sees and truly knows.[76]

Logos ascending into unity moves from the eloquence of many words, to fewer words and finally to no words at all: 'the more it climbs, the more language falters, and when it has passed up and beyond the

71 M. Th. I 3 (1000c-1001a). The liturgical facet of the unifying experience of the Mystical Theology is brought out by A. Louth, op. cit. 101 9: see note 16 above).

72 M. Th. II (1025b) and III (1033c).

73 Like Plotinus, Dionysius uses the image of the sculptor chipping away at a statue in order to bring forth its inner beauty to illustrate the kind of purification involved in *aphairesis*, see Enn. I 6, 9, 6; see M. Th. II (1025a-b).

74 M. Th. I 1 (997b-1000a), trans. 135; see also C. H. III 3 (165d) and E. H. III 5 (401a-b). According to Vanneste's interpretation, the kind of purification advocated by Dionysius is primarily intellectual and not moral; he concludes that the practice of *aphairesis* is not a Christian one, see Le mystère de Dieu, 230.

75 M. Th. I 3 (1001a), trans. 137.

76 M. Th. II (1025a), trans. 138: 'I pray we could come to this darkness so far above light! If only we lacked sight and knowledge so as to see, so as to know, unseeing and unknowing, that which lies beyond all vision and knowledge'.

ascent, it will turn silent completely, since it will finally be at one with Him who is indescribable.'[77] It is in this sense that Dionysian theology can be understood as dependent upon Scripture, although the movement from logos takes us into the realm of silence, a silence which is no longer dependent upon words of any kind—even the most divine and illuminating. It is clear, therefore, that mystical theology in the Dionysian schema is the culmination of the journey of Moses; it is not an alternative way to God which can bypass either hierarchy or Scripture, and it does not function as a tool for the deconstruction of all concepts.

Perhaps if it were possible to retranslate the works of the Pseudo-Dionysius and somehow 'decaffinate', as it were, the very obvious Neoplatonic elements in his writings, he would emerge as an orthodox champion of Christian theology. However, even with their strong Neoplatonic themes, the works of the Pseudo-Dionysius successfully penetrated the intellectualism of the Latin West. In perpetrating one of the greatest intellectual forgeries of all times, Dionysius ensured the survival of an approach to the theological and exegetical disciplines without which the scholasticism of the West would have been greatly impoverished.

In the end, however, the concerns and perspectives of the Pseudo-Dionysius are those of the fifth century and sometimes appear quite alien to our twentieth-century minds. Perhaps any attempt to rehabilitate his method of exegesis would be a fruitless task, for what von Balthasar has said is, at least in some measure, true: we have lost the sense of the mysterious in our lives and in our theology: we no longer appreciate the mystery hidden in the depths of scriptural symbols.[78]

Two years ago I saw a kingfisher for the first time. I was so enthralled that I wanted to find out more about this minute flash of brilliance. But none of the artists' reproductions in the books I looked at was able to catch its magnificent colour. It is called kingfisher blue: we have named our colour after the bird, for no other words can describe its unique, ineffable iridescence. The Fathers of the Church, in similar fashion, were aware that the unique mystery of the Godhead was accessible, at least partially through the sacred texts, but in the end, words lose their meaning: 'bright darkness', 'ineffable word', 'silent music': these are the conceptions which point us in the right direction, back to the Mystery of God.

---

77   M. Th. III (1033B), trans. 139.
78   See his comments in Science, Religion and Christianity, London 1958, 100f.

Origen and the Literal Interpretation of Scripture

GERARD WATSON

Despite the title, I should begin with something which is perhaps too obvious to point out in a context such as this: Origen was not a dogmatic literalist. He will of course try to show where need be that the literal truth of Scripture is possible, even when it may run the risk of incurring ridicule from non-believers. But he knows that there is more than one way of stating the truth, and he will emphasize with some subtlety that this fact is recognised by Christians and pagans alike. Allegory is an alternative way of stating the truth used by both pagans and Christians. Origen does not want to sound superior to his pagan readers, and certainly not to his more simple-minded Christian ones, but he does wish to suggest that the verification of almost any story is not a simple matter and certainly not to be taken for granted. Without labouring the fact, he indicates that the apparently simple acceptance of reports may in fact involve complicated philosophical processes, not noticed by the unreflecting. So, for instance, when attempting to defend stories found in the Gospels which his opponent Celsus is inclined to mock at, he says: 'Before we begin the defence, we must say that any attempt to substantiate almost any story as historical fact, even if it is true, and to produce complete certainly about it, is one of the most difficult tasks and in some cases impossible.' [1] Here in fact, but as I said, without labouring it, Origen is referring to a well-known Greek philosophical position, one fundamental to Stoic epistemology. The Stoics maintained that an impression on the mind coming from the senses will be reliable if it permits *katalêpsis*, a real grasp of the object. To be acknowledged, the impression must be from an existing object, clear and distinct. Sextus Empiricus reports that they held that it must be imaged and stamped in the subject, in order that all the characteristics of the presented objects may be reproduced with artistic exactitude.[2] Various criteria must be called into play in establishing the truth of a presentation; the new piece of information must fit into the so far established world picture, and *katalêpsis* cannot take place without proper reasoning, however rapidly this is done.

1   C. Celsum 1,42. 2   Cf. Adv. math. 7,250

So even in this brief allusion to a central Stoic position on the criterion of truth Origen is suggesting that even the most banal facts cannot
be taken for granted. The critical mind must be applied to all stories,
Greek and Christian. But this does not imply the complete rejection of
stories that have been told, Greek or Christian. In the lines which immediately follow on Origen's allusion to the rigorous Stoic position on the
criterion, Origen refers to well-known stories from the Greek tradition,
such as the war at Troy or the Oedipus story, and comments: 'Anyone
who reads the stories with a fair mind who wants to keep himself from
being deceived by them, will decide what he will accept and what he will
interpret allegorically, searching out the meaning of the authors who
wrote such fictitious stories, and what he will disbelieve as having been
written to gratify certain people'. He adds immediately: 'We have said
this by way of introduction to the whole question of the narrative about
Jesus in the Gospels, not in order to invite people with intelligence to
mere irrational faith, but with a desire to show that readers need an
open mind and considerable study, and, if I may say so, need to enter
into the mind of the writers to find out with what spiritual meaning each
event was recorded.'[3]

There are a couple of points here to which we must return, notably
allegory and the spiritual meaning. But what I want to emphasise primarily is both the subtlety and the conciliatory nature of Origen's
approach. The Christians take important matters on faith. But do not all
sensible people? Thinkers of much greater perspicacity than Celsus
accept that difficulty is to be expected on obscure questions. Origen has
just referred to Plato's discussion of the immortality of the soul in the
Phaedo, where he ends the dialogue with a story or picture of the after-
life which is meant to add force to the arguments adduced earlier in the
discussion. Yet Plato ends the story by saying (14c): 'Of course no reasonable man ought to insist that the facts are exactly as I have described
them. But that either this or something very like it is a true account of
our souls and their future habitations—since we have clear evidence that
the soul is immortal—this, I think, is both a reasonable contention and a
belief worth risking.' Origen summarises this by saying: 'Plato says that a
sensible man will not be confident about such obscure questions.' 'And',
he adds, 'Chrysippus, who always gave an account of the reasons which
influenced him, refers us to people whom we might find to give a better
explanation than himself.'[4] Chrysippus the Stoic was regarded as one of
the most learned and acute thinkers in antiquity. The implication is
clear: the best minds of the Greeks as well as of the Christians have taken
things on faith. Celsus is being unreasonable in demanding clear logical
proof of everything.

3   C. Celsum 1,40.   4   Ibid.

Yet Origen was well aware that Celsus was not alone in criticizing the Christians for their reliance on the words of their sacred books and dismissing it as simplistically literal. Celsus see Christianity as anti-intellectual and afraid of argument. It represents foolishness as a good thing (1,13), it appeals to the stupid, the ignorant, the uneducated, to slaves, women and little children (3,44). 'It is successful only among the uneducated because of its vulgarity and utter illiteracy' (1,27). 'Some do not even want to give or receive a reason for what they believe, and use such expressions as 'Do not ask questions; just believe'(1,9).

Origen of course was not the first Christian to have to endure such assaults. As Chadwick has pointed out,[5] Origen's predecessor, Clement of Alexandria, had also to confront the pagan critic who scorns faith as an unreasoning opinion. And the tradition of scepticism was a long one even within the boundaries of Greek Philosophy alone. So Origen was not breaking new ground in his reply to Celsus on problems of interpretation, and, typically, he draws on a number of sources. He says, first of all, that if everyone could afford to devote all their time to philosophy, this is what they ought to do (1,9). 'It is in harmony with Scripture to say that it is far better to accept doctrines with reason and wisdom than with mere faith' (1,13). In fact, it can be shown from Scripture that 'the divine Word also exhorts us to study dialectics' (6,7). Christianity provides a wonderful field for applied philosophy, and with some people 'we do all we can to approach them with rational arguments 'by questions and answers', as Plato has prescribed (6,10).

But, secondly and realistically, 'there are some people to whom we preach only an exhortation to believe, since they are incapable of anything more' (6,10). 'Partly owing to the necessities of life and partly owing to human weakness, very few people are enthusiastic about rational thought'(1,9). It would obviously be foolish to wait until the majority might devote themselves to the study of rational argument when they might immediately 'be helped by the belief that they are punished for sin and rewarded for good works' (1,9). 'The task of those of us who give an intelligent account of Christianity is simply to deliver our hearers from stupidity as well as we can and to make them sensible' (4,72).

So Origen admits that we teach some people to believe without forcing them to think out the intellectual credibility of their reasons. But, and this is his third and most important point, in practice others do the same, even if they do not admit it. When someone, for instance, decides to join a particular philosophical school, be it Stoic, Platonist, Peripatetic, Epicurean or whatever, he does so on an act of faith that this is the best school, rather than because of an exhaustive comparison of all the pros and cons. And not only in philosophy: whoever goes on a voyage,

5   Early Christian Thought and the Classical Tradition, Oxford 1966, 51f.

or marries, or begets children, or casts seeds into the ground does so in the faith that things will turn out for the better (1,11).

Here again Origen is 'spoiling the Egyptians'.[6] He is saying that the Christians act like normal reasonable people when they give their assent to propositions from their own tradition. It is also worth noting here that both sides, pagan and Christian, in the early centuries were inclined to use the argument from authority, particularly the authority given by the antiquity of a position. Origen repeats time after time (taking a theme from Jewish apologetics) that divine revelation in the Scriptures is so much older than Greek thought.[7] Reconciliation is possible. 'If the doctrine is beneficial and its intention sound and if it has been stated among the Greeks by Plato or one of the Greek wise men and among the Jews by Moses or one of the prophets and among the Christians in the recorded words of Jesus or utterances of one of his Apostles, we are not to suppose that any objection to the saying uttered by Jews or by Christians can be based on the fact that the doctrines were also set forth by the Greeks and particularly if the writings of the Jews are proved to be earlier than those of the Greeks' (7,59). According to Jerome, Origen compared 'the maxims of the Christians to those of the philosophers' and confirmed 'all the dogmas of our religion by extracts from Plato and Aristotle, from Numenius and from Cornutus'.[8]

I began by emphasizing that Origen was not a dogmatic literalist. But the important complementary point should be added that Origen regarded himself primarily as an exegete, an expounder of the Scriptures rather than as a systematic theologian or a Christian philosopher, although he was of course both. But the exposition of the Scriptures was the centre of his life. To expound the Scriptures faithfully one must first make sure that one has a reliable text of the Scriptures to expound, and in his commentaries and homilies he pays careful attention to the variant readings of the manuscripts. Hence one of the most remarkable of his scholarly works, the *Hexapla*. But before turning briefly to that, let me at least refer to his works on Scripture. I say 'refer', because even to list these works would exhaust the patience of even the most dedicated biblical scholar.[9] Jerome's incomplete list ranges from 13 books on Genesis, through the Old Testament, to works on the New Testament including 25 books on Matthew and 32 on John, not to mention homilies on various works. Many of these writings are now lost: this, of course, is the fate of many writings from the ancient world, but it is sad to record that in the case of Origen, perhaps the greatest of the early Greek Christian fathers, the loss may have been due to the misunder-

6   See Chadwick's note ad loc. and Reid on Cicero, Acad.II, 109.
7   Cf. 1,20; 4,31; 4,36; 6,7; 7,28; 7, J.S. Reid, The Academica of Cicero, London 1874, 30.
8   Letter to Magnus, quoted in Crouzel, Origen, 39, English transl.
9   For a list see Crouzel, op.cit., reporting Jerome.

standing, or malice, of later Christians. Yet we have some indication of the detailed nature of Origen's commentaries from the books that have survived. Book One of the *Commentary on John*, for instance, comments only on the first five words of verse one, chapter one. Book Two gets on to verse 7 of chapter 1. The fifth book took him to verse 17 of chapter one.

The *Hexapla* was not a commentary as such, but it too has not survived as a whole. The word means 'six columns', and we have references to it from Origen himself and others, as well as several fragments. Before going into the rather strange title we should recall another obvious but sometimes not sufficiently emphasized point about Origen: he was a citizen of Alexandria in Egypt. Alexander the Great had swept down through the Near East in 332 BC, and in 331 founded this, the first of many Alexandrias. Within ten years he was dead, but his city survived, and, under the Ptolemies, flourished. Ptolemy, one of Alexander's generals, had proclaimed himself King of Egypt in 304, and Egypt was soon the strongest power after the division of Alexander's empire. Egypt was a country with a long history, and a strong sense of that history, a developed culture and social organization, long the object of Greek admiration and curiosity. Under the Ptolemies Alexandria was to become a Greek city and to displace Athens as the centre of Greek learning. Greek was the common tongue, the *koinê*. That does not mean that all the inhabitants were true born Greeks: among the population there were the Macedonian Greeks and their camp followers, native Egyptians, and, a very important element, Jews.

Palestine was a small spot on the total map, but it was a key area, on the crossroads between North and South, East and West, controlling the overland routes and the outlets to the sea. The Ptolemies were keen to establish their power, and gradually did so, from 322 onwards. Jewish mercenaries served in Hellenistic armies, and, with slaves, were the biggest builders of the Diaspora in the Greek speaking world. There was then in the third century BC a strong Greek presence in Palestine, coming largely from Egypt. But there were also, of course, Jews in Egypt, and there had been for a long time—from perhaps as early as the sixth century BC. But the large settlements only really began in the wake of Alexander and under the Ptolemies. Jews were settled all over Egypt: their presence in Alexandria was particularly striking. There might have been between 120,000 and 400,000 Jews in Alexandria in the first century BC. By the time of Philo, in the first century AD, two out of the five quarters of the city were full of Jews, and there were Jewish synagogues right through the city. There was no question of a ghetto, although the Jewish community had a very definite organization.

A very important element in the Jewish population of Egypt were the mercenaries and the soldiers. The Greek language was adopted particularly quickly by them. They had clung to their religion, but their language was now more and more Greek. Ptolemy II (284–246) would have been interested in seeing that a translation of the Torah was provided and any possible trouble arising from religious discontent removed.

The importance of the Septuagint for the Jews of the Hellenistic period cannot be overestimated. It was a translation of the Old Testament which had been produced over a period of time, and which varied considerably in style and fidelity to the original. It was the Greek Bible for the Jews and was accepted as such by the Christians when they began to spread their gospel in the Hellenistic world of the first and second centuries AD. This take-over by the Christians naturally antagonized Jews who would be anxious to show that the Christians were misusing, by misunderstanding and mistranslating, their sacred text. Alexandria was a city with a long tradition of close attention to the text in hand, and it is there particularly that we can see the beginnings of textual criticism and the establishment of reliable texts as we know it. This activity had been particularly associated with the Museum and library instituted by Ptolemy I. There had worked great critics like Zenodotus, Aristophanes and Aristarchus, centuries before the time of Origen. Origen had been trained as a grammarian, and close attention to the letter of the text had become part of his nature. It may be that the letter killeth, but not if it is established that the letter is the word of God. Anything *apparently* fatal must in that case be properly interpreted. Alexandria was a melting-pot—native Egyptians, Greeks, Jews and, now, Christians. It is obvious even from the remarks of Origen himself that a great deal of discussion went on, philosophical, theological and scriptural, and particularly between the Jews and Christians. What exactly the Bible said mattered a great deal. The best possible text of the Old Testament had to be established. Even though many of the Jews, as we saw, depended on Greek for their knowledge of the Old Testament, it was obvious that where Hebrew was the original text this text must be provided. Origen among other things wished to supply Christians with a Septuagint text which could be used in controversies with the Jews. The result was the *Hexapla*, a work which eventually showed the Hebrew text and the various Greek versions in six parallel columns. This would have been an enormous work, and it is easy to believe that no copy of the entire original work was ever made. But it remained an important work: 'a milestone,' as Trigg says, 'in biblical scholarship that makes Origen the father of textual criticism of the bible in the Christian tradition.'[10] He was to be the inspiration of many others, not least Jerome.

The consciousness of the importance of the individual word, which is partly due to the inheritance of Alexandrian scholarship, helps to explain the vastness of Origen's commentaries on Scripture, insofar as

10   Joseph Trigg, Origen, London 1985, 82 ff.

we can judge them from what remains—*archê* and *logos* are good examples in John I. But the fact that each word in the Bible was chosen by the Holy Spirit meant, as Origen saw it, that we must often look further than the obvious meanings of the word, extensive as the range of these meanings might already be, in the case of *logos*, for instance. The result is that events recorded in, say, the Gospels, which may sound entirely credible as they stand to us, are subjected by Origen to further analysis which gives the original story at best a secondary place. An example of this is the story of Jesus meeting the Samaritan woman at the well: it is really, according to Origen, an indication of the difficulty of arriving at a full understanding of John's Gospel. Similarly, the account in John 2: 13–17 of Jesus driving the money-changers from the temple with a whip of cords. Origen is not in favour of any literal cleansing of the temple: the cleansing of the temple is really the cleansing of the soul.

Origen of course is not attempting to give gratuitous offence to believers in the literal sense of the Scriptures: indeed, time and time again he shows his sensitivity to the demands of simple faith. Nor is he trying to bend over backwards to please pagan intellectuals who might look for displays of sophistication. Origen is simply aware that the truth is told in various ways, and he could point to Christ himself as the master who conveyed some of his most vivid messages in parables. The story of the Good Samaritan did not require an hour-long analysis to get its meaning over to anyone, Greek or Christian. But, as I mentioned at the start, the use of allegory was far from being a strange notion to the Greeks themselves, and from a very early stage, the fifth century BC at least, some philosophers specialised in explaining the 'hidden meanings' in what seemed straightforward story-telling in Homer, or in explaining away obscene passages in Homer and Hesiod. This continued down to the days of Origen, and his opponent Porphyry, the pupil of Plotinus, wrote a work with an allegorical interpretation of the Cave of the Nymphs in Homer. If Homer and Hesiod can be allegorized by the Greeks, the Old Testament can be seen by Christians as the presentation of Christ before His actual appearance on earth.

So Origen did not need to feel defensive in giving an allegorical or spiritual interpretation of Scripture, any more than Philo the Jew did before him. And his understanding of how words relate to realities was at least as subtle as that of any of his contemporary pagan philosophers. This awareness is not flaunted, and often indeed passes unnoticed, because he did not want to alienate either his Christian readers or the well-disposed pagans who obviously came to Origen in hope of some truth which they felt was eluding them. But Origen's sophistication in his approach to language is obvious in his treatment of Paul's word 'law' in the Epistle to the Romans. He is aware of the danger of treating all words as merely names, or of being taken in by the 'Fido-Fido' theory of meaning. There are words, things signified, and externally existing objects. Origen seems to have taken note of the Stoic theory of meaning and of the elaborate discussions that went on in that school. Yet, while using the technical terms and the associated useful distinctions, Origen does not allow his discussion to lapse into a desiccated philosophical discussion.

We are, then, according to Origen to expect sophistication from words, and particularly from the words of God as given to us in the Testaments, Old and New. The Old Testament is the foretelling of Christ, and to be understood from Him. Those who do not accept Christ have before their faces a veil which hides from them the true meaning of the Bible (2 Cor 3:4f). It is in this way that it is the letter which kills. God is veiled in mystery, and our way to Him must be through the symbolic language of the Bible. We must speak of God in human terms, but we must not take the anthropomorphisms literally. The pillar of cloud, the manna, the water spouting from the rock, the death in the wilderness which Paul refers back to in I Cor 10: 1–11 represent different things for us, like Baptism and the Eucharist, and he says 'that happened to them to serve as a figure, but it was written as a warning to us'. So it was for Christians that the Old Testament was written, and as Crouzel[11] says 'that affirmation necessarily implies a spiritual interpretation, for a good many of its precepts, those concerned with ceremonies and the law, are no longer binding on us in their literal sense'.

The revelation then that is in the Bible is Christ, the *Logos*, the Word of God. But this does not mean for Origen that details can be ignored. Origen did have a literal understanding of the inspiration of Scripture: as Crouzel again says[12] 'he thought of it rather like dictation'. Every word of the Spirit must have a useful meaning. So if a word is puzzling in one place in the Bible, the rest of it must be searched to throw light on the puzzle. On the other hand, the word might occur only once in Scripture, as is the case for a word in the Our Father, the word we translate as 'our *daily* bread', the *epiousion arton* of Matthew and Luke. This provokes an elaborate discussion of the adjective. Origen takes it to be connected with *ousia*, the philosophical term for the ultimate reality in things, something incorporeal in itself but the core of the other attributes. So the bread we are asking for in the Lord's Prayer is the wisdom and true reality which is the word of God.

Obviously, such discussions were not intended for simple Christians. Yet Origen never forgot that there were such Christians, and he never forgot his duty to them. That is part of the reason why he says that the Bible contains three levels of meaning, corresponding to the three-fold

11 Op.cit. 66f.   12 Op. cit. 71.

division of a person into body, soul and spirit. The bodily level of Scripture, the literal, is obviously helpful, but Origen, as we have seen, has always an eye ready for the other levels. For example, the first five chapters of Genesis can be read quite satisfactorily on a simple level as an account of the creation of the visible world. On the other hand, people with more complicated minds might be thrown by some of the statements in the early chapters of Genesis if the statements were to be taken literally. So Origen tries, in *Peri archôn* IV 3 for example, to explain how some of these statements should be understood. One could, for instance, hardly talk of the evening and the morning of the first day, when the sun did not even exist. Nor should we be encouraged to think that God, like a farmer, planted a garden east of Eden, or that He went for a walk in the cool of the day, as if He needed to stretch his legs. Similarly, in the New Testament, how would it be possible for the devil to take Jesus up into a high mountain in order to show him the kingdoms of the whole world? Where could you find such a mountain?

Origen was well aware that some Christians would regard such questions as disrespectful or even blasphemous. Origen's intention, of course, was quite the opposite: it was, as indicated before, to save the Scriptures from the mockery of those who were hostile as well as critical. But Our Lord himself has told us to be critical. And so, as Origen says in *Peri archôn* IV 3, 5: 'The exact reader will hesitate in regard to some passages, finding himself unable to decide without considerable investigation whether a particular incident, believed to be history, actually happened or not, and whether the literal meaning of a particular law is to be observed or not. Accordingly he who reads in an exact manner must, in obedience to the Saviour's precept which says, "search the Scriptures," carefully investigate how far the literal meaning is true and how far it is impossible.' Truths have been hidden in the Scriptures. But they have been placed there by God to encourage us to search, and to assure us that if we must seek, we shall also find.

There can be no question of trying to summarize here the achievement of Origen: I am sure that this conference will not pass without much reference to him, direct or indirect. He was, as I have said, badly treated by Christans of a later period who should have known better. But he was also much appreciated, not least by the Cappadocian Fathers, Basil and the Gregories. Through them and because of them, particularly through Ambrose, Origen was to have a decisive influence on perhaps the greatest of the Latin Fathers, Augustine. Augustine tells us in his *Confessions* how three main questions tormented him when he was a student in Carthage: the problem of evil, the nature of spirit, particularly God, and the problems arising from the Old Testament. When he came to Milan in the Autumn of 384 he went along to hear Ambrose preach—not as someone who still retained a marginal interest in Christianity, but rather as one professional going along to hear another and to judge whether he lived up to his reputation. The Manichaean (and his own) objections to the Old Testament began to disappear. 'I began to see that the Catholic faith, for which I had thought nothing could be said in the face of Manichaean objections, could be maintained on reasonable grounds: this especially after I had heard explained allegorically several passages of the Old Testament which, when I had interpreted them literally had "killed" me spiritually. Many passages of these books were expounded in a spiritual sense and I came to blame my own hopeless folly in believing that the law and the prophets could not stand against those who hated and mocked at them' (V 14,24). The credit for the fact that Ambrose could dissolve these difficulties goes back ultimately to Origen. Ambrose was a Roman who could read Greek fluently and knew the whole tradition of Greek Christian scholarship. As Brown[13] says: 'One thought runs through Ambrose's preaching: beneath the opaque and rebarbative "letter" of the Old Testament, this "spirit", the hidden meaning calls to our spirit to rise and fly away into another world'. The capturing of the questioning mind of Augustine and the turning of it to the service of the Church was perhaps the greatest achievement of Origen, the interpreter of Scripture.

13   Peter Brown, Augustine of Hippo, London 1969, 85

St Athanasius: De synodis and the Sense of Scripture[1]

VINCENT TWOMEY

The Trinitarian controversies in the fourth century were essentially concerned with scriptural interpretation. Though certain texts (such as Prov 8.22) were central to the debates, what was at stake was not simply any one text as such but rather Scripture as a whole. For Athanasius, the entire sense (*dianoia*, singular!) of Scripture testifies to the nature of Christ—and to His mission, intrinsic to which is Scripture itself. Accordingly, the interpretation of Scripture stands in reciprocal relationship to one's own relationship to, and so to one's understanding of, Christ. To convince his readers that the *homoousios*, though not itself a scriptural term, best preserved the sense of Scripture in the face of the threat of Arianism is the purpose of *De synodis*.

Already in *Contra gentes*, Athanasius had affirmed that '. . . the sacred and divinely inspired Scriptures are sufficient for the exposition of the truth . . .' Yet he also drew the reader's attention to writings of 'our blessed teachers,' study of which could be used 'in the interpretation of Scripture'[2]. The express purpose of that early work was to expound 'the faith in Christ the Saviour.' Scripture, in other words, is not absolutely self-sufficient,[3] it demands interpretation. Further, interpretation takes place within a tradition, that of 'our blessed teachers,' whose object is the 'ecclesiastical teaching',[4] the apostolic *paradosis*.[5] This tradition is above all handed on by 'the Fathers.' As we will see the latter term refers primarily to the Bishops in so far as they are the authoritative interpreters of Scripture.[6] The interrelationship between Scripture and Tradition is one

---

1 The original draft of this paper was intended as a contribution to Joseph Cardinal Ratzinger's Festschrift, but circumstances prevented me from completing it at the time. I would like to offer this revised version as a belated homage to my revered professor who introduced me to the unfathomable riches of the Church's living, divine-human, Tradition.

2 C. gent. 1, PG 25,4 A11–B1, translation by R.W. Thompson, Oxford 1971.

3 Even though Athanasius affirms: *esti men gar hikanôtera pantôn hê theia graphê* (De syn. 6,2, Opitz 234,26), the use of the comparative, as well as the context, confirms this.

4 C. gent. 6, PG 25,13 A10.

5 Cf. De syn. 47,4, Opitz, 272, 17; unless otherwise indicated, translations are mine.

6 Cf. De syn. 43, 1–3, Opitz 268, 16–17; 45, 5, Opitz 270, 15–18; see below 107–108.

of the main themes of *De synodis Arimini in Italia et Seleucia in Isauria celebratis.*

But what happens when, as was the case in the fourth century, a plethora of synods issued several synodal decrees with varying degrees of agreement? How are they to be interpreted? Where is the authoritative interpretation to be found? What is the nature of that authority? Nicaea was considered, at least by Athanasius, to have decided the matter, but those who found difficulty with Nicaea pointed out, among other things, that Nicaea itself seemed to have flatly contradicted a previous synod (Antioch) which no one disputed. Accordingly there was need for what might be called a hermeneutic of synodal decrees. In *De synodis* Athanasius attempts to provide such a hermeneutic modelled on the inter-pretation of Scripture itself.[7]

The interpretation of Scripture and tradition, including Church authority, arises from our need to know the truth revealed in Christ as witnessed by Scripture and handed on by the Church. Interpretation thus raises the question as to the possibility of theology. This, we will see, is the primary concern of Athanasius in his defence of the non-scriptural term *homoousios.*

The interpretation of the text of *De synodis* is the subject of this study.[8] Despite appearances to the contrary, it is not an easy text to fathom due to the interrelated themes and concerns of the writer just briefly outlined. Apart from noting the historical circumstances that occasioned its writing and the precise literary genre, the main analysis will be devoted to an attempt to uncover the inner structure of the text: the way the writer marshals the evidence, presents his arguments and deals with the various

7   With regard to Athanasius' interpretation of Scripture see T. F. Torrance, 'The Hermeneutics of St. Athanasius' in Ekklesiastikos Pharos 52,1 (1970) 446–468; 52,2–3 (1970) 89–106; 52,4 (1970) 237–249; H. J. Sieben, 'Herméneutque de l'exégèse dogmatique d'Athanase' in Ch. Kannengiesser (ed.), Politique et théologie chez Athanase d'Alexandrie. Actes du Colloque de Chantilly, 23–25 Septembre 1973, Paris 1974, 195–214 [see for earlier literature, especially that of Pollard and Kannengiesser; see also J. Pelikan, The Light of the World, New York 1962, 26–29]; Ch. Kannengiesser, 'Holy Scripture and Hellenistic Hermeneutics in Alexandrian Christology: The Arian Crisis' in Center for Hermeneutical Studies in Hellenistic and Modern Culture, Colloquy 41, Gradutate Theological Union and the University of California Berkely, California 1982; W. Schneemelcher, 'Der Schriftgebrauch in den "Apologien" des Athanasius' in idem, Reden und Aufsätze. Beiträge zur Kirchengeschichte und zum ökumenischen Gespräch, Tübingen 1991, 126–135.

8   There is a marked absence of studies devoted exclusively to De synodis. The critical edition of the text by H.-G. Opitz, Athanasius' Werke II, 1, Die Apologien, Berlin-Leipzig, 1945, 231–278, also includes a limited commentary on various points, mostly of a historical nature. Of particular interest is the study of H.J. Sieben, 'Werden und Eigenart der Konzilsidee des Athanasius von Alexandrien (+373)' in: idem, Die Konzilsidee der alten Kirche, Paderborn-München-Wien-Zürich. 1979, 25–67, esp. 45–52 which deals with the place of De synodis in Sieben's reconstruction of the evolution of Athanasius' thought on the nature of a council. Cf. also J. Gummerus, Die homöusianische Partei bis zum Tode des Konstantius, Leipzig 1900, especially pp. 163–168.

interrelated themes. The use of such a methodology would seem to offer the most promising means of approach to the thought of Athanasius.

BACKGROUND: THE SYNOD IN ITS HISTORICAL DEVELOPMENT

Since one of the main concerns of *De synodis* is to demonstrate the authoritative, definitive nature of Nicaea, it is however necessary to begin with a brief account—no matter how inadequate[9]—of the pre-Nicene understanding of episcopal or synodal authority.

Synodal authority is based on the authority of the individual bishop who as bishop of a local church is responsible directly for his own Church and indirectly for the one Church universal, the former being the actualization in a particular place and at a particular time of the latter. His authority was apostolic and collegial in nature due to his participation in the apostolic succession and his unique responsibility for handing on intact the apostolic teaching.[10] The bishop was in turn both dependent on and responsible for communion with the Church universal. Communion with his fellow bishops was originally established through mutual recognition (*Letters of Communion*[11]) which primarily involved agreement with regard to the content of the apostolic *paradosis*.[12]

With the expansion of the Church, the growth of heresy and differences with regard to liturgical discipline, the original interdependence of the bishops and their consciousness of responsibility for the well-being of the other churches[13] gradually found a new form of expression

9   For a more complete account, see especially Dom H. Marot, 'Vornikäische und ökumenisch Konzile' in: Dom B. Botte (ed.), Das Konzil und die Konzile, Stuttgart 1962, 23–51. The following sketch, incomplete though it may be, is none the less indispensable for an understanding of the nature of the problem faced by Athanasius and his contemporaries, one which Athanasius attempts to solve in De synodis. As J. Pieper once pointed out in The Silence of St. Thomas, London 1957, 52, '. . . an interpretation which does not reach the unspoken assumptions underlying the actual text must remain, in essence, a misinterpretation.'

10   Such a responsibility involved the right and duty to decide who ought, or ought not, to be admitted to the full life of the Church expressed in the Eucharistic communion. This is the origin of eccesiastical jurisdiction.

11   Cf. e.g. L. Hertling, 'Communio und Primat. Kirche und Papsttum in der christlichen Antike' in Una Sancta 17 (1962) 91–125.

12   'Als eucharistische Tischgemeinschaft verwirklicht an sich jede einzelne Gemeinde das ganze Kirchsein der Kirche, aber doch nur dadurch, daß sie mit allen anderen Gemeinden in Kommunionverbindung steht, die ihrerseits wiederum ohne die Einheit des gemeinsam geglaubten und bezeugten Wortes unmöglich ist. Das Netz von Kommunionen, das die Kirche demnach bildet, hat in den Bischöfen seine Fixpunkte; ihnen obliegt als der nachapostolischen Fortsetzung des Collegium apostolorum die Verantwortung für die Reinheit des Wortes und für die Rechtheit der Kommunion': Joseph Ratzinger, Das neue Volk Gottes. Entwürfe zur Ekklesiologie, Düsseldorf 1970 (2nd impression), 117; further literature indicated there.

13   As evidenced e.g in the intervention of Clement and Soter of Rome in the affairs of the Church in Corinth, the concern of Ignatius of Antioch for the various

in the development of synods in the latter half of the second century.[14] The object of these 'meetings and assemblies' was to establish unanimity[15] on disputed matters, a unanimity that was from the start presumed to be universal. This was particularly marked when assemblies of bishops took place throughout the world at the same time to discuss the same basic issues. The decisions of such assemblies were communicated to the other Churches—especially through the three main sees of Rome, Antioch and Alexandria—and their reception came to signify their acceptance by the whole Church, in a word: universal unanimity.

But from the beginning the nature of that unanimity was itself disputed. A mere majority opinion, or compromise agreement, was evidently excluded by the apostolic nature of the episcopal authority, as can be inferred from the response of Polycrates of Ephesus to Victor of Rome.[16] Justifying his stand, and that of the bishops of Asia who met under his presidency, the Bishop of Ephesus informs Victor that he had consulted Scripture and the tradition of the Fathers in full awareness of his own personal responsibility in conscience before God for preserving and handing on intact that *paradosis*. He also pointed to his communion with his fellow bishops who had never questioned his faith. In this context he quotes Acts 5,29: 'One must obey God rather than men.' Unanimity is not simply majority rule but, to quote Irenaeus, a union of soul and heart.[17] The message of Polycrates would seem to have been well received by Rome since half a century later, during the baptismal controversy, Cyprian, while defending the principle that every bishop is responsible to God alone, claims that he himself had learnt it from Rome.[18]

The same controversy provides us with an important witness to the growing awareness of the definitive nature of synodal decrees around the middle of the third century. Appealing to Rome to tolerate local customs approved by local synods at Iconium and Synnada, Dionysius of Alexandria appeals to Scripture to justify their authority: 'Do not remove your neighbour's boundary stone, which your fathers placed . . .' (Deut 19:14:).[19]

    churches in Asia Minor to whom he sent letters, and the letters of Polycarp to neighbouring churches.

14   Cf. Eusebius, HE V 23, 2 ; see also J. A. Fisher, 'Die antimontanistischen Synoden des 2./3. Jahrhunderts' in AHC 6 (1974) 241–273.

15   *Synodoi dê kai synkrotêseis episkopôn epi tauton eginonto, pantes te miâi gnômêi di' epistolôn ekklêsiastikon dogma tois pantachose dietyptounto* ... Eusebius, HE V 23, 2.

16   Cf. Eusebius, HE V 24,1–8; see G. La Piana, The Roman Church at the End of the Second Century' in Harvard Theological Review 18 (1925) 232–236 on the implications of Victor's actions for the understanding of tradition.

17   Cf. Adv. haer. I 10,2 (PG 7, 552B).

18   Cf. M. Bévenot, 'A Bishop is responsible to God alone (St. Cyprian)' in: Recherches de Sciences religieuses 39 (1951) 397–415.

19   Cf. Eusebius, HE VII 7,5, cf. Fisher, art.cit., 270–272; Dionysius is the earliest witness to the use of the *term synodos* for an assembly of bishops.

As we have seen, the source of all synodal authority was the apostolic succession, or rather to use the terminology of Ratzinger, the post-apostolic continuation of the *Collegium apostolorum*. The same source determined the special relationship between bishops of Sees claiming direct apostolic succession and their fellow bishops. In disputed matters concerning the faith, those Churches with direct apostolic succession ought to be consulted since the unadulterated apostolic tradition could *a fortiori* be expected to be found there. Pre-eminent among these, according to Irenaeus, was the Church of Rome, whose apostolic succession could be traced back to St Peter and St Paul.[20] But the Petrine authority was not limited to Rome. The growing recognition of Antioch and Alexandria in the course of the third century as enjoying special prominence within their respective spheres of influence was attributed to their Petrine traditions. Such a development may well have been conditioned by the political and cultural importance of the three cities, but the theological justification was ultimately, though not exclusively, based on the unique relationship between St Peter and the apostolic succession there—however strained, as in the case of Alexandria, whose special authority it would seem was traced back to St Peter via St Mark, his disciple and interpreter.

Thus we have noted two parallel developments, that of the local synods and that of the growing importance of Sees claiming Petrine succession, as well as a certain tension between both. In Rome the relationship of the Bishop to the local synod of bishops as something more than *primus inter pares* would seem to have been accepted from the very beginning.[21] A similar situation would seem to have emerged in Alexandria. But at Antioch the Novatian sympathies of Fabius of Antioch and, especially, the heretical teaching of the Bishop of Antioch, Paul of Samosata, called into question the principle about recourse to Sees of direct apostolic, especially Petrine, succession to resolve matters of dispute. Leaving aside the implications of these experiences in Antioch for the later Eastern attitude towards any special claims due to the Petrine succession in Rome itself,[22] what is of greater concern in this context is the way the local synod of bishops emerged in these controversies. The

20   Cf. Adv. haer. III 3,1–3; regarding this much disputed text, see I. Ortiz de Urbina, 'Patres graeci de sede romana,' in: OrChrP 29 (1963) 99–103; H. Grotz, Die Stellung der römischen Kirche anhand frühchristlicher Quellen, in AHP 13 (1975) 52–55; Roland Minnerath, 'La position de l'Église de Rome aux trois premiers siècles' in Michaele Maccarone (ed.), Il primato del Vescovo di Roma nel primo millennio, Vatican City 1991, 154–159; re the phrase *propter potentiorem principalitatem*, cf. Notes justificatives by Rousseau-Doutreleau in their SC critical edition of *Adv. haer.* (SC 210, 228–236), which also includes further literature.

21   See especially G. Roethe, Zur Geschichte der römischen Synoden im 3. und 4. Jahrhundert, 1937.

22   The existential roots of the later Eastern difficulties with the claims of Rome based on the Petrine succession may well be found here, in the 3rd century experience of heresy in the *Petrine* See of Antioch.

synods subjected the teaching of Fabius to scrutiny; later they excommunicated Paul of Samosata. The primacy of the synod over the incumbent of a See claiming direct apostolic, indeed Petrine, succession was established in fact.[23] But even in this case, it was the acceptance of the decisions of the Synod of Antioch by the See of Rome that finalized the matter even in the eyes of the imperial authority.

At the early stages of the Donatist dispute, the intervention of Constantine, prompted by the Donatists themselves,[24] introduced two new principles of synodal authority, that of the synod as a type of imperial court (and so in principle subject to the authority of the Emperor) and that of appeal to a numerically bigger synod, with the attendant danger of substituting majority opinion for unanimity. The former was implicitly rejected by Miltiades of Rome, in his interpretation of Constantine's instructions. The Synod of Arles (314) would likewise seem to have acted in a way that implicitly rejected the imposition of these new principles, not least by underlining the Petrine authority of the Bishop of Rome[25] Constantine's principles found a more receptive audience in the East.

Nicaea was unique. It was the first time, if we exclude the 'Council' of Jerusalem recorded in Acts, that a synod representing the entire Church could be assembled and the universal unanimity expressed in synodal form. It was also a celebration of the new status of the Church after centuries of peripheral existence in the *oikoumenê*, ranging from

23   It was only in the middle of the 4th century, and in very different circumstances, that the attempt was made—by the Eusebian bishops gathered again at Antioch—to articulate it as a principle and incorporate it into the incipient Canon Law. In reply Julius of Rome has recourse to, and develops, the traditional (Irenaean) principle. For a full discussion of the exchange of letters between Antioch and Rome, and the implication of same for the growth of both synodal and primatial principles, see Vincent Twomey, Apostolikos Thronos, The Primacy of Rome as reflected in the Church History of Eusebius and the historico-apologetic writings of Saint Athanasius the Great, Münster 1982, 374–425; the account of the events surrounding the synods at Rome and Antioch as given by H. C. Brennecke, Hilarius von Poitiers und die Bischofsopposition gegen Konstantius II, Berlin/New York 1984, 5–15 (based on Girardet) fails to convince.

24   Cf. W.H.C. Frend, The Donatist Church. A Movement of Protest in Roman North Africa, Oxford 1971, 141f.; T. D. Barnes, Constantine and Eusebius, Cambridge (Mass.)/London 1981, 56f.; with regard to the authoritative intervention of the Emperor in the internal affairs of the Church, cf. W. Kinzig, Novitas Christiana. Die Idee des Fortschritts in der Alten Kirlche bis Eusebius [Forschung zur Kirchen- und Dogmengeschichte, 58], Göttingen 1994, 558–559, who claims that the Church, up to the Synod of Sardica, took no offence and indeed repeatedly called on Constantine to intervene; for further literature, see his footnote 289.

25   See the Letter of the Synod of Arles to Pope Sylvester, preserved in Optatus (CSEL 26, 206–208); cf. T. Jalland, The Church and the Papacy. A Historical Study, London/New York 1944, 193–197; Twomey, op. cit. (note 23 supra) 212–213; Michele Maccarrone, '"Sedes Apostolica—Vicarius Petri." La perpetuità del primato di Pietro nella sede e nel vescovo di Roma (Secoli III–VIII)' in Maccarrone, op. cit. (note 20 supra) 278–280.

uneasy tolerance to active persecution, the most recent being one of the most severe. It was also a moment when the interests of Emperor and Church coincided.[26]

Though the theological disputes concerning the divinity of Christ continued to fester after 325, the authority of Nicaea as such, it would appear, only became a controversial issue at the Synod of Arles 353 when the Roman legates placed it at the centre of the discussion.[27] Synods, especially in the East, had produced alternative credal formulas, but they did not explicitly reject Nicaea.[28] That changed at Sirmium in 357 when the Nicene terms were rejected by the Synod.[29]

HISTORICAL CIRCUMSTANCES AND LITERARY GENRE

De synodis is one of the few Athanasian texts that can with some confidence be dated fairly accurately: after the death of the Emperor Constantius II, 3 November 361, and before the Alexandrian Synod of 362.[30] The immediate circumstances are also sufficiently well known[31] and,

26 With regard to Nicaea, see espcially Barnes, op. cit (note 24 supra), 208–219; C. Luibhéid, The Council of Nicaea, Galway 1982. The Bishop of Rome excused himself on the grounds of age and was represented by legates. Little attention has been given to the possibilty that the real reason may have been an awareness by Rome of the dangers to the independence of the Church implicit in the Emperor's increasingly active involvement in Church affairs.

27 See Twomey, op. cit. (note 23 supra) 483–485; J. N. D. Kelly, Early Christian Creeds, London 1960 (2nd ed.) 284, states however that the first hint of the new role the Nicene creed was beginning to play came in the letter (preserved by Hilarius, Frag. hist. 5,6, PL 10, 685f.) which Pope Liberius addressed to Constantius in 354.

28 In so far as these synods concerned Athanasius, it was primarily in connection with his claim to the See of Alexandria from which he had been deposed by the Synod of Tyre in 335. Though he consistently claimed that the ultimate motivation behind those who disposed him was their adherence to the Arian heresy rejected by Nicaea, his main attention was focused on what Sardica called the 'Eusebian heresy.' This was the Reichskirche as conceived by Eusebius of Caesarea, whose ultimate authority was the divinely appointed Emperor, and effectively executed by his namesake of Nicomedia by means of the newly conceived autonomous local synod. Athanasius rejected this transformation of the Apostolic Church into an Imperial Church by stressing the apostolic (and catholic) nature of the Church, the source of her independance vis-à-vis the State, and in particular by appealing in his own case to the *thronos apostolikos* at Rome with its Petrine succession and universal significance. With regard to the Eusebian understanding of the Imperial Church., cf. R. Farina, L'Impero e l'Imperatore cristiano in Eusebio di Cesarea, La prima theologia politica del cristianesimo, Zürich 1966.

29 See below, note 68.

30 Following Opitz (231; 258, note 21), who defends the unity of the text, against those (e.g. Robertson, Quasten, Sieben) who, claiming that par. 30–31 and 55 were later interpolations, suggest autumn 359. According to Ch. Kannengiesser, art. 'Athanasus der Große' in LThK, third edition, 1993, col. 1129, the Letter— Athanasius' longest work—was finished in winter 361 or at the beginning of 362.

31 See e.g. G. Bardy, Saint Athanase, Paris 1914, 154f.; Kelly, op. cit., 283f. and, especially, M. Simonetti, La crisi Ariana nel IV secolo, Rome 1975, 241f.

at least for our purposes, so non-contentious as to require but the briefest mention. The Letter was prompted by the twin synods of Ariminum and Seleucia (359), the history of which is outlined in the first part of the Letter. Ariminum was clearly pre-Nicene while Seleucia manifested the emergence of the Homoiousian party in the East under Basil of Ancyra who, rejecting the Arian tenets of Acacius of Caesarea (Homoeans), were evidently sympathetic to Nicaea but could not accept the *homoousios*.

The literary genre of *De synodis* is that of a Letter.[32] In it Athanasius sets out, if not to persuade the Homoiousian party to accept the key Nicene term, then at least to deal with their objections to it, which were indeed serious. But, as mentioned at the outset, this involved several issues which needed to be clarified. It is here that the methodology used by Athanasius is important to note. Repetition is one of the characteristics of his thought.[33] Each apparent repetition, however, contains a new emphasis, a development or an application of an earlier point. Such repetition is not arbitrary, but systematic. His systematic thought can be discovered by dividing the text up into its component parts. These are found to be pairs within pairs. Thus the Letter can be divided into two: Part I (par. 1–32), which poses the theological issues raised by the historical events and Part II (33–54) which attempts to solve the issues in a more theoretical fashion. Each of these (Parts I and II) is subdivided into two. The subdivisions within Part II are yet again subdivided. In this *De synodis* is similar in structure to his *Apologia secunda* and, in particular, the *Historia Arianorum*, both of which were likewise in the form of letters and had recourse to both copious documentary evidence and historical narrative, including fictional speech.[34] With regard to the style of Athanasius, Photius aptly comments that his writing is 'clear, unpretentious and plain, but strong,

---

32 It is difficult to ascertain who were the addressees of the Letter. The opening would seem to indicate that it was written for his followers, possibly the desert monks, while the second part of the Letter gives one the impression that he is directly addressing the various protagonists, in particular the Homoeousian party under Basil of Ancyra, though this may simply be due to the author's rhetorical style. According to Ch. Kannengiesser, Arius and Athanasius, Two Alexandrian Theologians, London 1991, x, 'Athanasius' literary legacy is, almost in its entirety, directed to audiences in the bishop's local church, and preferably to the Egyptian monks.'

33 Cf. his own admission of the need for repetition when speaking about the graciousness of God to humanity, De incarn. 20,3, SC 199,338; on the implications of this for Athanasius' theological and literary methodology, see D. Ritschl, Athanasius. Versuch einer Interpretation (Theologische Studien, Helft 76), Zürich 1964, 24–27; Twomey, op. cit., 266–267. With regard to his rhetorical method, see G. C. Stead, 'Rhetorical method in Athanasius', VC 30 (1976) 121–137, which article is severely critical of same.

34 Athanasius expressly draws attention to his recourse to fictional speech (De syn. 7,2, Opitz 235, 3–4) in order to clarify the intention (*dianoia*) of those to whom it is attributed.

full of content and vigorously consistent, with an originality which is truly amazing.'[35]

OUTLINE

Part I: De synodis 1–32

Athanasius opens his letter with an account, supported by relevant documents, of how the 'Arians' with the support of Constantius II attempted to call a second oecumenical synod, or council,[36] at Nicaea in order to undermine the first synod and substitute another credal formula for the Nicene Creed.[37] This raised the question as to the nature of synodal authority, in particular the definitive nature of its decrees. Behind this question lies a more profound one which the Arian party implicitly posed by daring to date one of their credal formulae, the so-called Dated Creed (Sirmium 359).[38] Is truth the product of ever renewed speculation (*zêtein*) which can be 'dated', and so relative, or is it timeless, absolute? Already in this, the first subdivision of Part I (par.1–14), Athanasius gives his readers an outline answer to both these questions. Truth is eternal, it existed even before the Prophets and always was, 'for before the foundation of the world God prepared it for us in Christ.'[39] And the authority of synods springs from the living faith (truth) of the bishops. Its objective is to present the teaching of the Fathers (Scripture and Tradition).[40] It rejects novelties and expresses itself through unanimity. Unanimity is, as we will see, the key concept. It is found for the first time in the fictional speech attributed to the majority of western bishops at Ariminum.[41]

35 As quoted by Ch.Kannengiesser, 'Athanasian and Peudo-Athanasian Legacy, Alfred Stücken's Athanasiana (1899) revisited' in N. el-Khoury, H. Crouzel, R. Reinhart (eds.), Lebendige Überlieferung. Prozesse der Annäherung und Auslegung. Festschrift für Hermann-Josef Vogt, Beirut-Ostfildern 1992, 149.

36 Throughout I have avoided using the term 'council' when rendering *sunodos* into English since 'council' implies a more technical understanding which was, at the time, only in the process of emerging.

37 Cf. De syn. 1, 4, Opitz 231, 15–232, 3; Simonetti suggests that the Semi-Arians were in fact those who called for such a synod.

38 Cf. De syn. 3,2, Opitz, 232, 26–30 text given in 8,3–7, Opitz 235, 21–236, 15.

39 De syn. 3,4, Opitz, 233, 4–5.

40 Cf. De syn. 8,2, Opitz 235, 16–18: 'While all the bishops were engaged in discussing the matter from the Divine Scriptures, these men [the Arian party] presented a paper and, reading out the consulate, demanded that its contents be given preference over every synod.'

41 Cf. De syn. 9, 2, Opitz 236, 25–26; the term used here is *homophrosunê*. It is of note that Constantine in his letter to Alexander of Alexandria and Arius (Eusebius, Vita Const., II,64–72 = Opitz, Urkunde 17) exhorts his addressees to a unity and unanimity (*homonoia*) that was little more than external conformity to a majority opinion, expressly excluding the need for unity of internal assent or judgement on what he considered to be a trifling matter (cf. Vita Const. 70–71 = Urkunde 17,

The second subdivision (par.15–32) is a history of the theological opinions of the 'Arians' and consists mostly of brief introductions to, and comments on, various 'Arian' documents arranged in chronological order, beginning with the *Thalia* of Arius[42] and ending with an account of the credal formula of Antioch in 361. Its purpose is to demonstrate how Arians fail to meet the criteria regarding the nature of truth and the nature of synodal authority which Athanasius had outlined in the previous subsection. In the final analysis their lack of agreement or unanimity quite literally deprived their synodal decisions of credibility.[43] Part I, in short, is mainly negative in its approach in so far as it is primarily aimed at showing how the Arian credal formulas and synods fail to match the required criteria concerning truth and synodal authority. Part II will demonstrate in a more positive way how Nicaea does in fact meet with the necessary criteria.

Part II: De synodis 33–54

Having clarified the theological issues that were raised by the history of the opinions of the anti-Nicenes, Athanasius now devotes his attention in the second half of the Letter to an analysis of the two related questions concerning the nature of truth and that of synodal authority in so far as they relate to the nature of Christ and the terminology used by Nicaea to express that mystery. In the first subdivision (par. 33–40), the question of truth, concerning the incomprehensibility of God, its perception and expression, is explored primarily by examining the implications of denying the suitability of the Nicene term *ek tês ousias*.

In contrast with that negative approach, the second subdivision (41–54) could be described as a positive approach where Athanasius applies

---

9–14). This is understandable in terms of Constantine's concern for political concord, cf. Barnes (note 24 supra), 212–213. In matters of faith, as he soon discovered, such an understanding of unanimity could not be accepted. For literature on the letter of Constantine, cf. Kinzig (note 24 supra), 563, note 301.

42   Cf. R. Williams, Arius. Heresy and Tradition, London 1987, 62–66, 101–103; Williams, 65–66, argues convincingly that the text is unlikely to be a 'neo-Arian' revision published in the 350s, as proposed by Kannengiesser, but rather the original text from the pen of Arius.

43   This is summarized at the conclusion of this subsection (De syn. 32): the documentation of the various synods amply demonstrates that the 'Arians' are enemies of the truth and of Nicaea: '. . . who, on [seeing] in every [synod] some things taken away and others added, but perceives that their mind is shifty and treacherous against Christ? . . . And the number of their [synods] and the differences of their statements [are] proof that those who were present at them, while at variance with the Nicene [creed], are yet too feeble to harm the truth' De syn. 32, 2; 32, 4, Opitz 260, 12–14; 25–27 (transl. Robertson). This entire section develops (with the aid of copious quotations from Arian sources) an objection first raised in Epistola Encyclica ad episcopos Aegypti et Libyae contra Arianos, 6, PG 25, 549 c10 – 552 c1.

the principles gleaned from the former to the question of the constitution and purpose of the Synod of Nicaea (41–47), and finally to the
question of the suitability of the disputed term *homoousios* to express the
mystery of Christ's divine nature (48-54). As mentioned above, the final
purpose of the letter was to convince his readers of the suitability of
using a non-Scriptural term to express the whole thrust of Scripture.

ANALYSIS OF THE TEXT

Part I (subsection 1)

Athanasius begins by assuring his readers that he wishes to relate what he
himself had seen or accurately ascertained about recent events. A new
'catholic synod'[44]—a universal council—was to have been held at Nicaea.
Those responsible were, according to Athanasius, intent on supplanting
truth with irreligion everywhere and confusing the whole world. But the
synod was, thanks to Providence, divided into two. 'But what defect of
teaching was there for religious truth in the Catholic Church, that they
should enquire concerning the faith (*peri pisteôs zêtôsi*) now and should
prefix the year's Consulate to their profession of faith?'[45] The central
issue here is the nature of truth professed by the Church. Athanasius
poured scorn on the Arians for appearing to be searching (*zêtein*) for that
truth of which bishops were the inheritors.[46] Christian truth is not
something novel that is discovered in our day by speculation, as it were,
for the first time.[47]

An examination of the implications of the so-called Dated Creed (3rd
Sirmium, 22 May 359)[48] allows Athanasius to elaborate on the nature of
truth as revealed in Christ. It also enables him to indicate what are the
limits of synodal authority, which is determined by that truth. What is
implied by dating a creed? There are two possible interpretations. Perhaps the 'Arians' took the Prophets as their model? They indeed gave
the date of when they announced their prophecy. But the truth they
proclaimed was eternal. They 'were not laying the foundations of divine
religion' as it was 'before them, and was always, for before the

44 De syn. 2,1, Opitz 232, 5.
45 De syn.3,1, Opitz 253.23–24 (Robertson).
46 Playing on the term 'cleric', who ought to be teachers (*didaskaloi*) rather than sear-
   chers (*zêtountes*), he accuses the Arians of running about seeking (*zêtein*) how best to
   learn to believe in Our Lord Jesus Christ. If they had faith, they would not have to
   search for it in this way. Seeing Christians, as it were, waking up from sleep and
   enquiring about (*zêtein*) how they should believe concerning Christ can only cause
   scandal to catechumens and amusement to the heathen; cf. De syn. 2,2–3; also 9,2.
47 Cf also De syn. 4,1, Opitz 233, 16–19.
48 De syn. 3,1 – 4,4; text: De syn. 8,3–7; commentators, failing to note Athanasius'
   purpose, tend to consider the attention paid to such a slight matter as dating
   their credal formula a bit exaggerated.

foundations of the world God prepared it for us in Christ.'[49] This is not speculation characterized by revision and novelty, but rather Revelation. Scripture (represented by the Prophets) witnesses to eternal truth.

But Scripture also provides another type of 'dating', identical to that which was used by the 'Arians', namely the imperial decree of Lk 2:1, concerning the census, something new, which had not existed previously. Now it is the claim of all heretics, such as the Montanists, that 'To us first was revealed . . . from us dates the faith of Christians.'[50] Thus Tradition is of necessity rejected by heretics,[51] since it witnesses to the immutability of truth.

What then is the role of a synod, especially one that is not only implicitly but explicitly oecumenical,[52] i.e. expressive of the catholicity of the Church?[53] Synods, Athanasius argues, are not casual, accidental events but, like Nicaea, are only convened for a pressing necessity or for a reasonable purpose. It is of note that, for Athanasius, the oecumenical nature of Nicaea was determined in the first place by the universal nature of the matters that occasioned it.[54] What reasonable cause could be used to justify the recent double synod (at Ariminum and Seleucia)? Where are the new heresies to be combated, who are the innovators?[55] The purpose of a synod is to confess how they believed that truth which existed before the foundation of the world, not to announce 'new' truths. Novelty, Athanasius affirms, is the opposite of Apostolic: 'what [the bishops at Nicaea] wrote was no discovery of theirs, but is the same as was taught by the Apostles.'[56]

---

49 De syn. 3,3–4, Opitz 233, 3–5 (Robertson); cf. Eph 4:1–9; this is an echo of what Kinzing calls the *Revelationsschema* (seit Anfang der Welt beschlossen—jetzt offenbart; op. cit., note 24 supra, 563), a common theme of the NT and the early Church with profound implications for the self-identity of the emerging Church, cf. Kinzig, 103f., 135 note 234, 196, 292, 348, 563.

50 De syn. 4,3, Opitz 233, 24–25 (Robertson); one may also note the irony implied in the reference to the *imperial* decrees of Lk 2:1, for such was, in the eyes of Athanasius, the type of creed issued by the neo-Arians with the authority of their patron, the Emperor Constantius.

51 Cf De syn. 4,4, Opitz 233, 26–30.

52 Cf. De syn. 5,2, Opitz 234.4; see also De syn 14, 4; 21, 1; 33, 1.

53 Cf. De syn. 5,3, Opitz 234, 10–11; the Synod of Ariminum (De syn.11,1) refers to 'the Catholic Synod and the Holy Church ....'

54 Cf. De syn. 5, 1–3, Opitz 233, 32–234, 13; Athanasius, stressed that Nicaea was called so that Easter could be celebrated 'everywhere' on the one day and that the Arian heresy be anathematized, heresy being the concern of the Church universal. Athanasius draws attention to the precise terminology used by Nicaea to describe the two different types of decision involved in these issues. With regard to the date of Easter, the term used was *edoxe*, 'it seemed good', but concerning the Faith, Athanasius stresses, they did not say 'it seemed good,' but *houtôs pisteuei hê katholikê ekklêsia*.

55 Athanasius, evidently, did not in principle rule out the possibility of a second catholic or oecumenical synod (council) like that of Nicaea.; cf. De syn. 6,1–2, Opitz 234, 14–26.

56 De syn. 5,3, Opitz 233, 12–13 (Robertson).

A genuine oecumenical synod thus has two chief characteristics, what could be called diachronic and synchronic unanimity, apostolicity and catholicity. Its teaching must be one with Tradition[56a] (*tas tôn paterôn paradoseis*) which is Apostolic in origin and at the same time reflect the universal agreement (*homophrosynê*) of the assembled bishops.[57] Unlike the relative notion of truth implied by the 'Dated Creed',[58] the decisions of the Fathers at Nicaea are definitive by nature (*hapax*)[59] since truth is eternal. Though he draws attention to the unanimity of over 400 bishops at Ariminum and most of some 160 at Seleucia, it is the chronological or diachronic unanimity which Athanasius stresses at this stage.[60] In a discussion on the implication of the terms 'Fathers', 'successors', 'teachers,' he roots the principle of Tradition in Scripture itself: 'The blessed Apostle approves of the Corinthians because, he says, "ye remember me in all things, and keep the traditions as I delivered them to you" (1 Cor 11:2) . . .'[61] Tradition is a process of calling to mind what had first been handed on by the Apostles. The Arians, by way of contrast, do not appear to fear the divine proverb: 'There is a generation that curseth their father (Prov. 30:11 LXX) and the threat lying in the law against such' (Ex. 21:16 LXX).[62] They also dissent from each other, not being of one mind (*mian tên gnômên*).[63]

The relationship between Scripture and the Creed confessed at Nicaea is worth noting. With regard to the Faith, Divine Scriptures are above all more than sufficient. But with regard to the matter disputed by the 'Arians', Nicaea suffices since the synodal 'Fathers' expressed the doctrine so well that anyone of upright heart (*gnêsiôs*)[64] who reads their words 'is able by means of them to call to mind (*hupomimnêskesthai*) the

---

56a Cf. De syn. 7, 1, Opitz 234, 33.

57 Cf. De syn. 9,2, Opitz 236, 21–29 the fictional speech attributed to the Bishops assembled at Ariminum. This is in sharp contrast with De syn 7,1 where Athanasius had described the hallmarks of a non-authoritative 'synod', namely, it transgresses the traditions of the Fathers, creates divisions among contemporary Bishops and has recourse to imperial support.

58 Quoted in full in De syn. 8.3–7, Opitz 235, 21–236, 15.

59 Cf. De syn. 9,2, Opitz 236, 27; the text of the Letter of the Western Bishops at Ariminum to Constantius II, as translated by Athanasius, appeals to the Emperor to allow the Bishops 'to abide by what has been defined and laid down by our forefathers, who, we venture to say, we trust in all things acted with prudence and wisdom and the Holy Spirit', De syn.10,10, Opitz 238, 18–20 (Robertson).

60 Cf. De syn. 13 –14, which brings the first subsection of Part I to a conclusion and at the same time serves to introduce the next subsection, which is a demonstration of the lack of unanimity among Arians by means of a history of their changing opinions.

61 De syn. 14,1, Opitz 241, 17–18 (Robertson).

62 De syn. 14,2, Opitz 241, 25–26 (Robertson).

63 Cf. De Syn. 14,3, Opitz 241, 27–30; the Decree of the Synod of Ariminum had already drawn attention to the fact that Ursacius, Valens, Gaius, Germinius and Auxentius had often changed their minds; cf. De syn. 11,1, Opitz 238, 36.

64 'Unvoreingenommen', acc. to Sieben, op.cit. (note 8 above), 48.

right belief in Christ (*eis Christon eusebeian*) announced in Divine Scripture.'[65] For Athanasius the believer who is open to the truth, will be *reminded* of the entire objective teaching of Scripture, which has worship of Christ as its end, when he reads the formula of Nicaea. Tradition is a calling to mind (cf. 1 Cor 11:2). It has distinct Platonic overtones.

Part II

Having demonstrated in the second subsection of Part I[66] that the synodal formulae of the 'Arians' failed to meet with the criteria demanded by truth revealed in Christ—its definitive nature—and by the nature of synodal authority—diachronic and synchronic unanimity that expresses this definitiveness[67]—Athanasius now takes up the objections to the Nicene formulae posed by the extreme Arians (in subsection I) and by the Homoeousians (in subsection II). The former objections raise fundamental questions regarding the nature of truth, hermeneutics in the strict sense of the term, while the latter concern the nature of synodal authority, the hermeneutics of authentic synodal judgements. Both are interrelated and both are in turn related to the question of the interpretation of Scripture.

Subsection I (De synodis 33–40)

The extreme Arians under Valens and Ursacius in the West and Acacios of Caesarea in the East objected to the terms of Nicaea (*ek tês ousias* and *homoousios*) as well as *homoioousios*, as troubling many people,[68] causing scandal[69] and above all being not only non-scriptural but alien to Scrip-

---

65 De syn. 6,2, Opitz 234, 26–30; the term *hupomimnêskesthai* may well echo 1 Cor 11:2, quoted in De syn. 14.1, as the scriptural basis for the Athanasian principle of tradition; later, acccusing the 'Arians' of being disobedient to their parents, Athanasius also alludes to Rom 1:34. The term *hupomnêsis* is used in exactly the same sense in Epistola Encyclica ad episcopos Aegypti et Libyae, 5, PG 25, 588, 48, c6. Sieben, ibid., 48, comments on De syn. 6,2 : 'Mitten im Feuer der Polemik ist hier dem Athanasius eine überaus glückliche Formulierung gelungen. Das Stichwort für die „Funktion" eines Konzils ist das „Erinnern" (*hupomimnêskein*) des in der Heiligen Schrift verkündeten Glaubens an Christus. Der Terminus bestätigt seinerseits, daß die tragende Vorstellung der Konszilsidee des Athanasius die „*Paradosis*" ist: Wenn das Konzil theologisch verstanden wird als Paradosis im acktiven und passiven Sinne des Wortes, dann wird der formale Akt dieses Vollzugs durch „Erinnern" umschrieben.' It seems to this reader that the formula is not simply an accidental insight that occurred to Athanasius, despite his polemics as it were, but flows logically from his understanding of the nature of Christian truth. See below 114–115, note 149.

66 A detailed analysis of this subsection is not demanded in this context. The reader is referred to the outline given above, p. 94.

67 *Epeidê de houtôs autoi pros te heautous kai pros tous pro heautôn dietethêsan...* (De syn. 33.1, Opitz 260, 28.).

68 Cf. the so-called Blasphemy of Sirmium 357, (text: De syn. 28.6); the 'Dated Creed" of Sirmium 359 (= De syn. 8,7), Seleucia 359 (= De syn. 29.3).

69 Constantinople 359 (text: De syn. 30,8).

ture.[70] For Athanasius what was at stake was the very possibility of *theologia* as such—God as He is in Himself—as compared with *oikonomia*, His creative and redemptive activity. To exclude any reference to *ousia* in speaking about God, as demanded by the extreme Arians, would be to deny the very possibility of *theologia*. It would also undermine the whole purpose of the divine *oikonomia*: God's self-revelation and our divinization.

The objection that the Nicene terms scandalized and troubled people was easily dismissed by pointing to the fact that the oecumenical synod—i.e. bishops representing the entire *oikoumenê* at Nicaea—found as little offence in the terms as the 400 and more bishops assembled at Ariminum. The cause of scandal is not to be found with with the terms but with the perverseness (*kakonoia*) of those who misinterpret them.[71] Likewise many read Scripture wrongly (*kakôs*) due to their evil disposition (*kakophrosynê*), like the Pharasees who were scandalized by the Lord's teaching or the ignorant and depraved minds of those who found fault with Paul (cf. 2 Pet 3,16).[72] The ultimate scandal, of course, is the Cross (1 Cor 1:23) which to us who believe is 'Christ the Power of God and the Wisdom of God' (1 Cor I:24).[73] Likewise for those who worship Christ[74] the terms of Nicaea cause no scandal; they are rather advantageous to those who read them with a right disposition (*gnêsiôs*); they also undermine all heresy (*asebeia*).[75] What really offends the Arians is the condemnation of their heresy by the terms used at Nicaea.

From the foregoing we learn about the centrality of the role of subjective faith (*eusebeia*, understood as worship of Christ) in interpretation of either Scripture or the Synod of Nicaea. It is the presupposition for any interpretation. It also implies a certain way of thinking and speaking about God, as Athanasius now indicates in a series of texts which are so crucial to an understanding of the thought of Athanasius that they demand rather extensive quotation and commentary.

---

70 At Sirmium 357 Valens, Ursacius, Germinius and Potamius introduced the objection to the use of the terms *ousia*, *homoousios* and *homoioousios* on the grounds that Scripture makes no mention of such terms and that they are beyond human understanding (cf. text: De syn.28.6, Opitz 257, 6–7); Sirmium 359 (= De syn. 8,7, Opitz 236, 11–13) decreed that, not being contained in Scripture, *ousia* ought never to be used of God; the Acacian party went further at Seleucia 359 (De syn. 29.3, Opitz 257, 35–258, 2), and described *homoousios* and both *homoioousios* as alien to Scripture; Constantinople 360 (= De syn. 30,8 Opitz 259, 12–16) rejected outright any further use of *ousia* on the basis that Scripture makes no mention of it.

71 Cf. De syn. 33,2, Opitz 261, 7.

72 Cf. De syn. 33,3–5, Opitz 261, 7–18.

73 Cf. De syn. 34,2, Opitz 261, 25–27; on the Cross, see M. Tetz, 'Das kritische Wort vom Kreuz und die Christologie bei Athanasius von Alexandrien' in: C. Andresen, G. Klein (eds.), Theologia Crucis—Signum Crucis, Festschrift für Erich Dinkler, Tübingen 1979, 224–465.

74 *tôn . . . eusebountôn eis ton Christon* . . . (De syn. 34,1, Opitz 261, 20).

75 Cf. De syn. 34,2, Opitz 261, 28–29.

Why do the Arians reject the term *ek tês ousias* and yet say that the Son is generated from the Father? Do they mean what they say, or are they simply using terms in a nominalist sense that has no correspondence with reality?

> 34,4: If, when you name the Father or utter the name God, you do not signify reality (*ousia*) or understand Him Who Is according to Being (*ousia*), as Him whose being is that He is (*auton ton onta hoper esti*), but signify something else about Him, or at any rate inferior, which I do not wish to mention, you indicate in this way that you should not write that the Son was 'from the Father' but 'from those things about Him or in Him.' The result is that, refusing to say that God is truly Father and thinking materially (*sômatikôs*) of Him who is simple, you consequently make Him composite, and so become the authors of a newer blasphemy. Thus of necessity you conceive the terms Logos and Son not as Being (*ousia*) but simply as names[76] and further, with regard to these names, hold your own views. Consequently what you say is not what you believe to exist but what you consider does not exist.

The term *ousia* refers to Being in the absolute sense, ultimate reality.[77] To refuse to use such a term with regard to the Father and the Son is to reduce talking about God to opinions that do not correspond with reality, since God is deemed to be in principle unknowable. The terms 'God', 'Father', 'Son' then simply become names or labels about which one may speculate at will. Such speculation must of necessity be materialist and immanentist. This is audacity of the Sadducees and those whom the Greeks called atheists, Athanasius insists, following his predecessor Dionysius. If the terms 'Father' and 'God' do not signify the very Being of Him who Is, but something else, then one must logically deny that creation is the handiwork of the true God who Is, since it posits some other cause.[78]

> 35,2: But if, when we hear 'I am who am' (Ex 3:14 LXX) and 'In the beginning God created heaven and earth' (Gen 1:1 LXX) and 'Hear O Israel, the Lord your God is one' (Deut 6:4 LXX) and 'Thus says the Lord the Creator' (2 Sam 7:8 LXX and others), we understand nothing other than the simple and blessed and

---

76 Cf. De decretis 16,1, Opitz 13, 19–21; Or. c. Ar. II 37, 38, PG 26, 225 A f.

77 Robertson in his Prolegomena (note 8 above) xxxi notes: 'The Platonic phrase for the Divine Nature, *epekeina pasês ousias*, adopted by Origen and Athanasius *contra Gentes*, appears to retain something of the ideas of *ousia* as implying *material* existence; and this train of association had to be expressly disclaimed in defending the Nicene formula.' Since in contemporary English 'substance' is even more heavily freighted with material asociations, while 'essence' (the term favoured by Robertson) is understood mostly as a pure abstraction, the term 'Being' has been used throughout to translate *ousia*, except where the context should demand otherwise.

78 Cf. De syn. 35,1, Opitz 262, 5–7.

incomprehensible Being itself of Him who Is (*autên tên haplên kai makarian kai akatalêpton tou ontos ousian*)—even though we are unable to comprehend whatever it is that He is (*ho ti pote estin*)[79]— yet hearing the terms 'Father' and 'God' and 'Creator' (*pantokratôr*) we understand nothing else to be signified other than the very Being (*ousia*) of Him who Is.

To refuse to use the term *ousia* is to deny that we can know God and speak about Him in human language. Knowledge of God does not mean that the human mind can comprehend God, i.e *what* He is, but *that* He Is. We know Him as simple and incomprehensible. '[W]hen Scripture says 'God' we understand nothing else by it but the intimation of His incomprehensible Being (*ousia*) Itself, and that He Is, who is spoken of.'[80] Earlier in *Contra Gentes* Athanasius, true to the Alexandrian tradition, had used the term *akatalêptos*, as it were, to 'define' God: He whose nature is invisible and incomprehensible. He explicitly denied that God had allowed Himself to remain completely unknown (*agnôston*) to men, but has so ordered creation that He can be known through His works, quoting Rom 1:20 and Acts 14:15-17 in support.[81] 'That the soul is immortal,' Athanasius states, 'must also be included in the Church's teaching for the complete refutation of idolatry.' He concludes his demonstration of this teaching: 'So, therefore, the soul has an idea of the contemplation of God (*tês peri Theou theôrias echei tên ennoian*) and its own path, taking the knowledge and understanding of God the Word not from outside but from itself.'[82] To affirm the absolute unknowability of God—as expressly taught by Arius[83] and implied in the denial of

79   Professor T. Finan drew my attention to a parallel passage in Aeschylus, Agamemnon, 160: *Zeus, hostis pot' estin . . .*

80   De decretis 22,3, Opitz 18, 33–35. (Robertson); Ep. ad Monachos 2 (PG 25, 693 A14–B9); Or c. Ar. III, 63 (PG 26, 456, B11–13): '. . . we need only hear mention of God for us to know and understand that He is He-who-is' *hoti autos estin ho ôn.*' Regarding the Platonic influence on Athanasius' thought at this point, cf Pelikan, op. cit. (note 7 supra), 33; re De syn. 35 and De decret. 22, see also the comments of E.P. Meijering, Orthodoxy and Platonism in Athanasius. Synthesis or Antithesis?, Leiden 1968, 141–142.

81   C. gent. 35, PG 25, 69 A12–72 A12.

82   C. gent. 33, PG 25, 65 B2–4, transl. Thompson; cf. also Or. c. Ar. II, 78–79 (PG 26,312 B6 –316 B4) where Athanasius, in the course of his exegesis of Prov 8:22, describes the origin and exercise of man's ability to know God, namely the presence of created wisdom in him and in creation; cf. J. Roldanus, Le Christ et l'homme dans la théologie d'Athanase d'Alexandrie. Étude de la conjunction de sa conception de l'homme avec sa christologie, Leiden 1977, esp. 25–65; also A. Louth, 'The Concept of the Soul in Athanasius' *Contra Gentes—De Incarnatione*,' in: Studia Patristica XIII, Berlin 1975, 227–231, who points to neoplatonic influence or inspiration in C. gentes.; see also idem, The Origins of the Christian Mystical Tradition. From Plato to Denys, Oxford 1981, 70–80.

83   God is by nature ineffable (*arrêtos*) to all, including the Son, cf. the *Thalia* (De syn. 15,3, Opitz 242, 9). The editorial selection of this quotation from the Thalia, which

ousia[84]—leads logically to atheism[85] and to idolatry, since creation is no longer understood as leading us to God but to some intermediary. It also leads to a truncated anthropology: man is no longer defined as one who is made in the image of God and whose end is to know God.[86] The ultimate consequence would be affirm that Christ cannot be the revelation of God, as Athanasius later clarifies.

> 35,3: And if you too have said: 'the Son is from God', it is obvious that you have said : 'He is from the Being of the Father' (*ek tês ousias tou patros*).[87] Since however even before you the Scriptures declared that the Lord is Son of the Father, and before them, the Father Himself said: 'This is my Son the Beloved' (Mt 3:7)—and a son is not other than the offspring from his father—how is it not evident that the Fathers were right (*kalôs*) to say that the Son is from the Being of the Father, considering it the same as to say rightly (*orthôs*) 'of God' and 'of Being"? For all creatures, even if said to have come

he calls the 'Blasphemy of Arius', and which opens with the affirmation of the absolute ineffability of God, betrays the importance Athanasius attached to this aspect of Arius' teaching. The interpretation of the passage as given by Williams, op. cit. (note 42 supra) 64 seems accurate: '. . . although God remains unknowable we are enabled to have at least some "negative" knowledge about him because of the Son . . . the totally transcendent God is is not incapable of bestowing the grace whereby the Son and, on account of him, other creatures also 'see' the invisible Father, grasp the fact of his utter mystery and otherness.' Knowledge *about* God is not Christian faith as understood by Athanasius. For an illuminating discussion of the philosophical achievement of Arius, cf. Williams, 191–229. He concludes; 'A Plotinian style of negative theology is being quite skilfully deployed in defence of some very un-Plotinian conclusions' (288); cf. F. Ricken, 'Zur Rezeption der platonischen Ontologie bei Eusebios von Kaisarea, Areios und Athanasios' in Theologie und Philosophie 53 (1978) 321–352, esp. 341–342.

84   Sirmium 357 rejected the use of the terms *ousia* (Latin *substantia*), *homoousios* and *homoioousios* also on the basis that they were beyond the knowledge and understanding of men (*hoti tauta huper tên anthrôpôn gnôsin kai ton anthrôpôn noun esti* . . . De syn.28,6, Opitz 257, 7); see also Constantinople 360 (De syn. 30, 3, Opitz 258, 30.

85   For the occurrence of this theme in Athanasius, cf Newman, Selected Treatises, II, 354–357; see Th. F. Torrance, 'The Implications of Oikonomia for Knowledge and Speech of God in Early Christian Theology' in: F. Christ (ed.), Oikonomia. Heils-geschichte als Thema der Theologie, Oskar Cullmann zum 65. Geburtstag gewidmet, Hamburg-Bergstedt 1967, 223–238, with regard to the roots of such thinking in the theological method based on the *chôrismos* between the two cosmic realms (the *kosmos aisthêtos* and the *kosmos noêtos*) first articulated by Clement of Alexandria and developed by Origen in a way that eventually bore 'evil fruit in Arianism.' According to Torrance, Athanasius '. . . from the very start rejected entirely the *chôrismos* between the two cosmic realms..' and so perceived that '[s]ince *oikonomia* refers to the way God has Himself taken in His action for us and our salvation . . . it must be in strict accordance with that *oikonomia* that we are to think and speak of Him in all His ways and works . . .' (238).

86   See especially C. gentes 2.

87   The formula used in the creed of Nicaea.

into being from God, are yet not from God as the Son is from God;
for, though offspring, they are by nature things made.

Finding the correct terminology to express the mystery of the divine
generation will occupy the attention of Athanasius in the next subsection. The suitability of a term, its correspondence with the reality
expressed, will be the principle concern. It presupposes not only that we
can know God but also communicate that knowledge in speech, which
will always be as inadequate as it is indispensable. For the moment he is
intent on showing how the distinction between the two meanings of the
term *ek tou Theou* is supported by Scripture[88], in particular 1 Cor 8:6:

> 35,6: Though the Apostle says: 'One God, from Whom all things',
> yet he does not say this as reckoning the Son with 'all things'. But
> since some of the Greeks consider the creation to be assembled by
> chance from the combining of atoms[89] and spontaneously from the
> fusion of similar parts,[90] and to have no cause, and since others
> [consider] that it came from a cause, though not through the
> Word, each of the heretics has given free reign to his imagination
> and constructs myths about creation, on account of which the
> Apostle was constrained to use the phrase 'from God'.

> 35,7: And so that he might make known the Maker and make
> known the creation of all things by His Will, he then immediately
> adds: 'And one Lord Jesus Christ, through Whom all things,' by way
> of excepting the Son from 'all things'. (For all things that are said to
> be 'from God' come to be through the Son and it is not possible
> that those things that were made should have the same origin as
> their Maker.) [This he does in order to] teach that the phrase 'from
> God' signifies something so very different, when used of creatures
> (*epi tôn poiêmatôn*), from what it means when used of the Son. For
> the One is offspring, the others are creatures. And therefore the
> Son is the distinct Offspring of Being (*idion tês ousias gennêma*), while
> creatures (*ta dêmiourgêmata*) are the handiwork of the [divine] Will.

Aware of the different senses of the same phrase 'from God', Athanasius
continues, Nicaea used the term *ek tês ousias* to express with greater
clarity (*leukoteron*) what Scripture teaches. 'From this the true reality of
the Son's relationship to the Father is made known.'[91] We are therefore
faced with the stark alternative: 'If He is Son, He is not a creature; is He
is a creature, He is not Son.'[92] With this argument the doctrinal core of

88 He points out that Gen 1:1 and Ps 103:4 use the term *poieô*, not *gennaô*, to
    describe God's creation of the material and the spiritual universes.
89 Democritus, Epicurus.
90 Anaxagoras.
91 De syn. 36,2, Opitz 263, 3–4.
92 De syn. 36, 2, Opitz 263, 10–11; see below n.128; to deny that He is true Son is to
    deny Baptism which is administered in the name of the Father and of the Son, not
    of Creator and Creature (Opitz 263, 11–12).

this subsection is complete. But what may be the most important characteristic of Athanasian thought has emerged, his doctrine of creation, central to which is the absolute distinction between God and His creatures[93]. In the above exegesis of 1 Cor 3:6 it provides him with his hermeneutical key.

Then follows a fierce attack on the extreme Arians, beginning with a demonstration of how, though they refused to use the Nicene terms because they were unscriptural, yet they themselves had used a string of terms likewise not found in Scripture. His polemics against the Arians, in particular George of Cappadocia, Acacius, Eudoxius and Patropolus[94] —ridiculing them for their own contradictory and unscriptural statements—does however contain an important hermeneutical principle, namely that 'although one may utter unscriptural terms, it makes no difference so long as his sense is religious' (*heôs eusebê tên dianoian echei*).[95] While the heretics, like the Devil, can use Scripture to their own purpose, Paul on the other hand can use texts from profane writers in a completely religious sense (*eusebê*)—such as in Tit 1:12, Acts 17:28, 1 Cor 1:33—since he, 'the teacher of the nations in faith and truth' (1 Tim 2:7), has 'the mind of Christ' (1 Cor 2:16), and that which he speaks he voices in a religious way (*kai ha lalei met' eusebeias phtheggetai*).[96]

Contrasting the irreverent use of language by the heretics with the deep reverence of the Nicene Fathers, Athanasius likewise affirms that their understanding (*dianoia*) of Christ was sublime; theirs was a Christ-loving religious attitude (*philochristos eusebeia*).[97] Knowledge of the Truth is only possible for those with the proper subjective disposition, that of adoration of Christ (*eusebeia*), like that of Paul and the Nicene Fathers. This in turn implies that a genuine understanding and grasp of Truth demands a mental process by which the concepts derived from human or created experience (offspring, radiance, light) are radically reinterpreted when applied to the transcendent God.[98]

The final objection of the extreme Arians was that the Nicene terms were obscure. The attitude of mind revealed by their rejection of Nicaea on this ground is that they are unwilling to know the truth. Such is the mark of heretics who logically reject whatever they do not understand in Scripture. Christians, on the other hand, may admit

---

93 According to L. Bouyer, L'Incarnation de l'Église—Corps du Christ dans la théologie de saint Athanase, Paris 1943, 134, the distinction between the Creator and His creatures is the fundamental principle of Athanasius' theology; cf. G. Florovsky, 'The Concept of Creation in Saint Athanasius' in: Studia Patristica IV, Berlin 1962 [TU 81], 36–57.

94 The text also witnesses to the extraordinary familiarity of Athanasius with Scripture, e.g. his use of 1 Tim 6:5; 1:7; Prov 7:22, Ez 16:25 in De syn. 37,1; 39,2.

95 De syn. 39,2, Opitz 265, 14.

96 Cf. De syn. 39,3, Opitz 265, 21.

97 Cf. De syn. 39,4, Opitz 265, 25.

98 Cf. De syn. 39,6, Opitz 265, 30–266, 4; this Athanasius develops in De syn. 42,1.

that they do not understand certain words, but, rather than rejecting them, they will look for someone who will explain them: 'For those things we do not understand in the words [of Divine Scripture] we do not reject but rather seek out (*zêtoumen*) those whom the Lord has revealed and from whom we think fit to learn.'[99] The true religious disposition is thus marked by humility—and by a searching which is radically other than that which Athanasius had earlier castigated in the Arians. This theme allows him to move to the climax of the Letter where he addresses those who have genuine difficulty in accepting the term *homoousios*, though they believe what it expresses.

Subsection II (De syn. 41–54)

This subsection is by far the most compact and complex text in the whole Letter. Athanasius first demonstrates the binding authority of the Nicene definition (par. 41–47 = a), and then discusses the meaning and suitability of the term *homoousios* (48–54 = b). Both topics are interrelated.

a) Athanasius now turns to the Homoiousian party under the leadership of Basil of Ancyra, to be treated as 'brothers with brothers' with whom the only dispute concerned the use of the term (*homoousios).* Far from suggesting that the term as such is of secondary importance, his whole energy and skill is devoted to demonstrating that the term is the most suitable (*harmozontôs*)[100] to express the Reality which the Homoiousian party affirm with inadequate terms, and is in fact indispensable for counteracting the Arian heresy.

The starting point is the agreement on both sides on the *ek tês ousias*: they too confess that the Son is from the Being of the Father, not from another substance (*hupostasis*); that He is not a creature but rather the genuine offspring by nature (*gnêsion kai phusei gennêma*), eternally with the Father, being Logos and Wisdom.[101] 'Like' being an ambiguous term, 'like-in-Being' (*homoioousios*) does not altogether express 'of the being', though when both are taken together what they signify is *homoousios.*'

The reason Athanasius can state so firmly that the party of Basil of Ancyra holds the same as the Nicenes is the evidence he had from the

---

99 De syn. 40,3, Opitz 266, 10–12; Meijering, op. cit. (note 80 supra) 183 notes that the young Athanasius wrote his early apologetic double work, at least partly, *zêtôn*; 'To Athanasius there was no real doubt what the truth is: the Bible as he saw it interpreted by his ecclesiastical teachers.' However one may ask whether Meijering was fair to the originality of Athanasius when he adds: 'His *zêtêsis* was not more than the gathering of new arguments for what he already believed to be true.'

100 Cf. De syn. 41,6, Opitz 267, 18.

101 Cf. De syn. 41,2, Opitz 266, 32–267, 2; Athanasius characterized the relationship between Father and Son as *to gnêsion tou huiou pros ton patera* (De syn. 41,3, Opitz 267, 5).

Synodal Letter of Basil of Ancyra (358).[102] Though in controversy they reject those who treat the Son as a creature, when they themselves use human language (son and father) they do so with the recognition that 'God is not as man is and the begetting of the Son is not the same as human generation but is such as is proper (*prepousa*) to God and is fitting for us to conceive (*hêmas harmozousa noein*).'[103] In a word, Basil and his fellow bishops share the same theological methodology as the Nicenes. Their fear is that the *homoousios* could give rise to anthropomorphic misrepresentation of the divine generation. Athanasius claims that this is ruled out by the fact that the Son is the Father's Word and Wisdom, 'whence we learn the impasssibility and indivisibility of such a generation from the Father.'[104]

> 42,1: Accordingly, as in using the term 'Offspring' we do not think in a human fashion, and though we know God to be Father we do not entertain any [quasi-]material ideas concerning Him, but hearing such illustrations and terms we conceive of them appropriately in relation to God (*harmozontôs . . . peri Theou nooumen*): for God is not as man; likewise when hearing the term 'of one Being' we are obliged to transcend (*huperbainein*) all sense perception and according to the divine Proverb 'understand by the understanding what is set before us'[105] so as to recognize that not by will but in truth He is genuine Son from the Father, as Life from the Source, Radiance from Light.

Having previously shown that to refuse to speak of the Son in terms of *ousia* was to deny the possibility of *theologia* in the strict sense of the term, Athanasius here outlines briefly what the latter entails. Based on the principle of *ou gar hôs anthrôpos ho Theos* it involves a definite process of thinking about God by which the mind transcends human experience and concepts, a method he will apply below.[106] For the moment he is intent on denying that the term *homoousios* implies quasi-material or corporeal concepts but rather intends to express what the Homoiousians

---

102 Preserved in Ephiphanius, Haer. 73,5, 4–7; Opitz (ad loc.) comments that the term *homoioousios* was never found in the Letter from Ancyra, though Hilary in his De synodis presupposes the discussion about both it and the *homoousios*. Whether or not the term was mentioned is really beside the point that Athanasius wishes to make, namely that the Letter shows the right theological presuppositions or method.

103 De syn. 41,5, Opitz 267, 13–15.

104 De syn. 41,8, Opitz 267, 21–23.

105 . . . *noêtôs noein ta paratithemena hêmin*, Prov 23:1 (LXX), transl. as given in Robertson; the use of this text by Athanasius is not in the literal sense it has in the original.

106 Cf. also De decret. 10, 4–6, Opitz 9, 19–32; Or. c Ar. 23 (PG 26, 60 B11–C6); For A. Louth, 'Reason and Revelation in Saint Athanasius' in the Scottish Journal of Theology, 23 (1970) 393–396, Athanasius developed what could be called a theory of analogical predication of attributes by recognizing Him who is the subject of his speech; see note 135 infra.

evidently accepted with regard to the term 'Offspring' ; the meaning (*ho nous*) of both is one.[107]

Homoousios was a term with a history, and it is precisely the materialist (Gnostic?) understanding of the term as understood by Paul of Samosata and condemned by the Synod of Antioch 268 which presented serious obstacles for the Homoiousian party. Athanasius attempts to demonstrate that it is capable of a non-materialist sense and can express transcendent Being. But first of all another obstacle must be overcome: the formal rejection of the term by a Synod whose authority no one doubted: Antioch in 268. To answer it Athanasius has to develop a hermeneutics of synodal decrees.

> 43,1: . . . But since, as they themselves say (I myself did not receive the actual letter), the Bishops who condemned the Samosatean had decreed that the Son of God is not 'of one being' with the Father, and since further, also out of reverence and honour for those who made this decree, they are thus disposed to the term, it is well to consider this point carefully with them.

> 43,2: On the one hand, to make these [Bishops at Nicaea] conflict with those [of Antioch] is indeed unbecoming, for all are Fathers; on the other hand, to distinguish them as though the latter spoke well whereas the reverse was true of the former would be impious, since all have fallen asleep in Christ. It is not right to be contentious by comparing the numerical strength of those assembled, lest the greater number [at Nicaea] appear to put the fewer [at Antioch] in the shade. [It would be equally invidious to] compare their antiquity, lest those who went before them [Antioch] seem to eclipse those who came after them [Nicaea]. 43,3: For all, as I said above, are Fathers; and yet the three hundred [at Nicaea] did not decree something they considered novel (*neôteron*); nor did they arrogantly take it on themselves to use unscriptural terms but rather, drawing on the Fathers, they too made use of their terminology.

It is significant that the term *synodos* does not appear. What is stressed is that the authority of the bishops who assembled at Antioch and Nicaea is equally binding. Neither numerical strength nor antiquity as such is decisive, but rather that 'all are Fathers . . . all have fallen asleep in Christ.' The Fathers are those bishops who remained in communion with the universal Church all their lives. The reference to their death in Christ indicates the definitiveness of their witness to the Faith. It also alludes to the source of their authority: their personal witness that cannot be established simply by majority opinion. 'All were charged with the embassy of Christ [cf. Eph 6:20] . . .'[108] Tradition is, likewise, not antiquarianism

107 Cf. De syn. 42,2, Opitz 268, 13–14.
108 De syn. 45,2, Opitz 269, 24–25.

but continuity, as implied in the very term 'Fathers',[109] which in turn rules out novelty. Arguing *a priori* Athanasius affirms that, since all are Fathers there cannot be any real opposition between their teaching, only an apparent one.

The obvious source for credal terminology is Scripture, the source of Tradition. But, in the absence of suitable terms in Scripture, the Fathers at Nicaea, according to Athanasius, turned to Tradition, namely the positive usage of the term by the two Dionysii, the Bishop of Rome and the Bishop of Alexandria, who were even earlier than Antioch.[110] Their authority—not mentioned but, in all likelihood, presumed[111]— was particularly significant. It was Petrine.

But one is still left with the problem of apparent contradictions in Tradition, specifically, the rejection of the term by Antioch and the full endorsement of the term by Nicaea. In reply, Athanasius points to the apparent contradictions in Scripture, such as Paul's conflicting state- ments on the meaning of the Law.[112] As no one would accuse Paul of inconsistency but admires how suitably (*harmozontôs*) he wrote to each of his addressees, in like manner one ought to search for the meaning intended by the two synods (*tên dianoian autôn ereunân*) when they used the same term in different ways and so discover the agreement (*tên homonoian*) of both. Athanasius then proceeds to indicate the reason why Antioch said that Christ was not 'of one being', while Nicaea had even greater reason to assert that He was 'of one Being.'[113] Bishops today ought not to find fault with the interpretation (*hermêneia*) of the term adopted by former bishops, just as the latter would not reproach their pre- decessors; each Synod had sufficient reason for saying what it did.[114] However at Antioch, where the disputed term was incidental to Paul's

---

109 Cf. De decret. 27,4, Opitz 24, 4–5; see Sieben's nuanced account of the different ways the term 'Fathers' was used by Athanasius in his writings, op. cit. (note 8 supra) 39f, note 59.

110 Cf. De syn. 43,4, Opitz 268, 27–29; an excerpt from Dionysius' Refutation and Defence is quoted in 44,1–2, where the latter also mentions the unscriptural nature of the term.

111 Later Athanasius refers to the Synod of Rome presided over by Dionysius (cf. De syn. 45,1, Opitz 269, 23–24).

112 Rom 7:14; 7:12; 8:3; Heb 7:19; Gal 3:11; 1 Tim 1:8 are quoted, and briefly commented on, in De syn. 45,3, Opitz 269, 26–37.

113 According to De syn. 45,4, Opitz 269, 37–270, 4, Paul of Samosata presented his fel- low Bishops with the alternative of either accepting his understanding of the divinity of Christ or reverting to a [possibly Gnostic] conception of Father and Son as two substances which derived from a third, common substance that preceded them. It was this understanding of *homoousios* that Antioch had to reject. Nicaea used the same term, understood in a radically different sense from that proposed by Paul of Samosata, to express the unity of Father and Son as affirmed in Jn 10:30 and Jn 14:9, two key texts for Athanasius' defence of Nicaea. According to Opitz, Athanasius' information about Paul of Samosata was not precise.

114 Cf. De syn. 45,5, Opitz 270, 15–18.

heresy, the bishops, while not arriving at accuracy about the term, had, with regard to the Divinity of the Son, affirmed that He who existed before all things had taken the form of a servant (Phil 2:7) and had become flesh (Jn 1:14).[115] At Nicaea, faced with the teaching of Eusebius of Caesarea, Arius and their followers, who effectively placed the Son among the creatures, the bishops had to clarify the nature of the unity of Father and Son. Rejecting any suggestion of a unity of likeness, or a unity brought about by unanimity (*symphônia*) of doctrines and teaching,[116] they, 'bringing together the sense (*dianoia*) of the Scriptures,' had to affirm that the Son was 'of one Being' with the Father and so clear up this point.[117] It is the very precision (*akribeia*) of this term, Athanasius claims, that exposes the Arian heresy and refutes their subtleties which only confuse the simple.[118] Thus the Arians dread that phrase, which the Fathers decreed as a bulwark (*epiteichisma*) against all their impious notions.

To demonstrate the use of a non-scriptural term, and one moreover that was interpreted in different ways by different teachers, Athanasius discusses the various meanings attributed to the term *to agenêton* by Ignatius of Antioch and other writers who are not identified.[119] We accept what they say, because 'we know their faith in Christ.'[120] The same acceptance should be extended to the Fathers at Antioch and Nicaea.[121] It is imperative to preserve a good conscience towards the Fathers, from whom we, their children, have received the traditions and the teaching on religion.[122]

In brief, when interpreting synodal decrees, the same principles of interpretation apply as is the case with Scripture. This of course presupposes that they are genuine synods which meet the criteria he outlines, namely that they are called for a genuine cause and that they manifest diachronic and synchronic unanimity. The relationship between Tradition, as represented by the synods, and Scripture is such that Tradition, calling to mind the truth witnessed to by Scripture, clarifies that truth in the face of attacks by heretics. And it does so definitively. Tradition is based on unanimity rooted in the living faith of the Fathers and their office as bishops. Later, in *De decretis*,[123] Athanasius compares the Fathers

---

115 Against Paul of Samosata, who denied his pre-existence; cf De syn. 45.6, Opitz 270, 19–26.

116 As proposed, e.g., by the credal formula of Antioch 341 (cf. De syn. 26,6).

117 Cf. De syn 45,7, Opitz 270, 26–271, 8.

118 Cf. De syn 45.8, Opitz 271, 8–10.

119 Cf, De syn. 46, 2–47,1; Newman refers to a similar passage in Clement of Alexandria, Strom., VI 7 (PG 9, 280B), cf. Select Treatises of St. Athanasius, London 1895, note 5. Opitz, ad loc., comments that this discussion is not pertinent to the theme, which he presumably takes to be the *homoousios*. It is in fact very pertinent to the actual theme of Athanasius at this stage, namely the legitimacy of using such terminology, which admits of different interpretations.

120 De syn.47,2, Opitz 272, 2.

121 Cf. De syn. 47, 2, Opitz 272, 8–10.

122 Cf. De syn. 47,4, Opitz 272, 16–18.

123 De decr 4, 4, Opitz 4, 8–10 (Robertson), possibly written c. 363/364, as I have argued elsewhere (see note 23 supra 313f, footnote 100).

to the Prophets: 'For though they lived in different times, yet they one and all tend the same way, being prophets of the one God, and preaching the same Word harmoniously.'

(b) Having answered objections of a formal nature to the term *homoousios*, Athanasius now turns to its meaning, to a demonstration of its suitability as a theological expression. We have seen that the exclusion of the term *ousia* was considered by Athanasius to be tantamount to the denial of the possibility of *theologia* in the strict sense. Here he presents a sketch of that *theologia*: how can we speak reasonably (*eikotôs*), i.e. in a way that is fitting (*prepei*), about the unity of Father and Son? A brief outline of this section gives us a glimpse of his strictly theological argumentation, his recourse to reason.

He begins with an either/or already alluded to above. Either the Son is by nature a creature, though surpassing them in grace, or 'He is the genuine Offspring from the Being of the Father, in which case it follows that He is inseparable from Him, being connatural (*homophuê*), because He is begotten from Him. Accordingly He is reasonably called "of one being"'[124] Since He is not Son by participation (as implied by sharing in grace, however much it may surpass grace in other creatures), 'but by reason of Being is the Father's Word and Wisdom, and this Being is the Offspring of the Father's Being and its Resemblance, as the radiance is of the light,[125] how can one otherwise understand His own words: 'I and the Father are one' (Jn 10:30), and 'He who sees me sees the Father' (Jn 14:9)'? Their unity cannot be considered in terms of an agreement (*symphônia*) of beliefs, as is the case of the Saints and Angels who are thus one with God, but rather must be conceived in terms of Being.[126] Created beings who may be in agreement with their Creator (through physical laws, grace or truth) may lose that union and forfeit heaven. 'But the Son, being an offspring of Being is One in Being, Himself and the Father who begets Him.'[127]

Then follows a list of Scriptural texts, that witness to the equality of the Son with the Father; in them what is said of the Father is also said of the Son, apart from being called Father.[128] It is a masterly exposition, brief and

---

124 De syn, 48,2, Opitz 272, 25–28. Stead, art. cit. 129, considers such argumentation a 'crude alternative', which is understandable since he believes in 'an immeasurable interval which separates the divine from the human level' (Stead, 130). In other words Stead shares the same, basically quasi-materialistic understanding of God which Athanasius (rightly) rejects.

125 De syn. 48,3, Opitz 272, 28–30.

126 Cf. De syn 48,4–5, Opitz 272, 32–273, 7.

127 . . . *ho de huios ek tês ousias ôn gennêma têi ousiai hen estin autos kai ho gennêsas auton patêr*, De syn.48,5, Opitz 273, 9–10. This theme is developed more fully in Or. c. Ar. III; cf. Bouyer, op. cit (note 93 supra) 114–119, who claims that, for Athanasius, the error of considering the unity of the Father and the Son as a moral unity was not simply one of the Arian errors, but their principal error.

128 Cf. De syn. 49,1–5, Opitz 273, 11–274, 8.

to the point, where he weaves texts from, allusions to, and events in, the Old and New Testaments into one continuous argument. Beginning with the words of Christ Himself, 'All things that the Father has are mine' (Jn 16:15), he shows that the Son shares all the titles of the Father: God, Light, Everlasting, Lord. Then he shows that both are equally worshipped by the Angels and honoured by all. The Son is Truth from Truth and Life from Life, as of a Source, that of the Father. With this, the text becomes more intricate. Like the Father, the Son raises the dead, is spoken of as God in the OT, forgives sins, and whose kingdom is an everlasting kingdom.[129] In short, what Scripture says of the Father, that is said of the Son, apart from being called Father.

Then Athanasius turns to examine the logic of denying that the Son is 'of one Being' with the Father in the light of the above evidence from Scripture.[130] It could lead to the denial of the Oneness of God, since it must of necessity posit another being, foreign to the Father yet possessing the divine properties, in other words, a second god.[131] 'For if what is the Father's is by nature the Son's, and the Son Himself is from the Father, and because of this oneness of Divinity and Nature He and the Father are one, [so that] "he who has seen the Son has seen the Father", it is reasonable (*eikotôs*) the He be called "of one Being" by the Fathers, since it does not pertain to what is other in being to possess such [characteristics].'[132] Oneness by participation (grace which deifies) is impossible, since He who deifies us cannot be Himself deified (*theopoioumenos*).[133]

The reason why some decline to use the term *homoousios* is what Athanasius calls the 'Greek interpretation',[134] namely that the term would imply three beings, one pre-existing being from which the other two, Father and Son, are generated, thus making them brothers. But this is not logically necessary, as in the case of any only-begotten child (with reference to Jgs 11:34; Lk 7:12). But generation must not be conceived in a human way, nor may the *homoousios* be understood in a corporeal sense. If creation cannot be understood in a human fashion it is even less fitting (*prepei*) so to conceive divine generation: '. . . rather it is necessary to distance ourselves from things which have an origin, abandon entirely human images and all things sensible, and ascend to the Father, lest in ignorance we take the Son from the Father and count

---

129 Most probably a rejection of the tenets of Marcellus of Ancyra whose support for the Nicene creed, to put it mildly, did little to encourage the Eastern bishops under Basil of Ancyra to accept the Nicene formulae.

130 Cf. De syn. 50,1–3, Opitz 274, 9–24.

131 Cf. De syn. 52,1, Opitz 275, 27–34.

132 De syn. 50.3, Opitz 274, 21–24.

133 Cf. De syn., 51, 1–2, Opitz 274, 25–33.

134 He seems in fact to develop the objections which he said earlier (see above, note 110) had been made by Paul of Samosata and rejected by the Synod of Antioch; they may have been Gnostic in origin; cf also De syn. 52,1; on Gnosticism see e.g. G. Filoramo, A History of Gnosticism, Cambridge-Oxford 1990, esp. 56–67.

Him among His own creatures.'[135] Here again we meet the negative
theology of Athanasius. It serves to introduce his exegesis of two titles
attributed by Scripture to the Son: He is Image (*eikôn*) and Impress
(*charaktêr*) of the Father.[136]

If, as the Gnostics taught, there were two gods, or if the Son had some
other mode of divinity (*tropos theotêtos*) He would not be the image and
likeness of the Father. One could then say that He was 'unlike'.[137] But if
the Divinity of the Father is one and unique, and if the Son is His Word
and Wisdom, one does not say there are two gods united in mutual
agreement, '. . . but rather One God, there being one form (*eidos*) of
Divinity, as is the case with the light and the radiance.'[138] The latter is
illustrated by Gen 32:31 LXX[139] and demonstrated from the Old Testament. When the Prophets said that 'the Word of the Lord came to me,'
they recognized the Father revealed in Him.[140] Why then hesitate to call
Him 'of one Being', who in likeness and divinity is one with the Father,
appears as does the Father, and is the illuminating and creative Power
most specific to the Father (*to phôtistikon kai dêmiourgikon to idiaitaton tou
patros*), without whom the Father neither creates nor is known (Col
1:16.17)?[141] As the sun and the radiance are not two lights, even less the
Father and the Son are two divinities. 'Since the nature of the Son's
relationship to the Father is even more indivisible than the indivisibility
of the sun and its radiance, and since divinity is not added to the Son but
rather the divinity of the Father is in the Son, so that he who sees the
Son sees the Father in Him (cf. Jn 14:9), why should such a one not be

---

135 De syn.51,7, Opitz 275, 23–26; in Ep. ad Monachos 1 (PG 25, 692 B1–8),
    Athanasius confesses: '...for as much as I wished to write about, and forced myself
    to understand, the divinity of the Logos, to this extent the knowledge receded far
    from me; and only to the extent that I knew myself to be left behind, to this
    extent did I seem to comprehend. And not only was I unable to write even that
    which I seemed to understand but that which I wrote became less than the weak
    shadow of the truth which arose in my mind . . .' Athanasius' awareness of the
    inadequacy of human thought to grasp, and of human speech to express, the
    mystery of God is acute; cf. C. gentes, 2 (PG 25,5 C8–11); In illud 'omnia . . .' 6
    (PG 25, 216 C7 – 220 B7); Or. c. Ar. I 23 (PG 26,60 B11–C1); Ep ad Serap. I 20 (PG
    26,577 B2 –C6); see Carabina, Above p. 64, on Plato's Seventh Letter (341 c-d).
136 Cf. De syn. 52,1; re *eikôn*, see 2 Cor 4:4; *charaktêr*, Heb 1:3.
137 Cf. De syn 52,1; this is, of course, the understanding of Acacius of Caesarea and
    his party.
138 De syn. 52,1; Newman remarks in a footnote to his translation that *eidos*, generally
    applied to the Son, is synonymous with *hupostasis*, but here is synonymous with *ousia*
    or *phusis*. 'Indeed in one sense nature, substance and hypostasis are all synonymous,
    i.e. as one and all denoting the Una Res, which is Almighty God. The apparent
    confusion is useful as reminding us of this great truth', Robertson, op. cit. 478.
139 Cf. De syn. 52,2, Opitz 275, 34–276, 2: 'for this was seen by the Patriarch Jacob, as
    Scripture says, "The sun rose upon him when the form of God (*eidos tou Theou*)
    passed by".'
140 Ex 3:16 is quoted in support.
141 Cf De syn. 52,3, Opitz 276, 9–10.

called "of one Being"?'[142] Athanasius thus rounds off his theological exposition of the *homoousios* with a reference to the second of the two scriptural texts with which he began.

Finally he looks at the term itself, its suitability. Having established that those who used the term did so without blame, one may still ask whether it is necessary (*chrē*) to use it at all, is it valid and suitable to apply it to the Son? He begins by showing how 'like' is unsuitable, since it is predicated of outward appearances and qualities, whereas with beings we speak not of likeness but of identity.[143] Men may be like in external appearance but in their being they are of one nature (*homophueis*). On the other hand a dog is not said to be unlike man, but rather is of a different nature. They are not of one nature, of one substance (*homoousios*). To speak of like according to being is to indicate like by participation, likeness being a quality that may inhere in being. This would be proper to creatures since they become like to God by participation as indicated by 1 Jn 3:2.[144] Like-in-Being (*homoioousios*), since 'like' indicates resemblance to reality, would signify sonship by participation, thus denying that He is either Truth, or Light, or by nature God.[145] Hence '. . . if He is not by participation, He is, by nature and in truth, Son, Light, Wisdom, God . . . and may be validly said to be not 'Like-in- Being' but 'of one Being'.[146]

For such reasons, Athanasius concludes, the Synod of Nicaea was right to decree, and the bishops fittingly (*prepei*) said, that begotten from the Being of the Father, the Son is 'of one Being.'[147] After a brief summary of the main arguments, he brings his Letter to a close with an appeal to his readers:

> 54,3: Remaining on 'the foundation of the Apostles' (Eph 2:20) and holding fast to the Traditions of the Fathers, pray that, from this time on, all remaining strife and rivalry may cease, the foolish searchings (*zēteseis*) and all empty argumentation of the heretics may be condemned; that on the one side the ill-omened, murderous heresy of the Arians may disappear, and that on the other the Truth may flare up in the hearts of all, so that everyone everywhere may 'say the same thing' (1 Cor 1:10) and think the same thing, and that, no Arian blasphemies remaining, it may be recited and confessed in every church: 'One Lord, one faith, one Baptism' (Eph 4:5) in Christ Jesus Our Lord, through whom to the Father be glory and power for ever and ever. Amen.

---

142 De syn. 52,5, Opitz 276, 18–20.
143 De syn. 53,2, Opitz 276, 24–26.
144 De syn. 53,3, Opitz 276, 30–33.
145 Cf. De syn. 53,4, Opitz 276, 33–277, 1.
146 Cf. De syn. 53,5, Opitz 277, 2–3.
147 Cf. De syn. 54,1, Opitz 277, 6–7.

CONCLUSION[148]

The final doxology highlights the burning passion of Athanasius: his passion for the Truth. It is not abstraction, though reasoning as such plays a not insignificant part in his theology, but knowledge of the living God, incomprehensible by nature, who makes Himself known through His Image and Impress, the Word through Whom all things were made and through whom we who believe are deified. Knowledge of God is only possible through the Faith proclaimed by the Apostles and handed on by the Fathers, the bishops who have the ultimate responsibility to interpret the Word of God and preserve it intact from attacks by heretics. The living faith of the bishops is the source of their unanimity, both spatially and temporally, which in turn is the source of their synodal judgements. But such unanimity must be one of conviction, rooted in conscience, a oneness of heart and mind. The gloss Athanasius adds to the words of 1 Cor 1:10 in the doxology is significant: one in heart involves one in mind. The whole thrust of *De synodis*, the care he takes to examine every possible objection, either to the authority of synods or to the terms of Nicaea, had as its ultimate objective: to persuade, to lead to the truth and so to genuine unanimity.

But also the question as to the nature of truth itself is a constantly recurring theme within the Letter. Indeed it is more, it is the hermeneutical pivot around which every other theme revolves. The defence of the use of the term *ousia* was based on the very possibility of theology in the original strict sense of the term, being able to speak about God in a way that corresponded to His Reality. But also his interpretation of synodal decrees was based on the nature of truth, as a result of which he was able to articulate, however tentatively, for the first time in the history of the Church, a theology of synodal authority which is oecumenical by nature.[149] The *sine qua non*, however, for any genuine interpretation of

148 *De synodis*, it seems to me, presents us with an outline sketch of all the major themes that Athanasius will later develop more fully in De decretis, De sententia, and above all in the Orationes (see note 122 above, regarding the need to revise the dating of these texts). The present study, limited though it may be, would seem to offer some confirmation for my thesis. There is no indication in the text of the other works being available, no reference to earlier writings. Many central ideas (such as the exegesis of Prov 8:22 or the argument from deification) are only mentioned in passing or would appear to be at the embryonic stage of their development. See also notes 76, 106, 109, 123, 127 supra.

149 Despite its undoubted achievement, Sieben's account of Athanasius' concept of an [oecumenical] council can only be accepted with the following reservations: (a) Sieben's interpretation of the texts is at times marked by the author's rather negative approach to, and basic distrust of, Athanasius, an approach still marked by the shadow cast by Schwartz (and others) over Athanasian studies and which has only recently been corrected; cf. in particular the work of M. Tetz, 'Zur Biographie des Athanasius von Alexandrien' in ZKG 90 (1979) 304–338. As a result, Sieben's analysis takes as its starting point the unproven, not to say dubious, assumption that

either Scripture or Tradition (including synodal decrees) is, according to Athanasius, *eusebeia*, variously translated above as worship of Christ, adoration, religion, a true religious attitude. This is the subjective presupposition of any genuine interpretation: union with God in Christ. A related term is *gnêsios*, indicating a proper disposition, a good conscience. Truth is not knowlege about some object but illumination,

Athanasius, the opportunistic *Kirchenpolitiker*, originally defended Nicaea primarily to bolster his own position [cf. Sieben, 27]. (b) Sieben fails to appreciate sufficiently the different roles that Nicaea played in the two major phases of the controversies surrounding Athanasius, the first (after 335) when he was locked in battle with the Eusebian party in his efforts to establish his claim to the See of Alexandria, Nicaea being essentially a background issue, and the second (after 353) when the Nicene creed came to the forefront. As I argue elsewhere (see note 23 supra), the first phase was marked by the reaffirmation of the apostolic nature of the Church, and so her independence and freedom, in the face of the threat posed by the Eusebian *Reichskirche*. The freedom of the Church was understood as a consequence of her apostolic nature and for this reason it became for Athanasius an essential characteristic of authoritative, ecclesial synods. But it also arises from his understanding of truth and the centrality of freedom of conscience in that understanding. Sieben, however, claims: 'Was Athanasius zum Anlaß wurde, freie Konzilien zu fordern, war gewiß weniger eine Reflexion über die Menschenwürde oder das Wesen der Religion, wie er selber anzudeuten scheint, als vielmehr die klare Erkenntnis, daß der Arianismus durch Staatsmacht die Oberhand gewonnen hatte: *dia tês exôthen exoúsias* [45]. Siebens interpretation der Epistula Julii ep. Romae (Apol. sec. 21–35; Opitz 102,12–113,25) is particularly misleading: 'Synodalbeschlüsse sind nicht schlecthin endgültig' [33]. Neither Julius nor Athanasius indiscriminately applied this fundamental principle to synodal decisions as such (i.e. including matters concerning the Faith) but only to those decisions of a legal nature where the issue was one of justice not truth. [Cf. also note 54 above where Athanasius draws attention to the different types of decision made by Nicaea.] The recourse on the part of Julius to Canon V of Nicaea, which Sieben explicitly disregards, is indeed of central significance for a correct understanding of the text (see Twomey, note 23 supra, 374–425, esp. 413–421). There the revision of previous synodal judgements was necessitated by the claims of justice, a principle Julius maintains was upheld by Nicaea. (c) A revision of the generally accepted chronology of Athanasius' various works (Sieben follows Camelot and Roldanus), as already suggested, might result in a more nuanced understanding of De decretis. Thus e.g. the conferring on the Faith of the Nicene synod, and so on its formulations, the dignity and authority of the *paradosis*, the divine Tradition,—as found in De decret. 27, and which on the basis of the generally accepted chronology would seem out of place—could not be dismissed simply under the suspicion (*Verdacht*) that it was simply a polemical salvo against the Arians [cf. 39]! (d) While Sieben's conclusion articulates well many of the central ideas of Athanasius concerning synbodal decrees, yet it is marred by what would seem to be the hermeneutical error mentioned by Pieper (note 9 above), namely the failure to see what the author may well indeed have taken for granted. For example, Sieben contrasts the references to the divine inspiration of the Council of Nicaea (expressly attributed to the Holy Spirit) in the letters of the Emperor Constantine with the absence of any similar references in Athanasius. Leaving aside the interesting question as to who might have inspired Constantine (Ossius of Cordova?), perhaps the more reasonable assumption is that, for his own political purposes, the Emperor used a commonly accepted assumption shared by all. Similarly the definitive nature of Nicaea seems to be the knowing God. To know and speak of God one has to be pure in mind.[150] Living union with God in Christ through the Holy Spirit is the source of all true interpretation: 'In Thy Light do we see Light.'[151]

The interrelationship between Scripture and Tradition, one throwing light on the other, is adumbrated in the introduction to the doxc ogy: the Church is to remain on the foundations of the Apostles and hold fast to the Traditions of the Fathers.[152] Throughout *De synodis* the inter-

one common theme in all the writings of Athanasius, one that he articulated more and more expressly in the course of the years, climaxing in the Epistula episcoporum Aegypti et Libyae nonaginta (PG 26, 1029–2048). There we find the quotation from Prov 22:28: 'Do not change the eternal boundries fixed by your Fathers', a parallel text to Deut 19:14 which, as noted above (note 19), had been used by Dionysius of Alexandria a century earlier with a similar meaning. Sieben notes that Prov 22:28 had also been used (together with Dt 32:7) by Eusebius of Caesarea to justify the motto: *dei hepesthai tois patrasi* (Contra Marc. I 4, GCS 20,26). In other words, we may well be dealing with a common assumpton of ancient origin. The 'astonishing silence' of Athanasius concerning the role of the Holy Spirit [cf. Sieben, 66] may not be so surprising after all. (f) Finally, Sieben is surely right to reject any trace in Athanasius' thought of some new form of synod or council known as oecumenical and so automatically, in some 'mechanical' way, infallible. However, it must be said that to look for such a notion in Athanasius is misplaced since it misses the real concern of Athanasius: Truth. As an expression of the *paradosis*, Nicaea, like every genuine synod, has an *a priori*, and so an absolute, claim to Truth. But like Scripture, synodal decrees concerning the faith, once they possess the marks of apostolicity and catholicity, diachronic and synchronic unanimity, are definitive, though they invite interpretation. Tradition is a living reality.

150 'But in addition to the study and true knowledge of the Scriptures are needed a good life and pure soul and virtue in Christ, so that the mind, journeying in this path, may be able to obtain and apprehend what it desires, in so far as human nature is able to learn about God the Word. For without a pure mind and a life modelled on the saints, no one can apprehend the words of the saints. For just as if someone wishes to see the light of the sun he cleanses and clears his eye, and purifies it until it is similar to what he desires, so that as the eye thus becomes light it may see the light of the sun . . .", C. gentes. 57 (Thompson).

151 Ps 35:10 LXX (quoted e.g.in De decret. 12,2; Or. c. Ar. I 12, PG 26, 37 A7–9; III 59. PG 26, 448 B14–15); the psalm text accurately captures his thought, as found in the text from C. gentes. quoted in the previous note; cf. also Ep. ad Serap. I 19, PG 26,573 C8–D3; In illud 'omnia mihi tradita sunt,' 2, PG 25, 212 A8–11; see Pelikan, op. cit. (note 7 supra), 75–111.

152 The formula used by Athanasius later was: '. . .let us look at the tradition, teaching and faith of the Catholic Church from the beginning, *which the Lord gave, the Apostles preached, and the Fathers kept*. Upon this the Church is founded . . . (Ep. ad Serap. 28, PG 26, 593 C13– 596 A1, transl. Shapland, my emphasis). The translator's own interpretation of this text, however, is not entirely convincing, cf. C. B. R. Shapland, The Letters of Saint Athanasius Concerning the Holy Spirit, London 1951, 133– 134; see also Ad Afr. 1: '. . . concerning the sound Faith which *Christ bestowed upon us, the Apostles preached, and the Fathers* who met at Nicaea from all this world of ours, *have handed down* (PG 26, 1029 A6–9;transl. Robertson, my emphasis); cf. Ad Adelph. 6 (PG 26, 1080 A10–B1). Newman's observation is still valid '. . . [Athanasius] assumes that there is a tradition, substantive, independent and authoritative, such as to supply for us the true sense of Scripture in doctrinal matters—a tradition carried on from generation to generation by the practice of catechising, and by the ministrations of

pretation of Scripture was the model for the interpretation of Tradition, while Tradition (dogma) called to mind, clarified and preserved the content of Scripture. Dogmatic tradition itself, however, is understood in the dynamic sense of being open to development. This is the ultimate implication of the fact that, in the analysis of the meaning and suitability of the disputed term *homoousios*, those who were at the time responsible for handing on that faith—Athanasius, Basil of Ancyra and their fellow bishops—had to defend that faith at the bar of reason, in harmony with the entire sense of Scripture.

Athanasius' use of Scripture in *De synodis* is marked first of all by fidelity to the letter. For all the parties to the dispute the divine inspiration of Scripture was beyond question. What is most striking is his astonishing familiarity with the whole of Scripture in detail, often weaving scraps of texts, generally given accurately, into the argumentation, some of which might otherwise be considered obscure, and on one occasion even coarse.[153] He notices the Lucan redaction of Mk 9:42 (=Lk 17:2).[154] He pays close attention to the terminology of Scripture (e.g. that used for God's creative activity, or the Pauline terminology of 1 Cor 4:9). But at other times he simply alludes to texts and to events in Scripture to evoke a familiar concept. As far as the question of the nature of the Son is concerned, the Old Testament is as significant as the New. The Alexandrian tradition was familiar with the identity of Christ with the Word of God who spoke to Moses and the Prophets. It was a tradition which all parties to the dispute shared, though their interpretation differed. And so he could on one occasion demonstrate the unity of Father and Son by a litany of texts, allusions and events from both the Old and the New Testament. But two texts may be singled out, since for Athanasius they in particular express what he, in other writings, called the *skopos* of Scripture, the Rule of Faith which is the hermeneutical key to interpreting Scripture:[155] 'I and my Father are one' (Jn 10:30), and 'He who has seen me

---

Holy Church,' Select Treatises (note 119 supra) II, 250. A. Louth (note 106 supra) 392 succinctly comments, 'Scripture and Tradition are interwoven: each intrepreted by the other.'

153 Pelikan, op. cit. (note 7 supra), 31, describes the theological method advocated by Athanasius in the latter's discussion of biblical *paradeigmata* as 'the collation of biblical images'. Kannengiesser, op cit. (note 30 supra) col.1130, aptly comments: 'Ohne schulmäßige Kommentare aufzusetzen, vermöchte es [Athanasius] eine originelle hermeneutische Haltung in allen seinen Werken zu veranschaulichen.'

154 See De syn. 2:4, Opitz 232, 29–31.

155 In the Orations, Athanasius explicitly states that using 'the scope of that faith which we Christians hold, and using it as a rule, [we] apply ourselves, as the Apostle teaches, to the reading of inspired Scripture. ....Now the scope and character of Holy Scripture, as we have often said, is this, - it contains a double account of the Saviour; that He was ever God, and is the Son, being the Father's Word and Radiance and Wisdom and that afterwards for us He took flesh of a Virgin, Mary Bearer of God, and was made man', Or. c. Ar. III 28–29 (PG 26,385 A1–14, Newman); for a com-

has seen the Father' (Jn 14:9). The *homoousios* affirmed the possibiliy of knowing the Father in Christ.[156]

But on the other hand, the whole argument of *De synodis* was to persuade his readers to go beyond the letter, not into allegory but into theology.[157] The *homoousios* was the guarantee, not only of fidelity to Scripture and Tradition, but of the possibility of theology in the strict sense of the word: to think and speak about the incomprehensible God revealed in Christ. But to do so in a way that was based on the transcendence of God as implied in the doctrine of creation: God is not as man is.

mentary, see Sieben 'Herméneutque' (note 7 supra) 205–214, who argues persuasively that here Athanasius develops a principle first articulated by Origen, De principiis IV 2,7. 'Athanasius' doctrine of the Logos arises out of the exegesis of the Scriptures, although at the same time it affects the doctrine of Scripture and determines its proper and regular interpretation,' Torrance, op. cit. (note 7 supra) 447; cf. Schneemelcher, op. cit. (note 7 supra) 131–2.

156 Cf. C. Schönborn OP, Die Christus-Ikone. Eine theologische Hinführung, Schaffhausen 1984, 21–27.

157 If this is to be inderstood as the necessity of expressing the faith in terms of Platonic ontology, a necessity due to the challenge posed by Arius, Meijering (note 80 supra) warns us that '. . . Orthodoxy and Platonism, both on the surface and in the depth of Athanasius' thought, are in antithesis to each other, viz. in the antithesis of true worship and idolatry. The true worship which is found in orthodox faith is, however, expressed in Platonic terms . . .' (131) And yet Meijering concludes: 'We regard as the most fascinating aspect of Athanasius theology the constant use he makes of Platonic ontology. We venture to say that in doing so Athanasius has sensed a truth which he never frankly admitted: there are certain affinities between Platonism and the Christian faith' (185). Ricken, op. cit (note 83 super) 343, broadly summarized his finding as follows: 'Seine [=Athanasius] Platon-Rezeption stellt eine Synthese dar zwischen dem Analogie- und Teilhabedenken, das für Eusebios kennzeichnend ist, und dem Anliegen der Arianer, die Tranzendenz des Schöpfers gegenüber dem Geschaffenen eindeutig auszusagen.' See the comments by Carabine, 64 supra. Our analysis has revealed that what Williams, op. cit. (note 42 supra), 236, says about the Church at large, was certainly the over-riding motivating force for Athanasius: 'There is a sense in which Nicaea and its aftermath represents a recognition by the Church at large that *theology* is not only legitimate but necessary'. A. Louth (note 106 *supra*), 353, draws attention to the role of *reason* in Athansius' interpretation of Scripture within Tradition: to discover the sense (*dianoia*) or purpose (*skopos*) of Revelation, and in 'the development of what can almost be called a theory of the analogical predication of attributes.' Further, he affirms: 'There must be no possibility of imagining that [for Athanasius] theology begins with mere assent, rather than believing worship. . . This situating theology in the context of prayer holds together the whole of Athanasius' theology' (395). Athanasian hermeneutics can be summed up in a quotation from Ad Serap. I 20, (PG 26,577 B1–2, Shapland): 'For tradition, as we have said, does not declare the Godhead to us by demonstration in words, but by faith and by a pious and reverent use of reason (*en pistei kai eusebei logismôi met' eulabeias*)'.

Maximus Confessor: On the Lord's Prayer

NICHOLAS MADDEN

Here it is my intention to look at a Father of the Church at work and to try to grasp what he had in mind as he wrote his commentary on the Our Father. It becomes immediately obvious, on examining the *Pater Noster*,[1] that Maximus Confessor is an exponent of the exegesis which is 'entirely centred on the mystery of Christ to whom all the individual truths are referred in a wonderful synthesis.'[2] We have here a commentary that is markedly allegorical and does not neglect the tropological and anagogical corollaries that characterize Alexandrian exegesis. Maximus would think of his use of the Our Father as most significant in a liturgical context. We have to visualize him then in the ecclesial assembly, worshipping God in the language of the Lord's Prayer and doing so with the privileged insight of a mystic. For all that, he expresses himself in a typically Byzantine way. In his *Mystagogia*, a commentary on the liturgy, he says that the Our Father is 'the symbol of filial adoption which was communicated to us by the gift and grace of the Holy Spirit.'[3] In that work the term 'symbol' is used to indicate a presence of, together with a participation in, the mystery that surpasses that of the Old Testament dispensation, but which has not achieved the fullness of the *eschaton*.[4] This is to make a quasi-sacramental claim for the efficacy of the use of the dominical prayer in the liturgy. The earnest tone of the writing in the *Pater Noster* echoes the mind of a man striving to realize and express the splendour of the gift communicated to him in this 'symbol'.

It is the intention of Maximus in writing the *Pater Noster* reverently to explore seven of the innumerable 'mysteries' conferred on us by

1 The Greek of the Expositio Orationis Dominicae by Maximus Confessor is to be found in Migne PG 90, 872D–908D. It is referred to in the footnotes as Or. Dom. and is named in the text of this essay as *Pater Noster*. Translations are mine.
2 Instruction on the Study of the Fathers of the Church in the Formation of Priests, Rome 1989, 27.
3 Myst., PG 91, 696c.
4 R. Bornaert, Les Commentaires Byzantins de la Divine Liturgie du VIIe au XVe Siècle, Paris 1966, 83–124.

God through the redemptive incarnation of his Son. The 'mysteries' are theology, sonship by grace, equality of honour with the angels, participation in divine life, restoration of nature to itself, purification from the 'law of sin' and the abolition of the tyranny of the Evil One. While the teaching on the 'mysteries' is an exegesis of the seven petitions of the Our Father, the 'mysteries' do not correspond exactly to the petitions. 'Theology', with its reference to the 'Father' of the invocation and to the 'Name' and 'Kingdom' of the first two petitions is a commentary on the mystery of the Trinity, while 'sonship by grace' implies these elements of the Our Father but with a different emphasis. In the course of his work Maximus deals with the 'mysteries' three times. The first treatment of the text of the Our Father is from a Christological point of view, the third, much briefer, approaches the petitions primarily from an ascetical angle, while the second exposition, which forms the bulk of the work, combines both the Christological and ascetical viewpoints. In this paper, we shall look at the first or Christological commentary.[5]

THEOLOGY—THE INVOCATION, FIRST AND SECOND PETITIONS

> The Word made flesh teaches theology in that He reveals the Father and the Holy Spirit. For the whole of the Father and the whole of the Holy Spirit were substantially and perfectly in the whole of the Son, even made flesh, although they themselves were not made flesh. The Father delighted in, and the Spirit cooperated with, the Son who himself effected his incarnation. For the Word remained in possession of his intelligence and his life; He was comprehended by no one at all in substance except by the Father alone and by the Spirit, but He was united hypostatically with the flesh because of his love for man.[6]

The first and most obvious comment to be made is that the *Logos* is the subject of all the sentences in the exegesis from a Christological point of view, so that grammatically we are left in no doubt that the Word is meant to dominate not only this section but the whole treatise, which holds true even when some anthropological aspects of Maximus' thought are given a more complete elaboration. Without more ado it can be said that *Logos* is the synthetic principle of this introductory commentary. The *Logos* is presented as the source of the seven mysteries conferred on man, so that man's being and destiny are totally bound up with the *Logos* and without Him man is for Maximus unintelligible. Christology is the key to Maximian anthropology and the inextricable quality of the treatment of these themes reflects their ontological

---

5   Or. Dom., PG 90, 876C–881A.
6   Ibid., 876CD.

coherence. This finds its explanation in the mystery of the Incarnation where humanity and divinity are united in Christ with the qualifications spelt out so firmly by Chalcedon, principles that operate at the very foundation of Maximus' system, explanatory not only of the mystery of the Incarnation, but of the whole relationship of creation to God.

We are not surprised then to find that the *Logos* teaches theology (*theologia*). Maximus is here concerned with the mystery of the Blessed Trinity in so far as it is communicated to man in Christ. We do not find an abstract treatment of the mystery but sufficient elaboration to enable us to identify Christ, the *Logos* incarnate, as one of the Three in One, who puts on humanity by hypostatic union. In the rapid summary of this section of his commentary[7] Maximus identifies the Son with the 'Name' of the prayer and the Holy Spirit with the 'Kingdom' and he elaborates this further in the second part. The Trinitarian context of the whole treatise is emphasized in this way and leads us to consider that Maximus wants all his subsequent reflections to be related to and understood in terms of what we know of the Trinity in its immanence and its economy. The hallowing of the Name and the coming of the Kingdom are given a firm anthropological interpretation in the main commentary in terms of *logos*/reason and the *praotês*/meekness.[8] There we find *logos* associated with *epithumia*/desire and *thumos*/anger. The Platonic triad takes on a complex of meanings that enables our author to distinguish between the faculties of the soul and their disordered use as passions. He transposes *logos* from being the innate 'ruling principle' to being the divine *Logos*, so that the ascetical implications of *logos*, clarified in its bearing on desire and anger, is thrown into relation with the divine order and human integration is recognized as a hallowing of the *Logos*. We would seem to have here the *vivens homo gloria Dei* of Irenaeus articulated in a different idiom. Maximus thinks that the virtues ensure that the *Logos* is present in the life of the Christian, not merely because He is the source of the *logoi*, but that in some way in his uniqueness He communicates to them a participation in the Sonship that became the ground of his humanity in the hypostatic union and which constitutes them in the freedom of their personhood. This is paralleled by the introduction of *praotês* | meekness with its evangelical connotations. Gregory of Nyssa had taught that the request for the coming of the Kingdom was asking for the Spirit, an interpretation which Maximus accepts here. Since the Spirit has promised to rest on the meek and humble, meekness assumes in human life a function that complements that of *logos*. Dalmais has pointed out that in the *oeuvre* of Maximus *praotês* and *agapê* are easily identified.[9] Meekness is used here to emphasize man's dependence on

---

7   Ibid., 881ᴀʙ.
8   Ibid., 885ʙᴄ.
9   I.-H. Dalmais, Un traité de théologie contemplative: le commentaire du Pater Noster de saint Maxime le Confesseur, RAM, xxix, 1953, 123–159.

the Holy Spirit to become his true self, so that it connotes a wise passivity. It is assigned the function of ensuring that the man who possesses it will enable the Kingdom to come, that is, allow the Spirit to act freely in his life. It is tied to the notions of human freedom, synergy, stability and ultimately man's becoming a person. We find adumbrated here a well known Maximian polarity of principle (*logos*) and mode (*tropos*), nature and person, in the context of the economic intervention of the Son and the Spirit in human life.

It is the being and life of the incarnate *Logos* that is presented to us as revealing the mystery of the Trinity, because He remains in possession of his 'intelligence' (*ennous*) and of his 'life' (*zôn*) in His incarnation, with the Father and the Spirit delighting in and cooperating respectively, even if it is the person of the *Logos* who effects the incarnation by assuming human nature. We discover the economic Trinity because it enters our life through Christ. The distinctness of the persons is emphasized by the use of their individual names, while their *perichôrêsis* is stressed in the epithets applied to the *Logos*: *ennous* and *zôn*, where *nous* designates the Father and *zôê* the Spirit in their comprehension and penetration of the *Logos*. This has an Augustinian ring about it. While it is difficult to establish a clear dependence of Maximus on Augustine, there can be little doubt but that the former is here concerned with the theological structure of the Christian soul and finds that man in his maturity is so identified with God that he perceives his *nous, logos* and *zôê* to provide a way of speaking of the inner life of God. Even more, their interaction is in some way an expression of that life so that their source and energy are more truly proper to God than to participating man. We may note too that they are said to be in the Logos incarnate *ousiôdôs/* substantially, and that He is comprehended by them *kat' ousian*. This refers to the substance and nature of the Godhead, so that the coinherence and mutual indwelling of the three persons, while it is in the hypostatic realm, is required by their equally possessing the same divine Being. In what follows Maximus is preoccupied by unity, so that here he is drawing attention to the principle of unity in the mystery of God himself, the divine *ousia* which has its created counterpart in the *physis* shared by men and which has to be restored to its proper place and function in human life. The revelation of the Father and of the Spirit in the incarnate Word is significant for man because he becomes 'son' and shares in divine life; man participating in the *Logos* will become analogously *ennous* and *zôn*. In the thought of Maximus the humanity of the *Logos* is caught into the hypostatic *ad Patrem* that is his in the Trinity and which is the source of the anointing of his being and activity as man with *agapê*. The *agapê*, which flows from the *Logos* and which is poured into the heart of man by his Spirit, so transforms the human's 'mode of existence' that his per- son gradually emerges in all its splendour, revealing him to be a son in the Son.

Finally, divine love for man—*philanthrôpia*—is thrown into relief here. It is given as the ultimate reason for the hypostatic union on which depends the possibility of the manifestation of the Trinity implied in *deiknus*. There is no source behind this source to account for man's being drawn into the mystery of God's own life.

SONSHIP BY GRACE—INVOCATION, FIRST AND SECOND PETITIONS

The Logos gives adoptive sonship, conferring through the Spirit in grace from above the birth which transcends nature. The guard and preservation of this in God is the free choice of those thus born, which cherishes sincerely the grace bestowed, and by the practice of the commandments carefully cultivates the beauty given through the grace; by emptying themselves of the passions they appropriate the divine to the extent that the Word of God himself, having emptied himself voluntarily of his own pure glory by economy, became and was truly a man.

Theology and Sonship by Grace are treated concurrently so that thematically they are correlative, self-communication of God being realized in the filial adoption which the *Logos* effects. Here we have two complementary themes, adoptive sonship (*huiothesia*), characterized by the notions of grace, beauty and the divine, together with free choice (*proairesis*), explicated in the ideas of cherishing, cultivating and appropriation. It is the *Logos* who bestows adoptive sonship. He is personally responsible for man's being endowed with this gift. The gratuitousness is underlined by 'in grace' (*en chariti*). 'The birth which transcends nature' derives from the *Logos* but it is not understood in a typically Western way. Since the Greek Fathers saw human sonship of God primarily in the personal order, Maximus is reminding us that man has a twofold relationship to the *Logos*: that of hypostasis to Hypostasis and that of the objective coincidence of the energy of the *Logos* and of man in *physis-*nature. By breaking his relationship to the *Logos* in the personal order through the Fall he incapacitated himself for cooperating with Him in the order of *physis*. The restoration of man to his pristine condition is said here to be *hyper physin*, above nature: it is beyond his own capacity to achieve and it is, besides, in the hypostatic order, so that he becomes one on whom God can look as a person in dependence on the person of his Son. The *Logos* gives sonship *anôthen*, from above, that is from his own sonship in which man participates by the enjoyment of that *pleon ti*, that something over and above which he aborted so tragically in the Fall. By being restored to personhood he is restored to sonship. His rebirth is the birth of a son, a *gennêsis*. Part of the newness, which is implicit in the *sarkôsis*, enfleshment, is that sonship is now conferred on man from within the realm of human nature, into which the *Logos* has entered 'because of his love for man', so that human nature can never again be deprived of the personal presence of the *Logos* now realized *kath' hypo-staton*, in the hypostatic order.

It is important to note here the function of the Spirit. It is through the Spirit that adoptive sonship is given by that birth from above in which man emerges as a person. The concept of person here should be understood in a dynamic way: it implies a process of hypostatic becoming which is expressed in free activity, so that the Spirit is introduced as the immediate source of the energy that brings about man's sonship through the synergy that requires the exercise of man's freedom. Although Maximus does not mention it here, we know from elsewhere in his work that the upshot of that synergy is *agapê*/charity, poured into man's heart by the Spirit, ensuring that his exercise of free choice is loving.[11] This is brought out in the complementary theme of *proairesis*, free choice, which is said to be proper to those born in God, a birth given by the *Logos* through the Spirit and throwing man into a filial relationship with the Father. The dynamic character of this sonship, and the function of free choice in its evolution, is underlined by attributing to the latter the guarding and preservation of the grace which it 'cherishes sincerely'. This is a right orientation, a willingness to correspond to the grace, a kind of promptitude in accepting the gift of God which must precede every other vital manifestation of the exercise of freedom. It is the right use of freedom that cultivates the beauty of sonship through the practice of the commandments. The energizing of the commandments by freedom and the reciprocal informing of free choice by the commandments issues in a splendour proper to divine filiation. Finally it is free choice that appropriates divinity, the grace of sonship of God, by the emptying of the passions that result from the Fall and which mar man's being and impede his becoming a person in the full sense because of the submergence of his freedom in disordered self-love, orchestrated in the many forms of desire and aggression. Free choice is presented here as the key to being human from a subjective point of view and on it depends entirely the reception, and growth, of the grace of sonship implanted in man by the *Logos* through the Holy Spirit. Maximus introduces a favourite theme here: *tosouton-hoson*, by which he expresses his insight into the reciprocity of the exchange implied in the mystery of the Incarnation, and analogously in the divinization of man.[12] God becomes man to the extent that man becomes God. This is realized *par excellence* in the *Logos* incarnate and by participation in those endowed with *huiothesia*.

---

10   Or. Dom., PG 90, 877A.
11   See J.M. Garrigues, Maxime le Confesseur, Paris 1976, 176–199.
12   Ambig., PG 91, 1084CD; 1113BC; 1288A.

EQUALITY OF HONOUR WITH THE ANGELS—THIRD PETITION

He has made men equal in dignity to the angels. Not only because, 'having pacified through the blood of his cross . . . things in heaven and things on earth' [Col 1:20], and having made ineffectual the hostile powers that fill the region lying between heaven and earth, He showed that, as regards the distribution of divine gifts, the festal gathering of earthly and heavenly powers was one because human nature joins in singing with great joy the glory of God in one and the same will with the powers on high, but also because, after the fulfilment of the economy on our behalf and having ascended with his assumed body, He united heaven and earth through himself and joined the sensibles to the intelligibles and showed them to be one created nature whose extremes are bound to it by virtue and full knowledge of the First Cause . . . He shows, I think, by what He accomplished mystically, how, on the one hand, the *Logos* unites what is separated, and on the other, how the absence of the *Logos* separates what is united. Let us learn then to strive for the *Logos* through virtuous activity in order to be united not only to the angels in virtue but to God in spiritual knowledge by detachment from things.[13]

In his treatment of this theme we find Maximus making use of another tradition and seeking to understand salvation as the establishment of some kind of parity between man and the angels. At the same time he integrates the insights of Dionysius the Areopagite to give us a vision of human destiny as a vocation to cosmic liturgy. Again it is the Incarnate *Logos* who achieves this by having made peace through the blood of his cross between those in heaven and those on earth, by having undone the evil spirits, denizens of some vague world between heaven and earth, by having formed into one a heavenly choir of men and angels, and by ascension, having entered definitively into the angelic world and thus made way for the entry of those He saved in the integrity of their human being, body and soul. The use of *logos* is to the fore here and Maximus employs it with considerable subtlety, binding together both Origenian and Dionysian ideas, as Dalmais says wittily, in a 'union without confusion'. The notion of will (*thelêma*) is prompted by the petition of the Our Father on which this section is a commentary.

The overriding concern here is that of unity, and the principle of that unity is said to be *thelêma* and *logos*. Again the *Logos* is credited with having achieved this unity in Himself and with communicating it to man. We note too that the mysteries of the incarnate *Logos* are thrown into relief so that there is no question of a merely philosophical principle as the ground of this unity, nor can we predicate an *a priori* unity in

13 Or. Dom., PG 90, 977A–C.

the treatment of this petition, but rather it is based on the data of revelation and is moulded by them. Maximus has already referred to his incarnation (*sarkôsis*) and to his self-emptying; here we are reminded of his having perfected the Economy by fulfilling his human existence by the paschal mystery. The cross is mentioned, the resurrection is implied, and the ascension is affirmed explicitly, so that we are being confronted with the historical Christ. It is He who made men of equal dignity with the angels: He showed that the multitude of earthly and heavenly powers are one and that He united heaven and earth, intelligibles and sensibles.

The implication is that it is first of all in the *Logos* incarnate that human nature celebrates with the angels the glory of God. The possibility of that concelebration relies on the unity obtaining between the powers of the heavenly and earthly orders, evidence for which is here adduced as a festal gathering 'in one and the same will'. The 'Thy will be done' of the Our Father is realized in this way. The *thelêma* of God finds a response in the created *thelêma* of men and angels. Maximus distinguishes *thelêma physikon*/natural will, and *thelêma gnômikon*/personalized will, and we might think of him as emphasizing the former here because of his reference to 'human nature'. Christ does not have *gnômê* in the developed theology of Maximus because the term is reserved for defective human will. Here he finds a common term to cover Christ, angels and men. The emphasis is on *physis* and *logos*, and *thelêma* is undoubtedly capable of sustaining this connotation. The affinity of *ousia*/substance and *physis*/nature entitles us to draw attention to the possibility of an emphasis on a principle of unity analogous to that hidden in the splendour of the Godhead. Just as in the language of the Trinity we find proof of Maximus' holding that, while *perichôrêsis* was hypostatic, unity is grounded in one *ousia*, so here he would seem to suggest that the one *thelêma* ordained by God for men requires a principle of unity in one 'created nature'. The union that involves personal *proairesis*/free choice, to be dealt with under 'restoration of nature to itself' below, will accept this physical basis for volitional unity brought about by the infusion of charity.

The incarnate Word is also said to have united heaven and earth, the sensibles and intelligibles. These are two of the five great unifications attributed to the incarnate *Logos* by Maximus.[14] He is said explicitly to have united heaven and earthy 'through Himself', having ascended with an assumed body. The reference to the 'body' is calculated here, as this dimension of created being is stressed in the third mediation, while soul and its activities, here virtue and knowledge, are given emphasis in the fourth mediation. The fact that human nature re-echoes the glory of God with the powers on high in one and the same will demonstrates that angels and men are one 'as regards the distribution of divine gifts'. This participation in a divine liturgy presumes being and well-being, *nous* and

14   See L. Thunberg, Microcosm and Mediator, Lund 1965, 396–454.

thelêma, nature and personal existence. But Maximus is here emphasizing unity and he develops this in his treatment of the way in which the
Logos incarnate united the separate heaven and earth, intelligibles and
sensibles, a process that converges in the idea of *logos*. The mention of
the First Cause in this doxological context is an indication that what
both the sensibles and intelligibles have in common is their createdness,
and it is the *logos* of this that they discern as binding them in common to
the created love of God in his *Logos*. 'The divine principle which holds
the entire creation together is that it would have non-being as the
ground of its being.'[15] *Physis*/nature is the locus of the intersection of the
activity of the *Logos* and of men. It is the objective order in which synergy
takes place, where the personal activity of the *Logos* and created persons
concurs in keeping with the uncreated *logoi*. This is realized especially in
this case where the *logos* of being drawn from nothing and of being
endowed with spirit is shared by angels and men. *Thelêma* is invited to
adopt this truth as its own, to be consistent with the *logos* of nature and
to give vent to this in a concerted paean. The created nature is one, and
in that sense it has one *thelêma*. The *Logos* is related to the angels then in
precisely the same way as He is related to men: a like synergy that is free
and consistent obtains between them and the *Logos* on an objective
basis. This basis is the commonness of their 'having non-being as the
ground of their being'. Here Maximus is suggesting that *logos* through
praxis/virtuous activity will enable man to appreciate this fact and so
release his will for the praise of God. From another point of view it is the
very condition of *logos* realized as virtue that is the will of God, and the
fact that this is attained presumes that man's *thelêma* is in concord with
that of the angels and ultimately with that of God.

Maximus speaks of 'full knowledge' (*epignôsis*) and 'with spiritual
knowledge' (*gnôstikôs*) in this context. 'Full knowledge' is said to depend
on *logos* through *praxis*. This knowledge is a form of contemplation but
falls short of *theologia*, contemplative knowledge of the Holy Trinity. It is
the apprehension of the *Logos* behind the common *logos* of the sensibles
and intelligibles, which in turn manifests the First Cause or is identified
with the First Cause. The exercise of knowledge is not strictly within the
realm of *praxis* nor is it designated as *aretê*-virtue. So it seems that our
union with God *gnôstikôs*, in spiritual knowledge, is not effected directly
by *praxis*, but that *praxis* must precede this knowledge and accompany it,
in the sense that the elevated knowledge in question would be impossible without the detachment from passionate involvement and carnal
modes of apprehension which are its necessary preliminary. We know
that in another context *logos* mediates between sense perception
(*aisthêsis*) and the exercise of *nous* in spiritual knowledge. Since Maxi-

15 Idem, 427. This is Thunberg's formulation of the thought of Maximus in
    Ambig., PG 91, 1312B.

mus does not introduce the notion of *nous* here, we can take it that *logos* usurps its function in this context and is a way of describing man's capacity for insight into the ultimate intelligibility of the cosmos by grasping its foundation in the *Logos*. Working backwards then we find that *logos* is a principle of being, order and intelligibility with its ontological ground in the *Logos*, and by means of which the whole created order is sustained and given coherence. This is actuated by the exercise of *logos* by human agents, something that issues in a participation in the incarnate *Logos* and with Him unites men to angels in worship. The whole scale of referents resonates in the term *logos*: faculty, principle of nature, *Logos* in person, and as such it points to a unity that is ultimately grounded in the *ousia*-substance of God.

PARTICIPATION IN DIVINE LIFE—FOURTH PETITION

> The *Logos* imparts a share of the divine life by making Himself food in a way that He understands, as they do who have received from Him such a noetic sense that by the taste of this food they know by spiritual knowledge truly that 'the Lord is good' [Ps 34.8]. It is He who imbues with a divine quality those who eat so that they may be deified, since He clearly is and is called the bread of life and strength [cf. Jn 6:48; Ps 78:25].[16]

Again the obvious concept in this section is that of *Logos*, which is the subject of the sentence and is the basic idea running through every consideration as well as linking this statement with the other six 'mysteries'. The *Logos* is here identified with the 'bread' of the petition and the language of the prayer is interpreted as another facet of the communication of the innumerable divine mysteries, recapitulated in seven, discerned by Maximus in the Our Father. In giving us his *Logos*, God has given us everything and whatever the commentator has to say is bound to be another aspect of that basic endowment, throwing into relief yet again the immeasurable love God has shown us in Christ. The idea of participation is brought out in 'imparts' (*poieitai metadosin*) and 'imbues' (*metakirnôn*). This terminology is calculated to bring home the presence of the *Logos* in those to whom He communicates Himself and who participate in Him, so that the relationship of men to the *Logos* is not merely an extrinsic dependence but an immanent realization. The indwelling of the *Logos* in men in some way constitutes them as men, by imparting to them divine life because of the divine quality in which they participate by eating the bread that the *Logos* provides, and which enables man to participate in the *Logos*. The participation through eating ensures that the *Logos* is within, communicating *logos* as the

16   Or. Dom., PG 90, 877c.

foundation of divine life shared. It is the Incarnation that ensures that the *Logos* is within the created realm, in a way identified hypostatically with human nature, so that any Neoplatonic associations that the term *logos* carries with it in this context, and which help to elucidate the Christian mystery in terms of participation, must be counterbalanced by the fact of the Incarnation and its wholly unforeseen character as a mode of presence in and to man from a philosophical point of view. The ontology here is the ontology of the mystery of 'Christ in you the hope of glory', where ontology, as Riou reminds us, is not metaphysics so much as a synonym for the mystery itself. We are dealing with a mode of presence that eludes philosophical categories, a mode by which the *Logos* incarnate can be so intimately present to man as to be the life of his life, the ground of his Christian being, something conveyed by images of vine and branches, head and members of a body, ultimately due to a hypostatic relationship, with its associations of synergy and enhypostatisation. If *Logos* is embodied in man, then man too becomes *zôn*-alive.

It is divine life that the incarnate *Logos* imparts to man. The *Logos* is alive with the personal perichoretic presence of the Holy Spirit, even in his Incarnation, so that in communicating life to us He is bound to do so by a communication to us of 'life' in the Trinity itself. Our life in dependence on his immanence as bread/*Logos* implies the presence of the personal source of life in the Trinity with whom we cooperate synergetically in a loving *perichôrêsis*. This ensures that we are imbued with a divine quality that is a participation in the *Logos* and is activated in knowledge and love. Thus we are gathered into the divine interplay of the Persons in the Trinity as well as being participators in the divine nature. The divine quality was given 'so that they may be deified' (*pros theôsin*), may share in the life of the Trinity. In the present dispensation this is primarily the exercise of *agapê*, the dominant factor in Maximian anthropology, so that *zôê* and *agapê* are almost synonymous. Perhaps *zôê* connotes the exercise of *agapê*, its actualization, by which *theôsis*, with a view to which the divine quality is bestowed, is realized. This association of *agapê* and *zôê* shows the link with the *zôn* of Maximus' commentary on the 'first mystery' above, where the Word remained in possession of 'life', and the reference to the life that is presented antithetically to death below in the commentaries on 'restoration of nature to itself' and 'abolition of the tyranny of the Evil One'.

The notion of *poiotês* would seem at first sight to evoke essential, natural associations as if the entity communicated had in some way a role in relation to *physis*/nature and *ousia*/substance in an Aristotelian schema, so that the *Logos* would then be credited with imparting to man an entitative habit by which his basic nature would be modified to become the principle of an activity, not merely proper to man, but properly divine. It would be a divine quality given for deification (*theôsis*), a word that connotes not merely a static predisposition, but energy, nature expressing itself in living activity. The grammatical root of *poiotês*/quality links it to *pôs*-mode, and so to the Maximian *tropos* which is personal, so that *theia poiotês*/divine quality indicates a personal endowment rather than a merely natural one. This is a way of saying that what the *Logos* is doing for us, by feeding us with himself, is giving us the possibility of becoming persons who appropriate and innovate nature in such a way that man's primordial relationship to the *Logos* is not merely as a partner in objective activity but is a relationship that is hypostatic and intersubjective. If *theôsis* is understood to be the culmination of the process of the evolution of man under the influence of the Holy Spirit, then we can think of this quality as *theôsis* in the making; it is *pros theôsin*, it is dynamically ordered to deification. Man is fully constituted as a person in relation to the *Logos*, but that actuation requires the intervention of the Holy Spirit with its connotations of hypostatic synergy and *perichôrêsis*, so that the person in act is the living person. This is a dynamic and existential concept.

This becomes evident in the use of simple language where 'I am' refers to the person, 'I have' to the nature, and 'I do' to the living activity by which the agent is what he becomes and becomes what he does. In the thought of Maximus man is *eikôn*/image as 'I am' and 'I have'; he is *homoiôsis*/likeness as 'I do'. The possibility of being what 'I do' is already present in what 'I am' and what 'I have'. It is to that possibility that *eikôn* primarily refers while *homoiôsis* intends actualization. *Theôsis* in the present text refers to *homoiôsis*. An advantage of this way of thinking is that 'I' is common to the three ways of looking at the concrete man, and by isolating different relationships for clarification we avoid the suggestion of fragments bound into a whole and leave the sovereignty of the unique person intact. 'I am' and 'I have' refer primarily to man's relation to the *Logos* and his character as *eikôn*; 'I do', not discarding 'I am' and 'I have', refers above all to the relationship to the Holy Spirit who energizes man in his personal evolution. The 'divine quality' then seems to refer to the hypostatic aspect of man rather than to his nature, although it necessarily implies it. There is not a renewal or modification of the *logos physeôs*, the principle of nature. That awaits reappropriation by man renewed by the Spirit. The principle of nature is innovated in two phases: by a quality for deification (*poiotês pros theôsin*) and deification (*theôsis*). Man the image is invited to likeness.

In his dealing with the *Logos* from this point of view Maximus mentions 'spiritual knowledge'. The object of the knowledge is that 'the Lord is good'. This in turn is the way in which those who eat know how the *Logos* makes Himself to be 'food'. As we have seen, we can interpret *epignôsis* as knowledge of the *logoi*, the principles of being and eventually of the only *Logos* from whom and to whom the *logoi* are derived and return. *Epignôsis* in this context seems to be of a more developed kind. It is undoubtedly a spiritual knowledge, something proper to *nous*, but it partakes too of the properties of *aisthêsis*/perception. This has the immediacy of sense knowledge, its experimental character, except that at this stage the knowledge has to do with the highest object of man's perception, the Lord.[17] It is the *Logos* who gives this knowledge. He is the source of this intellectual perception, and this is bound up with the tasting of the food which is the *Logos* himself, the 'bread of life and strength'. 'Taste' corroborates the notion of *aisthêsis* and strengthens our impression that knowledge here is mystical in character and transcends the logical categories, whose obliqueness it forsakes for direct apprehension of the Lord. Everything is ultimately derived from the *Logos*, and here Maximus is primarily concerned with the experience, so that we can take it that the fact that the *Logos* as bread is apprehended in this way is what conveys to man so convincingly that 'the Lord is good'. To taste the food is to have 'intellectual' perception that the food, that is the *Logos*, is good. This kind of immediacy in knowledge presumes that it is taking place with another kind of relationship than that demanded in the noetic apprehension of the *logoi* and even of the *Logos* noted in the previous section. Here the apprehension takes place within the relationship of *agapê*.

We have to remember too that Maximus describes the bread as 'of life and power'. *Dynamis* is a divine attribute made manifest in Christ and through Him in the Christian life of grace.[18] It is the power of God expressed in his operation and here issuing in the divine quality that makes *theôsis* possible. Christ Himself is the *dynamis* of God. To participate in Him is to participate in that power. The Holy Spirit is the *dynamis* of Christ and it is through this power that ultimately deification is achieved. Finally it should be noted that nowhere in this commentary does Maximus identify the ' bread' with the Eucharist.

RESTORATION OF NATURE TO ITSELF—FIFTH PETITION

He restores nature to itself. This was not only because He was made man and kept free-will dispassionate and submissive to nature but because He annulled the hatred by nailing to the cross the record of the sin by which nature was implacably at war with itself [cf. Col 2:14]. Neither was free-will shaken in any way from its proper basis in nature with regard to those who crucified Him. On the contrary, it chose death instead of life on their behalf, which shows the voluntary character of the passion, ratified by the love of the one

17 See Qu. Thal., PG 90, 621d–624A; Myst., PG 91, 669CD; Ambig., PG 91, 1112D–1113A; 116D.
18 See Clement of Alexandria, Paed., 2, 8, PG 8, 488A; Eusebius of Caesarea, De eccl. theol., 3, 17, PG 24, 1042A; Ignatius of Antioch, Ep. ad Rom., 32, 2, PG 5, 688B.

who suffered. Having called those who were far away and those who were near, that is obviously those who were under the Law and those who were outside the Law, and having broken the wall of partition, that is having clarified the Law of the commandments with his teaching, He created the two into one new man, making peace [cf. Eph 2:14-18] and reconciling us through Himself to the Father and to one another. Since our will is no longer at loggerheads with the principle of nature we can be steady in free-will as well as in nature.[19]

Now we are presented with the vision of the *Logos* restoring nature to itself and so creating one new man. We find here Maximus' insight into the personal way in which the *Logos* effected this, and into the implications that this has for the rest of men. Again the evidence is found in Scripture and is interpreted by means of fundamental anthropological concepts in the Maximian system: *physis*/nature and *gnômê*/free-will. The implication is that nature was in some way estranged from itself and is in need of reconciliation with itself. Nature here is considered to be the basis of *gnômê*, it is that on which *gnômê* is founded, that from which it springs. It is the ground of *gnômê*. This nature was implacably at war with itself because of the sin which Christ nailed in record to the cross. The source of the division is clearly defined when we are told that the new unity achieved by Christ is because 'our will is no longer at logger-heads with the principle of nature'. The notion of ground is evoked too when we are assured that 'we can be steady in free-will as well as in nature'. The adhesion of *gnômê* to *physis* would ensure the stability of *gnômê* and the unity of men with one another and with the Father through Christ in the Holy Spirit. Nature, as it is presented here, is what men hold in common and what the *Logos* took hold of hypostatically in his Incarnation. Maximus obviously thinks of nature as a unity and a principle of unity. Nor does he suggest that it has its source of division in itself, but rather in the wills that tear it asunder and make it to be at war with itself, where will, being a constituent element of nature itself, must be thought of as having a personal determination. If we think of *gnômê*/will as the immediate source of man's wrong use of his freedom and his setting in train the baneful effects of his perversity, then we realize that *gnômê* is man's capacity for freedom, marked by his *hypostasis*, that the divisions in nature, created as one, are due to personal waywardness on the part of man.

The *logos physeôs*/principle of nature is the immanent source of what man has, or even of what he is, in contrast to who he is. *Gnômê*/will on the other hand is presented here as subject to inconsistency: it is liable to change and to becoming the source of fragmentation and disorder.

19   Or. Dom., PG 90, 877D–880A.

The will is subject to passions and the possibility of revolt and of being prised away from its basis in nature. It is even thought of as opposing nature and the principle of nature. The principle of nature is thought of as normative and foundational. This is because it is rooted in the *Logos* and in some sense indefectibly so. *Gnômê* on the other hand bespeaks a possibility of failure and while it too must signal acceptance of the primacy of the *Logos*, we know from man's history that through it he has attempted to throw off this 'given', this ontological necessity.[20] Here Maximus is suggesting that *gnômê*, and more radically its hypostatic source, will be in a proper relationship to the *Logos* if they accept the exigencies of *logos physeôs*.

Maximus puts the hypostatic union at the basis of the unification of man visualized in this section: *genomenos anthrôpos*. There could be no rift in nature as the result of the abuse of freedom in his case since He personally is the *Logos* from whom the *logos physeôs* of his humanity is derived and who imparts a personal impress to his use of will; in the language of this phase of Maximus' theology his *gnômê* was indefectible as well as his *logos physeôs*, since it is rooted in Him who is *Logos*, so that inconsistency in the use of his human will would imply some kind of inconsistency in the divine *Logos* himself.[21] This is unthinkable, so that the principle that is deployed in the whole of this Christology is applicable here too: 'to speak in general, all that is natural in Christ has also, joined to its principle (*logos*), the mode (*tropos*) which is above nature'.[22] Besides, in his divine and unique hypostasis there is no place for fluctuation and hesitation. So He ' kept free-will dispassionate and submissive to nature'. Likewise it was not in a state of revolt from *physis* nor shaken from its basis in *physis*. Christ's personal human will was in perfect harmony with the totality of his nature as a man and, beyond that, with its ground which was Himself in person. Maximus appreciated the historical unfolding of that perfection, especially in its expression in the Passion, where hypostatic union takes on its historical dimensions and retains its transcendent consistency, even to the acceptance of death in order to give life to man.[23]

We can take it from what Maximus says here that he considers the unity of man in himself as basic to the reconstruction of the fragmented universe and to the restoration of man's proper relationship to God. He sees this achieved in and exemplified by the incarnate *Logos* Himself in whom two natures are united in one person. It is that astounding and

20 *Gnômê* has the mark of *hypostasis* and *tropos*; See Ambig., PG 91, 1217ab; 1280a; 1289BD; Opusc. 20, PG 91, 236BD.
21 For Maximus' later view of *gnômê* see Pyrr., PG 91, 308C. For a comprehensive treatment of this question see M. Doucet, La Dispute de Maxime le Confesseur avec Pyrrhus, unpublished thesis, Montreal 1972.
22 Pyrr., PG 91, 297D–300A.
23 See F. -M. Lethel, Théologie de l'Agonie du Christ, Paris 1979, 86–121.

unprecedented union that makes the other unities possible. This is achieved in man analogously. Man becomes a true person when *gnômê* and *physis* are co-ordinated in the way that we find outlined here. This signals the restoration of man to his proper relationship with the *Logos* both as *physis* and as *hypostasis*, and it can be added that *hypostasis* has a priority in this new condition which entitles man to participate in the unifications wrought by the incarnate Word. In his case we find one hypostasis and two natures so united that He can restore to unity male and female, inhabited earth and paradise, heaven and earth, intelligibles and sensibles, God and creatures. The Word articulates this historically by his virginal birth, his entry into paradise with the good thief, his ascension, his recapitulation of all created powers, and finally by sitting in his humanity at the right hand of the Father.[24] The possibility of these unities obviously hangs on the union of divinity and humanity in the one hypostasis of the Word. In an analogous way we can claim that man's becoming mediator, in dependence on Christ, will necessitate his achieving personality in the way suggested in this section, not forgetting the role of the Holy Spirit in ensuring that we become sons in the Son.

PURIFICATION FROM THE LAW OF SIN—SIXTH PETITION

By not allowing sensual pleasure to precede His incarnation for our sake, He makes nature free from the law of sin. For his conception took place paradoxically without seed, and his birth was supernaturally unaccompanied by physical rupture. This means that when God was born, He tightened the bonds of his Mother's virginity by a birth that transcended nature. In those who are willing and who imitate his self-chosen death by mortifying their earthly members in the realm of sense He frees nature from the power of the law which dominated it [cf. Col 3:5]. For the mystery of salvation is for the willing, not for the coerced.[25]

Maximus now addresses the question of the removal of obstacles to the divine beneficence in man's regard. The *Logos* is again given the initiative. It is He who primarily establishes nature in freedom from 'the law of sin' and who destroys the tyranny of the Evil One. This requires the willing cooperation of man, but, consistent with his practice in dealing with the previous petitions of the Our Father and their associated mysteries, Maximus will deal with that more fully in the main part of his work. Here he concentrates on the Christological dimension. The fact that the *Logos* is the subject of the principal statements is itself bond enough with what has gone before. We are meditating on further aspects of the dyad *kenôsis-theôsis*, self-emptying and deification.

24   See Ambig., PG 91, 1308c–1312a.
25   Or. Dom., PG 90, 880ab.

At a glance we can see that for our author there is a connection between pleasurable procreation and 'the law of sin', which is the equivalent of the 'temptation' of the Our Father. The manner of the conception and the birth of the incarnate *Logos* have a direct bearing on the abolition of the 'law of sin'. The usual 'corruption' that marks human birth was not realized in the case of Mary. In fact Maximus claims that her virginity was in some way enhanced. He then transfers his attention to the death of Christ, saying that He frees nature from 'the law of sin' in those who willingly imitate his voluntary death. Men cannot be born free from this law as Christ was, but by being baptized into his death and living consistently with that they can be reborn and progressively rid themselves of this impediment to their identification with the *Logos*. The mortification which was inculcated in the previous sections is now seen in relation to purification from the 'law of sin'.

In order to grasp more fully what Maximus is saying here we must look more closely at his teaching on sin and particularly on the *archaia parabasis*/the ancient transgression, of which any other sin is in some way a dark reflection. Maximus finds the abuse of free-choice at the core of Adam's sin. Man was created with the gift of self-determination in the image of God and it was God's intention that he should grow in his likeness through the proper exercise of freedom: 'every "reasonable" creature is the image of God; but only those who are good and wise are in his likeness'.[26] Since he was by nature endowed with will, the exercise of man's freedom was to have been in keeping with his godward nature; it was to have been *hê kata physin autexousiotês*, naturally self-possessed and self-determining. This exercise of freedom was intended as the human way of attaining to God:

> For thus must man have been in the beginning: in no way distracted by what was beneath him or around him or near him, and desiring perfection in nothing except irresistible movement, with all the strength of love, towards the One who is above him, that is God.[27]

This was to have been the manner in which man willingly entered the cosmic movement of all creation to God. Man's failure was the outcome of the corruption of his power of free-choice, his *proairesis*.[28] The repercussions from this area are the disorders to be found in his nature: animal generation, passibility and death. While for Maximus sin is the transgression of a divine commandment, this juridical notion has an ontological dimension. 'Evil has its being in non-being,'[29] to quote

---

26 Carit., 3, 25, PG 90, 1024c.
27 Ambig., PG 91, 1353c.
28 Qu. Thal., PG 90, 405c.
29 Gregory of Nyssa, De anima et resurrectione, PG 46, 93b.

Gregory of Nyssa. Maximus echoes this and concludes that man's substituting creatures for God is to grasp at minus-being in the place of
being. 'Evil is the failure of the operation of the powers that are in
nature to attain its end'.[30] It cannot be identified with any of the known
categories of being. The enormity of the primeval sin is revealed for
Maximus in the fact that it is precisely man's capacity for God that he
recklessly turns to creatures. He abuses *nous*.[31] Creatures are 'the something besides the end' which man pursues by the '"unlogical" movement
of his natural powers',[32] which is Maximus' alternative definition of evil.
The notion of 'pleasure' is central to this conception of the Fall. There is
a place for *theia hêdonê*, but here pleasure is a component of the disorder
of sinfulness. It is bound up with the abuse of free-choice and the per-
version of the *nous* which are fundamental to this understanding of the
archaia parabasis. It is an epiphenomenon of man's substitution of the
created for the Creator and itself becomes the object of his desire. In the
Pater Noster we find that it plays an essential part in the defective manner
of human generation that followed man's transgression. The *Logos*
becomes man without being caught into this fallen process and thus He
can institute a new order of things. We find an elaboration of the process of the Fall in *Quaestiones ad Thalassium* where creation is figured as
the tree of the knowledge of good and evil, about which we are told that
'considered spiritually it contains knowledge of good, but when taken in
a bodily way it induces a forgetfulness of divine things'.[33] Man could have
had a proper appreciation of the created order and used it appropriately if he had first participated in the grace of deification. This he
would have attained by partaking of the tree of life, that is by appre-
hending and using the *logoi* of creation instead of gorging himself on the
'delights of sense' without due recognition of what is primary. Because
man failed to maintain his relationship with the Logos in the personal
order, he was unfitted to co-operate with Him in the order of nature.

In the following excerpts from the *Ambigua*, Maximus contrasts the
modes of generation that characterize man before and after 'the
ancient transgression':

> The first man was condemned to have a bodily generation, inde-
> liberate, material and perishable, since God rightly judged him
> who willingly preferred what is inferior to what is superior. He
> exchanged a generation that is subject to passion, servile and con-
> strained like that of the beasts of the earth, brutish and mindless
> for a generation that would be free, impassible, holy and the object

30   Qu. Thal. PG 90, 253AB.
31   Ibid., 628AB.
32   Ibid., 253B.
33   Ibid., 257c–260A.

of choice. He preferred dishonourable materialization with brute beasts to divine and ineffable honour with God.[34]

Man's aspiration to be like a god has reduced him in some way to the condition of the beasts, where with them he wallows in *symparenulêsis/* materialization. Elsewhere we find that the pleasure associated with this inferior mode of propagation is stressed and the consequent paradoxical pain and death thrown into relief:

> Adam, the first parent, because he transgressed the divine commandment, introduced into nature besides the first another principle of generation consisting of pleasure indeed, but through pain ending in death. In keeping with the advice of the serpent he invented a pleasure that did not succeed in foregoing pain, but rather one which turned into pain. He caused all those begotten in the flesh like him, through the wicked principle of pleasure, to be rightly made subject to him, with death through pain as their end.[35]

There is some kind of solidarity between Adam and those begotten of him in the flesh. This in turn is dependent in some way on 'the wicked principle of pleasure', which is synonymous with the fallen mode of propagation, so that the changed condition of man is transmitted to his successors precisely because of the way in which he begets his children, not as sons of God, but as the offspring of the will of the flesh and of the will of man. Elsewhere he says that 'all those begotten of Adam are conceived in sin, liable to the condemnation of the forefather'.[36] The 'sin' here does not mean that the act of begetting is a sin, but it means that it takes place in the state of 'sin' that is consequent on the 'ancient transgression'. In this state the passions have replaced the 'principle of nature' as the ground of decision and so make part of 'the law of sin' by analogy with the law of nature. For Maximus, transgression, sin and passibility are bound together in a causal sequence.

In the *Pater Noster* it is precisely by not allowing pleasure to precede his incarnation that the *Logos* frees nature from 'the law of sin'. In other words, because He was 'the seed of his own flesh'[37] He could become man without being caught into the tragic dialectic of generation and corruption, of pleasure and pain, in which man found himself since the sin of Adam. Commenting on a passage from Gregory of Nazianzus on the conception of Christ where he affirms the consubstantiality of the Logos with us in human nature, but making a crucial distinction with regard to how the Logos possesses that nature in contrast to fallen man,

34 Ambig., PG 91, 1348A.
35 Qu. Thal., PG 90, 632B.
36 Qu. Dub., PG 90, 788AB.
37 Ambig., PG 91, 1037A.

Maximus says: 'in no way did He have in his members a law which is derived from the transgression, contrary to the law of the spirit.... In no way is the law of sin in his members whose generation was not through seed. Rather it was the law of divine justice shining forth to determine us, and which abolished perfectly that which befell our nature through the transgression'.[38] The children of Adam have in their members 'a law which is derived from the transgression', that is 'the ancient transgression'. The 'sin' which is derived from that transgression is present in mankind. It is the basis of 'the law of sin' which is a parody of 'the law of nature' fundamental to man's being and destiny. There is an intimate bond between 'the law of sin', identified with 'proneness to sin', and generation 'through seed'. Because the *Logos* is not subject to this kind of generation, He is not subject to 'the law of sin'. His norm is 'the law of the spirit', 'the law of *nous*', 'the law of divine justice'. His *logos physeôs* as man becomes the ground of 'the law of nature' in Him because of the indefectible character of the 'possessor of nature', that is of human nature, in his case. For this Adam and his progeny have substituted 'the law of sin', where passion becomes the alternative to reality, so that the life of fallen man, to the extent that it is not founded on his 'principle of nature', is untrue. The rebirth of men as sons of God does not coincide with their physical birth. It is initiated in baptism and has to be progressively appropriated by a death to 'the law of sin'. A new order has begun with the conception and birth of the Savour, 'a man above men' who brought the integrity of the *Logos* to bear on the exercise of human freedom.[39]

THE EVIL ONE—SEVENTH PETITION

He destroys the tyranny of the Evil One who dominated us by deceit. By casting at him as a weapon the flesh that was vanquished in Adam He overcame him. Thus what was previously captured for death conquers the conqueror and destroys his life by a natural death. It became poison to him in order that he might vomit up all those whom he had swallowed when he held sway by having the power of death [cf. Heb 2:14]. But it became life to the human race by impelling the whole of nature to rise like dough to resurrection of life [cf. Rom 11:15–16; I Cor 5:6–7]. It was for this especially that the *Logos*, who is God, became man—something truly unheard of—and voluntarily accepted the death of the flesh.[40]

Maximus continues to deal with the providential overcoming of whatever impedes the progress of man to deification. He is concerned

38   Opusc. Theol., PG 91, 240D–241B.
39   See Qu. Thal., PG 90, 505C.
40   Or. Dom., PG 90, 880B–881A.

with the problems of sin, corruption and death, and their undoing through the beneficence of Christ, but here the whole tragic dilemma of man is given a new dimension by the introduction of the Evil One. There is a subtle play on the ideas of death and life which makes for continuity with what Maximus has said in the previous section where he presented us with the vision of the incarnate Word annulling 'the law of sin' by his paradoxical generation and birth and the culmination of his sanctifying life in his passion and death. Here we are reminded that it was for the purpose of salvation that 'God becomes man and voluntarily accepts the death of the flesh'. He willingly takes on Himself punishment for sin, so that by his unjust sufferings our just punishment may be nullified. He took on the wholeness of our human condition, becoming flesh but without sin, so that the incorruption of his free-choice might rectify our subjection to passion. Maximus emphasizes the redemptive and vicarious character of his death: 'giving Himself as a redemption and exchange on our behalf', He the innocent one, who has been born in a manner that clearly demonstrated his sinlessness, had taken on through love not merely our common humanity but also the consequences of our corrupted use of freedom. Maximus asserts that Christ destroys the life of the Evil One, presumably in men, 'by a natural death', and further on that He accepted death voluntarily. It would be the achievement of Maximus to clarify how the incarnate *Logos* saved us not merely by the exercise of divine freedom but by his human will as well.[41] This teaching is adumbrated here.

The specific characteristic of the 'mystery' which Maximus addresses here is Christ's victory over the Evil One. In the previous section he described how we can participate in redemption by imitating Christ's willing death. This is elaborated here to include the outcome of a mortified life in a resurrection made possible by 'the first-born from the dead'. The tragic condition of fallen man is reversed by the incarnate Word, the deceiver is deceived and mankind no longer languishes in thrall to the Evil One, subject to death because of sin. *Sarx*/flesh is central to the intricate pattern of opposites. Vulnerable in its weakness, it is the means of undoing the strength of the adversary because of its assumption by the *Logos*, who being sinless was able to negate the wages of sin, death. The beating of the Evil One at his own game of deceit is emphasized in a passage in the *Quaestiones ad Thalassium*,[42] where Maximus comments on the Lord as 'a worm and no man': it is the *Logos* who destroys the Evil One; it is by the very flesh which the devil overpowered through sin, the sting of death, that he is in turn overcome; the release from the diabolical realm of death is expressed as a vomiting on the part

41   See Lethel, op. cit. (footnote 23), 92.
42   Qu. Thal., PG 90, 713A.

of the Evil One, the deceived serpent. We find the equivalent of the 'bait' of the *Ad Thalassium* in the 'poison' which acts as emetic in the *Pater Noster*; the notion of 'weapon' in the latter finds its counterpart in the 'fish-hook' of the former which is explicitly made to image 'the Divinity', something that the Evil One cannot stomach. The 'deceit' was 'the hope of divinity' in man, to be like gods, which is disappointed to the extent of tasting death, the essential flavour of meontic being. It is now that Maximus takes the argument forward in a positive way: the flesh of the Word 'became life to the human race by impelling the whole of nature to rise like dough to the resurrection of life'.

In a remarkable passage in the *Ambigua* our condition as 'food for death' is accounted for by Adam's failure to feed on the *Logos*, who is described not merely as 'bread' but also as 'the tree of life'.[43] Maximus states clearly the deeper significance of death when he says that 'separation from God is properly death, and sin the sting of death. In consenting to it Adam at the same time became exiled from the tree of life, from paradise and from God; of necessity bodily death followed'.[44] Then he adds: 'He who says "I am life" is properly life. He, in his death, led back to life him who had been made dead'. It is Adam who separates himself from God, the same Adam who failed to nourish himself on the *Logos*. Adam breaks his essential bond with the *Logos* and as a consequence is deprived of the proper interaction of his nature with the energy of the *Logos*, which becomes tragically obvious in 'the bodily death' which followed of necessity. Death is voluntary separation from the living God and the sin of the forefather was instrumental in delivering up 'the whole of nature as food for death'. The outcome of this for the human race is that 'death lives throughout all this space of time'; man cannot find within himself the resource to deliver himself from this fate, but what is impossible to man is possible to God. The *Logos* himself, who is the source of life, enters the human condition, taking on the fullness of humanity, but without sin. There can be no deflection of energy between his person and the nature He assumed. Since the incarnate Word was never separated from God by sin, He can change the meaning of death and lead men back to participate in the resurrection which crowned his passion and death. In the following passage, having referred to the incarnation and passion, Maximus writes:

> And having willingly gone down to the heart of the earth where the Evil One kept us in thrall, swallowing us through death, and having drawn us back up through the resurrection and leading this whole conquered nature up to heaven, He is indeed our 'rest', 'healing' and 'grace'. He is 'rest' because He abrogated the law of besetting

43   Ambig., PG 91, 1156c–1157a.
44   Carit., 2, 93, PG 90, 700ab.

servitude in the flesh because of a time-bound life. He is 'healing' in that He thoroughly cures the fracture of death and corruption by resurrection. Finally, He is 'grace' as the dispenser of adoptive sonship through faith, and of the grace of deification in keeping with one's worthiness.[45]

Here Maximus deftly enumerates the final significant phases of salvation and indicates how they are to be appropriated by man. It is the Word through his condition of being *sarx*/flesh who becomes 'life to the human race'. His resurrection makes the resurrection of the race a real possibility. But man must respond to this initiative by faith and so become 'son', and he must earn deification by 'worthiness' and so be restored to the tree of life, to paradise and to God, from all of which he was exiled by the 'ancient transgression' and personal sin. In the perspectives of this final 'mystery' Maximus sees this salvific achievement as 'destruction of the Evil One who dominated us by deceit'.

In conclusion we can listen to Maximus himself on what Scripture means to him: 'The mystery of the taking of flesh by the *Logos* has the force of all the enigmas and types of Scripture, and the knowledge of creatures visible and "intelligible". And whoever has understood the mystery of the cross and burial has understood the *logoi* of the aforementioned matters. Whoever has been initiated into the ineffable power of the resurrection has understood the purpose for which God initially gave sustenance to all things'.[46] For him the mystery of Christ is the unique object of the spiritual sense of Scripture; it is not so much a case of understanding something of Christ through the Scriptures as of understanding the Scriptures through Christ, and beyond them the whole of the created realm. He will when required have recourse to the literal sense, but at the other end of the spectrum he maintains that 'the *logoi* of all beings are contained by the Word of God, while It is not contained by any being'.[47] For Maximus the language of Scripture rests on an inverted apex, but opens out to infinity.

---

45 Qu. Thal., PG 90,700AB.
46 Cap. Theol., PG 90, 1108AB.
47 Qu. Thal., PG 90, 249A.

Allusions and Illusions: St Ephrem's Verbal Magic in the Diatessaron Commentary[1]

CARMEL McCARTHY

It is only in recent decades, and with good reason, that Ephrem of Nisibis has been re-established as one of the great theologian-poets in the Christian tradition.[2] This belated recognition is due in part to the inaccessibility of his works which were written in Syriac, and which, until recently, were poorly served by modern editions and translations. But it is perhaps due even more to the fact that, for too long, Church historians have tended to look at the Church through western eyes, focusing only on its Graeco-Roman origins. While it is true that most of the out-standing figures and literature of early Christian history are associated in some way with the area surrounding the Mediterranean seaboard—the great centres of Rome, Ephesus, Alexandria and Antioch—it is nonethe-less important to remember that another great Christian tradition existed alongside that of the Mediterranean, rooted in those ancient lands dominated by the mighty rivers of the Tigris and Euphrates.

To assume that the early Christian tradition was limited to its Greek and Latin expression would be to distort historical reality, and to weaken greatly our understanding of the roots of Christian theology and spirituality. In the third and fourth centuries, and possibly even earlier,[3] there existed in the regions of Mesopotamia and Syria a distinctive, independent branch of Christianity, ascetic in outlook and

---

1 This article will be included in the Martin McNamara Festschrift, and is being reproduced here with the kind permission of the Festschrift editors.

2 S. P. Brock characterises Ephrem as 'the finest poet in any language of the patristic period' in The Syriac Fathers on Prayer and the Spiritual Life, Michigan, 1987, xv, while Robert Murray evaluates him as 'the greatest poet of the patristic age, and perhaps, the only *theologian-poet* to rank beside Dante' in Symbols of Church and Kingdom, Cambridge 1975, 31.

3 Cf. L. W. Barnard, 'The Origins and Emergence of the Church in Edessa during the First Two Centuries A. D.,' VigChr 22 (1968) 161–175, who argues that the history of the Church in Edessa can be pushed back into the first century, and that it was strongly influenced by an early Jewish-Christian Gospel tradition. R. Murray argues that the Christianity of Aphrahat and Ephrem had as its main base a breakaway movement from the Jewish community in Adiabene, cf. Symbols of Church and Kingdom, 7–8.

strongly influenced by Jewish ways of thought. The language of this community was Syriac, a form of Aramaic not far removed from that spoken in first-century Palestine, and their concern was with the meditative, poetic and ascetical dimensions of the Christian experience rather than with its intellectual formulation. Its thought patterns and modes of expression were distinctively Semitic and in close continuity with the spiritual and cultural context from which the Gospel emerged. The two major authors of the fourth century, Aphrahat and Ephrem, attest this Semitic form of Christianity, to be distinguished in many respects from the Christianity of the Greek and Latin-speaking world of the Mediterranean seaboard. Perhaps the simplest way of distinguishing this form of Christianity might be to characterize its approach as being primarily symbolic and synthetic, whereas the Greek approach is more philosophical and analytical in character. It would have been only from the fifth century onwards, in the aftermath of the Chalcedonian and post-Chalcedonian controversies, that the Syriac-speaking Churches would have been rapidly exposed to hellenization, with the result that no subsequent authors would have escaped from Greek influence of one kind or another.

Yet one must not imagine too sharp a divide between the Semitic approach and that of Ephrem's contemporaries who wrote in Greek and Latin. When it is remembered that, by the fourth century AD, Hellenistic cultures would have been present in the Middle East for over half a millennium, and that in the third and fourth centuries Syriac was the third international language of the Church, one could expect that no Syriac writer of Ephrem's time would have been totally unhellenized, nor would any Greek Christian writer of that time be totally unsemitized. As Sebastian Brock puts it, 'it is simply a matter of degree.'[4]

It is therefore important to reserve the term *Syriac Orient* for specifying that earliest flowering of Syriac-speaking Christianity as yet essentially uninfluenced by either Greek or Latin thought forms. Brock is quite adamant in insisting that to the familiar pair of Greek East and Latin West there should be added a third component of Christian tradition, the Syriac Orient.[5] But he immediately adds that none of these three traditions was totally isolated from the others, for not only do they have common roots in the gospel message, but throughout their existence they have always interacted with one another, directly and indirectly, and often in unexpected ways.[6]

---

4   The Luminous Eye. The Spiritual World Vision of St. Ephrem, Rome 1985, second edition: Kalamazoo 1992, 143.
5   S. P. Brock, The Syriac Fathers, xxxiii.
6   In a paper presented to the International Conference on Patristic Studies in Oxford 1987, 'From Ephrem to Romanos,' Studia Patristica 20 (1989) 139–151, S. P. Brock has examined this interaction in the area of poetry by taking Ephrem

Ephrem's exegetical style is a testimony to how much both he and the Church for whom he wrote were at home in the Scriptures. In his *Diatessaron* commentary the Gospel text as he encounters it in that Gospel Harmony is his starting point, but he displays great freedom and at times unpredictability in what he chooses to comment on. Sometimes he quotes a lot of Gospel text with brief comment. At other times he takes off and develops his reflections and theology at length, with little or no Gospel text serving as the immediate basis. He has the freedom of a bird to move at will over the vast range of Scripture and select whatever text pleases him in the execution of his task. In this sense his commentary is deeply biblical. To illustrate a particular point he can sometimes call up a wide range of texts from both New and Old Testaments, in the form of *testimonia,* or proof texts. At another time he will interweave scriptural events by way of allusion and typology rather than by direct *quote,* thereby demonstrating the particularly Semitic nature of his thought patterns and language.

At one level it can be argued that Ephrem has a very coherent theological vision, with certain key concepts and themes recurring again and again. Yet, from another point of view, because his approach is not expressed in any systematic or logical (Western) form, it is essentially dynamic and fluid.[7] Hence the title of this study!

There are two concepts in particular however which are fundamental to Ephrem's theological framework, and which intertwine in a myriad of both predictable and unpredictable ways. These are his uses of symbolism and typology. Through the centrality of these concepts Ephrem's theology is profoundly sacramental in character. Everything in the created world has the potential to act as a witness and pointer to the Creator. Everything is imbued with a hidden power or meaning (*ḥaylā kasyā*), and it requires the eye of faith to penetrate into the inner spiritual reality. It is worth noting in passing that by developing this positive linkage between the outer material world and inner spiritual reality, Ephrem is very far from those Christian writers who, under Neoplatonic influence, tended to devalue the material world.

Another way of understanding the coherence of Ephrem's use of symbol and typology would be to note how, for him, the fundamental distance between God the Creator and his creation is in fact impassable as far as any creature is concerned, and that any statement about God

and Romanos as representatives of Syria's two great literary traditions, Syriac and Greek, and, set within the framework of the fourth to the first half of the sixth century, he has focused on 'the possibility (I would say probability) of the transmission of literary motifs in the other direction, from Syriac to Greek' (p. 144). Cf. also W. L. Petersen, 'The Dependence of Romanos the Melodist upon the Syriac Ephrem,' Studia Patristica 18,4 (1990) 274–281, who argues in favour of a Syriac original for Romanos' compositions.

7   Cf. Brock, The Luminous Eye, 21.

would be impossible had not God himself taken the initiative and bridged the chasm.[8] From Ephrem's perspective God's mode of revelation is essentially threefold. He has revealed Himself in the first instance by means of types and symbols which are operative in both Nature and Scripture. An excerpt from his fifth poem on Paradise sums up succinctly what Ephrem has to say about these two main vehicles for communication through symbols. Scripture (*ktābā*) and Nature (*kyānā*) indeed constitute God's witnesses:

> In his book Moses described
> > the creation of the natural world,
> so that both Nature and Scripture
> > might bear witness to the Creator:
> Nature, through man's use of it,
> > Scripture, through his reading it;
> they are the witnesses
> > which reach everywhere,
> they are to be found at all times,
> > present at every hour,
> confuting the unbeliever
> > who defames the Creator.[9]

Further illustrations from the *Diatessaron* commentary of how nature and scripture bear witness to the Creator and become symbols of the hidden power within will be discussed at a later point below. God has revealed Himself, in the second instance, by allowing Himself, the Indescribable, to be described in Scripture in human terms and language, or, to use Ephrem's terms, by his 'putting on names.'[10] Finally, the climax of God's self-revelation takes place in God's 'putting on the flesh,' or 'putting on the body' in the supreme mystery of the Incarnation. In this threefold process of revelation the use of symbol and type is both crucial and extremely rich and varied.

Two extracts from Ephrem's poetry confirm how central this approach is to his theological vision, and can also serve as a point of entry into his use of symbolism and typology in the *Diatessaron* commentary:

> In every place, if you look, his symbol is there,
> > and when you read, you will find his types.
> for by him were created all creatures,
> > and he engraved his symbols upon his possessions.

8 Cf. Brock, Hymns on Paradise, 41.
9 Cf. Hymns on Paradise, no. 5 (translation: S. Brock, 102).
10 This 'incarnation' of God into human language is most fully described by Ephrem in Hymn 31 in the collection On Faith, which begins with the lines: 'Let us give thanks to God, who clothed himself in the names of the body's various parts: Scripture refers to his ears, to teach us that he listens to us...' (translation of S.P. Brock, Hymns on Paradise, 41).

When he created the world,
   he gazed at it and adorned it with his images.
Streams of his symbols opened, flowed and poured forth
   his symbols on his members.[11]

In fact Ephrem at times felt almost overwhelmed with the super-abundance of symbols. In musing on the episode in Judges where Samson finds that a swarm of has taken up residence in the carcass of the lion he had killed, Ephrem wrote:

Was that a symbol?
This Jesus has made so many symbols for us!
   I am sinking amid the waves of his symbols!
He has pictured for us the raising of the dead
   by every kind of symbol and type.[12]

It comes as no surprise therefore to find that the most distinctive and pervasive characteristic of Ephrem's literary style in the commentary is this frequent use of symbolism and typology. He uses a variety of different terms in this regard more or less interchangeably, but the central one is *rāzā* which can be translated as either 'mystery' or 'symbol.' The word *rāzā* is of Persian origin, and is first attested in Dan 2:18, where its meaning in that context is 'secret.' It occurs also in the Qumran writings, and is probably the Semitic word underlying Paul's use of *mystêrion* in Rom 16:25 and elsewhere. By Ephrem's time *rāzā* had taken on a wider variety of meanings, and when he uses it in the plural it refers to the liturgical 'mysteries' or 'sacraments'. As a typological term *rāzā* 'symbol' draws attention to the link or connection between two different modes of reality. It is crucial to remember that for the early Syriac Fathers, and Ephrem in particular, their use of symbol was much stronger and dynamic than modern usage.[13] For them a symbol actually participated in some mysterious way within the spiritual reality it was pointing towards. This is worth keeping in mind, in particular when Ephrem is using symbols from the material world, given the view of certain early Christian writers influenced by Neoplatonism.

Side by side with *raza* are two other Syriac words that frequently recur in Ephrem in an almost interchangeable sense: *tupsā* and *yūqnā*, both instantly recognisable as Greek loan words for *tupos* and *eikôn*. Generally speaking, types for Ephrem are to be found in Scripture, while symbols and images are in nature, but he is by no means consistent in this usage.[14] His developed theory of typology, with its levels of mystery/

---

11 On Virginity 20, 12, translated by K.McVey, Ephrem the Syrian, Hymns New York/Mahwah 1989, 348–349.
12 Carmina Nisibena 39, 17. Cf. R. Murray, Symbols of Church and Kingdom, 292.
13 Cf. Brock, Hymns on Paradise, 42.
14 Cf. McVey, op. cit., 349n.

symbol and inner truth (*shrārā*) fits well with that of the early Fathers in general. His use of *shrārā* corresponds fairly closely to that of *alêtheia* in the fourth Gospel,[15] while his third level, that of eschatological fulfilment, is also quite traditional. It was common enough practice in both Jewish and Christian apocalyptic circles to picture the eschatological paradise in the imagery of the first.

Types and symbols therefore are a means of expressing relationships and links, of disclosing, in so far as that is possible, what is mysterious and hidden. Operating in several different ways, they bring out hidden connections full of meaning between the Old Testament and the New, between this world and the heavenly, between the New Testament and the sacraments, between the sacraments and the eschaton.[16] In each case they 'reveal' something of what is otherwise 'hidden', they uncover some aspect of the inner truth or *shrārā* which is present in creation and Scripture.

Although the *Diatessaron* commentary is essentially a prose work, Ephrem's poetic genius expresses itself in many forms of rhythmic balancing between personalities, institutions and situations, whether similar or divergent.[17] Since examples of his symbolic imagery occur on practically every page it will be necessary to be selective, and focus more especially on two frequently recurring typologies in the commentary, that of the First Adam-Second Adam typology which played a very prominent role, not only in Ephrem,[18] but in early Syriac Christianity as a whole, and secondly, the theme of the election of the Gentiles in place of the former Israel, 'the nation and the nations.'[19]

Ephrem's favourite term for the Incarnation is that God in Christ 'put on a body,' a phrase already deeply rooted in the early Syriac tradition as a whole. It is to be found in the *Acts* of Judas Thomas and in Aphrahat, and occurs in the *Diatessaron* commentary with regular frequency, especially in the first chapter which begins with theological reflections on the prologue of the fourth Gospel:

> Why did our Lord clothe himself with our flesh? So that this flesh might experience victory, and that [humanity] might know and understand the gifts [of God]. For, if God had been victorious without the flesh, what praise could one render him? ... Thus, the Word came and clothed itself with flesh, so that what cannot

---

15 Cf. Murray, Symbols of Church and Kingdom, 292, who mentions the works of Melito and Origen as sources for this approach also.

16 Cf. S. P. Brock, Hymns on Paradise, 42.

17 Cf. L. Leloir, Ephrem de Nisibe. Commentaire de l'évangile concordant ou Diatessaron. SC 121, Paris 1966, 31.

18 Cf. L. Leloir, Doctrines et méthodes de S. Ephrem d'après son commentaire de l'évangile concordant (CSCO 220, Louvain 1961), 42–44.

19 Cf. Murray, Symbols of Church and Kingdom, 41–68, for the origins of this theme in early Judaeo-Christian circles.

be grasped might be grasped through that which can be grasped, and that, through that which cannot be grasped, the flesh would raise itself up against those who grasp it.[20]

By means of the clothing imagery, that of the putting on and taking off of clothing, Ephrem develops for his readers a coherent image of salvation history, in which the Second Eve and the Second Adam reverse the effects of the Fall which had been brought about by the self-will of the First Eve and the First Adam. The eschatological Paradise is far more glorious than the original Paradise. At Baptism, understood as the re-entry to Paradise, the Christian puts on 'the robe of glory' with which Adam and Eve had been clothed in Paradise before they were stripped naked as a result of their self-will. Hymn 23,13 from the Nativity cycle illustrates the clothing imagery very effectively:

> All these changes did the Merciful One effect,
> . stripping off his glory and putting on a body;
> for He had devised a way to reclothe Adam
> in that glory which Adam had stripped off.
> He was wrapped in swaddling clothes,
> corresponding to Adam's leaves,
> he put on clothes instead of Adam's skins;
> He was baptized for Adam's sin,
> He was embalmed for Adam's death,
> He rose and raised up Adam in his glory.
> Blessed is He who descended,
> put on Adam, and ascended.

Ephrem makes use of this First Adam-Eve/Second Adam-Eve typology in a different way in II, §2 to highlight the virginal conception of Jesus, using very skilfully balanced contrasts:

> [Mary] gave birth without [the assistance of] a man. Just as in the beginning Eve was born of Adam without intercourse, so too [in the case of] Joseph and Mary, his virgin and spouse. Eve gave birth to the murderer,[21] but Mary gave birth to the Life-Giver.[22] The former gave birth to him who shed the blood of his brother, but the latter to Him whose blood was shed by his brothers. The former saw him who was trembling and fleeing[23] because of the curse of the earth, the latter [saw] Him who bore the curse *and nailed it on*

---

20 I, §1. For the translation here and elsewhere from the commentary, cf. C. McCarthy, Saint Ephrem's Commentary on Tatian's Diatessaron, An English Translation of Chester Beatty Syriac MS 709 with Introduction and Notes, Oxford 1993.
21 Gen 4:1 records the birth of Cain, who later murdered Abel.
22 This is one of the words Syriac typically uses for Saviour.
23 Cf. Gen 4:10–14.

his cross.[24] The virgin's conception teaches that He, who begot Adam without intercourse from the virgin earth, also fashioned the Second Adam without intercourse in the virgin's womb. Whereas the First [Adam] returned back into the womb of his mother,[25] [it was] by means of the Second [Adam], who did not return back into the womb of his mother, that the former, who had been buried in the womb of his mother, was brought back [from it].

In the section commenting on the Temptations the contrast between Adam and Christ is done through the Semitic imagery of 'corporate personalities.' This is prefaced by an extended review of Christ's life showing how at each stage of his life he overcame Satan personified in the form of Death:

Take note therefore how the Living One sought to refute death in every kind of way. He was an embryo, and while in the womb [death] was not able to destroy Him. [He was] an infant and while growing up, it was not able to disfigure Him. [He was] a child and during his education it was not able to confuse Him. [He was] a young man, and with its lustful desires it was not able to lead Him into error. [He was] instructed, and with its wiles, it was not able to overpower Him. [He was] a teacher, and because of his intelligence, it was not able to refute Him. [He was] vigilant, and with its commands, it was not able to turn Him aside [from his purpose]. [He was] strong, and in killing him, it was not able to frighten him. [He was] a corpse and in the custody of the tomb, it was not able to hold Him. He was not ill, because He was a healer. He did not go astray, because He was a shepherd. He did not commit error, because He was a teacher. He did not stumble, because he was the light. This is the perfect way that the Christ opened up for his Church, from the beginning through conception until the completion of the resurrection.

Ephrem then shows how Christ, by overcoming Satan's wiles in his own incarnate body, wins victory for the Church, which in a mysterious corporate sense is his body. Christ thereby reverses the lot of humanity, condemned to death through the First Adam:

If the Church therefore is his body, as Paul his witness has said,[26] then believe that his Church has journeyed through all this without corruption. Just as, by the condemnation of the one body of Adam, all bodies died and continue to die,[27] so too, through the victory of this one body of the Messiah his entire Church lived

24   Col 2:14.
25   That is, the earth.
26   Cf. Eph 1:23.
27   Cf. Rom 5:12–21.

and continues to live. So, just as [it was] because these bodies themselves have sinned and are themselves dying, that the earth, their
mother, was also accursed,[28] so too, because of this body, which is
the Church without corruption,[29] its earth is blessed from the
beginning. The earth is the body of Mary, the temple in whom it
was sown.[30]

The earth, which is now blessed because of Christ's victory for his
Church, is in fact Mary's body, Christ's temple, and she is called blessed
precisely in contrast to the earth which was cursed. Although not explicit, there is a hint at the end of the passage that Mary, the new Eve, is the
mother of all the redeemed and sinless, by virtue of Christ's sinlessness.[31]

Apart from other brief references in the main body of the commentary it is in the context of the Passion that the First Adam-Second Adam
typology is most developed. In reflecting on the Agony in the Garden,
Ephrem contrasts the 'members' of Adam and of Christ (understood as
'corporate personalities') as follows:

> Every human person carrying the visible sign of the First Adam
> in his body became food for death, but everyone who carried the
> sign of the Second Adam in himself became lord and destroyer
> of death. The one, in tasting [the fruit], loosened his will and
> submitted it to his body. He weakened it so that it became food
> for death. But the Other, through the energy of his will, har-
> dened his body so that it would resist the mouth of death.[32]

Jesus' surrender to the Father's will contrasts with Adam 'who resisted
the will of the Creator and followed the will of his enemy.'[33] Our Lord,
he tells us, 'sweated to heal Adam who was sick' and 'remained in prayer
in this garden, to bring [Adam] back into his own garden again.'[34]

A focal text for Ephrem's symbolic theology is John 19:34, the pierc-
ing of Christ's side, for through it he illustrates a host of interrelated
typologies.[35] The lance and the side of Christ bring to mind the cherub's
sword,[36] and the First Adam's side/rib which gave birth to Eve in a myste-

---

28   Cf. Gen 3:17–19.
29   Cf. Eph 5:25–27.
30   Cf. IV, §§14–15.
31   Cf. R. Murray, Symbols of Church and Kingdom, 84. After commenting on the
     greetings of Gabriel and Elizabeth, Ephrem ends the passage with a traditional
     contrast of Eve and Mary: '… because the first mother was cursed, this second
     mother was therefore addressed with blessed names' (IV, §15).
32   Cf. XX, §8.
33   XX, §9.
34   Cf. XX, §11.
35   Cf. R. Murray, 'The Lance which Re-opened Paradise: A Mysterious Reading in
     the Early Syriac Fathers,' OCP 39 (1973) 224–234.
36   Although Gen 3:24 speaks of a sword, and John 9:34 of a lance, Syriac writers
     frequently use the same word for both to bring out the typology more effectively.

rious way. The side of Christ also points forward to the sacraments of Baptism and Eucharist, as well as to the mysterious birth of the Church. In a marvellously crafted lyrical outburst which interweaves all these themes in typical allusive fashion Ephrem proclaims:

> I have run towards all your members, I have received all [possible] gifts from them, and, through the side pierced by a lance, I have entered into Paradise enclosed by a lance.[37] Let us enter through the pierced side, since it was through the rib that was extracted [from Adam] that we were robbed of the promise.[38] Because of the fire that burned in Adam—it burned in him because of his rib—it was because of this that the side of the Second Adam was pierced, and there issued forth from it a stream of water to extinguish the fire of the First Adam.[39]

Then, in more sober fashion he continues his commentary, first on the significance of the blood that flowed forth, and then on the water, after which he sums up John 19:34 as follows:

> *There came forth blood and water*, which is his Church, and it is built on Him, just as [in the case of] Adam, whose wife was taken from his side. Adam's rib is his wife, and the blood of our Lord is his Church. From Adam's rib there was death, but from our Lord's rib, life.[40]

One final passage from the *Diatessaron* commentary illustrates yet again how skilfully Ephrem grafts a number of allusions into one central typology. Since Christ's body is compared with the fruit of the tree in this passage it is possible to see the Church as an antitype of the garden, even if only implicitly:

> Just as it was said to Adam, *The day on which you eat of it you will die*,[41]—he did not die however on the day when he ate it, but [instead] received a pledge of his death through his being stripped of his glory, chased from Paradise and haunted daily by [the prospect of] death,—so too, in like manner, with regard to life in Christ, we eat his body instead of the fruit of the tree, and we have his altar in place of the garden of Eden. The curse is washed away by his innocent blood, and in the hope of the resurrection we await the life that is to come.[42] Already we walk in a new life, for these [the body of Christ and his altar] are the pledges of it for us.[43]

This contrast between the two Adams which Ephrem loves to develop is matched in frequency by another key typology in his writings, that of

---

37   Cf. Gen 3:24.   41   Gen 2:17.
38   Cf. Gen 2:21–22.   42   Cf. Rom 8:23–25.
39   XXI, §10.   43   Cf. XXI, §25.
40   XXI, §11.

'the nation and the nations.'[44] The replacement of God's chosen people by a new people, the Gentiles, is a theme which has an understandably high profile in early Judaeo-Christian circles. In Robert Murray's view, the calling of the Gentiles constitutes (with the person of Christ and the Cross) one of the three main themes of typological exegesis of the fourth-century Syriac Fathers.[45]

Two traditional techniques or literary forms in particular feature in the development of this theme: typological parallels, of which there is no shortage in Ephrem, and lists of *testimonia*. The fact that Ephrem occasionally uses *testimonia* or chains of proof-texts illustrates how he, along with other fourth-century Syriac Fathers, and some Greek and Latin Fathers, are all heirs to a tradition already attested in both the New Testament and Qumran.

The *Diatessaron* commentary on the entry into Jerusalem contains a special kind of typological comparison reflecting a tradition of oral teaching not unlike the Good Friday *Improperia*.[46] Elements from Ezek 16:9–13 are contrasted with details in the Passion in short rhythmic phrases. The passage is lengthy but worthy of being quoted at some length:

> *Untie the donkey and bring it to me.*[47] He began with a manger and finished with a donkey, in Bethlehem with a manger, in Jerusalem with a donkey. This is like, *Rejoice Daughter of Zion, for behold your king is coming to you, just and lowly, and seated on a donkey.*[48] But [the daughter of Zion] saw Him and was troubled. She looked at Him and became sad. He, the Merciful One, and the Son of the Merciful One, had spread his benevolence over her like a father, but she conducted herself as perversely towards him as she had done towards the One who had sent Him. Not being able to abuse the Father, she displayed her hatred against his Only-Begotten.
>
> [The daughter of Zion] repaid Him with evil for the immensity of his grace. The Father had washed her from her blood, but she defiled his Son with her spitting.[49] The Father had clothed her with fine linen and purple, but she clothed Him with garments of mockery.[50] He had placed a crown of glory on her head, but she plaited a crown of thorns for Him.[51] He had nourished her with choicest food and honey, but she gave him gall.[52] He had given her

---

44 Syriac uses the same word *'ammā* in the singular for God's chosen people, and *'amme* (plural) for the Gentiles.
45 Cf. Murray, Symbols of Church and Kingdom, 41.
46 Cf. XVIII, §1.
47 Mark 11:2; Matt 21:2.
48 Zech 9:9.
49 Cf. Ezek 16:9; Matt 26:67.
50 Cf. Ezek 16:10,13; Matt 27:28.
51 Cf. Ezek 16:12; Matt 27:29.
52 Cf. Ezek 16:13; Matt 27:34.

pure wine, but she offered Him vinegar [soaked] in a sponge.[53]
The One who had introduced her into cities, she drove out into
the desert. The One who had put shoes on her feet, she made
hasten barefoot towards Golgotha.[54] The One who had girded her
loins with sapphire, she pierced in the side with a lance.[55] When she
had outraged the servants [of God] and killed the prophets, she
was led into captivity to Babylon, and when the time of her punishment was completed, her return [from captivity] took place.

But, now that she has stretched forth her hands against the Son
and crucified the Son of the living [God], her house has been
uprooted and her altar overturned, just as the prophet had said,
The holy city shall be destroyed,[56] together with the king who is to come.
And she will lie there in ruins until the completion of judgements.

Thus, for Ephrem the coming of Christ revealed God's hidden plan
for the salvation of the nations, but it also brought a tragic catastrophe
for the 'former nation.' This theme of catastrophe, and of the Jewish
people's replacement by a new people, the Gentiles, runs like a con-
necting thread through the entire Gospel commentary. It is often
embedded in rather bitter anti-Jewish invective. Indeed it is no secret
that Ephrem was very anti-Jewish in his writings, and seldom lost an
opportunity to express this bias.[57] His comments on Jesus' parable about
the unclean spirit in Matt 12:43–5 illustrate these various points with
great ingenuity. After explaining the text's primary meaning as a
warning not to let faith die after initial conversion (XI, §5), Ephrem
then expands in allegorical fashion as follows:

> *When the unclean spirit goes out of a person.*[58] [The Lord] was com-
> paring Israel to a madman possessed by a spirit, and Himself to the
> likeness of a physican . . . Because He poured out his grace
> among them, idolatry fled before Him, and their paganism took
> off into the Gentiles. And it was as if they, when the time was
> fulfilled, were healed of the illness of error. Their idolatry betook
> itself far from the rays of the Life-Giver, and through the constraint
> of his miracles the people's paganism deserted them.[59]

---

53   Cf. John 19:29.
54   Cf. Ezek 16:10; Matt 27:33.
55   Cf. Ezek 16:10–11; John 19:34.
56   Cf. Dan 8:11–12; 9:26–27; 11:31–39.
57   Cf. R. Murray, Symbols of the Church and Kingdom, 68: 'It must be confessed with
     sorrow that Ephrem hated the Jews. It is sad that the man who could write the magis-
     terial Commentary on Genesis, with the command it shows of the tradition which
     still to a great extent united Christians and Jews, could sink to writing Carmina
     Nisibena 67.'
58   Matt 12:43.
59   XI, §6.

However, this unclean spirit of idolatry could find no rest among the Gentiles, because these had heard God's voice. For this Ephrem gives a short testimony in a series of passages from Isaiah, followed by the conclusion of the allegory, that the evil spirit returned to the Jews, and God gave them over to their enemies:

> For the Gentiles also heard the voice of Him who said, *All who are thirsty, come to the waters;*[60] and also, *The Gentiles will hope in Him,*[61] and, *I have given you as a covenant for the people and a light for the Gentiles.*[62] Because *the desert* of the Gentiles had become pools of water,[63] the [evil spirit] did not find rest among the Gentiles. Wherefore, *I will go back to my former house,*[64] this [spirit] and its seven companions, and so it entered and took up residence among this people, according to the number of days of the week, and did away with all its religious observance . . .
>
> [The evil spirit] rejected them again in the days of our Lord, for it found them full of envy toward their Saviour. But this [time] their evil deed was worse than the former one. They requited the prophets with slaughter, and hung Christ on the cross. Consequently they were thrown away like a vessel for which there was no use.[65]

It is in the commentary on the Passion that the tragedy of the Jews and their replacement by the Gentiles reaches its climax. Simon of Cyrene is seen as representing the Gentiles, while the Jews, through placing the cross on Simon,[66] symbolize their voluntary rejection of Christ:

> *After He had taken the wood of his cross and had set out, they found and stopped a man of Cyrene,* that is, from among the Gentiles, *and placed the wood of the cross on Him.*[67] It was only right that they should have given the wood of the cross voluntarily to the Gentiles, [since] in their rebellion, [the Jews] had rejected the coming of Him who was bringing all blessings. In rejecting it themselves, in their jealousy, they cast it away to the Gentiles. They rejected it in their jealousy and the Gentiles received it, to their [even greater] jealousy. For [the Lord] approved the welcoming Gentiles, thus provoking jealousy amongst their contemporaries through [the Gentiles'] acceptance.[68]

60 Is 55:1.
61 Is 11:10.
62 Is 42:6; cf. Is 49:6.
63 Cf. Ps 107:35.
64 Matt 12:44.
65 XI, §§7–8.
66 In the Gospel narrative it is the soldiers who do this, cf. Matt 27:32 and parallels.
67 Cf. Matt 27:32; Mark 15:21; Luke 23:26; John 19:17.
68 XX, §20.

This relentless censure of the Jews finally reaches a dramatic finale in his commentary on the rending of the temple curtain:

> *The curtain was torn.*[69] [This was] to show that [the Lord] had taken the kingdom away from them and had given it to a people who would bear fruit.[70] Alternatively, He was indicating, through the similitude of the torn curtain, that the temple would be destroyed because his Spirit had gone forth from it. Since the High Priest had wrongfully torn his robe, the Spirit tore the curtain to proclaim the audacity of the pride [of the Jews], by means of an action on the level of created beings.[71]

In the strictly analytical sense philosophical reflections will not be found in Ephrem, yet his recurrent wrestling with the reasons why the Jews rejected their Lord reflects how concerned he was also with the question of freedom and free will. In analysing the text of Matt 11:11, *The least of these [latter] who preach the kingdom of heaven is greater than [John]*, in IX, §§16–17, Ephrem concludes that John the Baptist's greatness was conferred on him and was not the result of free will, whereas, in the case of ordinary human beings, the role of their free response, their free will, is highlighted.[72] The mystery of human freedom and free will is illustrated too in the number of times Ephrem returns to grapple with why Judas should have betrayed the Lord.[73]

There are numerous other examples which show the extent to which Ephrem's mode of theological discussion is essentially couched in symbolic and typological dress. For instance, in contrasting the angel's annunciation to Zechariah with that to Mary in I, §11 of the commentary, Ephrem develops a number of insights. Zechariah goes to the angel because his child is destined to be inferior to the angel, whereas it is the angel who comes to Mary, since her child will be the angel's Lord. Moreover, the angel did not go to Elizabeth, since Zechariah is the true father of John. Gabriel did not go to Joseph however since Mary alone gave birth to her first-born. In III, §17 Ephrem uses the theme of being espoused near a well of water to draw together three separate Old Testament betrothals[74] as types of the Lord's betrothal to his Church through his baptism in the Jordan waters.

In commenting on the Sermon on the Mount in VI it is not surprising to find Ephrem focusing at length on the *Antitheses* and related

---

69   Mark 15:38.
70   Cf. Matt 21:43.
71   XX, §4.
72   Cf. VI, §§5,7; X, §2; XI, §12; XIII, §7.
73   Cf. IX, §14; X, §§5–6; XIV, §12; XVII, §§7, 13; XX, §§12, 18–19; and particularly Ephrem's discussion of the text: It would have been better for him if he had never been born (Matt 26:24) in XIX, §1f.
74   The betrothals of Rebecca (Gen 24:1–67), Rachel (Gen 29:1–21) and Zipporah (Ex 2:16–21).

texts[75] since these already belong to this central Semitic mode of expression through parallelism.[76] Although the paragraphs devoted to the *Antitheses* are of varying length, they constitute the longest single section of his commentary on the Sermon on the Mount,[77] and develop in depth a central theme in Ephrem's writings, the creative tension between God's grace and his righteousness or justice.[78] In the development of this theme Ephrem uses a variety of images and concepts which he places in parallelism with each other. An extract from §11b illustrates this point particularly well:

> When justice had reached its perfection, then grace put forth its perfection. *An eye for an eye* is the perfection of justice but, *Whoever strikes you on the cheek, turn the other to him*, is the consummation of grace. While both continually have their tastes, He proposed them to us through the two [successive] Testaments. The first [Testament] had the killing of animals for expiation, because justice did not permit that one should die in place of another. The second [Testament] was established through the blood of a man, who through his grace gave Himself on behalf of all. One therefore was the beginning, and the other the completion.

Ephrem frequently develops more than one interpretation for a given text, particularly texts that seem contradictory or ambivalent to him. A good illustration of this occurs in VIII, §14 where he quotes Matt 10:34: *Do not think that I have come to bring peace upon the earth*, and then immediately asks how this can be reconciled with Col 1:20, *He came to reconcile those things which are in heaven and those which are on earth*. His answer is nuanced. He begins by quoting two other passages from the Pauline letters which state that Christ did bring peace,[79] but then shows how different faith responses to Christ resulted in various kinds of divisions.[80] There are interesting variations offered in XIV, §7

---

75 Cf. Matt 5:20–48 (You have heard it said ... but I say to you). Cf. S. P. Brock, The Harp of the Spirit. Eighteen Poems of Saint Ephrem, second enlarged edition, San Bernardino, California 1984, 10–13 for an examination of Ephrem's creative use of typological exegesis in his extended meditations on Scripture.

76 Cf. C. McCarthy, 'Gospel Exegesis from a Semitic Church: Ephrem's Commentary on the Sermon on the Mount,' Tradition of the Text, Studies offered to Dominique Barthélemy in Celebration of his 70th Birthday, edited by G. J. Norton and S. Pisano, OBO 109, Freiburg und Göttingen 1991, 103–123, especially 114–117.

77 §§4–15.

78 S. P. Brock holds that this is one of the many Jewish traditions, found only outside the Bible in post-biblical literature, not attested in any other Christian source apart from Ephrem and some other early Christian Syriac writers; cf. S. P. Brock, The Luminous Eye, 20.

79 Eph 2:14 and Gal 6:16.

80 There is a lengthy discussion in XV, §§9–11 on how Jesus could say 'No one is good except God' to the rich man (Mark 10:18), but elsewhere refer to himself as 'the good shepherd' (John 10:11). In XVIII, §15, he explores the seeming

as to why Peter wanted to build three tents on the occasion of the Transfiguration. Similarly, in reflecting on Gethsemane, Ephrem suggests many different reasons as to why Jesus should have been fearful and sorrowful, to the point of asking that the chalice of suffering be removed from Him (XX, §§1–7).

Although the *Diatessaron* commentary is essentially a prose work, it is rich in poetic imagery and metaphors. Of Jesus' birth Ephrem writes: 'At his radiant birth therefore a radiant star appeared, and at his dark death there appeared a dark gloom' (II, §24). His description of the awe and amazement experienced by the angels in heaven at the sight of Jesus eating with sinners is eloquent: 'Angels stand and tremble, while tax collectors recline and enjoy themselves; the watchers tremble at his greatness, while sinners eat with him' (V, §17b). There are some beautiful reflections on the richness of God's word in I, §§18–19:

> Who is capable of comprehending the immensity of the possibilities of one of your utterances? What we leave behind us in [your utterance] is far greater than what we take from it . . . Many are the perspectives of his word, just as many are the perspectives of those who study it . . . His utterance is a tree of life, which offers you blessed fruit from every side ... The thirsty one rejoices because he can drink, but is not upset if unable to render the source dry. The well can conquer your thirst, but your thirst cannot conquer the fountain.

While best appreciated in their original Syriac formulations, Ephrem's puns and word-plays testify to a richly fertile, and at times playful, imagination. In commenting on Zechariah's disbelief in I, §13, he notes that '[God] who can close an open mouth can open a closed womb.' In VII, §18 the woman who was a sinner 'could scoff at the cunning thoughts of him who had been scoffing at her tears,' while at the same time the Lord 'was judging the secret [thoughts] of one who thought that He [the Lord] did not even know those that were manifest' (VII, §10). At the well in Samaria Jesus 'asked for water, that He might give water, under the pretext of water' (XII, §16). In VII, §7 Ephrem describes the woman who had a haemorrhage as 'she who had wearied physicians and she whom the physicians had wearied.' The force of the interplay between the images of sleeping and waking in VI, §25 in relation to Jesus' calming of the storm is difficult to capture fully in translation: 'He that was sleeping was awakened, and cast the sea into a sleep, so that by the wakefulness of the sea which was [now] sleeping, he might show forth the wakefulness of his divinity which never sleeps.' After commenting on the Lord's recommendation to cut off one's hand or foot if it

contradiction in how Jesus could say in Matt 24:36, 'Not even the Son knows the day or the hour,' in view of the intimate knowledge between Father and Son expressed in Matt 11:27, 'No one knows the Father except the Son.'

offends,[81] Ephrem wryly observes in VI, §7 that 'Herod's right hand was Herodias, and instead of cutting it off and casting this unclean hand away, he cut off and cast away a holy head.'[82] Pharaoh drowned in the waters in which he himself had drowned the infants (IV, §12).

Pithy admonitions and observations are plentiful. In VI, §18a he advises: 'Nourish your soul with the fear of God, and God will nourish your body.' Elsewhere, in that same paragraph, he notes that 'Anxiety tortures the soul, and the money that one accumulates injures oneself.' In XV, §12 there is an economy of words in the statement that 'Not [all] who are living are alive, nor are [all] those who are buried dead,' as also in XXI, §15: 'He died to our world in his body, that we might live to his world in his body.' Indeed there is a touch of humour in XIX, §13: 'Our Lord's words, *As I have loved you*, can be explained, Let us die for each other; but we do not even want to live for one another!'

Occasionally he includes extended reflections which are more spiritual in nature, such as those contained in VII, §§3–12. In this section he has been commenting on the woman who had a haemorrhage and who touched Jesus' cloak from behind.[83] He then develops a keenly argued reflection on various kinds of touching and their spiritual benefits. Other extended reflections occur in VIII, §§3–4 in the context of the peace greeting[84] and in X, §8 in relation to the sinful woman.[85]

Reading through Ephrem's commentary one comes across a number of interesting and sometimes unusual observations. In his pen-portrait of Simon Peter in IV, §20 we learn that Peter was timid, because he was frightened at the voice of a young servant girl, and poor, because he was not able to pay his own tax, and stupid, because he did not know how to take flight after denying the Lord. In VI, §24a, the motive Ephrem attributes to the rich young man in his aspirations to follow Jesus is that 'one who performs such deeds must possess much money'! In commenting on the phrase, *Are not two sparrows sold for a penny?*, he observes in a practical vein that things sold in bulk like vegetables are of lesser value.

In the early Christian centuries Edessa was a centre with a certain reputation for healing and medicinal skills.[86] Disease and illness were a source of constant anxiety and preoccupation in the ancient Near East, and the search for cures and healers is a theme recurring in the literature from these times.[87] Syrian Christians it seems devoted much of their energies to medicine, and in later centuries they were to become renowned for their role as the transmitters of Greek medical science to

81   Matt 18:8.
82   The beheading of John the Baptist, cf. Matt 14:3–11.
83   Mark 5:24–34.
84   Luke 10:5.
85   Luke 7:36–50.
86   Cf. J. B. Segal, Edessa, The Blessed City, Oxford 1970, 71f.
87   The Abgar-Addai legend has the search for healing at its centre.

the East, and for their status as physicians at the Persian court.[88] Edessa's many springs and their healing properties were well known. It is interesting therefore to note how the theme of healing is a frequent one for Ephrem, in which he often contrasts the divine healing powers of the Lord with the rather powerless ones of human physicians.[89]

Another characteristic trait of Ephrem is his keen eye for nature and his readiness to see therein the reflection of the Creator.[90] In commenting on the miracle at Cana in V, §§11–12, he points out that the Lord, in creating the wine, did not go outside of creation, but instead transformed the original creation 'to make it known that He was its Lord.' The imagery he uses in describing nature testifies to his alert powers of observation, particularly in relation to birds,[91] and the natural phenomena such as lightning and wind.[92] Linked with Ephrem's approach to nature is his insistence on trusting in divine providence. The Lord, he says, wanted his disciples 'not to be dragged down by the anxiety of the world, but rather to rely on the heavenly bread, and to reflect on what is above rather than on what is on earth' (VI, §18a).

In conclusion therefore, just as one will have difficulty in finding a fully systematized theology in Ephrem, so too one will look in vain for a fully developed set of hermeneutical principles.[93] To illustrate the richness of his approach, and the fact that for him the Scriptures are like an ever-flowing fountain whose wellsprings of meaning can never be exhausted, one could do no better to conclude than by letting him speak for himself:

> If there were [only] one meaning for the words [of Scripture], the first interpreter would find it, and all other listeners would have neither the toil of seeking nor the pleasure of finding. But every word of our Lord has its own image, and each image has many members, and each member possesses its own species and form. Each person hears in accordance with his capacity, and it is interpreted in accordance with what has been given him.[94]

---

88   Cf. M. W. Dols, 'Syriac into Arabic: The Transmission of Greek Medicine' in Aram 1 (1989), 45–52.

89   Cf. V, §23; VI, §14; VII, §§2, 7, 12, 16–17, 19, 21; X, §7a; XIII, §2f.

90   For a fuller treatment of the relation between the Bible and nature in Ephrem's exegesis, see for example, P. Yousif, 'Symbolisme christologique dans la Bible et dans la Nature chez saint Ephrem de Nisibe (De Virginitate VIII–XI et les textes parallèles)', Parole de l'Orient 8 (1977–1978) 5–66.

91   Cf. IV, §8c, VI, §§ 17a, 18a, VIII, §§6, 12, XI, §13 and XII, §16.

92   Cf. I, §32 and X, §13.

93   In his article, 'Exegetical Principles of St Ephraem of Nisibis,' P. Yousif has set about presenting 'the general shape of Ephraem's exegetical principles in a short, comprehensive and logical way' (p. 301), using the Diatessaron commentary as the most important source, but making reference also to the other extant biblical commentaries of Ephrem (cf. p. 296).

94   VII, §22.

APPENDIX

EPHREM THE SYRIAN

Short Biographical Outline

306   Born in Nisibis, on the borders of the Roman and Persian empires.

325f.   Appointed Chief Exegete of the Catechetical School in Nisibis by Bishop Jacob of Nisibis, recently returned from the Council of Nicaea.

363   Fled from Nisibis with most of the Christian population to escape persecution by the Persians.

363f.   Spent the remaining ten years of his life (aged c. 57–67) in Edessa, as a deacon serving the Church there in many capacities (preacher, theologian, composer of melodies, choir-master, poet and famine-relief worker).

373   Died on 9 June, having actively relieved famine distress in Edessa in 372.

Ephrem's Writings (five main categories)

(a)   *Scriptural Commentaries:*
        Extant in Syriac: Genesis, Exodus, the Minor Prophets, part of Isaiah and the Diatessaron.
        In Armenian: Genesis, Leviticus, Joshua, Judges and Kings, and certain letters of St Paul.

(b)   *Controversial Writings:* against Marcion's followers and other heretics.

(c)   *Works in Artistic Prose:* notably the *Discourse on Our Lord*, and the *Letter to Publius*.

(d)   *Verse Homilies:* the most important of which is the collection of six on *Faith*.

(e)   *Hymns:* of which at least five hundred survive. These were collected together into separate cycles in the early fifth century.

Recent English Translations of Some of Ephrem's Works

Brock, S. P., The Harp of the Spirit. Eighteen Poems of Saint Ephrem, second enlarged edition, San Bernardino, California 1984.

Brock, S. P., St. Ephrem the Syrian, Hymns on Paradise and Commentarium in Genesim, Section 2, New York 1990.

McCarthy, C., St Ephrem's Commentary on Tatian's Diatessaron. An English Translation of Chester Beatty Syriac MS 709 with Introduction and Notes, JSS Supplement Series 2, Oxford 1993.

McVey, K. E., Ephrem the Syrian: Hymns, Classics of Western Spirituality, New York/Mahwah 1989.

IV Select Bibliography

Brock, S. P., The Luminous Eye: the Spiritual World Vision of St Ephrem, Rome 1985, Kalamazoo 1990.

Brock, S. P., The Syriac Fathers on Prayer and the Spiritual Life, Michigan 1987.

McCarthy, C., 'Gospel Exegesis from a Semitic Church: Ephrem's Commentary on the Sermon on the Mount,' in Tradition of the Text, Studies offered to D. Barthélemy on the occasion of his 70th Birthday, edited by G. Norton and S. Pisano, OBO 109, Freiburg/Göttingen 1991, 103–123.

Murray Robert, Symbols of Church and Kingdom, Cambridge, 1975.

St Augustine on the 'mira profunditas' of Scripture: Texts and Contexts

THOMAS FINAN

What we call the City of God is the one witnessed to by that Scripture which, manifested by no choice impulses of human minds but by the guiding power of God's supreme providence, surpasses all the writings of all mankind, and in consequence of its supreme divine authority has subordinated to itself every genre of human genius.'[1]

'It is in point to notice also the structure and style of Scripture, a structure so unsystematic and various and a style so figurative and indirect that no one would presume at first to say what is in it and what is not. It cannot, as it were, be mapped or its contents catalogued; but after all our diligence, to the end of our lives and to the end of the Church, it must be an unexplored and unsubdued land, with heights and valleys, forests and streams on the right and left of our path and close about us, full of concealed wonders and choice treasures.'[2]

'The Bible's claim to truth . . . excludes all other claims . . . The world of the Scripture stories is not satisfied with claiming to be an histori-cally true reality—it insists that it is the only real world . . . let no one object that this goes too far, that not the stories but the religious doctrine raises the claim to absolute authority; because the stories are not . . . simply narrated "reality." Doctrine and promise are incarnate in them and inseparable from them; for that very reason they are fraught with background, and mysterious, containing a second, concealed meaning.'[3]

I have used these three extended quotations as an overture to my theme. One of the authors is ancient, two are modern. Two of the authors are religious and theological writers. The third is a secular schol-ar of European literature from its earliest beginnings down to modern times—under the rubric of 'the representation of reality in western literature.' The significance of that rubric is in the underlying question: What *is* reality?, and consequently, what is an adequate 'representation' of it in literature?, and consequently further, what is an adequate 'inter-

1   St Augustine, De civ. Dei., XI 1; cf. his De doctrina Christiana, II 42,63.
2   John Henry Newman, An Essay on the Development of Christian Doctrine, Image Books ed., New York 1960, 90f.
3   Erich Auerbach, Mimesis, Anchor Books ed., New York 1957, 12.

pretation' of the representation? To use St. Augustine's terms,[4] is a *res* (thing) or the *verbum* (word) representing it, merely a thing or a fact, and the word merely a nominalist naming of it? Or is the thing or the fact something more than its mere facticity? Is it in some sense also a *signum* (sign) pointing to a reality beyond itself, or even, in the stricter sense of symbol, embodying, incarnating, revealing while concealing another reality beyond itself? The same question obviously arises about the dimensions of meaning of the *verbum* itself as *signum* to the *res* represented.

The terms of the distinction are ancient, but the distinction itself is familiar to us in the terminology of contemporary literary criticism and theory. It is the distinction between the literature of two-dimensional factual realism and the literature of multi-dimensional levels of reality and the corresponding multivalent levels of meaning in the medium of its representation. That is a distinction first formally made by Aristotle, in his perennially canonical *Poetics*. In chapter 9 he makes a famous distinction between history and poetry. 'The poet and the historian differ not by writing in verse or in prose . . . The true difference is that one relates what has happened (the facts—*ta genomena*), the other what could potentially happen. Poetry, therefore, is a more philosophical thing and of weightier import than history; for poetry tends to express universal truths, but history particular facts and events.'

To realise the full import of this statement we need to attend to some of its terms. 'History' in classical antiquity was a 'literary' as well a 'scientific' genre, and Aristotle was not unaware of its search for causes and meaning as well as facts and events. The distinction he is pointing to is in the mode in which causes and meaning are sought and set out in history—by explicit 'scientific' analysis of the facts rather than by multivalent poetic embodiment of 'universal' meaning in what is sometimes called the 'concrete universal' of the facts themselves. And 'concrete universal' is an apt term to bring out what Aristotle meant by poetry expressing 'universal truths' (*ta katholou*). He did not mean abstract general 'concepts' ungrounded in concrete particular percepts. His aesthetic theory is a particular application of his general metaphysical system, and in that system it is well known that he transferred Plato's universal 'ideas' from the transcendent world of 'forms' to the immanent world of concrete particulars.

That Aristotelian principle provides a close analogy to the exegetical principle which insists that the 'fuller' meaning of Scripture be rooted in the literal and historical truth of word and event. And Aristotle also links up with Auerbach on that theme. Auerbach's title, 'Mimesis', is borrowed from Aristotle's generic definition of poetry and art as *mimêsis*, conventionally translated as *imitation*, with its attendant connotation of

4   De doctrina Christiana I 2,2 f.

merely realist fidelity to the surface appearance of phenomena, instead of what is really meant, namely 're-presentation' of phenomena in such a way as to 'interpret' them, to express their *inner* nature and meaning. Aristotle has often been misunderstood in the former of these two senses. And, of course without the benefit of Aristotle at all, it is now a commonplace of literary history that in the tradition there is a classification of literature corresponding to each of the two meanings—to use contemporary terms: 'realism,' and 'symbolism' (multilayeredness) in the largest and loosest sense of that word.

The general relevance of Auerbach to our theme is twofold. First he finds this division into realist and symbolic or multivalent present in a line of critical classification that runs through the representation of reality in western literature from its very beginnings. Western literature of course is a river flowing from the confluence of two earlier streams, the Judeo-Christian and the Greco-Roman. Secondly, he finds this dividing line of critical classification already most incisively in the very earliest literature of the two originating streams, the Bible and Homer. And, interestingly, he finds it through purely *literary* analysis of texts, without benefit yet of the later technical classification of scriptural meanings into literal and figurative and the famous four levels of significance—literal, allegorical, tropological and anagogical.

We cannot here go into the details of the literary analysis of his sample texts. The main results of the detailed analysis may be stated in two very important points. There is, firstly, in Old Testament narrative, as compared with Homer, the awesome penumbra of implied but unexpressed 'background' and 'mystery' against which characters and events are presented, and out of which they are seen to emerge. And, secondly, there is the corresponding penumbra of 'background' and 'mysterious' significance which the narrative is made to imply, and not just imply but demand—the demand of a claim to universal and absolute Truth.

'The decisive points of the narrative alone are emphasized, what lies between is non-existent: time and place are undefined and call for interpretation; thoughts and feelings remain unexpressed, are only suggested by the silence and the fragmentary speeches; the whole . . . remains mysterious and "fraught with background."'[5] 'The Bible's claim to Truth is not only far more urgent than Homer's—it excludes all other claims.'[6] 'The Old Testament . . . presents universal history: it begins with the beginning of time . . . and will end with the Last Days . . . Everything else that happens in the world can only be conceived as an element in this sequence; into it everything that is known about the world . . . must be fitted as an ingredient of the divine plan . . .', and

5   Auerbach, op. cit., 9, commenting on the command to Abraham to sacrifice Isaac in Gen 22:1 f.
6   Id., 12.

this, he goes on to say, is possible only by 'interpretation.'[7] St. Augustine hardly expressed similar ideas more powerfully, as we shall see.

In comparison with such Old Testament narratives of events and characters, 'whose depth of background is veritably abysmal'[8], the world depicted by Homer has of course its own depths, even to the tragic dimension. And even though 'he does not need to base his story on historical reality, his reality is powerful enough in itself; it ensnares us, weaving its web around us...' But 'this "real" world into which we are lured, exists only for itself, contains nothing but itself; the Homeric poems conceal nothing, they contain no teaching and no secret second meaning. Homer can be analysed . . . but he cannot be interpreted. Later allegorising trends have tried their arts of interpretation upon him, but to no avail.'[9]

In sum, and as a starting point for an investigation into the literary representation of reality in European culture, we have two styles representing two basic types. 'On the one hand fully externalised description . . . all events in the foreground, displaying unmistakable meaning, few elements of historical development and of psychological perspective; on the other, certain parts brought into high relief, others left obscure . . . suggestive influence of the unexpressed, "background" quality, multiplicity of meanings and the need for interpretation, universal-historical claims, development of the concept of the historically becoming . . .'[10]

Auerbach carries forward this 'concept of the historically becoming' from the Old Testament to its culmination in the New Testament. And there—still by purely literary analysis—he finds the same dimension of dark penumbral 'background' and 'mystery', and the corresponding dimension of abyssal depths of suggested meaning, and the same absolute demands of its truth. The same, but more finally absolute than the Old Testament could ever be, based as it was on the sense of 'promise' and 'historical becoming' as unfulfilled. That fulfilment was in the Incarnation, the embodiment of the Infinite itself in one unique concrete individual Being, one unique 'concrete universal'— 'harshly dramatised through God's incarnation in a human being of the humblest social station, through his existence on earth amid humble everyday people and conditions, and through his Passion which, judged by earthly standards, was ignominious. . . .'[11]

Auerbach chooses the dramatic scene of St. Peter's denial (in Mark's version) to illustrate the agonizing and even tragic implications of confrontation with such an embodiment of unsoundable 'background' and 'mysterious' depths of meaning. (He might also have chosen many confrontational scenes in John's Gospel . . .). 'Peter is called to the most

7   Id., 13.   10   Id., 19.
8   Id., 10.   11   Id., 36.
9   Id., 11.

tremendous role . . . how tremendous it is, viewed in relation to the life a fisherman from the Sea of Galilee normally lives, and what enormous "pendulation" [Harnack's word—*Pendelausschlag*] is going on in him!'[12] And Peter's experience is itself a universal—it applies to every other occurrence in the New Testament. 'Every one of them is concerned with the same question, the same conflict with which every human being is basically confronted and which therefore remains *infinite* and eternally pending'.[13] By the Incarnation of the Timeless in time, in 'Christ the power of God and the wisdom of God,'[14] a transformation of earthly reality and historical existence has taken place whose full meaning and development 'progresses to somewhere outside of history, to the end of time or to the coincidence of all times, in other words upwards, and does not, like the scientific concepts of evolutionary history, remain on the horizontal plane of historical [i.e. merely *intra*-historical] events.'[15]

It is within that incarnational context, with its transvaluation of the values of the concrete real, that Augustine broke the Greco-Roman connection between levels of literary style and the corresponding levels of reality as they understood them—the high or grand, the middle, and the low. In Christianity even the 'low' is 'high' or 'grand' because it has an eternal, and therefore infinite dimension and implication. 'When we are speaking of the eloquence of those men whom we wish to be teachers of things which will liberate us from eternal evil or lead us to eternal good . . . whether in extended speech or in conversation, whether in treatises or in books, whether in long letters or in short, they are great things. Unless, perhaps, because a cup of cold water is a small and most insignificant thing, we should also regard as small and most insignificant the promise of the Lord that he who gives such a cup to one of his disciples "shall not lose his reward".'[16]

This was what Augustine could not yet understand when he turned to the Scripture after his first 'conversion'—to the quest for 'immortal wisdom'. 'They seemed to me unworthy to be compared with the majesty of Cicero. My conceit was repelled by their simplicity, and I had not the mind to penetrate into their depths.'[17] Looking back even on

---

12 Ibid.
13 Id., 37—italics mine.
14 1 Cor 1:24, a recurring text in Augustine.
15 Auerbach, op. cit., 39.
16 De doctrina Christiana, IV 18,37; Matt 10:42; cf. the famous quotation by Longinus, On the Sublime, chap. 9, from the Genesis creation narrative, to illustrate the capacity of a single sentence to express the sublime: 'The lawgiver of the Jews, no ordinary man—for he understood and expressed God's power in accordance with its worth—writes at the beginning of his Laws: "God said"—now what?—"Let there be light," and there was light: "Let there be earth," and there was earth.'
17 Conf. III 5,9; on Augustine's initiation into Scripture see Anne-Marie la Bonnardière, L'Initiation biblique d'Augustin, in (edited by the same author) Saint Augustin et la Bible, Paris 1986.

his own earliest philosophical writings, the Cassiciacum *Dialogues,* he sees that 'the writing was now in your [God's] service, but during this breathing-space still smacked of the pride of the schools.'[18] Even his friend and fellow convert thought at first 'it would be in some sense lowering to put into my writings the name of Jesus Christ'[19]—the name without which not even a philosophical work could ever wholly satisfy Augustine,[20] and in whom alone, doubly revealed, in the flesh and in the Scriptures, his first conversion to the quest for 'immortal wisdom'[21] was to be ultimately fulfilled. For 'philosophy' means love of wisdom, but wisdom is with God,[22] and it is in Christ there indwells corporeally the whole plenitude of divinity.[23] Even the secular book that 'converted' him to the quest of 'immortal wisdom', Cicero's now lost exhortation to the philosophic quest, the *Hortensius,* by its critique of all the innumerable schools which used the 'great and fair and honourable name' of philosophy to lead men's minds astray, 'illustrates the wholesome advice given by the Spirit through your good and loving servant: "Make sure that no one traps you and deprives you of your freedom by some secondhand, empty, rational philosophy based on the principles of this world instead of on Christ".'[24]

Christ being the central and total meaning of Scripture in Augustine's exegesis of its fuller sense,[25] the foregoing illuminates our opening quotation from *The City of God,* and anticipates *in nuce* so much that we shall find Augustine asserting about Scripture as inexhaustible in its

18   Id. IX 4,7.
19   Ibid.
20   Conf. III 4,8.
21   Id. III 4,7.
22   Id. III 4,8; Job 12:13.
23   Id. III 4,8; Col 2:9.
24   Id. III 4,8; Col 2:8, in Jerusalem Bible version.
25   See e.g. Contra Faustum, XII 27: *Christus mihi utique illorum librorum* . . . (I find Christ everywhere in those Books . . .); cf. the even more forceful remarks in XII 39 on the futile ingenuity of 'a certain Philo', attempting to interpret Scripture without Christ, 'in whom he did not believe,' and thereby only succeeding in showing 'what a difference it makes whether you refer everything to Christ, with reference to whom everything was truly said in this way, or, ignoring Him, you hunt after no-matter-what conjecture with no-matter-what ingenuity of mind . . .' In other—and very contemporary—words, the whole of Scripture is meaningless without its fulfilment in Christ, see Hans Urs von Balthasar, The Glory of the Lord, Edinburgh 1982, vol. I, 658: 'For the eyes of faith, the "riddle of Israel" does not exist . . . The figure is legible, but only on Christian presuppositions. Israel and Christianity form one single figure, carved in bold relief from the block of world-history—a figure whose higher centre is the God-Man . . .'; this in a context where much of profound interest is said about the true meaning and permanent validity—even necessity—of the traditional figural exegesis of Scripture: 'We have no choice . . . but to characterise all Old Testament existence . . . as an existence *in typo.* Thus, it is a foreshadowing of Christian existence, but at the same it is the *reality* whereby all human existence assumes a form oriented towards Christ'—ibid., 654.

potential meaning. This potential inexhaustibility is in fact anticipated in one of the Cassiciacum *Dialogues*. 'What is it that we ought to call by the name of Wisdom except the Wisdom that is God's? But we have also learned on divine authority that the Son of God is none other than the Wisdom of God' [1 Cor 1:25] . . . But what do you suppose Wisdom to be except Truth? For this too has been said: "I am the Truth"' [Jn 14:6]. It is Christ then who is Wisdom and Truth, and if He is the whole meaning of Scripture we can once more see the ground of the absolute claim made for Scripture in our opening quotation from *The City of God*. But we can see it fully only if we understand the full significance of the terms wisdom (*sapientia*) and truth (*veritas*). They do not resonate much in English but they are high metaphysical concepts, as fundamental to Augustine's philosophical and theological thinking as they are to his personal existential drive towards absolutes.

Truth is the eternal, immutable, absolute, infinite subsistent Reality, a Truth which is the Ground and the Condition of all other realities and of all other truths, and is also the source of the light by which we know reality and its truth. Plato had already said as much in his simile of the sun for the Supreme Reality that is the Form of the Good. 'What gives the objects of knowledge their truth and the knower's mind the power of knowing them is the Form of the Good . . . The Good therefore may be said to be the source not only of the intelligibility of the objects of knowledge, but also of their being and reality . . .'[26] 'He who knows the Truth knows that Light, says Augustine of his first mystical experience, (Plotinus-influenced, but 'with [God] as my guide'), and he who knows that Light knows eternity.'[27] 'This mysterious Sun radiates its light into our inner eyes. By its light is true every truth we utter, even when, with still ailing or only half-opened eyes, we tremble to turn boldly towards it and look upon it wholly face to face.'[28]

We have Augustine's theory of knowledge already in germ, as elaborated for instance in the *De magistro*. There it is established by what one might call strict 'phenomenological' analysis, proving that all perception of truth is in the light of, conditional upon—by 'consulting', to use his own recurrent term—an unconditioned, absolute a priori Truth. This principle itself takes even philosophical analysis to the point where 'faith' too is necessary, for the ultimate a priori cannot itself be 'proved'![29]

26   Rep. 508e and 509b.

27   Conf. VII 10,16.

28   De beata vita, 35—the concluding phrase clearly alluding to the experience of Conf. VII 10,16, where in the dazzle of the Light 'you beat back the weakness of my gaze by the intensity of its radiance upon me, making me tremble with love and with dread.'

29   Elaborated in De utilitate credendi—written specifically against the Manichean 'intel-lectual' insistence on accepting truth, even Christian truth, only as rationally demonstrated and not as based merely on the faith of orthodox Christianity.

This gives the rationale for Augustine's much-quoted principle from Isaiah 7:9 (in the version he knew): 'Unless you believe you will not understand.'[30]

But in whom or what are we to believe in the quest for Truth? Whose shall be the teaching, who the teacher-master who will initiate us? What is 'written with divine authority' provides the answer: 'You must not allow yourselves to be called teachers, for you have only one Teacher, the Christ' (Matt 23:10).[31] What is meant is not extrinsic teaching but interior enlightenment by the indwelling Christ of Eph 3:16f, that is, the Christ of 1 Cor 1:24, 'the immutable Power and sempiternal Wisdom of God.'[32] This epistemology will underpin not just his philosophical thought but his scriptural exegesis as well, with its vast assertions of the inexhaustible meanings of Scripture. And concerning that range of meaning the whole passage of Eph 3:16 f. is significant, for it provides an ontological as well as an epistemological basis for that range. Through the indwelling Christ 'you will . . . have strength to grasp the breadth and the length, the height and the depth, until, knowing the love of Christ, which is beyond all knowing (*gnôseôs*), you are filled with the total plenitude (*pan to plêrôma*) of God.'[33] As commentators point out, the relevant terms here, 'grasp', 'breadth' etc, and *plêrôma*, are technical terms borrowed from Greek philosophy, evoking both the *cosmic* dimension of Christ and the ungraspable range of what is to be known about Him.

When to that cosmic dimension of Christ we add Augustine's already noted sense of Christ's omnipresence in Scripture, and when to those dimensions we add his epistemological significance as the Light, so to speak, in whose light we shall see light,[34] we glimpse again the vast background to our opening quotation from *The City of God*, with its categorical assertion that Scripture 'surpasses all the writings of all mankind, and in consequence of its divine authority has subordinated to itself every genre of human genius.'

That is but one of many such statements, which are found in greatest concentration and in their most developed form in the *Confessions* and in the *De doctrina Christiana*. They are statements that attribute to Scripture a certain *mira profunditas*,[35] an awesome[36] profundity. They are

---

30 De mag. XI 37.
31 See De mag. XIV 46; cf. Conf. V 6,10: 'You, O my God, had taught me in secret and marvellous ways. That it was You who taught me, I believe: for it is the truth and there is no teacher of truth (*doctor veri*) save You, no matter where or when it may happen to shine.'
32 De mag. XI 38.
33 Cf. Eph 1:23 on 'the plenitude (*plêrôma*) of Him who fills the whole creation.'
34 Ratified in any case already by Jn 1:9: 'The Word was the true light that enlightens every man, and He was coming into the world'—or any other way we choose to read it!
35 Conf. XII 14,17.
36 This rendering is not too strong, as we shall see.

statements that attribute to Scripture not just two senses, a literal and a figurative, not just the four senses of the traditional classification (although of course he does use that classification), nor yet even a 'plurality' of senses in some definable and delimited sense. They are statements which entirely transcend such classification, and attribute to Scripture an unlimited, inexhaustible, indeed infinite, potential of meaning. They recur throughout the *Confessions* from the moment of his 'conversion' to philosophy and its quest of 'immortal wisdom.'

At that point 'I resolved to make some study of the Sacred Scriptures and find out what kind of books they were. But what I came upon was something not grasped by the proud, nor revealed to children either, rather something lowly in access but, once entered, sublime and enveloped in mysteries (*excelsam et velatam mysteriis*).'[37] As we noted earlier from the context, he was not yet of a mentality capable of entering or bending his proud neck to take the necessary steps.[38]

It was the preaching of Ambrose in Milan that enabled him to enter, by revealing the fuller, figurative sense of Scripture and so unblocking also the Manichean objections to the apparent anthropomorphisms and other problems of Scripture. Augustine's reaction expresses the same ideas as before, but now in more elaborate and enthusiastic terms.

> Now that I heard them expounded so convincingly, I saw that many passages in those books, which had at one time struck me as absurdities, must be referred to the profundity of mystery.[39] Indeed the authority of Scripture seemed more to be revered and more worthy of devoted faith in that it was at once a book that all could read, and read easily, while yet it preserved the majesty of its mystery (*secreti sui dignitatem*) in a more profound interpretation (*in intellectu profundiore*): for it offers itself to all in the plainest words and the simplest expressions, yet demands the closest attention of the most serious minds.[40]

Augustine's confessional analysis of the meaning and the quest of his life from the past to the present is completed by a quest into the future, through a meditation on Scripture, on 'the wondrous things of thy Law' [Ps 118:18], for the analysis and the quest are in the light of Him 'in whom [the mystery of God the Father, *mysterium Dei Patris*] are hidden

---

37 Conf. III 5,9; Augustine likes the metaphor of veiling/unveiling—ultimately from 2 Cor 3:16 ff—see De utilitate credendi III 9; Contra Faustum XII 11.

38 Conf. III 5,9.

39 *Sacramentorum altitudinem*: see C. Couturier, '"Sacramentum" et "mysterium" dans l'oeuvre de Saint Augustin', in H. Rondet et al., Études Augustiniennes, Paris 1953, 161–274; cf. von Balthasar, op. cit., vol. I, 548: 'Even if we would not attribute to Scripture a sacramental and eucharistic structure in the strict sense, as Origen usually seems to do, we must still maintain the closest kind of connection between Scripture and Sacrament.'

40 Conf. VI 5,8.

all the treasures of wisdom and knowledge.'[41] This projection into the future through Scripture implies by itself the totalizing range of meaning he attributes to Scripture. For the range of the *Confessions* themselves, with their quest for 'immortal wisdom', is a 'totalizing' range—from the mystery of his origins in the dark backward and abysm of time,[42] forward into the abysm of futurity in destined eternity.[43] The same totalizing range is implicit in the part of Scripture chosen to be meditated on in the three concluding books of the *Confessions*—the creation narrative in the opening chapter of Genesis. Ever since Philo, down even to Eriugena in the *Periphyseôn*, that narrative provides the framework for exposition of the total order, origin and destiny of creation and of human existence under the Creator. And that is precisely the range of Augustine's opening prayer in *Confessions* XI 2,3: 'O Lord complete thy work in me, and open these pages to me . . . Let me confess to Thee whatever I shall find in your Books . . . from the first "beginning" in which You made "the heavens and the earth," up to our everlasting reign with Thee in thy Holy City.'

And again Christ is the source and the ground[44] of this totality, and the light by which it is understood. He is the Word 'by which You made all things[45] . . . It is through Him that I beseech you . . . through Him "in whom are hidden all the treasures of wisdom and knowledge." It is those treasures [or, variant, Him] that I seek in your Books. It is of Him that Moses wrote[46]: this He himself says, this He says who is Truth[47] itself.'[48]

It is in the account of his sojourn at Cassiciacum in preparation for Baptism in *Conf.* IX 4 that we find Augustine's first full 'discovery' of Scripture and the depth of the meaning he found in it. The account is a rhapsody on the Psalms, composed around a meditation on Psalm 4 in particular. The tone is intensified by the realization of how wrong the Manicheans had been about Scripture—the Manicheans with

---

41   Conf. X 43,70; Col 2:3.

42   See the questioning in Conf. I 6,9: 'And before that again [existence in his mother's womb] . . . my God? Was I somewhere or someone?'

43   See Conf. XIII 36,51: 'You rested on the seventh day, to let us know in advance by the word of your Book that we too, at the end of our works . . . will rest in You in the Sabbath of eternal life'; cf. the conclusion of The City of God.

44   See Conf. XI 3 ff on the question of what is meant by the statement that 'in the beginning' (*in principio*) God made heaven and earth (Gen 1:1); the explanation culminates in the interpretation of *principium* not as a temporal beginning but as an ultimate metaphysical principle, an eternal reason or logos (*ratio aeterna*) identified with the eternal *Logos* that is Christ, on the basis of a reading of Jn 8:25: 'They said therefore to Him: Who are you? Jesus said to them: The *principium* (*arkhên*), O God, in which You made heaven and earth, in your Word . . .' (Conf. XI 9,11).

45   Cf. Jn 1:3.

46   Cf. Jn 5:46.

47   Cf. Jn 14:6.

48   Conf. XI 2,4.

whom he had himself been 'a blind bitter barker against Writings all honeyed with the honey of heaven and all luminous with your light . . .' (IX 4,11). The language is at times that of the higher states of prayer, or even of mystical experience. 'I was speaking with myself and to myself in your presence out of the intimate feeling of my spirit. I was in awe and dread . . . I heard and trembled . . . *inhorrui timendo . . . audivi et contremui*' (IX 4,8f). 'Oh if they could but see the internal eternal (*internum aeternum*) which . . . I had tasted . . . I cried out as I read these things aloud and recognized their truth within me. And I no longer wanted to fragment myself in earthly goods, devouring time and devoured by time, since in the simplicity of the eternal (*aeterna simplicitate*) I now had other corn and wine and oil' (IX 4,10; Ps 4:7).

'Behold, O Lord my God, how much I have written on those few words, how much, I ask You! What stamina, what time, would be required to study all your Books at such a rate!'[49] The few words in question are the first two verses of Genesis—they have taken up two whole Books of the *Confessions* (XI–XII). Those few words have raised, and Augustine has found answers to, all the ultimate metaphysical questions about the nature of reality, Creator and creation, the transcendent spiritual world and the material phenomenal universe, the nature of eternity and of time, of being and of the nothingness from which being is created, of 'form' and that almost ungraspable entity, the 'primal matter' which is the substrate of 'form.' 'If one could call it "a nothing which is something" and "a being which is non-being", that is what I would call it. And yet it *was* in some way, in order to receive those visible and organised forms.'[50] His heart indeed 'is hard wrought in the poverty of my present life when the words of your Scripture knock on its door,' and the poverty of human understanding uses more words in asking questions than in finding the answers.[51]

It is out of this sense of mystery and unsoundable depths of meaning that Augustine breaks into one of his lyrical, even mystical, apostrophes to Scripture. 'Wondrous is the profundity (*mira profunditas*) of your oracles. We see their surface before us enticing us as children. But wondrous is their profundity, my God, wondrous their profundity! To look into them is to experience a shudder, the shudder of awe and the trembling of love—*horror honoris et tremor amoris*.[52] This is the language of the sacred, the holy, the *mysterium tremendum*.[53] The fact that Augustine could have borrowed the terminology from Plotinus[54] does not invalidate the experience. We have seen him use the same terms about the mystical

49   Conf. XII 32,43.
50   Id. XII 6,6.
51   Id. XII 1,1.
52   Id. XII 14,17.
53   See e.g. Rudolf Otto, The Idea of the Holy, Oxford 1923, repr. 1973.
54   E.g. Enn. I 6,4.

experience in Milan.[55] He uses that language in an even more explicit and extended passage in *Conf.* XI 9, 11, meditating on the realisation that Christ, the *Logos,* is the *Principium* in whom God created heaven and earth.

> Who will understand this? Who will explain it? What is that which shines upon me intermittently and strikes my heart without wounding it?[55a] I am on fire and draw back in dread (*inhorresco et inardesco*) . . . It is Wisdom, Wisdom itself, that in those moments shines upon me, cleaving through my cloud . . .

In case we be tempted to regard such language as unique and excessive, or just rhetoric, let us put beside it a summary statement from a modern theologian.

> It is a pity that both orthodox Protestant and Catholic biblical scholars often speak as if the human, historical and philological content of Scripture formed a closed world, and that the divine or 'spiritual' sense begins only beyond it. The saints realised how the infinite shines directly through the fearful intensity of the prophets, of Jesus, of Paul and of John; how the human word and gesture are but a thin film before it...'[56]

It is to be noted too that Augustine's sense of the inexhaustible potential of the meaning of Scripture, though perhaps more powerful, explicit and frequent in his expression of it, is but a link in a millennial tradition, based both on professional exegesis and on contemplative study in the spirituality of *lectio divina.*[57] Henri de Lubac's vast explora-

---

55 Conf. VII 10,16: *contremui amore et horrore.*
55a Cf. St John of the Cross, Canciones del Alma . . . (Song of the Soul . . .),
       O cautery most tender!
       O gash that is my guerdon! (tr. Roy Campbell).
       ¡Oh cauterio suave!
       ¡Oh regalada llaga!
56 Hans Urs von Balthasar, Science, Religion and Christianity, London 1958, 102; cf.
       112 on 'the abyss of silence from which springs the Word of God . . . All the words
       . . . all the gestures and deeds of Jesus Christ are not only surrounded by silence,
       they are steeped in the ineffable, drawn from silence . . .'; also 99 on the same idea:
       'The Fathers worked on this golden background [symbol of the infinite in iconic
       art]. They had the feeling for the dialectic of that which is always greater . . .'; cf.
       also, by the same author, First Glance at Adrienne von Speyr, San Francisco 1981,
       101: 'Every single sentence which seen from without has a finite meaning, to be
       precisely differentiated from other sentences, partakes . . . of an infinity always
       inherent in divine Truth. Without ceasing to have a *definite* meaning, every sentence
       shares as the word of God in the divine quality of the ever-more, ever-greater, and
       consequently ever-inexhaustible.' That amounts not just to a parallel with Augustine,
       but to a magisterial summary of Augustine's scattered but connected assertions, and
       of his ultimate reasons for them.
57 See e.g. von Balthasar, The Glory of the Lord, I,659; also Jean Leclercq, The
       Love of Learning and the Desire for God, Mentor Omega ed., New York 1962.

tions[58] save us the labour of hacking our own way through those woods with all their thickets and undergrowth. We can cull our own florilegium from one section of his research in particular—headed precisely with Augustine's phrase, *mira profunditas*.[59] Scripture is 'an infinite forest of meanings'—*infinita sensuum silva*. It is a treasury of the Holy Spirit, with riches as infinite as He is. It is 'an unplumbed abyss', 'an ocean immeasurable, wide and deep',[60] and so on. It is of interest to an Irish reader to get the flavour of the tradition as expressed in a résumé of Scotus Eriugena. He works with the concept of a double divine revelation—in Scripture and creation. Both are 'sacrament and symbol' for us. Each of them is 'a letter, a visible and sensible aspect', which however, must be transcended to attain to the 'spirit' (*intellectus*) of the one and the 'reason' (*ratio*) which runs through the other. 'Starting from the "simplicity of the letter and of the visible creation" we must let ourselves be led thus by degrees "right to the summit of contemplation"',—'to the pure and invisible beauty of Truth itself', *ipsius Veritatis*.[61] This is the frame and the scale of ascent for Augustine too in the study of Scripture.[62]

It is important to note that it is not only in the descants of 'enthusiasm' in the *Confessions* that we find Augustine's assertions of the all-encompassing meaning of Scripture. He had already stated the principle in the earlier *De doctrina Christiana*, written as a systematic handbook to professional exegesis. 'The knowledge collected from the pagans, although some of it is useful, is also little as compared with that derived from the divine Scriptures. For whatever one has learned outside them is censured there if it is harmful, and if it is useful it is found there. And . . . moreover he will find there in much greater abundance what can be learned nowhere else at all, but only in the wondrous sublimity and the wondrous humility (*mirabili altitudine et mirabili humilitate*) of those Scriptures.'[63]

Another passage in the same work (III 27,38) comes close even to the expressions we find in the *Confessions*. It has the additional interest of being late, written in Augustine's old age in 427 or 428, more than a quarter of a century after the *Confessions* and the greater part of the *De doctrina Christiana*, which was left unfinished in 396 at III 25,35. It thus shows the permanence of Augustine's exegetical principles. And more than that, it confirms his conviction about their validity. For at the time of completing the *De doctrina Christiana* he was writing the *Retractationes*, a rereading, and revision where necessary, of his *opera omnia*.[64]

58 In Exégèse Médiévale, Paris 1959.
59 Op. cit., Première Partie, vol. I, 119 f.
60 Ibid. 119 f.
61 Ibid. 121 f.
62 See De doct. Chr., II 7,9–11.
63 Op. cit., II 42,63; note the recurring motif of Scripture's combination of *altitudo* and *humilitas*; on De doctrina Christiana see Madeleine Moreau, 'Lecture du *De Doctrina Christiana*', in Anne-Marie la Bonnardière, op. cit., 253–285.
64 Retractationes II 4,30.

The section in III 27,38 is concerned with passages of Scripture where 'from the same words not one but two or even several meanings can be understood,' without the exegete being able to decide 'what meaning was intended by the author'. The exegete may take any or all of those possible meanings provided they are not invalidated by some other passage in Scripture, and provided also that he who is scrutinizing the divine utterances does make an effort to arrive at the intention of the author, 'through whom the Holy Spirit composed that Scripture'. But even if he fails and takes a meaning different from that intended by the author his interpretation is valid if compatible with any other passage in Scripture.

> For in fact the author himself may well have seen that same additional meaning in those same words that we are trying to understand. And certainly the Spirit of God, who worked through that author, foresaw without any doubt that that particular meaning too would occur to the reader or the hearer. Nay, more, He *provided* for its occurring to him, for that meaning too is grounded in Truth—*veritate subnixa*. In fact, what more rich and generous provision could have been divinely made in the divine words than that the same words be interpretable in several ways made acceptable by the witness of other no less divinely inspired passages?[65]

*   *   *

That passage takes us to an important question, the same question asked by opponents of Augustine's exegesis:[66] how do we know that Scripture has this range of meaning? What is the rationale of such interpretation? We have touched on some elements of the answer earlier, but the question demands to be examined more closely. It occupies Augustine at great length in *Conf.* XII 14,17ff. but he poses the question already at the start[67] of the three Books of reflection on the creation narrative. How are we to know what Moses really meant by 'In the beginning (*principium*) God made heaven and earth?' The answer is, by consulting that supreme Truth, *Veritas*, as in *De doct. Chr.* III 27,38, the full transcendent dimensions of which we have explained already, dimensions epistemological and ontological, as identified with Christ the *Logos* and the ultimate metaphysical *principium*. But here Augustine himself sketches the epistemology that leads up to that *principium*. Moses is gone and we cannot ask him what he meant. If he were here we could ask him, but if he answered in Hebrew we would understand nothing. If he spoke Latin then? We would know what he *said*, 'but whence should I know whether what he said was *true*? And if I did know it, would it be from him that I knew it? No, it would be from within myself, in the

65   Cf. the same idea in *Conf.* XIII 24,37.
66   See *Conf.* XII 14,17.
67   *Conf.* XI 3,5.

inner retreat of my own thought, where the Truth which speaks neither Hebrew nor Greek nor Barbarian would say to me without lips or tongue or sound of syllables: "he speaks truth".'[67a] It is the epistemology elaborated in the *De magistro,* in which the teacher does not teach the student in the sense of conveying knowledge from one mind to another. Rather, as in the Socratic-Platonic maieutic,[68] he helps the student to *see* truth by himself, by 'recalling' to him, 'reminding him' of, that transcendent, subsistent Truth which is the ultimate presupposition of all truths, and without which their truth could not be recognized.[69] 'These [truths] we know, thanks to You, and our knowledge compared with your knowledge is ignorance.'[70] 'Let him hear You speaking within who can . . . "You have made all things in your Wisdom",[71] and that is the *Principium,* and it is "in" *that* "Principium" [i.e. the *Logos,* Christ], that You have made heaven and earth.'[72] 'For it is true, Lord, that You made heaven and earth. It is true that the *Principium* is your Wisdom *in* which You "made all things.".'[73] That is, in the transcendent but also immanent and omnipresent 'cosmic' (as we have called him earlier) Logos-Christ.[74]

67a Conf. XI 3, 5.
68 See e.g. Plato's Meno, 81b f. on 'teaching' Pythagoras' theorem!
69 See the concluding summary in De mag. XIV 45 f.
70 Conf. XI 4,6.
71 Ps 103:24.
72 Conf XI 9,11.
73 Conf. XII 19,28; Ps 103.24.
74 Cf. the poetry of G.M. Hopkins—on which see von Balthasar, The Glory of the Lord, vol. III, Edinburgh 1986, 353–399; there is of course an analogy between the sensibility that can recognize the inexhaustible or even transcendent significance of the aesthetic experience and that of understanding the Scriptures in their transcendent height and depth—see von Balthasar, The Glory of the Lord, passim, also George Steiner, Real Presences, London 1989, passim; Augustine of course was a professor and lover of literature, and himself a poet in prose, and he too points up the analogy in De utilitate credendi, VI 13; it is an analogy of current contemporary interest—see e.g. Paul S. Fiddes, Freedom and Limit: A Dialogue Between Literature and Christian Doctrine, London 1991; one point of the analogy is well made in a sentence by Jean Leclercq, op. cit., 265: 'The extreme frontiers of literature . . . open into the whole realm of the ineffable'; cf. Karl Rahner, Poetry and The Christian, in his Theological Investigations, vol. IV, Baltimore and London 1966, 357–367. And despite the appearances of his theoretical anti-art puritanism, in 'the long-standing quarrel between philosophy and literature', Plato recognized the point in his practice— resorting to his literary 'myths' when dialectical reasoning reached its own frontiers—see e.g. J.A. Stewart, The Myths of Plato, New York 1905. In fact Plato himself anticipated Augustine's assertions about Plato and the Platonists, that 'there are none who have come closer to us than they have' (De civ. Dei VIII 5), and, if they were alive today, 'with the change of only a few words and ideas they would become Christians, as so many more recent Platonists of our own times have done' (De ver. rel. IV 7): the anticipation is in the fact that Plato too, when reason's raft had taken him as far as it could, hoped for 'some stronger vessel, some divine revelation (*logou theiou tinos*) on which to voyage with less risk and in

That is the basis of his sustained and detailed argument in *Conf.* XII 14, 17ff against those opposed to his totalizing interpretation of Gen 1:1, 'In the beginning God made heaven and earth,' as meaning that 'in his Word, co-eternal with Himself, God made both the intelligible and the sensible worlds, or in other words, both the spiritual and the material creation,' that is, the total universe of being, transcendent and phenomenal.[75] Whether Moses did mean that or not, it is still *true*, as is clear to all whom God has enabled to see such matters with an interior eye, 'and who believe unshakeably that Moses, the servant of God, spoke in "the Spirit of Truth".'[76] And in any case, 'even if Moses himself were to appear and say: "This is what I meant", even then we would not see its truth but would have to take his word and *believe* it.'[77] That statement is based on Augustine's theory of knowledge, already explained. 'If therefore we are in no disagreement about the Light itself of the Lord our God, why should we dispute about the thought of our neighbour, which we cannot see in the same way as we see the immutable Truth [which is above our minds, i.e. as their Light]?'[78]

Augustine carries this criterion of truth even further in *Conf.* XIII 29,44 and XIII 31,46. There in the context of the truth of judgements about the goodness of creation (Gen 1:31, and with the Manicheans in mind), he says that when the human mind judges truth and value under the light of the Word and the inspiration of the Holy Spirit it is God himself who judges in us.[79] 'You say to me, for You are my God and You speak with strong voice to the inner ear of your servant . . . : "O Man, it is clear that what my Scripture says it is I who say . . . Thus, what *you* see through my Spirit I see, just as what *you* say through my Spirit I say".'[80]

The Manicheans are wrong about Scripture and the goodness of creation, 'because they do not see your works through your Spirit, nor recognize You in them.'[81] 'But as for those who see those things through your Spirit, it is You who see in them . . . And I am moved to add: Assuredly "no one knows the things of God except the Spirit of God."[82] How then do we know, we too, "the gifts given us by God"?[83] The answer

---

greater security' (Phaedo 85d); cf. J. Pieper, 'Gottgeschenkte Mania. Eine Platon-Interpretation', in IKZ Communio 23 (1994) 260–270.

75   Conf. XII 20,29.
76   Ibid.; Jn 14:17.
77   Conf. XII 25,35.
78   Ibid.
79   See the note to III 31,46 in Les Confessions de Saint Augustin, Livres VIII–XIII, Bruges 1962, and its reference to Franz Koerner, 'Deus in homine videt', in Phil. Jahrb. 64 (1956) 166–217.
80   Conf. XIII 29,40.
81   Conf. XIII 30,45.
82   1 Cor 2:11, but see the whole context for the full implications in Augustine as well as Paul.
83   Id. 2:12.

is given me: when we know things through his Spirit, even then "no one knows them except the Spirit of God". For just as it has been rightly said to those who would *speak* in the Spirit of God, "It is not you who speak",[84] similarly to those who *know* in the Spirit of God it is rightly said: "It is not you who know".[85]

In the course of the argument that begins in *Conf.* XII 14,17ff Augustine eventually prefers the higher Truth of charity to contentious argument—'"which is to no profit except to the subverting of the listeners"[86] . . . And our Teacher knows well on what two precepts He hung "the whole law and the prophets".'[87] And Scripture itself 'prescribes nothing but charity' and proscribes nothing but its opposite, 'cupidity.'[88]

But Augustine brings in another remarkable supporting argument, one that is also more easily graspable—despite the fact that it is so far-reaching, and even anticipatory of some powerfully stated contemporary exegetical principles.[88a] The gist of the argument is that a book like the Bible, composed in a particular time and place but, as the Word of God, intended to be not only authoritative but universally meaningful over space and time to all men in all ages and situations, such a book must have an ever-inexhaustible potential of meaning. That is the simple summary, but without quotation *in extenso* we miss the power of the argument —as indeed we miss also Augustine's own trained and practised sense of literary and semiotic complexity.

> I cannot think that Moses your most faithful servant was given lesser gifts by You than I should have wished and longed to have for myself if I had been born at the same time as he, and You had settled me in the same place, to dispense by the service of my heart and my language those Writings which for so long after, from such a summit of authority, were to benefit all nations and throughout the whole world to overtop the words of all the doctrines produced by falsehood and pride.[89] If I had been Moses at that time, I would wish therefore, had I been then what he was and You had enjoined on me the writing of the Book of Genesis, I would wish to be granted such a skill in writing and such a way with weaving words that those who cannot yet understand how God creates would still not reject my words as beyond their capacity; and again that those who do already understand would find in the few words of your servant any truth they had already attained by their own thinking;

---

84   Matt 10:20.
85   Conf. XIII 31,48.
86   2 Tim 2:14.
87   Conf. XII 18,27; Matt 22:40.
88   De doct. Chr. III 10,15.
88a See n. 56 and n. 213.
89   Recall Conf. III 4,8 on the debasing of the noble name of 'philosophy' by the discordant schools.

and if in the light of Truth some other person saw some other truth
I would wish that it too could be seen in those same words of mine.[90]

That wish he expresses again in *Conf.* XII 31,42, in terms more explicit
about the inexhaustible meaning of Scripture. 'For myself—and I say this
without fear and from my heart—had I to write something of supreme
authority I would prefer so to write that my words should resonate with
any truth that anyone could find on these matters—I would prefer that to
having my words express one true meaning so clearly that they excluded
all others . . .' And at this point he cannot believe that a man as great as
Moses was not thus gifted. 'Yes, of course, when he was writing those
words he did discern and think of all the truth we have been able to find
in them, as also all that we have not—or not yet—been able to find in
them, and yet is in there to be found.'

Augustine the artist has an innate sense of the complexity and the
depths of reality and thought, and of the polysemy of language that tries
to express them—and often is unable to express them.[91] 'I know that the
corporeal signifies in multiple ways what the spirit understands in one
way only, and conversely, that the spirit understands in multiple ways
what the corporeal signifies in one way only.'[92] The statement is made in
the course of a long reflection on something he finds very strange, why
it is only the *human* and *animal* creation that is bidden to 'increase and
multiply' in Gen 1:28. 'What can this mean? What kind of mystery is
this? . . . It cannot be that you imply nothing particular by it . . .'[93]
'What then am I to say, O Truth, my light? That the fact means nothing,
that the expression was used without any particular meaning? Never! . . .
Far be it from the servant of your Word to say such a thing.'[94] If we
consider the nature of things in their literal sense the phrase 'increase
and multiply' applies to all things born of seed. But if we take the phrase
in a figurative sense (*figurate*)—'which in my opinion was rather what

90   Conf. XII 26,36.
91   See De catechizandis rudibus X 14 ff on the various kinds of writer's block and
     their remedies! And in II 3 a glimpse of his own labour pains: 'Myself too, I am
     nearly always dissatisfied with what I compose . . . I want the hearer to under-
     stand what I understand myself, and I feel that I do not so express myself as to
     succeed. The main reason is that the intuitive conception floods my soul with
     the rapidity of a lightning flash, while the expression is slow, long and very
     unlike the original intuition; and while the expression is unfolding the intuition
     has already disappeared into a hidden retreat . . .'
92   Conf. XIII 24,36.
93   Conf. XIII 24,35; Augustine insists on the significance even of details; in Con.
     Faustum XII 37 he asks: 'What are we to believe about so many things done
     outside any usage of nature and without any necessity of the business in hand?';
     he goes on to list examples in 38 f., the creation of Eve from the side of the
     sleeping Adam, the details of the construction of the ark, the order to Abraham
     to sacrifice his son, etc. The answer to his question he finds in 1 Cor 10:6: 'All
     these things were done as figures, types and symbols for ourselves.'
94   Conf. XIII 24, XIII 24, 36

Scripture intended'—then we find the hermeneutics of the *multiple* meaning in the *one* and of the *one* meaning in the *multiple*.

> What is in question is that kind of increasing and multiplying in which one meaning is expressed in multiple ways and one expression is understood in multiple meanings; and that kind of increasing and multiplying we find only in signs made corporeally and in things conceived intellectually . . . In that blessing then [Increase and multiply] I understand that You have granted us the faculty and the power both to express in multiple ways what we have conceived intellectually in the mode of a single idea, and to understand in multiple ways what we have read darkly expressed in a single mode.[95]

We do not necessarily have to accept the reasoning that led up to this insight in order to accept its validity. The polysemy of great literature, the inexhaustibility of the 'classic', is a commonplace of modern[96] literary theory and criticism[97]—even before its excesses of 'interpretation' outdo those of the maligned allegorizers of Scripture!

It is in the light of such principles that the more flowery passages are to be understood. In XII 27,37 he compares Scripture to a spring—though enclosed in a confined space it is more abundant, and from its many streams waters a wider territory, than any one of those streams on its own however far they flow. Likewise, 'the narrative of the dispenser of your Word, meant to serve many who would later discourse upon it, from brevity of utterance sets flowing streams of limpid truth from which everyone can draw for himself such truth as he can find therein, one person this, another that, but in the exposition of it demanding much longer windings of words.'

95 Conf. XIII 24,37.
96 Even though the insight itself is as ancient as Longinus; one of the marks of the authentic 'sublime' is that it 'disposes the mind of the reader to high thoughts (*megalophrosunên*), and leaves his intellect with more to think on than is contained in the mere words, op. cit., 7,3; cf. 35,2 ff: 'What then was the vision that inspired these godlike writers . . . ? . . . The universe itself . . . is not wide enough for the range of human speculation and intellect . . . Other literary qualities show their authors to be merely human, but the sublime lifts us close to the high thoughts of a god;' it has been suggested that Augustine knew this work: see L.J. van der Lof, 'Verbricht Augustin das Schweigen des Klassischen Altertums um Ps-Longinus?', Vigiliae Christianae, XVI (1962) 21–33.
97 Of the many references that could be given see William F. Lynch, Christ and Apollo: The Dimensions of the Literary Imagination, New York 1960. Its particular interest is that it constructs a theory of the levels of meaning in literature on the double basis of the philosophical doctrine of the analogy of being and the traditional four senses of Scripture; and of the latter he makes solid sense—see e.g. 165 and 187 ff, with which pages cf. de Lubac, op. cit., Première Partie, II, 630 ff, 643 ff.

Or again, expressing once more his constant motif of the combined simplicity and depth of Scripture, it is a nest for 'the poor unfeathered nestling' (XII 27,37), while for others its words are no longer a nest, but rather a leafy orchard in which they find hidden fruits and flutter joyfully around them, gazing, chattering and picking. 'For when they read or hear these words of yours , O God eternal, they see that all times past and all times to come are over-arched by your changeless abiding . . . Those things they see, and they rejoice in the light of your Truth, to what little extent they are able to see it here below' (XII 28,38).

*   *   *

We have been analysing at some length the concept of Truth in Augustine, and the epistemology, ontology, and hermeneutics through which he finds it 'totally' in Scripture—to the extent, as we saw at the beginning, of subordinating to itself every other product of human genius.[98] To understand more fully these assertions of all-inclusive and absolute Truth in Scripture we need to look at them in a larger context and in a less dialectical, more 'existential' or experiential mode.

To take the latter first, we have already glimpsed it in the phenomenon of Augustine's 'conversion' to 'philosophy' with its quest for immortal wisdom in *Conf.* III 4,8—'not this or that philosophical sect but Wisdom *itself* whatever it might be,' and not just in an abstract intellectual mode, but to be 'loved, sought, attained, seized and passionately embraced.'[99] The Manicheans cried 'Truth, truth!' and spoke much of it, 'but it was nowhere in them.'[100] 'O Truth, Truth, from how deep within me did I sigh for You from the very marrow of my soul.'[101] Ten years later, in the throes of philosophical scepticism, he is tormented[102] by the realisation of how little progress he has made since that nineteenth year of his life when he first 'began to burn with a passion for the pursuit of Wisdom.'[103] Perish all else, all the vain distractions and empty ambitions of life! 'Let us devote ourselves to the sole pursuit of truth. Life is a poor unhappy business, death is uncertain, and suppose it crept up on us suddenly—in what state will we go hence, and where then shall we learn what we neglected to learn in life?'—if death itself be not the end of everything.[104]

98   See n.1 above.
99   Language which anticipates the ultimately mystical dimension of Augustine's quest—cf. VII 10, 16; X 7, 11.
100 Conf. III 6,10.
101 Ibid.
102 Although now with a dawning hope in Christianity, after hearing Ambrose on Scripture: 'I shall plant my foot on that step where my parents set me as a child until I find the clear light of Truth (*perspicua Veritas*); but where am I to look for it?'—Conf. VI 11,18.
103 Ibid.
104 Conf. VI 11, 19.

At this stage he is speaking from among a group of like-minded friends, all troubled by the same problems as Augustine, and detesting the distractions of the cares and troubles of life in the world. It was in that situation that they discussed the project of pooling their resources to withdraw from the world and live the common life in a community devoted to the pursuit of truth in a life of philosophical thinking and contemplation.[105] The project and the terms may sound strangely parallel to the Christian contemplative religious life.[106] And so in fact the project was, and is. For such philosophical communities were well known in the ancient world, from the Pythagorean communities down to, for instance, that of Plotinus in Rome.[107] There are two reasons for the parallel, the nature and goal of philosophy as understood in the Greco-Roman world, and the process by which its truth and goal were understood to be attained, especially in the Platonist tradition. In that tradition the finality of philosophy was religious, in a sense of philosophy we are no longer familiar with: the Absolute, not only, as the ultimate cause and ground of being but as the source of the light of truth about it—in a Supreme Being, the Form of the Good, the One, God. And that not in a merely abstract conceptual mode of knowledge, but ultimately in unmediated vision and experience. Understood in that demanding sense,[108] it is not surprising that the ultimate Reality, and the ultimate Truth of philosophy, was not thought to be found at the end of a syllogism but only at the end of the *askêsis* of a 'way', a way of life, the 'philosophic life,' the *bios philosophikos*.[109] In that sense early Christian writers could refer to Christianity as the 'true philosophy.'[110] It is in that sense that there could be the experience of conversion to philosophy. It is out of that sense there could develop the philosophical *genre* known as the *protreptic*, an 'exhortation' to such conversion. That was the genre of Cicero's *Hortensius*, which 'converted' Augustine.

Thirteen years later, after conversion to Christianity, it is still to 'philosophy' that he sees himself called in the Cassiciacum *Dialogues*,

---

105 Conf. VI 14, 24.

106 Which in fact was Augustine's own final project on returning to Africa after conversion and Baptism—Conf. IX 8, 17.

107 See Porphyry's Life of Plotinus; cf. Pierre Courcelle, Recherches sur les Confessions de Saint Augustin, Paris 1950, 178 f.; relevant too of course is Augustine's own sojourn with his group in Cassiciacum, from which issued his first philosophical Dialogues in the months between his Christian conversion and Baptism.

108 Implicit in Conf. III 4.

109 See e.g. the account of the 'ascent' in Plato's Symposium, 209e f.; cf. his Seventh Letter, 344b, on the long way to the moment when 'at last in a flash understanding . . . blazes up, and the mind . . . is flooded with light'; cf. Augustine, De civ. Dei IX 16, quoting Apuleius to the same effect; Plato describes the *bios philosophikos* and its rationale in the Phaedo, 62d ff, and cf. Rep. 474b ff.

110 A term the lost understanding of which brought suspicion on Erasmus when he revived it! In an earlier age Clement of Alexandria could call one of his works the Protrepticus—to the 'true philosophy.'

and it is to 'philosophy' that he 'exhorts' their dedicatees. 'Wake up, wake up!,' he cries to his friend Romanianus (whom he had himself inducted into Manicheanism), inviting him to give up worldly pursuits and falsehoods for the life of true philosophy'.[111] He has just done that himself, withdrawn into the bosom of philosophy, *in gremium philosophiae*. It is she that has delivered him wholly from 'that abyss of irreligion (*superstitione*) into which I had precipitated you along with myself . . . It is she who promises to show us the most true (*verissimum*) and invisible God, and already has begun to do so in stages, as it were through luminous clouds.'[112] This 'showing' is 'promised from the philosophy to which I invite you, the truth proclaimed to those who love it, and far removed from the profane, in the richest of all the oracles of knowledge'[113]—obviously the Scriptures. And for that enlightenment of Romanianus Augustine prays daily to 'the Power and the Wisdom itself of the Supreme God, revealed by the Christian mysteries as none other than the Son of God.'[114]

Five years later, in 391, the quest, the problem, and its scriptural solution are set out much more systematically in the *De utilitate credendi*, written to one Honoratus to win him back from the Manichean heresy into which Augustine himself had led him. The quest is the quest for Truth, *Veritas*, 'for which as you know, we burned with a passionate love from earliest adolescence.'[115] The problem is to prove that the Manicheans are wrong in attacking 'those who follow the *authority* of Catholic *faith*' rather than *reason* in the quest for truth, to prove that believers, before they are capable of perceiving 'that truth which is seen only by the purified mind . . . are strengthened precisely by *believing*, and prepared for the God who alone will enlighten them.'[116] That was the only reason that kept Augustine himself with the Manicheans for nearly nine years— their promise to 'compel' no one to *believe* before truth was investigated by, and made accessible to, the light of reason:[117] And 'who would not be seduced by such a prospect, especially the soul of an adolescent hungry for truth, even to the point of pride and garrulity in argument with learned men in the schools?!'[118] The solution is twofold—to establish the necessity of *believing*, and to establish that it is Scripture which is to be believed.

The necessity of believing does not mean eliminating reason, but establishing the *priority* of believing—Augustine always conjoins both

---

111 See A.D. Nock, Conversion, Oxford, pb. ed. 1961, chap. XI on Conversion to Philosophy; Paul Aubin, Le Problème de la 'Conversion', Paris 1963.
112 Contra Academicos I 7, 3; cf. De beata vita, I 1 ff.
113 Id. I 1, 1.
114 Id. II 1, 1.
115 De util. cred. I 1.
116 Id., I 2; cf. Con. Faustum XII 46.
117 Ibid.
118 Ibid.

ways to the truth, 'authority' and reason, *auctoritas* and *ratio*.[119] The priority of believing exists at different levels, from the *moral* inability of reason
to attain supreme Truth, up to that *philosophical* necessity of believing
which emerges from the implications of epistemology—namely that
reason itself depends on belief in its ultimate unproven and unprovable
presuppositions.[120] The same argument is used in *De utilitate credendi*, at
different levels of its application. Firstly at the highest philosophical
level, in XIII 28f. The search for Truth and Wisdom implies the a priori
belief that despite the variety and the dissensions of philosophical schools,
it does exist. 'For what, I ask you, is it that we are in search of with such
effort and desire? What is it that we want to attain? Where is it that we
want to arrive? Is it to somewhere we do not even believe to exist or concern us? There is nothing more self-contradictory and preposterous than
such a state of mind!'[121] And in any case, given the drive of 'philosophy',
both in Platonism and in Augustine's own Christian Platonism, towards
the visionary and experiential level of knowledge already noted, a higher
illumination is necessary. It is belief, faith, that provides the *askêsis*
towards that illumination.[122]

Lower down the scale, faith is implied even in the choice among
the options of where to look for the answer to the quest.[123] And on the
lowest and broadest plane of all Augustine demonstrates at length the
extent to which all human life, individual and social, is based on
knowledge not known as *proven* but accepted on trust, belief, in other
words faith.[124]

When it comes to making a choice of the 'authority' (*auctoritas*) in
which to put one's faith, Augustine is fond of the argument from the
authority that accrues to Scripture and Christianity from the fact of their
universal diffusion throughout the world—that fact cannot be without
providential significance. This argument is made more explicit in *De
utilitate credendi*. In view of man's need of an 'authority', 'what more
indulgent and generous could be done by God than that the very

---

119 E.g. De ordine II 98, 26 ff, De vera religione XXIV 43 ff; in the former, loc. cit.,
   he is explicit: 'Of necessity we are led to knowledge in two ways, by authority and
   by reason. Temporally authority comes first, but in logic reason has priority.'
120 See n. 30.
121 Loc. cit., 29; cf. XIV 30, and the occasional modern argument that 'rational'
   science presupposes 'faith' in the 'rationality' of its object, i.e. the universe, in
   general and in its particulars.
122 See n. 116; cf. De util. cred. XVI 24: 'It is therefore perverse and preposterous to
   want to *see* Truth in order to purify your spirit, when in fact it is the other way
   round—you purify your spirit in order to see.'
122 See e.g. De util. cred. VII 14 ff.
123 Id. X 23—XII 26.
124 See e.g. De vera religione III 3–5, Conf. VI 5, 8 and 11, 19; XI 2,3: 'No, it is not
   for nothing that You have willed so many umbral and mysterious pages to be
   written . . .'

Wisdom of God himself, authentic, eternal and immutable . . . should deign to become man?'[125] 'This, believe me, is the soundest *auctoritas* . . . this is the *conversion* to the true God from the fate of this world. It is the sole *auctoritas* which moves those who lack wisdom (*sapientiam*) to hasten towards it.'[126] And its claims are doubly supported, 'in part by miracles, in part by the multitude of its followers.'[127] Moreover, whatever is in its Scriptures, 'believe me, is lofty and from God: in them is truth entirely, together with a discipline (*disciplina*) finely adapted to the renewing and restoring of souls: so well regulated in fact that nobody can fail to draw from it to the measure that answers his own needs, provided only that he comes to draw from its well with devotion and reverence, as true religion demands.'[128]

* * *

We have been sketching the larger and wider context of Augustine's quest, within which his truth-claims for Scripture are better understood. We now come to a more systematic setting out of the exact measure of that 'truth entirely' which is the measure both of his own quest and of the context of Scripture.

To set that out as briefly and succinctly as possible, we can draw upon a multi-volume work by a contemporary philosopher, Karl Jaspers on *The Great Philosophers.*[129] Among the 'greats'—great because they are the great founders and perennially fertilizing fountains of thought—along with Parmenides, Socrates, Plato, Plotinus *et al*, he includes St Augustine.[130] But what more exactly constitutes their greatness—including, necessarily, that of Augustine? *Qu'est-ce que la grandeur?* Jaspers asks.[131]

The answer is in a certain totality and universality of range. 'The great man is like a reflection of the *whole* of being, *infinitely interpretable*. He is its mirror or its representative . . . He lets himself be guided by the all-inclusive (*l'englobant*) . . . greatness is there where the real . . . becomes by this distant reflection a symbol of the *whole* . . . greatness is that which has something of the *universal* in it . . . '[132] 'From the great thinkers there emanates an energy which makes ourselves grow by our

---

125 De util. cred. XV 33.
126 Id. XVI 34.
127 Ibid.
128 Id. VI 13.
129 Die Grossen Philosophen, in the original German; I refer to it in the French translation, Les Grands Philosophes, Paris 1972.
130 In vol. 2—to the full dimensions of Augustine's thought, reason and 'authority', philosophy and revelation in Scripture.
131 Vol. 1, 20.
132 Ibid., italics mine.
133 Id. 22, italics mine.

own freedom: they fill us with the world of the invisible, whose *figures* they unveil and make visible, the world and its figures whose language they enable us to read.'[133] 'The existence of the Greats is like a guarantee against nothingness (*le néant*). To see them is itself a satisfaction beyond compare.'[134]

In such passages we already find expressions which we have found in or ourselves used about, St. Augustine on Scripture, e.g. 'infinitely interpretable', *interprétable à l'infini*. And to develop his idea he quotes *in extenso* the great passage in the first-century Longinus' *On the Sublime* which we have already referred to and quoted from.[135] The passage not only expresses that 'wholeness', 'all-inclusiveness', and sense of the 'infinite' that are Jaspers' criteria of greatness. It is also expressed in language characteristic of Longinus' work as a whole, the language of the trans-conceptual drive to unmediated *vision* of the 'whole'. 'For greatness produces *ecstasy* rather than mere persuasion in the hearer; and the combination of wonder (*thaumasion*) and astonishment (*ekplêxis*) always proves superior to the merely persuasive and graceful.'[136] We have already noted this dimension in the 'philosophy' of Platonism and of Augustine.

The relevance of the above to the wider context of St Augustine's sense of the ever-inexhaustible meaning of Scripture is that nobody provides better expressions of Jaspers' criteria of greatness—'wholeness' or totality, 'all-inclusiveness,' 'universality'. There is no need to cite again all the passages that imply precisely *interprétable à l'infini*. We can now draw attention to more precise philosophical statements of them.

One of the Cassiciacum *Dialogues* is the *De ordine*. Its theme is stated in the opening sentence: 'to seek out the order of the universe (*ordinem rerum*), and to conform ourselves to it, as befits all existents, to seek out the order of the *whole* (*universitatis*) which contains and governs this world . . .' It has been remarked that all is not orderly in Augustine's book about order, but only the holistic range of the question concerns us here. And towards the end he gives us a résumé, 'lest anyone think we have embraced too vast a subject.'[137] The ultimate principle of order is in 'that supreme law and supreme principle of order in the universe.'[138] That supreme law and supreme principle is one of the transcendentals of all being, unity. Every existent is an ordered unity, a one. That metaphysical fact can be explained only by ascending to an ultimate all-ordering, transcendent One. And the ascent is through—again—an *askêsis* of study leading to the wisdom (*sapientia*) 'by which one becomes capable of understanding the universal order, that is, of discerning the two worlds [the material and the spiritual] and the Father himself of

134 Id. 23.
135 Id. 24; see n. 96.
136 Longinus, op cit., I 4.
137 De ord., II 18, 47.
138 Ibid.

the universe, whom the soul knows only in knowing how far it knows Him not.'[139]

Some four years later, in 390, all this is expressed in a much more analytic and systematic way in what amounts to Augustine's first ordered *summa* of his thought to date, the *De vera religione*, written to convert Romanianus, on foot of a promise made to him in the course of his 'protreptic' to him in *Con. acad.* II 3,8.[140] Here, from the opening sentence, the dimensions of 'true philosophy' and of 'true religion' are equivalently defined as identical. 'The way of every good and blessed (*beatae*) life is established in the true religion, in which the one God is worshipped, and in which, by reverent purification of spirit, we come to know the Ground and Principle (*principium*) of all existents, the *principium* by which the universe (*universitas*) begins, is completed, and contained.'[141] In Greek 'philosophy' only the Platonists came to that realisation, that 'there is one God, superior to our minds, by whom all life and the whole universe was made'[143]—through his Truth, *per ejus Veritatem*.[144] But Platonism failed to achieve the *auctoritas* and the universality of Christianity and its Scriptures.[145] If Plato were asked today how the soul could be purified for the seeing of 'the immutable form of [all] things . . . he would reply, I believe, that this can be achieved by no man, or by no human teaching, but only by interior illumination from the Power itself and the Wisdom of God.'[146] The only *Principium* and the only light to it is the One declared in St. John's Prologue—the *Principium* through whom 'all things were made, and without whom nothing was made.'[147] It is in this holistic sense that he interprets the Trinity itself as the *Principium* (*arkhê*) of all things. For . . . 'we need to know the following three things about every created being: who made it, by what means, and why?'[148] The pre-eminence of Plato and the Platonists is due to the fact that they seem to have had a conception of God that enabled

---

139 Ibid.
140 Cf. De vera rel. VII 12.
141 Id. I 1; *principium* of course translates not only Gen 1:1 and Jn 1:1, but also the age-old Greek term for the ultimate metaphysical ground of reality, 'a*rkhê* of all things', e.g. Plotinus in Enn. I 3, 1; VI 9, 3; VI 9, 5; in its triadic nature of One, Nous and Soul it is replaced by the Christian Trinity see Conf. VII 9, 13 and De civ. Dei VIII 4 ff—with which cf. De vera rel. XVI 32 f.
142 They 'represent the closest approximation to our Christian position,' De civ. Dei VIII 9.
143 De vera rel. II 2.
144 Id. III 3.
145 Id. III 4 ff.
146 Id. III 3; 1 Cor 1:24; cf. Conf VII 21, 27, in conclusion to his reflections on what St. Paul on Christ had to offer, but not the Platonists: 'In astonishing ways these truths penetrated the very core of my being as I read that least of your apostles; I had considered [or read] your works and been stricken with awe (*expaveram*)'.
147 De vera rel. III 4.
148 De civ. Dei XI 24; cf. XI 21.

them to find in Him the Cause of existence, the Principle of understanding it, and the Order according to which life should be lived.'[149] And that is the rationale of their triple division of philosophy into metaphysics, logic and ethics. All other philosophical systems must yield to the Platonists, who 'recognize the *true* God as the Author of being, the Source of the light of truth about it, and the Dispenser of the beatitude [that is its purpose].[150] But do not these three questions (Who? How? Why?) and their answers intimate the revealed Trinity?[151] They do—their very necessity makes creation itself an image of the Trinity.[152] More specifically in the attribution of the respective roles of the Three Persons in Creation. The Father is the source, the Son-and-Word is the means and the light, the Holy Spirit is the purpose—the Good and its correlative Beatitude.[153]

'It is the Trinity, whole and entire, that is intimated in its works. And it is from the same Trinity that the Holy City, the celestial city of the holy angels, derives her origin, her form, and her beatitude. For if we ask *whence* she is, the answer is that it is God who founded her; and if we ask whence her wisdom, the answer is that it is God who illuminates her; and if we ask whence her beatitude, the answer is that it is in God she has her joy. By *subsisting* in God she has her degree of being; by *contemplating* Him she is enlightened; by *cleaving* to him she has joy. She is, she sees, she loves. She is strong in God's eternity, she shines in God's truth, she is blissful in God's goodness.'[154]

* * *

Such are the dimensions, holistic, 'totalizing', infinite indeed, of the cadre within which only, as we have said, Augustine's assertions of the inexhaustible meaning of Scripture, its *mira profunditas*, can be adequately understood. It remains to show, in conclusion, that he does explicitly situate the study of Scripture within such a comprehensive 'philosophical' framework. That can be shown from his own manual on the methodology of Scriptural exegesis, the *De doctrina Christiana*, already referred to. In a way, and within the limits of its purpose, it too is a little *summa* of Augustine's thought, in so far as the axes and outlines of that thought are expressly used here to draw the 'horizon' within which Scripture is to be studied professionally.[155]

149 Id. VIII 4: cf. XI 24 f, and De vera rel. XVI 32 f.
150 De civ. Dei VIII 5.
151 See e.g. id. XI 23.
152 Id. XI 24 ff.
153 Id. XI 24.
154 Ibid.; cf. De vera rel. XII 26 on the destiny of fallen mankind restored: 'It will return from multiplicity and mutability to the unchanging One, reformed through the Wisdom itself unformed but through whom all things are formed and informed, and it will have joy in God through the Holy Spirit, who is the Gift of God.'
155 And for how insistent he is on 'professionalism' see the Prologue, and II 8, 12 ff.

The whole first Book is devoted to drawing that horizon—in fact an infinitely receding horizon. And once again it is coloured by Platonist 'philosophy' adapted to the purposes of the 'true philosophy', but it is not to our own purposes to dwell on that here. All learning concerns either existents (things, *res*) or their signifiers (signs, *signa*). Book I will deal with *res*.[156] It goes on to deal with them by establishing the ontological scale of *res*, the great chain of being, as it were, and the corresponding great scale of *values* in the scale of being of the existents. The scale of values is determined by Augustine's fundamental distinction between things to be 'enjoyed' (*frui*) and those to be merely 'used' (*uti*).[157] The terms are defined. 'To "enjoy" something is to cleave to it for its own sake [i.e. its own intrinsic value, as an end in itself]. But to "use" something is to employ it merely as a *means* to the obtaining of that which you love [i.e. because it has its own intrinsic value, and is an end in itself].'[158] The *res* to be enjoyed make us blessed (*beatos*), while the *res* to be merely used are such because they are only the means that keep and sustain us on the way to that blessedness (*beatitudo*), 'in order that we may attain and adhere to the *res* that make us blessed (*beatos*).'[159]

But in Augustine *beatitudo*, blessedness, is an *absolute* value, the absolute end in itself.[160] It is logical then that only the absolute Reality has this absolute intrinsic value. 'Consequently the things to be "enjoyed" are the Father, the Son and the Holy Spirit, self-identical Trinity, the unique and supreme Reality . . . if "Reality" it be and not rather the *Cause* of all realities—if even "Cause" it may be called. For it is not easy to find a name appropriate to such a transcendent Reality . . . one God from whom all things, through whom all things, towards whom all things.'[161] That is the 'horizon' and that is the whole meaning (*summa*) of Book I, and the whole meaning of Scripture and of God's whole temporal dispensation is to enable us to know this absolute Reality and to attain to its absolute Value.[162]

Such emphasis on absolutes might seem to short-circuit *contingent* realities, with their truth and value, and the range of truth he attributes to Scripture in the passage already quoted from *De doct. Chr.* II 42,63. We must recall a number of corrective factors. Firstly there is his constant insistence, especially against the Manicheans, that the scale of being is a

156 De doctrina Christiana I 2, 2.
157 I 2, 3.
158 I 4, 4.
159 I 3, 3.
160 See e.g. earlier references to the repose of the 'eternal Sabbath' in which both the Conf. and the De civ. Dei culminate; and of course the much-quoted Conf. I 1, 1: 'You have made us oriented towards Thyself, and our heart is unquiet until it repose in Thee.'
161 I 5, 5; Rom 11:36.
162 I 35, 39.

scale of *degrees* of being, from the highest to the lowest, every level of which has its corresponding degree of truth, goodness and value.[163] We recall too the Trinitarian imagery already referred to in *De civ. Dei* XI 24f. Similarly the supreme creative Wisdom itself pervades all creation, 'reaches with power from end to end of the world ordering all things in beauty.'[164] Created reality is everywhere so transparent to that informing, ordering, and consequently beautifying Wisdom that it provides one of Augustine's principal proofs for the existence of God, by ascent from the image to the Reality.[165] And its aesthetic dimension is such that von Balthasar can include St. Augustine among the great theologians of *glory*.[166]

Finally, in *De doct. Chr.* II 19,19 ff, Augustine sets out at length and in detail 'a matter of supreme importance' as a 'professional qualification' for the study of Scripture—the study of the complete curriculum of the Greco-Roman ideal of liberal education, in the humanities, science, and philosophy. Not of course as though those disciplines were an ultimate end in themselves, but rather as steps intrinsic to the scale of being and truth. They are a necessary propaedeutic in the ascent of the mind to the supreme Being and Truth from which they derive.[166a] Understanding is not complete until the searcher understands 'on what *ground* those things are "true" which he has only "sensed" to be true, and on what ground those things are not only true but immutably true which he has understood to be immutably true.'[167] That demands turning round to see all particular and partial truths in the light of 'the ultimate immutable Truth which is *above* the human mind' as the Source of its light.[168] That is the unique God 'from whom he knows that all things have their being.'[169] He who does not know that can appear 'learned' (*doctus*), but by no manner of means 'wise' (*sapiens*)![170]

All this is Platonist-coloured, but Augustine has already been at pains to set it out systematically on a uniquely scriptural foundation in *De doct.*

---

163 See e.g. Conf. VII 11, 17; 13, 19 and 15, 21.
164 De libero arbitrio, II 11, 124; cf. Wis 8:1.
165 Id. II 8 ff; and cf. Rom 1:20, also echoing Wis 7:22 ff.
166 The Glory of the Lord, vol. II.
166a Cf. De ord. II 10, 28 f.; De musica VI; the latter 'demonstrates how from corporeal and even spiritual but still mutable rhythms we arrive at the immutable rhythms (*numeri*) which are the attributes of the immutable Truth, so that by those mutable rhythms the invisible perfections of God are revealed to us in their stamp on created things'—Retractationes, I 6.
167 De doct. Chr. II 38, 57.
168 Ibid.; cf. Conf. VII 10, 16.
169 De doct. Chr. II 38,57.
170 Ibid.; cf. Plato, Rep. 551b f, and 531f. on 'dialectic', the ascent from the hypothetical axioms of the individual sciences to the ultimate non-hypothetical precondition of truth, the axiom-of-all-axioms, and the pages on it in A.E. Taylor, Plato, London, 1960 ed., 291f.; also Plotinus, Enn. I 3, and Augustine himself, already in De ordine II 11, 30f.

Chr. II 7,9–11.[171] Its purpose there is, again, to outline the framework within which Scripture is to be studied and interpreted, in particular the epistemological (and morally conditioned) levels at which its meaning is to be sought. They are on an ascending scale of seven stages, based on what we have come to know as the seven gifts of the Holy Spirit—taken from Ps 110:10 and Is 11:2–3. They are, in ascending order: the reverential fear of the Lord, piety, knowledge, fortitude, counsel, understanding, and at the summit, wisdom. Augustine sets out the framework also to make clear which level of interpretation he is going to speak about in his present work—that of *knowledge, scientia,*[172] the third stage.

It is at the fourth and following stages that 'higher' insight begins. The fourth is the turning point, literally a turning, a 'conversion'[174]— 'away from transient things and towards the eternal, that is, towards the Unity unchanging and self-identical that is the Trinity.'[175] 'When one has glimpsed it glowing in the distance, within the narrow limits of his capacity, and discovers that the weakness of his sight cannot endure such light,'[176] he then enters on the fifth stage—one of deeper spiritual purification.[177] At the sixth stage he 'purifies that eye by which God may be seen—in so far as He can be seen by those who die to this world . . .'[178] At this stage that Light begins to appear more certain (*certior*), and more tolerable (*tolerabilior*), but still only 'through a glass darkly.'[179] The seventh and last step is the ascent to wisdom, 'which gives him the supreme joy (*perfruitur*) of peace and tranquillity,'[180] in other words the *beatitudo* that is the concomitant of the supreme *Veritas* and *Sapientia.*[181] ' "The fear of the Lord is the *beginning* of Wisdom" . . . From it to transcendent subsistent Wisdom these are the steps. . . .'[182]

More than twenty years later, as he approaches the completion of one of his greatest works, speculative, spiritual and psychological, the subject

171 Described as 'pièce maîtresse de la synthèse augustinienne' in an extended note on the passage in Oeuvres de Saint Augustin, vol. XI, Le Magistère Chrétien, text, translation and notes by G. Combès and M. Farges, Paris 1949, 568–570; see references there to the numerous other *loci* in Augustine on the same theme—the steps of 'ascent.' It should also be observed at this point that the concepts of *veritas* and *sapientia* (Greek *sophia*), which we have used so much, are not only Greek and philosophical but also profoundly biblical, as any concordance shows.
172 De doct. Chr. II 7, 10 and II 8, 11.
173 On the difference between *scientia* and *sapientia* see e.g. De Trinitate XII 14, 21 ff.
174 *Se avertens convertit...*
175 De doct. Chr. II 7, 10.
176 Cf. Conf. VII 10, 16.
177 De doct. Chr. II 7, 11.
178 Ibid.
179 Ibid.; 1 Cor 13:12.
180 Ibid.
181 See e.g. Conf. X 23, 34, on *beata vita, quae non est nisi gaudium de veritate.*
182 De doct. Chr. II 7, 11.

is still that transcendent Wisdom—and based still on Is 11:2–3.[183] 'It is this contemplative wisdom that the Scriptures, in my opinion, call "wisdom" exclusively (*sapientiam proprie*), and specifically distinguished from "knowledge" (*scientia*): the wisdom of man indeed, but acquired only from the One who, by our participation in Him, can make the rational and intellectual soul truly wise.'[183a] And, extraordinarily in such a work and after such a span of time, he relates that wisdom to the decisive event of his reading Cicero's *Hortensius* some forty years before. The passage is worth quoting, because it gives us the savour of what a 'protreptic' was, and gives us an insight into why this particular one had such a definitive effect on Augustine.

'This is the contemplative wisdom that Cicero commends [although he does not know its source, as Augustine has noted] at the end of his dialogue *Hortensius*, when he says':

> This is our great hope as we ponder night and day, and sharpen the understanding which is the fine point of the mind (*mentis acies*) and take care it does not get blunt, that is to say as we live in philosophy; either that we will have a cheerful sunset to our days when we have completed our tasks, and an untroubled and quiet quenching of life, if this capacity of ours to perceive and be wise is mortal and fleeting; or else, if we have eternal and divine souls, as the ancient philosophers agreed, and they the greatest and by far the most brilliant, we must suppose that the more these souls keep always to their course, that is to reason and to passionate enquiry, and the less they mix themselves up in the tangled vices and errors of men, the easier will be their ascent and return to heaven.[184]

The culminating Book of the *Confessions*, XIII, is also organized in seven stages, based on the seven days of the creation narrative. In their figurative meaning[185] they also are stages of ascent, from the dark formlessness (*informitas*)[186] illumined and informed by the light to which it turned and clove on the first day,[187] up to the 'renewal of the human spirit in [God's] "image and likeness",' so that 'submitting itself to Him alone it needs no human *auctoritas*.'[188] But between those two extremes of darkness and the unmediated light of God's *auctoritas*, there is

183 De Trinitate (AD399–419), Book XIV.
183a Id. XIV 19, 26; on the distinction between *scientia* and *sapientia* see also Conf. XIII 18, 23.
184 Ibid.; translation, with slight modification, by Edmund Hill, O.P., in Saint Augustine: The Trinity, New York 1991.
185 Summarized in Conf. XIII 34, 49.
186 See n.50 to Conf. XII 6,6 above—in the total context of XII 3,3 ff, on the *informitas* referred to in Gen. 1:2: *terra erat invisibilis et incomposita*; see also XIII 3,4; 5,6; 12,13, and many other *loci* in Augustine.
187 Conf. XIII 3, 4.
188 Id. XIII 34, 49.

established the mediated '*auctoritas* of [God's] Book.'[189] And already in
its opening two verses the Trinity is glimpsed 'darkly.'[190] For God, who
made the heavens and the earth, is the Father. And the 'Beginning'
(*Principium*) in which He made them is the '*Principium* of our wisdom,
the *Principium* which is your Wisdom born of You, equal to You and co-
eternal.'[191] And looking further, 'behold, your "Spirit was borne over the
waters" . . . There, my God, is your Trinity, Father, Son and Holy
Spirit, Creator of every creature.'[192]

Augustine repeatedly describes the *auctoritas* of Scripture figuratively
as a '*firmament* of authority,' *firmamentum auctoritatis*,[193] an analogy based
on the figurative sense of Gen 1:6–8, on the dividing of the waters above
the heavens from those below by a firmament or vault.[194] Augustine sees
the figurative sense of the waters above and the waters below as referring
to the inhabitants of the lower material world and those of the transcendent immaterial heaven. In that higher world the supercelestial hosts
of the angels 'do not need to lift their eyes to this firmament [of
Scripture] and to get to know your word by reading it. For they always
behold your face, and in that face they read your eternal will without
utterance in syllables of time.'[195] Not so those who live in the world of
time and materiality, on pilgrimage through it, and seeing only in a glass
darkly. They need a mediating *auctoritas*. And that is 'the firmament of
your Book, the firmament of your ever concordant words, which you set
over us by the ministry of mortal men.'[196] By their very mortality the
auctoritas of the sacred writers has become all the greater and more
universal. For while they lived their words were not widely known. But by
their death 'the reinforcing firmament (*solidamentum*), the authority of
the words You sent out through them, was stretched out sublimely and
universally over everything that lies below.'[197] The preachers of this Word
of God pass from this life, but 'his Scripture is stretched out over the
peoples to the end of time.'[198] And we should complement the life of
action in the world by rising to the delights of contemplating that Word
of life . . . firmly established in the firmament of Scripture, from there

189 Ibid.
190 Id. XIII 5, 6; cf. 1 Cor 13:12.
191 Conf. XIII 5, 6.
192 Ibid.; cf. XIII 11, 12.
193 Id. XIII 15, 16; cf. 18, 22.
194 Ibid.
195 Id. XIII 15, 18.
196 Id. XIII 15, 16.
197 Ibid.; and once again, the characteristically personal, lyrical 'confessional' grace-
       note: 'I know not Lord, I know not any words of such "pure alloy" [Ps 11:6],
       none that could so powerfully move me to confession . . . or call me to worship
       You for your own sake alone.'
198 Conf. XIII 15, 18.

to shine on the world, as do the heavenly bodies from the earthly firmament.[199]

Insight into the full dimensions of Scripture's meaning depends precisely on a contemplation based on a distinction parallel to that constant motif of Augustine which we noted earlier: Scripture's fusing of surface simplicity for the simple with inexhaustible depths of meaning for the more intellectually and spiritually advanced. That is the distinction between the 'spiritual' and the 'carnal' (*spiritales et carnales*) members of the Church—for there too 'God has created a "heaven and earth"'![200] The distinction is based on a number of Pauline texts, especially 1 Cor 2:10–3:3 and Rom 7:14. We need not here go into all the complexities of that distinction in Augustine.[201] For our purposes 1 Cor 3:1f suffices—in its total context:[202] 'Brothers, I myself was unable to speak to you as people of the Spirit (*spiritalibus, pneumatikois*): I treated you as people of the senses (*carnalibus, sarkikois*), still infants in Christ. What I fed you with was milk, not solid food, for you were not yet ready for it. . .'

The reference to the Spirit is to be given its full value: for, as is clear from both Paul[203] and Augustine, the reference is to a charism, a gift of the Spirit, if not even of mystical insight. 'It is no longer the voice of the Apostle that speaks, but yours in him, You who sent your Spirit upon him from on high, through Him who ascended up on high, and opened the floodgates of his gifts that the rush of the river might make your City joyous,' the City for which '"the friend of the Bridegroom" sighs, having already the "first fruits of the Spirit" within himself.'[204] It is in the Pauline context of the charisms of the Spirit that Augustine speaks of the *spiritales* in *Conf.* XIII 18, and distinguishes specifically the 'word of knowledge' from 'the word of wisdom' (1 Cor 12:8). The 'word of knowledge' deals only with those sacred signs (*sacramenta*) that are subject to temporal change. It differs from 'the radiant light of wisdom' as the stars of night differ from the dawning of the day.[205]

It is the charism of the *spiritales* to speak this 'word of wisdom' about the deeper depths of Scripture. Theirs to 'shine in the firmament' that

199 Id. XIII 18, 22.
200 Id. XIII 12, 13.
201 See the extensive note to Conf. XIII 12, 13 f in ed. cit.
202 E.g. 1 Cor 2:13: 'We speak not in the learned words of human wisdom (*sapientia, sophia*), but in the way the Spirit teaches us ...'; and cf. 1:13 f. on philosophical speculation contrasted with the Wisdom of God.
203 Cf. 1 Cor 12–14, and Conf. XIII 18, 23.
204 Conf. XIII 13, 14; Jn 3:29 and Rom 8:23; on 'the first fruits of the Spirit,' *spiritus primitias*, see the use of the expression in Conf. IX 10, 24 to evoke Augustine's and Monica's mystical experience at Ostia: 'While we were talking of these things together and longing for [the region of inexhaustible abundance where You graze Israel for ever on the pastures of Truth], for one brief instant, for one whole beat of the heart, we did come into contact with it; we sighed, and leaving the first fruits of our spirit bound to it, we returned to the time-bound sound of our own voices...'
205 XIII 18, 23.

'the heavens may recount his glory,' and thus 'divide the light of the perfect—though not yet the light of the angels—from the darkness of the little ones—though not the darkness of those without hope.'[206] The *spiritalis* is of the new creation of '"man renewed in the knowledge of God according to the image of Him who created him," and having become *spiritalis* he "judges all things"—all things, that is, which it is permissible to judge—and he himself "is judged by none".'[207] 'All things, that is, which it is permissible to judge!' For even the *spiritales*, even if in authority themselves, 'judge not the spiritual truths which shine "in the firmament": it is not for man to judge so sublime an *auctoritas* . . . They may not judge that Book of yours, even when something in it is unclear; rather do we *submit* our understanding to it, and hold it as a certainty that even what is closed to our eyes in it is said with the rightness of Truth.'[208]

And in this matter of 'judging' there is a wider range of implication then meets the eye at once. So often in Augustine what appears to be philosophical is found to be also scriptural, and *vice versa*. Here 'judging' is a scriptural term. But it is also Augustine's technical term in epistemology—and the metaphysical implications he finds in it. We looked at Augustine's epistemology earlier, in particular the argument from the necessity and immutability inherent in any *particular* truth—best illustrated in mathematical truths[209]—to the requirement of a ground and precondition of that necessity and immutability in an absolute, transcendent Truth, eternal, immutable and unconditioned.[210] The argument becomes a proof of the existence of God, with whom that Truth is identified and who is the ultimate unconditioned 'axiom' of all the merely provisional though apparently 'necessary' axioms on which the various theoretical disciplines hang.[211]

This argument is more immediately intelligible in one of Augustine's favourite areas of its application, in comparative 'judgements' of *value*, as in ethics and aesthetics. To judge that something is morally better or aesthetically more beautiful than another implies immediately a non-empirical, *a priori criterion* of judgement, which by fairly simple analysis is shown to depend on an *absolute* criterion. We see the ethical argument in *De libero arbitrio* II 9,100 ff, succinctly stated in II 10,113; and again in *Conf.* X 20,29 ff, succinctly in X 23,33. There is a fine statement of the aesthetic argument in *Conf.* VII 17,23:

206 XIII 19, 25; Ps 18:2f.
207 XIII 22, 32; 1 Cor 2:15.
208 XIII 23, 33.
209 See e.g. De libero arbitrio II 8, 79 ff.
210 An argument already developed in the Soliloquia, II 1, 1ff—*si quid verum est, veritate utique verum est*, I 15, 27.
211 So stated already in Solil. I 8, 15.

> I was seeking to understand on what ground I approved the
> beauty of corporeal things, and on what principle I made a valid
> judgement . . . when I said: 'This *ought* to be so, that *not* so.'
> Enquiring then on what *basis* I judged when I judged in this way,
> I had found the immutable and true eternity of Truth.

He goes on to trace the actual steps in the argument—

> to find out what light suffused the mind when, without hesitation
> or doubt, 'it proclaimed that the immutable was to be valued above
> the changing. From where in fact did it know of the immutable at
> all? For unless it had in some sense known it, the mind could not
> possibly judge it with such certainty to be valued above the mutable.
> And in the flash of a trembling glance my mind arrived at *That
> Which Is—id quod est* absolutely.'

That is the penumbra to Augustine's quoting of Paul's terminology of
'judging'. That is the sense in which, by analogy, Scripture is the
'firmament', the absolute and universal *auctoritas*, under and in whose
light the *spiritalis* 'judges all things'—but not Scripture itself, rather does
Scripture 'judge' him. Only here below of course, for 'there are other
"waters" above this "firmament", I believe, waters immortal and beyond
all earthly corruption and transience. May they praise your name!'[212]

*   *   *

We opened these pages with an 'overture' of sample thematic texts,
ancient and modern. It would be appropriate to conclude with a 'coda'.
I take one from the late contemporary far-firing Apollo to whom I have
already referred more than once—Hans Urs von Balthasar. It is a passage written in this twentieth century that could have been written by
Augustine in the fourth.

> Thus we can risk making the general proposition that the mean-
> ing of Scripture (where it is in process of development) journeys
> along with history, and this journeying is attested to not merely
> externally but in the details of its text. Of course this raises the
> problem of how this journeying of the word is related to the
> closing of objective revelation at the end of the apostolic age and
> to the completeness of the canon of Scripture. The 'closing' as
> such arises from the definitive and unsurpassable character of
> the divine Word uttered in Jesus; but the fact that the word is
> henceforth present in world history in this fullest form, capable
> of *infinite* assimilation and *interpretation*, is in truth not a 'closing'
> at all but the widest imaginable 'opening'.[213]

212 Conf. XIII 15, 18.
213 Theo-Drama, vol. II, San Francisco 1990, 105—italics mine, in a section on
    Theodramatic Hermeneutics, 91 f.; cf. nn. 56, 88a and 89 above.

The rainbow arc of which that passage is one earthing spans a space even vaster than that from Balthasar to Augustine. Its other earthing is in the Old Testament itself and in pre-Christian Jewish interpretation of it. And that in two stages. Firstly, it appears to be now accepted (*sit venia profano!*) that the Old Testament Scriptures as we have them are the end-product of a process of revising and editing that began already in the sixth-century BC post-exilic period. 'This means that the beginnings of scriptural interpretation are to be looked for within the Scriptures themselves. Scholars now recognize that the making of the Scriptures was already a hermeneutical process in which earlier biblical materials were rewritten in order to make them intelligible and applicable to later situations.'[214]

The second stage in this Jewish, and pre-Christian, hermeneutical process was its systematizing in the professional *Midrash* exegesis of the established texts of the Old Testament. Its core significance for our present purposes is that same ever-inexhaustible openness of Scripture to that ever-inexhaustible interpretability that has been our theme. And its rationale links up with much that we have been saying on that theme— even with certain contemporary approaches to metaphysics.[215] In the first place it is based on the realization that the word of revelation is the Word of God, and therefore of the Transcendent and Infinite—and therefore in the written Scriptures adapted to and 'translated' into the mode of the finite idiom of human language, which inevitably 'conceals' as much it 'reveals' of the infinity and the mystery and the inexhaustibility of the transcendent Word and Reality in the silent depths of which it originates.[216] Therefore, 'Once God has spoken; twice have I heard this.'[217]

In the second place there is the often neglected linguistic factor, in the verbal and syntactical structures of the Hebrew language in which the Old Testament Scriptures were written, so different from the analytic, unidimensional, linear logic of our western languages. 'We must leave the translations, however worthy of respect they may be, and return to the Hebraic text to reveal the strange and mysterious ambiguity or polysemy which the Hebraic syntax permits. In this syntax the words co-

214 Gerald L. Bruns, 'Midrash and Allegory: The Beginnings of Scriptural Interpretation,' in Robert Alter and Frank Kermonde (eds.), The Literary Guide to the Bible, London, Fontana Press ed. 1989, 626; see 638 for remarks on St Augustine in that line.

215 I have in mind such philosophers as Jaspers and Heidegger, with their sense of 'comprehensive', enveloping (*englobant*), transcendent-immanent Being, and of man as the locus of 'openness' to it, as it is revealed-and-concealed in its 'cyphers'; cf. also von Balthasar again, in The Glory of the Lord, passim.

216 See e.g. Emmanuel Levinas, 'Revelation in the Jewish Tradition', in Seán Hand (ed.), The Levinas Reader, Oxford U.K. and Cambridge U.S.A., 1992 repr., 205 f; it is worth noting that Levinas, like Augustine, is a notable philosopher as well as a commentator on Scripture.

217 Ps 62.11, quoted by Levinas, art. cit., 194.

exist, rather than falling immediately into structures of co-ordination and sub-ordination, unlike the dominant tendency in the "developed" or functional languages.'[218]

Consequently—

> the specifically Jewish exegesis of the Scriptures is punctuated by these concerns: the distinction between the obvious meaning and the one which has to be deciphered, the search for this buried meaning and the one which lies deeper still, contained within the first. There is not one verse, not one word, of the Old Testament, if the reading is the religious one that takes it as Revelation, that does not open up an entire world, unsuspected at first, in which the text to be read is embedded. . . . These scribes and doctors. . . would try to extort from the letters all the meanings they can carry or bring to our attention, just as if the letters were the folded wings of the Holy Spirit, and could be unfurled to show all the horizons which the flight of the Spirit can embrace.[219]

218 Levinas, art. cit., 193; cf. the professional qualifications laid down by Augustine in De doct. Chr. II 11, 16.
219 Levinas, ibid., 194; it may be noted too that in the context of this ever-inexhaustible interpretability Levinas in this article also addresses the necessary question of how to give reason its rights (like Augustine), and how to avoid subjectivity in inter-pretation. Cf. Josef Pieper, 'What Does It Mean to Say "God Speaks?"', in his Problems of Modern Faith: Essays and Addresses, Chicago 1985, 117–148.

Augustine's Exegesis of the First Epistle of John

EOIN G. CASSIDY

Written while at the height of his powers, the *Tractatus in Epistulam Iohannis* consists of ten sermons completed between Easter and Pentecost of AD 407.[1] It is small in volume in comparison to the two other commentaries on which he was working simultaneously, namely, the *Enarrationes in Psalmos* and the *Tractatus in Iohannis Evangelium*. Nevertheless, the *Tractatus in Epistulam Iohannis* is rightly regarded as a highly significant piece of writing. It both contains Augustine's most sustained treatment of the motif of *caritas* and constitutes what is generally recognised as the high point of his spiritual writings. No less an authority than Henri Rondet has remarked that, 'Si le précepte de la charité est la clé de l'Ancien et du Nouveau Testament, les *Tractatus in Primam Iohannis* sont la clé de l'exégèse spirituelle d'Augustin'.[2]

Augustine's commentary on 1 Jn has been in recent years the focus of a number of detailed studies, the most celebrated being Paul Agaësse's introduction to the *Sources Chrétiennes* edition of Augustine's commentary on 1 Jn published in 1961;[3] Dany Dideberg's *Saint Augustin et la Première Épître de Saint Jean*, 1975,[4] and Francis de Beer's *L'Amour est Dieu*, 1979.[5] These studies, particularly that by Dany Dideberg, offer the reader a detailed textual comparison of 1 Jn with Augustine's *Tractatus in Epistulam Iohannis*. In consequence, this paper takes a narrower focus and will limit itself to an examination of two issues: the influence on Augustine's exegesis of 1 Jn of the Donatist conflict, and Augustine's theology of *caritas*. The study of these issues is designed to offer the reader an insight both into the context within which Augustine under-

---

1 Cf. D. Dideberg, Saint Augustin et la Première Épître de Saint Jean, Paris 1975, 44–46.

2 H. Rondet, 'Thèmes bibliques, Exégèse augustinienne', Augustinus Magister. Congrès International Augustinien, Paris 1954, iii, 236.

3 P. Agaësse, Saint Augustin, Commentaire de l 1a Première Épître de S. Jean, Paris 1961.

4 D. Dideberg, Saint Augustin et la Première Épître de Saint Jean: Une Théologie de l'Agapé, Paris 1975.

took this particular work of interpretation and the 'pre-understanding' which Augustine brings to all exegesis.

In treating of the topic of Augustine's exegesis of 1 Jn there are a few preliminary questions which must be briefly addressed: had Augustine access to any other commentary on 1 Jn, what was the text of the Bible upon which he based his commentary, and what was Augustine's method of composing and delivering sermons?

Considering the importance of this text for our understanding of the early Christian treatment of the motif of love it is surprising to observe that the only other commentary on this letter which is found in the Fathers of the Church is that written by Clement of Alexandria. Unfortunately, we only know of this work through a Latin translation by Cassiodorus.[6] Given the fact that there is no evidence to suggest either that there existed a Latin translation of Clement's commentary predating that of Cassiodorus or that Augustine had access to the original Greek commentary, we can with a fair degree of certainty rule out any suggestion that Augustine's commentary was influenced by that of Clement or any other of the Fathers.

Regarding the text of the Bible which Augustine would have utilized as he prepared his commentary, the extant manuscripts of Augustine do not allow us to say with absolute certainty which Latin text he is using. However, from a study of comparative versions of the families of the *Vetus Latina* we know that Augustine is using a text that is pre-Vulgate and one which belongs to the T family. The proof is that when T breaks with V Augustine with few exceptions follows T.[7] Where Augustine departs from all known forms of the text, something which he frequently does, this is more likely to be accounted for by the fact that he is citing from memory. What must be recognized is that the homilies were in all probability not written in advance by Augustine but were transcribed by *notarii* who were present in the church as he preached.[8]

At the outset, in examining the exegesis of 1 Jn contained in the *Tractatus in Epistulam Iohannis* it is important to draw attention to the fact that this work cannot be regarded as a commentary in the strict sense of the term. Apart from the fact that the content of the work is influenced to no small extent by the need to counter the Donatist heresy and, in this context, by the need which Augustine felt to

5   F. de Beer, L'Amour est Dieu: La première Épître de Saint Jean selon Saint Augustin en 10 Sermons, Strasbourg 1979.

6   A Latin translation of the commentary by Clement of Alexandria entitled 'Adumbrationes in Epistolas Canonicas' has been reconstructed from Cassiodorus and is to be found in GCS 17 (1909), 203–215. Cf. also the reference to this work in Cassiodorus, De Institutiones, Oxford 1936, 29 lines 16–22.

7   Cf. I Jn. 2,18 where Augustine reads with T. (*puera* as against V. (*filiali*), ed. Walter Theile, Vetus Latina, 1965, 284.

8   Cf. R. J. Deferrari, Augustine's Method of Composing and Delivering Sermons, American Journal of Philology, 40(1922) 193–219.

emphasize the primacy of charity, there is the obvious fact that the *Tractatus* is not a biblical commentary as such but rather a series of homilies which were addressed to the people of Hippo.

It is necessary to reflect briefly on the way in which his method of composing and delivering sermons affected his exegesis of 1 Jn. It seems fairly clear that, although well prepared, Augustine's sermons were delivered extempore and without notes. As mentioned above, they would have been taken down by *notarii* as they were spoken. Consequently, what we have today are copies of the transcripts of the notes of these *notarii*. Furthermore, there is evidence that these transcripts were not extensively revised by Augustine. This is not meant to call into question the accuracy of the commentary which we possess, but merely to alert us to the fact that its content is clearly influenced by extraneous factors, one of which would have been Augustine's sensitivity to the receptiveness of his congregation to the message which he wished to impart. Finally, there is need to keep in mind that the sermons were delivered in a liturgical setting and, in this respect, that these particular homilies were delivered during paschal time and thus contain references to specifically paschal themes.

The constraints imposed by the homiletic form on Augustine's exegesis of 1 Jn can be seen by comparing the structure of the homilies with that of 1 Jn. Apart from digressions imposed by the liturgical calendar such as that on the Emmaus theme in Homily Two and another on prayer in Homily Six, the pastoral concerns of Augustine are evident in the way that his commentaries on the later chapters of John's epistle—ones which stress the importance of love in the Christian community—are far more detailed than the earlier ones. Furthermore, in some of the homilies Augustine either develops themes which are only briefly alluded to by John, such as the motifs of hope and desire in Homily Four, or introduces themes which are not to be found at all in the epistle such as the Pauline motif of the Body of Christ which provides the focus for Homily Ten.

THE PRINCIPLES UNDERLYING AUGUSTINE'S EXEGETICAL METHOD

In attempting to unravel the principles underlying Augustine's exegetical method we are fortunate to possess *De doctrina Christiana*, a detailed and highly informative treatment of this issue.[9] Although it is outside the scope of this paper to reflect at any length on the exegetical principles proposed in this work, it is nevertheless important that we alert ourselves to some of the more important points which he makes. This is par-

---

9 Cf. Madeleine Moreau, 'Lecture du "De doctrina Christiana"', in A.M. La Bonnardière,ed., Saint Augustin et la Bible, Paris 1986, 253–285.

ticularly the case when we advert to the importance of scriptural exegesis in the life and ministry of Augustine. For him the task of exegesis was no mere academic exercise. In fact, it was precisely the young Augustine's inability to interpret the Bible which so manifestly hindered the process of his conversion. He had to struggle to overcome the prejudice fostered by the Manicheans that the Bible was 'quite unworthy of comparison with the stately prose of Cicero'.[10] The struggle was one which was only resolved when in his early 30s he heard Ambrose interpret the Scriptures allegorically and, 'grew more and more certain that it was possible to unravel the tangle woven by those who had deceived both me and others with their cunning lies against the Holy Scriptures.'[11]

Mastering the rules of rhetoric was for Augustine the first indispensable step in the work of exegesis. Armed with the skills of the rhetorician he believed that one could be alert to the tropes in the Bible, thus enabling the interpreter to recognize the difference between the literal and allegorical meaning of an image or passage. This was of capital importance for Augustine as he was constantly alert to the allegorical or what he would regard as the spiritual meaning of a passage.

Given his background as a rhetorician it is not surprising that much of what he understands by the rules of rhetoric are to be found in the writings of Cicero. Nevertheless, he did not slavishly follow Cicero. In Book Three of *De doctrina Christiana* Augustine treats at length in a favourable manner of the seven rules for discerning the allegorical use of language in the Bible put forward by the Donatist Tyconius. For example, accepting the rule entitled 'The Lord and His body'[12] allows one to spot the unity underlying the meaning of certain related images such as the bride and the bridegroom. The rule entitled 'Of Species and Genus'[13] allows one to recognize the universal extension of certain references such as that suggested by the image of the city of Jerusalem. Finally, the rule entitled 'Of Times'[14] alerts one to the symbolic use of synecdoches and numbers in the Bible, something to which Augustine was particularly sensitive.

Although Augustine never underestimated the importance of learning the discipline of rhetoric he repeatedly states that the Bible is only accessible to faith, which he understood as the movement of love. For Augustine the principle of first importance in exegesis is always charity, and it is this principle alone which enables one to comprehend the spiritual meaning of a passage from the Scriptures. As he says, 'Scripture teaches nothing but charity, nor condemns anything except cupidity.'[15] Or again, 'Whoever, therefore, thinks that he understands the divine Scriptures or any part of them so that it does not build the double love of God and of our neighbour does not understand it at

---

10   Conf. III 5,9.
11   Ibid., VI 3, 3.
12   De doctr. Christ. III 31,44.
13   Ibid., III 34,47.
14   Ibid., III 35, 50.
15   Ibid., III 10,15.

all.'[16] If charity is the key to unlocking the meaning of Scripture then understanding the true meaning of love is the indispensable first step in the task of exegesis. It is this conviction which gives credence to the view that a study of the *Tractatus in Epistulam Iohannis* not only gives one an insight into Augustine's understanding of John's treatment of the motif of love, but even more importantly, it gives one a privileged insight into this exegetical principle which underlies all of Augustine's commentaries on the Bible.

THE ATTRACTION FOR AUGUSTINE OF THE FIRST EPISTLE OF JOHN

Unquestionably, the principle reason which attracted Augustine to 1 Jn was his conviction that love is the unique object of Scripture. The first Letter of John is written to reassure his readers that in reciprocal love they live in God and are thus guaranteed salvation. Augustine never ceases to repeat this message. Whether writing against the perfectionist and ascetical ethics of early Gnosticism or against Judaism, John is concerned above all to impress upon his readers that the affirmation of the divinity of Jesus is the sine qua non of communion with God and that reciprocal love is the key to communion with God.[17] In a succession of beautiful images, repeated throughout the Epistle, he affirms that those who love their brothers know God, live in God, are born of God, see God, love God, and are in the true God.

The emphasis on fraternal love in 1 Jn and the community context within which the Epistle was written clearly resonated with both the spirituality of Augustine and the pastoral and monastic setting of his homilies. However, this was not the only thing which would have attracted Augustine to the Epistle. What cannot be disputed is that 1 Jn is also a closely argued critique of all forms of moral elitism, and Augustine was not slow to recognize that moral elitism—a classical feature of Gnosticism—bore clear similarities with the Donatists of the early 5th century. Consequently, it is not surprising that John's insistence on the folly of saying that 'we have no sin in us'[18] and the emphasis on the necessity of grace 'not our love for but God's love for us'[19] found a sympathetic response from one such as Augustine who in his conflict with Donatism was struggling against precisely the same tendencies.

Finally, one should remark the emphasis on teleology which one finds in 1 Jn and the images which John uses to describe the goal of human fulfilment—images which Augustine translated as *contemplatio Dei*,

16   Ibid., I 36, 40.
17   Cf. Ph. Perkins, The Johannine Epistles, Dublin 1979, xiii–xvi; 3–7.
18   1 Jn 1:8.
19   Ibid., 4:10.

adhaerere Dei, and *amor Dei*. It is not only this stress on teleology which would have resonated with Augustine's classical philosophical background but also the images used by John. In particular one notes the way in which John links the love of God with the vision of God. Even the briefest perusal of the Augustinian corpus will reveal that his whole spirituality is based on such a vision whereby the love of God is inseparable from the vision of God.

THE INFLUENCE OF THE DONATIST CONFLICT ON AUGUSTINE'S EXEGESIS OF 1 JN

First confess, then love

The principal theme of 1 Jn is the union of believers with God, a union which is premised on three conditions: renunciation of sin, brotherly love, and faith in Jesus Christ. Chapter One verses five to ten focuses upon this first condition. As John says, 'If we say that we have no sin we deceive ourselves and the truth is not in us.'[20] Faithful to this emphasis Augustine in Homily One, verses four to eight, gives prominence to the need to confess or admit one's sinfulness. Furthermore, just as John in Chapter Three, verses three to nine, returns to this theme, so also Augustine when commenting on this passages in Homily Four, verse three.

In some respects, however, the focus of their deliberations on this theme is different. John is arguing primarily against a form of Gnosticism which did not give full recognition to the sacrificial or atoning nature of Christ's death and resurrection—the denial of the truth of God's redeeming love that is revealed in those who say that they are sinless. Augustine, on the other hand, focuses on the psychological state of those who say that they are without sin and consequently, he interprets these passages from 1 Jn in that light. Commenting on the passage he says,

> If then you confess yourself a sinner the truth is in you, for the truth itself is light. . . . First of all, then, confess and next, love . . . for charity alone can quench transgression. Pride quenches charity: humility strengthens it: charity quenches transgression.[21]

According to Augustine, what is revealed in the attitude of those who refuse to accept their sinfulness is pride and it must be remembered that he consistently held that pride was the sin which most effectively destroyed the possibility of communion with God. The pertinence of this stricture against pride must be seen in the context of the conflict with the

20   Ibid., 1:6
21   In Iohannis Epistulam, tr. I 6.

Donatists. From Augustine's point of view the conflict was rooted in the the assumption by the Donatists that they were more worthy than their fellow Catholics who had apostatized during the persecutions.

In this context therefore it is not surprising to note that the whole thrust of Augustine's commentary on that passage from 1 Jn focuses on the importance of humility and the recognition that pride is the root cause of all schism.[22] Nevertheless, to illustrate to his listeners that this is a faithful interpretation of the spirit of 1 Jn Augustine goes to some trouble to propose John as a model of humility and to show that 1 Jn 2:1 can be interpreted in the light of that vision:

> See how John himself keeps humility . . . Schisms arise when men say, we are righteous; when they say, we sanctify the unclean, we justify the wicked, we ask, we obtain. But what said John? 'If any man sin, we have an advocate with the Father, Jesus Christ the Righteous One.'[23]

Augustine saw in these passages from John a recognition that confession and love—both instances of grace—are the two essential moments in the movement of the soul to God. For Augustine what is common to both is that interior attitude that is signified by humility. His criticism of the Donatists was that they lacked this essential ingredient either to confess that Jesus is the Christ our advocate, or to love Him. They lacked humility.

The love of unity

Towards the end of the first Homily Augustine begins his commentary on the second condition of sharing in the divine life proposed by John (Jn 2:3–12), namely, preserving the commandments of love. In the course of these passages John utilizes a beautiful series of images to highlight the importance of the opposition between love and hatred. These are light and shade, life and death, sight and blindness. Augustine's writings abound in references to these Johannine images, all of which for Augustine stress the centrality in the Christian ethic of fraternal love. However, paradoxically, in his Homilies on 1 Jn Augustine is not primarily interested in emphasizing the importance of this distinction between love and hatred of the brethren but is concerned rather to focus on that quality which distinguishes this love from hatred.

For Augustine, embroiled in conflict with the Donatists, it is the refusal to break the unity of love and the readiness to forgive which

---

22 Cf. *In Iohannis Epistulam*, tr. I 8. Augustine's emphasis that love is incompatible with pride is to be seen ibid., tr. VIII 6–9.

23 Ibid., tr. I 7. The importance which Augustine attached to the virtue of humility is well documented. In particular cf. T.J. van Bavel, 'L'Humanité du Christ comme lac parvulorum et comme via dans la spiritualité de saint Augustin', *Augustiniana* 7 (1957) 245–281.

are the yardsticks that measure the genuineness of one's love. Few
themes occupy a more central place in his homilies on 1 Jn than this
opposition between those who cherish the unity of love and the love
of unity and those who wish to sunder it. The idea that one could love
Christ without seeking to preserve the unity of the members of the
one body was an unfailing source of scandal for him. In Homily One,
verse twelve, one gets a flavour of precisely what Augustine means:

> He cannot be in Christ, who is not in Christ's Body. It is they who
> desert either Christ or the Church who take offence. But we can
> see that in him who loves his brother there is no offence; for the
> lover of his brother endures all things for unity's sake. In the
> unity of charity brotherly love consists.[24]

This is a theme to which Augustine will constantly return in the
course of his homilies. In fact the whole of Homily Ten is focused
upon the destructiveness of attempting to break this unity of the Body
of Christ. The treatment of the motif of the Body of Christ in Homily
Ten is arguably the high point of Augustine's analysis of this Pauline
theme, one which, many would argue, is the focus around which
Augustine's theology is constructed.

In Augustine's mind, the refusal by the Donatists to preserve the unity
of the Church was based on their refusal to forgive those who had
apostatized during the persecutions. It is not therefore surprising that,
in these Homilies, he should also stress the link between love and forgiveness as he does in tr. I 9 and tr. VII 3. It also explains the stress which
he, unlike John, places on love of enemies and not just the love of the
brethren. In the context of Augustine's commentary on 1 Jn the extensive treatment of these themes is an illustration of how, in the midst of
the Donatist controversy, Augustine will use his Homilies on 1 Jn to
develop themes which clearly transcend the limits of strict exegesis but
which allow him to meet the pastoral needs of his congregation.

Affirming Christ not just in words but in deeds and in truth

Few passages in 1 Jn receive a more detailed commentary than the following one from Chapter Three verse eighteen: 'My Children, our love
is not to be just words or mere talk, but something real and active'.
Augustine's version reads *Filioli, non diligamus verbo tantum et lingua sed
opere et veritate*. In Homily Six and Seven Augustine proceeds to explain
what John meant by the phrase 'loving in act and in truth'. Drawing on a
variety of passages from the Letters of St Paul which stress the importance of the subjective intention of the person, Augustine makes the
point that John wishes to emphasize that to love truly it is not sufficient

24 Ibid., tr. I 12.

merely to accomplish charitable acts.[25] Here again one sees Augustine's concern to focus on the psychological state or the interior attitude which animates the charitable actions. It is a concern which reflects his own recognition of the importance of the will, one expressed so succinctly in that phrase from the Confessions, *pondus meum amor meus*.[26] The stress on the intentionality of the action is one which is also clearly influenced by the need to counter the claims of the Donatists to be the authentic followers of Christ. Augustine pursues this theme in Homily Six by drawing on the image from the Beatitudes of the 'pure in heart' which is one of the most widely used images from the Scriptures to be found in the Augustinian corpus. The way in which Augustine takes the liberty here to interpret a difficult passage from 1 Jn by using examples taken from a wide variety of scriptural sources illustrates an important exegetical principle of Augustine not so far adverted to, namely, the unity of the Scriptures. Augustine's exegesis of the Bible was always animated by a recognition that underlying the diverse styles of the different books of the Bible one sees the hand of the one divine Author.

Augustine's commentary on the distinction between loving in word and in deed, which is also to be found in that passage from 1 Jn quoted above, is one that occupies major portions of the third, sixth, and eighth Homilies and one that is also treated in the fifth and seventh Homilies. It was to provide Augustine with one of the main hermeneutical keys with which he unlocks the message of John for his listeners. It enables him to demonstrate wherein lies the basis of the critical Johannine distinction between those who belong to Christ and those who are antichrists, a distinction which is dealt with at length in 1 Jn 2:18–29 and 4:1–6. The point which John is making in these passages is that unless one affirms Christ in the flesh—against Gnostic or Jewish beliefs—one is not of Christ. With characteristic sharpness Augustine develops this Johannine theme to counter Donatism by pointing out that if one denies the Body of Christ or indeed any of the members of the Body one is in fact denying Christ in the flesh—one is an antichrist. Even if the Donatists profess in word that Jesus is the Christ, nevertheless, by their deeds, they are denying that very same profession of faith. The refusal to love the Church or any members of the Church is as much a denial of Christ in the flesh as anything presumed in any Gnostic or Jewish polemics, against which John's distinction between those who belong to Christ and those who are antichrists was directed.

25   Cf. Dideberg's book, cited above, 99–106.
26   Conf. XIII 9,10.

No one who has been begotten by God sins

In 1 Jn 3:9 one finds the following passage,

> No one who has been begotten by God sins
> because God's seed remains inside him,
> he cannot sin when he has been begotten by God.

It does not take much imagination to recognize the difficulty which this verse posed to Augustine in the context of the Donatist crisis. Although meant by John to point out to Gnostic perfectionists the worthiness or holiness of the Christian community, it could easily be misinterpreted to mean that anyone in serious sin is automatically excluded from the Body of Christ and would need to be rebaptized. However, Augustine in Homily Five, verses one to four, turns the argument on its head to make one of his most telling criticisms of the Donatist schism. He agrees that there is a sin, not all sins but a particular sin, which cannot be committed by those begotten by God, and that is the sin against fraternal love. It is certainly a telling argument against the Donatists and one which is arguably faithful to John's use of this phrase, because John in the following ten verses (1 Jn 3:10–19), explains the use of this phrase by highlighting the fact that what distinguishes the children of God from the children of the devil is their love rather than hatred of the brethren. Augustine devotes the whole of his fifth Homily on 1 Jn to emphasizing this link which John makes between the love of God and the love of the brethren.

CARITAS: THE EXEGETICAL PRINCIPLE UNDERLYING
AUGUSTINE'S COMMENTARY ON THE FIRST EPISTLE OF JOHN

If the need to counter the Donatist schism was an important influence on the way Augustine interpreted 1 Jn, it is no less true that the spirituality of Augustine which was centred on the motif of *caritas* provided the lens through which he interpreted this Epistle and indeed the reason why he chose it as the subject of his homilies. Nothing illustrates this better than to quote Augustine himself:

> But I chose it (1 Jn) more particularly because what it specially commends to us is charity. The man who has in himself that of which he hears must rejoice at the hearing.[27]

Again, in the seventh homily Augustine comments on the following celebrated verses from 1 Jn 4:7–9,

> My dear people
> let us love one another

27   In Iohannis Epistulam, Prologue.

> since love comes from God
> and everyone who loves is begotten by God
> and knows God.
> Anyone who fails to love can never have known God,
> because God is love.

Augustine concludes his commentary on this verse in the following manner,

> If nothing else were said in praise of love, in all the pages of this epistle, nothing else whatever in any other page of Scripture, and this were the one and only thing we heard from the voice of God's spirit—'For God is Love'—we should ask for nothing more.[28]

To understand how Augustine interpreted this Johannine statement that God is Love one can do no better than to look at the way he describes the personality of Christ. It is the image of the Christ as a physician which is most representative of Augustine's references to Christ in his Homilies on 1 Jn and it is above all this image which allows him both to restate this idea of John that God is love and to express his own understanding of the character of that love. To understand Augustine's preference for this image one has only to reflect on the fact that throughout his life Augustine was acutely conscious of the need which every person has to be healed by Christ—that one cannot be the instrument of one's own salvation. However, it was not only his own personal experience which would have dictated his preference for this image. What Augustine found in 1 Jn was a perspective similar to that rooted in his own experience. It is one which is clearly expressed in the following passage from 1 Jn 4:8–10:

> . . . God is love.
> God's love for us was revealed
> when God sent into the world his only Son
> so that we could have life through Him;
> this is the love I mean;
> not our love for God,
> but God's love for us when He sent his Son
> to be the sacrifice that takes one's sins away.

It is not only Augustine's commentary on these verses in the seventh Homily[29] which illustrates his fidelity to this view of God's love. The whole ten homilies are marked by this Johannine vision. References to God as the physician occur in tr. II 1; tr. IV 4; tr. V 5; tr. VIII 10; tr. VIII 11; tr. VIII1 4; and tr. IX 9. It is an image which both reflects the idea of God as Love and also offers an explanation of the Incarnation in terms of that healing

---

28 Ibid., tr. VII 4.
29 In Iohannis Epistulam tr. VII 5–9.

love. Furthermore, the stress on the image of the physician reminds Augustine of the Johannine emphasis on the need for grace—that we can only love God because God loved us first. As Augustine states,

> What manner of love is this, that transforms the lover into beauty!
> God is ever beautiful, never ugly, never changing. He that is ever
> beautiful, He first loved us—and loved none that were not ugly and
> misshapen. Yet the end of his love was not to leave us ugly, but to
> transform us, creating beauty in place of deformity. And how shall
> we win this beauty, but through loving Him who is ever beautiful?
> Beauty grows in you with the growth of love; for charity itself is the
> soul's beauty.[30]

One would go far to find a finer passage which, when describing God, links the motifs of Beauty and Love to portray the working of grace in the human soul. It is a passage which marks the high point of Augustine's mature spirituality.

THE MEANING OF CARITAS AS FRATERNAL LOVE

Given the perspective just noted it is not surprising to find Augustine emphasizing that love takes its meaning from the nature of Christ's love for us, and that our task is to imitate that love, something which he stresses in tr. VII 9; tr. VIII1 1; and tr. IX 3. In this context it is the benevolence of Christ's love which ought to be the primary characteristic of fraternal love.

Love as benevolentia

The most sustained treatment of this theme is to be found in Homily Eight, verse five, where Augustine reflects on the absence of any reference to the love of enemies in John's description of perfect love. In contrast to John's treatment of love in his first Epistle Augustine's homilies on 1 Jn dwell at some length on the importance of this command of Christ to love one's enemies. As Augustine notes, John prefers to stress the importance of being prepared, in imitation of Christ's love, to die for the brethren.[31] This is also an ideal on which Augustine places considerable emphasis. On no less than four occasions in the course of his commentary he mentions it, and on each occasion it is placed before his listeners in continuity with John as the perfection of love.[32] However, unlike John, Augustine is keen to emphasize that the perfection of love in dying for one's brethren is an ideal which must be seen in the context of the universal extension of love which is expressed in Christ's com-

30   Ibid., tr. IX 9.
31   Cf.1 Jn 3:16.
32   Cf. ibid., tr. V 4; tr. VI 1; tr. VII 7; tr. IX 4.

mand to love one's enemies.[33] This Augustinian emphasis can be partly explained due to the conflict with Donatism which preoccupied him at this time. As he frequently remarked, the Donatists could not be regarded as followers of Christ because the essential mark of Christ's love is its universal character—a love which extends even to enemies. Despite this difference in emphasis which Augustine adverted to, he does not see any inconsistency between his stress on the love of enemies and the absence of any reference to this by John in his first Epistle. This is the case because Augustine recognized that in the first Epistle of John one is offered a privileged insight into the kernel of love as preached by Christ namely, its benevolent character. As he says:

> Do not think that John has given no charge concerning love of one's enemy; for he has said much of brotherly charity, and it is always the brother that you love. Let your desire for him be that he may be your brother. And if that is what you desire in loving your enemy—that he may be your brother—when you love him, you love a brother. You love in him not what he is, but what you would have him be.[34]

Augustine was fond of quoting the passage from Jn 15:15, ' I call you friends not servants because I have made known to you all that I have learnt from my father.' The benevolent love desires the intimacy of the relationship described by friendship:

> Men are not to be loved as things to be consumed, but in the manner of friendship and goodwill, leading us to do things for the benefit of those we love. And if there is nothing we can do, goodwill alone is enough for the lover.[35]

Love deserves to be reciprocated not out of any meanness but rather so that the equality and the intimacy of true friendship may be fully perfected. In this context the absence of any reference to the love of enemies in 1 Jn is not so strange, because, as Augustine recognizes, Christ's love of enemies, and consequently ours also, has as its goal the intimacy of friendship. All love including the love of enemies is consequently to be seen in the light of the command to love one's neighbour.

The perfection of love is a love in which there is no fear.

When John treats of the perfection of love in Chapter Four he places the ideal of the perfection of love in an eschatological setting and speaks of it as a love where there is no fear. As he says,

33 For a detailed treatment of this theme see Dideberg, op. cit., 67–73.
34 In Iohannis Ep., tr. VIII 10.
35 Ibid., tr. VIII 5. An extensive treatment of the benevolent character of love is to be found in Enarrationes in Psalmos CXXXII (AD414/5). Note also Sermo XXIII 8 (AD413).

> In love there can be no fear,
> but fear is driven out by perfect love.[36]

Augustine's commentary on this theme in Homily Nine, verses two to eight, is justly celebrated as a masterly example of the technique of holding in balance ideas which would seem to be contradictory.[37] It is not only different ideas but also conflicting biblical passages that he has to reconcile, because, as he remarks, the text from Psalm 19:9 which reads 'the fear of the Lord is pure, enduring for ever', seems to be in direct conflict with the passage quoted above from 1 Jn.[38] Augustine poses the problem in terms of the need to resolve an apparent conflict in the Bible. However, the tenor of his remarks suggests that the problem could be more accurately stated in terms of a conflict between the different psychological perspectives of John and Augustine. If this intuition is accurate the real conflict is between the psychologist in Augustine who recognizes the complexity and in many cases the importance of fear, and the exegete in him who is faced with the clear statement that perfect love and fear are mutually exclusive. He resolves the issue in an ingenious manner by having recourse to the simple device of splitting fear into chaste and unchaste fear, a solution which allows both views to co-exist. Chaste fear which is akin to reverence is ultimately identical with love and thus endures for ever, whereas unchaste fear, as 1 Jn says, is driven out by perfect love.

The value of these passages lies in the way they show us how Augustine resolves apparent conflict between biblical texts. In addition, they show us the way in which Augustine will use the Scriptures to qualify the biblical texts which seem to contradict his vision of the psychological make-up of the person.

THE IMPORTANCE OF LOVE

Love and do what you will (Dilige et quod vis fac)

The first epistle of John abounds in references to the importance of love but nowhere is this more clearly illustrated than in this passage from Chapter Four which was quoted earlier,

> My dear people,
> let us love one another
> since love comes from God
> and everyone who loves is begotten by God and knows God.

---

36 1 Jn 4:17–18.
37 For a detailed treatment of this theme cf. de Beer, *L'Amour est Dieu*, op. cit., 238–244.
38 *In Iohannis Epistulam* tr. IX 5; see also tr. IX 2 where Augustine quotes the passage from Psalm 11:10:'The fear of the Lord is the beginning of wisdom.'

> Anyone who fails to love can never have known God,
> because God is love.[39]

Augustine in his Homilies on 1 Jn treats at length of the importance of love. However, it is in his comment upon this passage in Homily Seven, verse eight, that one finds the phrase 'Love and do what you will' (*dilige et quod vis fac*)which is arguably the most celebrated and without doubt the most controversial of all Augustine's statements on love. It is repeated, although in a slightly different form, in Homily Ten, verse seven, 'Love and you cannot but do well' (*dilige, non potest fieri nisi bene facias*).

How are we to understand these phrases? Well, the first thing that must be said is that they are clearly not intended and cannot be interpreted as offering a licence to his congregation to act in whatever way they wish. The context in which both these passages occur, namely, that there are times when out of love one must accept the difficult task of correcting one's brethren, could not be less amenable to this interpretation. I suggest that we can only understand them in the context of Augustine's attempt to interpret faithfully the perspective of 1 Jn, namely, that love is of God and that in consequence, all actions motivated by love unite us to God. However, the way in which Augustine expresses this Johannine perspective offers us an unrivalled insight into his theory of the significance of love in the context of his analysis of human nature. It is one which is worth pursuing.

Augustine was not one to deny the objective character of the moral ideals which are universally desired by the heart that is 'restless until it rests in Thee, O Lord.'[40] However, the characteristic Augustinian stress is always on the interior attitude or intention which lies behind the doing of the act. Augustine's belief is that a person is defined in terms of his or her interior attitude or in terms of what he or she loves or desires—love is the weight of the soul (*pondus meum amor meus*).[41] It is a perspective which reflects the importance of the will in Augustine's psychology of the human person. What must not be forgotten is that it was Augustine's genius to be the first to give prominence to the centrality of the will in defining the person, and furthermore, that it was this insight which marked his distinctive contribution to classical philosophy. This is the context within which one must situate the importance of love for Augustine, and specifically the phrase 'Love and do what you will'. The quality of the moral character of the person cannot be evaluated other than by analysing the quality of the interior attitude which motivates that person's choices.

The emphasis which Augustine placed on the importance of the will can be illustrated by adverting to the way in which he will repeatedly

---

39 1 Jn 4:7–8.
40 Conf. I 1,1.
41 Ibid., XIII 9, 10.

remind his readers of the importance of the biblical phrase 'Blessed are the pure in heart'.[42] Spiritual growth was consistently identified by him as a process of listening to one's heart, a listening which demands a movement of one's focus from what is exterior to what is interior, and one which provides the only path by which one can progress spiritually —ascend from what is lower to what is higher. While never doubting that God is to be found in the exterior world, in the beauty of creation, the characteristic Augustinian emphasis is that God is always to be found in the interior of the person. This perspective is well illustrated in the following passage from Homily Three, verse thirteen, where Augustine comments on the reference in 1 Jn 2:20 to the role of the Holy Spirit in the process of spiritual discernment and growth:

> . . . those whom the Holy Spirit teaches not inwardly, go home untaught. Outward teachings are but a kind of helps and promptings: the Teacher of hearts has his chair in heaven. Let Him speak to you within.

The full significance of this passage becomes apparent when we recognize that the interior teacher—the Holy Spirit—is Love. In listening to the dictates of love, *dilige et quod vis fac*, we are doing nothing other than listening to the interior teacher who is God himself.

The eyes of the heart are purified by love

One of the more revealing passages on the importance which Augustine attaches to love in the period in which he delivered his homilies on 1 Jn is the reference in Homily Nine, verse ten, to the eyes of the heart being purified by love.[43] The passage from Mt 5:8, 'Blessed are the pure in heart for they shall see God', was one, as mentioned above, much beloved by Augustine. From his earliest days it allowed him to integrate Neoplatonist philosophy with Christian spirituality. Almost without exception Augustine identifies purity of heart with the acceptance of faith. Although there are references, mainly in his later writings, to one being purified by faith working through love, the passage just quoted is the first reference in Augustine's writings to the belief that one is purified through love.[44] It is a significant pointer to the increasing importance which Augustine in his mature writings attached to the role of fraternal love in the process of spiritual growth. It is also an indicator of the importance of his commentary on 1 Jn in the context of the development of his mature spirituality, one which is based on his recognition of the centrality of *caritas*.

42   Mt 5:8.
43   Cf. also In Iohannis Epistulam tr. III 2; tr. IV 5; tr. VII 10–11.
44   The only text in Augustine's writings dated prior to AD 407 which links the virtue of purity of heart to fraternal love is Ad Galatas 5:6 (AD 394).

Anyone who lives in Love lives in God

As mentioned earlier, one of the concerns of John as he wrote this Epistle is to reassure the young Christian community. The way in which he does this is by assuring his readers that if there is fraternal love in the community they will attain the fulfilment universally desired, namely, salvation. Augustine's Homilies are faithful to this perspective of 1 Jn. He stresses that the way to God is through fraternal love and that the proof that one is begotten by God is that one loves the brethren. The particular Augustinian emphasis is on the idea that love makes us like God,[45] and that through fraternal love we will see God.[46]

The importance of his commentary on 1 Jn can be seen in the way in which he will subsequently use these Johannine images to explain the Pauline motif of *imago Dei*, one which was much beloved by him. His reflections on 1 Jn helped him to recognise that it is precisely in love that we image God who himself is Love.

Another issue which preoccupied Augustine at this period was how to explain the goal of *contemplatio Dei* and, in this context, the relation between loving and seeing God. Monastic spirituality, as it developed in the early Church, had tended to situate the role of the active life or fraternal love primarily in the context of the necessary preparation for the goal of *contemplatio Dei* rather than as an essential component of the goal itself.[47] As can be seen from the following passage from Homily Seven, verse ten, Augustine's understanding of the relationship is very different:

> My brothers, one does not love what one cannot see. Why then, when you hear the praise of charity, are you stirred to acclaim and applause?

While recognising that there is a difference between this life and the next, Augustine saw that the difference cannot be accurately described as that which may be supposed to exist between a life of fraternal love and a life of contemplation. In the last analysis seeing and loving are identical to the eyes of Augustine, and in this context fraternal love can

---

45   In Iohannis Epistulam, tr. IX 9–11.
46   Ibid., tr. V 7; tr. VII 10; and tr. X 6.
47   Cf Basil, Epistle XXII and CCXCV, both of which are addressed to monks. The emphasis is either on renunciation or obedience to the apostolic way of living. In a lengthy treatment by Jerome of the relative merits of the anchorite and cenobitic ideals in Epistle CXXV there is no mention of the positive value of community. Note also the discussion as to why the community life is important in Cassian, De institutis cenobiorum IX 7. The answer offered by Cassian is that it teaches one patience. Gregory in his Funeral Oration in memory of Basil v.62 has a lengthy treatment of the respective merits of the anchorite and cenobitic ideals. The danger from pride in the solitary life is stressed, as is the practical usefulness of the community life. However, in the final analysis it is the solitary life which, being more tranquil and stable, leads one to union with God.

only be described in a form of contemplation in the midst of action.[48] This of course is highly significant having regard to the emphasis which Augustine places on fraternal love in his monastic rule, and it marks what is undoubtedly the single most important contribution made by Augustine to the development of monastic spirituality.

CONCLUSION: GOD IS LOVE AND LOVE IS GOD

The final and most important theme in the Homilies, is that of the unity of the love of God and the love of neighbour. The context for the discussion of this issue in the commentary is the passage from 1 Jn 4:20:

> Anyone who says I love God and hates his brother is a liar, since a man who does not love the brother that he can see cannot love God whom he has never seen.

In a previous work from his early years Augustine interpreted this verse to show the importance of fraternal love as a preparation for the love of God.[49] But what then is the status of the love of neighbour? Is the neighbour just to be loved as a means to our end? In this case are we really loving our neighbour at all? It is clear from his writings that in Augustine's early ministry the emphasis was placed firmly on the primacy of the love of God, but increasingly as his life progressed, and without doubt owing to the influence of the monastic life, he came to stress the centrality of fraternal love.[50] However, it is only in the course of his Homilies on 1 Jn that the issue is finally resolved to his satisfaction. The key passage is Homily Nine, verse ten, which is a commentary on the above text from 1 Jn.[51]

> Does it then follow that the one who loves his brother loves God also? Of necessity he must love God: of necessity he must love love itself. He cannot love his brother and not love love itself : he cannot help loving love. And if he loves love, he needs must love God: In loving love he is loving God. You cannot have forgotten

48   In Sermo CIV; ibid., CLXIX, and in In Iohannis Evangelium tr. CXXIV Augustine compares the biblical figures of Martha and Mary, Peter and John to illustrate the difference between the active and the contemplative life—the former reflecting life as it is lived in this world, and the latter reflecting life as it will be lived in eternity. In no case is fraternal love equated exclusively with the active life.

49   Cf. Ad Galatas 4:5 (AD 394).

50   'Before all else, live together in harmony, being of one mind and one heart on the way to God. For is it not precisely for this reason that you have come to live together?', Regula ad servos Dei I,2 (AD 397), trans. Raymond Canning, The Rule of Saint Augustine, London 1984, 11. Cf. also Epistula LXXIII (AD 404); In Iohannis Evangelium, tr. LXX 4, (AD 407)

51   Other texts from In Iohannis Epistulam which reflect this perspective include tr. IV 6; tr. VII 6; tr. VIII 4 and 12; tr. IX 2; tr. X 3.

the words that came a little earlier. 'God is love'. If God is love, whoever loves love loves God. Therefore love your brother and have no other care.

It is a truly remarkable passage which unites the love of God and love of neighbour with the deceptively simple remark that when you say God is love you are also saying love is God. This insight into the unity of the love of God and the neighbour was one which Augustine never lost.[52] Furthermore, it also answers the problem for Augustine as to why John in the Epistle stressed only fraternal love and not the love of God—there is no conflict when one recognizes that not only is God love but love is God.

The other great pillar upon which he rested his conviction of the unity of the two loves is the Pauline image of the Body of Christ. No other image receives anything like as much prominence both in these Homilies and indeed in all of Augustine's writings as that which he accords to the Body of Christ. This is particularly noticeable in the final homily which is actually structured around an analysis of this motif. In this homily Augustine utilizes the image of the Body of Christ to highlight the identity between love and unity—to emphasize the point that he who professes to love must work to preserve unity. In continuity with the emphasis which is to be found in the Pauline epistles, Augustine insists that he who professes to love God must love the Church which is the body of Christ and that he who loves God must seek to unite the whole of mankind in the community of the body of Christ which is the love and unity of Christ himself. The importance of the link between the love of unity and the unity in love which is constitutive of a Christian community was one which Augustine never lost an opportunity to stress. Not only did it serve as the focus of his criticism of the Donatists but it equally provided the locus around which his monastic rule was constructed.[53]

There are very few passages in Augustine's writings that express with such intensity the intimate nature of the goal of unity in love as that which is to be found in Homily Ten, verse three.

> But John, having just spoken of the Son of God, now speaks of God's sons. It is because the sons of God are the Body of God's only Son; because He is the head, and we are the members, that the Son is still one. Therefore to love the sons of God is to love the Son of God; to love the Son of God is to love the Father; none can love the Father unless he love the Son; and he that loves the Son loves also

52 Cf. In Iohannis Evangelium tr. XVII 8 (post AD 417)
53 For a detailed treatment of significance of this theme in the Regula ad servos Dei, see Eoin Cassidy, 'Le rôle de l'amitié dans la quête du bonheur chez S. Augustin', J. Follon et J.McEvoy, eds., L'Actualité de la Pensée Médiévale, Philosophes Médiévaux, Louvain 1994, Vol.31, 171–201, esp. 189–193.

> the sons of God. These sons of God are members of God's Son; and he that loves them, by loving becomes himself a member. Through love he becomes a part of the structure of Christ's body. And thus the end will be one Christ, loving himself, for the love of the members for one another is the love of the Body for itself.

In the last analysis it is the Christological focus of this theme which offers the only appropriate context which can explain the central place which the motif of unity in love has in Augustine's spirituality. Augustine's commentary on I Jn is imbued with the importance of the goal longed for in the prayer of Jesus at the Last Supper 'that they may be one as I and the Father are one.[54] It is this goal of unity in love that provides Augustine the exegete with the interpretative key to understanding this First Epistle of John. Not surprisingly, it is also the key to interpreting Augustine's own spiritual writings.

---

54 Jn 17: 21.

The Symbol gives Life: Eucherius of Lyons' Formula for Exegesis

THOMAS O'LOUGHLIN

When he died, in the mid-fifth century, Eucherius of Lyons' fame had already spread throughout the Latin world. Time only enhanced his reputation as a wise bishop and learned writer; and for a period of roughly seven hundred years his two little treatises on exegesis were among the basic textbooks of the West: copied, read, referred to, and cited wherever the Scriptures were studied. More recent history has been less kind to him: the rise of scholasticism in the twelfth century left his books behind as overly simple and outmoded, and he disappeared from among 'the illustrious'[1] of the tradition. While I doubt if there is a single work of exegesis between AD 600 and 1,000 without traces of his work and method, he is now unknown.[2] When his name is mentioned, even among historians of theology, the response is often 'who?' Indeed, apart from notes in general histories,[3] I have been able to locate less

---

1   Gennadius at the end of the fifth century considered him such in his De viris illustribus 63[64] (PL 58,1096–1097) and later Isidore wrote of him in his De viris illustribus, XXVIII 38 (PL 83,1098): *Eucherius, franciae episcopus, elegans sententiis, ornatus in verbis, edidit ad Hilarium Arelatensem antistitem eremi deserta petentem unum opusculum de laude eiusdem eremi luculentissimum, et dulci sermone dictatum, in quo opere laudamus doctorem, et si pauca, tamen pulchra dicentem. 'Brevitas' ut ait quidem, 'laus est interdum in aliqua parte dicendi, in uniuersa eloquentia laudem non habet.'* On this material, cf. H. Koeppeler, 'De uiris illustribus' and Isidore of Seville', Journal of Theological Studies 37(1936)23 and 32.

2   Evidence to justify this statement can be found in M. McNamara, 'Plan and source analysis of Das Bibelwerk: Old Testament' in P. Ní Chatháin and M. Richter eds., Irland und die Christenheit: Bibelstudien und Mission, Stuttgart 1987, 84–112; and J.F. Kelly, 'Eucherius of Lyons: Harbinger of the Middle Ages' in E.A. Livingstone ed., Studia Patristica , Leuven 1989, XXIII,138–142.

3   Even these are uneven: O. Bardenhewer, Patrology, ET: T.J. Shahan, Freiburg 1908, 518–519 has a fine overall introduction surveying studies up to that time; L. Clugnet in the Catholic Encyclopaedia V, 595 although based on this ed. of Bardenhewer, ignored the fact that a critical edition had been prepared in 1894 and gives the name of his longest work as 'Institutiones' instead of Instructiones. P. de Labriolle, History and Literature of Christianity from Tertullian to Boethius, ET: H. Wilson, London 1924, has only a footnote on page 425 on the exegetical material; B. Altaner, Patrology, ET: H.C. Graef, Freiburg 1960, has just one sentence on page 541, while the F.L. Cross and E.A. Livingstone in the Oxford

than half-a-dozen articles on his exegetical works in the last hundred years[4] Hence, my task in this paper is to introduce this man whose importance in the development of the Latin tradition is virtually unknown. I propose, first, to look at the man, his family and friends; then to look at the salient features of the shorter, and more popular, of his works: the *Formulae spiritalis intellegentiae*;[5] and, finally, to suggest why he should be seen as a major force in the history of Latin theology.

BACKGROUND

Husband, father, monk, bishop and friend

This 'greatest of the great bishops of his time', as Claudianus Mamertus described him[6], was born into what appears to have been a Christian family sometime in the latter half of the fourth century.[7] The family was

Dictionary of the Christian Church, 478 and A. Neuwirth in the New Catholic Encyclopaedia V, 621 more or less follow Bardenhewer; among other reference works only one is outstanding: R. Etaix, 'Eucher de Lyon' in the Dictionnaire d'Histoire et de Géographie ecclésiastiques XV, 1315–1318; the best recent accounts are by A. Hamman in A. di Berardino (ed.), Patrology, ET:P. Solari, Westminster MD 1988, IV, 504–507 and S. Pricoco in the Encyclopaedia of the Early Church (= Dizionario Patristico e di Antichità Cristiana), Cambridge 1992, I, 295 which has the most up-to-date bibliography on the topic; surprisingly J. Pelikan, The Christian Traditon: The Emergence of the Catholic Tradition, Chicago 1971, makes no mention of him.

4   G. Bardy, 'La littérature patristique des "Quaestiones et responsiones" sur l'écriture sainte', Revue Biblique 42(1933)14–22 [this article also contains the only examination I have found of the work of Salonius]; J.G. Hirte, Doctrina scripturistica et textus biblicus S. Eucherii Lugdunensis Episcopi , Diss. Rome 1940 [I have not been able to get access to this thesis; cf. F. Stegmüller, Repertorium Biblicum Medii Aevi, VIII, 407]; C. Curti, '"Spiritalis intellegentia"', nota sulla dottrina esegetica di Eucherio di Lione' in A.M. Ritter ed., Kerygma und Logos, Göttingen 1979, 108–122; I. Opelt, 'Quellenstudien zu Eucherius', Hermes: Zeitschrift für klassische Philologie 91(1963)476–483; G.M. Pintus, 'Il bestiario del diavolo: l'esegesi biblica nelle Formulae spiritalis intellegentiae di Eucherio di Lione', Sandalion 12–13 (1989–1990) 99–114,

5   The standard edition used is that of C. Wotke in CSEL 31(1894) 3–62; this edition will be used throughout this paper and it will be cited as 'Formulae', followed by section number; it has been taken for granted by all, except R. Etaix, loc. cit., 1317, who have studied or mentioned Eucherius that this edition has the text as it left Eucherius and that it has replaced the longer text of the Formulae found in PL 50,727–772. I have reservations about both texts, see below pages 247–248 and 250–251, all translations, unless otherwise noted, are by the present author.

6   De statu animae II 9 ed. A. Engelbrecht, 1885, CSEL 11,135: *magnorum saeculi sui pontificum longe maximus* . . . ; on Eucherius in Claudianus, cf. P. Courcelle, Late Latin Writers and their Greek Sources, ET: H.E. Wedeck, Cambridge MA 1969, 240 and 245.

7   Cf. J.R. Martindale, The Prosopography of the Later Roman Empire (A.D. 395–527), Cambridge 1980, II, 405.

of the senatorial class and fully part of that refined culture we associate with late imperial Gaul. His Latin is, perhaps, the best testimony to this: it has a refinement that echoes Ausonius, a delicacy like that of Paulinus of Nola, and that crispness of expression which made these writers admired models of prose for the students of the early Middle Ages. We know that he was a relative of the patrician Priscus Valerianus, for he dedicated his *De contemptu mundi* to him, and so was connected to the elite in oratory, literature and law.[8] He married Galla and they had two sons, Salonius and Veranius, and two daughters, Consortia and Tullia.[9] Later (possibly around the year 410) they disposed of their goods and as a family withdrew to the island monastery of Lérins, for that other episcopal family, Paulinus of Nola and his wife, addressed a joint letter to both Eucherius and Galla there about that time.[10] The education of their sons was entrusted to his friend, the founder of Lérins, Honoratus, and both Vincent of Lérins and Salvian of Marseilles appear to have taught them.[11] Eucherius loved this island retreat and the famous description of its beauty, a blend of Genesis 2 and the classical garden of the poets, is from his pen.[12]

Christian Gaul as a centre of learning tends to be overlooked because of its towering neighbours: the north Italy of Ambrose, the north Africa of Augustine, the east of Basil, Nyssa, Nazianzen, Chrysostom, not to mention the ubiquitous Jerome. But it was in Gaul, between Hilary of Poitiers (c.315–367) and Caesarius of Arles (470–542)—a period of nearly two centuries, that the most sustained effort in Christian scholarship took place. There, through a succession of bishops, teachers, writers and councils, the external form of the Latin Church took shape.[13] The lives of Eucherius and his two sons well exemplify this: all three were bishops, two were writers, and all three took part in the development of Christian law. Eucherius' quiet in Lérins ended when he was elected to the see of Lyons sometime in the 430s, and shortly after that Salonius became bishop of Geneva and Veranius bishop of Vence (*Vinctium*). Eucherius presided, alongside another friend, Hilary of Arles, over the Council of Orange (*Arauscanum*) in 441, and may be the Eucherius mentioned in the text that contains the statutes of the

8   Ibid., 1142–1143.
9   Martindale (op. cit. 405) considers the information on the daughters less than certain.
10   Epistola 51; cf. Martindale, op. cit., 491.
11   Cf. Martindale, op. cit., 973 and 1155.
12   De laude heremi XLII (Wotke, 192): *Lerinum meam . . . Aquis scatens, herbis virens, floribus renitens, visibus odoribusque iucunda paradisum possidentibus se exhibet.*
13   Cf. M.L.W. Laistner, 'The influence during the Middle Ages of the Treatise "De vita contemplativa" and its surviving manuscripts', in Miscellanea Giovanni Mercati (Studi e Testi 122), Vatican 1946, II, 344; J.F. Kelly., loc. cit., has also drawn attention to this formative role in suggesting that Eucherius should join the group that E.K. Rand picked out as 'founders of the middle ages'.

Council of Arles c. 455, which dealt with the problem of monastic authority on Lérins. We know that Salonius was there, and after that he disappears from history. Veranius was one of a group of bishops who wrote to Pope Leo in 450 on legal questions, and may have been still alive in 470 if he is the same Veranius then referred to by Faustus of Riez.[14]

Eucherius was also fully part of Gaul's rich theological culture. Apart from his own works (five books, a letter and some fragments are extant[15]), his son Salonius wrote some exegetical works very much in the style of his father;[16] and both were known to most of the other writers connected with Gaul in the period.[17] John Cassian was a friend of Eucherius and dedicated the second part of his *Collationes* to him.[18] Salvian and Eucherius exchanged letters and he dedicated his *De gubernatione Dei* to Salonius. Salvian praised Eucherius' prose style, and said that his writings were an ornament of the Church as models of learning that helped both teachers and students.[19] As to that other major figure we associate with Lérins, Vincent, our evidence for direct contact is more tenuous. At the beginning of the *Instructiones* he tells Salonius to study the Scriptures and to try to be like 'those most holy men . . . Honoratus . . . Hilary . . . Salvian and Vincent' whom he associates with Lérins.[20] The other link with Vincent is a tradition, already mentioned, that he was one of the sons' teachers.[21] It is inconceivable that they did not know one another. It is in this tradition of Vincent, Salvian, and Cassian that Eucherius saw himself (even if he expressed this with the usual formula that he was the lesser follower[22]) and, more importantly for us, it is within the world of these writers, each preparing short texts that were to become classics, that we must situate Eucherius' writings.[23]

---

14 Epistola II (A. Engelbrecht ed. 1891, CSEL 21,165); and cf. Martindale, op. cit. 1155; it should be noted that Faustus is himself one of this group of Gallic writers, for although born in Britain, he spent time in Lérins as a monk (c.424–433) before becoming bishop of Riez, and he throws further light on the whole group in that he attacked Augustine indirectly on several occasions in order to show that human freedom and nature were not as devastated by Original Sin as the more rigorous followers of Augustine held it to be, cf. M. Simonetti, 'Faustus of Riez', in the Encyclopaedia of the Early Church, I, 320–321.

15 CPL (editio altera), nn. 488–493.

16 Ibid., n. 499.

17 A simple way to glimpse the vitality of this learned Christian culture is to look at the contents page of PL 50: Cassian, Fastidius, Vincent, Eucherius, Hilary, among others.

18 Praefatio secundae partis [Conlationes XI-XVII]: *O sancti fratres Honorate et Eucheri* (M. Petschenig ed., 1886, CSEL 13,311).

19 Epistola VIII ad Eucherium, 2 (PL 53,168)

20 Instructiones ad Salonium, praefatio 66.

21 Cf. Hamman, op. cit., 504.

22 Instructiones, ad Salonium, praefatio 66.

23 Since this paper is being written in Ireland it is interesting to recall that it was at this period that the mission of Palladius to Ireland was recorded by Prosper of

In the wake of Augustine

No Latin writer in the fifth century can be discussed in isolation from the Bishop of Hippo. This is especially true of southern Gaul where the arguments of Augustine against Pelagius and Julian seem to have been debated with special fervour. After all, it was there that the councils were held—Eucherius may have been present—which affirmed Augustine's position and which, still today, are cited as positions in the systematic theology of grace. For this paper, one consequence of this interest in Augustine in Gaul is of paramount importance: whether or not a writer quotes Augustine directly, we can presume the availability of his major works to that writer. So, even if a writer had not read Augustine, since Augustine's theology was part of the common currency in theological circles, how a writer stands in relation to Augustine is a crucial question and may illuminate his own thought for us.[24] So what of Eucherius ?

Eucherius is linked by several scholars to those writers who sought to mitigate the extremes of Augustine's position on grace and have been variously labelled 'semi-pelagians', or the like, for their trouble. Thus, if Cassian is a 'Semi-something' regarding grace and at times appears to favour Julian against Augustine—one thinks of the optimism of *Collatio* XIII where the initiative to good resides in the will and grace is an *incrementum* to this good intention, and if Eucherius can be linked with him, then he too is to be seen as opposite to Augustine.[25] With regard to Scripture the situation is more complex: for while he does not quote Augustine by name he clearly followed him. Eucherius stated in the *Instructiones* that his aim would be to follow the most illustrious teachers,[26] and clearly he considered Augustine to belong to this group. Recently Joseph Kelly has shown how Augustine's exegesis was followed on certain specific points by Eucherius, but it is in questions about the overall approach to Scripture that the greatest similarities occur; although it is equally true that these Augustinian ideas were to be subtly, yet decisively, changed by Eucherius. Thus it was Augustine's exegetical agenda that probably inspired the structure of Eucherius' manuals, even if he used a different approach to the senses of Scripture. Certainly, it

Aquitaine, and it is in this period that the mission of Patrick took place. Over the years many have speculated on links between Patrick and Lérins and many more have spent time casting doubt on such speculations, but surely both sides of this argument miss the central point: Patrick was in contact with a vibrant, and widespread Christian culture, whether he was in a particular place or not is irrelevant, for it is not a case that Christian learned culture only existed in monastic pockets such as Lérins.

24 Kelly, loc. cit., has done some of the spadework on this question.

25 de Labriolle, op. cit., 422–432, is an example of this position; cf. my comment on Faustus of Riez, n.14, above.

26 The solution to problems shall be *non ex meo ingenio sed ex inlustrium doctorum iudicio* (Instructiones ad Salonium, praefatio 65); and cf. Kelly, loc cit., 139.

was that agenda that led to them being so highly valued by later generations. So, in exegesis at least, it is difficult not to see him as Augustine's heir and, perhaps, disciple.

The most obvious link between them is in their semiotics. In the *De doctrina Christiana* Augustine proposed a theory for the understanding of Scripture as a system of signs. This he saw as an instance of a larger pattern in human life, for it is through signs that humans come to knowledge and come to an understanding of God. Humans know of God through signs (*signa*) which point to realities (*res*) which are beyond and above them. For Augustine this sacramentalism was basic to faith. The unseen is pointed to by the seen and human life involves the raising of the mind continuously from its corporeal starting point to the higher realities: this is the pattern of all knowing, including religious knowing. Truth (God) himself stands beyond all things, which are his creation, and all things point beyond themselves towards him. Thus the universe is in its totality a sign of God and each part of it can be a pointer towards his Being, Power and Wisdom. Since all reality points beyond itself, Augustine lives in a double universe: it is what it is, and it is a pointer to what it is not: God or the things of God. This same sacramental process is operative in the Scriptures. For they record the signs by which God communicates himself and are themselves signs communicating a message to us. Thus the basic religious skill is to be able to read the signs and understand what they point to, be these signs in the universe or in the Book. One can only read the Scriptures with understanding when one knows that it (1) does contain signs that have to be interpreted and (2) what the signs mean. So one only knows the meaning of the sound written *bos* when one knows that that sound has significance as a sign (i.e. it is more than a noise) and when one knows that *bos* means an animal which eats grass in a field.[27]

Augustine's hermeneutic is not restricted to the correct interpretation of texts: it applies to anything that can act as a sign; but texts do have a priority and it is with their correct exegesis that he is primarily concerned. The priority of a text in learning of things divine follows from the fact that it is God's chosen means and the most explicit way of communicating a message over a span of time: He has given humanity a Law written in a Book. The Law was communicated to Moses and to the Apostles; the text is the record of this in writing. As a conventional system of signs it points to God in two ways. First, it can record what God has said to us, the signs he has given to us directly in language: the exegete must know how to interpret such statements in such a way that one does not fall into contradictions and in a way that is worthy of God, for he often uses obscure and difficult images in this communication.

---

27 De doctrina Christiana I, passim; the particular example is found at II 10, 15 (ed. I. Martin, 1962, CCSL 32).

Examples of this category of signs would be oracles in the Prophets or the sermons of Christ in the Gospels. Second, the language of the Scriptures can be a record which draws attention to the other signs in the fabric of the universe or in history that have been used by God: the description of the creation, the history of Israel, the geography of events, and the events of Christ's life fall into this category. In this second case there is a continual interplay between physical reality and the text: reality is acting as a sign telling us of God, and this is recorded in a further set of signs, the language in the Book. These, the thing which is the sign and the record in writing, illuminate one another. Thus, for example, our understanding of the universe is enhanced by reading the account of the creation in the Book, but we cannot understand the Book without knowledge of the things it mentions. Only by reading the Book can one know that the creation is the unique specific willed act of God, and so know that an atomism such as that postulated by Democritus or an eternal universe such as Aristotle postulated is incorrect. However, only one who has studied the creation through different arts can appreciate the beauty and order of the divine handiwork.[28]

Augustine moved in a sign-filled universe and so whether he was looking at the creation or reading the Book he could be said to be living at two levels: the actual and the sign level.[29] Indeed, in some passages he conceived the Christian life as moving through one level to the other; for humans are beckoned *per corporalia ad incorporalia*.[30] Augustine's conviction that these formed two interdependent worlds was best expressed

---

28 I omit detailed references in this survey of Augustine as it is given here as background to Eucherius; for the specific places in Augustine where this semiotics is spelled out, cf. J.C.M. van Winden, 'In the Beginning: some observations on the patristic interpretation of Genesis 1:1', Vigiliae Christianae 17(1963)105–121; and T.J. van Bavel, 'The Creator and the Integrity of Creation in the Fathers of the Church especially in Saint Augustine', Augustinian Studies 21(1990)1–33.

29 Augustine made this explicit when he wrote about the senses of Scripture. Most writers after Philo used between three and four senses (literal, allegorical, and moral) and this was to some extent codified using the example of Jerusalem in the writings of Jerome and given added detail by Cassian. Most writers have assumed that Augustine shared this three-fold approach to the senses of scripture. However, as H. Caplan ('The Four Senses of Scriptural Interpretation and the Medieval Theory of Preaching', Speculum 4 (1929) 282–290) has pointed out, Augustine had essentially a two-fold approach: the historical and the sense-beyond-the-historical. That said, Augustine's actual exegesis is often indistinguishable from the method of Philo. Indeed, modern writers who see no difference in his approach to the senses of Scripture are at least in harmony with the tradition going back to Eucherius, and which continued right through the Middle Ages, of interpreting Augustine as if he saw the senses of Scripture in the same way as Philo, Ambrose and Jerome. To set Caplan's work in context, cf. C.W. Jones, 'Some Introductory Remarks on Bede's Commentary on Genesis', Sacris Erudiri 19 (1969) 135–141.

30 Cf. my 'Knowing God and Knowing the Cosmos: Augustine's Legacy of Tension', Irish Philosophical Journal 6 (1989) 42–44.

in the programme he suggested for Christian education in the *De doctrina Christiana*. All the skills that enable us to understand the universe must be studied (the *artes liberales* such as arithmetic, music, astronomy), and along with these the skills to enable us to understand language and writing must be acquired (grammar, rhetoric and logic). Then if the sign is in nature or recorded in a book it can be understood.[31] With reference to the Scriptures which form the focus of this whole educational process certain other special studies must be undertaken.[32] These may be generic, such as learning Greek or Hebrew, or specific studies dealing with especially obscure passages or signs. These particularly obscure passages can be broken into two groups: (1) enigmatic passages where one text 'apparently' contradicts another, and (2) obscurities of language or fact. Into this latter group fall such things as words from Hebrew carried over into the versions, matters of chronology, and of the special sign-values of things such as places, numbers, animals, plants or stones when these are mentioned in the Scriptures. What was needed here was manuals classifying, listing and explaining these things. Augustine was glad that some such works had already been written, for example by Eusebius, and suggested that the other guides to obscure signs should be written as soon as possible.[33] In this he set forth a plan of work that was eagerly taken up in subsequent generations.[34] Augustine set great store by this enterprise: the manuals would not only explain the obscure, but would show that many 'contradictions' were just results of our ignorance and that many passages we might dismiss as insignificant or unworthy were full of value. The task required learning, careful empirical observation in the case of places, animals and the like, as well as diligent study of the Scriptures. The significance of these signs is then uncovered by comparing what Scripture says in one place with what is found in another. By this method of comparison Scripture illuminates itself, and the specific interpretations of particular signs is given an objective validity.[35] It is within this understanding of Scripture, and with this task and this method in mind, that Eucherius set to work in both his exegetical manuals.

31   Cf. E. Kevane, Augustine the Educator, Westminster, MD 1964.
32   On how the Scriptures formed the core of Augustine's curriculum cf. G. Howie, Educational Theory and Practice in St Augustine, London 1969.
33   Augustine mentions this need on several occasion in the De doct. Chr. II 16,24; II 29,45; II 29,54; II 32,50; II 39,59 (where he mentions grouping them in classes and praises those already produced by Eusebius).
34   I have examined in detail the plan of Augustine for dealing with *aenigmata* in my article 'Julian of Toledo's Antikeimenon and the Development of Latin Exegesis', Proceedings of the Irish Biblical Association 16 (1993) 80–98; on the question of obscure things operating as signs in the Scriptures and of the need for manuals dealing with these, I have examined this in 'The Exegetical Purpose of Adomnán's De Locis Sanctis', Cambridge Medieval Celtic Studies 24 (1992) 37–53.
35   De doct. Chr. II 6,8; II 9,14 and II 12,17.

Other intellectual factors

Christian Gaul in the fifth century presents us with two contradictory aspects, and in emphasizing the links between Eucherius and Augustine's educational writings, we are apt to see only the culture, civilisation, learning and scholarly *otium* of that society. But there is a another aspect to their culture and theology. For just as they did not share the later Augustine's pessimism over human nature vis-à-vis grace, neither did they share his optimism regarding the value of secular studies. They exhibit a darker attitude to human learning and scholarship which is a variant of that contempt for learning that can be found in the writings of Ambrose and Jerome[36], and which Augustine is anxious to refute in the *De doctrina*.[37] This low opinion can be found in many writers of this period, for instance Cassian,[38] but it received its most developed expression in Eucherius' *Epistola de contemptu mundi et secularis philosophiae*.[39] There he stated his low opinion of learning that was not explicitly devoted to sacred things: secular studies were vain and the philosophers were to be shunned. Their place was to be taken by the new monastic wisdom of asceticism and the study of Christian truths (*Christiani dogmatis studia*)[40] This had diverse consequences for his exegesis.

The value of human learning

This shift is most obvious in two connected areas: (1) the inherent worth and value of the external world in comparison to the realities of salvation; and (2) the importance and value of the actual text of the Scriptures, as against any spiritual interpretation, in mediating the Word of God. This issue is further complicated by the fact that neither Eucherius, the medieval tradition following him, nor most modern writers on the history of exegesis, were aware just how radically he changed the focus of Augustine's teaching.[41]

Augustine had viewed the creation as a real gift to be appreciated and valued as it was from God. It was through (*per*) this corporeal world that one could see the things of God which became visible in an illumination

---

36 Ambrose's Hexaëmeron relishes the contrast of futile human learning and divine revelation (cf. my 'Aquae super caelos (Gen 1:6–7): The First Faith-Science Debate', Milltown Studies 29 (1992) 100–103); the frenzied tirade (*sub specie visionis*) of Jerome, who juxtaposes Christ with Cicero in Epistola XXII, is so well known as to need no comment.

37 Praefatio.

38 Cf. Courcelle, op. cit., 231.

39 PL 50,711–726.

40 Ibid., 724.

41 Cf. the references to Caplan and Jones in above.

42 Cf. E. Portalié, A Guide to the Thought of St Augustine, ET: R.J. Bastian, Chicago 1960, 109–114; I give this as a token reference to the question of 'Divine Illumination'—I give it fully aware of its age (1902) and that it has been criticized as

given by God in grace.[42] The world is here, now, because God wills it, and there is another world, which we are called to participate in, whose reality is pointed to from within this world. This world is no mere *signum* to another world, but a *res* in itself which is also a sign. Augustine carefully avoided any implication that this world was not a 'real' one in comparison with some other 'spiritual' world, or any implication that this world was not a place where God's creative action was present and of importance. Such notions were avoided as hinting at some sort of dualist error. There is a tension in Augustine between, on the one hand, the seriousness with which this world is to be approached and, on the other, its lack of importance when compared to eternity. But he, on the whole, never reduced the problem to a simple choice: the perfection of eternity versus the transience of material existence.[43] This nuanced approach disappears in Eucherius where the two-tier universe of Augustine (a-reality-which-is-also-a sign and a-higher-reality-which-is-pointed-to) became the much simpler two-tier universe of the physical (matter-mutation-transience) versus the spiritual (immaterial, unchanging, eternal) world. For Augustine the universe is a reality in itself that manifests the power of the Creator and so points back to Him; in Eucherius it is but a token of what is the real, and it is a token which, if taken seriously as a reality in itself, may become a fatal curiosity. In this attitude to the world around us Eucherius was the unwitting inheritor of the secular philosophers he consciously shunned. This two-tier view is typical of a major part of the tradition of Greek philosophy in the early centuries of Christianity, in some sense 'Platonic' in its contrast of the real-eternal-spiritual world with the world that we see. To concentrate on this world is to be in slavery to matter and mere images of something higher. Wisdom is freedom from this slavery to images and involves abandoning this world for the perfect immaterial world of the Forms. This two-tier universe is also in a sense 'Aristotelian' in that it harnesses Aristotle's physical dualism of the sublunary and superlunary worlds as a model and exemplar of the contrast of physical and spiritual. Thus the contrast of the world of change, corruption and matter with a higher world of perfection and eternity (the heavens) is analogically similar to the transience of all this world's existence and Heaven. Unwittingly, this view had adopted many of the religious themes of various philosophic cults which were themselves the object of attack.[44]

---

being 'a very Thomist' reading of Augustine: however, unlike many more detailed studies of Augustine's theory of knowledge, it brings out one aspect of that theory which, while of little apparent importance to those whose main concern is epistemology, is of central concern here: that Augustine's approach to knowledge cannot be separated from his understanding of the dependence of the creature on the Creator in grace.

43   Cf. my 'Knowing God and Knowing the Cosmos: Augustine's Legacy of Tension', loc. cit. passim.

44   Cf. Courcelle, op. cit., 224–236.

By the time this dichotomy reached Eucherius it already had impressive credentials within Jewish and Christian writings. Philo had adopted a similar system and, importantly for our topic, had developed a theory of exegesis that dove-tailed closely with it.[45] The same view had emerged in several of the Greek ascetical writers who had used it as an underpinning for the new ascetical monasticism.[46] Along which paths these ideas reached Eucherius is a question we are not, and perhaps never will be, able to answer fully; but that they reached him in this latter form we can be certain. Eucherius at the beginning of the *Formulae* says that his concern is with a spiritual as opposed to a physical understanding and that the spiritual is to be preferred precisely because while the spiritual gives life, the opposite kills. This dichotomy he expresses by way of an accommodation of 2 Cor 3:6 where 'spirit' is taken to be 'the spiritual', and as 'spirit' is opposed in the text to 'letter', so 'spiritual' is opposed to 'physical'.[47] He developed this division a little later when he said that sacred studies could be divided into (1) practical and (2) the theoretical. This classical dyad of *theoria* and *praxis* corresponds to the actual everyday life (*vita actualis*)—concerned with moral correction—and the contemplative life (*vita contemplativa*) concerned with the things of Heaven and the interpretation of the Scriptures.[48] In this, as Courcelle has shown, his direct source is Cassian who in turn is quoting Evagrius of Pontus.[49] Needless to remark, this ascetical vision of the material world and these categories for understanding the spiritual world which these writers, Eucherius in particular, were so insistent upon, and which they were eager to contrast to 'pagan' and 'secular philosophy', are almost wholly derived from the very sources they are meant to oppose.[50] In so far as these categories would later become commonplaces in Latin exegesis, Eucherius is an important bridge between Neoplatonic religious theory and Latin thought in the Middle Ages.[51]

45 V.F. Hopper, Medieval Number Symbolism, New York 1938, 47.
46 Courcelle, op. cit,, 224–236.
47 *Formulas spiritalis intellegentiae conponendas tibique mittendas . . . quibus perceptis in omnia scripta diuina facile se ad intellectum sequax sensus intenderet. Nam cum 'littera occidat, spiritus autem vivificet', necesse est ad illa spiritalium interiora sermonum spiritu vivificante penetrari*, opening sentences of the Praefatio, 1.
48 *Omnis autem disciplina nostrae religionis ex illo duplici scientiae fonte manavit, cuius primam practicen secundam theoreticen vocaverunt, id est actualem et contemplativam; unam, quae actualem vitam morum emendatione consummet, aliam, quae in contemplatione caelestium et divinarum scripturarum disputatione versetur.* Praefatio, 5.
49 Courcelle, op. cit., 232–233, n.57.
50 Ibid. ch. 5,1, 224–236; Courcelle repeatedly points out the irony that they opposed 'pagan [=Greek] philosophy' at every turn while unconsciously adopting the very categories which would ensure that they would view Christianity through the eyes of later Greek religious philosophy.
51 The distinction *actualis-contemplativa* is characeristic of early medieval exegesis, and it has been noted by many authors; some have even seen it as a special quality of Irish exegesis (cf. B. Bischoff, 'Turning-Points in the History of Latin

The focus of exegesis

The other area where Eucherius departed from Augustine in favour of a more Platonic view is in his approach to the 'senses of Scripture'. On this topic there has been a wealth of writing in recent decades and it is this aspect of Eucherius's work that has received most attention. I do not propose to cover this ground again, but only to point out a strange anomaly: his agenda for a manual is clearly inspired by Augustine, yet its contents conform to an agenda that owes more to Jerome and Cassian than it does to the theory of interpretation that led Augustine to desire manuals. This whole discussion on the senses of Scripture has been further complicated by the practice, already established by medieval writers, of discussing Jerome's, or some other writer's approach, as 'favouring the literal' or 'the allegorical'. However, while these early writers did use these terms, they did not use them with anything like the systematic precision with which these were used in the medieval period—and we should be cautious about overly precise statements about their use even then. It must be borne in mind when we discuss the senses of Scripture that it is only with Eucherius refining Cassian that anything like a systematic format emerges. Eucherius outlines his system at the beginning of the *Formulae* : first in knowing are the divisions of philosophy—the divisions of physical, ethical and logical; which in turn correspond to natural, moral and rational; and which in turn are related to historical, tropological and anagogical senses of Scripture.[53] The terminology has earlier roots, but as a unified theory explicitly applied to scriptural interpretation Eucherius marks an important development in the history of Latin exegesis and we must be careful about anachronistic retrojection of any neat system of labels, such as those which became commonplace in the Middle Ages, to earlier Latin writers.[54]

Eucherius' terminology was common to most writers of the period: the same division of knowledge is found in Augustine;[55] however, in

Exegesis in the Early Middle Ages', Proceedings of the Irish Biblical Association 1 (1975) 86 [='Wendepunkte in der Geschichte der lateinischen Exegese im Frühmittelalter', Sacris Erudiri 6 (1954)]); its actual importance in that exegesis needs, however, to be more fully examined: the distinction is used repeatedly to import a Platonic dualism of heaven-earth, spirit-flesh, sacred-secular and with the implication that these can be further parallelled with good-bad, of God-of the devil; in support of my argument I would point to the use of the distinction in a very obviously Platonic way by Eriugena in his Homilia in prologum sancti evangelii secundum Joannem (SC 151, É. Jeauneau ed. 1969).

53   Formulae, praefatio, 4–5.
54   In Carolingian works, for example, borrowing directly from Eucherius' Formulae, the commentary on a particular passage is often divided up literally under a rubric: *historialiter, spiritaliter* and *moraliter*, cf. my 'Adam's Rib and the Equality of the Sexes: Some Medieval Exegesis of Gen 2:21–22', Irish Theological Quarterly 59 (1993) 44–54.
55   E.g. De civitate Dei IV 4 and XI 25; and cf. Courcelle, op. cit. 232–233, who points to the origin of the division in Eucherius.

the way he applied it to Scripture—identifying the 'physical-natural-historical' with the 'literal', and the others with the more valuable 'spiritual' senses—he gives his whole approach a direction away from Augustine. Writers such as Jerome and Augustine were deeply aware of the need for several different senses if the Scriptures were to be understood. For Jerome this was necessary so that a valuable spiritual truth could be derived from what else might seem to be the dead letter. Thus we could characterize the need for additional senses in Jerome as programmatic—these senses were needed because of the very nature of Scripture. For Augustine, on the other hand, this need was practical and apologetic: unless other senses were invoked in solving particular problems of exegesis, the Scriptures might seem contradictory or full of seemingly irrelevant details.

Jerome's most celebrated comment is in his *In Ezechielem* where he explained what he took the word 'Jerusalem' to mean under the various senses:

> *Quattuor autem modis intelligi potest Jerusalem: vel haec quae Babylonio et Romano igne succensa est; vel coelestis primitivorum; vel Ecclesia quae interpretatur 'visio pacis'; vel animae singulorum quae fide cernunt Deum. Illudque quod plerique de coelesti Jerusalem interpretandum putant, Ecclesia non recipit, ne omnia quae in presenti prophetia contexuntur, ad coelestium fortitudinum ruinas atque cruciatus, et restitutionem in pristinum statum suscipere compellamur.*[56]

These four meanings of 'Jerusalem' as the city that can be burned down, the Church, the believer's soul and the heavenly city, are strikingly similar to the example of the need for fuller spiritual understanding of Scripture that is found in John Cassian where Jerusalem is the Jewish city, the Church, the heavenly city and the human soul as a moral subject.[57] Whether Jerome and Cassian are related to one another historically is not my concern; at the very least they are linked conceptually. In both the desire is to the get beyond the letter (which is directly related to the material and historical) as quickly as possible. Only when one realizes that, when Scripture speaks of 'Jerusalem' one need not be seriously concerned with a city in Palestine with a particular history, and is able to get beyond this level, does the real meaning of Scripture reveal itself. Jerome is often fretful that the historical and literal is but a veil to be passed through, while Cassian situates his comments in a passage which is explicitly concerned with 'spiritual knowledge', and in the following chapter he points out that we must leave the 'practical' for this higher knowledge. This contrast and

56 In Ezechielem 4,16 (PL 25,125); and cf. R.E. McNally, The Bible in the Middle Ages, Westminster, MD 1959, 54.
57 Conlatio XIII, 7–8.

division is further strengthened by citing Prov 31:21 and 22:20, in their LXX form.[58] The effect of this is to suggest that truth is double wrapped and one must remove outer covering (the literal/ historical) before one knows what one is dealing with; and then there are three aspects to the inner hidden truth (allegorical, anagogical and tropological). Then by an examination of Paul's interpretation of the Old Testament in Gal 4:22–27 he suggests that his method is identical to that of the Apostle's, and this functions as a proof for his scheme.

Augustine gave several accounts of what he considered to be the different levels of meaning that were to be found in the Scriptures.[59] Perhaps his most systematic explanation is to be found in the *De utilitate credendi* where he outlines (1) an historical (the facts of history), (2) an aetiological (exegesis by finding causes), (3) an analogical (the congruence of Old and New Testaments), and (4) an allegorical (figurative explanation).[60] Apparently closer to the approach of Jerome and Cassian is the admonition at the beginning of the *De Genesi ad litteram* where the reader is told to note in Scripture the (1) things of eternity which are communicated, (2) the facts of history which are recounted, (3) the future events which are foretold, and (4) the moral precepts which are set out. What distinguishes these approaches is that the first three senses in each case are implied in the literal text itself and accessed through the study of the text and the direct study of events and facts that the text records. So while Jerome and Cassian see the text and its historical details as something to be passed early on in exegesis, for Augustine it is the central focus and is only left when it has been exhausted and there are still problems remaining. It is this approach that he exemplifies for students in the *De doctrina Christiana* where he shows how a knowledge of language solves some questions, a knowledge of the liberal arts, of history, geography, zoology, mineralogy other questions, a study of the relationship of one text to another still more questions, and finally when these earlier approaches are abandoned—then we can speak of allegory in Scripture.[61] While the resulting exegesis from either school may appear very similar, at least to us, the intention behind it is vastly different: for Augustine all these external facts are the free work of the Creator and all that occurs in history is part of the work of his providence and as such has a status greater than human conjecture and must never be dismissed.[62] It is because this

---

58   Cassian's own use of Scripture here, and of these two verses in particular, needs fuller examination.
59   Caplan op. cit.,285
60   De utilitate credendi 5–7 (J. Zycha ed. 1891, CSEL 25, 7–9).
61   De doctrina Christiana II, passim; and cf. my 'The Exegetical purpose of Adomnán's De Locis Sanctis', loc. cit.
62   De doct. Chr. II 29,45–46; and II 32,50.

examination of the Scriptures requires exact information gathered in the field, from books, and from a minute study of the use of words and things mentioned in the actual text of the Scriptures that he recognized the need for manuals. Augustine was glad that some were already in existence—and perhaps forestalling a criticism that these were not the more interesting of books either to write or to read, added that those who have provided them had performed a 'truly valuable service to the Church' (*non sane parvum beneficium*)[63] from people like Eusebius;[64] others were being produced—indeed later he praised the work of Jerome in this regard;[65] others were still needed on such things as numbers, places, customs, animals, trees, plants, minerals and other things: when they are produced they will be most useful in solving the problems (*aenigmata*) of the Scriptures.[66]

It was this aspiration of Augustine, carried out using Jerome's approach to the Scriptures, that inspired the *Formulae* and insured its high reputation during the early the Middle Ages. Eucherius approached his task with a 'Platonic' two-tier view of the universe and a similar 'Platonic' view of Scripture regarding the division between letter and spirit. Each attitude would reinforce the other and the resulting vision would become a common-place of Latin thought.

THE FORMULAE

The concept of a 'formula'.

The word '*formula*' has a range of meanings in Latin somewhat comparable to its various uses in modern English: it can mean a legal document, be part of a fixed process, or describe a part of liturgical ritual.[67] None of these well evidenced uses fully explains why Eucherius chose it as the title of his book or why he says in the preface that he is sending a work on the *formulae* which go to make up a spiritual understanding. However, from the various uses of the word we can say, with some certainty, that Eucherius intended it to convey the notion of a series of little pictures that would make the message of the text clear by being used in a fixed and orderly way. In legal documents the word means a fixed rule, method and process for carrying out a case, and in particular a rule of evidence on which an enquiry is conducted. This clearly fits the purpose of the book. The book is

63   Ibid., II 16,23.
64   He was probably thinking of his Chronici canones and his onomastic works.
65   De doct. Chr. IV 7,15 which he wrote in the late 420's and long after the earlier books of the De doctrina.
66   Ibid., II 29,45.
67   Lewis and Short, A Latin Dictionary, Oxford 1879, 769 s.v.; and J.F. Niermeyer, Mediae Latinitatis Lexicon Minus, Leiden 1976, 446–7, s.v.

intended to give an inquirer a fixed and definite guide for finding out what is the implied signification of a particular word or passage in Scripture.

From a later writer, Adomnán of Iona, we see that the word *formula* means a little picture that makes clear an obscure point in a text.[68] This gives us another hint as to its meaning here: it is a collection of small pictures that can be used to see through to the hidden meaning in the Scriptures. Eucherius takes, on the whole, visible things in Scripture and overlays them with another layer of more spiritual pictures. The Scripture text is a series of coded signs and it can be dissected into its individual signs and then, using this book of fixed codes, it can be deciphered and its real meaning made plain, each new meaning corresponding to an item in the text.

It is helpful to keep a visual notion of exegesis in mind when reading Eucherius. The text uses names of visible things: parts of the body such as head or hands, things like money or chariots, or visible activities like sitting or running. These belong to the visible corporeal world and point beyond to the unseen world: the book allows us to glimpse through these visible bits-and-pieces the bits-and-pieces of a higher world. The book is the collection of these glimpses and is a map for seeing the unseen within the seen.

The range of the work

In the book as edited by Wotke[69] there are ten sections of varying length: section 9 (on Jerusalem and things connected with it) has the largest number of entries at 73, while sections 1 (on referring to parts of the Lord's body) and 10 (numbers) have the fewest—each with 24. All in all there are 465 items covered in the book.[70] Thus from the first it looked like a series of things, gathered in classes and explained, exactly what Augustine had asked for.[71] Some comments on these sections shows how this work fits into the agenda of fifth century interpretation and how it is typical of much medieval writing not only in exegesis, but on liturgy, and in the broader sphere of religious writing and art.

The first section deals with the application to God of names from parts of the human body and the application to God of things that humans use. He mentions 'eyes', 'ears', 'mouth', 'word', 'arm', 'right hand', 'womb', 'feet' and 'footsteps' as names relating to a human body used of God; and of things he lists various weapons (e.g. 'arrow'), instru-

---

68 Adamnanus, De locis sanctis I 2,2; 18,1; 23,19 (L. Bieler ed. 1965, CCSL 175).
69 Wotke's edition is much shorter than the text in PL; on the problems of the edition and the need for a new edition see 250–251 below.
70 The sections have respectivly: 24; 39; 68; 70; 34; 39; 68; 26; 73; and 24 entries.
71 De doct. Chr. II 39,59.

ments (e.g. 'rod' and 'chariot', and other things such as 'coals', 'smoke' and 'fire'. This roughly corresponds to what Augustine deals with under the 'First Rule of Tyconius' which relates to interpreting Scripture in terms of the Lord and his body.[72]

Here we see the simplicity, as well as the limitations,of the approach. There is no discussion of the nature of anthropocentric images for speech about the ineffable, nor any justification for them. The author was clearly little bothered by such images and there is no hint that there are difficulties with such uses of language. Augustine had pointed out that while such images were inadequate, they were necessary and to think one could avoid them involved one in a contradiction.[73] Eucherius saw them as having direct, if metaphorical, significance and they could be decoded into clear and direct language. At no point does he suggest that his explanation of an 'obscure' term is still, in relation to God, but a cipher. There is a stark pictorial positivism: God is such-and-such but hides himself in obscure images. The faithful soul can know what reality lies underneath these metaphors. The Christian with spiritual understanding can see into the depths of reality and can even see God. Thus God's 'arm' and 'right hand' stand for the instruments by which he does all things; the 'womb' of the Lord is that through which his Son is brought forth; and his 'footsteps' (*vestigia*) are the secret signs he has left in his works.[74] In this last example Eucherius touches on a favourite Augustinian theme, that God can be known from his *vestigia* in the creation.

In the second section Eucherius explains things that are 'above the earth' (*de supernis creaturis*): first things like clouds, thunder and lightening; then things relating to angels (e.g. thrones), the heavenly bodies (sun, moon, and stars), and then meteorological phenomena such as snow, ice, the winds, and the cardinal directions. This material strikes us as quaint and, at first sight, its position of importance in the work, and its detail (39 items and some with two different meanings: one good and another bad), is inexplicable. However, here we get a far better insight into Eucherius' world than in his discussion of more obviously religious images such as the 'right hand of the Father'.

The first point is that this material relates to the most magnificent and most awesome parts of the material world. It was not only in Scripture,[75] but in the everyday knowledge of ordinary people, whether Christian or not, in the late Roman empire that the phenomena of the sky (the weather and objects in the heavens) were believed to be meaningful

---

72   Ibid., III 31,44.
73   Ibid., I 6,6.
74   Formulae I, lines 11–16 and 19–29.
75   E.g. Acts 2:19 (And I will show wonders in the heaven above and signs on the earth beneath, blood, and fire, and vapor of smoke); or Dan 6:27; Lk 21:11; Rev 13:13; the notion of the heavens as the proclaimers of the divine work is too widespread to be covered in a note.

communicators of things divine. They stood as signs and pointed out the eternal. In the world of Eucherius few doubted, Augustine being one of this small minority, that all such matters were of major religious value.[76]

Moreover, we see the intellectual-scientific world of Eucherius in this section. We do not think of the 'winds' as distinct 'things'—to us they are but convenience names for a major force in our weather. For instance, by 'that's a cold east wind!' what we mean is that the phenomenon of wind is particularly noticeable on a certain day—we may not even bother to check the direction: a cold wind is an 'east wind' from whichever direction it comes! But to Eucherius the different winds are 'things' each with its own specific nature and qualities. Similarly, with the directions of the compass: to us they are only reference points in our plotting of place; but they are more than names to Eucherius. There is a reality, 'the south' and so forth, and when these words are used in Scripture they are 'things' with an added significance and not just verbal metaphors.[77] To dismiss these points as merely footnotes in the history of scientific thought does not do justice to their importance in understanding Eucherius' view of Scripture. If Scripture refers to winds and cardinal points and considers them real things—a position certainly held by Eucherius and most probably held by the scriptural authors too, then one does not see Scripture as using poetic images but as using the real world as a set of encrypted messages. Thus the first and obvious meaning of any reference to natural realities is a literal reading of 'the facts', and it is this state of affairs which exists in the real world that forms the *datum* from which all the other 'senses' spring. There was no need to see any distinction regarding knowledge between what was contained in the Holy Book and the reality people saw around them.[78] We today are surprised by this literalism and how they used the Scriptures as a source of information about the external world, and vice versa. It reminds us of contemporary fundamentalism.[79] However, there is a crucial difference: the literalism which produced a book like the *Formulae*, and which it in turn did so much to propagate, was a coherent response to all the then known 'facts' and at no point did it generate contradictions of fact. The claim, therefore, for the inspiration and authority of the Sacred Text stood in continuity with, and in an apologetic mode could rely on the support of, the rest of human knowledge. The fundamentalist position is the exact opposite of this: the incoherence and discontinuity between human

76 Cf. my 'Astrology and Thirteenth Century Philosophy', Milltown Studies,33 (1994) 91.

77 I have examined the role of wind and cardinal points in the religious universe of the Middle Ages in 'The Quincentenary of Schedel's Map of the Creation: A Turning point in the Development of the Modern Mind', Milltown Studies 31 (1993) 46–47.

78 Cf. my 'Aqua super caelos (Gen 1:6–7): The First Faith-Science Debate', loc. cit.

79 Often there is an uncanny similarity between the questions asked in the early medieval period and the answers they produced and the literature of contemporary fundamentalist sects.

knowledge and the 'facts' in the Book is its *datum*. The authority of the Book is, in the modern case, neither a guarantee alongside the process of knowing nor a consequence of knowing, but the 'fact' that is to be known and against which all other 'facts' are to be judged. Furthermore, while Eucherius and those who came after him saw an interplay between the Scriptures and external 'facts', to the fundamentalist the trade is only one-way: the text can dictate to the rest of knowledge, but the rest of knowledge cannot challenge an interpretation of the text. To the fundamentalist, but not Eucherius, if and when the 'facts' are in agreement with the text, it is not primarily a help to understanding the text but an instance which demonstrates the reliability of the whole book and hence its divine authority.

We see in this section that deriving a sacred message using the *Formulae* is not limited to the study of the Scriptures; for just as it is made up of icons derived from reality, so the things themselves are icons of a spiritual reality. When one reads in the book that the sun stands for Jesus Christ or the moon for the Church this not only decodes references to these things when they are found in the book, but the actual sun and moon are, when seen in the sky, images that remind one of higher spiritual realities. Thus while one walks home on a wintry evening one can see the sun, moon, stars, clouds, frost and snow and feel the wind, and all these phenomena can be understood as pointing to another higher and hidden universe. Of this other world only seen in faith the Christian was as much a part as he was part of the wintry scene around him physically. The sun was the Sun of Justice: Jesus Christ who lights up the world; the moon was the Church to which the man belonged and which shone out amid the darkness of this world because it reflected Christ to the darkened world. In the Church there were the teachers who shone like stars and the mysteries which were veiled from human sight (clouds); while round about there were those who acted with justice (snow) and others hardened in their sins (frost).[80]

One further note should be made on how this picture-for-picture, thing-for-thing exegesis impacted on the life of the Church: it was intimately connected to the liturgy. Whether the interpretations given by Eucherius were derived from the liturgy, or whether the liturgy's use of the same symbolism is derived from Eucherius is a complex matter and beyond the scope of this paper. However, it should be noted that there are a great many overlaps, not just in this section but throughout the *Formulae*, between images interpreted here as biblical and similar uses in the liturgy. Furthermore, many scriptural texts used as antiphons, and the like, in the liturgy for particular feasts are also found as illustrative texts in Eucherius. Examples in this section are Ps 18:2 for the feasts of the Apostles and Dan 12:3 for the feasts of Doctors. This relationship

---

80 Formulae II.

with the liturgy deserves a full study, not least in view of the fact that both the liturgy and Scripture can be 'read' within the same cognitive framework and, indeed, have a remarkably similar content. Such a study if it examined not just the individual images employed, but looked at how the liturgical and scriptural imaginations coincided in the period after Eucherius might take us far closer towards understanding the development of the Latin theological mind in the early medieval period than either approach individually.

The third and fourth sections of the *Formulæ* deal with earthly things (*de terrenis*) and animals (*de animantibus*). Under these headings are mentioned geographical features like rivers and mountains, trees and fruits, stones and metals, and there is a detailed list of animals. These two sections correspond most closely to the most specific of Augustine's lists of items he wanted catalogued: places, animals, plants, trees, stones, metals 'and other things mentioned in Scripture'.[81]

The fifth (the significance of names derived from human offices) and the sixth section (the significance of imagery derived from the human body) are both classifications not explicitly mentioned by Augustine for lists and so stand somewhat apart from the rest of the book. In the fifth section there is the significance of human being (*homo*), man (*vir*), woman (*mulier*), virgin (*virgo*), of authority figures such as king (*rex*), of family relations such as brother (*frater*) and wife (*uxor*), and of 'occupations' such as poor person (*pauper*) and shepherd (*pastor*). What is most interesting about this group is the number of times that the Church is the thing pointed to.[82] In no other section is this ecclesial dimension so apparent and, even where it is not mentioned, most of the titles in the list are understood implicitly in terms of the Church in that they point to different roles, ministries or ecclesial realities like Baptism.[83]

The sixth section lists parts of the human body from head to toe and from the internal organs to the footsteps that are left behind when we walk. Compiling a list of the parts of the body was of great value within his exegetical framework, as this body imagery is so frequently used in Scripture and there was the precedent that Paul used such imagery allegorically in his letters. However, there are some surprises in the list in what is left out: rib (*costa*) and heart (*cor*) are not mentioned.[84] Likewise there are no references to the genitalia and there is no reference to female bodily parts: the human body which Eucherius considers here is a *male* body.[85]

81   De doct. Chr. II 39,59.
82   In 6 of the 34 items the Church is given as the thing signified.
83   In addition to the six explicit references to the Church there are 11 or 12 references to ecclesial realities.
84   I have considered some aspects of body imagery, and of the rib in particular, in medieval exegeis in my 'Adam's Rib and the Equality of the Sexes', loc. cit.
85   It could be argued that there is an exception, for he treats of the word '*venter*' which we usually take to mean 'womb' (Formulae VI); however, the primary meaning of

The seventh section deals with various things that are used in the Scriptures. He looks at things like bread, wine, oil, salt, honey, linen, fire, shadow, items of furniture, keys, money, and again at various precious stones (e.g. pearls) and metals (gold, silver, bronze, iron and lead). This section follows Augustine's pattern exactly as 'it gathers all the other things that Scripture uses as signs.'[86] Indeed, just as he repeatedly mentioned the need of a list of metals and stones so here some of the material already covered in the section on earthly things is repeated. The section here also has another interest: many of the things explained here were originally used explicitly in Scripture as symbols, and so even today we would ask what are these a metaphor of. However, it is not easy to think ourselves back into his theological world. Two examples suffice to demonstrate this. He asks what is the meaning of 'keys' (*claves*)? We would probably imagine this allegory in terms of '*virtus clavium*' and then perhaps authority, papacy or faculties to absolve. However, their first signification is that of an opening to spiritual knowledge on the basis of Lk 11:52: 'Woe to you legal experts, for you have taken away the key of knowledge . . .'; and its second meaning is the virtues of justice, mercy and piety on the basis of Mt 16:19: 'To you I give the keys of the Kingdom of Heaven'.[87] The second example is the meaning of 'money' (*pecunia*). For Eucherius this stands for the divine words on the basis of Mt 25:27: 'You should have given my money to the bankers'.

The eighth section is concerned with verbs and nouns that are formed from verbs (*de variis verborum vel nominum significationibus*). This covers activities such as '*vigilare*' and '*dormire*' and events like '*ascensus*' and '*descensus*'. It differs from the other sections in that the basis of classification here is grammatical rather than real.[88] And, like section five, it covers a genus of ideas not specified by Augustine as important for an understanding of Scripture.

The last two sections of the *Formulae* are fully in line with the agenda of Augustine: section nine deals with Jerusalem and the temple *cultus* and a few other places; section ten deals with the significance of numbers in Scripture. Elsewhere I have examined how the significance of places held a special place in Augustine's agenda for manuals and that he used places as examples of how such works would help in exegesis.[89]

this word is something like 'belly or 'stomach'—the meaning 'womb' is a derived and more specialised meaning—and that it should be taken in the more general senses is clear in that he takes it to be 'the capacity to reason' on the basis of Hab 3:16 where a male says 'I tremble inside my stomach' (*venter meus turbatus est intra me*).

86 De doct. Chr. II 39,59
87 Formulae VII.
88 Although we cannot exclude the possibility that they are grouped in this way as they all could be part of that genus of 'things' called 'actions'.
89 In all his lists of the manuals that should be produced places top the list; he uses them as examples in II 16,23; III 35,50 and 36,52; cf. 'The Exegetical Purpose of Adomnán's De Locis Sanctis', loc. cit.

This theme had already been explored by Eusebius in his *Onomasticon*, translated into Latin by Jerome,[90] and, as we have already noted, it was a place, Jerusalem, that both Jerome and Cassian took as an example of the different types of exegesis. That any understanding of Scripture involved knowing why places had certain names was a basic truth accepted by all exegetes for a long period before and after Eucherius.

Since so much has been written on the significance of number symbolism, arithmology and numerology in exegesis it warrants no special comment here.[91] As with place-names, only more so, all were agreed that numbers were significant in understanding Scripture: a secret language which pointed to mysteries. However, it should be noted how closely this followed the Augustinian agenda. Augustine repeatedly stressed in *De doctrina Christiana* how important numbers were and how desirable to have a proper list of them. Indeed, at one point he indicated that he wanted the various things listed in classes 'and the same thing to be done for those numbers mentioned in Scripture'.[92] As examples of this he had given meanings for 3, 4, 7, 10, 12, 40, 46, 46, and 153. Eucherius gave meanings for twenty-four numbers and so has the distinction of being the first Latin theological writer to produce a formal guide to Christian number symbolism.[93] Likewise, it is worth noting that while in these two last sections of his book Eucherius was part of a tradition of listing places and numbers for exegetical purposes he has an importance of his own: his explanations are often different from those of his predecessors and very often it was these explanations that became the standard ones for his successors.[94]

Method

All of Eucherius's writings, but especially his two manuals, manifest a very definite scholarly care and method. Indeed, this precision and

90   Cf. my 'Adam's Burial at Hebron: Some Aspects of its Significance in the Latin Tradition', *Proceedings of the Irish Biblical Association* 15 (1992) 66; it is quite possible that Augustine had seen the Latin translation by the time he came to finish the De doctrina Christiana as he at that time praises Eusebius' chronological work, also translated by Jerome.

91   One of the best overall surveys is still Hopper, op. cit.; a survey of more recent work can be found in J. MacQueen, Numerology: Theory and Outline History of a Literary Mode, Edinburgh 1985.

92   II 16,25; II 16,26; II 28,42; II 39,59—where having suggested that the various things should be put in classes he suggested that there is a special listing of numbers; and III 35,50–51.

93   The numbers he covered are: 1–10,12, 14–16, 22,24, 30, 33, 40, 42, 50, 60, 72, and 100.

94   For example on the number 10 he says this is the Decalogue on the basis of Ps 143:9 (following Augustine, De doctrina Christiana II 16,26), but he also gives a meaning to 15 as the number of steps in the Temple; this I have not found earlier than him, but have found after him—moreover this is one of the very few cases where he did not give a citation to support his interpretation.

detachment, on first appearances, puts us more in mind of someone in the early scholastic rather than the later patristic period. One feature of this method stands out: his desire that the interpretation he gives should be not his interpretation but should be the hidden meaning of the thing itself as Scripture wants it to be interpreted. Augustine had pointed out that the best way to interpret Scripture was with Scripture: let it interpret itself, and in that way one could be sure that the interpretation was not an arbitrary opinion. This was to be done by a careful comparison of passages, and what was obscure in one place might be clear in another.[95] This was the very basis of the *Formulae*, for in almost every case the meaning that is given is supported by a citation that makes his interpretation clear. Eucherius was conscious that there were eminent precedents for his conviction that this was an excellent method and one sure to bring one to the truth. Paul had interpreted allegorically (Gal 4:24), and so there was a pattern for his task, and on occasion Paul had written in an explicitly symbolic way, as when he said that 'the head is Christ' (1 Cor 11:3; Eph 4:15 and 5:23). But above all he saw himself in a pattern of exegesis used by Christ himself when he explained the parables allegorically. Here was incontrovertible proof of the validity and dignity of his procedure and the rationale for the work involved in extending it from these items to cover all the images in Scripture. Needless to say whenever Christ or one of the scriptural writers gives a meaning for something it is this meaning that Eucherius follows. Thus for 'field' (*ager*) he says '[this stands for] the world, as in the Gospel "the field is this world"[Mt 13:38]'; and for 'head' (*caput*): 'his [i.e. a man's] head is Christ, as the Apostle says: "the head of the man is Christ"[1 Cor 11:3]'.

Eucherius' desire was for a sure method of exegesis based on what the sign really means and not on human convention; but the price of this simple and sure method was that of assuming that images, symbols, metaphors, and anything else that could be noted as an image in Scripture, had a fixed meaning or set of meanings in the manner of words. To consider a polyvalence of meaning would defeat his project. At best, and in very few instances, an image could have two meanings, one when related to God and another to humans, or one related to a good act and another related to an evil act, but still the essentially fixed quality is maintained. It is clear that Augustine never intended his method to be used in such a simple and rigid way. From the examples he gives in the *De doctrina Christiana* we can see that whenever he considers an image he knows that it has many possible meanings as a sign: the skill of the exegete is to find the most appropriate.[96] With Eucherius any hint that images were not just a second code language disappeared:

95   De doct. Chr. II 6,8; II 9,14; and III 28,39.
96   Ibid., II 6,7; II 10,15; II 41,62; III 1,1;III 36,52; IV 21,45.

symbols were reduced to direct propositional coherences. For Eucherius
the logic of exegesis was that an object in the text stood as the direct sign
of another reality in the manner of a simple hypothetical syllogism: if A
then B; and in those cases where it had two meanings (e.g. one good,
another bad): if A and if x, then B, and if A and if y, then C—allowing
that the relationship between the variables x and y is itself fixed.[97]
Because of this Eucherius can be considered a major force in the development of propositional exegesis. Furthermore, if one takes the view
that the characteristic of Latin theology from the period after the
Fathers almost until today is its fascination with propositions as the form
of theology—and even of Revelation—then the *Formulae* must take
much of the credit for encouraging this development.[98] After the
Formulae, exegesis not only had a fixed method—the different senses
outlined in the preface to the work—but a fixed content: it used a
language whose conventions were established by God and learned by
believers. Exegesis was now the simple matter of applying a technology.

Is this a case of Eucherius reducing Augustine? The history of
theology is littered with less brilliant disciples simplifying, and thus
corrupting, their masters' intentions, yet here I believe we have an
exception. Certainly Augustine did not foresee that in implementing his
agenda the interpretation of Scripture would become so formalized, but
this result was implied in his desire for manuals, and it just so happens
that Eucherius in adhering to his agenda brought it to the surface.
Augustine was impressed by the 'decoding' of the parables that was to be
found in the Gospels—here clearly was a proof that things had symbolic
meanings. More importantly, when he came to express his desire for
manuals he took place-names as the example of how background
knowledge was essential for the full meaning of the text, again with
apostolic authority in Jn 9:7.[99] But in such cases there can be only one
meaning—the actual one given in the text in the case of explanations of
the parables, and the literal meaning of the place-name, its linguistic
etymology, such as was supplied in the *Onomasticon* of Eusebius. Thus in
the very hope of manuals that would give the meaning of 'things' there
is a latent notion that there is a one-to-one signification between the
factual and the deeper/hidden meaning. Eucherius was the hard-
working careful researcher who not only fulfilled his brief well, but who
brought to light dangers in the method we do not see in the master's
work, and of which Augustine seemed to be unaware.

---

97 I examine this question in detail in my 'Augustine's Exegesis and the Evaluation
    of Logic in Medieval Theology', Collectanea Augustiniana V, forthcoming.
98 I have examined this in my 'Julian of Toledo's Antikeimenon and the
    Development of Latin Exegesis', loc. cit.
99 De doct. Chr. II 16,23.

AFTERLIFE OF THE *FORMULAE*

The focus of this article has been to introduce Eucherius as someone whose contribution to the development of Latin theology has been overlooked and who should be more fully studied. But this question turns on just how great an impact he had on the Latin tradition. Answering this presents two difficulties. First, the question's size—it would have to look at almost every theological writer before the thirteenth century and in most of the great MS repositories, even before one looked at the impact of his ideas—it would require many years' work and a book-length monograph. Second, despite the confident tone of many histories of Latin theology, since so much of the material for the period between Eucherius and the twelfth century still lies unedited, or in inadequate editions, any judgement of his impact is at best provisional. What follows is really no more than notes.

The attraction of Eucherius

What made Eucherius attractive in the turbulent period after the fifth century? That he was popular there is no doubt for by the early sixth century Cassiodorus in his encyclopaedia, the *Institutiones*, mentions Eucherius' works among the handful of introductory works on Scripture that every student should know.[100] We have already seen how in the lists of theologians Eucherius is mentioned with approval as a *vir illustris* and significantly Isidore mentions that he wrote with *brevitas*. This desire for *brevitas* is something that appears again and again in writers before the Carolingian renaissance and often it is the only aspect of a writer's style that is picked out for comment.[101] Here I believe is the key to his popularity. The *Formulae* is a neat little book: only 59 pages in the CSEL edition. It was easy and inexpensive to copy, easy to read, and held the promise of every handbook: in any

---

100 Cassiodorus, Institutiones I 10 (R.A.B. Mynors ed., Oxford 1937, 34) where it is put among 5 basic works: the Rules of Tyconius; the De doctrina christiana; Adrianus; and Junilius; much work remains to be done on the role of this list in medieval biblical studies but the following must be noted: A. Souter. 'Cassiodorus' Copy of Eucherius' Instructiones', Journal of Theological Studies 14 (1913) 69–72; B. Smalley, The Study of the Bible in the Middle Ages, Oxford 1941, 17; and Courcelle, op. cit., 355, 370–371 and 374 where he suggests that this scheme may help us identify MSS from Vivarium; whether or not it could identify a particular MS tradition is open to question; however, it certainly could be a useful tool for understanding the make-up of otherwise seemingly diverse collections of material - I suggest as an example St Gallen 908 (CLA 7,953–965) which in many ways reflects the agenda of Cassiodorus: on this MS cf. C.D. Wright, 'Apocryphal Lore and Insular Tradition in St Gall, Stiftsbibliothek MS, 908' in P. Ní Chatháin and M. Richter eds., Irland und die Christenheit: Bibelstudien und Mission, Stuttgart 1987, 124–145.

101 Cf. J.N. Hillgarth, 'Towards a Critical Edition of the Works of Julian of Toledo', Studia Patristica 1 (1957) 42; and his introduction to CCSL 115, xix.

situation it could provide an answer. Its physical convenience was matched by its academic usefulness: in a small book one had a sure method for understanding and preaching without recourse to long, and hard to get at, books. Anyone with a copy could set out to work on their own with confidence: exegesis could be a straightforward, almost mechanical, process. At a time when the educational structures that had trained men such as Ambrose and Augustine were but a shadow of their former glory, a work like the *Formulae* is even more appealing than that of the *vade mecum* to the student: it put a tool into the hands of preachers that did not require great academic skill, or great ability, to use well.

Another aspect of Christian preaching at this time is also significant. Evangelization was still incomplete among the people that were indigenous to the area that had formed the Roman Empire, and at the same time there was the need to preach to those who entered that area from without. This process can be seen as the Church taking over one *cultus* and replacing it with another. In point of fact this was the Church replacing one universe of symbolism with another.[102] Thus the sun cults were replaced by the Sun of Justice, the feast of the *Sol invictus* became Christmas, and on down the line to the fertility symbols in fields and the spirits who guarded wells. But such a symbolic transference requires a coherent set of new symbols. We have already seen that using this hermeneutic one can read both the universe and the biblical text in a similar way: in applying this hermeneutic the Scriptures gave explanation to the universe around the people, while the universe dove-tailed with, and provided and explanation for, both the Scriptures and the Christian faith. It is my belief that the *Formulae* played a key role in this process: for while we expect to find its use in Scripture commentaries, we should remember that it is just as much used in the allegorical interpretation of the liturgy, and bits from it turn up in all sorts of contexts connected with popular religion. The impact of the *Formulae* in medieval iconography is a topic that is only now beginning to receive attention. Indeed, it is possible that its greatest use in preaching was not in explaining scriptural texts, but in contributing to a new Christian imagination for the world around us.

The links between the imagery-system of the *Formulae*, Scriptural exegesis and liturgy are especially interesting. As sacramental theology developed in the West it took on a very formal and fixed aspect where all its images could be expressed in a propositional way and mysteries could be regulated by law. Indeed, in Latin theology when we think of things acting as signs in a fixed relationship to a spiritual meaning we think of the sacramental system. The extent to which he directly contributed to this system is something beyond the present state of our knowledge—

---

102 This view of evangelization as the replacement of one symbolic universe by another I take from J.N. Hillgarth, 'Popular Religion in Visigothic Spain' in E. James ed., Visigothic Spain: New Approaches, Oxford 1980, 52.

but that he contributed to the intellectual framework that eventually produced Latin sacramental theology there can be no doubt.[103]

Diffusion

In looking at the spread of the *Formulae* I want to show that while it is unknown to us, by and large, that was not the case for any theologian or preacher in the early medieval period.

Direct evidence: MSS and re-workings

From before the end of the ninth century 10 MSS are extant with this work.[104] While arguments from the number of extant MSS are weak as they depend to a large extent on the serendipity of survival, we should notice that very few works of 'minor figures' survive in anything like this quantity from this period. We are on safer ground when we look at the distribution of the MSS in terms of their origins: southern France;[105] northern France;[106] upper Rhine;[107] Britain[108]; northern Italy;[109] and central Germany.[110] And, we should not forget that in many cases this information is based on old catalogues and that this number should therefore be viewed as conservative. All these early MSS exhibit other interesting features: in nearly all of them there are other introductory works in exegesis (glossaries, simple sets of *quaestiones et responsiones*, and the like) and many show signs of having been prepared specially for the

---

103 It should be noted how frequently this work appears in canonical texts: e.g. The Collectio canonum hibernensis XVIII 1,a (H. Wasserschleben ed., Leipzig 1885, 55); and cf. F. Brunhölzl, Geschichte der lateinischen Literatur des Mittelalters, Munich 1975, 191; and my 'Adam's Burial at Hebron', loc.cit., 77.

104 This is the number of MSS of the work given in the index by R.A.B. Mynors to CLA [=Codices Latini Antiquiores] in CLA Supp.,[75].

105 Paris B.N. Lat. 9550 (CLA V 589)—possibly from Lyons, s.VI-VII (this is codex P in Wotke's edition); the fact of the extensive survival of MSS—but not their geographical distribution—was mentioned by Pricoco, loc. cit.

106 Leyden Univ. Bibl. Voss. Lat. F.82 (CLA X 1581) from the Paris region; what is contained in this MS is an excerpt from Eucherius and while he is not mentioned in the entry at n. 1581 he is mentioned in the index by Mynors, CLA Supp. [75]; cf. n. 113 below.

107 St Gallen 225 (CLA VII 928) and 230 (CLA VII 933) (this is codex G in Wotke's edition).

108 Zürich Z XIV 30 Nr,II (CLA Supp.1778).

109 St Gallen 908 (CLA VII 965) cf. n. 100 above; Milan, Ambros. I, 101 sup (CLA I 6)—mid-eighth century from Bobbio; and Rome, Sessorianus 77(2107)(CLA IV 423)—this MS dating from the second half of the eighth century is from North Italy and was written in uncial—but it is an uncial that has all the characteristics of a Caroline display script; this is the venerable codex which Wotke believed on the basis of its use of the uncial to be the oldest surviving MS and upon which he based his edition, cf. 115 below.

110 Vatican City, Biblioteca Apostolica Vaticana, Lat. 553 (CLA III 352)—eighth-ninth century from a Germanic area.

schoolroom or other didactic purposes,[111] or at least for purposes of study.[112] All of which indicates that this was not just a work that was copied *ne pereat*, but one which was highly valued and widely used.

Another indication of the popularity of the work is the number of re-workings that can be found that either abridge the whole work or just copy sections or parts of sections. When consulting MSS *in situ* it is instructive to note those snippets of information that are used to fill a blank page or half-page at the end of a larger work. Often these take the form of a table of words or a short glossary: I have noticed that the *Formulae* often supply these snippets.[113] Moreover, we know that the whole work was abridged at least twice. The text that has been used throughout this paper is that edited by Wotke in CSEL which is considerably shorter than that which is found in PL 50. Wotke believed that the MS on which he based his edition was from the sixth century and that it represented the original in its brevity[114]—longer versions were the result of accretion and additions. However, that MS, Sessorianus 77, is of a much later date and actually represents an abridgement.[115] Another abridgement exists in an eighth century Reichenau MS and is entitled *Glossae spiritales secundum Eucherium episcopum*.[116] As regards the text printed in PL—based on a seventeenth century edition whose MS base it probably would be impossible to establish—there is evidence that Wotke's basic judgement was sound and that the text does contain many additional entries. Thus the PL text provides further evidence for the fluctuating state of the text in its MS tradition. Such fluctuations, what-ever headaches they may cause editors, are invaluable to the historian of theology. For a text that is being shortened, added to, glossed, and copied with several layers of scribal errors shows that the text was in demand, in use, and of practical value in the work of the theologian. The spread and number of the MSS, along with the state of the text— indicating much thoughtful use, is mute but crucial evidence that we are dealing with an important item in the evolution of Latin theology.

---

111 It is worth noting that in the ninth century the *Instructiones*, Book II, became a standard part of the apparatus of the study-Bibles known as 'Theodulf's Bibles', cf. J.J. Contreni, 'Carolingian Biblical Studies' in U.-R. Blumenthal ed., Carolingian Essays, Washington 1983, 79.

112 St Gallen 908 is a case in point: cf n. 100 above.

113 I wish to draw attention to this fact in the hope that others in the field may, follow-ing this suggestion, notice such and inform me. I have noticed this phenomenon in Laon, St Gallen, Verona, Paris and Karlsruhe MSS: I do not wish to be more precise at this time as so much work remains to be done in searching out such material and then presenting it to the public; CLA X 1581, cf. n. 106 above, is a good example of how excerpts of the work were incorporated in collections of other works.

114 CSEL 31, editor's preface, vii-viii.

115 Cf. R. Etaix, loc. cit., 1317; and cf. n. 5 above; for details of Sessorianus 77 cf.n. 109 above.

116 CPL *editio altera*, n. 495.

Direct evidence: Works inspired by Eucherius

Eucherius's work is the earliest example we possess of someone taking up Augustine's agenda. This agenda was taken up by many others in the centuries that followed and in different formats: from the travelogue of Adomnán's *De locis sanctis* to the adversarial method of Julian of Toledo's *Antikeimenon*.[117] However, one very definite method that is copied is that of lists of words, arranged in some order, explained with supporting evidence. Here I shall draw attention to just one of these: as late as the twelfth century Garnier of Rochefort in his *Allegoriae in universam sacram scripturam* takes over almost every item from Eucherius, adds many more of his own, and arranges the whole work alphabetically.[118] This pattern of re-using and extending Eucherius can be found with lists of animals, plants, numbers, and stones.

Direct evidence: Pseudo-eucheriana

Another indication of the impact of Eucherius is that he was considered sufficiently worthy to have later exegetical works attributed to him. A major study of Genesis, another of Kings, and a short work on the Holy Places, were attributed to him until well into this century.[119]

Indirect evidence

The evidence of the influence of Eucherius from citations from the *Formulae*, or the use of distinctions (especially such common-places as '*theoria/actualis*', or a system of labels in exegetical works following that found in the preface to the *Formulae*) is so widespread that any attempt to detail it would be but random notes. However, the extent of this use of Eucherius can be seen by looking at references to him, or to distinctions which he made common, in any survey of medieval exegetical material.[120]

---

117 I have taken these two examples as I have written elsewhere on how each follow Augustinian criteria; however, one could pick a great many works from the 6th or 7th centuries which in one way or other tried to fill the need for manuals; pride of place in these attempts must go to the various works of Isidore.

118 PL 112, 849–1087; in PL this work is attributed to Rabanus Maurus, on this cf. P. Glorieux, Pour revaloriser Migne: Tables rectificatives, Mélanges de Science Religieuse, IXe Année, Cahier Supplémentaire, Lille 1952; and cf. Brunhölzl, op. cit., 332.

119 Cf. the note by E. Dekkers in CPL, *ed. altera*, after item n. 498 for an account of the research that led to the rejection of many works attributed to Eucherius in the past; for further detail on his spuria see my 'On dating the Pseudo-Eucherius's De situ Hierosolymis: The Insular Evidence', Revue bénédictine, forthcoming.

120 A suitable example is B. Bischoff's 'Turning-Points in the History of Latin Exegesis in the Early Middle Ages', loc. cit.; the criticisms of this by C. Stancliffe, 'Early "Irish" Biblical Exegesis', Studia Patristica 12 (1975) 365–366, strength-tens my point here: that these exegetical materials are representative of Europe-wide trends at the time.

Why did it disappear?

It may seem strange that a work that was so popular for so long should not only fade from the limelight but disappear altogether. Here we meet the distinction between the manual/textbook and 'the masterpiece', (i.e. a work written by a major shaping force in theology). There is a curious relationship between the theologian of genius and his writings: the quality of Augustine's writings gives Augustine authority; then, within the tradition, that authority held by Augustine as the wise and holy doctor gives an authority to everything written by him. Thus, Augustine's writings retained a currency precisely because of who their author was. Not so with practical manuals: by their nature their glory as tools does not automatically rebound on their authors. Their authority is not in their inherent genius or that of their author, but in their practical use in doing a job. One does not read the *Formulae* for its own sake, but in order to read a more difficult book or write a homily. Its value is in its service to another task and once that task is performed the means are passed over. Here lies the reason behind the disappearance of the *Formulae*. Its destiny was to be superseded by what it would bring about. So in time, better and more complete manuals made their appearance and the *Formulae* looked primitive by comparison. The new scholastic methodology needed manuals of its own, and although the *Formulae* had in its own way contributed to the formation of that method, it was now too simple in its analysis of terms and in its semiotics.[121] Finally, it was perhaps a victim of its own success: so many of its explanations passed into common stock of Christian and theological images that it seemed to do no more than narrate the obvious. For whatever reasons it ceased to play a significant role in theology, and we can never completely explain changes in the history of ideas, we should remember that for approximately 700 years it was a standard tool-of-the-trade and there are but a handful of works whose academic shelf-life comes near, much less surpass, that.[122]

Some Urgent Issues

Wotke's edition of 1894 was a model of editing for its time, however, several developments have rendered it obsolete and a new edition is

---

121 Cf. G.R. Evans, The Language and Logic of the Bible: The Earlier Middle Ages, Cambridge 1984; while Eucherius is not mentioned, in chapters 4 and 6 dealing with the developments in the theory of signification it can be seen how simple is the semiotic theory underlying the Formulae.

122 In n.1 above I drew attention to the fact that by the end of the fifth century Eucherius already had a place in that sequence of works *de viris illustribus* (cf. J. Quasten, Patrology, Utrecht 1950, i, 1–2); he still had that place in the mid-12th century, for the Anonymus Mellicensis writes in his De scriptoribus ecclesiasticis: *Eucherius in divinis scripturis admodum exercitatus scribit Quaestiones in Regum* [cf. n. 119 above]. *Scribit nihilominus de forma spiritualis intellectus; et interpretatione nominum. Habetur et alius liber ab eo conscriptus, qui inscribitur De quaestionibus difficilioribus.* (PL 213,975).

badly needed. The most important of these developments is in palaeography. Wotke based his edition, which departed in major respects from the text published in PL, on the assumption that one MS, Sessorianus 77, represents a sixth century 'pure' tradition of the *Formulae*. But this MS is now recognized to be of a much later date and to contain a shortened version of the *Formulae*.[123] Furthermore, Wotke's intention was to establish by critical editing the 'original' text of the work and for this he used just five MSS: four of which were essentially checks on Sessorianus 77. Since then many new MSS have come to light and those he used have been re-evaluated.[124] Since this work was a school book its text fluctuated far more than a more literary work of theology: thus the endeavour to establish the 'original' text—if such reconstructions are possible—is only part of the task facing the editor. We need to know how in various places and at specific times the text was being used, added to, or shortened. The new edition will have to exhibit the complete MS deposit for the work: thus we may be able to see the use of the manual evolving in actual teaching. Every manual becomes the private research tool of its owners/users; what is needed is as full an account as possible of how the manual originally produced by Eucherius was used over time. This task is an awkward one and may seem an unnecessary amount of labour for an edition of so small a work: however, to judge it by standards that would be applied to a theological work that was intended for reading and study, for example a letter by Jerome or a short tract by Augustine, is to ignore the special position these works had in a formative period in the history of Latin thought. Such an edition may enable us to see the changes and developments as they took place and not just in their concluding phases in the ninth century or later. It may also enable us to relate other works to particular text-families and MS-families of the *Formulae* allowing us to be more precise about the materials available in particular places at particular times.

The present edition has no *apparatus fontium* to enable us to see where Eucherius himself is seeking out a meaning for a sign in Scripture and where he is following earlier writers in giving a designation. A new edition would provide an opportunity for adding this and other material, by way of *apparatus*, which would enable us to situate Eucherius more accurately within the tradition.

CONCLUSION

Eucherius belongs to the very end of late antique civilization. He is a Janus character: he looked back to the urbane world of late Gaul's upper classes and its confident church. He lived in a civilization in rapid

---

123 Cf R. Etaix, loc. cit., 1317 and nn. 5 and 109 above.
124 Cf. nn. 105, 107 and 109 above.

change: the breakdown of the imperial government, the invasions, and even the sack of Rome. The Church too was changing rapidly. Its theology was becoming dominated by the thought of the older Augustine and its theological agenda was being changed for ever. It was changing socially as well: new peoples, new numbers, new pastoral demands in preaching and communicating. Moreover, its spirituality was being transformed under the influence of the new ascetic monasticism. Eucherius reflects all these changes: his work both preserved earlier strands and anticipated the developments of the medieval period. Though the successor to the greatest Latin Fathers, his view of revelation and his method of exegesis exhibits a new formalism and a new caution in thought. His desire for simple guides and sure proofs ensured that his work would be in constant demand, but also reflects a period of academic, if not intellectual, poverty. Today, his work is forgotten and, when it is read, easily dismissed; but this judgement, and I am not in disagreement with it, should not blind us to the fact that in a very different age his work played a crucial role in making us what we are.

ACKNOWLEDGEMENT

I am in the debt of many scholars in the production of this article: in the first place to the Dean of the Faculty of Arts of University College, Dublin, Dr Fergus D'Arcy, for a travel grant in 1992 and 1993 which enabled me to study certain manuscripts of Eucherius *in situ* and to consult other materials not available in Ireland—without this assistance this paper could not have been written.

I must also thank others who have helped me on various points: Dr L.E. Boyle O.P. (Prefect, Biblioteca Apostolica Vaticana); Prof. Dr H.J. Frede (Direktor, Vetus Latina Institut, Beuron); Dr. M.M. Gorman (Milan); Dr. J.F. Kelly (John Carroll University, Ohio); and Dr K. Schmuki (Stiftsbibliothek, St Gallen): the usual disclaimer applies.

Patristic Background to Medieval Irish Ecclesiastical Sources

MARTIN MC NAMARA

SOME DEFINITIONS

In this paper I use the term 'patristic' in the strict sense, as referring to writings on Christian matters from roughly the end of the first century to the close of the seventh (AD 100–700). In the Latin West Isidore (c. 560–636) is generally taken as the latest of the great writers of the patristic period, the last of the Fathers, although Bede (c. 673–735) is often included in this period also, as he is in the *Corpus Christianorum, Series Latina*. With the same *Corpus Christianorum, Continuatio Mediaevalis*, I take the term medieval to cover ecclesiastical texts from the eighth to the fifteenth century.

The writings to be considered as patristic or medieval are those connected with ecclesiastical matters, whether they be orthodox or heterodox, and this either entirely or partially. These sources may be apocrypha, Bible texts, exegesis, homiletical, grammatical texts, computistics or others besides.

PATRISTIC AND MEDIEVAL IRISH ECCLESIASTICAL LITERATURE

From the definition given at the outset, it follows that the early part of Irish Church history falls within the patristic period, that is the period prior to AD 700 (735), thus including St Patrick, Columba of Iona (died 597), Columbanus (died 614), Adomnán (died 704), Laidcend (author of the *Eclogae of Gregory's Moralia in Iob*) and his contemporary, the Irish Augustinus, author of *De mirabilibus sacrae scripturae* (about 665); the anonymous Irish author of *De ordine creaturarum* (AD 675–700); Aileran Sapiens (7th century), and the anonymous Irish authors of a number of other works besides. Like Isidore and Bede, many of these Irish writers also depend heavily on earlier patristic writings.

From the later medieval period (AD 700–1450) we have in Latin a rich heritage of works which are of Irish origin or with Irish connections, written either in Ireland or in Irish circles on the Continent. The Hiberno-Latin section of this ecclesiastical literature is at present being closely studied by scholars from different countries, for instance Ireland, Great Britain, France, Germany, Spain, Italy, Belgium, Holland,

Japan, Canada, the United States of America. It is becoming increasingly recognized that the writings in question constitute a rather closely-knit body of literature with characteristics which both give it internal cohesion and set it off from the mainstream of continental European tradition. While the bulk of the literature originated in the period 650–800, it continued to be produced through the ninth to the twelfth century.

By about the year 900, vernacular Irish tended to replace Latin as the language of the Irish schools. Not, of course, that Irish was not earlier used in ecclesiastical learning. Quite the contrary. From about 700–750 we have a rich corpus of Irish glosses on St Paul's Epistles in the renowned Würzburg manuscript and also from c. 800 in the commentary on the Psalms in the Bobbio Codex now at Milan (Amb C 301 inf.). From the later period, particularly from the eleventh, twelfth and thirteenth centuries, we have Irish texts on a variety of theological subjects (e.g. the Creed, the sacraments, Doomsday, the general resurrection), the sources of which have not as yet been properly investigated.

ARGUMENTS IN FAVOUR OF AWARENESS OF PATRISTIC BACKGROUND

There is a variety of reasons why Irish patristic scholars could profitably make themselves conversant with post-patristic Irish tradition. One is the very valid contributions patristic studies have to make in helping identify the sources of this Irish tradition, in any of its many branches such as apocryphal literature, canon law, biblical exegesis, theological speculation, etc.

Another reason is that any particular branch of learning could profitably interest itself in the history of its own particular discipline in Ireland itself. Thus, philosophers could contribute to the history of philosophy in Ireland, and among Irishmen and women at home and abroad; biblical scholars could do likewise for the history of biblical studies. Likewise for patristic scholars in Ireland with regard to the patristic period of Irish Church history and the use of the Fathers of the Church in the Irish tradition.

Closely connected with what has just been said is the identification of the sources of Irish ecclesiastical culture. Most students are well acquainted with the work done on the sources of British literary tradition, for instance by J. D. A. Ogilvy in *Books Known to the English, 597–1066*, and the current projects intended to bring information on the matter up to date, e.g. *Fontes Anglo-Saxonici. A Register of Written Sources used by Authors in Anglo-Saxon England*, and *The Sources of Anglo-Saxon Literary Culture*, which latter takes up and follows its immediate predecessor J. D. A. Ogilvy. Working along similar lines it may be possible to identify the patristic works known to the Irish AD 450–1200 (or 450–1450).

Further reasons for interest in this Irish tradition is the contribution this may have to make to patristic studies. Some of the Irish texts may help in the critical edition of certain patristic writings. This point has been made in particular with regard to Sedulius Scottus (who wrote c.850). In his commentary on Matthew Sedulius explicitly cites many authors, and clearly not from memory, but rather using a manuscript. For this reason the commentary can be used *codicis instar* by the editors of the Latin Fathers. Bengt Löfstedt has so used it for the textual criticism of the commentaries on Matthew by Jerome and Hilary, the *Homiliae in Evangelia* of Gregory the Great, Augustine's *De sermone Domini in monte*, and the Gospel commentaries and sermons of Bede.[1] Another Irish work replete with citations from earlier and patristic writings is the *Collectio Canonum Hibernensis*. And there are others besides.

A similar reason for interest in this Irish medieval tradition is that it may help us reconstruct lost writings of the earlier patristic age. In his essay 'Wendepunkte in der Geschichte der lateinischen Exegese im Frühmitteralter' ('Turning Points in the History of Latin Exegesis in the Earlier Middle Ages')[2] Bernhard Bischoff remarks that, given the conditions prevailing, it is understandable that the older literature was for a long time available to the Irish only in a selection which depended on chance, and which included literary works regarded with suspicion, as well as unknown and forgotten ones. He instances Pelagius' expositions on the Pauline Epistles from the biblical commentary literature, and fragments said to be from the 'Gospel according to the Hebrews' from the Apocrypha. We shall expand on these two points below.

Not all the patristic texts and doctrine in the Irish tradition are by way of citation or excerpt. Sometimes in the Irish compositions the patristic texts are transformed in what appears to be a new synthesis, whether in cosmology, eschatology or whatever. The active involvement of patristic scholars in the study of Irish texts of this nature is highly important and altogether desirable, principally for the identification of the patristic sources and influences. Without contact between the two branches of learning the ultimate sources may for long remain unidentified, and particular syntheses and points of teaching may be regarded as specifically Irish whereas in reality they may have deep patristic roots.

The particular patristic texts used in Irish sources can have importance in attempts to understand the early Irish Church and to determine what particular foreign influences were at work there, whether these be Eastern or Western, and if Western, what particular area in the West, for

---

1 B. Löfstedt in Aevum 62 (1988) 169f.; in Orpheus 9 (1988) 96f.; in Arctos 21 (1987) 61f., and 22 (1988) 9ff. See also B. Löfstedt, Sedulius Scottus. Kommentar zum Evangelium nach Matthaeus, vol. II, Freiburg im Br. 1991, 648.

2 B. Bischoff, 'Wendepunkte in der Geschichte der lateinischen Exegese im Frühmittelalter,' Sacris Erudiri 6 (1954) 189–281, at 268f. (§§34A, 34B); reprinted in Bischoff's collected essays, Mittelalterliche Studien I, Stuttgart 1966, 205–273.

instance Spain, Visigothic Spain, northern Italy, Bobbio, Gaul, the area of Lyons, Britain. Before any real progress can be made in this field, a thorough analysis of the sources of the Irish tradition is required.

IRISH MATERAL TO BE EXAMINED AD 450–1450

The Irish material to be examined in research work of this nature spans an entire millennium—from the coming of St Patrick to the eve of the Reformation. The material is in Latin and in vernacular Irish. Of the older Latin texts to be examined, some were composed in Ireland and others apparently in Irish circles on the continent. With regard to the contents of this material, whether in Latin or Irish, we have apocryphal writings, biblical glosses and commentaries, grammatical writings, computististical texts, homiletics, hagiographa as well as theological treatises. In many cases, of course, there is no clear-cut distinction drawn between these different classes. Theological issues, in particular, are often treated in the biblical commentaries. Nor is it to be forgotten that some, if not many, of the writings we class as apocrypha originally served as a vehicle for theological opinions.

We shall now take some examples from the different classes of these writings to illustrate the relationship of Irish tradition with the patristic past.

APOCRYPHA

The second Christian century is currently a period of special interest for scholars. A recently founded review is dedicated to that century alone.[3] One of the features of the second century of our era was the production of works which we would regard as apocrypha. In a number of instances these originated in heterodox or only marginally orthodox groups, with the result that some of them have survived only in fragments or in citations. Of the many apocryphal writings from this early period we can restrict ourselves to a few: the Protevangelium of James, the *Transitus Mariae*, the Acts of John, some Jewish-Christian Writings (the Gospel of the Ebionites, the Gospel of the Nazareans, the Gospel according to the Hebrews [or: 'Of the Hebrews']), and the Pseudo-Clementine literature.

Two narratives on the Infancy of Christ have survived in Irish translation, both in fifteenth-century manuscripts. One of them is found as an independent item in the *Liber Flavus Fergusiorum*, the other as part of a

---

3   Second Century 1 (1981). See also C. Osiek, 'Second-Century Church Writers,' in The New Jerome Biblical Commentary, R. E. Brown et al. (eds.), London 1989, 1346–1350, (§80, 34–63).

larger Biblical and New Testament history in the *Leabhar Breac*.[4] The *Liber Flavus* text contains the narrative from the birth of Mary to the birth of Christ. The first section of this, from Mary's conception as far as the journey of Mary and Joseph from Nazareth to Bethlehem for the census, is a translation of a Latin text of the *Protevangelium* of James. It presents evidence that a Latin version of at least a good part of this work was circulating in Ireland until the later Middle Ages. The second part of this Infancy Narrative is related to what M. R. James calls 'the Special Source' of a Latin Infancy Gospel published by himself in 1927 from two manuscripts (BL Arundel 404 and Hereford, Library of the Dean and Chapter 0.3.9).[5] This source covers events from the journey to Bethlehem to the advent of the Magi. Because of the nature of its description of the birth of Christ (as light), James believed it was Docetic in origin and surmised that it was from the apocryphal Gospel of Peter. This view has had very few followers. A section of this Latin Gospel coincides verbatim with a citation on the Magi given by Sedulius Scottus as from the 'Gospel according to the Hebrews'. Because of this some scholars believe that the 'Special Source' is from this second century apocryphal writing, or more probably from the other Jewish-Christian work 'The Gospel of the Nazareans.' Even this opinion is not without serious difficulties. Whatever of its relation with second century apocrypha, it seems likely that the Latin work itself originated in the West (probably South Germany) before AD 800. It remains for future research to trace its earlier history, and in this examination the Irish evidence is important. The *Liber Flavus* text contains only part of this source, ending as it does before the advent of the Magi. The *Leabhar Breac* text goes further, with the narrative of the shepherds and of the Magi.

Irish texts of the *Transitus Mariae* are found in fifteenth-century manuscripts.[6] It appears, however, that the form of the apocryphon which these manuscripts contain represents one that is earlier than the Greek recension B (John of Thessalonica's *Homily*). This would seem to indicate that the original of the Irish texts must have come to Ireland in the seventh century.

In the *Liber Flavus Fergusiorum* there is a piece headed 'Beatha Eoin Bruinne,' containing episodes from the life of the Beloved Disciple.[7] A colophon in the text says that this was translated from Latin into Irish by Uighisdin Mac Raighin of the Canons Regular of Saint

---

4   The Leabhar Breac text has been edited: E. Hogan, The Irish Nennius from L. na hUidre and Homilies and Legends from L. Breac, Todd Lecture Series, Royal Irish Academy, Dublin 1895, 38–85.

5   M. R. James, Latin Infancy Gospels. A New Text, with a Parallel Version from the Irish, Cambridge 1927.

6   See McNamara, The Apocrapha in the Irish Church, Dublin 1975, 1984, 97, 122f..

7   See McNamara, ibid., 83 (95–98).

Augustine in Holy Island, Lough Ree. Uighisdin, we know, died AD 1405. The sources behind the Irish can be identified. One is the well-known *Apostolic History* of Pseudo-Abdias (or Pseudo-Melito). For one of the episodes of the Life, however (concerning the sinful priest Seuesp; Greek Xeuxis), the only known witness is the fourth-century Greek Oxyrhynchus papyrus no. 850.

The Pseudo-Clementine *Recognitions* can be dated to the third century (AD 211–231), and are regarded as of Jewish-Christian origin. They were known in the West through the Latin translation of Rufinus. There is a citation from Book 8 of the *Recognitions* (in Rufinus' translation) in the work of the unnamed Irish scholar known as Anonymus ad Cuimna-num, *Expositio Latinitatis*. This work, however, from c. AD 730 was probably written at Bobbio, not in Ireland, and for Cuimnanus, 'cloister' bishop and abbot of Bobbio. However, in the Irish (Hiberno-Latin) Reference Bible (from c. 775–800) there are some citations from *Recognitions* Book 3 (3, 27–28) and possibly also from Book 1. It will be a matter for future research to determine to what extent, if any, the Pseudo-Clementine *Recognitions* were known in Ireland.

What I have noted above are but a few examples of the bearing Irish tradition may have on the study of the original texts and on the transmission of the early apocryphal literature. Ireland has preserved a rich corpus of New Testament apocryphal writings. This is being studied at the moment with a view to critically editing the individual pieces and the individual texts, situating each item within the larger context of its proper transmission history.

THE FATHERS: MAINSTREAM TRADITIONS, AUGUSTINE, JEROME, GREGORY

Irish exegetical tradition is, generally speaking, solidly based on the great western Fathers: Augustine, Jerome, Gregory, Cassiodorus, Isidore. The same can be said for the homiletic and theological tradition. This is already clear from the writings of Columbanus, and is becoming ever clearer as source analysis of the exegetical material is being carried out. Thus, for instance, the Irish commentaries on Matthew are heavily dependent on Jerome's commentary and on Augustine's *De sermone Domini in monte.*

It goes without saying, however, that only detailed source analysis of the available material will permit us to give a full and satisfactory picture of the situation, with regard to the writings of the Fathers known and used by the Irish, and as to whether they knew them directly from full texts of their works or from excerpts and collectanea.

APPONIUS' COMMENTARY ON CANTICLES

There is a rich Christian commentary tradition on the Canticle of Canticles. From the Greek tradition we have the commentary of Origen and some others. Two homilies on Canticles by Gregory the Great are known.[8] Other homilies on Canticles ascribed to him are spurious. Bede also wrote an exposition of Canticles that was to become widely used in the medieval West.[9]

A very full commentary on Canticles was composed by Apponius. This work has been transmitted in full and in an abbreviation. Apponius uses Jerome's Vulgate and follows the exegesis of Origen and Hippolytus. His intention is to give a christological interpretation of Canticles, considering it exclusively from the spiritual point of view. He also seeks to bring out in his exposition the relationship of Christ with the Church from the beginnings of history. He is interested in the destiny of the Jewish people, and sees in Canticles the history of divine revelation from creation to Doomsday, including the conversion of the Jewish people. He also understands Canticles as speaking of the union of Christ with the faithful, perfect, soul and of the very special union of the Word with the human soul of Christ.

Various views have been put forward regarding the date and nationality of Apponius. One (held by J. H. Baxter and the Bollandist Paul Grosjean) was that the writer was an Irish scholar of the seventh century. A more commonly held opinion was that Apponius was a Syrian Jew, converted to Christianity, who wrote in Rome in Latin about AD 391–415.

Apponius' commentary has recently been critically edited by B. de Vregille and L. Neyrand.[10] From their analysis of the work these editors believe that the author was a westerner, not a Syrian or a Jew. He may have been a Roman, but could well have been from northern Italy. The early fifth century suits as a date for the work. The first explicit evidence for the existence of Apponius' commentary is apparently Bede. Apponius' work, contrary to earlier opinion, was not known to Cassiodorus (died c. 580) or to Gregory the Great (d. 604). The manuscript evidence indicates that the work was transmitted in the early Middle Ages through insular sources, that is British and Irish.

In the available Hiberno-Latin commentary material the only work drawn on as a source for the understanding of Canticles was Apponius' exposition. These writers knew the complete work, but drew especially on the abbreviated form, known from its opening words as *Veri amoris*. We have texts from it in the Irish Reference Bible (late eighth century)

---

8 Homiliae II in Canticum Canticorum, PL 79,47; CCL 144.
9 Bede, In Cantica Canticorum allegorica expositio (PL 91, 1065–1226; CCL 119B [1983]).
10 B. de Vregille and L. Neyrand (eds.), Apponii in Canticum Canticorum Expositio, (CCL 19), Turnhout 1986.

and in some other works.[11] The editors note that on the continent Apponius' work was diffused principally from Anglo-Saxon centres.

A question not yet settled is how to explain the early history of Apponius' commentary on Canticles. A theory attempting to do justice to the known facts would be that Apponius' work (composed in the early fifth century) lay hidden in Italy, unknown to Cassiodorus and Gregory the Great. This may have been in northern Italy; it may even have been in the monastery of Bobbio. The commentary must have been brought to Ireland and England from Italy in the eighth century at the latest. It is not to be excluded that the abbreviation was made in Ireland, since similar abbreviations of patristic writings were being made by Irish scholars already in the seventh century, for instance Laidcend's *Eclogae moralium in Iob*.[12]

The Canticle of Canticles seems to have been a popular work in Ireland, at least in Céli Dé circles. In the *Teaching of Máel Ruain* (par. 29) we read:

> When a person was at the point of death, or immediately after the soul had left him, the *Canticum Salomonis* was sung over him. The reason for this practice was that in that canticle is signified the union of the Church and every Christian soul. (*As e dob fhath chuige sin de bhrigh gorb ceangal na heaglaisi agus gacha hanma Criostuidhe ciallaigther san chaintic sin.*)

PSALM EXEGESIS: CHRISTOLOGICAL AND HISTORICAL

That the early Irish Church was conversant with the christological interpretation of the Psalms is beyond doubt. In fact, the oldest series of Psalm headings is that in the Cathach of St Columba (c. AD 650), which for this reason is known as 'the Columba Series.' This series is characterized by its christological orientation. The *Commentarioli* of Jerome and the *Expositio Psalmorum* of Cassiodorus, among others, were also used in Ireland. In this sense Ireland was in the mainstream Christian tradition of Psalm exegesis.

Any attempt to understand the Psalms as if they spoke only of Christ or the Church is forced to ignore a wealth of evidence from the Psalms themselves, literary and otherwise. And yet this attempt was widely made in the Christian Church, east and west. As is well known there was a strong reaction to the tendency in the fourth century from Diodorus of Tarsus (died c. 390) and his student Theodore (c. 350–428), later to become bishop of Mopsuestia in Cilicia. Theodore wrote a commentary on the Psalms in which only four of them were regarded as direct

---

11 See M. McNamara, 'Early Irish Exegesis: Some Facts and Tendencies,' in Proceedings of the Irish Biblical Association 8 (1984) 57–96, at 71–73.
12 Ed. M. Adriaen, Lathcen filius Baith, Eclogae de moralibus Iob quas Gregorius fecit (CCL 145, 1969).

prophecies of Christ, that is Pss 2, 8, 46 and 109 (in the Septuagint and Vulgate numbering). This approach to the Psalms was short-lived in the Greek world. Theodore's commentary, however, survived in the Syriac Church and also to a certain extent in the West, thanks to the translation of it made by Julian of Eclanum. After his expulsion from his see of Eclanum (in Apulia, southeast Italy) in 417, because of his refusal to condemn Pelagianism, Julian journeyed to the East and enjoyed the hospitality of Theodore's brother. He translated Theodore's commentary into Latin. An abbreviation of this Latin translation was later made. What remains of the full Latin translation of Julian, as well as of the abbreviation of it, has been transmitted almost exclusively by Irish sources. Julian ended his days in Sicily c. 455. His Latin translation of Theodore's commentary, and the abbreviation of this, must have reached Ireland in the seventh century at the latest. It is the principal text used in Irish exegesis of the Psalms, and its Antiochene tradition gave a very definite direction to Irish Psalm exegesis, which retained a strong interest in historical exegesis and tended to interpret the Psalms against the background of Jewish history rather than as direct prophecies of Christ.

By what route or intermediaries Julian's Latin translation of Theodore's commentary and the abbreviation of it reached Ireland has not yet been determined. Their introduction to Ireland may have been in some way connected with the influence of Pelagian circles. As we shall presently remark, Pelagius' own commentary on the Pauline Epistles enjoyed great prestige in Ireland and is cited by name (*pil., Pelagius*) in Irish texts.

Irish Psalm exegesis of the historical approach is not just of the Antiochene kind we find in Diodorus, Theodore or Julian. In Irish sources, notably the manuscripts Vatican, Palatinus Latinus 68 and Rouen, Bibl. mun. A. 14 (the Double Psalter of St Ouen), we find another form of historical Psalm exegesis in which none of the Psalms is understood as a direct prophecy of Christ. It is not clear whether this form of exegesis derives from some early patristic source as yet unidentified, or whether it originated and developed within the schools of Ireland and Northumbria. In any event, whether of Irish or other origin, its beginnings are to be set within the patristic period.

PELAGIUS ON THE PAULINE EPISTLES

Pelagius himself was more probably a Briton than an Irishman.[13] While there does not appear to be evidence for use of his theological writings

13 For bibliography on Pelagius see M. Lapidge and R. Sharpe (eds.), *A Bibliography of Celtic-Latin Literature 400–1200*, Dublin 1985, 2–20; 3–8; D. Dumville, 'Late Seventh- or Eighth-Century Evidence for the British Transmission of Pelagius.' *Cambridge Mediaeval Celtic Studies* 10 (1985), 39–52; M. Forthomme Nicholson, 'Celtic Theology: Pelagius,' in *An Introduction to Celtic Christianity*, James P. Mackey (ed.) Edinburgh 1989, 386–413. For Pelagius and Ireland, J. F. Kelly, 'Pelagius, Pelagianism and the Early Irish,' *Mediaevalia* 4 (1980, for 1978), 99–124.

in Ireland, Pelagius' commentary on the Pauline Epistles was used in the Irish schools, and furthermore under the real name of its author.[14] From the material available to us on this matter we can say that the chief authority drawn on in the Irish schools for the exposition of Paul was Pelagius in his original unexpurgated form, but also in one or other ot the revised editions of his commentary, particulary that known as *Pseudo-Primasius*. To take but one example, from the best-known Irish text with glosses on Paul, that is *Codex Paulinus Wirziburgensis* in the manuscript Würzburg, Universitätsbibliothek M. p. th. f. 12, containing the Latin text of the Pauline Epistles (including Hebrews) together with numerous marginal and interlinear glosses, both in Irish and Latin. The chief source of the glosses is Pelagius' genuine commentary. It has been reckoned that in all there are 1311 glosses of Pelagian origin here, and Pelagius is cited by name 957 times. We should also note, of course, that Pelagius is not the only source used. Other authors cited by name are Origen (in Rufinus' translation) 21 times, Hilary (by which the Ambrosiaster is meant) 29 times, Jerome 116 times, Augustine 11 times. Since this use of Pelagius in Irish sources has already been treated of on more than one occasion, it need not detain us here.

Pelagius did not accept that the Epistle to the Hebrews was by Paul, and has left us no commentary on it. The absence was made good by a commentary on Hebrews in the Pelagian tradition by an anonymous author. Two forms of this commentary are known to us, one of them in the manuscript Sankt Gallen, Stiftsbibliothek 73 (with siglum G in the study of Pelagius's work). In his 1954 essay on Irish commentary material,[15] B. Bischoff advanced arguments in favour of an Irish origin for this work. The commentary (from the St Gallen manuscript) had been already edited by H. Zimmer,[16] who attached great importance to it because of his particular position on what he believed was Pelagian influence in early Ireland. The St Gallen MS 73 is not in Irish script, but Zimmer believed that the original from which it derives was brought by the Irish monk Moengal from Bangor/Luxeuil to Sankt Gallen. More recent studies have indicated that there was a transmission of Pelagius on the Continent quite independent of any Irish influence and that there was a similar transmission in Anglo-Saxon Britain.[17] Doubts have been cast on the presumed Irish origins or affiliations of St

---

14   See a summary of the evidence in M. McNamara, 'Early Irish Exegesis: Some Facts and Tendencies,' Proceedings of the Irish Biblical Association 8 (1984) 57–96, at 79–84.

15   B. Bischoff, 'Wendepunkte'(cf. note 2 above); Sacris Erundiri 6 (1954), 189–281, at 268f (34A, 34B); Mittelalterliche Studien I, 205–273.

16   H. Zimmer, Pelagius in Irland: Texte und Untersuchungen zu patristischen Literatur, Berlin 1901.

17   See H. Frede's position summarized in Proceedings of the Irish Biblical Association 12 (1989) 90–94; also D. Dumville, art. cit. (note 13 above).

Gallen 73, most recently by Hermann Frede who thinks that it originated in southern France, probably Provence, in the first half of the seventh century.[18] The last word on this matter, however, has not been said. Liam Breathnach, of the School of Irish Studies, Trinity College, Dublin, has very recently drawn attention to the fact that a ninth-century Irish law tract cites a text of the Epistle to the Hebrews together with the corresponding gloss for this particular commentary.[19]

ESCHATOLOGY: TIDINGS OF THE RESURRECTION (SCÉLA NA
hESÉRGI)

In the Irish manuscript Lebor na hUidre (c. AD 1100), pp. 34a–37a, we have what can be regarded as a medieval Irish synthesis on the resurrection. It is an interesting text from our present point of view in that on close examination it shows very strong dependence on patristic texts.[20]

With regard to the date of the Irish text, the first editor, W. Stokes[21] says that on linguistic evidence the text cannot have been composed much before the date of the manuscript, then in 1904, taken to have been the end of the eleventh or the beginning of the twelfth century.

Very little study of the text or of its sources has been done since it was first edited.[22] In Stokes' opinion: 'Next to the Vision of Adomnán . . . and

18 See H. Frede, Kirchenschriftsteller. Aktualisierungsheft, Freiburg im Br. 1988, 23; McNamara, Proceedings of the Irish Biblical Association 12 (1989) 92f.
19 See L. Breathnach's note in Proceedings of the Irish Biblical Association 16 (1993).
20 Editions: R. I. Best and O. Bergin, Lebor na hUidre. Book of the Dun Cow , Dublin 1929, 82–88; J. O'Beirne-Crowe, Scéla ne hEsérgi. A Treatise on the Resurrection, Dublin 1865 (with English translation; a work of little value); W. Stokes, 'Tidings of the Resurrection,' Revue Celtique 25 (1904) 232–259 (text, with English translation, introduction and some notes); P. Walsh, in Mil na mBeach, Dublin 1911, 69–78 (text only, with notes, 122–125). For studies on the text see J. F. Kenney, The Sources for the Early History of Ireland, Columbia Univrsity Press 1929; with addenda by L. Bieler, New York 1966, 738; St. John D. Seymour, Irish Visions of the Other World, London 1930, 121.
21 W. Stokes, 232.
22 Seymour (see above note 20) cites as follows from the opening paragraph (§1; Revue Celtique, 235): 'Heaven and earth will be shaken, and all the elements that are therein. They will be dissolved and melted by the heat of the Fire of Doom; but all those, after being smelted and purified by the Fire, will be cast into a form more beautiful by far than the form in which they existed. The glowing Fire of Doom will burn all the sinners and the impious. But it will do no hurt to the bodies of the righteous, for that Fire will be like a soothing rain to the saints, but will consume the sinners.' In like strain, he comments (p.121), runs a passage from the Leabhar Breac, on the Creed, edited by E. Hogan (Todd Lecture Series 6, 33): 'The whole world, from the rising to the setting of the sun, shall be in one fiery blaze. Sinners shall be weeping and crying, lamenting and grieving, throughout that flame, while it will not at all hurt the righteous.' Similarly, the Fifteen Tokens of Doomsday (which he dates as probably not earlier than the thirteenth century, and possibly

the Tidings of Doomsday this tractate is the most important document now existing for the study of the eschatology of the medieval Gaels.'[23] His words were repeated almost verbatim by James Kenney a quarter of a century later (1929).[24] Forty-six years after Kenney's work, the text was listed among Irish apocrypha by M. McNamara.[25] As to sources for the piece, Stokes admitted that he was too unfamiliar with patristic and medieval eschatology to point them out with confidence. He notes, however, that the Irish writer seems to translate from a nameless person whom he calls 'the author' (*in t-augtar*) in §14, the 'authority (*augtartas*) in §33; 'the sage' (*in t-ecnaid*) in §§30, 36, 37. The Irish writer quotes, or refers to, the Bible in §§2, 8, 10, 16, 27, 28. Augustine is expressly mentioned, Stokes notes, in §12, and that saint's *De civitate Dei* is drawn upon in §11. The refutation by St Gregory (Stokes adds with a question mark: Nazianzenus) of the heretical opinion of Eutyches in §10, Stokes admits he has not traced.

The sources for most of the Irish text can, in fact, be traced. The two principal ones are St Augustine (principally) the *De civitate Dei*, and the *Moralia in Iob* of Pope Gregory the Great. The source analysis of the forty paragraphs of the text is given below as an appendix.

GENERAL CONCLUSION ON SOURCES OF SCÉLA NA hESÉRGI.

The author is heavily dependent, whether directly or indirectly, on Augustine's *De civitate Dei*, and less so on the same author's *Enchiridion*; likewise for two sections on Gregory's *Moralia in Iob*. What is not clear is whether the Irish (tenth? eleventh?) century author is drawing directly on these patristic writings or on some later patristic or early medieval synthesis of eschatology based on these authors, and citing them by name. A less extensive synthesis may have already been used by the compiler of the Irish Reference Bible, c. AD 775–800. An argument in favour of the use of such a synthesis by the Irish author is that he refers to material from both as coming from 'the sage,' and cites a text from 'the authority' (on *Praestigia*) found in neither. His principle 'authority' may have been the synthesis drawing from both Augustine and Gregory, and containing other material besides.

---

later). F. Mac Donncha has a brief reference to this text, which he describes as containing philosophical questions of little interest to the ordinary people; cf F. Mac Donnacha, Seanmóireacht in Éirinn ó 1000 go 1200,' An Léann Eaglasta in Éirinn 1000–1200, M. Mac Conmara (ed.), Dublin 1982, 93.
23   Stokes, 232.
24   Kenney, 738 (see note 20 above).
25   M. McNamara, The Apocrypha (see note 6 above), 141 (§107).

TIDINGS OF DOOMSDAY: SCÉALA LÁI BRÁTHA

Another interesting text from our point of view is that headed 'Scéla Lái Brátha' ('Tidings of Doomsday'), of which only one copy has survived (Lebor na hUidre pp. 31b–34a).[26]

No precise date has been assigned to this Irish piece. Stokes has called it 'Early-Middle-Irish'. It may be from the eleventh century. F. Mac Donncha believes it is one of a set of eleventh-century homilies, possibly composed by Mael Iosa Ó Brollcháin (died 1086).[27] Gearóid Mac Eoin has recently shown that the author of the homily is using phrases from the verse composition *Saltair na Rann,* generally taken to have been composed composed AD 988. This fits in well with an eleventh-century date for this homily.

Lebor na hUidre, we may note, is in two main hands—A and M [=Mael Muire), probably from the eleventh century. It has sections from another hand, regarded as an interpolator or reviser (H), who wrote the homilies. R. Thurneysen assigned the work of the interpolator to the thirteenth century.[28] The reviser is now, however, regarded as probably Mael Muire (mac Céileachair mac mic Cuinn na mBocht), who died 1106. The present text with *Scéla Lái Brátha* is in the hand of the reviser.[29]

The text is in the form of a homily. We first have the exordium (1–7), with an indication of the divine author (3) and the human author (4).[30] Next (5–7; 9–11) comes the biblical text to serve as the basis of the reflection (Matt 24:30; 25:32–46). In 8 and 12 we have enumerations: the six kinds of mercy 'by which the heavenly kingdom is bought' shown by the righteous to Christ (in hunger and thirst; in need of guesthouse or without raiment; in sickness and captivity), and their opposites through which hell is attained. Next (13–14) comes a question and answer: 'It is asked in the Holy Scripture when it is that the Lord will come to the judgement of Doom, and how he will come, and wherefore

26 Editions: R. I. Best and O. Bergin, Lebor na hUidre. Book of the Dun Cow, Dublin 1929, 77–81 (text only); W. S[tokes], 'Tidings of Doomsday. An Early-Middle-Irish Homily,' Revue Celtique 4 (1880) 245–257, 479 (text with English translation); P. Walsh, Mil na mBeach, Dublin 1911, 62–69 (text, with vocabulary, without translation). Studies: Seymour, Irish Visions, 107, 108, 122, 161, 162 (see note 20 above); D. N. Dumville, '"Scéla Lái Brátha" and the Collation of Leabhar na hUidhre', Éigse 16 (1975–1976) 24–28; F. Mac Donncha, 'Medieval Irish Homilies,' Biblical Studies (=Proceedings of the Irish Biblical Association 1), 59–71; id., Seanmóireacht, 77–95 (see note 22 above); see H. Oskamp, 'Notes on the History of Lebor na hUidre,' Proceeding of the Royal Irish Academy, 65C, 1967, 117–176; 'On the Collation of Lebor ne hUidre,' Ériu 25 (1974), 147–156; 'Mael Muire: Compiler or Reviser?,' Éigse 17 (1976), 177–182.

27 Mac Donncha, 'Medieval Irish Homilies,' 61, 67f (see note 26 above); Seanmóireacht 79, 93 (see note 22 above)

28 See Best and Bergin, xvi–xviii (see note 20 above).

29   See Éigse 15 (1973–75), 277–278.

30 On this see Mac Donncha, Biblical Studies, 61–63 (see note 26 above).

he will come.' (13). The answer is given (14) with citations (or rather paraphrases of the text) from Ps 49:3 and 49:5.

After this (15–18) comes a description of the four groups (*cethri budni*) into which the human race will be divided in the day of Doom, the first two to be assigned to hell, the other two to eternal bliss in heaven. One in each group (the *mali non ualde* and the *boni non ualde*) will first be judged; the other two (*mali ualde* and the *boni ualde*) with go to their destiny without being judged.

At the end of the description of the fourth group (the *boni ualde*, not named) something seems to have been lost in the text, which passes to a description of hell (19–22). This is followed by a description of heaven (23–25), following by the ending (*peroratio*) (26).

The Division of Souls:[31] *boni ualde; boni non ualde; mali ualde, mali non ualde*

The following is the essential part of the *Lebor ne hUidre* Irish text on the division of souls on the Day of Doom, in Stokes translation:

> 15. It is certain, then, that there will be made four troops of the human race on the Day of Doom. Now a troop of them shall be brought to judgement and shall go after their doom to pain and punishment. . . . This is the name of that folk in the Scripture, *mali non valde*, that is bad, but not greatly bad.
> 16. Another troop of them will not be brought to judgment, but to hell they will go at once, without adjudication at all then. . . . This is the name of that troop, *mali valde*, that is, what is worst of the human race.
> 17. Another troop of them will be brought to judgment, and they will go after their judgment unto reward. . . . This, then, is the name of that troop in the holy Scripture *boni non valde*, that is, 'good who are not greatly good'.
> 18. Another troop of them, however, will not be brought to judgment, but unto heaven and all golden rewards they will go at once without adjudication at all. With them it is not enough of good to fulfil everything that the divine Scripture enjoins on them to do, so that they abound through their own virtues . . . [:] they do more of good than what is enjoined on them in the divine commands. It is to them . . . that Jesus pledges and prophecies this great good . . . 'Since you have left for me', saith Jesus, 'every good thing that ye had in the world . . . come ye now . . . that ye may be along with me on twelve thrones, without adjudication on you. Ye are judging the human race.'

---

31 See Seymour, 'The Eschatology of the Early Irish Church' in Zeitschrift für Celtische Philologie 14 (1923) 191–197.

The fourfold division of souls and the designation of these as *boni ualde, boni non ualde; mali ualde, mali non ualde* are both widespread in medieval Irish writing on eschatology. We have a fourfold division in the Vision of Tundal (AD 1149), even if only two have explicit designations, i.e. *mali non ualde* (XV) and the *boni non ualde* (XVI). The grouping and terminology is already found in the (Irish) *Liber de numeris*[32] (probably composed in the late eighth century), even though there the grouping is given under the number three. The first occurrence is on the division of faith: *Tribus tamen principalibus modis spes recta esse intelligitur, id est in ualde bonis et in ualde malis et in his qui nec ualde boni nec ualde mali* (III, 11). And again with regard to the last judgment in III,18: *Tres turmae in iudicio erunt: id est ualde boni, id est angeli Dei et sancti; ualde mali, id est daemones et impii; nec ualde boni nec ualde mali. Et hi tales per ignem purgabuntur.*

In the *Catechesis Celtica* (Reg. lat. 49) we have a text very similar to that of *Scéla Lái Brátha*. This is a tenth century MS, apparently written in Britain or Ireland although in Caroline minuscule, not in Irish script. In ff. 50–51 we have a passage on the second coming of Christ, following on the text of Matt 19:16–30. The second coming will be in majesty, as foretold in prophecy (citing Ps 96:3; 49:3 and Is 13:9 following the LXX text, not the Vulgate). The text of Matt has Celtic/ Irish readings. It speaks of the last judgment as follows:[33]

> IIII familiae quae ascri(bentur) in iudicio. Duae familiae ex eis non uenient in iudicio, id est *boni ualde et mali ualde.* Sedebunt enim impii statim cum diabolo, sicut sedebunt iusti et perfecti cum Christo. Aliae duo familiae uenient ante iudicem, idest *boni non ualde et mali non ualde.* Et iudicabit illas, atque illis dicetur: ITE et VENITE. Resurget impius ut damnetur, iustus ut iudicet.

The terminology for each of these four groups seems to be have come (ultimately at least) from Augustine's *Enchiridion*, chapter 110.[34] Terminology apart, however, the content of what is said on these four groups seems clearly to depend on Gregory, *Moralia in Iob* 26,27, 50

---

32   See R. E. McNally, Der irische Liber de numeris, Munich 1957, 54f., with reference to other texts.

33   Ed. A. Wilmart, Analecta Reginensia , Vatican City 1933, 110.

34   In this text of the Enchiridion (ch. 110) Augustine is treating of 'the benefit to the souls of the dead from the sacraments and alms of their living friends. . . For there is a manner of life which is neither so good as not to require these servces after death, nor so bad that such services are of no avail after death; there is, on the other hand, a kind of life such as not to require them; and again one so bad that when life is over they render no help. . . . When, then, sacrifices either of the altar or of alms are offered on behalf of all the baptized dead, they are thank-offerings for the very good (*pro valde bonis*), they are propitiatory offerings for the not very bad (*pro non valde malis*); and in the case of the very bad (*pro valde malis*), even though they do not assist the dead, they are a species of consolation for the living.'

(PL 75,378–379). Gregory, commenting on Job 36:6 (*Sed non saluat impios, et iudicium pauperibus tribuit*) writes:

> *Reproborum alii judicantur, alii non judicantur.—Duae quippe sunt partes, electorum scilicet, atque reproborum. Sed bini ordines eisdem singulis partibus continentur. Alii namque judicantur et pereunt, alii non judicantur et pereunt. Alii judicantur et regnant, alii non judicantur et regnant. . .*

(50) There are in truth two classes, namely, of the Elect and the reprobate. But two ranks are comprised in each of these classes. For some are judged and perish; others are not judged and perish. Some are judged and reign; others are not judged and reign. They are judged and perish, to whom it is said in our Lord's declaration, *I hungered, and you gave me not to eat; I thirsted, and you gave me not to drink.* . . . To whom it is before said, *Depart from me, you cursed* . . . But others are not judged in the Last Judgment, and yet perish. Of whom the Prophet says, *The ungodly do not rise again in the judgment.* And of whom the Lord declares, *But he that believes not is judged already.* And of whom Paul says, *They who have sinned without the Law, shall perish without the Law.* Therefore even all unbelievers rise again, but to torment and not to judgment. For their case is not then examined; because they come into the presence of their strict Judge, with the condemnation already of their own unbelief. For those who retain their profession of faith, but have not works in accordance with it, are convicted of sin, in order to their perishing. But they who have not enjoyed the sacraments of faith do not hear the reproof of the Judge at that last ordeal; for, condemned already by the darkness of their own unbelief, they do not deserve to be condemned by the open reproof of Him whom they have despised.

(51). But of the class of the Elect, some are judged and reign. As those, who wipe away with their own tears the stains of their life, who, atoning their former misdeeds by their subsequent conduct, conceal from the eyes of their Judge, with the cloak of alms deeds, whatever unlawfulness they may have ever committed. To whom . . . the Judge says at his coming: *I hungered, and ye gave me to eat Come, ye blessed.* . . . But others are not judged and yet reign; as those, who surpass even the precepts of the Law in the perfection of their virtues; because they are by no means satisfied with fulfilling that which the Divine Law enjoins on all, but with surpassing eagerness desire to perform more than they would learn from general precepts. To whom it is said by the voice of the Lord: *Ye have left all and have followed me . . . you shall sit upon twelve thrones, judging the twelve tribes of Israel* [Matt 19:28]. . . . These, therefore, are not judged in the Last Judgment, and yet reign, because they come as judges together with their creator.

Gregory's text, in §§50 and 51, adduces scriptural support for its various statements on those who are to rise and not rise on the Day of Judgment. The piece, in fact, seems built around certain Scripture texts and is an attempt to synthesise biblical evidence on these points. The principal texts are as follows:

> They shall be judged and perish, those to whom it is said: 'Depart. . .' [Matt 25:42, 43; 25:41].
>
> They shall not be judged and perish, as in Ps 1:5 ['The wicked shall not arise in judgement'], and Jn 3:18 ['The one who does not believe is already judged']; also Rom 2:12.
>
> For the elect (Mor. §51) some shall be judged and reign, as in Matt 25:35 ['I was hungry. . .'] and 25:34 ['Come. . .'].
>
> Others of the elect shall not be judged and reign, *qui etiam praecepta legis perfectione virtutum transcendunt*, e.g. those who have left all, who shall sit and judge [Matt 19:28; also Is 3:14; Prov 31:23].

It seems clear that Irish eschatology is in the tradition of that of Pope Gregory's *Moralia*. A comparison of the texts of the Irish 'Tidings of Doomsday' (*Scéla Lái Brátha*) with Gregory's *Moralia* given above makes it clear that ultimataly the text behind the Irish composition is Gregory, even though the precise designation of each group is later (and possibly of Irish origin) and the author of the homily is also drawing on the language of *Saltair na Rann*.

An indication that this text from Gregory's *Moralia* might have been also used with awareness of its origin, and ascription to its true author, can be seen in the Cracow Catechesis no. 13 (MS Cracow, Cathedral Chapter 43; now 140 Kp, from c. AD 800, Verona or environs), also found in other texts, principally Karlsruhe, Aug. CXCVI (9th century), as chapter 15. This collection of homilies seems (like the *Catechesis Celtica*) to have been connected with Ireland, and to have Irish affiliations, if not an Irish origin. The particular catechesis which here interests us is a homily or exposition on Matt 25:31: *Cum uenerit Filius hominis in maiestate sua et omnes angeli cum eo, tunc sedebit super sedem maiestatis sue.*[35] It goes on to speak of the coming in majesty, as foretold in prophecy (Ps 49:3; 96:2–3 cited). In the exposition of Matthew's text it cites from Jerome's commentary by name. It then goes on to say (p.106, MS reading followed):

> *Gregorius dicit in Moralibus Iob: In quattuor partis diuident homines in die iudicii. Prima pars apostolis et similes eorum qui non iudicabuntur, sed illi iudices erunt, sicut dixit Dominus de illis:* Sedebitis et uos super sedes duodecim iudicantes duodecim tribus Israel. *Secunda pars bonorum communis iusti, qui iudicabuntur sed in regnum ibunt. Tertia*

---

35 A critical edition of this homily, edited by Dr Tom L. Amos, is to be published in *Proceedings of the Irish Biblical Association* 17 (1994).

pars malorum impii, qui non crediderunt Deum de quibus dicit in psalmo: Ideo non resurgunt impii in iudicio [Ps 1:5], *quia non iudicabuntur sed tollentur ne uideant gloriam Dei. Quarta pars peccatores de quibus* neque peccatores in consilio iustorum

Duration of the Day of Doom: the commentators' views

At the beginning of the section on hell in the homily *Scéla Lái Brátha*, the Irish text says on the lost (19): 'And they shall separate from the delight of this world which they loved, and from the faces of heaven's household (*Ocus frignúsib muintire nime*), that is, of the Angels and of the Saints and of the Righteous, after they have been a thousand years in the fire of Doom. For that is the length of Doomsday as the commentators of the holy canon declare (*mar innisit trachtaireda na canoini nóimi*). An identification of the commentators in question might help identify some of the writer's sources that have influenced him. While the canonical text commented on is not indicated, it presumably has to do with the *mille anni* of Apoc 20:2–7.

THEOLOGY: PATRISTIC ROOTS OF DESIGNATION 'BRIGID' (ITA) MARY OF THE GAEL'

A well-known Irish designation for St Brigid of Kildare is 'Brigid Mary of the Gael.' This is because she was regarded as mother of Jesus, as Mary was. St Ita and other Irish saints were so regarded in Irish tradition. We can trace the Irish custom of so designating St Brigid back through many centuries. Medieval continental Christians knew of it as an Irish custom. J. Henning notes that in Erfurt the 'Scoti' were abused by a poet in the thirteenth century for calling St Brigid 'Mother of God.'[36] We can go back far beyond this, however. In his book, Mary. A History of Devotion in Ireland,[37] Peter O'Dwyer remarks that the earliest reference to Our Lady found in an Irish source (Latin or vernacular Irish) seems to occur in a prediction on Brigid's birth in an Old Irish text which on linguistic grounds can be dated to c. AD 600. The Old Irish text in which it occurs is recognized as a difficult one, and has been translated as follows by M. A. O'Brien:[38]

> A fair birth, fair dignity will come to thee thereafter from thy children's descendants, who shall be called from her great virtues, truly pious Brig-eoit; she will be another Mary, mother of the great Lord (*brigeoit fhir-diada. Bid ala-maire-Coimded mathair*).

36　See J. Henning in Irish Ecclesiastical Record 61 (1943)190.
37　Dublin 1988, 32f.
38　M. A. O'Brien, 'The Old Irish Life of St Brigit,' Irish Historical Studies 1 (1938–39), 123–34; 343–53; at 348.

The general idea of Brigid and other Irish saints, notably Ita, sharing in Mary's motherhood of Christ has been discussed by the late Professor James Carney[39] and P. O'Dwyer.[40] Carney sees the biblical foundation for the idea in Christ's words in Luke 8:21: 'My mother and my brothers are those who hear the word of God and put it into practice.' Carney finds the Irish understanding very much in keeping with Augustine's remark (on virgins) in *De virginitate*. *Et ipsae cum Maria matres Christi sunt, si Patris eius faciunt voluntatem.* ('And they, with Mary, are mothers of Christ, if they do the Father's will'). He comments: 'This whole mystical idea, which . . . is entirely orthodox, could only have arisen in a society already in the habit of honouring the actual mother of Christ.'[41]

The theology implicit in all this is developed at length in a homily, or catechesis, on Luke 11:27–28 ('Blessed is the womb that bore you . . .') in the collection of homiletic pieces in the tenth-century manuscript Vat. Reg. lat. 49, commonly known as the *Catechesis Celtica*. This item, if not the entire collection, seems to be of Irish origin.[42] In this text the woman in the crowd is understood as having said to Christ, or of him: 'I only wish you were my own son.' Christ's reply is that the woman need not envy Mary, Christ's own mother. She can become Christ's mother by obeying God's word. 'Indeed, blessed are they who hear and keep the word of God.'

> *Optas ut mihi mater fieres, quod est in potestate tua. Si enim uerbum Dei custodieris, mihi mater eris nec Mariae inuidebis. Beatior est enim Maria percipiendo fidem Christi quam capiendo carnem Christi.*

The text then cites Matthew 12:49–50 and 12:46; 'Stretching out his hand to his disciples he said: Behold my mother and my brothers. Anyone who does the will of my Father who is in heaven, he is my brother and my sister.' This is illustrated by a lengthy citation from Augustine (mentioned by name), *De sacra virginitate* 3,3 followed by another from 3,5:

> . . . *Sic et materna propinquitas nihil Mariae profuisset, nisi felicius Christum corde quam carne gestasset. . . . Item mater est eius omnis anima pia, faciens uoluntatem Patris fecundissima caritate in his quae parturit, donec in eis ipse formetur* (Reg. lat. f. 24rv).

---

39 See J. Carney, 'Poems of Blathmac Son of Cú Brettan,' in Early Irish Poetry, Thomas Davis Lectures, Cork 1965, 45–57, at 50f; idem, 'Old Ireland and her Poetry,' in R. McNally (ed.), Old Ireland, Dublin 1965, 147–172, at 166f.

40 P. O'Dwyer, op. cit. (at note 37 above) 32f.

41 Carney, 'Old Ireland . . .' (see note 39 above) 167.

42 On this text of the Catechesis Celtica see M. McNamara, 'Sources and Affiliations of the Catechesis Celtica (MS Vat. Reg. lat. 49),' in Sacris Erudiri 34 (1994) 185–237, at 225–228.

LAW OF NATURE: SALVATION OF THE UNBELIEVER

From the preceding section on the designation of St Brigid (or, indeed, of any faithful believer) as mother of Christ, we can see that by the seventh century the early Irish Church had developed a theology from reflection on the word of God and in dependence on its patristic heritage. The same seems to have been true with regard to the salvation of those who do God's will without having had the opportunity of hearing God's word through the Gospel.

One of at least two attitudes could be taken with regard to the salvation of those who died before the advent of Christianity, and both were possibly held in different sections of Irish Christianity as they were elsewhere in Christendom. One position was to regard one's pre-Christian ancestors as damned in hell. This seems to be the attitude adopted by the author of the Prologue of the Félire of Oengusso (c. AD 800) who states that 'great kings of the pagans wail ever in burning: the hosts of Jesus without a fall, they are joyous after triumph.'[43]

Quite a different attitude is adopted in the *Coras Bescnai*, the pseudo-historical prologue to the Laws of Ireland (the *Senchus Már*). This text is probably from the early eighth century, and contemporary with the *Senchus Már* as a whole. In this the ancient pre-Christian order is made to accept Christianity in the persons of the judge Erc of Slane and the poet (*fili*) Dubthach maccu Lugair. In a narrative of the encounter of St Patrick with the high king Lóegaire, and his advisers Dubthach is made to say:

> Each law is bound. It is in this that the two laws have been bound together. It is the law of nature (*recht aicnid*) that was with the men of Ireland until the coming of the faith in the time of Lóegaire son of Niall. It is in his time that Patrick came. It is after the men of Ireland had believed in Patrick that the two laws were harmonized, the law of nature (*recht aicnid*) and the law of the letter (*recht litre*). Dubthach maccu Lugair the poet (*in fili*) displayed the law of nature. It is Dubthach who first paid respect to Patrick. It is he who first rose up before him at Tara . . . Lóegaire, then, refused Patrick on account of the druid Matha son of Umor. He, the druid, had prophesied to Lóegaire that Patrick would steal the living and the dead from him . . . Dubthach maccu Lugair the poet (*in fili*) recounted the judgements of the men of Ireland according to the law of nature and the law of the prophets (*recht fáide*). . . . For prophecy according to the law of nature (*fáidsine a recht aicnid*) had

43 Félire Oengusso Céli Dé: The Martyrology of Oengus the Culdee, Prologue 61–64; ed. Whitley Stokes, London 1905 (reprint: Dublin Institute for Advanced Studies 1984), 19. A similar position with regard to Ireland's dead heroes (with the exception of Conchobar Mac Nessa) is expressed by the shade of Cú Chulainn in: Síaburcharpat Conculaind, Irish text ed. by K. Meyer in: Anecdota from Irish Manuscripts, Halle/Dublin 1910, 48–56, at 55–56.

prevailed in the judgement of the island of Ireland and her poets. Prophets among them, then, had foretold that the blessed white language (*bélrae bán biáid*, glossed *in léigind*) shall come, i.e. the law of the letter (and) that there are many things according to the law of nature that have reached what the law of the letter has not reached. Dubthach, then, showed (this) to Patrick. What did not contradict the word of God in the law of the letter and the conscience of Christians was harmonized in the order of judges by the Church and poets. All the law of nature was right except for the faith and its due, and (there was) joining of Church to state.[44]

Dubthach is presented here as the carrier of a particular theology on the relationship of the law of nature to the Gospel. This theme of *lex naturae/lex litterae*, or in Irish *recht aicnid/ recht litre* is found in vernacular Irish and Hiberno-Latin texts from the earliest period. The *recht aicnid*, *lex naturae*, or the 'law of nature' ('natural law') means 'morality arising from natural instinct',[45] and is used especially of the moral law before the Mosaic legislation.

The theology is based ultimately, it would appear, on Romans 2:14–15. It seems, however, to have been worked out in Ireland with probable dependence on earlier patristic tradition, the exact nature of which still remains to be determined. We have texts similar to that of Dubthach in the (roughly contemporary) Irish Reference Bible (c. 775–800). A first treatment of the subject occurs in an introduction to the Pentateuch, under the general heading '*De lege Moysi.*'

> ii. *Quod sunt leges principales, et unde incipit et finit unaquaque de eis? Leges quattuor sunt principales: lex nature et lex littere, lex prophetiae et lex euangelii. Incipit lex nature ab Adam usque Moysen; lex littere a Moyse usque ad Samuhel; lex prophetiae a Samuhel usque ad Iohannem Babtistam; lex euangelii ab Iohanne usque ad finem mundi.*
>
> iii. *Quot modis constat lex nature? Tribus: lex enim uel promittit aliquid, ut uir fortis petat premium; aut uetat, ut sacrarum uirginum nuptias nulli liceat; aut punit, ut qui cedem fecerit capite plectetur. Hoc lex nature facit.*

The text then goes on to treat under separate headings *De inuentatoribus legum* (for the Hebrews, Greeks, Egyptians, Athenians, Lacedemonians, Romans; using Isidore, *Etym.* VI 1,1–3). The next item is headed *De generibus legum*. Giving Jerome as authority, the text says that there are twelve *genera legum*. One is the law of nature:

---

44 Corpus Iuris Hibernici, ed. D. A, Binchy, vol. II, Dublin Institute for Advanced Studies 1978, 527, 14–529,4. Translation by K. McCone in: Pagan Past and Christian Present in Early Irish Literature, Maynooth 1990, 92. On this text see also K. McCone, 'Dubthach Maccu Lugair and a matter of life and death in the pseudo-historical prologue to the Senchus Már,' in Peritia 5 (1986) 1–35, esp. 1–5; also idem, in Pagan Past, 96f.

45 See Dictionary of the Irish Language, s.v. *recht*. col. 26, 48–49.

Item lex nature ut Paulus dicit: 'Cum gentes legem non habent, naturaliter ea que legis sunt faciunt. Isti enim legem non habentes ipsi sibi sunt lex' (Rom 2:14).

These Irish texts are clearly giving a theology of the law of nature based ultimately on Romans 2:14. How much this was elaborated in Ireland and how much came to the island already developed remains to be determined. The theology as found in the Reference Bible seems to depend on that of Eucherius of Lyons (died c. 449). Towards the end of his treatment of the book of Exodus in Book I of his *Instructionum libri duo* (XXXII) he poses a question and answers it:

> What is to be given as reply to those who inquire why God gave the law through Moses to one people alone, and this only after the lapse of many centuries?
>
>   That that law which is inborn in all people by the constitution of the natural law (*lex illa . . . quae omnibus gentibus constitutione naturalis legis innascitur*) was not offered to Jews alone is confirmed by the Apostle when he says: 'When the gentiles who do not have the law do by nature (*naturaliter*), in this wise while not having the law they are a law to themselves and show forth the work of the law written in their hearts' [Rom 2:14–15]. And for this reason it was not at a late hour (*sero*) that the Lord collected the law of innocence into ten words, when its origin had already gone before, implanted in the human breasts. Nor was it at a late date that he wrote again on tables of stone what he had earlier insculpted in the pages of the heart. Indeed before this law of Moses, nature had its law, through which it was easy (*in promptu erat*) to come to know God and the author of life and thus to love [Him], and practise justice and love towards the neighbour, on which two commandments the whole Law and the Prophets hang. Therefore they already were aware of that [law]: 'Anything that you want people to do to you, you likewise do to them. In this is the Law and the Prophets' [Matt 7:11]. And we shall also prove this by examples: Before this law of the letter, by that law of nature (*ante hanc legem litterae per illam naturae legem*) Abel is recognised as just, Enoch is snatched away, Noah is chosen, Abraham is called father of nations. For this reason, the law of Moses was not given at a later date, preceded as it was by the law of nature, through which there were many who were recommendable (CSEL 31, 1894, 76–77).

Eucherius in this seems to be dependent on Irenaeus, his predecessor in the see of Lyons (from c. 170–200). In his work *Contra Haer.* 4,22,2 Irenaeus writes:

> For it was not merely for those who believed in Him in the time of Tiberius Caesar that Christ came, nor did the Father exercise

his providence for the men only who are now alive, but for all men altogether, who from the beginning, according to their capacity, in their generation have both feared and loved God, and practised justice and piety towards their neignbours, and have earnestly desired to see Christ and hear his voice.

It is very probable that the theology, and even the texts, of Eucherius were available to the early Irish theologians as they worked out their solution to the question of the relation of their pre-Christian past to the Christian message. Part of the Irish past would have been a religion and culture in which the druids formed a central part. The non-Irish counterpart of the druids could have been the Magi from the east who visited the new-born babe at Bethlehem to pay him homage. In Irish tradition the Magi of this text are translated as 'druids' (*druí; draoithe*), and are looked on in a favourable light. The apocryphal writing referred to already, extant in Latin and in Irish translation, has a developed section on the Magi, in which these too are proud of their ancient tradition, which pointed the way to the King of the Jews they have come to worship. In this text Joseph asks the Magi how they had come to learn of the birth of Christ. They reply that as the Jews had their prophetical books, so had they theirs:

> *Dicunt ei Magi: Sunt apud nos [read: uos] scripture ueteres prophetarum Dei in quibus scriptum est de Christo . . . Item sunt apud nos antiquiores scripture scripturarum in quibus scriptum est de eo.*[46]

In the Irish rendering of this in the *Leabhar Breac*[47] the Magi reply as follows:

> 'Not hard to tell, said they, on account of its being in our old books and old writings from the time of the first man of us till today, that whatever be the times we should behold a star like this over our land, (we were) to go with it what way soever it would go, as it was a sign of the King of the world. For it is ourselves and the human race that are to be saved after his birth immediately'

Or in its variant form later in the same text:[48]

> 'We understood it, they said, from our own writings and from our ancient prophecy, which were from long ago in our possession predicting Christ. . . . [W]e will tell thee all from the beginning to the end as our fathers and our forefathers foretold to us from the time of the sons of Abraham of yore till this day'

This text is apparently connected with the old tradition that the Persian Magi had foretold the coming of the Saviour (Clement of

46   Ed. M.R. James, Latin Infancy Gospels, Cambridge 1927, 94; see also 89–90.
47   Ed. E. Hogan (see note 4 above), 82, 61f.
48   Ed. Hogan (see note 4 above), 92, 69f.

Alexandria), having learned of it from Balaam through the Chaldeans (Diodorus of Tarsus).

Since Sedulius Scottus cites a lengthy text on the Magi from this Latin apocryphon c. 850, we can legitimately presume that it was known in Ireland before AD 800, and when the theology of the law of nature, and certain pre-Christian expectations of Christ were being discussed.

Together with the traditions from Irenaeus, Eucherius and the apocryphal narrative on the Magi just mentioned, the 'Irish' synthesis may well have behind it earlier Christian thinking on the *Praeparatio evangelica* (cf. the *anima naturaliter christiana* of Tertullian). In fact, I believe, this text of the *Córus Béscnai* should be set in the larger context of the Christian reflection on the salvation of humanity (including the pre-Christian generations) by Jesus Christ, particularly as found in some pre-Augustinian writers, notably Irenaeus. Lactantius (c. AD 300) in *The Divine Institutes* 1,4 speaks of the testimony of the prophets to Christ; then (1,5) of the testimonies of (pagan) poets and philosophers, then (1,6) of other testimonies: of the Sibyls, of Hermes Trismegistus who 'wrote books, and those in great numbers, relating to the knowledge of divine things, in which he asserts the majesty of the supreme and only God, and makes mention of him by the same name as we use—God and Father'.

The text of Córus Béscnai has been examined in this larger context by Charles Donahue in two essays, 'Beowulf, Ireland and the Natural Good,'[49] and '*Beowulf* and Christian Tradition: A Reconsideration from a Celtic Stance.'[50] In this second essay (pp. 66f.) he says that the 'material is pre-Pelagian and pre-Augustinian. It found its way into Ireland via Gaul and Britain in the fifth century probably from the monasteries in southern Gaul and on the islands of the Tyrrhenian Sea.' The close relationship with texts of Eucherius of Lyons (a monk in Lérins before becoming bishop of Lyons) and Irenaeus would tend to confirm this view.[51]

APPENDIX: TIDINGS OF THE RESURRECTION (SCÉLA NA hESÉRGI)
SOURCE ANALYSIS

The source analysis of the *Lebor ha hUidre* text 'Scéla na hÉsergi' is as follows:

1–3. Introduction; contains some biblical citations and allusions (2 Pet 3:10; Dan 3:22).

4a. The Command to arise, which may be corporeal (voice of Jesus, or archangel) or incorporeal, that is the unspeakable power of the Lord.

---

49 Traditio 7 (1949) 263–277, esp. 266–274.
50 Traditio 21 (1965) 55–116, esp. 59–72.
51 On Irenaeus see also F. Vernet, in Dict. de théol. cath., vol. 7, 1927, esp. col. 2489–9 and literature given by C. Donahue. On the larger question of salvation see L. Capéran, Le problème du salut des infidèles. Essai historique, 2nd ed. Toulouse 1934.

The exact sources have not been identified, but in part they are biblical; cf. John 5:25, 28; Apoc 20:13 (sea gives up its dead); 1 Cor 15:32.

4b. Bodies to become reconstituted, to become again the persons they once were. This is a kind of summary of topics that will be treated in greater detail later. For this see *De civ. Dei*, XXII 20.

5. God sends his envoys, his angels, to the four corners; see Matt 13:41; 24:31; will bring dead into the air; see 1 Thes 4:16. For the devil gathering all the sinners I have identified no clear source or parallel.

6. The exact place out of which everyone's resurrection will be. Answer: out of their graves; if devoured by beasts, etc. where the Lord wills, but more likely from the place where they died. I have not found a source for this.

7–18. Abortives and monsters; excess matter; holy martyrs; no change of sex; no lust. The source for this section is St Augustine, principally his *De civ. Dei*.

7. Abortives and monsters. Augustine, *Enchiridion* 85 (*de abortiuis fetibus*); id., *Enchiridion 87 (monstra, bismembra)*; id., *De civ. Dei* XXII 12 (*fetus abortiui*).

8–9. At what age will their resurrection be?, with 30 and 33 as answer, citing Eph 4:11; Rom 8:29.

This text depends on *De civ. Dei* XXII 15,16: 'Will all the resurrected bodies attain the stature of Christ's body?', citing Eph 4:11. Augustine gives the age as at about 30 years. Here the Irish text gives both 30 and 33; in the parallel passage (34 below) only 30 years is given.

For 9 see *De civ. Dei* XXII 16.

10. Excess of matter, 'monsters, that have two bodies in one union' (*na torothair dano techtait da chorp i n-óen-accomol*), mentioning Job by name.

Augustine, *Enchiridion* 87: 'The case of monstrous births,' mentioning Jerome's letter, i.e. Letter 72, of Jerome to Vitalis the priest (written AD 398), on the case of Siamese or conjoined twins at Lydda.

The reference is probably to Job 19:26, 'And in my flesh I shall see God.' Gregory, *Moralia* 14,76 and 77 on this verse stresses the reality of the bodily resurrection, without mention of the problem treated of here.

11. The holy martyrs bear the traces of their wounds.

Augustine, *De civ. Dei* 22, 19 (end).

12–14. The excess of hair.

Augustine is mentioned explicitly in 12 as having treated of the subject, and in 14 mention is made of 'the author' (*in t-augtar*), who for the Irish writer is presumably the same person. Augustine treats of this particular 'problem' at length.

For 12 see *De civ. Dei* XXII 12; 19; *Enchiridion* 89. In XXII 12 Augustine poses the question; in XXII 19 he replies.

For 13: 'the opinion of some' on the excess of hairs: the reference is to Augustine, *De civ. Dei* XXII 19: 'Another solution.'

14: On the risen body, with mention of an opinion that God will give them what body he pleases, and mention of 'the author' (on the excess of hair). See Augustine, *De civ. Dei* XXII 20, with the title: 'The restoration of the whole body at the resurrection, no matter how its parts have been dispersed.' See also Augustine, *Enchiridion* 88, 89 (in substance as 14).

15. Apparently intended as a summary of what is considered essential in the discussion: 'So then this is probably what we should believe in the case: that the completeness of the whole human body is to be renewed in the resurrection, so that the soul united to it in that wise may receive whatever it deserves of punishment or rewards for their ill deserts or their good deserts.' This leads on to the recognition of legitimate doubt in 16.

16. Legitimate doubt on the matter is defended in this paragraph:

> For precaution then, and for avoidance of presumption, that is, of affirming what is not lawful to affirm, but what should properly remain in doubt, this variety of opinion exists. For though some of the mysteries of the resurrection are certain and manifest—for, according to the teaching of the apostle and the rest of the Scripture, the resurrecction itself is sure to come—yet others are uncertain and obcure. So that it is more prudent and wiser that they should be hoped for and supposed than that they should be boldly affirmed.

No precise source for this has been identified, but see Augustine, *Enchiridion* 87: 'That the bodies of all the dead shall rise again is certain beyond doubt.' This may imply legitimacy of doubt in matters beyond this.

17. Women will rise in the form of women.

This is from Augustine, *De civ. Dei* XXII 17.

18. No lust.

Thus Augustine, *De civ. Dei* XXII 17: *Non enim libido ibi erit quae confusionis est causa*, with reference to Gen 2:21.

19–20: That the risen body will be palpable.

The source here is Gregory, *Moralia* 14, 72–74 (on Job 19:26), who narrates at length his own debate with Eutychius, bishop of Constantinople, on the matter (Job 19:26): 'And I shall be again encompassed with my skin.' Whereas the 'skin' is expressly named, all doubt of a true resurrection is removed; in that our body will not, as Eutychius the Bishop of Constantinople wrote, be impalpable in that gloriousness of the resurrection, though more subtle than the wind and air: for in that gloriousness of the resurrection our body will be subtle indeed by the efficacy of a spiritual power, but palpable by the reality of its nature; whence also our Redeemer, when the disciples doubted of his resurrection, showed them his hands and feet, and offered his hands and feet to be touched. . . .' Gregory goes on to give Eutychius' opinion, and his own involvement in the public debate.

21,22,23: The risen body will be spiritual.

Gregory treats of this also, but here the Irish text returns to Augustine and *De civ. Dei.*

21 The risen body spiritual; harmony and oneness with the spirit. See *De civ. Dei* XXII 21 (beginning).

22. The risen body spiritual in the spiritual 'stations' (*isna sostaib*). Augustine, *De civ. Dei* XXII 21. See also Augustine, *Tractatus in Ioh.* LXVII, 2 (PL 35, 1812) (on John 14:1–2); in substance in the *Catechesis Celtica* (Reg. lat. 49, fol 43v; ed. Wilmart, pp. 68f.)

23. Risen body spiritual, changed from corruption. See *De civ. Dei* XXII 2; also *Enchiridion* 91.

24–25. The complete joy of the blessed after the resurrection. No envy or grumbling.

See Augustine, *De civ. Dei* XXII 30: 'The eternal felicity of the city of God in its perpetual sabbath' (last chapter of the entire work). Also Augustine, *Tractatus in Ioh* LXVII, 2 (PL 35, 1812) (on John 14:1–2); in substance in the *Catechesis Celtica* (Reg. lat. 49, fol 43v ; ed. Wilmart, pp. 68f.).

26. Everyone will recognize the other.

Exact source unidentified; but see *Vision of Adomnán* 13.[52]

27. Everyone will understand what shall be in the other's mind, illustrating through the example of Elijah and Elishah (4[2] Kgs 5:26).

This apparently depends on Augustine, *De civ. Dei* XXII 29, which also illustrates through the same example.

28. The blessed perform no other work beyond praising God; citing Ps 83:5.

This seems dependent on *De civ. Dei* XXII 30, which also cites Ps 83:5: 'Praise of God who is all in all. What other occupation could there be?'

29. The resurrection of the impious.

This is not in *De civ. Dei*, but see Augustine, *Enchiridion* 92: 'The resurrection of the lost,' but not quite as the Irish text: 'But for those who . . . are not redeemed, they too shall rise again, each with his own body, but only to be punished with the devil and his angels. Now, whether they shall rise again with all their diseases and deformities of body, bringing with them the diseased and deformed limbs which they possessed here, it would be labour lost to inquire. For we need not weary ourselves speculating about their health or their beauty, which are matters uncertain, when their eternal damnation is a matter of certainty . . .'

30. Resurrection of the lost, from death to death.

---

52 In the translation of M. Herbert: M. Herbert and M. McNamara, Irish Biblical Apocrypha. Selected Texts in Translation, Edinburgh: 1989, 140; § 12 in translation of C. S. Boswell, An Irish Precursor of Dante. A Study of the Vision of Heaven and Hell ascribed to the eighth-century Irish Saint Adamnan, London 1908.

Here what appears to be a citation is given from 'the wise man' (*in t-ecnaid*). The 'wise man' is also named in 36 and 37, and in 37 the source seems to be Gregory's *Moralia in Iob*. The text here, however, does not appear to be the *Moralia* of Job. It seems rather to be a summary of Augustine, *Enchiridion* 92 (the continuation of the text cited to the preceding paragraph): '. . . Nor nor need we inquire in what sense their body shall be incorruptible, if it is susceptible of pain; or in what sense corruptible if it is free from the possibility of death. For there is no true life except where there is happiness of life, and no true incorruption except where health is unbroken by any pain. When, however, the unhappy are not permitted to die, then, if I may so speak, death itself dies not; and where pain without intermission afflicts the soul, and never comes to an end, corruption itself is not completed. This is called in Holy Scripture "the second death" (Apoc 2:2).'

31–32. Death and Resurrection of the soul.

For these paragraphs see Augustine, *De civ. Dei* XX 6, entitled: 'The first resurrection and the second,' especially the end: 'There are thus two rebirths. . . . Similarly there are two resurrections: the first resurrection of the soul which is here and now, and prevents us from coming to the second death.'[53] The next chapter in *De civ. Dei* (XX 7) is headed: 'The two resurrections and the millennium. The descriptions of John in the Apocalypse and their interpretation.'

32. There are two resurrections. As in *De civ. Dei* XX 6.

33. What the general resurrection is not: 'Now the general resurrection which shall be beyond on the Day of Judgement is not the same as the resurrection which in the authority *(isind augtartas)* is called *praestigia*, that is an apparitional resurrection, like the pythonism (*esergi fuathaigthi, amal in pitóndacht*). Nor is it the same as the resurrection called *Revolutio* , that is the transmigration of souls in various bodies (*tathcorthe na hanma i corpaib ecsamlaib*), after the example of transmigrated persons (*iar ndesmirecht na tathcorthe*). Nor the resurrection called *Metaformatio*, that is transfiguration after the examples of werewolves (*tarmchrutad, iar ndesmirecht na comricht*). Nor is it the same as *Subductio*, that is subduction, as in the case of the prematurely dead (*fothudsestu .i. amal bite lucht in remeca*). Nor the resurrection called *suscitatio*, that is, the awakening of the dead by a miracle, after the example of Lazarus.'

I have failed to trace the source of this. The first example, at least (praestigia), is said to have been taken from the 'authority' (*augtartas*), presumably the work of 'the author' mentioned in 14. The source in 14 seems Augustine, or a work in which he was named. The 'authority' mentioned here in 33 seems to be the same work. I have failed to find any of this teaching in Augustine, however, or in Gregory's *Moralia*.

---

53 On this see B. E. Daley, The Hope of the Early Church. A Handbook of Patristic Eschatology, Cambridge 1991, 148–49.

34–35. Summaries; 34 is as in 8 and 9; 35 as in 17 and 18 above.

36. A text citing 'the sage' (*in t-ecnaid*) on creation, the sky, angels and the word of the Lord. The 'sage' has already been mentioned in 30, which appears to be a summary of Augustine, *Enchiridion* 92, and in 37 which appears to depend on Gregory's *Moralia in Iob* 14,70. Here in 36 the points of teaching ascribed to the sage seem closer to Augustine (*De cat. rudibus* chap. 25, 46) rather than to Gregory, *Moralia* 14,70.

37. Arguments in favour of the resurrection, ascribed to 'the sage' (*in t-ecnaid*).

As W. Stokes already noted,[54] this text seems to depend on Gregory, *Moralia* 40,70.

38. Conclusion.

The exact sources of this paragraph, if any, remain to be determined.

---

54   Stokes, 253, note.

The Irish Augustine's Knowledge and Understanding of Scripture

GERARD MacGINTY

The subject of this paper is not really a patristic text. It is, however, closer to home than any text of Origen, Philo or Maximus, and the subject is, in a sense, more manageable, for there is only one text of the Irish Augustine, whoever he may have been, that known as the *De mirabilibus sacrae Scripturae*. Sadly this is still only generally available in Migne Patrologia Latinae XXXV, 1861, 2149ff. Ultimately that text derives from the Maurist edition in the Appendix to their great edition of the works of St Augustine. The Maurists' text left much to be desired, but even so, the printing in Migne does not do it justice.

I have argued elsewhere for Irish authorship and for a location somewhere in the south of Ireland as the more *probable* place of writing. Further, I have argued for linking the teachers mentioned in the text with the circles deriving from Mo-Lúa of Clonfert Molua and the Upper Shannon Estuary, and have suggested that the *Cartaginenses* of the prologue to the text is a corruption of *Catagenses/Cataginenses*, the term certainly used in later centuries to indicate the community of Inis Cathaig[1]. The way the prologue is addressed inclines me to believe that the writer was perhaps some distance from his teachers. I have been tempted, at times, to think that he may have mildly compromised his *Roman* allegiance, this from other indices in the text! Whatever about all that, it is generally agreed that the work derives from a Hiberno-Latin context, and is very Irish both in its thought content and reference. It is further agreed today that the work was written in 655 AD.

Mirabilia is generally rendered 'marvels', but to judge by the contents of the work we are discussing, the sense taken should rather be of 'mat-

---

1 Cf 'The Irish Augustine: De Mirabilibus Sacrae Scripturae', in P. Ní Chátháin and M. Richter, Irland und die Christenheit / Ireland and Christendom, Stuttgart 1987, 70–83. The text could have been written in some very Irish centre in Britain, perhaps even on the continent of Europe. Recently S. Sanderlin, 'The Monastery of Lismore AD 638–1111', chapter 2 of W. Nolan and T.P Power, Waterford: History and Society, Dublin 1992, 27–48, prefers to place Augustine in Lismore, 33. I can hardly describe the description or discussion of my position by the authoress as serious. She is seemingly unaware of my having published on the matter.

ters which cause us puzzlement'. (If the work had been undertaken in the eighth instead of in the seventh century we might well have had a title referring to the *Aenigmata* of Sacred Scripture; *aenigmata* does not occur in the text). It is in what may be termed one of the main lines of Irish scriptural exegesis, in which, although approaches and treatments differed greatly, there was certainly a tendency to be obsessed with what we term *accidentalia...* This I greatly qualify further on in the case of the *De mirabilibus*, and, although I may criticize the Irish Augustine, I have a very considerable respect for him.

The work is made up of a short prologue and three books : I, On the Pentateuch; II, On Prophecy, i.e. the other Old Testament writings; III, On the New Testament. This third book is incomplete in all MSS.

KNOWLEDGE OF SCRIPTURE[2]

There are two major recensions of the *De mirabilibus*, a long, and plainly original one, and a short, or summary text. The long text in the better MSS is still manifestly Irish, although subjected to scribal 'doctoring', while the oldest MS of the short recension, written in Reichenau at the beginning of the ninth century[3], is much closer to the Hiberno-Latin tradition and this is all the more transparent because the scribe, or his exemplar's scribe, while clearly familiar with an Anglo-Saxon script, was not so familiar with an Irish one, which led[4] to manifest errors of copying. At the same time the actual texts of Scripture in this recension are frequently edited, which would be in accord with Carolingian zeal for the pure text of Scripture.

The books of Scripture Referred to and the Canon

The following are the books of the Old and New Testaments referred to and/or quoted from in the *De mirabilibus*: Genesis, Exodus, Numbers, Deuteronomy, Joshua, Judges, Samuel 1 and 2, Kings 3 & 4, Chronicles, Ezra, Nehemiah, Judith, Job, Psalms, Proverbs, Ecclesiastes, Wisdom, Sirach, Isaiah, Jeremiah, Ezekiel, Daniel, Jonah, Micah, Zekariah (?); Matthew, Mark, Luke, John, Acts, Romans, Corinthians 1 and 2, Galatians, Ephesians, Philippians, Colossians, Thessalonians 1, Hebrews, James, Apocalypse. According to my reckoning texts from twenty-seven of these are cited.

---

2   This study is based on my original Ph.D. thesis, but has been fully revised. My current work on the Old Testament of the Reference Bible has served to colour some of my judgements.

3   Karlsruhe Landesbibliothek : Augiensis CXCI, s. IXin. fol. 132–149v(150v). Cf Alfred Holder, Die Reichenauer Handschriften. I Die Pergamenthandschriften der Reichenau, Leipzig 1906, 432–433.(J in my apparatus criticus).

4   For instance, one recurrent misreading is of the Irish *et* for *ex*.

If one were to argue from silence to the author's canon of Scripture, then his canon would be quite reduced, but such a line of argument would be unwise. He does refer specifically to the 'divine canon' and this to exclude 1 and 2 Maccabees from his treatment[5]. Following St Jerome, then, certain parts of Daniel were not accepted by him as inspired[6]. For the rest, it would seem he had no difficulties; but, if we cannot argue from silence that he would reject certain books, neither can we argue that he accepted them. The simple, honest, and scientific position is to say we do not know.

No matter how we look at these findings we must accept that our pickings are rather disappointing for a work the title of which embraces the sacred Scriptures without qualification. To be of any scientific worth this paper must consider these matters in detail, setting out not only the chapters referred to, the problem texts in each Book of Scripture, but also each text cited with a study of the version of Scripture it reflects. The quotations can be variously assessed but I have examined one hundred from Old and New Testaments. These I shall treat of in summary fashion here, gathering them under the various text versions,—first for the Old and then for the New Testament; and follow that by my conclusions on the detailed study. The texts themselves, and my studies on them I give in appendix. I do not attempt to outline the various chapters of the differing Books to which some reference or other is made, the time allotted us does not permit it.

Texts from the Old Testament

In what follows, the references to the *De mirabilibus* are to Book and chapter, the chapter numbers being set out following my own critical edition of the text. Each reference is followed by an arabic number within parentheses, these numbers refer to the order of the texts in appendix, where they are treated in accordance with their position in the Bible.

We find texts corresponding with the contemporary critical Vulgate text[7] only for Gen 1:22—De mir III 10 (1); Num 24:17—III 4 (25), and

---

5   This was a widespread opinion in early times; Augustine's immediate source could have been Jerome, Prologus in libris Salomonis, 19–20, cf. Weber, 957, and for Daniel, ibid., 1341f. If Jerome's prologues were not known in Ireland, his Apol. adu. lib. Rufini, 2 (PL xxiii, 455), and for Maccabees equally Gregory the Great, Mor. in Iob, XIX 21 (PL 76, 119B), could have served as sources.

6   Cf. Weber, 1341 (?).

7   For the Old Testament I used:
     Vulgate: Biblia Sacra iuxta latinam uulgatam uersionem . . . , cura et studio monachorum Pontif. Abbatiae S. Hier., edita Romae 1926ss. (Vulgate); R. Weber, Biblia Sacra iuxta Vulgatam Versionem, Stuttgart 1969 (Weber); A. Grammatica, Bibliorum Sacrorum iuxta Vulgatam Clementinam Noua Editio, Typ. Polygl. Vat., MCMXLVI, (Clementine).

35:1—I 35 (26), both hardly more than phrases; Judg 16:3—II 31 (31); 1
Sam 28:19—II 11 (34). Then the *Clementine* Vulgate in Gen 8:3-4—I 8
(12); and 3 Kings 17:21—III 13 (37). Besides these few there are readings which offer a *reordered* or adapted Vulgate text—adapted in this
context means with omissions or glosses as well as possible reorderings:
Gen 3:14—I 2 (5); 7:11-12—I 6 (9); 8:2—I 6 (11); 8:5—I 7, 8 (13);
8:14—I 8 (15); 41:45—I 15 (17); Ex 13:22—I 34 (20); Num 22:28—I 34
(24); Josh 10:12ff—II 4 (28); Judg 6:37—II 5 (29); 6:40—II 5 (30); 1
Sam 16:23—II 10 (32); 19:23—II 10 (33); 2 Sam 24:15—II 13 (35); 3
Kings 17:1—II 15 (36); 18:17—II 15 (38); 18:18—II 15 (39); 18:24(?)—II
18 (40); 19:8(?)—II 19 (41); 4 Kings 4:3—II 23 (45); Job 9:10—I 1 (48);
28:1—I 24 (49); Wis 19:11—I 27 (58); Is 14:13f—I 2 (59); and, perhaps,
Eccles 1:10—I 17 (57).

The *Vetus Latina* then, and we have a handful of texts: Gen 3:19—I
2 (7); 7:11—I 8 (9)—the word order of this differs from the critical
edition; 21:17—I 13 (16)—this is the European text; Ex 13:19—I 15
(19); Num 11:31(?)—I 27 (23); Dan 3:49f(?)—II 28 (62). There are a
few more texts which could be either Vulgate or Vetus Latina, or are
mixed: Gen 1:28—I 3 (2); 3:17—I 4 (6); Ex 2:22—I 25 (18).

The *Gallican Psalter* is represented by Pss 77:24—I 6 (50); 77:24-25—I
23 (50); 98:6—I 25 (52); 109:3—III 5 (54); 148:7f—I 23 (56); and the
Roman Psalter or a mixed text by Pss 84:13—I 6 (51); 103:4—I 16 (53).

Finally there are those texts which, although presented as Scripture,
are very much the writer's own: Gen 2:2—I 1 (3); 2:3—I 1 (4); 8:1—I 7
(10); 8:5—I 6 (13 above); Ex 22:1—II 18 (21); Num 11:21f—I 27 (22); 4
Kings 1:9—II 20 (42); 1:10—II 20 (43); 2:9—II 22 (44); 7:1—II 23 (46);
7:2—II 23 (47); Ps 120:6—I 34 (55); Is 38:1—II 25 (60).

Texts from the New Testament

With regard to the texts from the New Testament[8] the situation is even
more confused, although, thanks to the apparatus of Wordsworth and

Vetus Latina. Die Reste der altlateinischen Bibel . . . hrsg. von der Erzabtei
Beuron. 2 Genesis, hg. von Bonifatius Fischer, Freiburg 1951-54 ; 25. Epp. ad
Thess., Tim., Tit., Philem., Hebr., hg. von H.J. Frede (1 Freiburg 1975. (VL).

P. Sabatier, O.S.B., Bibliorum Sacrorum Latinae uersiones antiquae seu Vetus
Italica, Paris 1751, (Sab.).

For the Septuagint : A. Rahlfs, Septuaginta, id est Vetus Testamentum Graece
iuxta LXX Interpretes, Stuttgart ed. 6ª, n.d., (LXX).

For the Hebrew : R. Kittel, Biblia Hebraica, Stuttgart 1925, (Hebrew).

For the Psalter: H. de Sainte-Marie, Sancti Hieronymi Psalterium iuxta Hebraeos,
Collectanea Biblica Latina xi, Vatican 1954; F. Merlo, Il Salterio di Rufino, Coll.
Bibl. Latina xiv, Vatican 1972; R. Weber, O.S.B., Le Psautier romain et les autres
anciens psautiers latins, Coll. Biblica Latina, x, Vatican 1953 (Roman Psalter).

8   For the New Testament:
Apart from Weber, Clementine, Sab., and VL listed above (n.7), I used the
following for reference:

White, the patristic reference is clearer. There are a few texts which may be judged those of the *critical editions* of the Vulgate: Mt 1:5–6—I 3 (63); 7:22—II 10 (67); Acts 3:6—III 18 (86); 7:49—I 5 (87); Rev 1:5—III 11 (99); then we have the *Clementine* Vulgate in Mt 22:30—I 2 (70).

We find a *reordered or adapted* Vulgate text in: Mt 4:4—I 23 (65); Lk 1:63—I 1 (75); 16:16—I 1 (79); Jn 3:8—I 34 (81); 8:44—I 2 (83); Acts 2:11—I 9 (85); 1 Cor 13:9—I 7 (90); Heb 11:30—II 3 (97); Rev 1:20—III 4 (100). Further there is a reading which reflects the *Itala* or Old Latin text: Lk 24:42—I 4 (80); and a series of readings which could be *either* Vulgate or Itala or mixed: Mt 4:17—I 2 (66); 8:20(=Lk 9:58)—I 6 (68); 23:35—III 13 (71); 25:41—I 2 (72); Lk 10:18—I 2 (78); Jn 5:17—I 1 (82).

Besides these there are texts which can have some contacts with tradition but otherwise are difficult to assign: Mt 3:17—III 5 (64); 10:9—III 18 (69); Mk 4:32—I 6 (73); Lk 1:18—III 1 (74); Jn 11:4—III 13 (84); 1 Cor 15:44—III 16 (91); 2 Cor 3:7—III 11 (92); 11:14—II 11 (93); Gal 3:19—I 23 (94); 1 Thess 4:17—III 8 (95); Heb 2:16—I 2 (96); 11:39–40—III 15 (98). Finally there is a text which seems wholly corrupt: Acts 20:10—III 13 (89).

Further to these various categories the question could be raised: is there any discernible patristic context for one or other of these categories or series of readings; put otherwise: does the text type revealed relate to the author's sources? The answer to this must be that if it does relate then such relationship is not readily discernible, whatever about individual texts.

General Conclusions on the Knowledge of Scripture

Any conclusions based on a survey of the knowledge of Scripture in the *De mirabilibus* entail a certain frustration:—

1. Quite frequently the form and word order of such quotations as there are would seem proper to the *De mirabilibus*, although one or other of them may have a patristic source.
2. It has been suggested that reliance on memory may have been responsible for some of the changes in the biblical texts quoted. This does not necessarily mean that it was *always* the memory of the Irish Augustine which was at fault, it could have been that of an author he was using.

J. Wordsworth and H.J. White, Nouum Testamentum DNIC latine secundum editionem S. Hieronymi, Oxford 1889–1954 (WW); as some of the Irish MSS are not well collated in WW I have referred to J. Gwynn, Liber Armachanus, Dublin 1913 (Armagh), and H.C. Hoskier, The Text of Codex Usserianus II r₂ (Garland of Howth), (Hoskier); A. Julicher, Itala, das neue Testament in altlateinischen Hberlieferung, I Matthäus-Evangelium, Berlin 1938, III Lucas-Evangelium, Berlin 1954, (Itala).

Then S. Sanday & C.H. Turner, Nouum Testamentum Sancti Irenaei, Oxford 1923.

3. Nonetheless, the frequency of the verbal changes and reorderings would suggest that, whatever about his sources, our writer was prone to act in that way, to think and quote *more suo.*
4. The writer's freedom with regard to his texts must also be remarked. He integrated his quotations into his own text, and this could result in his omitting words used earlier in the sentence or passage, and in various grammatical alterations.
5. Then there are the erroneous references and statements. It is difficult to explain all of these: now a memory lapse, then dependence on a corrupt source, e.g. defective copies of certain works of Jerome, and so on. To judge him by our standards we would have to say that there can be little doubt that certain Books of Scripture were not accurately known, if really known at all[9].
6. As regards the type of text used: a) in the Old Testament the readings have an Old Latin edge, but in the case of more Books the Vulgate text is witnessed to, although it is a reordered text. As one might expect, the texts from both Old-Latin and Vulgate relate to the European tradition, and, in the case of the Vulgate particularly, to the tradition of north-west Europe. With regard to the Psalter text it will be noted that I interpret the evidence rather differently to Martin McNamara, Psalter Text and Psalter Study in the Early Irish Church, PRIA 73 C 7, 1973, 260 and 262; b) in the New Testament the influence of the Old-Latin would seem more marked, but it is not always possible to distinguish between Old-Latin and Vulgate traditions. There are texts which contain elements of both traditions, and again there are texts which it is difficult to assign clearly to either or indeed any tradition.

THE UNDERSTANDING AND USE OF SCRIPTURE

General approach

The Irish Augustine was much inspired by the writings and ideas of Augustine of Hippo, (hence, perhaps, 'Augustinus' ?), and then, to a lesser extent, by the writings of St Jerome. There could also be *some*

9 I was unable to trace any reference to the following: Ruth, Tobith, Esther, Song of Songs, Lamentations, Baruch, Hosea, Joel, Amos, Obadiah, Nahum, Habakkuk, Zephaniah, Haggai, Malachi in the Old Testament, and to 1 & 2 Timothy, Titus, Philemon, 1 and 2 Peter, 1, 2 and 3 John, Jude in the New. It must also be pointed out that no *real* knowledge of the text of Leviticus, Chronicles, Ezra, Nehemiah, and Judith, particularly of the two first, and the last of these is witnessed to in the text. (In this connection Prof. Terence O'Reilly of UCC commented to me that I was reading Scripture with twentieth century eyes, not those of an earlier age. This arose over a query I put to him concerning John of the Cross's use and knowledge of Scripture. He cites Scripture very freely, and yet we know he read the Bible regularly and knew it well!)

influence of the Antiochene, or some related tradition, in both exegesis and theology, but, save to suggest some influence through Spain, I do not know how this came about, and I fear that researching the point might prove to be like chasing a will-o'-the-wisp (cf n.12).

What is striking is the power of synthesis and consistency which the *De mirabilibus* exhibits. The principle that God no longer creates having been accepted, for so Scripture was interpreted (I 1. from Gen 2:2–3), the purpose of the whole work is to develop the theme of God's governing by exploiting the native possibilities of his creatures. This was an original and courageous undertaking, and it has led to the comment that the *De mirabilibus* was the only original commentary on Scripture between Gregory the Great and the scholastics[10].

In the strictest sense the writer accepted the Scriptures as inspired, and the notion he had of inspiration was common to most of the Fathers, (and later to the medievals). No allowance was made for literary styles, and any clear dictum of Scripture is taken as an absolute, for Scripture cannot err. Such a fundamental stance imposes severe limitations on scientific enquiry, and almost ensures its complete inhibition[11].

The Scriptures are referred to as 'holy' and 'divine' (*passim*); the Books of Scripture have 'authority' (I 1), and Scripture does not lie (I 2, etc.). This approach meant that poetry, saga, satire and polemic were frequently given equal authority and universal validity. A more serious and fundamental flaw, though, was that no real allowance was made for the progress of revelation, (was there even such a notion about?), and the Old Testament was read consistently in the light of the New. A valid principle, that of explaining Scripture by Scripture, was pushed too far. We might say the error is one of emphasis, a onesided stress on the activity of the Holy Spirit, at the expense of the human agent. A consequence of this is that much of the resulting exegesis appears to us as an explaining *away* rather than an explaining *of* the scriptures. In the De *mirabilibus* III 4, by way of exception, we do find a seeming contrast of *in re* and *in spiritu*.

A good proportion of Book I is taken up with matter other than the 'marvels of Scripture'. On almost any pretext, particularly in the early chapters, comment is made on Scripture and its related problems. However, while the writer's treatment of his matter does tend to differ from chapter to chapter, his usual procedure is first to clarify the literal meaning of the particular text with which he is dealing, where he deems this necessary, and such clarification is normally by recourse to Scripture

---

10 So R.E. McNally, S.J., The Bible in the Early Middle Ages, Woodstock Papers, No.4, 1959, 30. This I should be inclined to view as perhaps an overly enthusiastic judgement.

11 See R.F. Smith, S.J., Inspiration and Inerrancy, in The Jerome Biblical Commentary, London 1968, 505, No. 29 and 513, No. 77(B), for the limited notion of inspiration and inerrancy which generally prevailed.

itself. This is followed by an attempt to explain the happening recounted in the light of his 'scientific' knowledge, in order to demonstrate that
no new creation was involved.

Explaining a point in Scripture Augustine, respects his text, has obviously considered it carefully, and is generally objective. On this level
his work, as a rule, manifests common sense and judgement, and his
opinions can, at times, be quite incisive.

The only forms of exegesis he mentions are the figurative and the
historical, both of which were of value in his eyes. He is fond of
moralizing from Scripture, but never explicitly referes to 'moral'
exegesis. It would seem that for him 'spiritual' and 'figurative' exegesis are one. It is dangerous to characterize without a very thorough
examination of the background, (a difficult undertaking in the 7th
century insular Church), but the following is an outline of the understanding of Scripture, as the writer would appear to have seen it:

First there is the historical or literal sense. It is not quite clear what
Augustine understood by this. In his Prologue he refers to *rerum . . .
gestarum rationem et ordinem*, yet Scripture is not confined to the mere nar-
rating of happenings, and we should, perhaps, understand his historical
sense to be simply what the text says, and, consequently, his historical
exegesis as a form of literal exegesis applied to the particular field he has
chosen to exploit[12]. He makes no attempt to rank such a sense or its exegesis above or below any other form. Because of the restricted nature of
the task he set himself, or had been set for him, he deliberately put aside
the second major form of exegesis he mentions,— *sepositis adhuc figurar-
um intellectibus*, and this for the reason that *spiritalium multiplex sensuum
intellectus habetur* of the many places touched on in his commentary,
(Prologue). Anyway, most authors had concerned themselves with the
mysticus allegoriarum intellectus, which is *figuralis expositio*, so there is no lack
of comment on the spiritual level (Prologue). These statements make it
rather hard to determine what were the other 'spiritual' senses Augustine
recognized, although in practice, as I remarked just above, the 'moral'
sense must have been one, and so it is that in the Prologue itself we have
a lesson drawn from incidents in the Old Testament for ourselves[13].

12   There may be influence of John Cassian in this. See his four senses of Scripture: i
     Historical/Literal; ii Allegorical/Christological; iii Tropological/Moral/Anthro-
     pological; iv Anagogical/Eschatological (R.E. Brown, Hermeneutics, in The Jerome
     Biblical Commentary, 612, No. 33). Cassian had a certain familiarity with Antioch-
     ene exegesis, but was hardly an Antiochene. The Antiochene note in the De
     mirabilibus is in part explained by the writer's purpose, but how far he was from the
     Antiochene tradition, at least as represented by Theodore of Mopsuestia, can be
     judged by the excellent survey article on the latter in P.R. Ackroyd and C.F. Evans,
     The Cambridge History of the Bible, I, CUP 1970, M.F. Wiles, 'Theodore of
     Mopsuestia as representative of the Antiochene School', 489–510.
13   So, in the Prologue lessons from Jonah, the prophet of Bethel and from Jeremiah:
     Plus namque periculi fugiens Ionas propheta in marinis fluctibus repperit, quam

It must be borne in mind that these senses were seen as in Scripture, not just read into it.

Some qualities of his approach

In the realm of scientific enquiry Augustine was hampered by the pseudo-science of his day. He is good when he confides in his own judgements and observations, although he never carried the latter as far as we should like; he is weak when, apparently, he relied on 'authorities'. He was interested in natural history, but it would be unreasonable for us to judge him by our standards. He was more scientific in his approach than Augustine of Hippo, particularly in his preparedness to observe critically, and, apparently, to experiment[14], in this preparing the way for Bede.

The work is one done by a believing Christian, its concern is a problem of faith, within faith: the problem of reconciling different teachings of Scripture on creation and God's governance. In a very real way the *De mirabilibus* can be viewed as a developed commentary on themes suggested by Wisdom 16–19.

Not only did Augustine wish to be Christian, he wished to be true to the Catholic understanding of his faith—*et si catholico sensui nihil repugnat*, III 4[15]. He would seem to have succeeded. The work is not marked by any note of 'devotional' warmth, but it is not intended as a work of devotion!

Some Points of Teaching

The one and triune God is and has been, I 1, and is the source of all things, which he created in time and out of nothing. His almighty power reaches down into the depths of natures, I 1, and here we have the ultimate explanation of the 'marvels'. Then the normal instruments or agents of his marvels, as well as of his regular governing of lower things are the angels, I 23, etc[16].

---

accusationis, si quod iubebatur impleret, in sermonibus populi sui pateretur, quod metuit. Propheta quoque altaris Bethel, quoniam laboriosi itineris famem et sitim ut sibi iussum fuerat, non perpetrauit, inoboedientiae uindicta mortem ipsam paulo post in uia saturatus inuenit. Ieremias uero adhuc puer nec litterarum doctrinam nec uirilis prudentiae uigorem, quando a Domino iussus est prophetare, habuit, sed quod praecepto oboediuerat, scientiam quam non habuerat, accipere promeruit.

14 Perhaps it would be more accurate to say 'investigate', so we find references to the shellfish on the skins of a whale, I 24, and to fossils, in the same chapter.

15 . . . *et si catholico sensui nihil repugnat,* . . . : III 4. There were many heresies about in the seventh century.

16 These teachings are derived from Scripture:

I 1 *Tunc ergo creator, nunc gubernator Deus intellegendus est, ac per hoc, etiam si noui aliquid in creaturis exoriri uideamus, non creare ibi nouam naturam, sed gubernare olim creatam Deus putandus est; sed ita est potens in gubernatione creaturae, qui condidit, ut ueluti naturam nouam creare uideatur, cum de abditis naturae sinibus, quod in illa latebat, depromit.*

There is no trace of either Arianism or of Spanish adoptionism in his Christology. His apparent use of *Sermo* as well as *Verbum* for the living Word of God reflects the earliest Latin tradition. A very imposing concept of Christ was present to his mind, and it could be that here alone we have a new creation, Christ as the new Adam formed from the Virgin (earth), yet the actual conceiving by the Virgin represented the exploiting of the possibilities of nature III 2, so it is a qualified new creation. There is a very sharp distinction drawn between Christ's divinity and his human body[17].

In connection with the justice of Christ we have a text on Abel, I 3, as the first just man, a type of the Saviour (*figuram gestare*), embodying the ideal of righteousness as a virgin, a martyr and a priest, (*cf* also III 6). As a statement this could hardly be more absolute[18].

The Holy Spirit, one in nature, will and operation with the Father and the Son, III 5, figures largely in the *De mirabilibus*[19].

God governs the world caring for his own, I 34, etc., so that the marvels are not random happenings. The ultimate aim is God's saving purpose with regard to mankind, *cf* I 17; I 20, etc.

The Church is mentioned as the body of the sons of God, III 3, and the new Israel, but it is primarily considered, it would appear, as an authoritative hierarchical institution; so III 18; I 33; I 28–31, etc. This is not without significance in the seventh century insular context[20].

> I 23 '*Panis*' autem '*angelorum*' cibus ille dicitur, non quod angeli, qui cibo non egent, isto saturarentur, sed quod per angelorum ministerium tale officium, sicut lex et cetera populo praebebatur, quae '*disposita per angelos in manu mediatoris*', tribuitur.
> In the text from I 23 the Maurists followed a slightly different reading: *illo* for *isto* and placed it before the *angeli* of line 1 here. This was in none of the MSS I used. However such a slight variant in no way affects the sense.

17 The text is very faithful to the terms of the New Testament. This emphasis on the distinction between the divinity and the humanity of Christ betrays a basic sympathy with the tradition identified with Antioch. On the use of *Sermo*, there are two interesting texts, one of which is particularly so because paralleling the use of *Verbum*: I 26 *diuini Sermonis consortio fruitus*; II 19 *Verbi dominici fruitus consortio*, and further III 6 *Sermo dominicus . . . hic Christi artus et neruos intus irrigabat.*

18 I 3 *Tota enim iustitia haec est: uirginitas, sacerdotium, et martyrium. Quae triplex iustitia in Abel primo fuit . . .*

19 III 5 treats of the baptism of Christ, the Holy Spirit under the appearance of a dove and the testimony of the Father to his Son. It emphasizes the doctrine of the Holy Trinity—*ut sic tota Trinitas eandem uoluntatem sicut haberet, ostenderet.*

20 E.g. III 3: *(Christus) enim est noui testamenti principium, filiorumque, qui ex noua lege nasceretur, exordium exstitit.* And III 18: *Ecce quanta est apostolica uirtus in Christo: sanum Ananiam dum Petrus arguit, per sermonis tantum imperium morte ligauit, et Tabitam mortis uinculo ligatam eadem imperii potestate dissoluit . . . (Ananias et Sapphira) . . . cito mortui sunt, ut apostolica auctoritas quanta esset, ostenderetur; et quam magnum peccatum esset, quod oblatum est, iterum ab ecclesia retrahere monstraretur . . .*
> I 28 to 33 are concerned with various protests against the divinely established order and how these were dealt with, and are concluded by the statement that (?) *uirtus nunc in Christo et in ecclesia continetur.*

There is manifestly much more which could be said, but I should like to end these points on an item which deals directly with the interpretation of Scripture. There are several instances in the Old and New Testaments of the dead being raised to life. Augustine is firmly of the opinion that, as yet, only one has risen from real death to eternal life, Christ the Lord, III 15. The others mentioned in the Scriptures as raised from the dead had only a likeness of death, cf III 13.

CONCLUSION

Such a sketch is manifestly no substitute for reading the treatise itself, but I hope to have said enough to lay the ghost in people's minds that the Irish Augustine was a seventh century rationalist or ecclesiastical rebel, and, equally, on the other hand, that he was both limited and ignorant. With the *De ordine creaturarum*, which manifestly derives *from* the *De mirabilibus* but with the advantage of access to and knowledge of the works of Isidore, it remains a worthy monument to a whole aspect of the Irish, or Irish-inspired, Church which would otherwise be unknown.[21]

APPENDIX: A DETAILED ANALYSIS OF THE TEXTS OF SCRIPTURE QUOTED

The scriptural versions referred to are listed in Notes 7 and 8 above. Sigla for the MSS of the De mirabilibus:

- O   Balliol College, Oxford: MS No.229, s.XIIex.
- R   Rouen, Bibliothèque Publique: MS No.665 (A 453), s.XII.
- B   Bodleian Library, Oxford: MS Rawlinson C153, s.XII.
- T   Troyes, Bibliothèque Publique: MS No.280, s.XII.
- P   Paris, Bibliothèque Nationale: MS Lat. No.1956, s.XIIex.*
- K   Pembroke College, Cambridge: MS 20, s.XIIIex.
- W   Worcester Cathedral Library: MS F.57, s.XIII.
- C   St John's College, Cambridge: MS. No.47(B25), s.XIIIex.
- X   Bodleian Library: MS Rawlinson C531, s.XIIIex.
- E   Emmanuel College, Cambridge: MS No.2, s.XIIIex.
- N   Naples, Biblioteca Nazionale: VI.B., s.XIII.
- Q   Paris, Bibliothèque Mazarine: MS No.640, s.XV.
- G   Tours, Bibliothèque Municipale: MS 247, s.XIII

21   Perhaps the most extensive and sympathetic study of the De mirabilibus published is M. Simonetti's De mirabilibus sacrae scripturae—Un trattato irlandese sui miracoli della Sacra Scrittura, in Romanobarbarica 4 (1979) 225–251. The author was not aware (?) of my thesis and editing of the text and is led astray on certain points by the text in Migne. In our different ways he and I are at one on many points of interpretation.

β   (J—Karlsruhe, Note 3 above, and A—consensus of most later
    MSS of the short recension.)
m   Maurists' text (m¹—Maurist edition, Paris 1836, III 2, 1837,
    2717–2790; m²—Migne, PL xxxv 1861, 2149ff).

Note :—(short hyphen) at the left indicates a change of reference,
save when the contrary is clear from the context, from my apparatus
for the De mirabilibus to those of the editions of the Bible to which
reference is being made.

Genesis

Reference to or comment upon matter from the following chapters is
found: 1–11, 13–14, 16–19, 21–22, 25, 28–29, 35, 37, 41, 45, 47, 49–50.
    The following must be noted:

7:20   *duodecim cubitis* for the height of the Flood over the moun-
        tains. I 5 m¹ 2726B / m² 2156.
        VL and Vulgate read *quindecim*; perhaps *xu* (*xv*) misread as *xii* (?).
22:13   addition of gloss *iubente angelo* to the offering of the ram. I 14
        m¹ 2735D/m² 2162. This represents an extra-biblical tradition,
        (whence?).
47:28   *annis xvi* for Jacob's stay in Egypt. I 15 m¹ 2736A / m² 2163.
        Hebrew, VL and Vulgate all read *xvii*.

Direct quotations:

1:22   *Crescite et multiplicamini et replete aquas maris.* (*implete* RK) III 10
(1)   m¹ 2787A / m² 2197.
        —Vulgate text. The reading *implete* is VL, where though, *replete*
        is found as a variant, *cf.* Augustine, De Gen. ad litt. and many
        others.
1:28   *Crescite et multiplicamini et implete terram.* (*replete* Q) I 3 m¹ 2724C
(2)   / m² 2155.
        —VL / Vulgate: *replete* is the main text of both, and in both
        implete is found as a variant.
2:2   *Et consummauit Deus omnia opera sua in die sexto.* (*in* om. Q;
(3)   *septimo* W^C) I 1 m¹ 2719B / m² 2151.
        —Proper (?) to the De mirabilibus; *die sexto* is a variant in
        VL(L) and the Vulgate (*sexto* ΣT²ΨF*), which read *septimo*.
2:3   *et benedixit diem septimum, quod in ipso requieuit ab operibus suis.*
(4)   (*quod*] *quia* E, *eo quod* Q; *in* om. Q; *requiescit* Q; post *ab* add.
        omnibus WNm) I 1 m¹ 2719B / m² 2151.

---

*   P₂—portion of the text repeated later in MS.

—Proper (?), closer to VL than to Vulgate.

—For *diem septimum* see VL; *ipso* is a variant with support in Augustine, De Gen. ad litt.; *requieuit* is VL; *quod* could be a misreading for *quia*; the omission of *omnibus* is in accord with LXX, see also Augustine, De Gen. contra Man.

3:14   *Maledictus tu inter omnia animantia et bestias terrae, super pectus*
(5)   *tuum gradieris, et terram comedes cunctis diebus uitae tuae.*
          (*omnia*] *cetera* N; *et*¹] *uel* WENQ; *cunctis*] *omnibus* m) I 2 m¹ 2721D / m² 2153.

—Vulgate text with, however, the *tu* of VL for *es*.

3:17   *Maledicta terra in opere tuo.* I 4 m¹ 2725C / m² 2155.
(6)   —Vulgate text, or possibly the European text of VL.

3:19   *Terra es et in terram ibis.* (*terram*²] *terra* OP) I 2 m¹ 2723A / m²
(7)   2153.

—VL in which *terra* is also found as a variant.

7:11   *secundi uigesima septima die mensis.* (*secundi*] *mense secundi* W;
(8)   *uigesima*] *decima* Q, *decimo* m; *septima*] *prima* TP, *septimo* m) I 8 m¹ 2731D / m² 2160.

—In the tradition of the VL, the order of words would seem proper (?).

7:11f *Rupti sunt omnes fontes abyssi magnae, et cataractae caeli apertae*
(9)   *sunt, et facta est pluuia quadraginta diebus et quadraginta noctibus.*
          (*aperti* XP₂) I 6 m¹ 2726C / 2156.
          Et rupti sunt omnes fontes abyssi. (*omnes*] om. m) I 6 m¹ 2727A / m² 2156.
          Et cataractae caeli apertae sunt et facta est pluuia. I 6 m¹ 2727C / m² 2156.

—Vulgate text, but close to the European text of VL. Note omission of *super terram* after *pluuia* in the first and longest quotation. The *Et* before *rupti* is found in the European text of VL.

8:1   *Inmisit Dominus uentum super terram et imminutae sunt aquae.*
(10)   (*misit* G; *deus* Q; *diminutae* m) I 7 m¹ 2729B / m² 2158.

—Proper (?), contact with VL in *inmisit*, and Vulgate in *imminutae sunt aquae*.

8:2   *Et clausi sunt fontes abyssi et prohibitae sunt pluuiae de caelo.* (*Et*¹
(11)   om. RBKWCXEQm; *prohibite pluuie sunt* Q) I 6 m¹ 2726C / m² 2156.
          Et clausi sunt fontes abyssi magnae, et prohibitae sunt pluuiae de caelo.
          (*magnae abyssi* Q; *magnae* om. β, I 6 m¹ 2727(A)B / m² 2156.

—Vulgate text without the *et cataractae caeli* after *abyssi* of Vulgate. The reading *magnae* proper (?). Note β, the short recension, tends more to the Vulgate.

8:3–4 *Post cl dies in mense vii⁰ uigesimo vii⁰ die mensis, in montibus Armeniae.*
(12)   (*in¹*] om. WE; *vii⁰ ¹*] *i⁰* E, *septum* Q; *vii⁰ ²*] om. m²) I 8 m¹
       2731D–2732A / m² 2160.
       —Vulgate rather than VL, v.g. *uicesima septima* (*uigesimo septimo*
       Clementine Vulgate) *die*, and *Armeniae. eadem archa requieuit*
       which concludes the sentence replaces the Vulgate *requieuitque*
       arca. An example, perhaps, of deliberate adaptation.
8:5   *aquae ibant et reuertebantur.* I 6 m¹ 2727B / m² 2156.
(13)   —Neither Vulgate nor VL, perhaps from Jerome, QQ sup. Gen.,
       but more likely confusion with Gen. 8:7 which refers to the raven!
       Aquae enim, inquit scriptura, *ibant et decrescebant.* (*decrescebant*]
       reuertebantur BTPm, *crescebant* P₂) I 7 m¹ 2728D / m² 2157.
       —Technically a paraphrase; without *enim* it is Vulgate.
       Prima die decimi mensis cacumina montium apparuerunt. (*mensis*
       decimi E; *mensis* om. WCm) I 8 m¹ 2732A / m² 2160.
       —From Vulgate (?), but almost wholly reordered.
8:13   *Prima die mensis primi aquae minutae sunt.* (*Et prima* m;
(14)   *imminutae* KQ) I 8 m¹ 2732A / m² 2160.
       —Proper (?), closer to Vulgate than to VL.
8:14   *mense secundo, uigesimo vii⁰ die mensis, terra arefacta conspicitur.*
(15)   (*uigesimo vii⁰*] *xxii⁰* C, *uigesima septima* m; *terra arefacta*] *arefacta*
       arua J, *arefacta terra* m; *aspicitur* J) I 8 m¹ 2732A / m² 2160.
       —Proper (?); related to the Vulgate but with some slight inver-
       sion and reading *conspicitur* for *est.* The reading of m partly
       restores the Vulgate word order.
       The reading *arefacta arua* of J is an echo of Jeremiah 23:10,
       arefacta sunt arua deserti, and see 25:37 ibid., *arua pacis.* The
       use of the term *arua,* which is a neuter plural, as a singular,
       reflects a love for exotica, (which are only half understood),
       and so could have been the original reading.
21:17 *Exaudiuit Dominus uocem pueri.* I 13 m¹ 2735C / m² 2162.
(16)   —European text of VL rather than Vulgate, but see GΣᴹΨᴮ for
       dominus and Φᴬ* for the omisssion of *enim/autem* in latter.
41:45 *Asenech filiam Putifaris sacerdotis Heliopoleos.* (*aserich* C(?Q);
(17)   *phutif(ph)aris* OBTPKCX, *phutepharis* R, *futifaris* G, *putifare* J;
       filiam post *heliopoleos* m; *heleopoleos* BCNQ, *heleopoileos* K, (*h*)*eleploeos*
       WE, *elyoploleos* G) I 15 m¹ 2736B / m² 2163.
       —Vulgate reads *Aseneth filiam Putiphare sacerdotis Heliopoleos*; the
       variant readings for the proper names are *asenech* ΛΜΦᴿᴬᶻᴾ ΘΨΩ,
       etc.; *phutipharis* Ωˢᴶ, rel., *putipharis* Ωᴹ; *elyopoleos* Ψᶠ. Many of the
       Western MSS of the Vulgate read *p(h)utiphares,* the termination
       in -*is* is represented only in some rather late MSS of the Paris
       tradition. (There are those who would assert that variations of *es*
       and *is* are of little or no significance.)

Exodus

Reference to or comment upon matter from the following chapters is
found: 1–4, 6–10, 12–19, 22–25, 31, 32, 34.
The following must be noted:

3:6,10   paraphrased into one text. I 16 m¹ 2737B / m² 2163.
An instance(?) of the writer's tendency to read the Old
Testament through the eyes of commentators.

14:21   a gloss added putting the staff in Moses' hand. I 17 m¹ 2738C
/ m² 2164. then the strong drying wind is called "freezing". I
20 m¹ 2741C / m² 2166.
The interpretation of the wind in this manner is found in
several of the Fathers.

16:1–3 combined with Numbers 11:4–6 with reference to the
murmuring of the people. I 27 m¹ 2746C / m² 2170.

23:16   interpreted in the light of the tradition which linked Pentecost
and the Alliance. I 26 m¹ 2746B / m² 2170. See Exodus 12:3,
19:1–2, 34:22; Leviticus 23:15–16; Deuteronomy 16:10.

Direct quotations: there are five discussed here.

2:22   *Et uocauit nomen eius Gersam dicens: quia aduena fui in terra*
(18)   *aliena.* (*Et* om. G; *gersan* KNGm, *iersam* J; *quia* om. J) I 25 m¹
2746B / m² 2170.
— From *Gersam* to *aliena* is the Vulgate text with the addition of
quia. In Exodus 18:3 the Vulgate reads *Gersan.* The *quia* may
reflect VL, as LXX has ὅτι, although the Greek has the present
tense (Sab.).

13:19   *Efferte ossa mea hinc uobiscum.* (*mea* om. WCN; *nobiscum* C; *uobiscum*
(19)   *hinc* m) I 15 m¹ 2736B / m² 2163.
Visitatione uisitabit uos Deus, et efferte ossa mea hinc uobiscum (*uos*]
nos (K?)W; *efferetis* W(N?)Q, *offeretis* E) I 15 m¹ 2736D / m² 2163.
—Not Vulgate, which has not *Visitatione.* Reading probably
reflects a VL text, (not in Sab.), as *Visitatione* corresponds with
the Hebrew, LXX and Gᶜ in margin; *et* omitted in the critical
Vulgate text, is read in GT
ΦΨᴮᴹΩˢᴶ, Hebrew and LXX.—Rather surprisingly the Maurists
give Genesis 50:24 for the biblical reference.

13:22   *columna nubis per diem numquam defuit, nec coram populo columna*
(20)   *ignis per noctem.* (*numquam defuit per diem* β; *numquam*] *quam
nunc* N; *coram populo* om. β) I 34 m¹ 2750C / m² 2173.
—Every word of this text is read in the Vulgate, but the clauses
have been completely inverted within themselves.

22:18   *Blasphemum non patieris uiuere.* (*blasphemium* BKCE) II 18 m¹
(21)   2764B / m² 2182.

—Text combined with or coloured by Leviticus 24:16 *et qui blasphemauerit nomen domini morte moriatur* ? The Vulgate of Exodus reads, *Maleficos non patieris uiuere.* The reading may be proper to our text, or may have a patristic antecedent.

Numbers

Reference to or comment upon matter from the following chapters is found: 11–12, 16–17, 20–24, 31, 33–34, 35.

The following must be noted:

11:7   paraphrased and combined with Exodus 16:31. I 23 m¹ 2743D / m² 2168. The reference is to the manna.

11:10   likewise paraphrased; combined with Numbers 11:18–20. I 27 m¹ 2746C / m² 2170. The text behind the paraphrase would seem to be that of the Vulgate.

31:6–8   interpreted as if Balac, king of Moab, were among the kings slain by Ph(F)inees. II 31 (34) m¹ 2777C / m² 2191. This is not in scripture, see Numbers 22–24. Confusion between Balac and Balaam ?

Direct quotations: I here discuss five possible ones :

11:21f   *sexcenta,* respondit, *peditum pugnatorum excepto innumerabili*
(22)   *uulgo huius populi milia numerantur. Numquid boum et ouium immensa multitudo caedetur? Aut ad saturationem innumerabilis turbae pisces maris in unum congregabuntur?* (*millia* post *sexcenta* m, post *pugnatorum* Q; *excepta* Q; *huius populi uulgo milia* Q; *boum*] *bonum* m²; *cederet* P; *ad*] *uel ob* Xᶜ; *innumerabili turbae* P, *innumerabiles turbae* E) I 27 m¹ 2746D / m² 2170.

—Hardly a direct quotation of Numbers ? The text has very tenuous contacts with the Vulgate. The *populi* may suggest a relationship with the Greek, see Sab.

11:31   *Ventus a Domino egrediens, arreptas trans mare coturnices ad castrorum*
(23)   *loca detulit . . . quantum unum die confici potest . . .* (*Ventus*] *Deinde* (?) *uentus* G; *coturnices trans mare* Q) I 27 m¹ 2746D–2747A / m² 2170.

—Close to the Vulgate but marked by omissions and inversions. The term which follows *potest* immediately in the text, although not quoted above, is *ortogometram* and is taken from the LXX (*ortugometra*), suggesting an Old-Latin source, (of which there is nothing in Sab.), at least in part.

22:28   *Et aperuit Dominus os asinae.* (*os asine dominus* G) I 34 m¹ 2749D
(24)   / m² 2172.

—This is the text of the *uersio antiqua* (Sab.). The Vulgate reads *aperuitque Dominus os asinae,* in which *que* is omitted by Λᴸ and L (Spanish).

24:17   *Orietur stella ex Iacob.* III 4 m¹ 2783A / m² 2195.
(25)   —Vulgate text but rather too short to be discussed.
35:1   *in campestribus Moab super Iordanem.* I 35 m¹ 2750C / m² 2173.
(26)   —Again the Vulgate text, but likewise too short for discussion.

Deuteronomy

Reference to or comment upon matter from the following chapters is found : 1–3, 8, 12, 16, 19, 29, 31, 34.
   The following is to be noted:
34:1,5 Moses is said to have died on Mount Nebo, having crossed
      montem Gay. I 35 m¹ 2750CD / m² 2174.
      This may be an erroneous reading of Jerome, Adu. Iou.I(PL 23,241B).

Direct quotation: I here discuss one possible one:

8:3   *non in pane solo uiuit, sed in omni uerbo quod de ore Dei procedit.* (*non*
(27)   om. N; *solo pane* KQGβm; *uiueret* Nβ, et additur *homo* EQGβ;
      in] *de* N; *quod—procedit*] *dei* J; *procedit de ore dei* Q; *dei ore* m) I 23
      m¹ 2745A / m² 2169.
      —Quoted in its Deuteronomical context the text, in fact, is
      much closer to the Vulgate traditions for Matthew 4:4, which in
      Weber reads: *non in pane solo uiuet* (= sZDGreek: *uiuit* cet.) *homo,*
      sed in omni uerbo quod procedit de ore Dei (the Clementine Vulgate
      reads *solo pane uiuit*). In a citation from memory the confusion is
      understandable, particularly as the text of Deuteronomy is itself
      rather confused, *non in solo pane uiuat* (*uiuit* CLM) *homo, sed in*
      omni uerbo quod egreditur (*procedit* l) *ex ore Domini* (*de ore dei*
      Clementine Vulgate). Some of the MSS have sought to reorder
      the text of the De mirabilibus in the light of the various recen-
      sions of the Vulgate. Note then, the writer's freedom with his
      text; since he had used *homo* earlier in the sentence he omitted
      it in the quotation. *dei* in place of *domini* is in accord with the
      LXX, as well as with Matthew.

Joshua

Reference to or comment upon matter from the following chapters is found: 3–6, 10–12.

Direct quotation: though presented as such, the one text is very free:

10:12s *Sol stetit contra Gabaon et luna ad uallem Achillon oboediente Domino*
(28)   *uoci hominis.* (*Achilon*] *haylon* K, *Hailon* m) II 4 m¹ 2754A /
      m² 2175.

—The actual biblical phrases are *sol contra Gabaon ... et luna contra uallem Ahialon ... oboediente Domino uoci hominis.* A text close to the Vulgate would seem to be behind this passage.

Judges

Reference to or comment upon matter from the following chapters is found: 2–4, 6–7, 11, 13–16, 19–20.

Chapters 6, 13 and 16 receive quite detailed treatment. Note in particular:

16:2–3 the text of which is in part close to the Vulgate but also differs widely from it, *in uertice montis qui respicit Bersabee . . .* The Vulgate (and LXX) read *qui respicit Hebron.* There are other contacts and differences in this passage. II 31 (34) m¹ 2778A / m² 2192.

Direct quotations: there would seem to be two/three such:

6:37   *siccitas in omni terra, et ros in solo uellere.* (*siccitatis in omni terra*
(29)   *siccitas* Q; *uellere* (?)W) II 5 m¹ 2756B / m² 2176.
6:40   *siccitas in solo uellere, et ros in omni terra fuit.* (*et* om. W; *ros* om.
(30)   W*) ibid.
        —In the citing of 6:37 the phrases of the Vulgate have been inverted, in that of 6:40 *fuit* has been transposed from the beginning to the end of the   quotation.
16:3   *ambas portae fores* II 31 (34) m¹ 2778A / m² 2192.
(31)   —This little phrase is found in the Vulgate, but otherwise the terms used to describe the incident are not from that version. Source?

Samuel

Reference to or comment upon matter from the following is found: 1 Samuel 4–7, 9, 12, 14, 16–20, 24, 26, 28, and 2 Samuel 2, 4–6, 8, 18, 23–24. Treatment is casual.

Note: 1 Samuel 28:19 is paraphrased very freely. II 11 m¹ 2760A / m² 2179.
        Samuel and not the Lord is made responsible for the handing over of the Israelites.

Direct quotations: three from 1 Samuel and one(?) from 2 Samuel.

1 Samuel:

16:23   *Spiritus Domini malus Saul arripiebat.* (*malus* om. β; *arripiebat*
(32)   *saul* Qβ) II 10 m¹ 2759C / m² 2179.

—*Spiritus Domini malus* is read in I*Ω[s] and in various editions, including the Clementine Vulgate. *Saul arripiebat* is an inversion typical of our text.

19:23　*Et factus est super eum Spiritus Domini, et ambulans prophetabat.*
(33)　　(*domini*] *dei* J) II 10 ibid.

　　　—*etiam* after *est* of the Vulgate has been omitted; *Domini* for *Dei* is the reading of ΣΛ, a number of other MSS and of the Clementine Vulgate; *ambulans* for *ambulabat ingrediens et*—typical freedom with the text.

28:19　*tu et filii tui mecum eritis.* (post *tui* add. *cras* β) II 11 m[1] 2760A /
(34)　　m[2] 2179.

　　　—This is the Vulgate text.

2 Samuel

24:15　*lxx uirorum milia.* (*lxxiii* P) II 13 m[1] 2761A / m[2] 2180.
(35)　　—Relates to the Vulgate text but has inverted *milia uirorum.*

Kings

Reference to or comment upon matter from the following is found: 3 Kings 6–7, 10–13, 15–19, 21; and 4 Kings 1–7, 13–14, 16–21, 23–25.

For these books the comment tends to be more developed, and the writer shows a marked predilection for Elisha.

Note the following paraphrases of texts from 4 Kings:

4:1–7　a very free paraphrase with a few words from the Vulgate. II 23 m[1] 2767A / m[2] 2184.

5:25–27 again very free and subtly different from the Vulgate while a fine piece. II 23 (24) m[1] 2768B / m[2] 2185.

7:1–2　part quoted, part paraphrased and part glossed. It is very difficult to determine the text used. II 23 (26) m[1] 2770A(B) / m[2] 2186.

Note further:

5:20–24 which differs greatly from the text of the Bible: Giezi brings two boys with him and brings back the money on horses. The first detail could be due to an Old-Latin mistranslation of the LXX, but the mention of horses suggests an Irish milieu (see C. Plummer, Vitae SS Hiberniae II 212). II 23 (24) m[1] 2768AB / m[2] 2185.

Direct quotations: I have identified six in each book:

3 Kings:

17:1 *Si ros et pluuia nisi iuxta oris mei uerba his annis erit.* (*Si non ros* m;
(36)   *et*] *aut* J; post *uerba* add. *in* Oβ, E(?); *erit*] *erunt* m) II 15 m¹
       2761D / m² 2180.
       —Vulgate text save for the very different word order.

17:21 *Reuertatur, obsecro, anima pueri.* III 13 (12) m¹ 2788B / m² 2198.
(37)   —The text of the Clementine Vulgate and of two Paris MSS,
       Ω^JM, but not accepted into the critical text.

18:17 *Tu quis es, qui conturbas populum Israel.* (*quis*] *ne* Q, om. β; post
(38)   *es* add. *ille* Q; *populum* om. β) II 15 m¹ 2762A / m² 2180.
       qui conturbas Israel. ibid.
       —Q has sought to align the first citation of this with the
       Vulgate but should have omitted *populum* as does the short
       recension and all the witnesses in the second citation. The
       first form is possibly proper (?) to our text as the Vulgate and
       LXX are in agreement.

18:18 *Non enim, inquit Helias, ego conturbo Israel, sed tu et domus patris tui,*
(39)   *quia dereliquistis legem Domini et seruis Baal.* (*enim* om. WCNQ;
       post *et¹* add. *omnis* J; *quia*] *qui* Q; *dereliquisti* OKQm, *reliquisti* C,
       dereliquis N, om. β) II 15 m¹ 2762A / m² 2180.
       —Taken as a quotation in spite of the *inquit.* Weber's Vulgate
       omits *enim* and *ego*—which latter is read by Clementine
       Vulgate and many MSS, see ΣΛΔΦ, Weber then reads *qui* for
       quia (Π^G has *quia*), and *mandata* for *legem*. For *seruis Baal* the
       Vulgate tradition reads *secuti estis Baalim*, but the shortened
       form would be typical of our text.

18:24 *Deus qui per ignem exaudierit, ipse totius populi Deus sit.* (*totius* om.
(40)   m²; *sit*] *esset* Q) II 18 m¹ 2763B / m² 2181.
       —Apart from the inverted word order in the first clause and
       the addition of *totius populi* (proper to the writer or some
       source of his?), this could be related to the Vulgate.

19:8   *in eius fortitudine, quadraginta diebus et quadraginta noctibus nihil*
(41)   *comedens, usque ad Choreb Dei montem ambulauit.* (*fortitudine eius*
       Q; *montem dei oreb* G) II 19 m¹ 2764CD / m² 2182.
       —Again perhaps, related to the Vulgate; *eius* replaces *cibi illius*
       and *nihil comedens* is a gloss, the other differences are in word
       order. (*Choreb* is found in the MS tradition of the Vulgate).

4 Kings

1:9   *Homo Dei, ut ad illum nobiscum exeas rex Ochozias,... iussit.* (*Dei*]
(42)   *diei* W; *exeat* N; *eas* Q) II 20 m¹ 2765A / m² 2182.
       —Very far from the texts of either Vulgate or LXX.

1:10   *ut inquis, si homo Dei ego sum,... in te nunc et in eos qui tecum sunt*

(43)   *caelestis flamma ardebit.* (*ut inquis* om. Q; *ego* om. KQ; *eos*] *omnes*
        Q) II 20 m¹ 2765B / m² 2182.
        —The phrase *si homo Dei ego sum* is the LXX reading here and
        that of the Vulgate in 1:12, but the rest of the text is very far
        from either version.

2:9   *Postula a me quod uis, priusquam me Deus a te transire et recipi*
(44)   *iubeat.* (*quod*] *quid* R(?Q); *me Deus*] *dominus me* Q) II 22 m¹ 2765D
        / m² 2183. It is from the same verse 2:9. *Spiritus qui in te est, fiat*
        dupliciter in me. (*duplex* Qm) II 23 (26) m¹ 2770C / m² 2186.
        —These are neither the Vulgate nor the LXX texts.

4:3   *Pete ergo, . . . mutuo a uicinis tuis uasa uacua non pauca.* (*mutuuo*
(45)   C) II 23 m¹ 2767A / m² 2184.
        —Related to the Vulgate (?), which, however, has not got the
        ergo and reads *omnibus uicinis*, as does the LXX.

7:1   *Cras eadem hora hac statere modius similae et ordei modii mercabuntur*
(46)   *in huius introitu urbis uno statere.* (*hac hora* RWCXENQ; *uno*
        statere Q; *ordei duo modii* WE, *duo modii ordei* Q) II 23 (26) m¹
        2770A / m² 2186.
        —Contacts with the Vulgate but some inversions of word order
        in the clauses and differences of terms. The phrase *eadem hora*
        hac is nearer to LXX but otherwise there is little relation to the
        latter.

7:2   *Tu haec oculis tuis uidebis, sed causa huius infidelitatis ex his comedere*
(47)   *non poteris.* (*haec*] *hoc* Q(?)) II 23 (26) m¹ 2770AB / m² 2186.
        —A very free development of the biblical text; the whole of
        this series from 4 Kings poses quite a problem.

Chronicles

There is *one possible reference* to 2 Chronicles 6:5–6, II 24 (27) m¹ 2771B
/ m² 2187. It is strange that 2 Chronicles 7:1 is not even mentioned.

Ezra

Reference to or comment upon matter from chapters 1, 6, and 7 is found.

Nehemiah

There is *reference* to the matter of chapter 8.

Judith

There is possibly *reference* to 4:17, see II 16 m¹ 2762C / m² 2181. The
evidence is not such as to help us determine the form of biblical text
used from Chronicles to Judith. The author's *real* knowledge of the

books in question, particularly of Chronicles and Judith, must be at least suspect.

Job

There is possibly *reference* to 26:8, see III 5 m¹ 2784C / m² 2195.

Direct quotations: I have noted two:

9:10   *Qui facit magna et inscrutabilia et mirabilia quibus non est numerus.*
(48)   (*scrutabilia* N; *quibus*] *quorum* Qm) I 1 m¹ 2719A / m² 2151.
        —A confused Vulgate text. *quorum* is the Vulgate reading. The
        critical Vulgate here reads *inconprehensibilia* but *inscrutabilia* is
        the reading of CXSΩ, one early edition, Gregory the Great,
        and, in the Vulgate itself, 5:9 and 37:5.
28:2   *Lapis . . . resolutus calore in aes conuertitur.* (*lapides* N; *uertitur*
(49)   β) I 24 m¹ 2745D / m² 2169.
        —The Vulgate reads: *solutus ... uertitur.* The reading *conuertitur*
        is found in E(Corbie).

Psalms

Reference to, *allusion* to or *comment* upon Pss 21, 104, 120, 131, 138, 147
is found.
Direct quotations: I here note eight:

77:24   *Panem caeli dedit eis* I 6 m¹ 2727C / m² 2157.
(50)   *Panem caeli dedit eis: panem angelorum manducauit homo.* (post
        *panem*¹ add. *inquit* Q) I 23 m¹ 2743D / m² 2168.
        —The Gallican psalter text.
84:13   *Et caeli dabunt imbrem et terra dabit fructum suum.* (*Et*¹ om. G) I 6
(51)   m¹ 2727C / m² 2157.
        —A conflated text. The second clause with the addition of
        nostra after *terra* would be that of the Gallican Psalter. The first
        clause would seem related to Zechariah 8:12, where the
        Vulgate reads *rorem* for *imbrem*. It may well be that citing from
        memory the writer confused the Psalm verse with Zechariah,
        so the change of order and *fructum* for *germen*, *imbrem* for
        rorem. See Jeremiah 14:22 and Ezechiel 34:26–27.
98:6   *Moyses et Aaron in sacerdotibus eius.* I 25 m¹ 2746B / m² 2170.
(52)   —The Gallican Psalter text.
103:4   *Qui facit angelos suos spiritus et ministros suos ignem urentem.* (*facis* β;
(53)   *suos—suos*] *tuos—tuos* RKJ, *suos—tuos* C(?E); *suos ·s· spiritus*
        G(?); *ignem urentem*] *flammam ignis* J) I 16 m¹ 2737C / m² 2164.

—From the Roman psalter, this is read as it stands in ΨB*. It is also found in ΘHKΛL and the Mozarabic psalter, as well as in Rufinus. Some influence of the Roman Psalter on certain MSS of the Gallican as regards possessive pronouns has been remarked.

109:3   *Ex utero ante luciferum genui te.* (*lucī* X) III 5 m¹ 2783D / m²
(54)   2195.
     —The Gallican Psalter text.

120:6   *nec sol per diem nec umquam luna per noctem exurit.* (post *diem*
(55)   add. *quem* Q; *numquam* (?K)C) I 34 m¹ 2750C / m² 2173.
     —Not Gallican nor Roman nor yet 'Iuxt. Hebr.'. It may be intended as merely an allusion.

148:7s   *Laudate Dominum de terra et reliqua usque uerbum eius.* (*et reliqua*]
(56)   *dra· et ·o ·a ·ignis ·grando ·etc.* G; *uerbum*] *faciunt uerbum* Q, *quae faciunt uerbum* m; in J the text is given in full: *laudate dominum de terra dragones et omnes abysi, ignis, grando, nix, glacies, spiritus procellarum qui faciunt uerbum eius.*) I 23 m¹ 2744D / m² 2169.
     —The abbreviated text is probably original, for the text was in everyday use. The text in J, orthography apart, is that of the Gallican Psalter. The reading of *qui* for *quae* is found in IWQ*O and others, and in the Roman Psalter.

Proverbs

There may be a *reference* to 8:29 which relates to the sea and its bounds, see I 7 m¹ 2729C / m² 2158.

Ecclesiastes

There is perhaps some influence of ideas with regard to the sun, 1:5–8, see I 7 m¹ 2731B / m² 2159.
Direct quotation: one (?):

1:10   *Nihil enim sole nouum, nec ualet quisquam dicere, hoc recens est.* (post
(57)   *enim* add. *sub* βm; post *dicere* add. *ecce* Jm; *recens hoc* C) I 17 m¹ 2738B / m² 2164.
     —If the *enim* were deleted then the text as read by m and J would be that of the Vulgate. This cannot be taken as the original reading, however, so that what we have here is a free citation from the Vulgate, not an exact one.

Wisdom

There is possibly *reference or allusion* to the matter of chapters 5, 10, 11, 16, 18. The later chapters of the book would seem to have influenced the writer heavily; this particularly as regards his view of the history of Israel and the comments he makes on some of the *mirabilia* he recalls.

Direct quotation: I have noted one:

19:11   *Nouam creaturam auium uiderunt* (*uiderunt nouam creaturam*
(58)   *auium* β) I 27 m¹ 2747A / m² 2170.

—The short recension has restored the Vulgate word order, which is typically inverted in the long recension (or main text).

Sirach

There is *reference* to the matter of chapters 18, 44, 46, and perhaps, 49. There is no posssibility of determining the biblical text used.

Isaiah

Reference to 45:1, see II 30 (33) m¹ 2777B / m² 2191, and 60:3, see III 4 m¹ 2781D / m² 2194.

Direct quotations: I have recognized two:

14:13f   *Sedebo in monte testamenti, in lateribus aquilonis: ascendam super*
(59)   *altitudinem nubium, et aedificabo thronum meum ad aquilonem et ero similis altissimo.* (*monte*] *sed* N; *similis ero* TP) I 2 m¹ 2721C / m² 2152.

—The Vulgate text, apart from the clause between the two conjunctions *et* and *et,* which is either a gloss which crept into the writer's text, or a phrase which became fused with his memory of it.

38:1   *Dispone domui tuae neque ultra uiues, sed morte morieris.* [*neque*
(60)   *uiues*] *quia non uiues ultra* m) II 25 (28) m¹ 2771D / m² 2187.

—The reading of m is an attempt to bring the text into line with the Vulgate, though not restoring the Vulgate's word order. Both Vulgate and LXX order the clauses differently; again we have a probable example of the writer's memory failing him.

66:1   See Acts 7:49–50.
(61)

Jeremiah

Reference is found to the matter of chapters 1, 21, 24, 25, 29. In a passage, II 26 (29) m¹ 2773C / m² 2188, which seems to depend on 4 Kings 24, two terms from Jeremiah 24:1 are introduced, scil., *inclusor* and *faber.* The latter does not appear in any form of the Vulgate tradition, but could ultimately derive from LXX *tektona* (?).

There is a possible conflation of Jeremiah 14:22 with Ps 84:13, but see Zekariah 8:12. I 6 m¹ 2727C / m² 2157.

Ezekiel

There is *reference* to 41:22 concerning the wooden altar in the vision of the temple, I 16 m¹ 2737C / m² 2164. The precise reference is to Jerome's Commentary in Ezechiel XII 41 (PL 25 403AB).

Daniel

Reference to or comment upon the matter of chapters 1, 2, 3, 6, 9, 14 is found; the last listed, 14, is rejected as uncanonical (II 29 (32) *ad finem*).

Note that 3:14–18 is virtually rewritten and heavily interpolated, II 28 (31) m¹ 2774BCD / m² 2189; and 3:91,92 in the same context is paraphrased, II 28 (31) m¹ 2775A(B) / m² 2190.

Direct quotation:

3:49s   *Angelus Domini descendit cum Azaria et sociis eius in caminum, et*
(62)   *excussit flammam ignis de camino, et fecit medium fornacis ut spiritum roris flantem.* (post *angelus* add. *autem* β; *caminum*] *fornacem* G; *camino²*] *fornace* G; *ut spiritum*] *quasi uentum* Am) II 28 (31) m¹ 2776A / m² 2190.

—Although this has no contact with Sabatier, the text must be judged as deriving from the Greek; *caminum* (*caminus*) is taken straight from the Greek and *spiritum* renders *pneuma*. The short recension variants added to those of G bring the text in line with ΣZMΦ and the Clementine Vulgate!

Jonah

Mention is made of his disobedience, 1–2:1, see Prologue m¹ 2717B / m² 2150; and the Hebrew tradition about him, as well as of his being swallowed by the whale, 2:1,11, see II 17 m¹ 2763A / m² 2181.

Micah

There is *reference* to 5:2, see III 4 m¹ 2782A / m² 2194.

Zekariah

?, see *Jeremiah*.

New Testament

Matthew

Reference to or comment upon material from the following chapters occurs: 1–4, 6, 8–11, 14, 15, 17, 18, 24, 27. Some of these references are merely in passing, others are more extended.

Direct quotations: nine, perhaps ten (?):

1:5–6   *Iesse autem genuit Dauid regem, Dauid autem rex genuit Salomonem.*
(63)   (*Yesse* Q, *gesse* G; *autem*[1] om. G) I 3 m[1] 2724A / m[2] 2154.
        —The Vulgate text. G's omission of *autem* corresponds with
        BFLU*XYZ in Wordsworth & White.

3:17   *Hic est Filius meus dilectus in quo sibi anima mea bene complacuit.*
(64)   (*anima mea sibi* C; *bene* om. Cm) III 5 m[1] 2783B / m[2] 2195.
        —It would seem a conflation of 3:17, 12:18 and Isaiah 42:1 all in
        Vulgate readings. Some source or a trick of the writer's memory?

(65)   4:4 see Deuteronomy 8:3 earlier, n.(27).

4:17   *Paenitentiam agite; appropinquauit enim regnum caelorum.*
(66)   (*appropinquabit* TPWENQ, *appropinquat* X; *enim* om. WEQ) I 2
        m[1] 2722D / m[2] 2153.
        —Either Vulgate or Itala. In this context the *-abit/ -auit* variant
        is not of consequence, but *-abit* is found in some MSS of the
        Vulgate, E*HOL[2].

7:22   *Nonne in tuo nomine prophetauimus.* (*nomine tuo* G) II 10 m[1]
(67)   2759B / m[2] 2178.
        —Wordsworth's & White's preferred reading for the Vulgate,
        it is that of EQR, (in WW, Q is the Book of Kells, R the Gospels
        of Mac Regol). In our context this is not without significance.
        Weber prefers the reading *nomine tuo* which is supported by most
        of the MSS. In the Itala, *tuo nomine* is in Ambrose and cfh.

8:20   *Volucres caeli nidos habent ubi requiescunt.* (*ubi requiescunt* om. G)
(68)   see Luke 9:58. I 6 m[1] 2727C / m[2] 2157.
        —A difficult text in the Vulgate tradition. WW and Weber both
        accept *tabernacula* as the reading in Matthew, *nidos* in Luke.
        Many MSS, however, read *nidos* in Matthew. *habent* has strayed
        from the preceding clause, its transfer was perhaps deliberate;
        the writer's freedom has been remarked. *ubi requiescunt* occurs in
        this form in Q(Kells) and g[1]; in FJERT etc., in the Itala, the
        reading is *ubi requiescant.* So, a mixed text.

10:9   *Nolite habere aurum neque argentum.* (*aurum habere* T; *neque*
(69)   *argentum* om. β) III 17 (16) m[1] 2790B / m[2] 2200.
        —Vulgate and Itala both read *Nolite possidere* and this is
        generally supported by the MSS. A citation from memory,
        then (?), *quoad sensum.*

22:30   *Erunt sicut angeli Dei in caelo.* I 2 m[1] 2723B / m[2] 2154.
(70)   —This is the reading of Kells, Mac Regol, Armagh and
        Hoskier among the Irish MSS of the Vulgate and is that of the
        Clementine Vulgate. WW and Weber prefer *sunt* to *erunt.*
        The text as it stands is also found in aur 1 of the Old-Latin
        MSS and in many of the Fathers.

23:35   *A sanguine Abel iusti usque ad sanguinem Zachariae.* (Immediately

(71)   repeated in the long recension; in the first citing *usque* om. W; post *Zachariae* add. *et reliqua* β) I 3 m¹ 2724A / m² 2154.
    —The Vulgate and Old-Latin reading.

25:41   *Discedite a me, maledicti, in ignem aeternam, quem praeparauit Pater*
(72)   *meus diabolo et angelis eius.* (*discedite*] *ite* G; post *me* add. *omnes* A; *quem—meus*] *qui preparatus est* Gβ) I 2 m¹ 2722A / m² 2153.
    —In the short recension J gives the Vulgate text as accepted by WW (but not Weber). The long recension text given above has a marked Old-Latin flavour. All its elements are to be found in various MSS of the Itala, although none give the text just as it is found here; *praeparauit* is read by d, ff² and Irenaeus⁴ alone. A text, then, quoted perhaps from memory (?).

Mark

Reference to 1:4–6 in III 1 m¹ 2779B / m² 2192.
Direct quotation:
4:32   *Possunt aues caeli habitare.* (*possint* m, *ut possint* J; *habitari* J) I 6 m¹ (73) 2727C / m² 2157.
    —*ut possint* is the Vulgate reading, but it should be followed by *sub umbra eius.* As it stands the text would appear proper to our text.

Luke

Reference or comment is found with regard to chapters 1–3, 6, 8–10, 23, 24.
Note: 1:8 apparently misunderstood, for in III 1 m¹ 2779A / m² 2191 it is stated that Zachary was offering the holocaust. This may be a fault of memory.
1:13ff   paraphrased, although not quite presented as that, see III 1 m¹ 2779AB / m² 2192.
Direct quotations: there would seem to be four, perhaps five such:
1:18   *Quomodo, respondit, hoc fieri potuerit, cum ego satis sim senex, et uxor*
(74)   *mea isto officio in iuuentute priuata in diebus suis prouecta aetate processit?* (*poterit* Q; *ego*] *ergo* K; *sum satis* Q, *sim satis* m; *sum* E; *suis*] *istis etiam* Q; *prouecta aetate*] *prouectate* B; *processerit* m) III 1 m¹ 2779A / m² 2192.
    —Far from the Vulgate or the Itala, it seems more a paraphrase than a quotation.
1:63   *Iohannes, dixit, nomen eius est.* (*est nomen eius* Xm) III 1 m¹
(75)   2779B / m² 2192.
    —*dixit* is erroneous, Zachary wrote the the name; otherwise this is the Vulgate and Itala text, but inverted; Xm restore the correct word order.

(76)   4:4 See Deuteronomy 8:3, (27), above.
(77)   9:58 see Matthew 8:20, (68), above.
10:18   *Vidi Sathanam sicut fulgur de caelo cadentem.* (*satanas* J) I 2 m¹
(78)   2721D / m² 2153.
        —*Vidi*, apart, (for *uidebam*), this is the Vulgate and Itala text. A
        citation from memory (?), influenced, perhaps, by the style of the
        Apocalypse, in which *uidi* and *audiui* occur again and again (?).
16:16   *lex et prophetia usque ad Iohannem fuerunt, ex eo autem regnum Dei*
(79)   *euangelizatur.* (*prophete* X(?), *prophetae* m; *autem eo* X; *eugelizatur*
        T(!), *euangelizaretur* K) III 1 m¹ 2779C / m² 2193.
        —the term *prophetia* occurs again and again in our text when
        we should expect *prophetae*. We find the same in other Irish
        writers of the period. (This I discuss in the notes to my edition.)
        The text is otherwise that of the Vulgate, with the additions of
        fuerunt and *autem*, both having a sonorous quality, and present
        here, perhaps, by assimilation to Matthew 11:12–13.
24:42   *piscis assi partem et fauum mellis.* I 4 m¹ 2726A / m² 2155.
(80)   —The text of adr¹ [e] of the Itala.

John

Reference or comment is found with regard to chapters 1, 2, 5, 9–11, 19.
Direct quotations: there are four:
3:8   *Spiritus Dei ubi uult spirat.* (*Dei*] *domini* KJ) I 34 m¹ 2750B / m²
(81)   2172.
        —Apart from the addition of *Dei/Domini* this is the Vulgate
        text.
5:17   *Pater meus usque modo operatur et ego operor* (*pater*] *ut in die septimo*
(82)   *pater* . . . T) I 1 m¹ 2720A / m² 2151.
        —The Vulgate and Itala text.
8:44   *Ipse ab initio mendax est et in ueritate non stetit* (*ueritate* ?G) I 2 m¹
(83)   2722B / m² 2153.
        —The second clause is the Vulgate text, the first clause would
        seem confused with 1 John 2:21ff. *mendax* for *homicida* is also
        found in Irenaeus.
11:4   *Haec infirmitas non est ad mortem, sed ut Filius hominis per eam*
(84)   *clarificetur.* (post *mortem* add. *ducens* β; *hominis*] *dei* Oβ) III 13
        (12) m¹ 2787D / m² 2198.
        —Not Vulgate. In the *clarificetur* there is contact with a tradi-
        tion of the Old-Latin, where is it found in three MSS, bcff².

Acts

Reference to or comment upon the matter of the following chapters is
found: 2, 3, 5, 7–9, 13, 20.

Note: 8:39, I 14 m¹ 2735D / m² 2162, where the "Western" text of
Acts is followed.
Direct quotations: there are four or five:

2:11   *Audiuimus eos linguis nostris loquentes magnalia Dei.* (post *audiui*
(85)   *mus* add. *enim* Q; *loquentes linguis nostris* W; *nostris linguis*
     RPTQ) I 9 m¹ 2733A / m² 2160.
     —Vulgate apart from inversion. Weber reads: *loquentes eos nostris*
     linguis, WW reads: *eos loquentes linguis nostris* (= Armagh).

3:6   *Surge et ambula.* III 18 (16) m¹ 2790A / m² 2200.
(86)   —Vulgate text, but too short for comparison.

7:49   *Caelum mihi sedes est, terra autem scabellum pedum meorum* (*est*
(87)   om. BKCXEm) III 5 m¹ 2784A / m² 2195.
     —Vulgate text of Acts, not of Isaiah 66:1.

20:9f *Et sublatus repertus est mortuus. Ad quem cum Paulus incubuit et*
(88)   *descendisset spiritus in eum, et complexus dixit, Nolite turbari, animam*
     enim in eo est. (*incubuit—eum*] descendisset (*Paulus* m) incubuit
     super eum QAm; *et*⁵ om. J; *spiritus* om. KJ; *et*⁵ om. X; *anima* m;
     enim] *eius* EG, post *enim* add. *eius* Qm, *ipsius* J) III 13 (12) m¹
     2788B / m² 2198.

20:10 *Anima illius in eo est* (*illius*] *eius* QG) III 13 (12) m¹ 2788C / m²
(89)   2199.
     —Text is manifestly corrupt. QAm strive to bring it closer to
     the Vulgate, which is the same as Armagh, although the latter
     reads *Paulus cum.*

Romans

Chapter 5 is *referred* to twice, and chapter 8 once.

1 Corinthians

There is *reference* to chapters 12 and 13.
Direct quotations: there are two:

13:9   *Ex parte cognoscimus et ex parte prophetamus.* (*agnoscimus* WNQ) I
(90)   7 m¹ 2731A / m² 2159.
     —Vulgate reads *enim* after *parte¹*. This *enim* ia omitted by
     Origen, Jerome, Augustine, gr**, and Irenaeus (see WW).

15:44 *Resurget corpus spiritale.* III 16 (15) m¹ 2789B / m² 2200.
(91)   —Critical Vulgate reads *surgit* (Weber and WW); Clementine
     Vulgate, some MSS, (including Armagh), and Fathers *surget.*
     resurget is found in Jerome and Augustine (see WW).

2 Corinthians

There is *reference* to chapters 3, 5, 12.

Direct quotations: there are two:
3:7   *non poterant filii Israel intendere.* III 11 m¹ 2787B / m² 2198.
(92)   —A free adaptation of the biblical text. Vulgate word order
        differs, and it reads *possent,* with variant *possint,* not *poterant.*
11:14   *se transferat in angelum lucis.* (*transfigerat* T, *transfigurat* Nm,
(93)   *transfert* CEβ, *transfigurat se* KQ(cf. N)) II 11 m¹ 2760B / m²
        2179.
        —KQ gives what is the Vulgate reading; N's reading is found
        in a number of early writers, (see WW).

Galatians

Direct quotation:
3:19   *disposita per angelos in manu mediatoris.* (*deposita* C) I 23 m¹
(94)   2744B / m² 2168.
        —*ordinata* not *disposita* in Vulgate, *disposita* is found in Irenaeus P
        and other Fathers (see WW).

Ephesians:
        there is *possible allusion* to 2:19, see III 5 m¹ 2784A / m² 2195.

Philippians:
        allusion to 2:7, see I 2 m¹ 2722C / m² 2153.

Colossians:
        reference is made to chapter 1 and, perhaps, chapter 2.

1 Thessalonians

Direct quotation: there is one:
4:17   *Rapiemur ad occurrendum Christo in aera.* (post *rapiemur* add. *in*
(95)   *nubibus* Qβ; *ad occurrendum*] *ad currendum* E; *obuiam* G) III 8 m¹
        2786B / m² 2197.
        —*ad occurrendum* is read by KAA in VL(Frede); *Christo* is read by
        Armagh, many MSS, Fathers, and is accepted by the Clementine
        Vulgate. It is also the reading of some Greek uncials. Taken as a
        whole, though, the text is rather far from either the Old-Latin or
        the Vulgate.

Hebrews

There are *references* to chapters 2, 4, 6, 7, 9, and 11(?).
Direct quotations: there are perhaps three:
2:16   *Non enim angelos sed Abrahae semen apprehendit Deus.* (*sed* ?N;
(96)   *Abrahae* om. Q; *apprehendat* (?X)N) I 2 m¹ 2722C / m² 2153.

—A paraphrase rather than a quotation.

11:30   *circuitu dierum septem* . . . *corruit* II 3 m^1 2753C / m^2 2174.
(97)   —*circuitu* is read by Armagh, FΦ and the Clementine Vulgate.
          Weber reads *circuiti. corruit* reflects *corruerunt*, read by Armagh,
          GΦ, others and the Clementine Vulgate.

11:39f   *Hi omnes testimonio fidei probati inuenti, non acceperunt repromis*
(98)   *sionem a Deo pro nobis melius aliquid prouidente uti ne sine nobis con-*
          summarentur (*inuenti*] *sunt* N, om. ß; post *inuenti* add. *sunt*
          P*WEQm, *sunt inuenti* K; *non*] *hi* E, *nam* N; *a* om. OQA; *aliquid*
          melius ß; *uti*] *ut* Eß, om. Q) III 15 (14) m^1 2788D / m^2 2199.
          —A (within ß) has this text in accordance with the Vulgate as
          read by WW and Weber. Among the MSS of the Vulgate f
          reads *inuenti sunt; uti* is witnessed to in the reading *huti* of C.
          The *a* before *Deo* is proper to the De mirabilibus,—its own
          addition or deriving from some earlier source?

James: *reference* is made to chapters 1 and 5.

Apocalypse

There are *references* to chapters 11, 17 and 20.
Direct quotations: there are two:

1:5   *primogenitus mortuorum* III 11 m^1 2787C / m^2 2198.
(99)   —The Vulgate text but too brief for comment.
1:20   *stellae septem ecclesiarum septem angeli sunt* III 4 m^1 2782D / m^2
(100)   2194.
          —Every word of this is found in the Vulgate, but the word
          order is quite different, so that it is difficult to determine
          what contacts it has.

(Note: I must acknowledge my debt to the Jesuit authorities of the Milltown Institute and the Abbot and Community of Roscrea for facilitating
my research by allowing me the use of their library facilities; and to Dr
Susan Anderson of UCLA, my confrère Fr Patrick Lyons and Francis
Lawrence for procuring copies of various texts for me; this is all apart
from the various libraries whose MSS I was privileged to be allowed to
consult when working on my doctoral thesis.)

Exegesis and the Book of Kells: the Lucan Genealogy*

JENNIFER O'REILLY

The Book of Kells was produced in a culture where the use and production of exegesis was long-established and sophisticated. Evidence is not confined to the sources and output of the Venerable Bede (673–735), impressive though this is. Both the early reception date of a wide patristic inheritance in Ireland and the impact of biblical and exegetical concepts and techniques on a large Hiberno-Latin literature have been increasingly recognized in recent years.[1] The difficulty has been to relate this material to an interpretation of the very different medium of insular illuminated Gospel books, partly because of the range of scholarly disciplines involved and partly because the attempt to identify pictorial exegesis in the decorative, stylized idiom of early insular manuscript art is far more hazardous than in the art of the Carolingian Renaissance or the late Anglo-Saxon Benedictine reform which more fully appropriated the conventions of representational art from the

* An early draft of this paper was given at the Trinity College Dublin conference on the Book of Kells in September 1992. It discussed pictorial exegesis in the Book of Kells with reference to several examples, but the version for the conference's Proceedings came to focus on one of these examples, the Lucan genealogy. The additional research was first presented at the Patristic Conference in Maynooth in June 1993. I am most grateful to members of the Patristic Conference for their helpful discussion and to Ms Felicity O'Mahony and Dr Bernard Meehan of Trinity College Dublin for their kind permission to publish here a shortened and slightly amended form of the finished paper, 'Exegesis and the Book of Kells: the Lucan Genealogy', The Book of Kells, ed. F. O'Mahony, Aldershot 1994, 344–397.

1   B. Bischoff, 'Turning-points in the history of Latin exegesis in the early Irish Church: AD 650–800', in M. McNamara, ed., Biblical studies. The medieval Irish Contribution, Dublin 1976, 74–160; J.F. Kelly, 'A catalogue of early medieval Hiberno-Latin biblical commentaries' (I), Traditio 44 (1988) 537–571; (II), Traditio 45 (1989–1990) 393–434; C.D. Wright, 'Hiberno-Latin and Irish-influenced biblical commentaries, florilegia and homily collections' in F.M. Biggs, T.D. Hill, P.E. Szarmach (eds.),The Sources of Anglo-Saxon literary culture: a trial version, Binghampton, N.Y. 1990, 87–123: I am grateful to Damian Bracken for this reference and for helpful discussion of the material.

Mediterranean world of Late Antiquity. Since the pioneering work of Patrick McGurk, however, there has been growing awareness of the antiquity of some features of insular Gospel book production too and of the variety of functions the decorative layout of the Gospel text can serve, not simply in embellishing the book as a precious liturgical object but in providing a visual structuring of the page, for example by marking punctuation, Eusebian sections and possibly lections. Iconographical studies have shown the possibility of reading a symbolic and expository element, not only in some of the whole-page illustrations in the Book of Kells, but in its abstract ornament and its sacred calligraphy.[2] Many distinctively insular decorative practices are already evident and, indeed, well-developed in the earliest of the extant illuminated Gospels, the late seventh-century Book of Durrow. The Book of Kells, which modern scholars variously date between the mid-eighth–early ninth century, therefore drew on a long insular tradition of Gospel-book production as well as on Early Christian and contemporary continental sources, including a wider range of representational images than any other surviving insular manuscript.

Many questions remain concerning the Book of Kells, including the exact date, place and circumstances of its composition: attempts to spot specific literary 'sources' of isolated images and decorative features therefore seem arbitrary, and dogmatic assertions about its meaning cannot be made. The growth in knowledge of early insular literary culture, however, does prompt the attempt to view the layout and decoration of the Gospel-text in the Book of Kells in the context of how Scripture itself was read. Insular biblical commentaries, compendia and homilies provide evidence of how well known certain patristic texts and rhetorical techniques were and which features evoked particular interest and received further development by insular writers. Bede's use of the patristic inheritance in his homilies notably illumines a living insular tradition of monastic *lectio divina* which is also evident in contemporary hagiography. The present paper considers the validity of reading some features of the decoration of the Book of Kells as an adaptation into visual form and an insular idiom of long-established exegetical themes and techniques whose interpretation reveals for an initiated audience the spiritual meaning concealed beneath the literal letter of the sacred text. The approach is here applied to the example of the Lucan genealogy.

---

2   P. McGurk, Latin Gospel books from AD 400 to 800, Les publications de
     Scriptorium 5, Paris 1961; 'Two notes on the Book of Kells and its relation
     to other insular Gospel books', Scriptorium 9 (1955) 105–107; S. Lewis,
     'Sacred calligraphy: the chi-rho page in the Book of Kells' in: Traditio 26
     (1980) 139–159; Otto Werckmeister, Irisch-Northumbrische Buchmalerei
     des 8 Jh. und monastiche Spiritualität, Berlin 1967; George Henderson,
     From Durrow to Kells. The Insular Gospel-books 600–800, London 1987.

In surviving insular Gospel books the tradition for the layout and decoration of Christ's genealogy in Lk 3:23–38 is far less developed than for the version in Mt 1:1–17. There is nothing comparable to the ornamented title-page opening of Matthew's *Liber generationis* which also forms the opening of his Gospel and of the Gospel text of the whole codex, nor is there any significant parallel to the decorative climax of the sacred *chi-rho* monogram in Mt 1:18 which habitually follows the Matthean genealogy in insular books. As early as the Book of Durrow, however, the genealogy had been treated as a distinct unit within Luke's text. The Hebrew names of Christ's ancestors were listed one beneath the other, each preceded by the formula *qui fuit*, meaning 'who was (the son) of X'. The three words of each entry were well spaced forming three vertical columns down the page and the listing could be continued in parallel on the same page to form six columns in all.

As with its treatment of the Matthean genealogy, the Book of Kells both expands established features of the insular tradition and goes beyond it. The columnar listing is retained but there is only one Hebrew name with its accompanying 'qui fuit' on each line so that the list is lavishly spaced over five pages, ff. 200r–202r (pl. 1–5). The repeated initial Qs, slightly enlarged or coloured in earlier examples, are in Kells decorated with prodigal variety and richness so that the Lucan genealogy, though not formally framed like the Matthean one in Kells, fol. 29v–31r, nevertheless presents a magnificent counterpart to its layout. Not only are the columns of words enlivened by touches of colour, ornament or calligraphic flourishes, but intercolumnar figures are introduced which have no precedent in surviving insular gospel books.

IONA

On the third folio of the Lucan genealogy is a curious hybrid figure of a man with arms crossed and contorted and with the lower body made up of interlace and two sets of fin-like projections (pl. 3). Because the figure grasps the final letter of the phrase 'Qui fuit' which precedes the Hebrew name Iona (= Jonah), Carl Nordenfalk read it as highlighting the name of 'Iona the prophet', and he speculated that 'it is quite likely that the artist wanted to draw attention to the place where the manuscript was written'.[3] The name Iona is not the only one to be so singled out on this folio, however: six birds also grasp the terminal 't' of the phrase preceding the names of six other ancestors in the list and the ambiguous crossed-arms gesture of the fish-man pointing both up and down could be read as indicating those birds which are grouped above and below him. Furthermore, as Nordenfalk himself later noted, the

---

3   C. Nordenfalk, 'Another look at the Book of Kells' in: F. Piel and J. Traer (ed.), Festschrift Wolfgang Braunfels, Tübingen 1977, 275–279, 278.

name of the island of Iona was not spelled thus in Hiberno-Saxon texts, so the fish-man could not have been intended as a visual pun on the name of Columba's island monastery. Nevertheless, Nordenfalk ingeniously suggested that 'the Irish scribe, knowing that *Ionas interpretatur columba* from Isidore, *Etymologiae* 7, 8, 18, was pointing to Jonah's name because it called to mind Columba in whose honour the Book of Kells may have been produced'.[4]

Paul Meyvaert also believes that the raised right hand of the fish-man 'undoubtedly has the purpose of directing our attention to the name Iona: it is a *nota bene* symbol containing a clue to the manuscript's place of origin'. He too cites the patristic exegetical device of translating Hebrew biblical names, a practice popularised by Jerome's *Liber interpretationis hebraicorum nominum* which interprets the name Iona as Columba. An abbreviated and corrupt list of Jerome's Hebrew names survives in a number of insular Gospel books. Dr Meyvaert makes the important observation, however, that the list of Hebrew names appearing in Luke's Gospel in a small sub-group of insular manuscripts including the Book of Durrow and the Book of Kells, does not have the spelling 'Iona' but 'Iori' (sic) columba mea'.[5] This would suggest that it was not the Hebrew names list copied out in the prefatory material of the Book of Kells itself that inspired the scribe-illuminator to draw attention to the name of Iona in the Lucan genealogy. Instead, Dr Meyvaert turns to two famous non-biblical Irish applications of the Iona-Columba interpretation.

In 615 Columbanus wrote, 'I am called Jonah in Hebrew, Peristera in Greek and Columba in Latin'; in correspondence he several times used the Hebrew name Iona of himself. Similarly, in the second preface to the *Vita Columbae* written before 700, Adomnán, ninth abbot of the island monastery of Iona noted 'what is pronounced *iona* in Hebrew and what Greek calls *peristera* and what in Latin is named *columba*, means one and the same thing'. Adomnán comments at length on the appropriateness of this name given to St Columba. Dr Meyvaert observes: 'From this evidence one can safely conclude that the scribe-illuminator is subtly indicating that the great name of Columba lies

---

4 Noted by S. Lewis, 'Sacred calligraphy' 139, n.1.
5 P. Meyvaert, 'The book of Kells and Iona', in Art Bulletin 71 (1989) 6–19, 6 n. 4. P. McGurk, 'An edition of the abbreviated and selective set of Hebrew names found in the Book of Kells' in: F. O'Mahony (ed.), The Book of Kells, 103–132. To the group of ten mss of insular origin or association which have the selective list of Hebrew names may be added B.L. Royal MS. I.A.XVIII which shares with the Book of Durrow, the Book of Kells and Poitiers B.Mun. MS 17 the further distinction of the *Iori columba mea* entry: see J. O'Reilly, 'The Book of Kells and two Breton Gospel books' in: C. Laurent and H. Davis (ed.), Irlande et Bretagne, Rennes 1994, 217–225.

concealed on fol. 201r of the Book of Kells' and that the manuscript 'can only have been produced in Columban territory.'[6]

Northumbria is excluded by this definition because the cult of Columba had been superseded there following the controversy over the dating of Easter.[7] Both Bede's *Historia Ecclesiastica* and the *Life* of Wilfrid show the Columban monks of Lindisfarne (which had been founded from Iona in the 630s) losing the debate at the Synod of Whitby in 664 about the relative authority of St Columba and St Peter.

COLUMBA

One difficulty with this interpretation of the significance of the fish-man figure in the Book of Kells is that the play on the Hebrew name Iona/ Jonah and its Latin version Columba was by no means confined to Adomnán's account of St Columba but was widely used in exegesis to describe St Peter, whose original name was Simon Bar-Jonah. Moreover the context for such discussion was exegesis of Mt 16: 15–19, the Petrine text which also figured largely in the insular literature of the Paschal controversy. The Hiberno-Latin pseudo-Jerome says of Peter's name Bar-Jonah, *id est, filius Iona, id est columba*; a commentary on Matthew from the eighth-century circle of Virgil of Salzburg has, *Petrus vocatur filius columbae quia iona columba interpretatur acsi dixisset filius sancti Spiritus est, quasi in columba Spiritus venit.*[8] Isidore's *Etymologiae*, well-known to Irish commentators, says *Simon Bar-iona in lingua nostra sonat filius columbae, et est nomen Syrum pariter et Hebraeum. Bar quippe Syra lingua filius, Iona Hebraice columba; utroque sermone dicitur Bar-iona.*[9] In his *Liber interpretationis hebraicorum nominum* Jerome briefly notes the meaning of the name Iona when it appears in Luke's Gospel, the Acts of the Apostles and the Book of Jonah: *Iona columba* or *Iona columba vel dolens.* In the section of St Matthew's Gospel however, Jerome comments more fully on Peter's original name: *Bariona filius columbae. Syrum est pariter hebraeum. Bar quippe lingua Syra filius, et iona columba utroque sermone dicitur.* Furthermore, in his Gospel commentary on Matthew, which was extremely influential with Irish exegetes, Jerome applies this interpretation of names to the Petrine text in which Christ says, 'Blessed are you Simon Bar-Iona' (Mt 16: 17). Jerome explains that Simon's acclamation of Christ in the preceding verse was inspired by the Holy Spirit, whose

6   Ibid. 9 n.10–12, quoting G.S.M. Walker (ed.), Sancti Columbani Opera, Scriptores Latini Hiberniae II, Dublin 1970, 2, 54 and A. Anderson and M.O. Anderson (eds.), Adomnán's Life of Columba, Edinburgh 1961, revised M.O. Anderson, Oxford 1991, 2–4.

7   'The Book of Kells and Iona' 9–10 n.14–16.

8   Expositio in IV evangelia, PL 30, 554; J.F. Kelly, 'Irish monks and the See of St Peter' in: Monastic Studies 14 (1983) 207–223, 217.

9   Etymologiae I, Bk. 7, 9:4.

son he was, as is shown in his name: the Holy Spirit is signified by a dove and *siquidem Bar Iona in lingua nostra sonat filius columbae.*[10]

If this exegetical tradition suggests that the fish-man figure on f.201r of the Book of Kells cannot, by itself, be read exclusively as a coded allusion to St Columba, does it have any significance or offer any comment on the text it decorates?

In an early commentary on the Acts of the Apostles, c. 709–716, Bede specifically refers to Jerome's list of Hebrew names and says, 'Wherever the sacred Scriptures give the names of things or persons with an interpretation, it certainly indicates that a more sacred sense is contained in them . . . Thus blessed Peter, on account of the grace of the same Spirit, was called Bar-iona, that is son of the dove'.[11] Bede's homily on the Chair of St Peter, which focuses on the Petrine commission in Mt 16, is of particular interest here in that it offers a number of parallels with Adomnán's account of St Columba. Bede says that the name *Simon Bar-iona,* meaning *filius columbae* in Latin, properly glorifies this perfect confessor of Christ's name because he was divinely inspired to recognize Christ's true identity with the acclamation, 'Thou art Christ, the son of the living God' (Mt 16:16). He was rightly called the son of a dove because the dove is a simple creature and *Simon Bar-Iona* followed the Lord with pious simplicity mindful of the command that the Lord's followers be prudent as serpents and simple as doves (Mt 10:6). Furthermore, adds Bede, because the Holy Spirit descended on the Lord at his Baptism in the form of a dove, one who is full of spiritual grace may properly be given the name 'son of a dove' or 'son of the Holy Spirit'.[12]

Similarly, Adomnán had drawn upon the patristic tradition of translating the Hebrew name Iona as Columba and also sought the significance of that divinely-given name in the authority of the Gospel. Like Bede, he refers both to the descent of the Holy Spirit in the form of a dove at Christ's Baptism and to the exhortation in Mt 10:6 that the simplicity and innocence of the dove be taken as a model for discipleship:

> Therefore a simple and innocent person (Columba) also was rightly called by this name, since he with dove-like disposition offered to the Holy Spirit a dwelling in himself.[13]

The play on the forms of Columba's name does not simply allow Adomnán to display his erudition and *urbanitas.*[14] The power of Adom-

10 Liber interpretationis hebraicorum nominum, CCSL 72, 140, 146, 124, 135. Commentariorum in Matheum, CCSL 77, 141.
11 Expositio Actuum Apostolorum, CCSL 121, 28; L.T. Martin (tr.), The Venerable Bede. Commentary on the Acts of the Apostles, Kalamazoo 1989, 52–53.
12 Opera homiletica, CCSL 122, 143–144.
13 Adomnán's Life of Columba, 4–5.
14 J.-M. Picard, 'The purpose of Adomnán's Vita Columbae', in Peritia 1 (1982) 176–177.

nán's claims here lies in his use of language traditionally used to exalt the discipleship of the Prince of the Apostles, not in order to lessen Peter's glory (the Columban monks at Whitby did not deny Christ's commission to St Peter), but to reveal Columba too as 'a man very dear to God and of high merit in his sight' on whom the grace of the Holy Spirit was poured out abundantly and in an incomparable manner.[15]

In a very different rhetorical register and nearly a century earlier, Columbanus had also assumed contemporary familiarity with the traditional exegetical interpretation of Iona-Columba when he frequently used it of his own name, even calling himself *Bar-iona* in a letter to Gregory I. This has recently been described as 'self-righteous' and 'intentionally offensive': 'the Irishman could hardly have expected a Pope to find his claim to be Bar-iona either clever or amusing'.[16] It does, however, point to a wider application of the Iona-Columba exegesis than that encountered so far and one which may well have some relevance in the attempt to read the fish-man symbol in the Book of Kells.

Columba and its various forms and diminutives—Colum, Colman and Columban—was 'very common among the Irish saints'[17] and exegesis of the Petrine and related texts makes it clear that *all* the faithful are called to be *columbae* or doves because at their Baptism they are filled with the Holy Spirit (albeit each according to his capacity). Whereas Bede and Adomnán show St Peter and St Columba respectively to have been very full vessels of the Holy Spirit, Columbanus in describing himself immediately follows the phrase *ego Bar-iona* with the self-deprecatory words *vilis Columba* and elsewhere in his correspondence repeatedly refers to himself as *Columba peccator*. Particularly when understood in the context of his idiosyncratic use of the authorial humility topos,[18] Columbanus seems to be saying that as a member of the Church he is a dove, his very name proclaims it, though he is a small and wretched one; far from abrogating the authority of *Simon Bar-iona* he presumes to offer advice and even admonition to Popes Gregory I and Boniface IV only in the interests of the Church's unity which St Peter represents. In exegetical parlance—and his letter of 600 is addressed to a great exegete whom he revered—unity was a very dovelike preoccupation.

As early as Cyprian's *De ecclesiae catholicae unitate*, which was well-known to insular commentators, the nature of the dove is allegorically expounded. The reason why the Holy Spirit came in the form of a dove is because doves are without rancour or bitterness, they fly in forma-

15 Adomnán's Life of Columba, 209.
16 J.F. Kelly, 'The letter of Columbanus to Gregory the Great' in *Gregorio Magno e il suo tempo*, Studia Ephemeridis Augustinianum 33, Rome 1991, 216, 218.
17 Sancti Columbani opera, xii n.3.
18 M. Lapidge, 'Columbanus and the Antiphonary of Bangor', in *Peritia* 4 (1985) 107–108.

tion, assemble and eat in one house, and are, in short, an image of unity and concord whose example the Church must follow, 'that we may imitate the doves in our love for the brethren'. In the second version of the text, Cyprian quotes the Petrine commission in Mt 16 to demonstrate that, although after the Resurrection the other Apostles also received the Spirit and shared in Peter's power, nevertheless 'It is on one man Christ builds his Church . . . in order to show that the Church of Christ is unique. Indeed this oneness is figured in the Canticle of Canticles when the Holy Spirit, speaking in the Lord's name, says, 'One is my dove, my perfect one'.[19] This classic text (Cant 6:8) is echoed in the very interpretation of the Hebrew name Iona not simply as *Columba* but as *Columba mea* in Jerome's list of the Hebrew names used in Luke.

Bede, who draws on Cyprian and the Song of Songs in his homily on the Chair of Peter, explains that although the same office is committed to the whole Church in her bishops and priests, the special way in which Peter was blessed and given the keys in Mt 16: 17–19 represented the unity of faith and fellowship of all believers. Playing on the interpretation of the name *Bar-iona* as *filius columbae*, Bede urges: 'if we imitate Peter's example . . . we also will be capable of being called blessed . . . on account of the gift of virtues we have received from the Lord, we will be called 'sons of a dove' and Christ himself, rejoicing with us in the spiritual progress of our souls, will say, 'How beautiful you are . . . your eyes are those of doves' (Cant 4:1).[20]

BAPTISM

The dove, a vessel or dwelling-place of the Holy Spirit, was a familiar image of the Church or the soul and could thus be applied to the particular examples of St Peter, Columba or Columbanus. Exegesis on the dove was not peculiar to exegesis of the Petrine text in Matthew 16 or to the traditional interpretation of Iona as Columba, however, but was found in two other important contexts: commentaries on the Gospel accounts of Christ's Baptism and catechetical and mystagogical works on the sacrament of Baptism. Ambrose's *De Mysteriis*, for example, links together the account of the descent of the Holy Spirit in the form of a dove at Christ's Baptism, the injunction of Mt 10:6 'be simple as doves' (which is directly applied to those who are baptized)

19 Cyprian, De ecclesiae catholicae unitate CCSL 3, 255–6, 252, note on authenticity of Primacy Text, 244–5. This work was used in the insular paschal controversy, e.g. Cummian's letter, M. Walsh and D. Ó Cróinín (eds.), De controversia paschali , Toronto 1988, 78–79 n. 151.
20 Opera homiletica CCSL 122, 146–147; L.T. Martin and D. Hurst (tr.), Bede the Venerable. Homilies on the Gospels I, Kalamazoo 1991, 204.

and the words of Cant 4:1, addressed by Christ to the pure soul of those regenerated in Baptism: 'How beautiful you are . . . your eyes are those of doves'.[21] This is one of a number of quotations about doves in the Song of Songs cited by Bede in a homily expounding Christ's Baptism and the sacrament it prefigured. Elsewhere he notes that the Holy Spirit by descending at Christ's Baptism as a dove 'does not represent merely its own innocence and simplicity, or that of Him on whom it descended, but likewise that of those who think of Him "in goodness and seek him in simplicity of heart" [Wisd 1:1]. The Lord himself says in praise of the piety that they share with one accord . . . granted by a spiritual grace: "One is my dove" [Cant 6:8] . . . The Church is appropriately given the name "the one dove of Christ" . . . for undoubtedly it is not because of her own merits, but because of a gift of spiritual grace she has received, that she is gathered into the unity of the Christian faith from many nations'.[22]

Any discussion of whether this exegetical chain of texts concerning the dove has any relevance to an interpretation of the hybrid figure apparently drawing attention to the name Iona on f.201r in the Book of Kells needs now to view both this exegesis and the figure of the fish-man in the context of the whole folio and in the larger decorated unit of text of which f. 201 forms a part. Two practical questions also need to be addressed: why is the fish-man accompanied by six birds to which he appears to be pointing? And why are these figures placed within the Lucan text of Christ's genealogy?

It is clear from the traditions briefly sketched here that the dove was universally regarded as an image of the baptized Christian soul or of the Church collectively, filled with the Holy Spirit. The key text in the exegetical chain and the unambiguous reason why the dove was so widely used as the image of the Holy Spirit filling the soul or the Church is that at Christ's own Baptism the Holy Spirit descended *in specie columbae*. This reason is quoted by Adomnán in the very next sentence after his play on Iona-Columba and forms the basis of his explanation of the suitability of the name Columba for one who 'with dove-like disposition offered to the Holy Spirit a dwelling in himself'. If, as seems likely, the Book of Kells was produced in a Columban monastery, the detail of the hybrid figure alongside the name of Iona would doubtless have had a particular significance but it could not have been an exclusive allusion to St Columba since all the baptized are called to be doves, to become the dwelling-place or temple of the Holy Spirit. At their Baptism and post-baptismal Confirmation the faithful are anointed with oil and chrism to signify their participation in Christ's spiritual

21 B. Botte (ed.), Ambroise de Milan. Des sacrements. Des mystères, SC 25, 168–176.
22 Opera homiletica, CCSL 122, 107–108; Homilies on the Gospels, I 151–152.

anointing with the Holy Spirit at his Incarnation, which was proclaimed at his Baptism by the descent of the dove and in the words of the Father, 'This is my beloved son'. In St Luke's Gospel alone the account of Christ's Baptism is immediately followed by His genealogy. In the Book of Kells the two lines of text concluding the Lucan baptism narrative are inscribed at the top of f.200r above the opening of the genealogy (pl. 1). The top line bears the words of the Father, *tu es filius meus dilectus*. The list of Christ's human ancestors thus immediately follows the revelation of his divine Sonship at his Baptism, a point also stressed at the end of the genealogy where Christ's earthly ancestors are traced back to Adam 'who was the son of God'.

Patristic and insular commentators were responsive to the theological implications of Luke's genealogy and its context. Following St Ambrose, an eighth-century Hiberno-Latin commentary on Luke's Gospel notes that the account of Christ's genealogy is placed after the account of the Baptism in order to demonstrate that God is Father not only of Christ but of all Christians through Baptism.[23] Bede's commentary on Luke's Gospel shows that the real significance of the coming of the dove at Christ's Baptism was its descent into his body, the Church; thus those who are baptized receive the Holy Spirit and become the sons of God.[24]

In the same Gospel commentary and in the context of discussing the importance of the number seven in Luke's listing of the seventy-seven generations of Christ's ancestors, Bede refers to the seven gifts of the Holy Spirit which Isaiah prophesied would descend on the Messiah (Is 11:2–3). Allusion to Isaiah's prophecy in the context of Baptism was a patristic commonplace. It is used by Ambrose, for example, to explain that the faithful also receive the spiritual seal of these seven gifts of the Holy Spirit at their own post-baptismal anointing with chrism at which they participate in Christ's anointing.[25] In his homily expounding Christ's Baptism Bede shows how the seven-fold nature of the dove, allegorically revealed in the Song of Songs, exemplifies the seven types of virtue

---

23 J.F. Kelly, editor of the Hiberno-Latin commentary on Luke, Cod, Vind. lat. 997, c. 780–85 (CCSL 108C), notes its dependence on Bede's Lucan commentary, c. 709–716, and other evidence of the early familiarity of Irish commentators with some of Bede's works: 'To study Hiberno-Latin exegesis without reference to Bede is to ignore not only an important source for the Irish exegetes, but also a part of the tradition in which they stood'; Bede's own use of earlier Hiberno-Latin works is also noted: 'Bede and Hiberno-Latin exegesis', in P. Szarmach (ed.), Sources of Anglo-Saxon Culture, Kalamazoo 1986; J. Kelly, 'The Hiberno-Latin study of the Gospel of Luke', in M. McNamara (ed.), Biblical Studies. The medieval Irish contribution (note 1 supra), 10–29.

24 Bede, In Lucae evangelium expositio, CCSL 120, 84; cf. Ambrose, Expositio evangelii secundum Lucam, CCSL 14, 81–82.

25 De sacramentis, SC 25, 74–75.

necessary to the life of the baptized: 'And this is rightly done because the grace of the Holy Spirit, who descended as a dove, is sevenfold'[26] The eighth-century Hiberno-Latin commentary on Luke's Gospel (which was influenced by Ambrose's Lucan commentary) interprets the evangelist's description of Jesus after his Baptism 'full of the Holy Spirit' as meaning the seven gifts of the Holy Spirit 'and of this fulness have we all received'.[27]

It has been seen that St Luke's Gospel uniquely connects Christ's Baptism and his genealogy and that the exegetical tradition emphasized both Christ's divine Sonship, made known in the words of the Father and the descent of the dove at his Baptism, and his human ancestry revealed in the genealogy. Commentators further noted the allusion of the dove to the descent of the Holy Spirit on the Church whose earthly members, reborn in Baptism, become sons of God. Related themes which also exist in other contexts were drawn into Ambrose's magisterial treatment of the Lucan Baptism and Genealogy: the exposition of the nature of the dove as an image of the Church or the individual soul filled with the Holy Spirit and the application of this image of the dove to all the faithful who in their Baptism and post-baptismal confirmatory anointing with chrism share in Christ's anointing with the seven-fold gifts of the Holy Spirit. Finally, the patristic interpretation of the Hebrew name Iona as *columba* had long been familiar in insular monastic culture and, in the *Life of Columba*, had found early expression in connection with a number of the exegetical themes itemized here. Seen from the perspective of exegesis on Luke's text and its themes, therefore, the possibility that the hybrid figure on f.201r in the Book of Kells may be a witty visual play on the Hebrew name Iona and its Latin meaning *columba* or dove, seems strengthened rather than diminished by his gnomic gestures. He is pointing both upwards and downwards, linking him to the six birds grouped directly above and below so that the whole column of figures may be read as seven 'doves' in all (pl. 3). A number of puzzles remain. Why, for example, is the central 'dove' depicted as half-man, half-fish? Is this just incidental, an idiosyncratic drollery, or is it integral to the meaning of the page suggested here?

THE SIGN OF JONAH

Françoise Henry's observation that the Hebrew name Iona in Luke's genealogy had itself 'probably suggested the fish-human figure' on f. 201[28] and Paul Meyvaert's comment that 'There may be a playful allu-

---

26 Opera homiletica, CCSL 122, 86.
27 Scriptores Hiberniae minores, CCSL 108C, 29.
28 F. Henry, The Book of Kells, London 1974, 200 and n.95.

sion here to Jonah and his whale'[29] tacitly depend on conflating Christ's ancestor Iona (about whom nothing is known) with the prophet Iona who was often depicted as a half-length figure emerging from the jaws of the whale or sea monster in early Christian art. In early Irish monastic circles the Hebrew name Iona certainly evoked the prophet of that name. Using word-play on his own name, Columbanus frequently and unambiguously likened himself to the prophet Jonah and his shipwreck, and Adomnán in interpreting St Columba's name says he 'received the same name as the prophet Jonah'.[30] The scriptural and exegetical associations of the prophet Jonah may, therefore, have some significance in interpreting the fish-man figure in the Book of Kells.

Jonah was cited by Christ in Mt 12:39–40; 16:4 and Lk 11:29–30 as the sign of the Son of Man, expanded in Matthew's version to a specific image of Christ's own death and resurrection. Because the faithful sacramentally participate in Christ's death and resurrection at their descent into the waters of baptism, from which ritual death they emerge to a new life, they too were in early exegesis likened to Jonah and his deliverance from the whale. In his commentary on the Book of Jonah, Jerome refers to Christ's Baptism to explain that the prophet's name means *columba* because *Spiritus Sanctus in specie columbae descendit.* He directly links Jonah's mission to the Ninevites with the risen Christ's injunction to his disciples to baptize all in the name of the Father, the Son and the Holy Spirit (Mt 28: 19).[31]

ROYAL PRIESTHOOD

Genealogy has an extremely important function in both the Old and New Testaments:

> The very interest in ancestry reflects Israel's tribal origins . . . Besides establishing identity, biblical genealogies are sometimes used to undergird status, especially for the offices of king and priest where lineage is important . . . to structure history into epochs and to authenticate a line of (cultic) office holders.[32]

The two versions of Christ's genealogy in the Gospels of Matthew and Luke received extensive exposition in patristic commentaries but were of particular interest for a clerical caste within barbarian society who shared many of the assumptions and techniques of the authors of biblical genealogies. Donnchadh Ó Corráin has shown that early Irish

29 'The Book of Kells and Iona' (note 5 supra), 6.
30 Sancti Columbani opera 19, 35, 55; Adomnán's Life of Columba, 3.
31 Commentarium in Ionam prophetam, CCSL 76, 380, 404.
32 R.E. Brown, The Birth of the Messiah, London 1977, 65.

churchmen themselves produced a vast corpus of genealogical material, shaped for ecclesiastical and political purposes.[33]

On the same page as the Iona figure in the Book of Kells is the name of Christ's ancestor David. Ambrose's Lucan commentary, followed by insular exegetes, explains that in Matthew's genealogy the descent is through David's son and royal heir, Solomon, but in Luke's version the sacerdotal line is traced through another of David's sons, Nathan.[34] Christ as a member of the royal house of Judah was not in the direct descent of the priestly tribe of Aaron (Num 3:3,10; Heb 7:14), but St Luke is at pains to explain that the Virgin Mary was the cousin of John the Baptist's mother, Elizabeth, who was 'of the daughters of Aaron' (Lk 1:5) and that Elizabeth's husband, the priest Zachariah, was descended through Abia from Aaron. Insular commentators document other examples of such links by intermarriage between the royal and priestly lines in order to show that Christ belongs in the flesh to both tribes and that in his assumed humanity He has the person of priest and king.[35]

The eighth-century Irish Reference Bible describes how Aaron, under the Law, was anointed to his office and thus became the first messias or christus. He is compared with Christ, the Anointed One, who was anointed at his Incarnation, however, not physically with oil or chrism like Aaron, but invisibly by the Holy Spirit as 'a priest for ever, according

---

33 D. Ó Corráin, 'Irish origin legends and genealogy: recurrent aetiologies' in T. Nybey, I. Pio, P. Sorensen, A. Trommer (eds.), History and heroic tale, Odense 1985, 51–96; K. McCone, Pagan Past and Christian Present in early Irish Literature, Maynooth 1991, 233–244.

34 Ambrose, Expositio evangelii secundum Lucam, I, CCSL 14, 82–3; cf. Bede, In Lucae evangelium expositio CCSL 120, 89–90. Also in the Hiberno-Latin tradition, e.g. in the commentary on the Matthean genealogy in Munich, Clm. 6233, f.22v, c. 770–780, and the commentary on the Lucan genealogy in the eighth-century Irish 'Reference Bible', Paris, B.N. lat. 11561, f.164v and Munich, Clm. 14277, f. 253r. I am most grateful to Dr Seán Connolly, who is editing the 'Reference Bible' New Testament, for making his transcripts of the genealogical material in these unpublished mss. available to me. Ambrose is the most important patristic source for the commentary on Luke in the Reference Bible but 'Ambrose's own source, Origen's Homilies on Luke, is known to the Irish exegete, in Latin translation, and the Alexandrian is cited by name', J.F. Kelly, 'Das Bibelwerk, organization und Quellenanalyse of the New Testament section' in: P. Ní Chatháin and M. Richter (ed.), Irland und die Christenheit (Stuttgart 1987) 113–123, 116. The contrast in Christ's descent traced through Solomon and Nathan was also perpetuated through the 'Monarchan' prologues prefacing insular Gospel books, including the Book of Kells. J. Chapman, Early History of the Vulgate Gospels, Oxford 1908, 230.

35 Ex dictis sancti Hieronimi (Munich, Clm. 14426), CCSL 108B, 229–230 and Bede, Opera homiletica, CCSL 122, 19–20 for royal and priestly inter-marriage.

to the order of Melchisedech' and also as a prophet and a king. It is this spiritual anointing which was made manifest at Christ's Baptism when the Holy Spirit descended in the form of a dove to the body of Christ, his Church. In this sense, all the baptized when anointed with chrism through which they sacramentally share in Christ's anointing are called to be prophets, priests and kings, as the liturgy also makes evident.[36]

There were other important factors in the particular association of Luke's Gospel with Christ's (and therefore with the Church's) royal priesthood. Luke's account of the Incarnation is symbolically prefaced by the scene of Zachariah, a priest of the Old Convenant, making an offering at the altar in the temple at Jerusalem. In Carolingian and late Anglo-Saxon Gospel books it is this scene, rather than the Annunciation, which is distinguished by its depiction in the spandrels or the initial of the Gospel incipit. In the illustrations of the sixth-century *Rabbula Gospels* Zachariah's symbolic function is acknowledged in his being paired with Aaron.[37] Following Ambrose, Bede notes that the appearance of an angel beside the altar of Zachariah's offering was to proclaim 'the coming of the true and eternal High Priest who would be the true sacrificial offering for the salvation of the whole world'.[38]

Ambrose in turn, like Origen before him, was drawing on the exegesis already well developed in the Epistle to the Hebrews which shows how Christ was called by God to be the new High Priest of the heavenly sanctuary superseding the Aaronic priesthood and the sacrifices of the Old Covenant and of the earthly tabernacle. The Epistle repeatedly cites

36 From commentary on Matthean genealogy, Paris B.N. lat 11561, f.138r, Munich Clm. 14277, f.219v. Angers 55 also gives other scriptural references for Christ's threefold anointing which is related to his Baptism and his title in the *tres linguae sacrae*: Christus, Unctus, Messias: *CCSL* 108B, 147–148. All three features are related in a commentary on the Incarnation in Verona, Bibl. Capit. LXVII (64), f.42r quoted by J.F. Kelly, 'The Hiberno-Latin study of the gospel of Luke' (note 23 supra) 21–22. See also Ambrose, De sacramentis, *CCSL* 73, 74–75. Isidore of Seville relates Aaron's priestly anointing to the anointing of Christ and of all the members of the Church as priests and kings, De ecclesiasticis officiis, CCSL 113, 106.
37 Florence, bibl. Medicea-Laurentiana (Plut. I, 56). C. Ceccheli, G. Furlani, M. Salmi (eds.), The Rabbula Gospels, Oltun and Lausanne 1959, Canon I, f.3v, pl. 9.2. After Aaron and Zachariah the Annunciation follows, accompanied by the O.T. priest Samuel with the oil for royal anointing, then Christ's Baptism, with the enthroned figures of David and Solomon. Early western representations of Zachariah at the altar reviewed by R. Walker, 'Illustrations of the Priscillian prologues in Gospel mss. of the Carolingian Ada school', in Art Bulletin 30 (1948) 1–10; W. Koehler, 'An illustrated Evangelistary of the Ada school and its model' in: Jnl. Warburg and Courtauld Inst. 15 (1952) 48–66.
38 In Lucae evangelium expositio, CCSL 120, 24; cf. Bede, Homelia II, 19. CCSL 122, 318–327, 323.

Christ's fulfilment of the Messianic prophecy from Ps 109:4, 'Thou art a priest for ever, after the order of Melchisedech' (Heb 5:6;10;6:20; 7:2,17). Melchisedech does not feature in Luke's list of Christ's ancestors because this mysterious priest-king was 'without father, without mother, without genealogy' (Heb 7:3). In Hebrews, however, the first of the repeated acclamations of Christ as 'Thou are a priest forever after the order of Melchisedech' is directly coupled with another prophetic text: 'Thou art my son: this day have I begotten thee' (Ps 2:7; Heb 5:5–6). Commentators, including Ambrose's work on Luke's Gospel, regularly noted the fulfilment of this prophecy in the Gospel accounts of Christ's Baptism when the Psalm words are alluded to in the proclamation of his divine Sonship. Exegesis on St Luke's combined account of Christ's Baptism and his priestly genealogy therefore regularly makes substantial use of the Epistle to the Hebrews' revelation of Christ as the divinely appointed great High Priest 'after the order of Melchisedech'. The image carried a further and widely known allusion to Christ's priesthood and sacrifice because the priest-king Melchisedech had offered bread and wine to Abraham (Gen 14:18), a standard type of prefiguring of the Eucharist which was frequently cited in commentaries on the Last Supper and on the Eucharist and recalled in the Roman Canon of the Mass.

The twelfth-century *Mosan Floreffe Bible* (London, B.L. Add. MS 17738) sets out the major themes of this exegesis in pictorial form at the beginning of St Luke's Gospel at the place reserved in earlier Gospel books for a literal illustration of Luke's account of Zachariah at the altar in the Temple.[39] On the double-columned page on f.187 the picture is positioned alongside the literal text of Luke's account of Zachariah but, with the aid of inscriptions, provides a detailed comment on its under-lying spiritual meaning. St Luke stands holding an emblem of his evangelist symbol, the winged calf, immediately beside a scene of the sacrifice of a calf on an altar by a priest of the Old Covenant. This blood sacrifice is superseded by the Crucifixion shown in the upper register of the picture and on the same central axis as the sacrificial altar below. The lance thrust which pierces Christ's side on the Cross parallels the knife thrust to the sacrificial calf on the altar below, which, under the Old Covenant, had to be made to repeated victims in expiation for sin. That Christ's Passion is to be seen as the priestly sacrifice of the New Covenant is made unambiguously clear by the addition of portrait busts with banderoles. King David quotes from his own Ps 109: 'Thou art a priest for ever after the order of Melchisedech', and St Paul, the pre-sumed author of the Epistle to the Hebrews, quotes from 9:12: 'But by his own blood He entered once into the holy place'. The inscription over the sanctuary arch which encloses the entire picture directly relates of Christ and the sacrificial calf.

39 G.W.H. Lampe (ed.), The Cambridge History of the Bible, vol. 2, Cambridge 1969, pl. 31.

The Book of Kells has no such didactic intent: its illustration will not teach what is not already known. Instead of attaching a coherent centralised design to the narrative of Zachariah in Lk 1 providing a clear commentary on it, the Kells artist has added enigmatic and apparently unconnected figures to the margins of a genealogy where they may be read by the casual eye as simply decorating or animating the page. But viewed in the context of the exegetical tradition just outlined they may also be seen as a series of pictorial cues both recalling and prompting a meditative reading of a mysterious text, namely the list of Hebrew names. Similarly, the author of the Hiberno-Latin commentary on Matthew's Gospel in Munich, Clm 6233, uses the bare list of Hebrew names and their etymologies as a series of hooks on which to hang exegetical chains of texts. Their precise relevance to the particular names against which they are positioned varies considerably—sometimes it is very close, sometimes it seems slight, forced or non-existent—but they are united in providing a series of insights into the nature of Christ within the framework of a genealogy whose very function is to elucidate that identity.[40]

On f.201v in Kells a figure with a chalice is placed over the name of Abraham (pl. 4). At the foot of the page is a small winged calf placed vertically, as in the evangelist symbol of Luke on f. 27v, where a cross appears in its halo. The patristic tradition of associating St Luke and his symbolic calf with the Passion and priesthood of Christ was very familiar in Hiberno-Latin exegesis on the four Evangelists.[41] Ambrose refers to the suitability of the calf as the symbol of St Luke precisely in his discussion of the Lucan genealogy which reveals Christ as a priest for ever 'according to the order of Melchisedech' : Ambrose observes that the calf always points to this sacerdotal mystery.[42] In Kells the calf is depicted with its back to the names of three of Christ's ancestors (Eber, Sala and Cainan) who merit no particular comment in exegesis. More important, perhaps, in explaining the calf's position on the page, is the fact that it is directly facing the ornament at the end of the genealogy on the facing page and that the calf's legs are outstretched so that its whole body forms a kind of bracket exactly spanning the depth of that decorative panel and visually relating the two.

---

40 The Hebrew names in Mt 1:4–5, for example, prompt succinct allusion to biblical texts on the Crucifixion as exaltation (linking Jn 12:32 and Phil 2: 8–11), on the body of Christ as the prophesied new sacrifice for remission of sin, on the Church drawn from the Gentiles and on Christ's royal and priestly lineage 'after the order of Melchisedech'.

41 R. McNally, 'The Evangelists in the Hiberno-Latin tradition' in A Hiergemann (ed.), Festschrift Bernhard Bischoff, Stuttgart 1971, 111–122.

42 CCSL 14, 83; cf. 5: in the prologue dealing with the priest Zachariah Ambrose also speaks of the calf as the symbol of Luke's Gospel which begins with a priest and ends with a victim.

The panel on f.202r is formed by entwined peacocks and a vine-scroll stemming from a chalice and partly conceals a bearded figure standing behind it (pl. 5). The idea that this is not simply a decorative endpiece but also carries the standard early Christian allusions of the motif to the Eucharist is strengthened by comparison with the decorative panel marking the *breves causae* of Luke which begins on f.19v with the words *Zachariae sacerdoti* (pl. 8). The opening letters, *Zacha,* clouded by ornament and enlarged on a panel to fill the width of the page, are ingeniously formed from an inhabited vinescroll stemming horizontally along the panel from a chalice, so that an allusion to the Eucharistic sacrifice of the new High Priest may be discerned, concealed in Zachariah's name.

THE TEMPLE

Ambrose's commentary on St Luke's Gospel contrasts the Aaronic priesthood represented by Zachariah with the eternal priest of whom it is said: 'Thou art a priest for ever'. Ambrose expounds this text as referring to 'the priest who is to come, whose sacrifice would not be like others, for he would not offer sacrifice for us in a temple made with human hands but he would offer propitiation for our sins in the temple of his body'[43] This draws heavily on the Epistle to the Hebrews ch. 9 which contrasts the blood sacrifices of the Levitical priesthood with Christ's redemptive single sacrifice of his own blood. The 'former tabernacle' is to be superseded by 'a greater and more perfect tabernacle, not made with hands, that is, not of this creation', as the new High Priest, 'Jesus is not entered into the [Holy of] Holies made with hands, the pattern of the true, but into Heaven itself, that He may appear now in the presence of God for us' (Heb 9:11, 24). But Ambrose links the Hebrews text to another important scriptural chain.

The earliest Christian preachers declared that the Lord who created heaven and earth 'dwells not in temples made with hands' (Acts 17:24, 7:48). To the Jews who demanded that Jesus give them some sign of the divine authority by which He had cleansed the Temple in Jerusalem, He replied: 'Destroy this temple and in three days I will raise it up'. They understood this literally. 'But he spoke of the temple of his body' (Jn 2: 19–22). During his trial before the chief priests his accusers said, 'We heard Him say, I will destroy this temple made with hands and within three days I will build another not made with hands' (Mk 14:58; Mt 26:61). The Jews failed to discern the spiritual fulfilment of his prophecy in the Crucifixion and Resurrection: 'Thou that destroyest the temple of God and in three days will rebuild it, save thy own self. If thou be the son of God, come down from the cross' (Mt 27:40; Mk 15:29).

43 Op. cit. 17.

Ambrose's contrast of the Old Covenant priesthood represented by Zachariah with 'the priest who is to come' depends on the Epistle to the Hebrews, some of whose themes have been traced here in the decoration of the last double-opening of Jesus' priestly genealogy in the Book of Kells, ff.201v–202r. But Ambrose's contrast of the Old Covenant sacrifice in the 'temple made with human hands' with the new priest's offering of 'propitiation for our sins in the temple of his body' also draws on the chain of Gospel texts, centred on Jn 2:19–22, which identify the new temple, the place of the divine presence, as the human body of Jesus.

Furthermore, Ambrose applies the image of the Temple not only to the incarnate body of Jesus but to the Church. Commenting on Luke's account of the Baptism, which points to the descent of the Holy Spirit on the Church at Pentecost, Ambrose pictures the birth, growth, composition and calling of the Church through the image of the Temple building, drawing on a chain of scriptural texts. He describes the Temple built by Solomon in Jerusalem as the type of the Church built by God and quotes Ps 126:1: 'Except the Lord build the house, they labour in vain who build it.' In particular he comments on the constituent phrases of two key texts in the chain. He calls on the faithful to be 'as living stones built up, a spiritual house, a holy priesthood, to offer up spiritual sacrifices' (1 Pet 2:5) and pictures this spiritual house as 'built upon the foundation of the apostles and prophets, Jesus Christ himself being the chief cornerstone in whom all the building framed together grows into a temple' (Eph 2:20–21).

Ambrose's interpretation of the Lucan Baptism and genealogy in terms of the new priesthood and Temple illumines the extraordinary picture in Kells which immediately follows the genealogy and precedes Luke's description of Jesus returning from his Baptism 'full of the Holy Spirit'. On f.202v a bust-length portrait of Christ is set on a smaller-scale church building (pl. 6 and Frontispiece). With metaphysical wit the picture gives a literal rendering of the Gospel image of 'the temple of his body', prompting the search for a spiritual interpretation. The image faces and is complemented by an elaborate framed display text of the opening words of Lk 4:1: 'Jesus full of the Holy Spirit' (pl. 7). This text and image positioned at the end of Luke's account of the Baptism and genealogy which together show Jesus to be Son of God and of human descent, thus reveal the Temple as the body or humanity of Jesus filled with the Holy Spirit. The rows of little figures beneath the building enable it to be read not only as the incarnate body of Jesus but also as his body the Church, made up of 'living stones' with Jesus as 'the chief corner stone'.

The visual ambiguities of the Temple picture in Kells mirror some of the multiple allusions of the exegetical chain of scriptural texts on the image of the Temple used by Ambrose in his Lucan commentary. The idea, central to Ambrose's use of the Temple image, that it can allude simultaneously to Christ and his Church is clearly stated in

Bede's homily on the chief Gospel link in the chain, Jn 2: 12–22. Referring to the Temple in Jerusalem Bede says, 'the temple made by hands prefigured Our Lord's most sacred body' but adds that it also 'pointed to his body the Church and to the body and soul of each one of the faithful (as we find in quite a few places in the Scriptures)'.[44] This mode of interpretation is set out more fully at the beginning of his allegorical exposition on the description of the Temple in 3 Kgs 5:1–7.51:

The house of God which King Solomon built in Jerusalem was made as a figure of the holy universal Church which, from the first of the elect to the last to be born at the end of the world, is daily being built through the grace . . . of its Redeemer. It is still partly in pilgrimage from Him on earth and partly, having escaped from the hardships of its sojurn, already reigns with Him in heaven where, when the Last Judgement is over, it is to reign completely with Him . . . to it belongs the very mediator between God and men, Himself a human being, Christ Jesus [1 Tm 2:5], as He Himself attests when He says, 'Destroy this temple and in three days I shall raise it up'. To which the evangelist by way of explanation added, 'But He was speaking of the temple of his own body' [Jn 2: 29, 21]. Furthermore, the Apostle says to us, 'Do you not realise that you are a temple of God with the Spirit of God living in you?' [1 Cor 3:16]. If, therefore, He became the temple of God by assuming human nature and we became the temple of God through his Spirit dwelling in us [Rm 8:11], it is quite clear that the material temple was a figure of us all, that is, both of the Lord himself and his members which we are. But [it was a figure] of Him as the uniquely chosen and precious cornerstone laid in the foundation [cf. Is 28:16, 1 Peter 2.6] and of us as the living stones built upon the foundation of the apostles and prophets, i.e. on the Lord himself [Eph 2:20, 1 Pet 2:5–7, I Cor 3:11] . . . the figure [of the temple] will apply to our Lord himself in some respects, in others to all the elect.[45]

44 Opera homiletica CCSL 122, 189; L.T. Martin and D. Hurst (tr.), Bede. Homilies on the Gospels II, Kalamazoo 1991, 8–9.

45 De Templo, CCSL 119A, 148. Translation used here is by Seán Connolly: I wish to thank Dr Connolly for generously making his work available to me before its publication. In De schematibus et tropis Bede explains that a single word or event may figuratively designate a mystical, tropological and anagogical sense at the same time. He cites the Temple as an example. Historically, it is the house built by Solomon; allegorically, it is the body of the Lord (Jn 2:19) or his Church (I Cor 3:17); tropologically it can refer to the individual faithful (1 Cor 3:16) and anagogically it signifies the joys of the heavenly dwelling (Ps 84:4): G.H. Tannenhaus (tr.), 'The Venerable Bede. Concerning figures and tropes' in J.M. Miller, M.H. Frosser, T.W. Benson (ed.), Bloomington, Ind. and London 1973, 120–121.

Bede's treatise shows the familiarity, within an early eighth-century insular monastic context, of the patristic tradition and, like the Kells picture, illustrates its highly creative reworking. It demonstrates that the Temple in Jerusalem prefigured both 'the temple of his body' (Jn 2:19,21) and the temple made of 'living stones' (1 Pet 2: 5–7; Eph 2:20) and shows that the use of the Temple as an image of the Church as the body of Christ does not simply refer to the Church on earth but to His Mystical Body, beyond temporal and spatial limitation: it includes the dead and those yet to be born. The faithful who died before the Incarnation are not regarded simply as part of the fabric of the Temple in Jerusalem which was superseded by the Christian Church: they are shown to be part of the single Body of Christ which will be completed only in the kingdom of heaven. Though Bede's treatise cannot be seen as the 'source' of the picture of the Temple in the Book of Kells, it can assist a clearer understanding of the conceptual connection between the image of the Temple on f. 202v and the iconography of the genealogy in the pages leading up to it, a connection which, it has been suggested here, reflects patristic exegesis of Luke's text. Seen within this exegetical tradition, the Temple image and its facing text in Kells transform a literal reading of the foregoing list of Hebrew names and reveals it as chronicling both the earthly ancestors from whom Christ took 'the temple of his body' in historical time *and* the spiritual ancestors of his Body the Church, still awaiting its completion at the end of time. From the moment of the Incarnation the 'temple of his body' is shown to be 'full of the Holy Spirit'; the revelation of this at his Baptism signifies that his Body the Church is also the habitation of the Holy Spirit.

ABRAHAM

Folios 201v–202r in the Book of Kells have already received some comment in the light of Ambrose's exegesis on the priestly genealogy and related themes in Luke contrasting the Old Covenant priesthood and repeated blood sacrifice in 'the former tabernacle' with the single sacrifice of Christ, the new High Priest, in 'the temple of his body'. The suggested connection between this exegesis and iconography and the picture of the Temple on the page immediately following the genealogy may now be considered further.

Directly above the calf in the inner margin of f.201v and facing the final page of the genealogy is a bearded figure reclining over the name of Abraham and alongside the names of Isaac and Jacob (pl. 4). In the New Testament, in early exegesis, liturgy and iconography Abraham is an immensely important figure of faith whose sacrifice of Isaac and reception of bread and wine from Melchisedech were seen as major prefigurings of the Eucharistic sacrifice. Although Melchisedech was often represented with bread and wine in Early Christian art there is no iconographic parallel showing him as a seated figure with only the chalice. Exegesis on Abraham however is of direct interest in deciphering the possible meaning of the figure in the context of Christ's genealogy.

In a solemn covenant the patriarch had received from God his new name Abraham, meaning the father of many nations (Gen 17:5), and was promised: 'in thy seed shall all the nations of the earth be blessed' (Gen 22:18). Already in the New Testament this is very fully interpreted, and in his commentary on the Lucan genealogy Ambrose quotes from Gal 3 to show that all the faithful, including Gentiles, are the children of Abraham: the seed of Abraham was his son Isaac, according to the flesh, but, according to the Spirit, it is Christ. All the faithful who have been baptized in Christ have put on Christ and therefore receive through Him the promise of the Spirit made to Abraham: 'There is neither Jew nor Greek . . . For you are all one in Christ Jesus. If you be Christ's then are you the seed of Abraham, heirs according to the promise' (Gal 3:29). Ambrose stresses that the patriarchs, including Abraham, Isaac and Jacob, lived before the age of the Law and lived in faith: grace precedes the Law and faith precedes the letter. The status accorded in the New Testament and patristic exegesis to Abraham and the other patriarchs who lived before the Incarnation and even before the Mosaic Law would have been of particular interest to a barbarian culture concerned with the fate of its own ancestors who had lived according to 'the law of nature' before their conversion to Christianity.[46] Ambrose shows the working of grace through the patriarchs quoting: 'Abraham believed in the Lord and it was counted to him for righteousness' (Gen 15:6; Gal 3:6; cf. Rom 4:3), and 'Your father Abraham rejoiced to see my day' (Jn 8:56).

In a considerable variety of contexts insular exegetes elaborated this interpretation. In the Hiberno-Latin commentaries on the Catholic Epistles, Abraham is *pater noster, id est apostolus non tantum carne sed et fide* or *pater nostrae fidei; filii Abrahae omnes fideles sunt.*[47] In the Irish glosses in the Würzburg copy of the Pauline Epistles Abraham is also seen as the father of all the faithful who spiritually inherit the promised blessing given to him.[48] Bede repeatedly returns to the theme:

> The house of Jacob [Abraham's descendants] refers to the universal Church; even though many of the faithful do not take their

46 D. Ó Corráin, L. Breatnach, A. Breen, 'The laws of the Irish' in: Peritia 3 (1984) 382–438, 390–396; K. McCone, Pagan Past and Christian Present, 71–72, 92–100.

47 Scriptores Hiberniae minores, CCSL 108B, 14, 65.

48 Rom 4:1, 12, 13, 16, 17. Univ. of Würzburg, M. p.th.f.12. L.C. Stern, Epistolae Beati Pauli glosatae glosa interlineali, Halle 1910; P. Ní Chatháin, 'Notes on the Würzbug glosses' in: Irland und die Christenheit (note 34 supra) 190–199.

physical origins from the stock of the patriarchs they are by Baptism reborn in Christ and so receive the heritage of the patriarchs.[49]

In the opening chapter of Luke's Gospel both Mary and the priest Zachariah recognize the coming of Christ as the fulfilment of God's promises made 'to Abraham and his seed for ever', 'to Abraham our father' (Lk 1:55, 73), and their testimony, enshrined in the Magnificat and Benedictus respectively, formed daily canticles in the monastic office. In a homily on Luke's text Bede shows that Mary properly names Abraham in particular in the Magnificat because:

> although many of the fathers and holy ones mystically brought forward testimony of the Lord's Incarnation, nevertheless it was to Abraham that the hidden mysteries of the Lord's Incarnation were first clearly predicted and to him it was specifically said: 'And in your seed all the tribes of the world earth will be blessed' [Gen 12:3] . . . However, 'the seed of Abraham' does not refer only to those chosen ones who were brought forth physically from Abraham's lineage but also to us who, having been gathered together to Christ from the nations, are connected by the fellowship of faith . . . We too are the seed and children of Abraham since we are born by the sacraments of our Redeemer, who assumed his flesh from the race of Abraham.[50]

Moreover, Bede shows that the divine promise made to Abraham does not end with the coming of Christ at his Incarnation but that 'to Abraham and his seed for ever' there will remain, until the end of the world, 'the everlasting glory of future blessedness'. Viewed in the light of this exegetical tradition, the genealogy of Christ is not only the record of a heritage but the sign of a continuing expectation; it is also the genealogy of the Church whose members, whether gentile or Jew, are reborn in Baptism and foretaste future blessedness in the sacrament of the Eucharist.

THE HEAVENLY BANQUET

On f. 201v in the Book of Kells the figure seated above the name of Abraham with his back alongside the names of Isaac and Jacob is raising a chalice, as though about to drink from it. The chalice is similar in shape and colour to the chalice from which the vinescroll stems in the genealogy's endpiece on the facing page (pl. 5). The eucharistic motif of the chalice, vine and peacocks was often used in Early Christian funerary art to allude to the eschatological banquet which the Eucharist

---

49 Opera homiletica, CCSL 122, 17; Homilies on the Gospels, I 23.
50 Op. cit., CCSL 122, 29–39; Homilies on the Gospels, I 41.

anticipates, and it is used in the scene of Christ in the heavenly liturgy on f.32v at the end of the Matthean genealogy in the Book of Kells. At the end of the institution of the Eucharist during the Last Supper, Christ promised the faithful He would celebrate that heavenly banquet with them:

> I will not drink from henceforth of this fruit of the vine until that day when I shall drink it with you new in my Father's kingdom (Mt 26:29).

In the Book of Kells these words in Matthew's Gospel are immediately followed on the facing page, f.114r, by an inscribed whole-page picture of Christ with priestly orant gesture, flanked by two figures and by chalices and vines. Like the Temple picture on f.202v, the image of the High Priest within the sanctuary offers an allusive visual metaphor of the incarnate and mystical Body of Christ and the incorporation of the faithful in Him.[51] In liturgy and exegesis the three patriarchs whose names seem to be highlighted by the reclining figure with raised chalice on f.201v in the Lucan genealogy of Christ and his Church are specifically associated with the promised heavenly banquet of Mt 26.29 because they are named in Christ's prophecy:

> Many shall come from the east and the west and shall sit down (*recumbent*) with Abraham and Isaac and Jacob in the kingdom of heaven (Mt 8:11).

The names of the three patriarchs, in specific allusion to this text and the heavenly banquet, are cited in a Mass for the dead in the Stowe Missal.[52]

The exegetical connection between the texts of Mt 8:11 and Mt 26:29 had been fully developed in Origen's allegorical interpretation of the Old Covenant priesthood and sacrifice in his important homilies on Leviticus. He describes Christ at the Last Supper on the eve of his Passion as the High Priest entering the sanctuary who will not drink the fruit of the vine until his priestly task is accomplished, that is, until he has brought his whole creation to perfection. Origen explains that therefore even the apostles and saints have not yet received their joy and that the faithful patriarchs of the Old Testament have still not received the completion of the promise made to them since they will 'not be perfected without us' (Heb 11:40). When the perfection is accomplished, the High Priest will drink the new wine 'in a new heaven and a new earth' and will 'gather up all the faithful together 'to build up that holy

---

51 J. O'Reilly, 'The Book of Kells, folio 114r: a mystery revealed yet concealed' in: R.M. Spearman and J. Higgitt (eds.), The Age of Migrating Ideas, Edinburgh 1993, 112–113, fig. 12.1
52 F.E. Warren, The Liturgy and Ritual of the Celtic Church, Oxford 1881, 248.

body which is the Church'. He who is the head of the whole body 'does not want to receive his complete glory without us, that is, without his people who are his body and members. For he wants to dwell in this body of his Church'. This interpretation of Mt 26:29, Origen says, glosses the text, 'many shall come from the east and the west and shall sit down with Abraham and Isaac and Jacob in the kingdom of heaven' (Mt 8:11):

> Abraham is still waiting to receive his perfection. Isaac is waiting, Jacob and all the prophets are waiting for us, that with us they may receive their perfect happiness. Here is the reason why this mystery is kept till the Last Day . . . For it is one single body that awaits its perfection, one body that is promised a future resurrection: 'There are many members, yet one body' [1 Cor 12:20].[53]

The quotation is from the classic description in 1 Cor 12:4–27 of Christ and his Church in terms of a single body with many members:

> For in one Spirit were we all baptized into one body, whether Jews or Gentiles, whether bond or free: and in one Spirit we have all been made to drink (1 Cor 12:13).

In the context of the interpretation already suggested here for folios 201v–202v in the Book of Kells, the figure with raised chalice may allude to the expectation of the heavenly banquet when the new High Priest, his priestly task accomplished, enters the second sanctuary and gathers Abraham, Isaac, Jacob, the prophets, the saints and all the faithful into a single body. That drawing together of the faithful into the Body of Christ is visualized in the picture of the Temple immediately following Christ's genealogy.

Christ's priestly descent, spiritually interpreted, reveals Him as the successor of the Aaronic priesthood, the eternal priest 'after the order of Melchisedech'. The figure partly concealed by the decorative endpiece of this Old Testament lineage on f.202r, waiting behind the eucharistic vinescroll and chalice, occupies exactly the same position on the page as the haloed priestly figure placed at the door of the sanctuary in the Temple picture on the verso.

The Old Irish treatise on the Mass appended to the Stowe Missal relates stages of the eucharistic liturgy to the successive uncovering of the mystery of Christ through history. The stage from the Introit to the

---

53 Homily 7.2, as quoted by H. de Lubac, Catholicism, London 1950, 256; cf. G.W. Barkley (tr.), Origen. Homilies on Leviticus, Washington D.C. 1990, 137; C. Bammel, 'Insular mss. of Origen in the Carolingian empire' in G. Jondorf and D. Dumville (eds.) France and the British Isles in the Middle Ages and Renaissance, Woodbridge 1991, 5–16 notes the survival of two seventh-century mss. from Gaul of Rufinus's translation of the homilies of Leviticus. Homily 9 is cited in Cummian's letter De controversia paschali c.632 (note 19 supra) and the Lucan commentary of the Irish Reference Bible frequently cites 'Origenes dicit' (note 34 supra).

Epistle and Gradual is regarded as 'a figure of the law of nature, wherein Christ has been renewed through all his members and deeds'; from the Gradual to the uncovering of the chalice 'is a commemoration of the law of the letter wherein Christ has been figured, only that what has been figured therein was not yet known'; from the uncovering of the host and chalice to the oblation 'is a commemoration of the law of the prophets, wherein Christ was manifestly foretold, save that it was not seen until He was born'. The full uncovering and elevation of the chalice then commemorates the incarnation of Christ and his glory.[54]

THE NEW CHOSEN PEOPLE

The 'living stones' arranged in regular courses on either side of the priestly figure on f. 202v, are shown to be beneath the Temple, which may be seen as 'built upon the foundation of the apostles and prophets' (Eph 2:20). The body of this priestly figure descends right to the foundation of the building and joins the two groups of people who face inwards to him and hence to each other. In his commentary on the Lucan genealogy Ambrose twice quotes Eph 2:14–18 to show that Gentiles and Jews are reconciled by the incarnate crucified body of Christ and now form part of his body, the Church, pictured as 'a holy temple', 'a habitation of God in the Spirit', with Jesus Christ himself being the chief cornerstone (Eph 2:20–22; cf. 1 Pet 2:5–8).

Gentiles and Jews then form part of his Body, the Church, pictured as 'a holy temple', 'a habitation of God in the Spirit', with Jesus Christ himself being the chief cornerstone' (Eph 2:20–22, cf. 1 Pet 2:5–8).

The themes of priesthood, sacrifice and the Temple which are featured in patristic and insular exegesis on Luke's account of the Baptism and genealogy of Christ, and which seem reflected in the iconography of the genealogy in the Book of Kells, thus reach a climax in the picture of the Temple. The royal and priestly lineage of Christ, inherited when He took on human flesh ('the temple of His body') is revealed to be that of his Church also. His Old Testament earthly ancestors are the spiritual ancestors of all those who, in Baptism, share in Christ's anointing as prophet, priest and king and who, whether Jew or Gentile, are reborn as sons of God to form the new Chosen People. These themes are also gathered up in the chain of scriptural texts on the Temple image used in Ambrose's commentary on Luke's account of the Baptism. Most notably, 1 Pet 2.5:9–10 addresses the faithful both as 'living stones built up, as a spiritual house' *and* as 'a chosen people, a royal priesthood . . . who in time past were not a people but are now the people of God'.

Seventh-century Hiberno-Latin exegesis of the Catholic Epistles highlights a number of ways in which the text of 1 Peter 2:5–10 was relat-

54 G.F. Warner (ed.), The Stowe Missal, London 1915, 40.

ed to themes already noted here in connection with patristic and insular exegesis on the Baptism and genealogy of Christ. In the *Commentarium in Epistolas Catholicas Scotti Anonymi* the 'living stone rejected by men' but now chosen by God to be the chief cornerstone of the spiritual building (vv. 4–8) is identified with Christ whose divinity was proclaimed in the words of the Father: 'This is my beloved Son'. The faithful are admonished to be 'as living stones built up, a spiritual house, a holy priesthood, to offer up spiritual sacrifices acceptable to God' (v.5); the commentary notes that each of the faithful is a member of the Eternal Priest of whom it was said: 'Thou art a priest for ever [after the order of Melchisedech]'.[55] The *Tractatus Hilarii in Septem Epistolas Canonicas* glosses the acceptable 'spiritual sacrifices' of the holy priesthood of the faithful as the offering of hymns, psalms and prayers (Col 3:16), and directly contrasts them with the unacceptable blood sacrifice of a calf. In this commentary's gloss on the individual phrases in 1 Peter 2:9: 'You are a chosen people, a royal priesthood, a holy nation', themes from exegesis of the Baptism and Lucan genealogy again appear: *genus electum: in Abraham; regale sacerdotium: in Aaron; gens sancta: id est in baptismo.*[56] The importance of Baptism in the formation of this new People of God, pictured both as a single body and as a holy temple or habitation of God, is again stressed in the early Irish glosses on Ephesians 2. The phrase in v.16, 'he might reconcile both (Jews and gentiles) unto God in one body', is glossed: 'by bestowing the gifts of the Spirit on all'[57]

These biblical images of the formation of the new Chosen People of God through Baptism were applied by insular writers to their own society. The text from Mt 8:11, for example, *Venient ab oriente et occidente et recumbent cum Abraham et Isaac et Iacob in regno caelorum'*, is quoted by St Patrick in each of his pastoral letters where those coming from east and west to join the patriarchs and 'banquet with Christ' in the heavenly kingdom are clearly identified by Patrick with recent converts, anointed with chrism, 'a people newly coming to belief whom the Lord took from the uttermost parts of the earth as long ago He promised through his prophets'. Patrick shows that the prophecy of Hosea 1:10 has been fulfilled through Baptism and the outpouring of the Holy Spirit on them:

> Those who were not my people I will call 'my people'. And in the very place where it was said: 'You are not my people', they will be

---

55 R.E. McNally (ed.), Scriptores Hiberniae minores I, CCSL 108B, 31–33, dated c. 650–90, the Tractatus Hilarii to c. 690–708, Bede's commentary on the Catholic Epistles to c. 708–709.

56 Op. cit. 82, 32.

57 See n.48; the middle wall of partition (v.14) is glossed as sin, which was between God and man, between body and soul. The word 'temple' in Eph 1:21 is glossed as 'the assembly of the saints; they are called a temple because Christ dwells in them, that is, it is a habitation for God'.

placuuest mes filius meus dilectus mihi·
bene · complacuit mihi·

Ipse ihserat incipiens quasi ad
horum triginta, ut putabatur filius

ioseph ⊸

Vi fuit heli

Vi fuit mathat

Vi fuit leui

Vi fuit melchi

Vi fuit iarine

Vi fuit ioseph

Vi fuit mathat hie

Vi fuit amos

Vi fuit nauim

Vi fuit esli

Vi fuit nagge

Vi fuit maath

1. The Book of Kells, fol. 200r

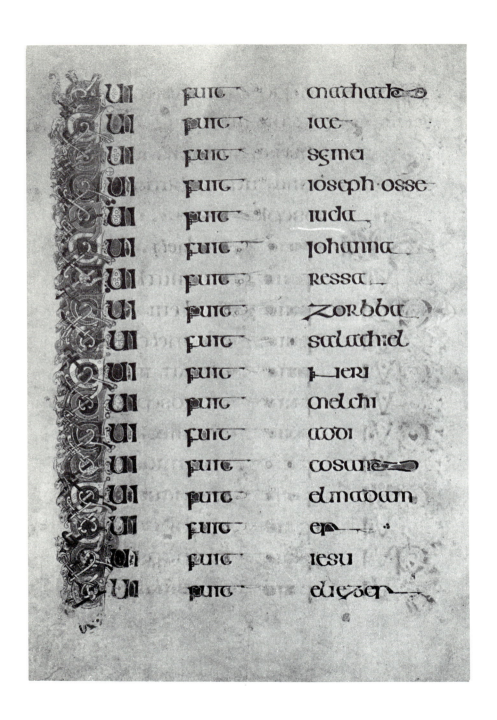

ui	fuit	mathate
ui	fuit	iae
ui	fuit	semei
ui	fuit	ioseph·osse
ui	fuit	iuda
ui	fuit	iohanna
ui	fuit	ressa
ui	fuit	zorbba
ui	fuit	salathiel
ui	fuit	ieri
ui	fuit	melchi
ui	fuit	addi
ui	fuit	cosun
ui	fuit	elmadam
ui	fuit	er
ui	fuit	iesu
ui	fuit	eliezer

2. The Book of Kells, fol. 200v

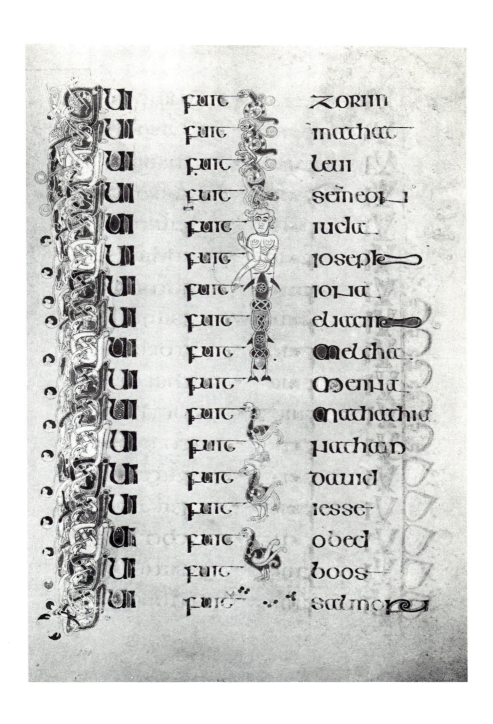

3. The Book of Kells, fol. 201r

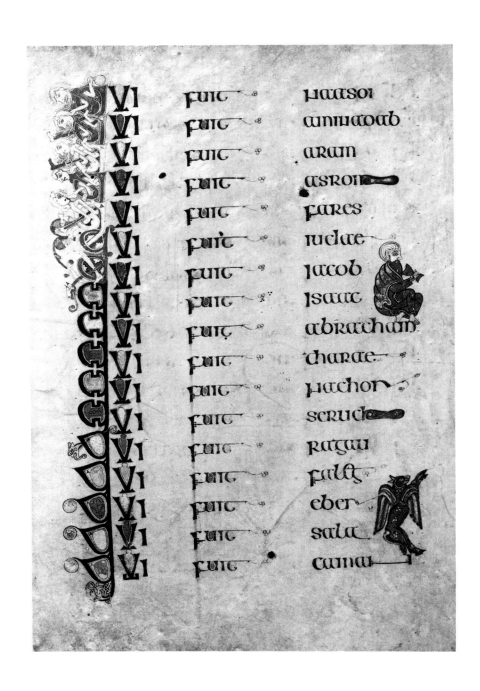

4. The Book of Kells, fol. 201v

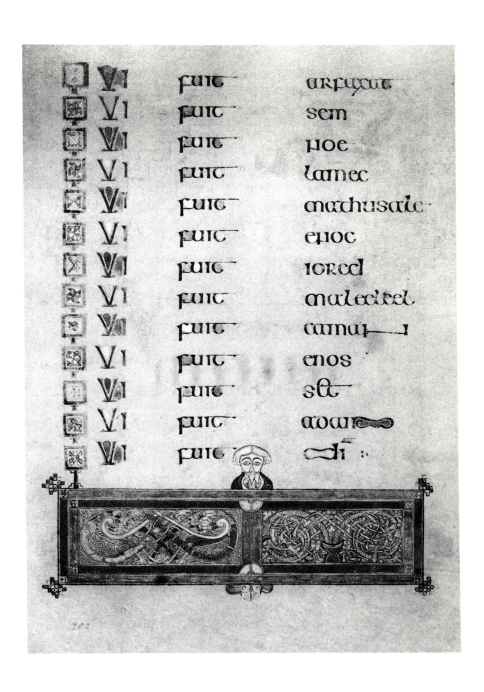

5. The Book of Kells, fol. 202r

6. The Book of Kells, fol. 202v

7. The Book of Kells, fol. 203

exponitur uescendi desiderio collocato &

quae rehabus fructus laboris & d̄n̄o magiste

rn doctrina seruetur

riae sacerdotii appa

ruit angelus & adnuntiauit ei filium ioha

nnem Eidem mariae adnuntiauit angelus

filium ihm toribus & uca

Natiuitatem ihu adnuntiat angelus pas

pit simeon puerum ihm & benedixit

dm & deanna professa bat

& annorum duodecim ihs intemplo doce

seniores asmum poenitez

Ubi iohannis baptizat populum bap

8. The Book of Kells, fol. 19v

called 'sons of the living God'. Consequently, then, in Ireland, they who never had knowledge of God . . . have lately been made a people of the Lord and called the children of God.[58]

The same Hosea text is cited in 1 Peter 1: 9–10 where the 'living stones' of the spiritual house, who are also a 'royal priesthood', are further identified as 'a holy nation, a chosen people . . . who in time past were not a people, but are now the people of God'.

Abraham, Isaac and Jacob, together with other patriarchs and the Old Testament prophets are related not only to the image of the Church as the body of Christ but to the other great New Testament image of the Church as a building or temple made up of the living stones of the faithful. The temple building image can refer variously to the Jewish Temple built in the city of Jerusalem in the Promised Land, which is a type or prefiguring of the Church, and also to the Temple in the heavenly Jerusalem described in Revelation. In some contexts it could be used interchangeably with the image of the heavenly city or paradisal promised land towards which the Church on earth is journeying in pilgrimage. The Epistle to the Hebrews describes Abraham, together with Isaac and Jacob as 'the co-heirs of the same promise', looking beyond their earthly inheritance 'for a city that has foundations whose builder and maker is God'; like other patriarchs and prophets they died 'according to the faith, not having received the promises but beholding them afar off' as pilgrims and strangers seeking a heavenly country: 'Therefore God . . . has prepared for them a city' (Heb 11: 10, 13–16). Bede, in his allegorical commentary on the Temple, shows that 'many of the patriarchs of the Old Testament attained such a peak of perfection . . . that they are not to be considered inferior to the Apostles'; although still separated from the mysteries of the Lord's Incarnation, nevertheless by their faith and preaching they were very near'. The patriarchs and prophets are accordingly visualized as part of the fabric of Solomon's Temple which is 'a figure of the holy universal Church'.[59]

The Epistle to the Ephesians shows that the Gentiles are reconciled in Christ to these chosen people of the Old Covenant, no more strangers and foreigners but 'fellow citizens and members of the household of God' (Eph 2:19). They are also visualized as forming part of the building fabric of the house or temple which represents the single community of the new People of God and is built upon the apostles *and* prophets. This image is animated by allusion to the Pauline image of the body as the temple or habitation of God so that the Church is seen as both building and body (Eph 2:20–22), as in the picture in the Book of Kells on f.202v.

58 D. Conneely, The Letters of Saint Patrick, Maynooth 1993, 71, 80.
59 De Templo, CCSL 119A, 161–162.

THE SECOND ADAM

In Luke's Gospel alone the line of earthly ancestors from whom Christ took his humanity is traced right back, beyond Abraham and the patriarchs, to Adam 'who was the son of God' (Lk 3:38). The genealogy ends with these words in the Book of Kells on f. 202r (pl. 5), and the image of the Temple appears on the following page (pl.6 and Frontispiece). Augustine's commentary on the image of 'the temple of his body' throws additional light on the appropriateness of the Temple image at this juncture of Luke's text. Augustine describes how Adam, who was both one man and the whole human race, was broken and scattered by sin but gathered together and renewed in Christ:

> because an Adam has come without sin that He might destroy Adam's sin in his flesh and that Adam might restore the image of God to himself. From Adam, therefore, is Christ's flesh; from Adam, therefore, is the temple which the Jews destroyed and the Lord raised up again in three days. For He raised up again his flesh . . . Our Lord Jesus Christ received his body from Adam, but did not take the sin of Adam—He took his bodily temple from him, not the iniquity which must be driven from the temple—but this flesh which He took from Adam . . . the Jews crucified. They destroyed the temple built in forty-six years and He raised it up in three days.[60]

The association of Adam and Christ with the image of the Temple had already been expressed in insular art. In an exegesis well known to Bede and to Hiberno-Latin commentators, Augustine noted that all peoples originate in Adam and that in the four letters of his name the four quarters of the earth are signified: the initial letters of the Greek words for east, west, north and south spell out the name of Adam.[61] The numerical values of the four letters of Adam's name add up to 46, the number of years it took to build the Temple in Jerusalem which Christ said he would raise up in three days (Jn 2:19–21). Cassiodorus had pictures of the Tabernacle and the Temple of Solomon in his *Codex Grandior* which Bede knew of, and referred to, in his own treatises on the Tabernacle and the Temple. In the *Codex Amiatinus* produced at Wearmouth-Jarrow, a large frontispiece diagram of the 'former Tabernacle' is inscribed with the names of the 12 tribes of Israel descended

60 In Iohannis evangelium tractatus, 124, CCSL 35, 108; J.W. Rettig (tr.), St Augustine, Tractates on the Gospel of John 1–10, Washington D.C. 1988, 222–224.

61 For Adam's name as a cosmic tetragrammaton in the Fathers, the Book of Enoch, Isidore's Etymologiae and in Hiberno-Latin exegesis, see R.E. McNally, 'The Evangelists in Hiberno-Latin Tradition' (see note 41 supra) 115–116.

from the sons of Jacob. Through the addition of a tiny cross over the Sanctuary entrance and the inscription of the Greek names of the four cardinal points which conceal the name of Adam and the number forty-six, the building also alludes to the Second Adam and the temple of his body which superseded the temple made with hands.[62]

In Ambrose's commentary on the Lucan Baptism it is precisely in the context of discussing Christ as the Second Adam from whose body on the Cross the Church was born, that he describes the Church by quoting from Eph 2, 1 Peter 2 and other texts in the biblical chain which picture the Church as the Body of Christ through the image of the Temple building. Ambrose notes that the name of Adam comes at the end of the Lucan genealogy, thus one made in the image of God (Gen 1:27) comes before his descendant who was the image of God. Adam, the created son of God, is 'a figure of Him to come' (Rom 5:14), that is the Son of God.[63]

The Pauline image of the individual member of the Church as the temple of God (1 Cor 3:17, 6:9; 2 Cor 6:16) is part of the very language of the baptismal rite where the sin of Adam is renounced and the devil expelled.[64] A long exegetical and catechetical tradition stressed the need for the baptized who have renounced the Old Adam and become sons of God to remain vigilant, under Christ, against the continuing assaults of the devil. This is prefigured in the Second Adam's own temptation by the devil in the desert and recalled in the Church's liturgy at the beginning of Lent. The tradition helps illumine the Kells picture of the Temple and its facing text, which are followed by the account of Christ's Temptation. The double opening may be read as showing the baptized Christian or the whole Church 'full of the Holy Spirit' and defended by Christ from the devil.

62 J.J.G. Alexander, Insular Manuscripts 6th to the 9th Century, London 1978, cat. 7, pl.23. For the uses of the Temple symbolism of 46 in Augustine and Bede, see W. Berschin 'Opus deliberatum perfectum: Why did the Venerable Bede write a second prose Life of St Cuthbert?' in: G. Bonner, D. Rollason, C. Stancliffe (eds.), St. Cuthbert, his Cult and Community to A.D. 1200, Woodbridge 1989, 95–102. For the Codex Amiatinus diagram see A.G. Holder (tr.), Bede, On the Tabernacle, Liverpool 1994, 92, n. 1 and frontispiece.

63 *CCSL* 14, 103–104.

64 Stowe Missal, F.E. Warren, The Liturgy and Ritual of the Celtic Church, Oxford 1881, 207, 210, 213; cf. Gallican sacramentary ordo for Easter Saturday Baptism with provision for exorcism of *omnes exercitus diaboli . . . ut fiat templum Dei sanctum,* J.M. Neale and G.H. Forbes (eds.), The Ancient Liturgies of the Gallican Church, Burntisland 1855, 269.

THE TEMPTATION

George Henderson has stressed the importance of the expulsion of the devil by Baptism for an understanding of the picture and has captured the sense of the pivotal positioning of the picture of the Second Adam in Luke's text:

> The Book of Kells picture, dominated by Christ in his Church, surrounded by his redeemed people, glorified by angels, easily confuting the black tempter, tackles the contents of the Gospel chapters before and after and gives full weight to the words displayed on the facing recto.[65]

Most modern scholars, however, have seen the picture on f.202v in the Book of Kells in isolation from the texts which precede it and have identified it as the Temptation of Christ. Carol Farr believes that the Kells picture 'almost undoubtedly depicts the Temptation on the Temple roof', although she transforms the traditional reading of the picture as a narrative illustration by viewing it in the context of Lenten liturgical themes and through exegesis of the Gospel account of the Temptation and of the Old Testament texts which it cites, particularly Ps 90.[66] Dr Farr shows how, in the Tyconian tradition of reading Ps 90 in terms of the figure of 'Christ the Head and his Body the Church', Augustine's commentary on the Psalm relates it not only to the Temptation of Christ but to the continuing temptation and ultimate triumph of his Church which, it is argued, is the theme of the picture in Kells. In this argument's detailed review of the familiarity in insular monastic culture of patristic exegesis on the image of the Church as the Body of Christ and on the related New Testament image of the Church as a spiritual building prefigured in the Tabernacle and the Temple of Jerusalem, there is much that is complementary to the interpretation of the picture suggested in the present discussion. Dr Farr herself points to several remaining enigmas, however, if the picture is seen primarily as a symbolic exposition of the Temptation narrative.

First, there is the question of why the Temptation should have received the extraordinarily elevated decorative status of a whole-page picture facing a framed display text. The placing of pictures within the

65 G.D.S. Henderson, Bede and the Visual Arts, Jarrow Lecture 1980, 17–18; From Durrow to Kells. The Insular Gospel Books 650–800, London 1987, 168–174: 'The emphasis in the Stowe Missal on the expulsion of the devil by baptism is sufficient in itself to explain the iconography of the Kells picture. It subsumes Christ's "Temptation" in the general victory offered by Christ to mankind', 174.

66 C.A. Farr, Lection and interpretation: the liturgical and exegetical background of the illustrations in the book of Kells (unpublished Ph.D. thesis, University of Texas at Austin 1989), 20, 74–112.

Gospel text (rather than at its opening or in the prefatory pages of the codex) is exceedingly rare in surviving early medieval Gospel books. Kells has two such pictures and, arguably, f.124r was reserved for a third which was not executed. F.124r faces an elaborate framed display text of Mt 27:38 from the account of the Crucifixion and the picture on f.114r, which has a framed display text on its verso, is also placed in a position of great theological importance, at Mt 26:30, after Christ's institution of the Eucharist at the Last Supper and before the account of the Passion.

Secondly, not only does Kells lavish apparently disproportionate decorative attention on the Temptation but chooses to do so in the context of Luke's Gospel rather than Matthew's, which was the version of the story read on the first Sunday in Lent in most known early lectionary systems. Nor is Kells entirely idiosyncratic in this respect. The opening of Lk: 4:1 which faces the Kells picture is also decoratively highlighted, though on a much more modest scale, in a number of other insular Gospel books. Dr Farr concludes that the Lucan version of the Temptation narrative was probably used as a lection for Quadragesima in some lost non-Roman liturgy.[67] While this may well be so and would have important implications for understanding the function of the image in the book and in the life of the community in which it was used, it is obviously difficult to demonstrate, as so little insular liturgical material remains and because the decorative structuring of texts in insular Gospel books seems to have served a variety of functions, not only liturgical.

Thirdly, the three Temptations of Christ are recounted in Mt 4:1–11 and Lk 4:1–13, but in Luke's version the Temple incident is the last of the three Temptations: it does not appear in the text of the Book of Kells, therefore, until f.204r, which is three folios after the Temple picture. Nor is the particular importance of the third Temptation (Lk 4:9–12) signified in the layout and decoration of its text on f.204r, in marked contrast to the embellishment of the opening of Lk 4:1 which actually faces the picture.

Finally, if the Temple picture on f.202v is seen as only referring forward, to the text of the Temptation, and if the decoration of Lk 4:1 on f.203r is explained as a structural break from the preceding text of the genealogy, it is difficult to explain why the picture is positioned *between* the end of the genealogy and the beginning of Lk 4.1 (pl. 5: Frontispiece, pl. 6).

In the present discussion it has been suggested that the layout and decoration of the Lucan genealogy and the Temple picture in the Book of Kells are related and that they are responsive to the theological significance of the Gospel text as perceived in patristic and insular exegesis. Ambrose devoted the whole of Book III of his commentary on Luke to

67 Op. cit., 141–161.

the text of the genealogy alone: the exegetical tradition of reading Scripture did not regard the list of Christ's ancestors as an awkward editorial intrusion into Luke's narrative of the Baptism and Temptation but as an integral part of an important statement about the identity of Christ and the collective personality of his Church. It is worth recalling at this point that commentators stress that Luke's juxtaposition of Baptism and genealogy sets out Christ's divine Sonship as well as his earthly ancestry, and that the indwelling or invisible anointing of the Holy Spirit begun at the incarnation was manifested on the eve of his public ministry when, at his Baptism in the Jordan, the Holy Spirit descended as a dove and the Father proclaimed 'You are my beloved Son' (Lk 3:22). The last verse of the Lucan genealogy again reveals Him to be 'the son of Adam, who was the son of God' (Lk 3:38), and the very next words of Luke's text specifically recall the Baptism before setting the scene for the Temptation: 'And Jesus full of the Holy Spirit returned from Jordan and was led by the Spirit into the desert' (Lk 4:1). Matthew's version, which continues directly from his account of the Baptism with no intervening genealogy, simply says, 'Then Jesus was led by the Spirit into the desert to be tempted by the devil' (Mt 4:1). Bede notes the difference in his Lucan commentary.

In the Temptation which immediately follows, the devil finally taunts Jesus to prove his divine Sonship ('If thou be the son of God . . .') by casting Himself from the top of the Temple and literally fulfilling the Messianic prophecy of Ps 90: 11–12. After the Temptation (Lk 4:2 2–13) Jesus returns to Galilee 'in the power of the Spirit' (4:14) and in the synagogue at Nazareth publicly reads from the Messianic prophecy of Isaiah 61:1–2: 'The Spirit of the Lord is upon me. Wherefore he has anointed me . . . to preach deliverance to the captives . . .', a prophecy Jesus claims has been fulfilled in Himself (4:18–21). Those present fail, like the devil, to 'see' who He is and demand 'Is this not the son of Joseph?' (4:22), which vividly recalls Luke's introduction to the genealogy: 'Jesus . . . being, as was supposed, the son of Joseph' (3:12). The irony continues, as only the devil or unclean spirit of a person possessed recognizes who Jesus is and acclaims Him: 'I know thee who thou art, the holy one of God' (4:34); other devils finally acknowledge his divine identity: '"Thou art the Son of God" . . . they knew he was the Christ' (4:41). An eighth-century Hiberno-Latin commentary on Luke illustrates contemporary interest in connections within the passage. It shows the fulfilment of the prophecy: 'The Spirit of the Lord is upon me' in the descent of the Spirit at the Incarnation and Baptism in the Jordan, and it notes that Isaiah's prophecy of 'deliverance to the captives' refers to the redemption of all people captive in Adam to the devil. The question, 'Is this not Joseph's son?' is directly linked with the taunt of the devil at the Temptation, 'If you are the Son (of God) . . .'[68] The sequence in Luke demonstrates the fulfilment of the prophecies of Ps 90 and Is 61: 1–2, but the largest prophecy is the genealogy itself which shows Jesus prefigured throughout the history of his people going back to the patriarchs before the Law, and indeed the whole of human history back to Adam.

THE SACRED MONOGRAM

The isolation of just the opening words of Lk 4:1 'Jesus full of the Holy Spirit' on f.203r in Kells would seem, therefore, not simply to be marking the reopening of the narrative after the genealogy but to be identifying the great theme of this whole sequence of Luke's text which reveals that Jesus of Nazareth is also Son of God, hence the picture of his human body 'full of the Holy Spirit'. Several insular Gospel books highlight this verse by the enlargement or other embellishment of the opening initial, word or line, but in Kells alone the opening words, *I[e]s[u]s autem plenus Sp[iritu]s S[an]c[t]o*, though written in abbreviated form, are enlarged to fill the whole page and are elaborately framed and veiled with ornament which elevates the text to the level of a Gospel incipit (pl. 7). The first two letters of Jesus' abbreviated name dominate the upper half of the page. The decoration of the *nomen sacrum* Ihs meaning Saviour, and the epithet 'full of the Holy Spirit' at the end of the Lucan genealogy may be seen as a counterpart to the treatment of his Greek title Christ (meaning the Anointed One) in the *chi-rho* monogram at the culmination of the genealogy in Matthew.

The Reference Bible's commentary on Matthew's genealogy reflects the Hiberno-Latin practice of showing how the two names Jesus and Christ and the two Gospel genealogies together reveal Him as human and divine, the Davidic Messiah and the Son of God, as king and priest. The very differences in the ancestral names, the number of generations and the direction of tracing descent in the two Gospel versions of Christ's genealogy help explain why they received such a burden of exposition to show that, properly read, they were in fact complementary revelations of the same truth. The mysterious latent power of names, genealogies and epithets to reveal identity was an important feature of patristic exegesis which touched a vital chord for insular and especially Hiberno-Latin commentators and received eloquent expression in the Book of Kells. The convention of writing the Greek title Christ and the Greek version of the name Jesus in Romanized versions of their initial letters with Latin endings offers some kind of cryptic calligraphic parallel to the common exegetical practice of expounding the significance of

---

68 CCSL 108C, 36, also 29 for the relation of Lk 4:1 to the theme of Baptism: the phrase *regressus est a Iordane* is associated with the four rivers of Eden rising from a single fount.

a name or title through its etymology and its Greek or even Hebrew equivalent. The primary function of the Xpi monogram on f.34r and of the Ihs monogram on f.203r in Kells was patently not as an aid to reading aloud. The splendour of the page and the difficulty of deciphering the veiled letter forms of its literal text compel the reader to pause and ponder the significance of the sacred names.

Remarkable though f. 203r is, the modern reader may feel it is less magnificent in conception than the *Chi-rho* design and is lacking in the kind of exegesis hidden on f. 34r in the embellishment of the name of Christ.[69] Among the display pages in the Book of Kells, f. 203r is unique in preserving the panelled vertical shafts of the first two combined letters, the 'I' and 'h' of the name of Jesus, as discrete elements, rather in the manner of earlier insular Gospel book incipits. A further unique feature is the curiously exotic six-lobed pierced ornament within the bowl of the 'h', the number six emphasised a second and a third time by concentric rings of dotting within the lobes, which in turn are encircled by three concentric circles of colour interspersed by decorative bands and with rectangular mounts marking off the outer band at three of its cardinal points. This abstract circular shape within the sacred name is, like the golden rhombus at the centre of the letter *chi* on f. 34r, the focal point of the design (pl. 7).

On the folio facing the Ihs monogram, the side panels of the Temple picture's frame have been rendered as stylised columns filled with golden ornament and with crosses in the place of bases and capitals, a device used for the capitals of the two columns supporting the arch over Christ in f. 114r. In the exegetical context in which the Temple picture has been located, the columnar frame may also be read as alluding to the two bronze pillars erected either side of the Temple entrance by Solomon (2 Chron 3:5). Bede has a detailed interpretation of this verse and of the multiple underlying meanings of the columns which can refer to the apostles and spiritual teachers who are pillars of the church (cf. Gal 2:9) and bulwarks of truth (cf. 1 Tim 3:15), and particularly to their drawing together both Jews and Gentiles, through Baptism, into the Church. The 'mystery of the material pillars' at the entrance to the Temple is also a reminder that 'both in prosperity and adversity we must keep the entrance to our heavenly homeland firmly before the eyes of our mind'. The great height of the pillars fittingly alludes to the spiritual ascent of the elect, 'that they may merit to see their Creator face to face, for they will have nothing further to seek when they reach Him who is above all things'. The capitals of the pillars in the Kells picture are on a level with the head of Christ and with the upper row of little figures ascending towards Him. Finally

69 S. Lewis, 'Sacred calligraphy: the chi-rho page in the Book of Kells' (note 2 supra) 140–151.

Bede reveals 'the more profound sense' of the two pillars when he discerns in the scriptural account of their dimensions an established sacred numerology, for concealed in the eighteen cubits of their height is the name of Jesus. Not only is eighteen the multiple of three and six, which carry their usual associations with the Trinity and the six days of creation, but 'the name of Jesus begins from this number among the Greeks. With them the first letter of this name means ten and the second eight'.[70] The column-like shafts of the first two letters of Jesus' name on f. 203r and the incorporation of the repeated motifs of three and six in the decoration of the letter 'h' may, therefore, conceal an arcane exegesis of the sacred name, identifying Jesus with the Temple and further linking word and image.

THE LANGUAGE OF PARADOX

Similarly, the striking ambiguities of the mixed visual metaphor on f. 202v facing the name of Jesus in the Book of Kells can yield a spiritual insight. The picture adopts a familiar exegetical technique in telescoping the New Testament image of the Temple with that of the body (1 Cor 12:12–27; Eph 4:15–16; Col 1:18) so that the Temple, which can denote the incarnate body of Christ is also revealed as representing the mystical Body of Christ, with Christ as its head, its members forming the 'living stones' of a curiously organic building which grows up into a Temple of the Lord (cf. 1 Pet 2:5–6; Eph 2:21).

Some of the features that may still puzzle us in the Kells picture also exercised the Fathers commenting on the texts which ultimately underlie this extraordinary image, because the scriptural chains themselves, read at a literal level, are often self-contradictory, irrational or bizarre. Augustine, for example, in his commentary on Ps 86, raises the question of how the Temple of God can be 'built upon the foundation of the apostles and the prophets' (Eph 2:20) when it was also written that 'other foundation no man can lay but that which is laid: which is Jesus Christ' (1 Cor 3:11)? Augustine replies with another paradox: the apostles and prophets are foundations in the sense that they sustain our weakness (lesser 'living stones' in the fabric of the building), but Christ is the foundation of all foundations, the pillar of pillars in this building. Both scriptural statements are spiritually true though literally incompatible. The small priestly haloed figure in the Kells picture, whose head is in the sanctuary but whose pillar-like body penetrates to the very foundation of the building which may also be read as being built upon the apostles and prophets, may be a pictorial equivalent of the exegetical attempt to resolve this paradox. Augustine also asks how Christ can be

70 CCSL 119A, 199. This interpretation of 18 is common in exegesis of Gen 14:14.

both the foundation and the keystone of this building, both at the base
and the top? He explains that, unlike bodies which have spatial limitations, 'the divinity is present in all places and the likeness of all things
can be applied to it, though in reality it is none of these things'. On the
contrary, all things have their reality in Christ. Augustine finds no incon-
gruity therefore, in the idea that 'just as the foundation of an earthly
building is at the base, so the foundation of the heavenly building is at
the top, in heaven'.[71] Rightly understood in *lectio divina* this building is
complemented, not contradicted, by the corporeal image of the Church
as the pilgrim body still on earth, its Head in heaven. Similarly, the large
portrait bust of Christ in the Kells picture may be read as both the head
of the body and as the cornerstone or keystone of the building.[72]

Such apparent contradictions and obscurities in Scripture were regarded as pointing to a hidden significance and attracted the particular
interest of exegetes. Augustine provides a second example of relevance in
considering the Kells Temple picture and its role in the larger decorative
unit formed by ff. 200r–203r. In the synoptic Gospels the disbelieving Jews
ask for a sign of Jesus' identity. He replies, 'A sign shall not be given [this
generation] but the sign of Jonah the prophet' (Mt 12:39, Lk 11:29).
However, in John's Gospel he does give another sign 'Destroy this temple
and in three days I will raise it up'(Jn 2:19). Augustine was drawn to
reconcile the two apparently contradictory signs given by Jesus, Jonah and
the Temple, in the significant context of explaining the spiritual blindness of those who failed to see the hidden God, the Lord of glory, in the
crucified and risen body of Jesus. He quotes Matthew's story of the sign of
Jonah and then says, Jesus also spoke 'through another similitude of this
same sign', and he quotes John's story of the Temple of Jesus' body: 'His
flesh was the Temple of the divinity hidden within. Whence the Jews
outwardly saw the Temple, the Deity dwelling within they saw not'.[73]

71   Augustine, Enarrationes in psalmos, 51–100, CCSL 39, 1198–1203.
72   G. Ladner, 'The symbolism of the biblical cornerstone in the medieval West'
     in Images and Ideas in the Middle Ages. Selected Studies in History and Art
     I, Rome 1983, 171–196, notes that the *lapis angularis* of Ps 117:96 (cited in
     the synoptic Gospels, Acts 4:11 and 1 Pet 2:7) is usually combined with Is
     28:16 and interpreted not exclusively as a coping stone but as a cornerstone
     or foundation stone (173). The *caput anguli* image was identified with Christ
     as head of of the Church in the body metaphor used in Eph 4:15 (194). C.
     Nordenfalk, 'Another look at the Book of Kells' (note 3 supra) suggests the
     possible influence on the Kells picture of an illustrated copy of Prudentius'
     Dittochaeum where 'the stone which the builders rejected' is raised to the
     top of the Temple in Jerusalem: 'Now it is the head of the Temple and holds
     the new stones together'. This may also explain the two Ottonian repre-
     sentations of the Temptation which, like Kells, show Christ as a half-length
     figure at the top of the Temple.
73   Enarrationes in psalmos, 51–100, CCSL 39, 843–845.

Reasons have already been considered here for supposing that the fish-man figure in the Lucan genealogy in the Book of Kells, f. 201, may well be an allusion to the prophet Jonah and to the meaning of his Latin name, *columba*, and signify that Jonah's established association with the sacramental sharing of Christ's death and resurrection in Baptism is particularly fitting in the context. It has been noted that the descent of the Holy Spirit as a dove at Christ's Baptism immediately preceding the genealogy signifies the descent of the seven-fold gifts of the Spirit into His body the Church. The individual soul thus becomes a dove (a *columba* or a Jonah) at baptism, that is, a vessel or habitation of the Holy Spirit, like Christ. Both Jonah and the Temple are signs given by Christ Himself in response to demands for proof of His divine power, yet in the Gospels both are explicitly interpreted as referring to his incarnate, crucified and risen body. In exegesis both the dove and the Temple are habitations of the Holy Spirit, both can be used as images of the individual Christian, both can also represent the unity of the whole Church, both are particularly associated with Baptism and with the spiritual life of the baptized.

The underlying spiritual similarity of dove and Temple is obscured by their manifest material differences. But it was precisely the puzzling decision of the Holy Spirit to descend in so small and simple a creature as a dove which prompted exegetical ingenuity in penetrating beneath the literal letter of scriptural passages about doves and finding that, spiritually interpreted, they revealed the dove to be a particularly appropriate vessel or habitation of the Holy Spirit. Ambrose raises this very question in his commentary on Christ's Baptism in Luke's Gospel, the same context in which he also explores the multiple allusions of the image of the Temple. Moreover, he directly compares the corporeal appearance of the Holy Spirit as a dove at Christ's Baptism with the invisible presence of God in the Temple.[74] In the Book of Kells the evident differences between the diverting 'Jonah' figure with six birds enlivening the column of Hebrew names on f. 201r, and the solemn whole-page picture of the Temple on f. 202v obscure the fact that they distinctively point to the same truth. They function as metaphysical conceits and, placed within the same decorative sequence in the Gospel text, can illuminate each other, like scriptural texts in an exegetical chain.

The Gentile Ninevites saved by Jonah's mission are often paradoxically identified with the Jews to whom Christ brought the means of deliverance from sin, enabling them to enter the Church through repentance and baptism. Christ's reference to Jonah occurs in both Matthew 12:39–45 and Luke 11:24–32 in the context of an exorcism and of Christ's teaching about an exorcized man who is repossessed by seven

---

74 CCSL 14, 72–4. M. Lapidge, 'Columbanus and the Antiphonary of Bangor' (note 18 supra) 108, n.18.

unclean spirits or devils and becomes their dwelling-place. Ambrose, in his commentary on Luke's Gospel, sees the seven devils as signifying the spiritually arid life of the unrepentant Jews, still living under the Law, contrasted with the seven-fold grace of the Holy Spirit which fills the baptized. In Bede's homily 1.12 already referred to, this Gospel passage is integrated into the time-honoured chain of texts linking Christ's Baptism and the sacrament of Baptism, the importance of the dove and the seven gifts of the Holy Spirit. By fasting in the desert after the descent of the dove at his baptism, Christ showed by example 'that after we have received the forgiveness of sins in Baptism, we should devote ourselves to vigils, fasts, prayers and other spiritually fruitful things, lest . . . the unclean spirit which had been expelled from our heart by Baptism may return and, finding us fruitless in spiritual riches, may weigh us down with a seven-fold pestilence and our last state be worse than our first.' Accordingly, Bede admonishes his readers to study and follow the example of the dove whose seven-fold nature described in the Song of Songs presents seven examples of virtue as 'the grace of the Holy spirit, who descended as a dove, is seven-fold'.[75] The story of the seven devils attached to the Gospel citations of Jonah is thus applied in some detail to the spiritual life of the baptized, who are continually threatened by the devil and continue to need the operation of the seven gifts of the Holy Spirit received in their post-baptismal anointing. How to remain a fitting habitation or temple of the Holy Spirit is, therefore, the purpose of the post-baptismal life. The Book of Kells' depiction of the devil driven from the bodily temple of Jesus' humanity simultaneously reveals Jesus' identity, 'full of the Holy Spirit', and the vocation of the baptized who are called to a life-long process of 'conversion' to become like Him (pl. 5: Frontispiece and pl. 6).

The theme has a particular importance for the *monastic* life which simply seeks more fully the perfecting of the seven gifts of the Holy Spirit granted to all the baptized. The eighth-century Hiberno-Latin commentary on Luke's Gospel which glosses the phrase in Lk 4:1, *Iesus autem plenus Spiritu sancto* as *id est, septem dona Spiritu[s] sancti habens, et de hac plenitudine . . . eius nos omnes accipimus,* sees the same verse's reference to Christ returning from the Jordan and going into the desert as a model for the monastic life: *Et hanc deserti regulam sancti monachi seque- bantur.* The devil in this desert, who once tempted and overcame Adam, will overcome the man who is earthly but will be overcome by the heavenly man; it is good, therefore, to flee the crowds of vices and seek the secrets of perfection.[76]

75   CCSL 122, 83–86.
76   CCSL 108C, 28–30.

IMAGES OF TABERNACLE, TEMPLE AND THE HEAVENLY JERUSALEM

If the illustrations in the Book of Kells were partly inspired by exegesis of the Gospel text and incorporate pictorial adaptations of rhetorical techniques, then the objectives of exegesis may offer some guide to the composition and function of the images. By this criterion, it seems unlikely that the picture of the Temple on f. 202v was intended as a static and didactic representation of theological or ecclesiological truths, or that it was intended to be read, in a manner more suited to some later medieval works, as an onion-layered series of fixed meanings denoting successively the body of Christ, of the individual faithful and of the Church. Patristic exegesis, in contrast, is concerned to show the *simultaneity* of such truths as aspects of a single truth and to show the continuing significance of the spiritual interpretation of the literal text for the present reader who is provided with images for *meditatio* and *imitatio*. The objective, using the image of the Temple, is nowhere more fully and clearly demonstrated than in the commentaries and homilies of Bede and especially in *De tabernaculo* and *De templo*, which are detailed allegorical commentaries on Exodus 24:12 – 30:21 and on 3 Kings 5:1 – 7:51 respectively.

Bede distinguishes between the temporary Tabernacle built by Moses in the desert, 'on the route by which one reaches the land of promise', and the Temple built by Solomon in the land of promise itself in the royal city of Jerusalem 'on an ever inviolable foundation until it fulfilled the task of the heavenly figures imposed upon it. For these reasons the former can be taken to represent the toil and exile of the present Church, the latter the rest and happiness of the future Church'.[77] Tabernacle and Temple cannot simply be equated with the Church on earth and in heaven respectively, however. Because the Tabernacle was made by the people of Israel alone it 'can be chiefly taken as a symbolic expression for the Fathers of the Old Testament and the ancient people of God'. The Temple of Solomon was also built long before the Incarnation but, because Solomon used the servants of Hiram king of Tyre in its construction, it may be seen as representing 'the Church assembled from the Gentiles', that is the new Chosen People. *Both* these Old Testament sanctuaries, however, when spiritually interpreted,

> can be shown in many ways to suggest symbolically both the daily labours of the present Church and the everlasting rewards and joys in the future and the salvation of all nations in Christ.[78]

The literal text of the Old Testament's detailed description of the construction, layout, dimensions, ornaments and furnishings of Taber-nacle and Temple therefore provides a rhetorical figure in which the nature of Christ and of his Church, past, present and to come, are delineated and

77 De Templo, CCSL 119A, 147–148.
78 Ibid., 148.

the reader finds a model of the spiritual life. The process of reading the figure to reveal this underlying significance is conducted and validated through reference to other scriptural texts.

The key links in the chains are set out in the opening section of Book One of *De Templo*. The house of God built by Solomon 'as a figure of the holy universal Church' refers both to Christ who said of the temple of his body, 'Destroy this temple and in three days I will raise it up' (Jn 2: 19–21), and to the faithful who are 'the temple of God' (1 Cor 3:16):

> If, therefore, He became the temple of God by assuming human nature and we became the temple of God through his Spirit dwelling in us [Rom 8:11], it is quite clear that the material Temple [of Solomon] was a figure of us all, that is both of the Lord Himself and his members which we are . . . of Him as the uniquely chosen and precious cornerstone laid in the foundation [Is 28:16] and of us as the living stones built upon the foundations of the apostles and prophets, that is, on the Lord Himself [Eph 2:20; 1 Pet 2:5–6].[79]

The texts Bede uses here to expound the Old Testament description of the Temple as a figure referring simultaneously to Christ's incarnate body, to the individual faithful and to the community of the new Chosen People, the Church, on earth and in heaven, are paralleled in Ambrose's much earlier use of the same array of texts to expound the figure of the Old Testament Temple used by Luke in the opening chapters of his Gospel.

Exegesis elaborated the importance of Tabernacle and Temple in Scripture as representing the whole complex relationship of the Old Covenant and the New, historically distinct, antithetical and yet mystically united. The more restrictive medium of pictorial art produced architecturally ambiguous representations of a single building which, through cryptic inscriptions or the larger context in which the image was positioned, could be read as referring simultaneously to Tabernacle, Temple and the heavenly Jerusalem. While the physical appearance of the single house-shaped structure on f. 202v in the Book of Kells does not seem to have been significantly influenced by the Old Testament descriptions of the fabric of Tabernacle and Temple, nevertheless it may reflect their treatment in the New Testament which strongly suggests their interrelatedness, their combined role in the whole history of salvation, and the sense that they are both but the copies or shadows of a heavenly reality (Heb 8:5, 10:1).

Descriptions of the heavenly Jerusalem in the Book of Revelation consciously evoke both Tabernacle and Temple.[80] The vision of the power

79 Ibid., 147.
80 B. Kühnel, 'Jewish symbolism of the Temple and the Tabernacle and Christian symbolism of the Holy Sepulchre and the heavenly Tabernacle' in Jewish Art 12/13 (1986–87) 147–168, 152.

of God filling the heavenly Temple (Rev 15: 5,8) recalls scenes of God taking possession of his Tabernacle in the desert (Ex 40:34–35) and of his Temple in Jerusalem (3 Kg 8:10–11; Is 6:4). The eschatological vision of the new Jerusalem in 'a new heaven and a new earth' is announced: 'Behold the tabernacle of God with men: and He will dwell with them. And they shall be his people' (Rev 21:3). Thus all three sanctuaries—the Tabernacle, the Temple and the heavenly Jerusalem (variously described as Temple or city)—represent the place where God dwells with his people.

RECAPITULATION

At the Incarnation the human body of Jesus became the new place of the divine presence. This is expressed in John's Gospel which compares Jesus with the Temple building in Jerusalem and presents Him as the new Temple. In Luke's Gospel the concept is expressed through his long introduction to the account of the Incarnation by the theme of the Old Covenant priesthood and Temple which Jesus came both to fulfil and to replace. Ambrose's development of Luke's own image and his use of the techniques of the Epistle to the Hebrews in comparing Christ with 'the tabernacle made with hands' explicitly incorporates John's image of 'the temple of his body'. Ambrose's continued use of the Temple theme in his exegesis of Luke's account of Christ's Baptism and priestly genealogy reveals the significance of the Incarnation by showing Jesus of Nazareth to be Son of God and 'full of the Holy Spirit', a concept which, it has been suggested here, is expressed by the Temple picture and its facing text in the Book of Kells showing the human body of Jesus as the Temple, 'full of the Holy Spirit'. The other readings of the Temple image which its context in the Book of Kells suggests—its allusion to the individual baptized and to the new Chosen People—explore the implications of the central theme and so lead to a renewed and more profound understanding of 'the body of Christ' as the incorporation of the faithful into the sacramental and mystical Body of Christ which transcends time and encompasses the Tabernacle, the Temple, the Church on earth and the heavenly sanctuary.*

* Sections omitted here explore the significance of the priestly figure shown within the Temple image, the idea of the Ark as a synecdochal representation of the Temple and compare the Book of Kells' use of scriptural metaphors of living stones, pillars, corner-stone etc. with their depiction in Anglo-Saxon mss. Finally, some of the scriptural and exegetical themes discussed in the paper are closely related to accounts of insular monastic life and Columban spirituality to suggest that a monastic reader familiar with Scripture through the liturgy and *lectio divina* might find in the Kells Temple picture both an image of the divine dwelling-place and an aid to meditation on the divine indwelling.

Index of Biblical References

The following are biblical references that appear in the text with the exception of those for Appendix A of 'The Irish Augustine's Knowledge and Understanding of Scripture' by Gerard MacGinty.

Index of Names

Abraham, 9–10, 11, 51n; allegory of two wives, 13–14, 17, 21; in Book of Kells, 334–6; in Philo, 39, 46
Acacius of Caesarea, 92, 98, 104, 112n
Ackroyd, P.R., 3n, 4n, 290n
Adam; First Adam – Second Adam, 148–52; sin of, 135–8, 140
Adiabene, 143n
Adomnán, 236, 249, 253, 263–4; Life of Columba, 318, 319, 323, 325
Adriaen, M., 260n
Adrianus, 245n
Agaësse, P., 201
Aileran Sapiens, 253
Alcinous, 67
Alexander, J.J.G., 343n
Alexander of Alexandria, 93n
Alexander the Great, 79
Alexandria, 4, 51, 52, 55, 79, 88, 89, 101, 114n, 143; Philo in, 41–3; predecessors of Philo, 43–6; synod of, 91; textual criticism, 80
Allen, H. T., Jr, 29n
Altaner, B., 221n
Alter, R., 198n
Ambrose, St, 223, 227n, 322; influence on Augustine, 1–2, 59, 83–4, 171, 182n, 204; Lucan commentary, 324–5, 327, 329–32, 334, 339, 343, 345–6, 351–2; Philo in, 58–9; senses of Scripture, 21
Ambrosiaster, 14
Amir, Y., 42n, 47n
Amos, T. L., 269n
Anaphora of James, 35
Anderson, A. and M.O., 319n
Andresen, C., 99n
Anonymus ad Cuimnanum, 258
Anonymus Mellicensis, 250n
Antioch, 88, 89–90, 143; Antiochene school, 21, 261, 289, 290n; synods, 86, 90, 94, 107, 108, 109

Aphrahat, 143n, 144, 148
Apocrypha, 255, 256–8
  Irish, 264
Apponius, 259–60
Apuleius, 183
Ariminum, synod of, 92, 93, 95, 97, 99
Aristarchus, 80
Aristeas, Letter to, 43–4
Aristobulus, 41, 43, 52
Aristophanes, 80
Aristotle, 78, 129, 164, 227
Arius, 93n, 94, 101, 109
Arles, synod at, 90, 91, 223–4
Armstrong, A.H., 61n, 64n, 66n
Arnaldez, R., 44n
Arnobius, 276
Aristeas, Letter to 43–4
Artapanus, 42n
Athanasius, 85–118
Athens, 61
Attridge, H.W., 39n, 51n
Aubin, P. 184n
Auerbach, E. 163n, 164–7, 165n, 167n
Augustine, Irish, 253, 283–93; knowledge of Scripture, 284–8; understanding and use of Scripture, 288–93
Augustine, St, 3, 14, 36, 223, 224n, 238, 243, 251, 255, 267, 271; on Adam, 342; authority of, 250; catalogue of earthly things, 240, 241; in Eucherius of Lyons, 225–8, 229, 236, 249; exegesis of First Epistle of John, 201–20; influence of Ambrose, 1–2, 59, 83–4, 171, 182n, 204; influence of Donatists, 201, 206–10, 219; influence of Origen, 59, 83–4; in Irish sources, 258, 262, 264, 277–81, 288; levels of meaning, 234–5; influence on Maximus Confessor, 122; on 'mira profunditis', 163–99; as philosopher, 62, 186–7; principles underlying exegetical method, 203–5; revelation in